WALDO EMERSON

Gay Wilson Allen

PENGUIN BOOKS

Penguin Books Ltd, Harmondsworth,
Middlesex, England
Penguin Books, 625 Madison Avenue,
New York, New York 10022, U.S.A.
Penguin Books Australia Ltd, Ringwood,
Victoria, Australia
Penguin Books Canada Limited, 2801 John Street,
Markham, Ontario, Canada L3R 1B4
Penguin Books (N.Z.) Ltd, 182–190 Wairau Road,
Auckland 10, New Zealand

First published in the United States of America by
The Viking Press 1981
Published in Penguin Books 1982

LIBRARY OF CONGRESS CATALOGING IN PUBLICATION DATA
Allen, Gay Wilson, 1903–
Waldo Emerson: a biography.
Includes index.
1. Emerson, Ralph Waldo, 1803–1882. 2. Authors,
American—19th century—Biography. 3. Transcendentalists
(New England)—Biography. I. Title.
PS1631.A7 1982 814'.3 82-10153
ISBN 0 14 00.6278 5

Printed in the United States of America by
Halliday Lithograph Corporation, West Hanover, Massachusetts
Set in CRT Garamond

The Preface of this book appeared originally in *Georgia Review*.

PENGUIN BOOKS

WALDO EMERSON

In addition to *The Solitary Singer: A Critical Biography of Walt Whitman,* Gay Wilson Allen is also the author of the distinguished *William James: A Biography,* among other books. Most recently, Mr. Allen has been Professor of English at New York University. He lives with his wife in Oradell, New Jersey.

Emerson, from a drawing by Samuel Rowse, 1857.

For
MALCOLM COWLEY
in gratitude
and admiration

Preface

Why "*Waldo* Emerson"?

Ralph Waldo Emerson disliked his first name, and his family and friends called him "Waldo" after he requested them to do so while he was in college—though even as a child he had signed one letter "R. Waldo Emerson."[1] In the first two chapters of this biography, "Ralph" is used as a first name because the boy's family still used it. He was named for his maternal uncle Ralph Haskins, and so far as is known he had no antipathy for his uncle; but he had *six* cousins named Ralph—two on his mother's side and four on his father's. This made it difficult for Ralph Emerson to attain an identity of his own, and even as a child he was an individualist.

The shift to "Waldo" in Chapter III marks important psychological changes in young Emerson. He was beginning to outgrow the daydreaming adolescence of his unpromising childhood and to acquire the identity which would later enable him to play a major role in the making of nineteenth-century American literature. "Waldo" obviously had an emotional appeal for him, probably because his Waldo ancestors were Waldensians who fled to England in the seventeenth century to escape persecution in Europe for their Protestant religion.[2] The first Emerson to emigrate to America was Thomas; his grandson Edward married Rebecca Waldo, the daughter of Cornelius, who had moved to Massachusetts during the great migration of the seventeenth century, though he was not a Puritan. Thereafter, Waldo was continued as a given name in the Emerson family, and the poet kept it alive by naming his first son Waldo.

The name Waldo Emerson should also have more favorable connotations for readers of this biography than the forbidding three names, which carry associations with the trinominal New England contemporaries Henry Wadsworth Longfellow, John Greenleaf Whittier, James Russell Lowell, and Oliver Wendell Holmes, whose genteel writings have not worn as well as Emerson's. For half a century their names have been eclipsed in American literature by Walt Whitman, Herman Melville, and Emily Dickinson, whose voices grow louder and clearer with each passing decade. Until recently that has not been true of Emerson, but he is beginning to take his rightful place in their company. Aside from his own merits, he is important for his influence on Whitman and Dickinson, and Robert Frost gratefully confessed his indebtedness. Recently critics have also begun to see his influence on Wallace Stevens and other modern poets. This suggests vital differences between Emerson and his fading New England contemporaries.

The need for a new biography of Emerson is not unrelated to the choice of *Waldo Emerson* as a title. Ralph L. Rusk's *Life of Ralph Waldo Emerson* has served well for three decades as the standard reference for the facts of Emerson's life, but it is weak on the intimate, personal life and in literary interpretation, which Rusk deliberately kept to a minimum. He did a prodigious amount of research, and most of the documents were available to him, though not quite all. Furthermore, the intellectual climate has changed so much in the past three decades that it is possible to see Emerson today in ways not possible when Rusk wrote his biography. Biographers now also pay more attention to social and intellectual background than Rusk did. His *Life* was, therefore, somewhat deficient both on the subjective and on the objective side.

Subjectively Emerson developed from an unhappy "ugly duckling" childhood, when his parents and teachers thought he was not as bright as his one older and two younger brothers, to a troubled adolescence and a moody, introspective young manhood. He grew up preferring solitary meditation to social activity. As a young Unitarian minister he was only partly successful because he disliked visiting and officiating at funerals and weddings, preferring to read, contemplate, and write in his own library.[3] To his congregation, theological questions had already been answered by the men who wrote the creeds and founded the traditions of their Church. All they expected from their pastor was a repetition of these accepted "truths" in soothing and encouraging sermons. But to Emerson nothing was settled; every inherited belief and custom needed to be examined in the light of modern experience and the individual conscience. To him the essential thing in the religious life was not conformity but a live relationship with God—the feeling that "God is, not was."[4] Inevitably this conviction led to conflict with Church officials, the custodians of tradition, and to Emerson's resignation from his pastorate.

Emerson's biography is a story of continuous struggle, physical and intellectual (until middle age), and refinement of his ideas in successive lectures, essays, and poems. Even the key words of his vocabulary changed subtly in meaning from year to year, or book to book, so that his meaning must always be derived from the context. Emerson's first book, *Nature* (1836), is often regarded as difficult, but it is much easier to understand if the reader is familiar with the preceding lectures on natural sciences and passages in the Journals of the period on the Neoplatonists. It was no accident that Emerson chose natural science for his first public lectures.[5] Contemporary geology, astronomy, and physiology were liberating him from the theological dogma he had been taught, and Neoplatonism suggested to him a theology for his own age.

In Emerson's fertile mind, the (seemingly) most unlikely sources fused in his own creations, such as Neoplatonism and the latest theories and discoveries in the sciences. The eighteenth-century Scottish "Common Sense" philosophy might seem incompatible with Plotinus and Plato, but Emerson's concept of the "moral sentiment" came from Adam Smith (*Theory of Moral Sentiments,* 1759), Richard Price, Thomas Reid, and Dugald Stewart, the very men whom Thomas Jefferson studied at William and Mary.[6] Emerson's theory of the "moral sentiment," therefore, though derived from Scottish philosophers and Neoplatonism, is as American as the Declaration of Independence. But the Scottish school prepared the way for Utilitarianism, which Emerson emphatically rejected, preferring the path of the Neoplatonists to "natural" truths.

This biography is not a source study, or a philosophical study, but wherever sources or interpretation of ideas are part of the story, they have been included. Waldo Emerson's thinking was complicated, but some of the complications and apparent paradoxes are more comprehensible in the context of his experience, and reading—creative reading—was part of his experience.

Another paradox is that during the first months of Emerson's pastorate of the Second Church in Boston he at times seemed to echo the Puritans, though he was always strongly anti-Calvinist.[7] This was partly because he was acutely conscious that for over a century Increase and Cotton Mather had presided over this very church, and he felt a sympathetic identification with them, though of course it was not the same building and several generations of ministers had succeeded the Mathers. The original building had been destroyed in 1775 by British soldiers, who used the wood to build fires during a cold Boston winter.[8] But in his Puritan inheritance, only partly rejected, Emerson bore witness to the survival of traces of Puritanism in American cultural history.

But how about Emerson's "mysticism"? This is a very ambiguous term, and whether it applies to Emerson depends upon the definition. In the sense that a finite mind can communicate with the Infinite Mind, Emerson was a mystic, for he believed that such communication was possible through prayer and meditation. And he had two or three experiences that might be called epiphanies: one in Charleston, South Carolina,[9] in his early manhood, and possibly the famous "transparent eye-ball" sensation described in *Nature,* though exactly when it took place is difficult to pinpoint. He also believed profoundly that in all great art

> These temples grew as grows the grass;
> Art might obey, but not surpass,
> The passive Master lent his hand
> To the vast soul that o'er him planned . . .[10]

This was, and remained, Emerson's idea of artistic "inspiration," but it says little more than any devout Christian believed about God's relation to the world He created—though not usually thought of as a theory in aesthetics. Emerson later rejected an anthropomorphic God and called his Deity Mind, Reason, or Over-Soul; but the traditional Christian belief in the subordination of matter to *soul* or *spirit* always remained the central assumption in his philosophy.

These basic assumptions were reinforced (though not initiated) by Emerson's reading of the Neoplatonists, especially Plotinus (the "certain poet" in *Nature,* as pointed out in Chapter XIII of this biography), and later of the "Indian Scriptures," from which he borrowed several Sanskrit terms, such as *Brahma* and *Over-Soul* (a translation of *At-Man,* the supreme and universal soul). These gave Emerson new terminology and metaphors, but not fundamentally new thoughts. Their influence on his art was extensive, but not on his "mysticism" (the mystery of God). In a chronological study of Emerson these influences are seen in their proper perspective. Each stage of his intellectual development prepared for the next. Emerson is a difficult author if the reader begins *in medias res* (as one is usually taught in college) instead of following the order of his unfolding experiences—his organic moral and intellectual growth.

Believing profoundly that the Christian conscience is an oracle, Emerson sought by introspection to find answers to moral problems. Through his close observation of his own mind he came to feel that a greater Mind was in some mysterious way thinking through him, or prompting his finite mind. This introspection led him to anticipate William James's description of the "stream-of-consciousness." Like James, too, he strongly suspected that the hidden source of consciousness was an *unconscious* mind in which his thoughts originated.[11]

In these observations and deductions Emerson anticipated later psychologists of the unconscious (Freud) or the subconscious (Jung). In *The Forgotten Language,* Erich Fromm says: "One of the most beautiful and concise statements on the superior rational character of our mental process in sleep is made by Emerson."[12] Fromm refers to the lecture on "Demonology," in which Emerson says, "Dreams have a poetic integrity and truth. . . . Wise and sometimes terrible hints shall in them be thrown to the man out of quite unknown intelligence."[13]

Although in his Journals Emerson many times described and speculated on his dreams, he was more interested in the relation of his subconscious to his waking mind, by which he experienced impulses and intuitions which he could not account for rationally. He came to feel that it was by this "doorway" that God entered his consciousness.[14] This is quite different, of course, from Freud's theory of the id and the subconscious, perhaps nearer to Jung's collective unconscious. But the important point is that Emerson was pioneering in psychology. It is important, too, that his confidence in the healthy effect of the harmony between his conscious and unconscious mind was an early example of psychiatric therapy. Many episodes in this biography show that it was good therapy for him, as in his recovery from (probable) tuberculosis in early manhood, from a nervous breakdown after his first wife's death and his resignation from the Second Church, and from the shock he experienced at the deaths of his brothers Edward and Charles and his son Waldo.

A common criticism of Emerson is that he denied the existence of evil. It is true that his view of life was not tragic, unlike that of William Faulkner, Robert Penn Warren, and other Southern authors (the Southern literary mind gravitates naturally to tragedy). But his philosophy of pain and evil has often been misunderstood. He did not say that they do not exist; rather, he said that they are not "real," meaning that they are finite and remediable. Tragedy is irremediable: it is predestined, inescapable, a permanent condition under which a fated person must live and die. Emerson was well aware of social injustice, political dishonesty, and human errors of judgment—as the following chapters will demonstrate. But he thought that rational judgment and moral action in response to the "inner voice" of conscience could at least ameliorate if not entirely eliminate these human evils, and often cure them.

Physical pain from accident or illness could also, Emerson believed, be blunted and endured by a courageous exercise of the will. This belief derived in part from his firm confidence in a benevolent Deity, and in part from his reading of Plutarch and other authors who praised stoicism. Both sources helped him endure his own residence in the "house of pain." When his son died, he lamented that he did not feel it more deeply, but actually the shock had numbed his nervous system. He felt so deeply that he could not feel. In fact, he never ceased to grieve for "that beautiful boy," the last coherent words he was heard to utter on his deathbed.[15]

A major concern to Emerson in his life and his writings was man's relation to nature, or the physical world. (*Nature,* like *soul* and *mind,* varies in meaning in different Emersonian contexts.) Leaving in abeyance his theories on the spiritual nature of matter, in which he anticipated what has been called "The Tao of Physics,"[16] Emerson was very much concerned with practical relations with nature. He was an ecologist before the word was used, though not quite to the extent that Thoreau was. The accusation in "The Sphinx" that man "poisons the ground" was undoubtedly intended in a practical as well as a philosophical way, though he was not so prophetic as to foresee the destructive use of pesticides. He was appalled, however, in 1848 by the industrial pollution he saw in England, and later in Pittsburgh.

Throughout his writings Emerson insisted that men and women must obey the laws of nature to avoid disaster, personally and collectively. Though optimistic in the long run about the future of the human race, he was pessimistic about contemporary men, and was severely critical of their greed, ignorance, and dishonesty. He refused to join social reform movements because he believed individual action was better than collective enterprise. Unless the individual could be improved, there was no hope for society. His own reform began with himself.

During his early years as artist and thinker, Emerson tried to remain aloof from political and social reform so that he might give full attention to his own mental and moral development, but his conscience inevitably drew him into movements promoting the abolition of slavery and the defense of a free society—more deeply than he usually gets credit for. In 1838 the removal of the Cherokee Indians from their ancestral lands by the United States government provoked him to write an indignant letter to President Van Buren.[17] He found it hard to believe, he said, that the American government could lie and steal and act brutishly. He learned that it could and did.

As early as 1844, in observing the anniversary of the emancipation of black slaves in the West Indies, Emerson delivered in Concord a masterful address on the evils of slavery.[18] His plan to buy the slaves from their owners could have averted the Civil War, which cost many millions in lives and property. A few years later the passage of the Fugitive Slave Law, requiring every citizen to assist in the capture and return of runaway slaves, destroyed all his respect for his former friend Daniel Webster. Emerson became so disillusioned about government, constitutions, and elected officials that he was for a time an anarchist.[19] This is also a side of Emerson which has received too little attention in previous biographies.

Readers of this biography will find much in Emerson's angry words of the 1850s to remind them of America in the 1960s. He denounced the war with Mexico as immoral, and slavery as a violation of every civilized principle of human rights. But this tumultuous period in his life was also progressive. Lincoln's Emancipation Proclamation restored Emerson's faith in the government.[20] Unfortunately, when his anger cooled, so did his creativity. Yet we can hardly begrudge Emerson a more relaxed life after his great efforts. The graceful way in which he accepted the handicaps of old age gives the last chapters of his biography a tone of Shakespearean romance, reminiscent of *The Winter's Tale*.

In Emerson's biography is mirrored the life of the American nation during his lifetime. Few men of the nineteenth century had more extensive knowledge of the period, beginning with the history of Concord, where the American Revolution began in sight of his grandfather, watching from an upstairs window in the Old Manse, and extending through the years of territorial expansion, the Mexican War and the Civil War, the settling of the West (which he observed on almost annual journeys to the new states and territories to lecture there), and ending with a trip by train to California in his old age. Emerson also made three trips to Europe, the last extending to Egypt. In his travels he met and won the friendship of most of the leaders of his day in literature, government, science, invention, and finance, whom he shrewdly evaluated in his Journals, letters, and lectures. He called traveling "a fool's paradise,"[21] but he found it no paradise, and his comments were not foolish.

In recent years several scholars and critics have rediscovered Emerson's importance as a poet, notably Hyatt Waggoner, Harold Bloom, Roy Harvey Pearce, and Joel Porte.[22] All of these have in one way or another contributed to the interpretative discussions of Emerson's poetry in this biography, but the clues provided by two earlier scholars served as springboards to the two characteristics emphasized in Chapter XXI, ecstasy and "the dance of the atoms." Professor John D. Yohannan has called attention to Emerson's translations from a German translation of Persian poetry.[23] These translations and an essay on "Persian Poetry" reveal that what Emerson most admired in the Persian poets was intoxication of the senses. Rereading Emerson's poems and his comments on the *gai science*[24] led to new appreciation of his theory and practice in poetry. In the past, critics of Emerson's poems have often overstressed their philosophical content and shown an undue preference for "Brahma" and "Hamatreya." They are superb of their kind, but not Emerson's only kind of poem.

The other scholar-critic who gave a valuable clue to the nature of Emerson's poetry was George E. Woodberry. In 1907 he observed that in his poems Emerson "conceives the energy of Nature as a Dionysian force . . . a dance of the atoms."[25] Thus, improbable as it may sound, Persian aesthetic inebriation and the bacchanalia of nature combined to give Emerson both subject matter and mode: rhythm, imagery, and tone. Woodberry was concerned only with the influence of science, but he also acutely observed that Emerson's poems "are autobiographical in a very strict sense."

Joel Porte, in a very perceptive biographical-critical study, calls Emerson the "Representative Man." That is a good title because his life did represent, both in example and in precept, the best in human nature.[26] But another term Emerson used was "the central man," a phrase that appealed to Wallace Stevens.[27] "The central man" was a Platonic concept: it takes the best attributes of a great many men to form an ideal man. If these qualities could be embodied in one man, he would be what Nietzsche, with confessed indebtedness to Emerson, called the *Übermensch,* popularly translated as "Superman," though literally "Over-Man."

Countless readers of Emerson's essays and poems have been stimulated to set higher goals for themselves and to believe in their own ability to achieve them. This teaching has often been debased by interpreting the goals to be material, making Emerson's "self-reliance" and "better mouse-trap" bywords for Rotarians, but his own life shows that that was not his meaning. It was, to use the term of Plato and Aristotle, "the good life." What is the *good life?* Emerson's biography gives the answer, partly in his own experiences, but more fully in his writings. "The good life," like "the central man," is never fully attainable, but Emerson came closer than most men—or most authors. For that reason John Dewey said that "when democracy has articulated itself, it will have no difficulty in finding itself already proposed in Emerson."[28]

Acknowledgments

My greatest debt of gratitude is to Mr. Malcolm Cowley, who encouraged me to undertake this biography and gave me his valuable critical advice on the manuscript; however, any shortcomings in the published work should be attributed entirely to me. My next greatest debt is to the Ralph Waldo Emerson Memorial Association, of which Mrs. Edith W. Gregg is president, for permission to use and quote from the vast collection of Emerson letters and manuscripts in the Houghton Library at Harvard University. Both Mr. W. H. Bond, librarian, and his staff in the Houghton Library have extended to me every aid and courtesy possible.

Of course my research was greatly aided by the publications of the leading Emerson scholars, past and present, but especially the editors of *The Journals and Miscellaneous Notebooks* and the *Early Lectures*. To supplement Ralph L. Rusk's edition of Emerson's *Letters* (incomplete) I examined the unpublished letters (including family correspondence) in the Houghton, and also the files of Professor Eleanor Tilton, who is preparing an expanded edition of Rusk's work. I have made such use as I could of the vast collection of letters and diaries of Mary Moody Emerson (Aunt Mary), but her handwriting is so extremely difficult to read that I often had to resort to the transcriptions (largely unpublished) made by George Tolman. Dr. Ethel Wortis gave me access to the letters and diaries of William Emerson, Waldo's older brother (the Columbia University Library now has a microfilm of this valuable collection). Since only a few of Emerson's sermons have been published, I read the holographs in the Houghton Library. Professor Joel Myerson generously shared with me the results of his research in Emerson's transactions with his publishers and statistics on the sale of his books. Professor Myerson also lent me proof sheets of his valuable study of *The Dial*, entitled *The New England Transcendentalists and the Dial: A History of the Magazine and Its Contributors* (1980). Mrs. Edith W. Gregg read the whole manuscript, gave additional information on Emerson's friend John M. Forbes, and supplied genealogical data. *The Diaries and Letters of William Emerson, 1743–1776,* by Amelia Forbes Emerson (Boston: privately printed, 1972), also yielded valuable genealogical information. *The Life of Lidian Jackson Emerson,* by Delores Bird Carpenter (Boston: Twayne Publishers, 1981), was received too late to be used, but the manuscripts in the Houghton Library on which the book is based had been examined.

The following persons read portions of the manuscript and offered helpful suggestions: Jerome Loving, Arthur Zeiger, Ray Gozzi, Arthur Golden, and Richard Ellmann. My wife, Evie Allison Allen, suffered through all versions in typescript and proof. Mrs. Katherine Lessersohn typed chapters at a crucial stage and corrected my own typographical errors.

For permission to quote from the following work I am grateful to the Harvard University Press: *The Journals and Miscellaneous Notebooks of Ralph Waldo Emerson,* edited by William H. Gilman, Alfred R. Ferguson, George P. Clark, Merrell R. Davis, Harrison Hayford, Ralph Orth, J. E. Parsons,

Merton M. Sealts and A. W. Plumstead, Vols. I–XIV, 1960–78; *Early Lectures of Ralph Waldo Emerson,* edited by Stephen E. Whicher, Robert E. Spiller, and Wallace E. Williams, 3 vols., 1964–72; *The Collected Works of Ralph Waldo Emerson,* edited by Robert E. Spiller and Alfred R. Ferguson, Vol. I, 1971; *One First Love: The Letters of Ellen Louisa Tucker to Ralph Waldo Emerson,* edited by Edith W. Gregg, 1962; Christopher Cranch's caricature of the "transparent eye-ball," by courtesy of F. DeWolfe Miller, the Harvard University Press, and the Houghton Library.

G.W.A.

Oradell, New Jersey
September 1980

Contents

List of Illustrations

Illustrations follow page 194.

Chronology

1803   May 25, born in Boston.

1811   May 12, father's death.

1812–17   Student at Boston Public Latin School.

1817–21   Student at Harvard College.

1821–26   Teaching school.

1826–27   October 10, approbated to preach; November 25, goes south for health, returns in June; December 26, meets Ellen Tucker.

1828   December 17, engagement to Ellen.

1829   March 11, ordination as pastor of Second Church, Boston; September 30, marriage to Ellen.

1831   February 8, death of Ellen.

1832–33   October 28, resigned pastorate; December–October, traveled in Europe; met Landor, Coleridge, Carlyle, and Wordsworth.

1834   January 6, first public lecture—beginning of new career; October 1, death of brother Edward.

1835   August 15, bought house in Concord; September 14, married Lydia ("Lidian") Jackson.

1836   May 9, death of brother Charles; September 9, publication of *Nature;* September 19, first meeting of Hedge ("Transcendental") Club; October 30, birth of son Waldo.

1837   August 31, "The American Scholar" address at Harvard.

1837–38   December–February, lectures on "Human Culture"; July 15, "Divinity School Address."

1838–39   Lectures on "Human Life."

1839   February 24, birth of daughter Ellen.

1839–40   December–February, lectures on "The Present Age."

1840–44   July–April, *The Dial,* edited by Margaret Fuller, Emerson, Thoreau.

1841   March 20, publication of *Essays* (First Series); November 22, birth of daughter Edith.

1841–42   December–January, lectures on "The Times."

1842   January 27, death of son Waldo.

1844   July 10, birth of son Edward; October 19, publication of *Essays* (Second Series).

1845–46   December–January, lectures on "Representative Men."

1846   December 25, publication of *Poems.*

1847–48   October–July, lectured in England; visited Paris.

1849   September 11, publication of *Nature, Addresses, and Lectures.*

1850   January 1, publication of *Representative Men.*

1851   Lectures on "The Conduct of Life."

1853   November 16, mother's death.

1854   Extensive lecturing in Midwest.

1855   July 21, "greeting" letter to Walt Whitman; lectures to antislavery societies.

1856   August 6, publication of *English Traits.*

1859   May 27, death of brother Bulkeley.

1860   December 8, publication of *The Conduct of Life.*

1862   January 31, address on "American Civilization," Washington, D.C.; talks with President Lincoln.

1863   May 1, death of Mary Moody Emerson ("Aunt Mary").

1867   April 28, publication of *May-Day and Other Poems.*

1868   September 13, death of brother William.

1870   February, publication of *Society and Solitude;* April 26, beginning of lectures at Harvard on "The Natural History of the Intellect," partially repeated in 1871.

1871   April–May, trip to California.

1872   July 24, house burned.

1872–73   October–May, trip to Egypt, with stops in London, Rome, and Paris.

1875   December, publication of *Letters and Social Aims* (dated 1876), edited by James Elliot Cabot.

1882   April 27, death and burial in Concord.

WALDO EMERSON

PART ONE

CHAPTER I

The Voice in the Garden

... I heard his voice ... (as Adam that of the
Lord God in the garden) ... and I vainly en-
deavouring to hide myself.[1]

I

In 1850 Ralph Waldo Emerson received an urgent request from Josiah
Quincy to write a memoir of his father, the Reverend William Emerson,
former pastor of the First Church of Boston and one of the founders of the
Athenaeum, the city's first library and museum. This request, conveyed to
the poet through his brother William, put Emerson in a quandary—and
an unpleasant frame of mind. To William he complained:

> But I have no recollections of him that can serve me. I was eight years old
> when he died, & only remember a somewhat social gentleman, but severe
> to us children, who twice or thrice put me in mortal terror by forcing me
> into the salt water off some wharf or bathing house, and I still recall the
> fright with which, after some of this salt experience, I heard his voice one
> day, (as Adam that of the Lord God in the garden,) summoning us to a
> new bath, and I vainly endeavouring to hide myself. I have never heard
> any sentence or sentiment of his repeated by Mother or Aunt [Mary
> Moody Emerson], and his printed or written papers, as far as I know, only
> show candour & taste, or I should almost say, docility, the principal merit
> possible to that early ignorant & transitional *Month-of-March,* in our New
> England culture. His literary merits really are that he fostered the Anthol-
> ogy & the Athenaeum. These things ripened into Buckminster, Channing
> & Everett.[2]

The tone of this complaint is highly revealing. Emerson's memory of his father was colored by fear, resentment, and a desire to be uncharitably candid. Of course at the age of eight he would have had a very limited understanding of his father's intellectual and professional merits, but his memories made him a harsh critic. Nothing in them could soften his recollection of that stern voice in the Eden of his vulnerable innocence.

The Monthly Anthology, which the Reverend William Emerson founded, and edited for a year and a half,[3] was indeed a mediocre literary production, but it was the forerunner of *The North American Review,* which would have considerable importance in the intellectual life of New England in the nineteenth century. Like the Athenaeum, it preceded the springtime of more gifted Unitarian authors such as Joseph Buckminster, William Ellery Channing, and Edward Everett, who in turn cultivated the ground for the flowering of Emerson's own literary generation. Culturally Emerson was certainly more indebted to his father than he realized, and probably he was also in mind and body, for he was said to resemble his father rather than his mother.

The Reverend William Emerson was a tolerant minister and polished gentleman, but his ethic of work and discipline derived more from Puritanism than from contemporary Unitarianism. A week before his fourth child's third birthday he wrote a friend: "Ralph does not read very well yet."[4] This was not a joke but a sober observation. Ralph was already enrolled in a private "Dame" school, though this was not unusual in Boston at that time, when children learned to read at the age at which twentieth-century children would be attending nursery school and doing finger painting.

In his sixth year Ralph was afflicted with a skin eruption, which his father treated by making the boy bathe in the ocean. He taught Ralph to swim by pushing him into the water and letting him swim for his life. That his son had not forgiven him for this forty years later, the letter to William vigorously testifies. By this time Emerson had also rebelled against all ritualistic religious authority and moribund intellectual conformity, both of which he associated in this same letter with his ministerial father. In a negative way William Emerson helped to make his son the strongest moral and literary personality of his generation. From his mother, Emerson inherited a tender conscience and an uncompromising moral integrity, which his Aunt Mary reinforced, but his Adamic spirit of disobedience to vested authority owed something to his father's dreaded voice of command.

On the day of Emerson's birth, May 25, 1803, the conduct of his father was entirely in character. In the morning he attended the Election Day sermon preached by one of his Boston colleagues; then he took dinner with the governor of Massachusetts.[5] On returning to the parsonage at three-fifteen in the afternoon, he found that his wife, Ruth, had given birth to a blue-eyed, towheaded boy. The urbane father dutifully and matter-of-factly recorded the birth in his diary. Probably Mrs. Emerson was having labor pains when he left the house that morning, but she would not have expected him to neglect his professional or social duties out of sympathy for her.

The Emersons named the baby Ralph, for Ralph Haskins,[6] Mrs. Emerson's prosperous younger brother, who at the time was somewhere on the Pacific Ocean in charge of a cargo of merchandise from China; and Waldo, for a family into which an Emerson had married in the seventeenth century.[7] The history of the Waldo family is vague, but they seem originally to have been Waldensians who sought religious asylum in England, succeeded as merchants in London, then joined the Puritan emigration to America.

Election Day was still a great occasion in Boston, as it had been in the earlier Puritan times, and the ceremonies continued next day. The Reverend William Emerson also entered in his diary that on May 26 he entertained the governor and other prominent guests in his home. Probably from her bed Mrs. Emerson gave instructions to the servants and to the women of her husband's congregation who volunteered to help prepare and serve the dinner. Three days later the father entered in the parish record that he had that day christened his son Ralph Waldo Emerson. It was Ruth Emerson's custom to carry the babies of the church in her own arms to the baptismal font, but it is likely that one of her sisters or her sister-in-law—her children's Aunt Mary—substituted for her on this occasion.

William Emerson, the personable minister of the First Church, lithe, handsome, rosy-cheeked, with blue eyes and sandy hair, stood nearly six feet in his knee breeches, black silk stockings, and well-polished boots.[8] In the pulpit his vestments were always immaculate: white lawn bands at his throat, and black silk gown held securely in place by a silk cord at his waist. His wife would not let anyone else iron his bands. On the street he wore a tricornered hat, carried a gold-headed cane, and walked with the confidence befitting his office as chaplain of the Massachusetts Senate and the Boston Artillery Company. He looked every inch a gentleman, and was the confidant and companion of the social and political elite of the city, who in religion might be Unitarian, Congregationalist, or Episcopalian, but in politics were rigid Federalists. In wealth and size Boston had lost first and second place to Philadelphia and New York, but it was still, with its population of twenty-five thousand, the dominant cultural influence in New England. India Wharf was piled with the products of the India and China trade. Fortunes were being made in the importation and selling of Oriental silks, textiles, ceramics, condiments, and other foreign products. (New England did not yet have its own textile factories.)

The pastor of the First Church was at ease in this mercantile society. Though well read, he did not take great interest in theology. He made no special attempt to "save souls" from eternal damnation, but was very active in civic causes of all kinds. The content of his sermons made no deep impression on his audience, but he read them with perfect enunciation in a charming baritone voice. He served on the School Committee, held meetings of the Singing Society in the parsonage, and participated in the activities of the Humane Society, the Agricultural Society, the Philosophical Society, the Massachusetts Historical Society, which he had helped to organize, the Society for the Promotion of the Study of Science, and the Anthology Club, which met once a month in his library to select the contents of the next issue of the magazine. He was also an overseer of Harvard College, and frequently inspected the annual "exhibitions" (public examinations of students) at Harvard and in the Boston schools.

The First Church, known affectionately as "Old Brick," was the oldest church in Boston, founded by the Puritans in the seventeenth century and first called "the Meeting House." Originally located on the south side of King Street,[9] after several moves it was now at Chauncy Place, off Summer Street. As Harvard College, which supplied the ministers, drifted away from Calvinism toward Unitarianism, the First Church softened its theology, though the belief in original sin lingered in the minds of some of its members. But it had lost little if any of its social prestige by the time Mr. Emerson was elected pastor in 1799, and the pews continued to be owned and occupied by the men who wielded power in Boston.[10] John Quincy

Adams, future President of the United States, was a member. His father, John Adams, recently defeated for a second term as President by that wild democratic upstart Thomas Jefferson, worshiped in the First Church whenever he felt like coming in from Quincy.

Ralph's mother, Ruth, the tenth child of the prosperous distiller John Haskins, was the quiet, patient, and dutiful wife a busy clergyman needed.[11] She was not conspicuous for beauty, yet her kindly dark eyes and pleasant face beneath dark hair won everyone's confidence. Though she bore eight children at intervals of one to two years, and lost three in their infancy, she never complained, regarding affliction and hardship as the will of Providence. Until her marriage in 1796, she attended the Episcopal Trinity Church, and would always be partial to her Church of England prayer book. She did not concern her mind with theology; her religious faith, though inherited, was private and intuitive. Yet no Puritan ever believed more devoutly in the absolute sovereignty of God, who punished or rewarded at His discretion.

Before her marriage Ruth Haskins began keeping a diary "to observe if I make progress in the Christian and divine life, or grow in the knowledge of the Holy Scriptures. . . ."[12] She wanted to record all of God's "providences toward my friends or myself, whether prosperous or adverse,—and conscientiously note down whatever appears to be for the glory of God, or the good of my own soul." She prayed for divine assistance in promoting and strengthening "vital piety and true religion in my own immortal soul!" Though such sentiments were the staples of pious church members of her day, she did not write them to impress any man or woman but preserved them in her secret diary as aids to her own moral perfection.

Mrs. Emerson was more devotional by nature than her sociable husband. Even after her marriage, and with all the burdens of motherhood, she retired to her room every morning after breakfast for an hour of reading the Bible, meditation, and soul-searching. Her husband regularly conducted family prayers before breakfast, and as soon as the children could talk, each one recited or read a verse of Scripture of his own choosing. These rituals satisfied the Unitarian minister, and after breakfast he took up his daily routine with a clear conscience. But no one dared disturb his wife at her private devotions, though after they were completed she returned to her domestic tasks with vigor and quiet efficiency. Her children obeyed her without scolding or nagging; in fact, she never raised her voice to anyone.

But her reserve and habitual restraint of emotion in speech and action also created an intangible atmosphere of remoteness.

Once when Ralph and his older brother William returned home several hours late, they were surprised to hear their mother exclaim, "My sons, I have been in agony for you!" Ralph "went to bed in bliss at the interest she showed."[13] Usually his mother kept her affections as secret as her silent talks with God. When members of the family were reunited after days or weeks of separation, they embraced, and discreetly rejoiced, but afterward they rarely touched each other. Having a saint for a mother was a calming influence—at times, even depressing—but, to anticipate Emerson's future doctrine of "compensation," every benefit has its opposite, its negative. From his father he inherited an unusually resonant voice and a sense of style in language; from his mother, an inhibited emotional life. Smiling would come easily to him, even when it concealed pain, but spontaneous laughter, seldom—and angry words only from moral, not personal, indignation.

II

When Ruth Haskins married the Reverend William Emerson, he was pastor of a church in a small village called Harvard, thirty miles from Boston and twelve from Concord.[14] His stepfather, the Reverend Ezra Ripley, had come over one Sunday in March 1792 to preach William's ordination sermon. Prospect Hill, a short distance from the village, gave a panoramic view of Mount Wachusett to the west and of Monadnock to the north, but beautiful scenery was almost Harvard's only distinction. It was a dull place for a man who had acquired literary tastes at Harvard College, was fond of music, and enjoyed the society of Boston. The seven years William Emerson spent in this remote village were lonely and discouraging. At times he thought of going to Washington, D.C., to start a new church on the most liberal principles imaginable. It would have "no written expression of faith, no covenant, and no subscription to articles, as a term of communion."[15] As he recalled this dream in a letter to his half brother, Samuel Ripley, "It was my plan, and still would be, in forming a new church, to administer the rituals of Christianity to all who would observe them, without any profession except such observance."

By teaching and farming on a small scale to supplement his meager salary at Harvard, Mr. Emerson managed to support his wife and their first child, a daughter, born in 1798, named Phebe Ripley (she died two years later). In May 1799 Mr. Emerson was asked to preach the Election Day sermon to the Artillery Company in Boston, to which the public was invited, and made such a favorable impression that he was offered the ministry of the First Church. Officials of the Harvard church demanded a thousand dollars for his release, which was more than twice his annual salary there, but the First Church met the demand, and in September the Emersons moved into the old parsonage on Summer Street.[16]

The parsonage was a yellow wooden house with a gambrel roof, half a mile from "Old Brick" at Cornhill. It stood well back from the street, in the midst of grounds covering two or three acres, large enough for an orchard and an extensive garden, almost a small farm. Elms shaded the house and tall Lombardy poplars lined the unpaved street. Nearby a cow pasture was available at low rent, and the Common, still being used as a community cow pasture, was only a short distance away. On both sides of the street were several fine houses with well-planted grounds, owned by leading merchants and professional men. Next door the orchard of Judge William Prescott, father of the future historian, was famous for its St. Michael pears. These made a lasting impression on young Ralph, who would always associate pears with his childhood—one of the pleasant memories, for there were many others which were not pleasant. In adult life, settled on his modest estate in Concord, he would win prizes at the county fair for his own fine pears.

In this semirural haven, five of the eight Emerson children were born: John Clarke, soon after his parents were settled in the yellow manse, in 1799; William in 1801; Ralph Waldo two years later; Edward Bliss in 1805; and Robert Bulkeley in 1807. Charles Chauncy was born in 1808 and Mary Caroline in 1811 in a new brick parsonage on the same street. John Clarke, never strong, died in 1807, and his younger sister in 1814.[17] Bulkeley was mentally retarded and would always have to be cared for. The other boys attended the same schools and shared the same pleasures and hardships. William, Charles, and Edward always excelled in their studies, but Ralph, stubbornly choosing his own pace, was only a mediocre student and a worry to his demanding father.

All the Emerson children shared in the household chores. Bulkeley, in spite of his mental handicap, carried in wood for the kitchen stove; William and Ralph drove the cow to pasture every morning before school, while Edward and Charles performed lighter tasks. When not carrying out their domestic duties or preparing their lessons, the children were expected to read such "improving" books as Charles Rollin's *Ancient History* or Jebb's *Sermons*. Novels were frowned upon, though Ralph did borrow and read several of Sir Walter Scott's. Mr. Emerson tightly supervised his children's studies. In 1806, during a brief absence from home, he sent these instructions to his wife, when William was five and Ralph three: "William will recite to you as he does to me, if you have leisure to hear him, a sentence of English grammar before breakfast,—though I think, if only one can be attended to, Ralph should be that one."[18] Not, evidently, because Ralph was a favorite, but because he needed the instruction more than William did. John Clarke was seven, and his father wanted him to "repeat passages from Addison, Shakespeare, Milton, Pope, etc."

Normal play was scarcely known to the Emerson boys. For relaxation they memorized poems or verses of Scripture, which they recited to their parents and to each other. Whatever outdoor playing they did was safely within the fenced grounds of the parsonage. They were forbidden to play in the street for fear of the "rude boys," toughs from Windmill Point ("Round Pointers" they were called), who passed through Summer Street on their way to the Common, or boys from South Boston who fought pitched battles with West Enders. Ralph never had a sled, and would not have dared use one on the frozen streets dominated by those "rude boys" so dreaded by his mother.[19]

Because the Emerson boys lived in an almost closed society, they were more dependent upon each other than is usual in a family of so many brothers, and the dependency also fostered loyalty.[20] Of course there were frictions, though in later years Emerson looked back on them as benefits. In 1866 he wrote in his Journal: "Best masters for the young writer and speaker are the fault-finding brothers and sisters at home [of course neither of his sisters lived long enough to become a critic] who will not spare him, but will pick and cavil, and tell the odious truth."[21]

Emerson did not, however, remember his father's criticism with gratitude. If Mr. Emerson was not Ralph's most severe critic, he was certainly the most feared. In 1810, during another absence, Mr. Emerson wrote his wife that he hoped Ralph, then seven, "regards his words, does not eat his dinner too fast, and is gradually resigning his impetuosity to younger boys."[22] The exact sense in which Ralph did not "regard his words" is not clear, but "impetuosity" suggests that he was quarrelsome and aggressive toward younger boys. At fourteen (the year he entered college), he still had this fault. "How is it, Ralph," his Uncle Samuel Ripley asked him, "that all the boys dislike & quarrel with you, whilst the grown people are fond of you?"[23] Perhaps it was a mystery to Emerson himself. "Now," he comments in his Journal, at the age of thirty-six, ". . . the old people suspect and dislike me, & the young love me."

III

When Ralph was only four years old his older brother John Clarke died, apparently of tuberculosis. In the autumn of 1805, in John Clarke's sixth year, his parents had sent him to Waterford, Maine, for instruction by his uncle and his aunt. Why the boy was sent to Maine is puzzling, but his mother complained of his indolence, and perhaps she thought the Ripleys could improve his habits. It is more than likely that his "weak lungs," of which his parents were already aware, were the cause of his lassitude, but tuberculosis was so little understood at the time that the most harmful remedies were often employed with the best intentions. Certainly the winter in Maine did John Clarke Emerson little good, and possibly much harm, for he died on April 26, 1807, a year after his return.

Ralph was too young to comprehend the full meaning of death. How it affected his mother is shown in a letter she wrote to her Maine sister-in-law the following August:

> My dear Sister, I have been endeavoring these three months past to bring my mind into such a state as to be able to write to you freely, and to unbosom my sorrow for the loss of our beloved and first-born, John Clarke. This dear boy is called from our embraces by our heavenly Father, who is infinite in wisdom and goodness. Therefore I will not complain, though I feel daily the agonizing pain arising from his loss, but little diminished by the length of time elapsed since his death. . . .[24]

Though Mrs. Emerson's consolation, in this case, sounds more like an emotional reflex than a deep conviction, she did, nevertheless, believe in the most literal sense that "our departed child" was now "an inhabitant of celestial glory in the presence of God, his Maker, and associated with angels and spiritual beings, where his infantile capacities will be continually ripening and expanding through the Ages of Eternity."

Mr. Emerson himself suffered a severe hemorrhage of the lungs the following year, but recovered sufficiently to take a lively interest in the building of a new church—a "New Brick" to take the place of "Old Brick," which was now in one of the busier and noisier parts of the city. The property at Cornhill (later Washington Street, near Court Street) was consequently becoming very desirable for business property. For this reason Mr. Benjamin Joy offered to build a new church at Chauncy Place and a brick parsonage diagonally opposite on Summer Street (and in addition three other brick dwelling houses, which the church could rent), in exchange for the Cornhill property and thirteen thousand five hundred dollars in cash. The new parsonage would be a great improvement over the old wooden one farther out on Summer, and the church officials were easily persuaded to accept the offer. Some members, however, were not pleased with the deal, and a satirist lamented:

> Farewell, Old Brick,—Old Brick, farewell:
> You bought your minister and sold your bell.[25]

("Bought" referred, of course, to the payment the First Church had made to the little church at Harvard to obtain Mr. Emerson's release.)

On July 21, 1808, the first service was held in the new church, and the pastor exhorted his audience to be thankful for the "new, commodious and beautiful edifice, where, in the silence of retirement, yet in the center of the territory of the metropolis, we may worship the Lord our God." But the parsonage was not ready for occupancy until November. It stood across the street from the governor's mansion, a fact which naturally enhanced its social prestige.[26]

The Emerson family had scarcely got settled in their new home before Mrs. Emerson gave birth to her last son, who was named Charles Chauncy for a previous distinguished pastor of the First Church. But the happiness of the family was shadowed by a steady decline in the Reverend William Emerson's health.

Ralph could hardly have been unaware of his father's increasing debility, though the family routines and rituals were little affected. Sabbath was rigidly observed from Saturday sundown until sundown on Sunday. Not only were all amusements forbidden, but even reading, visiting, writing letters, and all work not absolutely necessary. Cooking was kept to a minimum. The young children could not help but find the enforced idleness boring, but of course they attended Sunday school and two church services on Sunday. Then in the evening the deacons of the First Church and other friends gathered in the parsonage for a hospitable glass of wine or other spirits. Though the children were only spectators of these festivities, they could enjoy the cheerful atmosphere of the household. Then on Monday afternoon Mrs. Emerson regularly took all her children to the big house on Rainsford Lane to have tea with Grandfather and Grandmother Haskins. Delicious cakes and cookies were served with the best China tea.

On Thanksgiving the large Haskins family dined with the Emersons in the parsonage, and at Christmas the Emersons were entertained by the Haskinses.[27] The Puritan attitude toward Christmas still prevailed in Boston, and the day was meagerly observed (half a century later, Harvard College would still be holding classes on Christmas Day). But Mrs. Emerson had grown up as an Episcopalian, and she celebrated Christmas by taking her family to her father's house for a sumptuous dinner. Then on New Year's Day everyone went to Uncle Thomas Haskins's house, and on Twelfth Night to Uncle Kast Haskins's on Hanover Street.

One of the most festive of all Boston holidays was Election Day.[28] Originally, officials had taken office as soon as the votes were counted, but after the inauguration was moved to a later date, it was still called Election Day. With the Emersons this festival began with breakfast served to visiting ministers, including several from churches in nearby Cambridge, Newton, Charlestown, and more distant places. After breakfast each child was given ninepence to spend as he wished. It usually went for gingerbread sold at booths set up for the occasion. But even more exciting than Election Day was the Fourth of July, which was celebrated by speeches, parades, and the greeting of sunrise and sunset by the discharge of artillery on the Common and the ringing of church bells. After dark, firecrackers and Roman candles popped and boomed on the Common while rockets lit up the sky in bursts of fiery colors.

Of course the Common was also occasionally the scene of a public hanging, which many witnessed as if it were a great sporting event. It is unlikely that the Emerson boys were permitted to attend such a spectacle, but they would have heard excited accounts from people who were present. In the autumn of 1810 they were doubtless permitted to join almost the entire population of Boston in observing the mock-Indian "Feast of Squantum." Few authentic Indians were actually present, but Boston citizens played at being Indians. A contemporary diarist says that "mounted cavaliers, wearing white top boots and spurs, rode back and forth over the Common"[29] and the "best people of the town performed Indian rites." Food was cooked in the Indian style and attempts were made to simulate Indian costumes. Boston, "home of the bean and the cod," could be frivolous when it tried.

IV

By the beginning of 1811 William Emerson knew that his strength was failing rapidly, and he began to withdraw from as many obligations as he could. He resigned from the *Monthly Anthology* editorial board, thus hastening the demise of that publication the following June. He had to stop work on the history of the First Church, though some members of his parish used his manuscript for a *Sketch* which they published the following December. Previously he had published a *Selection of Psalms and Hymns,* the culmination of years of study and collecting.[30]

In February Mr. Emerson was so weary that he could only feebly rejoice over the birth of a "fat, black-eyed" daughter, who was named Mary Caroline and was destined to live only three years. Although his salary had nearly doubled since he had accepted the "call" to the First Church for fourteen dollars a week, plus rent and a supply of firewood, he had not been able to save anything, and he now worried about how his wife, with five boys and an infant daughter to care for, could manage without him. His physician advised him to take a vacation in Maine, and he left Boston on April 15 in a sloop bound for Portland.

Next day Mr. Emerson wrote his wife: "We had a tolerable day yesterday on board, though the air was rather too sharp to be on deck, where we were obliged to keep in consequence of a cabin crowded with bunks, kettles, fish, women, and crying children. When good Dr. Desher planned for me this voyage, he did not see the interior of Capt. Blanchard's sloop."

The sick man tried bravely to be cheerful, but he seemed to anticipate the inevitable, and, in fact, he never saw his family again. A few days before his death he wrote his sister Mary, who had come to Boston at his urging to stay with his wife:

> To my wife and children, indeed, my continuance upon earth is a matter of moment; as, in the event of my decease, God only knows how they would subsist. And then the education of the latter! But I am not oppressed with this solicitude. Our family, you know, have so long been in the habit of trusting Providence, that none of them ever seriously thought of providing a terrestrial maintenance for themselves and households.[31]

Death came to William Emerson in Portland on May 12, 1811. The doctors did not think that the hemorrhage of the lungs he had suffered three years before was related to his death at the age of forty-two. His body was returned to Boston for burial. At the end of the funeral sermon in the First Church, the Artillery Company of Boston led the procession to King's Chapel cemetery. Behind the uniformed artillerymen the hearse rumbled on the cobblestones, followed by the two oldest sons, William and Ralph, on foot; behind them slowly rolled more than fifty coaches of mourners. Ralph's most vivid recollection of his father's funeral was the dignity of this solemn parade through the streets to King's Chapel.[32]

The First Church was deeply sympathetic to Mrs. Emerson's plight, and the officials voted to pay her husband's salary of twenty-five dollars a week for a year and permit her to continue living in the parsonage during that time.[33] Actually, use of the house was extended beyond the year and an annual stipend of five hundred dollars was granted the widow for seven years. By that time some church members had begun to make anonymous donations. To raise money quickly, she sold her husband's library at auction. It contained Latin classics, good editions of the standard eighteenth-century authors, theological works of course, and some volumes of *The Spectator* and *The Tatler*. As a consequence Mrs. Emerson was not in immediate need, but she was deeply worried about becoming dependent upon the charity of her friends and relatives. It was the children, however, who suffered the greatest psychological shock at the loss of the stabilizing authority of their father, even if at times it had been painful. Fortunately, Mrs. Emerson's sister-in-law, Mary Moody Emerson, was willing for the present to stay with her to help with the "fatherless children," as Mrs. Emerson called them in her letters to her Maine relatives.[34] This Aunt Mary, though an erratic and often vexing companion to his mother, would become one of the strongest influences in the early life of Ralph Waldo Emerson.

CHAPTER II

The Hoop That Holds

> What is the hoop that holds them stanch? It is
> the iron band of poverty, of necessity, of auster-
> ity, which, . . . has directed their activity in safe
> and right channels . . . [1]

I

The Reverend William Emerson's eccentric sister Mary was staying at the parsonage at the time of his death, and she remained after the funeral for several months to help Ruth Emerson care for her six children: William, ten years old; Ralph, eight; Edward, six; Bulkeley, four; Charles, three; and Mary Caroline, three months old. Miss Emerson was thirty-seven, had some years before rejected her only offer of marriage, and now devoted her life to writing a spiritual diary, which she called her "Almanack," to reading such books on philosophy as she could borrow, and to visiting her relatives between bouts of quarreling with them. She had been a frequent guest in her brother's parsonage and was deeply attached to her nephews.

Mary Moody Emerson had an agile brain, a volatile character, and a very sharp tongue. In spite of her prickly personality, Ralph would always feel deeply grateful to her for instruction and encouragement during his youth. After her death in 1863, he wrote an affectionate memoir in which he tried to balance her faults against her intellectual and moral virtues:

> She had the misfortune of spinning with a greater velocity than any of
> the other tops. She would tear into the chaise or out of it, into the house
> or out of it, into the conversation, into the thought, into the character of
> the stranger,—disdaining all the gradation by which her fellows time their
> steps: and though she might do very happily in a planet where others

moved with the like velocity, she was offended here by the phlegm of all her fellow creatures, and disgusted them by her impatience. She could keep step with no human being.[2]

Miss Emerson also had a low center of gravity, for she was only three inches over four feet in height, which made it easier for her to gyrate. Also she was propelled by an overcharged ego, which had been building up resentment since her unhappy childhood. Perhaps, too, her disposition was partly inherited from her great-grandfather, the Reverend Samuel Moody, known as "Father Moody," a man of great physical vigor and moral determination. He kept as close watch as the early Puritan ministers over his parishioners. Sometimes his public criticism of them was so pointed that a member of his congregation would get up and leave the church, only to have Father Moody yell at him in an awesome voice, "Come back, you graceless sinner, come back!"[3] On Saturday nights he paid particular attention to the weaker brethren who could not resist the alehouse. He simply went in, dragged them out bodily, and sent them home with stern commands to reform. And he was equally fanatical in his personal charity, always willing to give away his last cent or his only coat—and on one occasion his wife's shoes!—to the needy.

Mary Moody Emerson was the fourth child of the Reverend William Emerson (Ralph's grandfather) and Phebe Bliss of Concord.[4] She was born on August 17, 1774, in the "Old Manse" (as Hawthorne would later call the house[5]), scarcely two hundred yards from the bridge where the historic battle took place the following year. She liked to say that she was "a babe in arms" at the Battle of Concord. Two years after her birth her father obtained permission from his church in Concord to join the American forces at Fort Ticonderoga, but delayed his departure until his wife was delivered of her fifth child (Rebecca). Then he carried two-year-old Mary, whom he called "Polly," to his mother in Malden to keep until his return from the war. But he did not return, for in less than a month he contracted "camp fever" (probably typhoid), and died in Rutland, Vermont, while desperately attempting to reach home. Three years later Polly's grandmother died, and she was taken by her Aunt Ruth (her father's sister) and Uncle Nathan Sargent in Malden.

Both Sargents were warmhearted, and they adopted Mary, having no children of their own, but the aunt was impractical, quick-tempered, and argumentative, and the uncle was constantly in debt. Polly could never forget the days when the whole family went hungry, or the times she was set to watch for the sheriff that her aunt might have warning in time to hide the silver. At a district school she obtained a smattering of education, but never learned to spell very well, though she became an omnivorous reader. At seventeen she experienced brief happiness with her oldest sister, Hannah, who had married William Farnham, a bookseller in Newburyport, Massachusetts. There she met a better class of people and had plenty of books to read. But in a few months Mr. Farnham died, and she was forced to return to Concord to live with her mother, who had married her first husband's successor in the Concord church, the Reverend Ezra Ripley. He had given Polly's mother a second brood of children. Here the peripatetic daughter helped care for her stepbrothers and -sisters and tried to prepare herself to become a governess. She lived in the Old Manse from 1793 to 1801, but the long separation from her mother had created uncongeniality, and Dr. Ripley did not sympathize with her philosophical interests. In 1801 Polly's Aunt Ruth remarried, her first husband having died. The second husband was Samuel Waite, a retired tanner in Malden. Polly returned to Ruth, and it was from Malden that her brother summoned her to Boston during his final illness.

II

Although William Emerson loved his sister Mary with all her faults, as he wrote her in 1806, she was nevertheless a constant irritant to him. The faults, he wrote, "I do not love, and will not tolerate as long as there is any hope of your forsaking them. One of them is an obscure style of writing, consisting of bloated figures, far-fetched allusions, and turgid words."[6] He also complained of her "illegible chirography" and "bad orthography." He begged her, "Recollect that your brother grows old . . . he delights in plain words, just thought, simple expressions, and right spelling." She had accused him, with her usual sarcasm, of indifference to her, and he resented both the charge and her language. She had also complained of her physical afflictions. "I grieve for your corporeal infirmity," he replied, but "You are not alone in affliction. Our little Ralph, whilst I have been playing bagatelle with you, lies seriously ill." This news doubtless made a deeper impression than his criticism of her "faults" and assurances of his love. The cause of Ralph's illness was not stated, but he was never a robust child and was often ill.

William Emerson and his sister were also at odds over theology. As a liberal Congregationalist drifting with the rising tide of Unitarianism, he rejected the Calvinistic doctrine of election and grace bestowed arbitrarily by a capricious God, angry with the human race because of the sin of Adam. He did believe that human nature was weak, but thought that by "good works" man could ensure his own salvation—with God's help, of course. Like other Unitarians he had to make a special effort to retain belief in the "atonement" and the divinity of Christ, but he did so by regarding Christ as the source of God's revelation to men, who by his example inspired men to live in harmony with God and each other. In the words of the historian of Unitarianism Conrad Wright, summarizing William Emerson's theology, Christ's "life of spotless purity counted most; his death became only a dramatic incident of perfect obedience."[7]

To Mary Moody Emerson such doctrines were wishy-washy, if not outright heretical. She professed contempt for Calvinism, but her concept of Deity was strongly Calvinistic, especially on the absolute sovereignty of God, whose anger human beings could assuage only by the most abject submission of will and by constant vigilance over their conduct. Her brother accused her of gross egotism, which her conduct certainly did exhibit in fantastic aberrations of decorum and lack of consideration for the feelings of others; yet she tried to overcome her pride and conceit by punishing her body. By asceticism, fasts, frequent prayers, and numerous self-denials she attempted to purify her mind and soul. At times the self-denial was so abnormal that it was masochistic—perhaps the real secret of her notorious eccentricities. A few extracts from her diary will show the extremes to which her religious devotion carried her, and the Calvinism from which she could never free her mind:

June, [*1806?*]: Such is the law of my constitution that there is something of necessity in my errors, when I am social. Therefore it seems my wisdom to avoid relaxation however stupid my life. Let me be but innocent and let others shine & inspire.[8]

In 1807 she was frequently contrite and penitent because she had lost her temper, descended to levity, or succumbed to "human influence" (as opposed to divine). For example:

March 12, 1807: Noon, What a day—so sacred, penitent for my past tri-fling. I swear in the name of Him who is my Mediator to renounce every pleasure & connection which wd. interrupt my communion—marr the grandeur of my prospects—and defile the purity of the Xian light. . . .

On the death of her sister Hannah:

[*March*] *16*, [*1807*]: How delightful is it to depart—to be where we be-hold the divine gov't more clearly. I envy almost her pain & distress—they are the corrections of God in wh. He embraces his chosen! . . . Merciful God. What is the death of a sister or all the friends I have, compared to offending Thee, to possessing a principle of disobedience—of—unlove— of presumption [*sic*]—all my cares of worldly interests vanish. Merciful God, where art thou when I am greedy of social life—afflict me, crush me, into the lowest cavern of the earth but preserve me from defiling my spirit.

Today Miss Emerson's asceticism seems pathological:

[*April?*] *15*, [*1807?*]: . . . in walking today I sinned by worldly tho'ts. Night. It is an awful symptom if we cannot in the presence of God prom-ise to renounce every indulgence of eating, sleep, dress, recreation, reading, study & friendship which appears *suspicious!* Oh, what awful hazards attend us ere we enter on *our rest.* . . .

[*April?*] *20*, [*1807?*]: . . . In retrospecting I find the cause of my backslid-ing to have been oftener from a relaxed state of the mind—a wish to amuse enliven or instruct has led me to social intercourse. . . .

Nov. 13, [*1812*]: Oh I hate to eat, for I perform nothing suffer nor enjoy nor feel nothing for piety truth sympathy. Yet it is mean to grudge myself the food w'h God prepares—for it is He who supports Angels. But I am all animal—all eat & sleep.

Dec. 2, [*1812*]: Why sd I grudge my board & clothes & sleep—The cer-tainty of death is a charter from every fear—*live* while we live—tomorrow we may be forever free from the grossness of a putrid carcase. . . .

What kind of influence would this frustrated anchorite, hating her "ani-mal" body and fantasizing death, have on the childhood of Ralph Emer-son? It would seem natural for him to be repulsed by her harshness and unpredictable moods, but apparently he was not, for he would always remember her with pleasure and smile at her outrageous acts, such as making a shroud to remind her of her mortality, and then wearing it for economy. Evidently another contradiction in her anomalous character was that she was capable of the most tender affection for her nephews. To the adult world she showed one side of her personality, and to children, another. Of course the children must be obedient, industrious, and show the proper reverence for God, but they need not do constant penance for their sins.

In spite of her idealization of humility, Aunt Mary believed that her nephews were "born to be educated" that they might become distinguished, though at the same time she jeered at a "frivolous desire for fame." Secretly she longed for them to become famous, and for that reason encouraged and prodded them to exert their abilities to the last ounce of their strength. Everything with her was extreme. Yet, that she did not warp Ralph's mind to her Calvinistic bias is quite evident from his later independence in creating his own religion—which in a climactic stage would alienate his Aunt Mary. Nevertheless, the subtle influences of his aunt would be reflected in his obsession for purity of motive ("disinterested love," he would call it), for privacy, for utmost freedom and self-reliance, for a tendency to idealize poverty and to exalt spirit over body.

For all his devotion to his Aunt Mary, Ralph would be the one nephew to hold back from pushing himself beyond his strength. His brothers would do that and shorten their lives. But he had a self-protecting frivolous streak in his character, what his father had called "levity" and he himself would later call "silliness." It was a kind of gift for humor, an ability to look at himself from the point of view of a detached bystander, to see his shortcomings not with the tragic regret of his Aunt Mary but as the comic failures of a limited person. This faculty insulated him against the most injurious influences of his God-obsessed aunt, while enabling him, in the metaphor of Samson's riddle, to gather honey out of the bitterness.

III

In 1811 Ralph was still attending a private elementary school on Summer Street. Little is known about these years, except that one of his teachers was Lawson Lyon, "a severe teacher, whose ruler and cowhide did active service," one of Ralph's classmates, Samuel Bradford, recalled half a century later. Whether Ralph ever felt the sting of the ruler or cowhide is not known; though perhaps not, for he never recalled these school days with bitterness.

At the beginning of 1812 Mrs. Emerson wrote her sister in Maine that she did not think her sister-in-law's "place could be supplied to these *fatherless children* by any one on earth. . . . & I hope she will not ever leave me except for a visit or a *good Husband,* while she lives."⁹ Yet within two or three months Aunt Mary had quarreled with Ralph's mother and departed for Concord. On the first anniversary of her brother's death she wrote her sister-in-law a letter which intimates one cause of the friction, and at the same time gives further insights into the character of Mary Moody Emerson—and, perhaps indirectly, that of Ruth Emerson. It was a long letter, as hers usually were, but its substance was that in spite of her brother's eagerness to make others happy, she could not help remembering his "defects," which she thought were the result of his defective view of the Gospels:

> Oh how differently would that ardent mind have left the world, had it viewed sin and human depravity as the Gospel, I think, represents them . . . The recollection of his last years and last days will always be gloomy, tho' I believe his piety and his endeavours to serve the interest of virtue, as far as they were disinterested, found acceptance, and that he is now sharing that salvation of which we know so darkly in this world. I make these remarks *because I love you,* and think the nearer the example is brought, the better. Your very great responsibility often fills my mind. Oh Ruthy, may you have grace to leave nothing undone to forming these children *to faith in a Redeemer, to humility and honesty* and disinterestedness.¹⁰

Except for the criticism of her husband, Mrs. Emerson probably agreed with the tenor of these pious assertions, but Miss Emerson did not spare her, either:

> Oh lay aside every anxiety for yourself and children to appear genteel; and while you exert every nerve to save the children from abject dependence on the world, you will at the same time enable them to bestow enough to keep the habit, or to implant the holy lessons of charity. Caroline—oh Ruthy, if her temper is not subdued, how great is your responsibility! I shall have no part in it any more.

Thus, in addition to other frictions, it seems likely that Aunt Mary and Ruth Emerson disagreed to the point of separation over Caroline's temper. When one remembers that the baby girl was only fourteen months old in May 1812, and would live only two more years (though of course not even "Cassandra" Mary Emerson could know that), the stern command to subdue her temper at all costs seems nothing short of monstrous. Whether or not Caroline was already suffering from some malady or dysfunction, she certainly could not have been a strong infant, and she probably cried a great deal because she was unwell. Furthermore, by what humane means could the mother *subdue the temper* of so young a child? Mrs. Emerson, in spite of her austere belief in discipline, had the instincts of a mother, which her maiden sister-in-law did not.

This letter also reveals another cause of friction between the two women. The widow is exhorted to stop trying to be "genteel," meaning, presumably, trying to keep up appearances in the social world of her late husband. In another passage of the letter, Miss Emerson confessed: "I have sometimes amused myself with the hope that Providence would put you in a place of independence and give you an earthly protector; but I have repented of this levity." In plainer language, Ruth Emerson, forty-three at the time of her husband's death, might still have a chance to remarry—ministers' widows often did—but it would be better for her soul if she lived in poverty and painfully struggled to provide a home for her six children by her own efforts. Actually, that struggle had already become very difficult, and worse would follow.

IV

The childhood world of Ralph Emerson was changing with disturbing rapidity. After vacationing in the summer of 1812 with his grandparents in Concord, he entered the Boston Public Latin School. Both the Latin School and the other grammar schools were publicly supported, but the main object of the Latin School was to prepare boys for college. (Girls did not attend college and were not permitted to enroll in the Latin School.) In 1812–13 the Latin School was in a state of turmoil for two reasons: the old brick building near the parsonage was being torn down, and the school was temporarily housed in a succession of inappropriate places; but even more upsetting was the conduct of the master, William Bigelow, who drank and beat the boys for minor offenses, or fancied ones. Finally a student rebellion in 1814 caused the school board to discharge Mr. Bigelow and to employ Benjamin Apthorp Gould, who promptly restored the school's reputation for excellence.

The major subjects in the Latin School curriculum were Latin and Greek, but a few of the boys supplemented these studies with more elementary instruction elsewhere. From eleven to twelve o'clock every day, Ralph took lessons in writing and arithmetic from Rufus Webb, master of a nearby public grammar school. Years later Emerson remembered having shirked Mr. Webb's instruction by spending his noon hour on the Common, "and being punished for it by imprisonment [at home] on bread and water."[11] He did learn, however, to write a fair hand, and as much arithmetic as he would need in everyday life, though he would never like mathematics.

The outdoors was far more interesting to Ralph than the schoolroom, and this preference for nature over books would later be evidenced in his writings, in his romantic attachment to nature, and more specifically in a great curiosity about all branches of science. The ocean was only a short distance from Summer Street, and one of the temporary homes of the Latin School was near the harbor. Ralph especially enjoyed collecting pebbles and shells cast up by the waves or discarded by the ships as ballast no longer needed. One day he found a piece of gypsum and discovered that it made sparks when stroked in the dark. He learned how to magnetize the blade of his knife so that it would pick up needles and small metal objects, and he was fascinated by this strange invisible power. Science was not yet taught in schools, though Mr. Gould did make geography interesting by playing a game in which a student would name a country and he would tell what important historical events had taken place there.

In the spring of 1813 Aunt Mary was with her relatives in Maine, where she had taken the youngest Emerson boy, Charles, her favorite—though Ralph was next in her affections. For some time Ralph had been corresponding with her, and on April 16 he tried to answer a question she had asked him in her recent letter about his daily routine. As an example he chose Friday, April 9. On that day he rose at five minutes before six, helped William kindle a fire, and set the table for breakfast. At a quarter after six he called his mother. After family prayers and a spelling competition among the brothers, they breakfasted at seven. From then until eight Ralph could play or read; then off he went to Latin School, where he was studying Vergil. From eleven o'clock until one, he attended the nearby private school mentioned above. Between one and two o'clock he went home, ate "dinner," and returned to the Latin School until late afternoon:

> after I come home I do mama her little errands if she has any then I bring in my wood to supply the break-fast room. I then have some time to play & eat my supper after that we say our hymns or chapters, & then take our turns in reading Rollin as we did before you went. We retire to bed at different times I go at a little after 8 & retire to my private devotions & then close my eyes in sleep & there ends the toils of the day.... R. Waldo Emerson.[12]

It was not until he reached college that the boy insisted on being called Waldo instead of Ralph, but this signature shows that he already preferred his middle name.

V

Early in 1814 Aunt Mary finally yielded to her sister-in-law's pleas for help and returned to Boston, temporarily interrupting Ralph's correspondence with her. But meanwhile Ralph had begun exchanging letters with the most learned woman of the period, Sarah Alden Bradford, later the wife of his half uncle, Samuel Ripley. Miss Bradford was at that time (though not in later years) a friend of Aunt Mary's, and Miss Emerson had probably called her attention to Ralph's precocious facility in rhyme. Miss Bradford had taught herself Latin, Greek, mathematics, botany, and "natural philosophy" (science) to the extent of books in the field available to her. Although her phenomenal reputation for scholarship was still some years in the future, it had already begun to grow; reason enough for Aunt Mary to cultivate her acquaintance. As an indication of the dimension of her mature fame, Moncure Conway reported that at Harvard he had heard the legend that Professor Asa Gray, the leading botanist in America, had called on Mrs. Sarah Bradford Ripley "and found her instructing a student in differential calculus, correcting the Greek translation of another, and at the same time shelling peas and rocking her grandchild's cradle with her foot."[13] (She was then living in Concord at the Old Manse, where she coached students who had been "rusticated," or temporarily suspended, from Harvard College.)

In one of his letters to Miss Bradford, Ralph enclosed his rhymed translation of the first eighteen lines of Vergil's *Fifth Eclogue*. She wrote him to "continue this versification," and suggested that he write her in Latin and Greek. On May 6, 1814, he replied that he was unable to write her in these languages, but would continue sending her verses in English. His rendering of lines 19 through 36 of the *Fifth Eclogue* ended with these verses:

> As vines themselves in grapes their beauty find,
> As the fair Bull of all the lowing kind,
> As standing corn does grace the verdant fields
> So to thy beauty every rival yeilds [*sic*];
> Since from our arms by fate thou hast been took
> Phoebus and Pales have our fields forsook.[14]

Both at home and at school Ralph was encouraged to continue his rhyming exercises. To think that he was a poet gave him his first pride in authorship and the confidence which he needed when he had no other distinction, for he was not good at games, and only passably satisfactory in his studies. He admired eloquence in the pulpit, but at this time showed only moderate ability in the declamation competition which Mr. Gould encouraged in his school.

In the early nineteenth century nearly every newspaper contained an "elegy," as piously and conventionally worded as the inscription on a tombstone. Of course Ralph tried his hand at these, too. His family especially admired the one he composed for his grandfather, John Haskins, who died on October 27, 1814:

> While round him gathered, all his children stand
> And some one holds his withered, pallid hand,
> He bids them trust in God, nor mourn, nor weep;
> He breathes religion, and then falls asleep.
> Then on angelic wings he soars to God,
> Rejoiced to leave his earthly, mortal load;
> His head is covered with a crown of gold,
> His hands, renewed, a harp immortal hold;
> Thus clothed with light, the tuneful spirit sings—
> He sings of mercy and of Heavenly things.[15]

John Haskins was a religious man, and of course his grandson did not have the least doubt that he had joined the angels. But this elegy gave no indication of the unusual man that John Haskins was. He had run away from home at sixteen to become a privateer during the hostilities among England, France, and Spain, when piracy against the enemy was patriotic. He was twice taken prisoner, once by a Spanish ship and once by a French vessel, and was rescued by an American one. After returning home he settled down in the distilling industry of his father and became a prosperous Bostonian.[16] Of course if his grandson had known this personal history he would not have been capable of using it in a literary way. When his three-year-old sister, Mary Caroline, died in the same year, Ralph did not write an elegy for her, though two years later he referred to her death in an elegy for a schoolmate's sister:

> Ne'er since my own loved sister met her doom,
> Has such a pang assailed my bleeding heart
> As when your sister felt the fatal dart.[17]

VI

Eleven-year-old Ralph Emerson must have felt at times in 1814 that his world was coming apart. He was now old enough to feel real grief over the death of his only sister and his Grandfather Haskins. His home life was also disturbed by his mother's having to give up the parsonage and take temporary refuge on Rainsford Lane with his Grandmother Haskins, uncles, aunts, and cousins. Later Mrs. Emerson rented a house on Bennet Street, intending to take in boarders, but that plan failed. On top of everything else, in the autumn an earthquake shook the town. It did no serious damage, but that an earthquake could shake the granite foundation of New England upset the boy's confidence in the permanence of his world. Moreover, it came on top of the fear of an invasion by Great Britain which had worried grown-up Bostonians for several months.

Up to this time the War of 1812, as the history books would later call it, had meant little to Ralph except remote battles, such as Oliver Hazard Perry's victory on Lake Erie and the two victories of the country's most famous battleship, the *Constitution,* against the *Guerrière* and the *Java* in 1812, which the young poet had celebrated in attempts at heroic poems.[18]

But now frightening talk about the British taking Boston made the war seem less remote. For several months everyone had been complaining about the high prices and the scarcity of sugar, coffee, tea, and cotton goods in the stores, a very tangible effect of the war.

The Embargo Act had brought New England shipping to a standstill, and the only commodities being imported were those smuggled in by the ships lucky enough to run the blockade. Knowledgeable people said President Madison was trying to crush the Federalist party in New England, and Boston's opposition to the United States government was almost as strong as its fear of the British Navy. Yet no one doubted that New Englanders would fight if necessary to repel a foreign invasion, and as this possibility grew, they began to make hasty preparations. Artillery and light infantry poured into Boston from surrounding towns, and local officials put many citizens to work on harbor defenses.

One summer day Mr. Gould took his Latin School students on a ferryboat to Noddle Island in the harbor to fill sandbags to be used in constructing barricades.[19] Looking back on this outing many years later, Emerson laughed at it, and remembered only the difficulty of obtaining drinking water to slake the boys' inordinate thirst. But in August 1814, after the British bombarded Washington, burned the White House, and captured the navy yard, no one thought the threat to Boston a joke.

Worst of all for the Emerson family were the scarcity of food and the high prices, at a time when Mrs. Emerson's income had already declined alarmingly. It was a serious matter when the price of flour went to seventeen dollars a barrel. But everything was outrageously dear—or unobtainable at any price. On September 20, 1814, Aunt Mary wrote her Maine relatives that "People of good judgment, at the head of society, think an invasion of this Town probable." She blamed the "affliction and humiliating war"[20] on the "apostasy" of her fellowmen—that is, as God's punishment for their wickedness. "We did not think of moving till last week," though friends had been advising it for some time. But now, "when we consider the price of wood & provisions which will be the consequence of the troops quart[er]ed already here it seems the best thing to go into the Country."

Grandfather Ripley (Aunt Mary's stepfather) had offered sanctuary in the Old Manse in Concord, but the small rooms of that old clapboard house would be uncomfortably crowded with the addition of the Emerson boys. Aunt Mary herself had "been desirous to try some new plan of life"—probably returning to the Maine relatives—"but Ruthy will not consent to our separation at this time. . . . I sd like to describe the garrison like appearance of this Town, the incessant echo of martial music, no day or night excepted, but I have no time on this paper, nor inclination."

Fortunately, Bulkeley was still in Maine, and William would enter college if his mother could make the financial arrangements. With the help of a scholarship fund from the First Church, the promise of board for waiting on table, and donations by friends and relatives, William was able to matriculate at Harvard in September. His aunt and mother, however, could not leave Boston until November. The three boys may have been sent to Concord earlier to enroll in school, though more likely they all took the stagecoach together sometime before Thanksgiving.

VII

Concord was only twenty miles from Boston, but the road was not very good and the trip took three hours by stagecoach. Going to Concord was not a new experience for Ralph, because he and his brothers always spent at least part of every summer in the Manse beside the famous battlefield and the slow-flowing Concord River, which ran, or sauntered, past the orchard back of the house. His father had lived here as a child during the American Revolution, in the house *his* father had built.

In fact, Concord had been founded by Ralph's ancestors, beginning with the Reverend Peter Bulkeley (1583–1659).[21] In 1635 he and Simon Willard obtained from the General Court of Massachusetts Bay Colony a grant of six square miles at Musketaquid, an Indian name meaning "river with grassy banks." The Indians of the region were peaceful, making this spot seem like a place of concord after the persecutions Bulkeley and Willard had known in England. Peter Bulkeley was a graduate of St. John's College at Cambridge University, and had succeeded his father as minister of the parish church in Odell, in Bedfordshire. But he regarded some of the ceremonies of the Established Church of England as superstitions, and had refused to use them in his church service. As a consequence Bishop Laud in 1634, in the reign of Charles I, suspended him.

Although the Reverend Peter Bulkeley had inherited considerable wealth and ranked with the landed gentry, he decided to emigrate to Massachusetts. Somehow he managed to liquidate his property and to take six thousand pounds with him, making him the wealthiest individual among the twelve families who first settled in Concord. His house was the first one built after the Meeting House was started. The church was organized on Congregational principles, like the one in Salem, and the members chose for their first pastors Peter Bulkeley and John Jones, another Cambridge graduate.

Several years later a doctrinal dispute in the church split the congregation, and Reverend Jones took about a seventh of the population of Concord (not all were church members) with him to Fairfield, Connecticut, leaving the Concord church entirely to Reverend Bulkeley and his followers. Edward Bulkeley succeeded his father as pastor. In the eighteenth century William Emerson, Ralph Emerson's grandfather, became pastor of this ancient church, over which Dr. Ezra Ripley now presided.

Ralph had heard some of this history from his Aunt Mary, who took great pride in her ancestors, and now he would live during the winter of 1814–15 in the house his grandfather had built near the North Bridge in about 1769. Ralph's grandfather had come to Concord in 1764 to succeed the Reverend Daniel Bliss, recently deceased. The new minister boarded with the widow of his predecessor, fell in love with her oldest daughter, Phebe, and married her the following year. Four years later he built the Manse beside the river for his "Phebe bird."

Grandfather Emerson (Aunt Mary's father) had played a very active role in the events that led up to the fighting at Concord and Lexington.[22] Possibly his grandson did not learn the full details until he began preparing his bicentennial address for 1835, but some of them he had certainly heard in childhood: how on April 19, 1775, his grandfather had wanted to stand with the minutemen guarding the bridge against the British troops who had come to destroy the military supplies concealed in Concord; how the officers had ordered him, a clergyman and noncombatant, to stay in the Manse with his frightened wife and four small children; and how his grandfather had watched from an upstairs window, rifle in hand, and seen the redcoats fire the first shot, killing two minutemen, and the return fire which killed two British soldiers and wounded four officers.

During the ensuing "Siege of Boston" the Reverend William Emerson tirelessly agitated in neighboring towns to stir up support for the Sons of Liberty, and at Cambridge visited the Continental Army being recruited by George Washington. The college buildings were used to house the troops, and Harvard classes were moved for a year to Concord. Then in August this patriotic minister had ridden off to Fort Ticonderoga to become chaplain to the northern division of the troops, under the command of General Gates. But, as already noted, he contracted a fever and died in Rutland while trying to return home.

After the loss of its pastor the Concord church invited various young ministers to preach on trial. One of these was Ezra Ripley, who had graduated from Harvard in 1776, when the college was in Concord. Members of the church had undoubtedly become acquainted with him during that year; they had liked him, and he was ordained as pastor of the church in 1778. Two years later he married the late minister's widow, Phebe Bliss Emerson. She was thirty-nine, with five children (though Mary, as mentioned earlier, was living with her Grandmother Emerson), and he was twenty-nine. Thus, Ezra Ripley was Ralph Emerson's step-grandfather. He was a small, lean, energetic man, with positive opinions and formal manners. He habitually wore a frock coat and a black stovepipe hat, and usually carried an umbrella tightly rolled. Having grown up on a farm, he took pleasure in cultivating the twenty-odd acres inherited by the widow Emerson, and did much of the work himself.

Reverend Ripley was an emotional preacher who took a personal interest in every member of his congregation—indeed, in every resident of the town. He was not a scholar, not even much of a reader. He divided his time and energies between his farm and parish duties, and was always ready to talk to anyone. When the fire alarm sounded, he grabbed his own pair of leather buckets and ran with the other volunteers to the fire. He faithfully attended town meetings, in which all municipal decisions were made, and spoke his mind.

During the autumn and winter of 1814–15 Dr. Ripley drove Ralph around town in his chaise, told him who lived in every house they passed, and often the history of the family.[23] In church he prayed for rain when it was needed, or returning health for any ailing parishioner. The ancient Meeting House was unpainted, uncarpeted, and unheated in the winter. Gray-haired deacons sat with austere dignity in a little box under the pulpit. The prayers were long, and the sermons longer. Dr. Ripley spoke as if the universe existed for the special benefit of his church and its members, and this was not far from his unshakable belief. In later years Emerson remembered assisting his step-grandfather in the hayfield as a storm approached. "We are in the Lord's hand," he exclaimed, and seemed to say to God, "You know me; this field is mine,—Dr. Ripley's—thine own servant."[24]

On Monday, February 13, 1815, news was received in Boston that England had signed a peace treaty with the United States. Within a few hours the welcome tidings had reached Concord, and a week and a half later Ralph wrote his freshman brother at Harvard how it had affected the town: "a smile was on every face, and joy in every heart."[25] A few days later the Court House steeple was illuminated and was plainly visible from the Manse. William tried to rise to the emotions expected of him in a letter to his mother: "Joy thrills through every vein, hope beats in every breast, pleasure beams in every countenance. Peace! O glorious, enraptured sound! The very thought sets the secret springs of every soul in motion."

To Mrs. Emerson peace meant the end of her exile from Boston. By the end of March, troops had left the city, and she and Aunt Mary could return, though her sons may have stayed a few weeks longer to finish the school term. Ralph, especially, liked attending school in Concord because his teacher praised him for his poetic compositions and frequently asked him to recite them in the classroom. On his last day in school he declaimed, by invitation, his "Valedictory Poem" to the assembled students and some townspeople. After saying farewell to his schoolmates and thanking his teacher, he apologized for Edward, "A Brother too by sickness long detain'd/ From study; at his loss is pain'd." Charles was greatly embarrassed to be included in the poem:

> Another brother small and younger too,
> New to the school and to its studies new,
> Has here received impressions of that kind,
> To banish all its dullness from the mind.[26]

The young poet, however, was more popular with adults than with his schoolmates, who may have resented his being the teacher's pet. His relations with them were tempestuous. One day his step-grandfather made him shake hands with two boys with whom he had quarreled, Elisha Jones and Frank Barrett. As Emerson later recalled the incident: "Dr. Ripley sent for them one evening to come to the house, and there made us shake hands: Aunt Mary asked me, 'Well, what did you say to them?' 'I did not say anything.'—'Fie on you! you should have talked about your thumb, or your toes, only to say something.' "

VIII

Mrs. Emerson's pleasure in returning to Boston soon gave way to the old worries about money. Her family on Rainsford Lane were willing to take her in if she would become their housekeeper, and she did try this arrangement for several months, but found it unsatisfactory. In early autumn a Boston merchant, Daniel P. Parker, offered her his furnished house, rent-free, while he made a trip to London.[27] She could take in boarders, and that income would help her feed and clothe her family. Beacon Hill was an excellent neighborhood, and she had several distinguished boarders, including Lemuel Shaw, later chief justice of Massachusetts (and the father-in-law of Herman Melville, not yet born). Dr. Ripley had tried to help by lending a "fresh" cow, which Ralph drove round the Common to a pasture on Carver Street.[28]

For several reasons Ralph was glad to be back in Boston. One was that Miss Sarah Alden Bradford took him to riding school when she went riding. Another was that it was easier to procure books in the city, either from the Library Society (the Athenaeum), in which his father's membership had been kept up, or from generous friends. He read Johnson's *Lives of the Poets* for the first time, and became curious about Abraham Cowley and John Donne, poets who had violated the neoclassical principles of versification and diction. Not yet having read Cowley or Donne, Ralph took Dr. Johnson's point of view and thought he disliked "Cowley for his uneven measure or rather no measure at all."[29] Johnson said he invaded the "rights of antiquity." Later, of course, Emerson himself would be strongly influenced by the seventeenth-century English poets, and their "uneven measure" would help to liberate him from the stereotyped heroic couplets he was still writing at this time.

In the autumn Ralph and Edward both attended the Latin School, and Edward quickly rose to first place in his class. Three days a week they attended Miss Sales's private school in French. Ralph liked the language and was soon reading stories in a French anthology. In January 1816, he began studying geography in the Latin School, and found it "almost a vacation" from Latin and Greek. But his "Lisping Muse" provided still better entertainment, and he continued to tease his serious-minded brother at Harvard with snatches of verse in his letters. William had commanded, "Ralph, don't make poetry till you have gone through Algebra."

In another January letter to William, Ralph quoted, almost as a warning, a couplet from a well-known poem by David Everett, "Lines Spoken at a School Exhibition, by a Little Boy of Seven Years Old":

> Don't view me with a critick's eye
> But pass my imperfections by.[30]

William approved, of course, of the interest Ralph took in the sermons he heard on Sunday, and liked to hear who had preached, what text he had used, and how it had been developed. Ministers were the Emerson boys' heroes, and the pulpit was their theater and arena of great deeds. William was more serious by nature than Ralph, and as the oldest son he felt greater responsibility for easing his mother's burdens, which that winter were the heaviest they had been. Ralph and Edward had only one overcoat between them, and on the coldest days only one could go to school. Other children observed this fact and teased them by asking whose turn it would be next day to wear the coat.[31] William helped the family by teaching in his Uncle Samuel Ripley's school at Waltham for four or five weeks at the end of the autumn term at Harvard.[32] At that time the college had a long winter vacation and permitted poor students to stretch it while they taught school.

After Mr. Parker's return from England, Mrs. Emerson gave up her boardinghouse on Beacon Street and moved at the end of September to another rented house on the same street,[33] and later to one on Hancock. Now, with rent to pay, the prospects were even darker. Bulkeley had come home from Maine. William had worked during the summer in a probate office, but even with his scholarship and what he could earn by waiting on tables at Harvard, he would still need some money. Furthermore, Mrs. Emerson had decided to send Edward to Andover Academy. Some of the Haskins relatives so highly approved of this plan that they may have helped out. Calvinism was still strong at Andover, and both Aunt Betsy

Haskins and Aunt Mary Emerson were pleased that at least one of the Emerson boys would be trained in the old faith.[34]

When Edward left for Andover on October 11, Ralph was recovering from bronchitis, and two days later Dr. John Warren told him that he "must have a blister on for ten days." In spite of the discomfort, this confinement at home gave him time to write long letters to Edward to allay his expected homesickness. In the first, dated October 15, he described the view from the basement window, for he supposed Edward "had no opportunity to take a minute survey" before he left—an indication that the family had just moved in.

> "The wide unbounded prospect lies before me"
> Imprimis then, a dirty yard
> By boards and dirt and rubbish marr'd
> Pil'd up aloft a mountain steep
> Of broken Chairs and beams a heap
> But rising higher you explore
> In this fair prospect wonders more
> Upon the right a wicket grate [gate?]
> The left appears a jail of State
> Before the view all boundless spreads
> And 5 tall Chimnies lift their lofty heads—[35]

James Elliot Cabot identifies the gate ("grate" was evidently a slip of the pen) as that of the Granary Burying Ground, and the jail as County Jail on Hancock Street,[36] which would place the house at the foot of Beacon Hill east of the Common, as shown on an 1814 map. Real-estate developers had decided in 1810 to cut down the top of the hill, on which a lighthouse beacon had stood for many years, and the work, which had started in 1811, was still uncompleted in 1816.[37] This would account for the mountain of rubbish in Ralph's rhymed description. No one could have enjoyed that dusty sight, but Aunt Mary found comfort, she said, in gazing out the window at the Burying Ground and longing to sleep there in peace.

Ralph was now writing a theme a week for Mr. Gould, and his last had been on astronomy.[38] The subject had come to him as he was crossing the Common one night and stopping to look up at the stars. Their immense distance made him feel small and light-headed. This may have been the emotional origin of that famous "mystical" passage in *Nature* in which the mature poet became a "transparent eye-ball." It was recalled in his Journal and finally elaborated in Emerson's first book, two decades after this childhood experience.[39]

During the winter of 1816–17 Ralph was beginning to have disturbing sensations in his dreams and daytime fantasies[40] which might be called, in the language of William James, "religious experiences."[41] They were probably brought on in part by his Aunt Mary's too-fervent teaching, and in part by his passing into adolescence. Many years later, in his Journal, Emerson would record the thought: "The age of puberty is a crisis in the life of the man worth studying. It is the passage from the Unconscious to the Conscious; from the sleep of the Passions to their rage."[42] In plainer language, he was becoming increasingly aware of sexual urges (wet dreams, temptations to masturbate, and waking sexual fantasies), which he had been taught, not only by Aunt Mary and his mother but by his whole society, to suppress at all cost. It was wicked even to dream of sex. The Puritans had insisted that a man who imagined carnal sin was already guilty of that sin, and Ralph was all too familiar with this doctrine. So, unable to keep erotic images out of his consciousness, he felt guilty, disturbed, even at times terrified. He concealed this anxiety, but secretly he turned, in the words of his later Journal entry on puberty, from "omnivorous curiosity to anxious stewardship." The turning from "faith to doubt," also mentioned in his Journal, would come later.

Politics did not interest Ralph very much, and he accepted without question the views of the Federalists who constituted Boston's respectable society. He was disappointed when James Monroe easily defeated Rufus King in 1816, but when the new President announced his intention of visiting Boston on July 2, 1817, the boy was as curious to see him as everyone else was.[43] Ralph stood for three hours on the Common with all the other schoolchildren of the city, waiting for the President to appear. The boys were dressed in blue coats and white breeches and wore an artificial red-and-blue rose in the left lapel. Most people thought it improper for girls to participate, but many from the public schools and a few from private schools also stood in line on the opposite side of the street.

Finally, guns at the fort boomed and the church bells began to ring. In a short time the white plume of the captain of the hussars came into sight, followed by his troops and the light horse cavalry. Artillery on the Common fired an eighteen-gun salute as the President, mounted on "an elegant horse which belonged to the Circus," rode up the Mall, followed by local dignitaries in carriages and chaises.

The Latin School had been given the place of honor, "and the President made his first bow to our school," Ralph wrote Edward, "who all took off hats and cheered. . . . He went through the Com[mon] to the Exchange [Coffee House] where after the addresses were delivered the company dined at *six*." But Ralph could not resist adding a partisan sour note: "People are not so pleased with J. Munroe [*sic*] as they expected." He did not say why.

Of more concern to the Emerson boys during the summer of 1817 was how Edward could return to Andover in the fall, how William could complete his senior year at Harvard, and how Ralph could enter Harvard—Mr. Gould said he was ready. Mrs. Emerson's boardinghouse was not flourishing, and she had had to dismiss her maid and her cook. In June, Ralph resigned himself to waiting another year before going to college. William decided to teach in his uncle's school in Waltham during September and October and then try to find a school of his own. He was employed to teach at a school at Kennebunk, Maine, probably obtaining the position with the assistance of relatives who lived there.[44]

In July, however, Ralph's prospects began to improve. The First Church assigned him the Penn legacy which William had held, and in August, during the exhibition preceding commencement, Mr. Gould told him that he had talked with President Kirkland and had obtained the appointment of "president's freshman" for him, which would pay his tuition and dormitory rent at Harvard. Perhaps he could also wait on table for his board. In addition to these arrangements, Uncle Samuel Ripley said Ralph could teach in his school during the winter vacation. And meanwhile Mrs. Emerson had found a more desirable house on Essex Street and the promise of four families to board with her. On September 1 she wrote Aunt Mary (still begging her to return) that the previous Thursday Ralph had walked to Cambridge to take the entrance examinations. On his return home on Saturday he was able to report that he had been admitted "without being admonished to study, (as was the case with many)." In other words, he was admitted without conditions.[45]

CHAPTER III

Two Educations at Harvard

... about 1825–35 students at Harvard College
and in the Divinity School were in actuality receiving two distinct and disparate educations;
one in the classroom ... and one in the dormitory.[1]

I

At fourteen Ralph Waldo Emerson was the youngest member of the Harvard class of 1821.[2] Tall, slender, and pale, this sandy-haired, blue-eyed boy
looked more precocious than he actually was. He had been well drilled in
Latin, had a smattering of Greek, and had read more widely than most of
his classmates, but he was so poor in mathematics that it is a wonder he
passed his entrance examination. Physically and emotionally he was an immature adolescent. His dignified manners and almost forbidding reserve
deceived strangers, but his brothers knew him for the dreamy, well-inten-
tioned, but rather frivolous boy he was. His older brother, William, was
only sixteen, but his awareness of his responsibilities had given him the
character and outlook of a grown man. Ralph teased him for being so serious and thought he had no sense of humor. Ralph's younger brother Edward was his favorite, a brilliant student, but at twelve he was not shocked
by Ralph's silly fancies and frivolous rhymes. William, Edward, and later
Charles competed for academic honors as if their lives depended upon
them, but Ralph lacked the competitive spirit, and for him sibling rivalry
was either so faint or so well concealed that it appears to have been almost
nonexistent.

Although William was a senior during Ralph's freshman year, he spent
very little time at Harvard. In the fall he taught a six-week term in his
Uncle Samuel Ripley's school at Waltham;[3] then he became master of his

own school in Kennebunk, Maine, during the winter and spring.[4] He returned to Cambridge in time to take his examinations and graduated with his class in August. Ralph appreciated William's sacrifices and admired his scholastic accomplishments, but he could not help snickering at William's extreme seriousness. On October 5, 1817, a few days before Ralph's classes began at Harvard, he wrote Edward at Andover: "I yesterday recieved [*sic*] a long letter from the Senior from Waltham and it is so humorous (though you stare at my saying *humorous* from his Deaconship) that I wish I could show it to you—"[5]

Ralph also teased Edward about studying in the stronghold of Calvinism. Aunt Betsy Haskins, he wrote, "is very much grieved she says that I go to *Cambridge* instead of *Providence* [Brown]—you guess the reason . . . I hope going to *Cambridge* will not prevent some future time my being as good a minister as if I came all *Andovered* from *Providence*[.]"[6] Though this statement leaves no doubt that Ralph expected to become a minister, like his father and numerous ancestors, he had as yet no sense of dedication; in fact, this assumption he docilely took for granted, knowing that it was expected of him by his mother and his Aunt Mary.

A theological revolution had taken place at Harvard a decade earlier, beginning in 1805 when a Unitarian, the Reverend Henry Ware, was elected to a senior professorship in divinity, and continuing the following year when the Corporation and the Board of Overseers chose the Reverend Samuel Webber for the presidency. In the words of Samuel Eliot Morison in *Three Centuries of Harvard,* Webber was a man "with liberal views verging on Unitarianism."[7] The rival candidate, Eliphalet Pearson (of course called by the students "the Elephant"), promptly founded Andover Theological Seminary, to the enthusiastic approval of rural New England. Until this break with Calvinistic orthodoxy, Harvard had been partly state-supported, but now the support was withdrawn and Harvard became a completely independent and private institution. To quote Morison again:

> On the positive side, the effect was far-reaching. Unitarianism of the Boston stamp was not a fixed dogma, but a point of view that was receptive, searching, inquiring, and yet devout; a half-way house to the rationalistic and scientific point of view, yet a house built so reverently that the academic wayfarer could seldom forget that he had sojourned in a House of God.[8]

Actually the Reverend Samuel Webber had few qualifications for the position to which he had been elected, but he died in 1810, and was succeeded by another Unitarian and Federalist, the Reverend John Thornton Kirkland, who became the most successful and popular president Harvard had ever had. He had grown up in poverty in the Berkshire Mountains and on the New York frontier, where his father was a missionary to the Oneida Indians. The Indians had called him "Fair Face," "and even as President," says Morison, "his countenance was that of a merry, rosy boy."[9] This was the charming gentleman, friend of the late William Emerson, who employed Ralph Emerson as his orderly, a position the students called "the president's freshman."[10]

Ralph's duties were to summon students to the president's office, keep a record of their leaving and returning to Cambridge, post notices, and run various errands, in exchange for a partial remission of college fees. President Kirkland lived in bachelor quarters on the second floor of Wadsworth House, and he assigned his freshman a room immediately beneath his study so that he could summon the boy by two taps of his heel on the floor. This arrangement considerably restricted his freshman's freedom of movement, but Ralph was glad to be able to earn part of his expenses. Harvard was the most expensive college in the country, the yearly minimum cost running to three hundred dollars, and wealthy students spent two or three times that sum.[11] Even with Ralph's petty office, a scholarship from his father's church, and gifts from friends of the family, there were always some debts for his mother to pay, such as the bills for his meals in the commons of University Hall before he was engaged to wait on table.

II

Harvard, founded in 1636, was the oldest college in the United States, and still retained some of its Colonial vestiges. The quadrangle formed by four brick and stone buildings occupied the original Yard, and until President Kirkland[12] began cleaning it up, it was untidy, with its ancient brewery, unconcealed privies in the southeast corner, the president's stable for his horses and cow, a large, smelly college pigpen, a vegetable garden, and unpaved paths connecting the buildings. For generations the students had annoyed the townspeople with their noise and pranks. Riots were not uncommon, and President Kirkland might have to rush out of his house in the middle of the night to quiet intoxicated students returning from Boston and yelling curses and insults at Cambridge citizens. Hazing was forbidden, but freshman-sophomore rivalry sometimes got out of control. The college had no organized games or athletic facilities as outlets for youthful energy, and it often spilled over in disorderly conduct, not infrequently at mealtimes. University Hall had four dining rooms with open oriel windows in the dividing walls. Students frequently threw balls of bread through these openings at each other, sometimes followed by anything else handy.

Life in the dormitories was both primitive and rowdy.[13] The rooms were heated by fireplaces, for which the students had to provide their own wood. A pump in the Yard was the only source of water. Wealthier students employed a servant to carry water, tend the fire, dispose of ashes, and keep their lamps filled with whale oil. But both rich and poor were often doused with buckets of water thrown from stair landings or poured on their heads from open windows. The windowpanes were frequently broken at night by stones thrown from the Yard.[14] Both the Yard and the dormitories were noisy, especially at night. Yet college rules assumed that the students were gentlemen. They were required to wear blue-gray tailed coats, similar in cut to a modern dress coat, and must never appear in public in shirt sleeves. They were strictly forbidden to attend the theater in Boston, or to patronize taverns unaccompanied by a parent or tutor, must be present at daily prayers, go to church on Sunday, and observe a "blue" Sabbath, which began Saturday evening.

Freshman Emerson's day began at six o'clock, when the college bell rang for prayers in chapel. Half an hour later he attended his first class, then breakfasted at seven-thirty in the commons with his class. His courses were in Latin, Greek, and "in English, History and Rhetoric." Instruction was given by tutors, recent graduates themselves, and stressed rote memory. Most students scorned their tutors, and anyone who was friendly with them was called derisively a "fisherman."

Many Harvard students had money, and social life in the college was more conspicuous than scholarship, though a few, like William Emerson, were studious. Wealthy students from Southern plantations set the social tone. In his biography of Emerson, Oliver Wendell Holmes remembered these *"elegans"* in their swallowtail coats and fine calfskin boots.[15] In his junior year Emerson would room with "the showy, fascinating John Gourdin" from Charleston, South Carolina. As the "president's freshman" Emerson got to know all members of his class, but he formed only a few intimate friendships. In fact, his first year at Harvard was a disappointment to him. The routine instruction bored him, and his poverty handicapped him socially. Harvard had no inspiring teachers, for Edward Everett and George Ticknor were still studying in Europe, and Edward T. Channing, who would become Harvard's most famous professor of rhetoric, would not join the faculty until 1819.

His boredom caused Emerson to begin his "second education" at Harvard in books not assigned, or even approved, by his tutors. William gave him a copy of Byron's *Childe Harold's Pilgrimage*. He was both repelled and fascinated by it, but it introduced him to contemporary British poetry, which he never heard mentioned in the classroom. He found other students who liked to read, too, and discussed with them his discoveries and enthusiasms. John Hill later claimed that Emerson introduced him to Shakespeare, Montaigne, Swift, Addison, and Sterne[16]—all too modern to be taught at Harvard. On long walks Emerson also talked of books with John Gardiner, a close friend since his Latin School days.

During the winter vacation Ralph took his turn at teaching in his uncle's school at Waltham. On January 20, 1818, he wrote Edward that he was instructing fourteen pupils, trying to keep them quiet and listening at intervals to their reading.[17] But he found this occupation a pleasant relief from Harvard, with time after school hours to rhyme, read, and learn to skate. The students had not yet "muzzled," or snowballed, him (pushed snow in his face). His Uncle Samuel had said he needed a new overcoat and sent him to the tailor, though he would rather have had the twenty dollars it cost to take to his mother. The exciting news about his uncle was that he was engaged to Sarah Alden Bradford.

After returning to Cambridge, Emerson was employed by President Kirkland to tutor his nephew Samuel Lothrop for the Harvard entrance examinations. But at the end of the term President Kirkland decided that Emerson needed the time for his own studies, for he was making an indifferent record. Mr. Gould, the Latin School master, heard this disappointing report, and, as Emerson recalled many years later, "He came to see me in my room, once or twice, to give me advice of my sins or deficiencies in mathematics, in which I was then, as I am now, a hopeless dunce."[18]

Before William returned from Maine he wrote Ralph that he would like to borrow someone's room on commencement day, August 26.[19] Commencement was a great occasion in Cambridge, with bands, parades, oratory, visiting dignitaries, and parties at the end.[20] Most graduating seniors gave dinners for their families and friends. The wealthier students had tents set up on the lawn by a caterer, who supplied ample food and drink. The previous year such a party had cost the family of one senior nearly eight hundred dollars, of which seventy-nine was for wine. But even a poor student such as William Emerson could not entirely ignore the traditional conviviality.

Ralph offered William his room in Wadsworth Hall, which he thought would be ample after removing the bed, borrowing chairs, and decorating with pictures and greens—"not to mention eatables." In a postscript he requested: "Remember when you go to Boston to ask Uncles to see that a relation of ours be kept quietly in B. on Commencement or else he will certainly be here as he asked very particularly about your part &c of me when he visited me last[.]"[21] Apparently Bulkeley was capable of taking an interest in his brothers' affairs, but he spoke in a very loud voice and his manners were embarrassing.

III

At the end of the summer of 1818 Ralph taught again in his Uncle Samuel's school for several weeks before beginning his sophomore year at Harvard.[22] During this time the Reverend Ripley married Sarah Alden Bradford, and Ralph was delighted to renew his acquaintance with her. To William, who had returned to his school in Maine, Ralph wrote his impressions of his uncle's bride. He had liked her since their correspondence during his childhood, and he now pronounced her "the finest woman I ever saw," whether cleaning lamps, making puddings, or reading German critics. She could explain Thomas Reid's *Inquiry into the Human Mind* or discuss the major philosophers with equal ease. She was never cross or indifferent, and was as "fond of *him* [her husband] as *he* of *her*." Uncle Samuel was a lucky man. Mrs. Ripley also advised Ralph in his reading, thus contributing to his "second education."

Emerson's sophomore year at Harvard was more interesting than his first had been. He roomed with William Dorr, a boy he liked, in 5 Hollis

House,[23] a more desirable location than his former room beneath the president's study. He did have to wait on table in the commons for his board, but between meals he was free. After chapel and a single recitation Saturday morning, students could leave the Yard until eight p.m., when they must be back in their rooms. Ralph usually walked the three miles to his mother's rented house in Boston to spend the day.

On Sunday all students must attend church, but otherwise there was nothing to do. By supper Sunday evening, everyone was ready for almost any kind of excitement. As a consequence, disorder in the commons during Sunday supper was not unusual. On November 1 the freshman and sophomore classes got into a playful fracas that developed into a riot. An anonymous mock-heroic "Rebelliad" memorialized some of the details:

> . . . Nathan threw a piece of bread,
> And hit Abijah on the head.
> The wrathful Freshman, in a trice,
> Sent back another bigger slice;
> Which, being butter'd pretty well,
> Made greasy work where'er it fell.
> And thus arose a fearful battle;
> The coffee-cups and saucers rattle;
> The bread-bowls fly at woful rate,
> And break many a learned pate . . .[24]

The professor of Greek, Dr. John Popkin ("Old Pop"), rushed out for President Kirkland, who came on the run and managed to stop the carnage. He immediately suspended four sophomores thought to be the ringleaders, whereupon the sophomore class held an indignation meeting under the Rebellion Tree, a large elm near the Yard where the Sons of Liberty had assembled before the American Revolution. Emerson shared the emotions of his classmates and joined them in plucking a twig from the Rebellion Tree and swearing to resist "Lord Bobo" (President Kirkland) until the suspensions were lifted. One of the leaders was George Washington Adams, son of the new Secretary of State, John Quincy Adams. He had just returned from London, where his father had been minister to Great Britain, barely in time to enroll in Emerson's class. He orated to his classmates, "Gentlemen, we have been commanded, at our peril, not to re-

turn to the Rebellion Tree: *at our peril we do return!"* This speech made
him an instant hero to his classmates, and when more students were suspended, the whole class staged a walkout.

Emerson simply trudged across the Boston toll bridge to his mother's,
where he remained for two or three weeks until the Harvard administration agreed to the return of the rebellious students, though some never
came back. Young Adams's grandfather, the second President of the
United States, said the rebels ought to be flogged. What Emerson's
mother thought is unknown, though she was probably more sympathetic
than Ralph's schoolmaster brother. But for Ralph the lasting result of this
burlesque around the Rebellion Tree was a feeling of comradeship for his
classmates which endured throughout his lifetime. Perhaps the episode
was also symbolic of his own incipient rebellion against authoritarianism,
for in the years ahead he would figuratively return to the Rebellion Tree
more often than any of his classmates. But he held no grudge against President Kirkland, who had been kind to him in several ways. The previous
January Ralph had exulted in a letter to William over an invitation from
Democratic President Monroe to the Federalist president of Harvard to
visit him in the White House. "Should you not like," Ralph wrote William, "to have been witness of the meeting of the two Presidents at Washington?"[25] Federalist Boston was confident that President Kirkland would
do honor to himself and New England when he met the man who looked
like a plowman, and, in Emerson's biased opinion, was little better than
one.

In his sophomore year Emerson joined the Pythologian Club (a literary
or debating society) and became its secretary.[26] He also organized a small,
intimate book club without a name, which met in its members' rooms to
read essays and poems to each other and drink a few glasses of wine. Each
member contributed a small sum of money to buy current periodicals,
such as *The Edinburgh Review* and *The North American Review,* which the
college library did not take, and recent volumes of poems and fiction by
Wordsworth, Coleridge, Byron, Scott, and others. This book club was another means by which Emerson acquired his "second education at Harvard."

Both because of his poverty and because of his natural reserve, Emerson
was not taken into any of the leading Harvard clubs, such as the bibulous
Porcellian (colloquially known as "the Pig") or the more bookish though

also convivial Hasty Pudding. But he was initiated into the Conventicle, formed after the rebellion in 1818, whose officers were called "archbishops," "bishops," and "parsons," though it was not in the least religious. These mock ecclesiastics were fond of wine, and Emerson wrote drinking songs for them. One of these was in derision of another freshman-sophomore dining-hall scuffle, which took place in Emerson's junior year. It began:

> You can say what you please of the current rebellion
> Tonight the Conventicle drink to a real one
> The annals of ages have blazoned its fame
> And Paeans are chanted to hallow its name.
>
> Derry Down[27]

IV

In his junior year Ralph Waldo Emerson decided to drop his first name, and his family and friends agreed henceforth to call him Waldo. He offered no explanation except his strong preference for his middle name, but the change was significant, because almost immediately he began to show signs of a newfound maturity of mind, as if he had actually acquired a new identity. His academic record did not improve significantly, but his prose style did. On January 25, 1820, he began keeping a journal, which both aided and recorded his intellectual growth. In fact, nothing he did in college would yield more far-reaching and lasting results than this simple matter of beginning a journal.

Waldo called his first Journal "Wide World," probably to indicate the inclusiveness of his interests, as he stated in his first sentence: "Mixing with the thousand pursuits & passions & objects of the world as personified by Imagination is profitable and entertaining."[28] He wanted to record his "new thoughts" lest he forget them. Later his Journal would become his literary bank, earning interest for future lectures, essays, and poems. He also compared it to a "Common Place book," and at times he used it to record quotations he wanted to remember, titles of books he had read or planned to read, and other information that might prove useful.

Though Waldo Emerson still expected to become a Unitarian minister, his instincts were already those of a writer, and keeping a journal was intuitive preparation. However, his ambition made him feel self-conscious and he made private jokes of his intentions. In a mock invocation to his journalizing he exclaimed, "O ye witches assist me! enliven or horrify some midnight lucubration or dream (whichever may be found most convenient) to supply this reservoir when other resources fail."[29] Then he apologized to Queen Mab for invoking the help of her enemies. He signed himself "Junio," and later invented other pseudonyms, such as "Edward Search." He found juvenile pleasure in these thin-veiled mysteries. He concocted the anagram "Tnamurya" for his Aunt Mary, whose letters he often quoted in his Journal.

In addition to his "Wide World" Journal Emerson also kept theme notebooks, into which he copied not only ideas and first drafts of his English themes but also compositions in verse and material for his Bowdoin Prize competition essays. He wrote fantasy adventures in Asia, poems on the death of "King Richard," and little Arthurian romances.[30] In these compositions he created vicarious heroes resembling Byron's proud Manfred and Caswallon in Henry Hart Milman's *Samor, Lord of the Bright City:* ". . . it is utterly against the order of things for a single man to presume to encounter all the prejudices & violence & power & war of the world . . . alone," yet some great men ignore both the scorn and the applause of the world to follow their own convictions. Waldo dreamed of being such a man and addressing a multitude with such courage and integrity that he would thrill his listeners, *"valde tremefacere eos"* (really make them shake).[31] Though Emerson would never become a spellbinding orator, his fantasy hero did forecast his own future in other ways:

> . . . let him ascend the pulpit for the first time not to please or displease the multitude but to expound to them the words of the book & to waft their minds & devotions to heaven. Let him come to them in solemnity & strength & when he speaks he will chain attention with an interesting figure & an interesting face. To expand their views of the sublime doctrines of the religion he may embrace the universe & bring down the stars from their courses to do homage to their Creator. . . .

Further insight into Waldo's mind at this time is provided by his letters to Edward, who was spending the winter months with relatives in Alexandria, Virginia, to escape the harsh effects of the New England climate on his lungs. Waldo wrote excitedly of having heard Edward Everett preach a

New Year's sermon in Bôston. Apparently his eloquence impressed Waldo more than his doctrine, though he did not question his hero's theology. Writing at the end of January, Waldo claimed he could still repeat half of the sermon word for word.[32] Preaching on the text "Brethren, the time is short" (1 Corinthians 7:29), Everett exclaimed apocalyptically:

> ... and in another life when Goodness and Happiness, those stranger sisters, shall meet together and know each other, where we shall stand upon the confines of another world and see creation on creation sweeping by to their doom, then we shall behold that time indeed is short[;] then we shall learn to pity little *man* piling up his monuments of marble and calling it *fame*. . . .

The tenor of the sermon was not only that the time was short for repentance, but also that God and all his angels would weep when the Recording Angel exclaimed "with the voice of destiny 'a soul is lost, seal up!' "

During the second semester of his junior year Emerson felt that a new era had dawned at Harvard with Everett's joining the faculty. He was right, though Everett alone was not responsible. One of President Kirkland's early decisions was to reform the system of instruction, entrusting it less to immature tutors and more to endowed professors. With funds donated by a Boston merchant he picked several promising recent graduates to study in Europe and return to appointments at Harvard. The first of these was a brilliant young Boston minister who had taken his A.B. at Harvard in 1811, the Reverend Edward Everett. Another was George Ticknor, who had recently taken his A.M. at Dartmouth. Both attended the University of Göttingen, one of the leading universities in Germany, which at that time led the world in scholarship. Everett took a Ph.D. in Greek language and literature, and Ticknor specialized in Romance languages. Both men stayed in Europe for two more years to travel and meet famous people. Everett ended his preparation by journeying through Greece on foot, "marvelling at the country and the ruins," as Morison says, "reading the inscriptions, and imbibing the beauty (but not, alas! the spirit) of Hellas."[33]

At Göttingen, Everett and Ticknor found complete intellectual freedom, where even a professor of theology could, and did, question the Bible as a repository of divine wisdom. Students were permitted to choose their own fields of study and to proceed at their own pace, attending lectures if they wished. Almost the only formal requirement for the Ph.D. degree was the writing of an acceptable thesis and passing a stiff oral examination on it and related fields. To Everett and Ticknor this made Harvard in comparison seem like a kindergarten. Neither would be able to change the basic structure of the Harvard system, but they did succeed in shifting the emphasis from recitation to formal lectures. Their students knew nothing about the comparative merits of Harvard and Göttingen but were awed by these learned men with the European polish.

In his college lectures Professor Everett used simple language and relied upon details and anecdotes to make his points, but in the pulpit "he gave the rein to his most florid and quaint affluent Fancy." The music and metaphors of his pulpit eloquence followed Emerson home, and not until some years later did he realize that "this was a pure triumph of Rhetoric. This man had neither intellectual nor moral principles to teach. He had no thoughts."[34] After attending Everett's inaugural address on April 4, 1820, Emerson tried to summarize it in his Journal, but could remember only that, though the ancient history of the Greeks was lost, "Every thing was handed down which ought to be handed down," and that "The greeks have left us a literature the most complete in all its parts which the world has ever known."[35] He resolved to study the language and read Herodotus, Aristophanes, and the Greek tragedies. This resolve soon weakened, though he did read these works later. But Professor Everett did not mention the one Greek author, Plato, who would have the profoundest influence on Emerson in his maturity.

The professor who really had most to teach Emerson was Edward Tyrell Channing.[36] A young lawyer and recent editor of *The North American Review,* he was appointed Boylston Professor of Rhetoric and Oratory in 1819, a position previously held briefly by John Quincy Adams. Channing was neither a scholar nor a famous author; his qualifications for the position were so little known that the students refused to march in a procession to honor his inaugural address in the college chapel on December 8, 1819. Emerson probably shared their attitude, for he did not mention Channing either in his Journal or in his letters to Edward. But President Kirkland had made a wise choice in his professor of rhetoric.

In his address on "The Orator and His Times" Channing anticipated some of the themes in Emerson's addresses two decades later. The style of oratory, Channing said, must be suitable for the time and society of the speaker. Greek and Roman orators, however great in their own day, should not be emulated in the United States in the nineteenth century. A democratic society does not need exceptionally gifted orators to inflame the passions of its citizens and sway them with baited words, but representative speakers whose honesty and simplicity of character would make their words carry conviction; character pleads louder than art. Channing was describing the public speaker Emerson would become, and doubtless influenced him in his achievements.

Channing was a good antidote for the influence of Everett. Emerson consulted him and received personal instruction in the spring of 1820 in the writing of an essay for the Bowdoin Prize. In his senior year he submitted themes every week for Channing's criticism. Channing and Everett combined, says Morison, to create "the classic New England diction—the measured, dignified speech, careful enunciation, precise choice of words, and well-modulated voice" which for many years was the mark of a Harvard graduate.[37]

V

It is unlikely that Emerson sought Professor Channing's advice in writing his poem "Improvement," delivered to the Pythologian Club the night of April 21, 1820. It was partly a prophecy that "Ages unborn must see the muses rear / The throne of universal empire here," and partly a condemnation of critics who praised inferior American poetry merely because it was nationalistic. He was not against literary nationalism, but third-rate poets should not be honored merely because they were American. He himself had not outgrown the heroic couplets of the prolix "Columbiads," but he was beginning to develop critical judgment. However, he had not yet found his poetic voice, and his notes for allegories sound more appropriate for Hawthorne than himself. On a Sunday afternoon in May he wrote in his Journal: "Would not Pestilence be a good personage in poetry for description? Wrapt in the long white robes of sickness, entering the town in her awful chariot. . . ."[38] The notion may have come from his reading the *Decameron,* which he withdrew from the Boston Library Society on May 13, 1820, and his continued absorption in Spenser's allegories. His independent reading was becoming wider and more miscellaneous, ranging from Isaac Barrow's *Sermons* to the *Works* of Ben Jonson and Juvenal's *Satires*.

Emerson's most concentrated reading in the spring and summer of 1820 was for an essay on "The Character of Socrates," which he planned to submit in July for the Bowdoin Prize.[39] For several months he read all the biographical and critical material he could find on Socrates in the Harvard Library, beginning with Xenophon, Plato, and Basil Kennett's *The Lives and Character of the Ancient Greek Poets*. Emerson believed that Xenophon and Plato were "faithful biographers" in presenting Socrates as a man of ideal moral character. He marveled that anyone in a pre-Christian era, without benefit of divine revelation, guided only "by the light of reason & nature could set forth a model of moral perfection which the wise in any age would do well to imitate." He believed that the charge of impiety which the Athenians made against Socrates was the attempt of a corrupt society to preserve its licentiousness.

Emerson also saw a parallel between the daemon ($\delta\alpha\acute{\iota}\mu\omega\nu$) of Socrates and "Inspiration in the prophets of God's revealed religion." Yet at the same time, "His plain sense, his peculiar mind which would reduce every thing however unpromising to the measurement of square & compass was little conversant with the poet's visions." These two views of Socrates curiously parallel the two sides critics would later find in Emerson himself, one pragmatic and the other mystical in a Plotinian-Platonic sense. Already, in fact, two of Emerson's favorite authors were, as we have seen, Montaigne, the tough-minded skeptic, and Plato, the idealist. To a considerable extent, then, Emerson's essay on Socrates was a self-revelation. And though he would never have to die for his convictions, as Socrates had, he would never compromise them, either. For this essay Emerson won second prize in the Bowdoin competition, and received twenty dollars. He was also one of the fifteen contestants in the Boylston oratorical contests held at the end of the term, and received one of the three "second" prizes—presumably in a three-way tie for second place.

VI

About a week before commencement, on August 24, 1820, Emerson observed "a strange face in the Freshman class whom I should like to know very much. He has a great deal of character in his features & should [be] a fast friend or a bitter enemy."[40] The editors of the new edition of *Emerson's Journals* note that Martin Gay was a young man from Hingham, Massachusetts, the same age as Emerson, though he had entered college two years later. On October 24 Emerson confessed:

> I begin to believe in the Indian doctrine of eye-fascination. The cold blue eye of [blank] has so intimately connected him with my thoughts & visions that a dozen times a day & as often by night I find myself wholly wrapped up in conjectures of his character and inclinations. We have had already two or three long profound stares at each other. Be it wise or weak or superstitious I must know him.

Throughout Emerson's senior year this face would continue to haunt him, though they never exchanged "above a dozen words." That Emerson was more than vaguely aware that the attraction had an erotic basis is indicated by his leaving the name blank in his Journal, or in other ways disguising the identity of the person so often in his thoughts. In one entry he thinks of burning his senior Journal because he had committed "to it more of what I may by and by think childish sentiment . . . which Somebody else may light upon."

Freud theorized that boys normally pass through a homoerotic stage at about the age of twelve. But Emerson was seventeen. It would appear that he was late in passing through this stage, or that he was bordering on homosexuality. But neither of these possibilities rules out another peculiarity in Emerson's emotional-intellectual life. The subject of ideal friendship, either with man or woman, would occupy his thoughts for many years, and almost invariably, whether in his private Journal or in public lectures and essays, he would prefer the ideal to the reality; indeed, at times, as with Martin Gay, he would seem to be afraid to test the reality against a cherished abstraction. This schoolboy infatuation was a forerunner of Emerson's later theorizing on love and friendship.

Finding more satisfaction in his daydreams than in action also kept Emerson from achieving a better record in college, and frequently caused self-disgust. Early in his senior year he confessed in his Journal (October 25):

> I find myself often idle, vagrant, stupid, & hollow. This is somewhat appalling & if I do not discipline myself with diligent care I shall suffer se-

verely from remorse & the sense of inferiority hereafter. All around me are industrious & will be great, [while] I am indolent & shall be insignificant. Avert it heaven! avert it virtue! I need excitement.[41]

A few days later Emerson called this tendency an "ugly disorder," perhaps "peculiar to myself," and he envied those not afflicted by it. If he was to attain the distinction to which his talents, in the judgment of a few friends and his own vanity, entitled him, this "lassitude & these desultory habits of thinking with their melancholy pleasure must be grappled with & conquered." Yet, "These soliloquies are certainly sweeter than Chemistry!"[42]

Though Harvard did not have a department of chemistry, John Gorham's two-volume *Elements of Chemistry* was a required text in a course in natural philosophy (physical science) taught to seniors by William Peck. By the second semester Emerson's opinion of science had improved, and he wrote in his Journal: "Of all the Sciences the Science of the Mind is necessarily the most worthy & elevating. But it cannot precede the others. Natural Philosophy & Mathematics must be sought in order to gain first the comforts of civilized life and then the data whence our moral reasonings proceed."[43] The latter was the clue to Emerson's growing interest in science, the foundation on which he would soon begin to construct a philosophy of nature and man's place in it.

During his senior year Emerson also took a course with Professor Ticknor on the history and criticism of French and Spanish literature.[44] Ticknor was a better scholar than Everett, but his bias against the French was revealed by some of his anecdotes quoted in Emerson's Journals, and it would take two visits to France before this particular student would discover that he liked the French people. But Ticknor's course, taught by formal lectures in the best German university manner, was thorough and probably the most demanding of any that Emerson took at Harvard.

The course that most deeply influenced him in his senior year was Professor Levi Frisbie's moral philosophy.[45] The textbooks were William Paley's *Principles of Moral and Political Philosophy,* Dugald Stewart's *Philosophy of the Active and Moral Powers of Man,* and Richard Price's *A Review of the Principal Questions and Difficulties of Morals.* Some of his Journal meditations show that Emerson was not yet free of Calvinistic doctrines on the degeneracy of man, which contradicted his poem on "Improvement":

"People prate of the dignity of human nature. Look over the whole history of its degradation & find what odious vice, what sottish & debasing enormity the degenerate naughtiness of man has never crouched unto & adored?"[46] Yet either Professor Frisbie or the assigned texts for his course encouraged Emerson to view human conduct idealistically: "utility is not essential to Virtue." When "in Morals we see Virtue what is it pleases us? not the Utility; but the idea of moral power & beauty which strike us as necessary to give birth to the action."[47]

On March 14, 1821, Emerson recorded in his Journal that he was "reading Price on Morals," and then summarized an idea in which Price anticipated Kant (though Emerson did not know Kant): "right & wrong are not determined by any reasoning or deduction but by an ultimate perception of the human mind."[48] (As the editors of *Emerson's Journals* point out, Price actually wrote "some immediate power of perception," which is even more "transcendental.") Since this intuition is not, Emerson noted, "capable of satisfactory proof," it should be supported by the best evidence attainable. This idea resembles Emerson's later "moral sentiment," though he would not, like Price, believe that "the Understanding" must be the "ultimate determiner." In the terminology of Emerson's later "Transcendentalism," the "Understanding" would mean the practical function of the mind, employing logic and rational analysis. The words "immediate power of perception" strongly suggest the intuitive "Reason" in Emerson's mature philosophy.

Other Journal entries during Emerson's senior year also show the direction of his mental development. During several days of illness near the end of March he contemplated the "chief use of temporary illness."[49] The Puritan doctrine had taught that God used afflictions both to chastise men for their sins and to warn them of the consequences. Emerson had outgrown this superstition, but his illness caused him to rededicate himself "to the great profession I have proposed to undertake . . . to give my soul to God & withdraw from sin & the world . . . to measure my conduct by the rule of conscience."

The following week, after he had recovered, Emerson wondered if his prayers had had any effect on his recovery. He decided that "the world is governed by Providence through the instrumentality of general laws which are only broken on the great occasions of the world or other portions of the Creator's works." This statement cautiously does not rule out miracles, but Emerson clarifies his thinking by adding: ". . . I think that it infinitely removes heavenly dispensations from earthly ones—this manner of giving gifts without expressing the reason for which they are bestowed & leaving it to the heart to make the application & to discover the Giver is worthy of a supreme, ineffable Intelligence." This seems to say that God is generous but ineffable, and He works by "general laws" rather than by special acts of individual kindness.

It was not in his courses that Emerson worked hardest in his senior year and did most to combat his tendency to idle and daydream. On March 7 the faculty assigned him a subject for a poem to be read at the exhibition exercises on April 24.[50] The subject was "Indian Superstition"—perhaps, Professor Kenneth Cameron conjectures, because a poem on "The Restoration of Learning in the East" by Charles Grant had won a prize at Cambridge University and had been reprinted in the United States. Of course the Harvard faculty did not expect an imitation, but Grant's poem had aroused interest in Indian thought. It is doubtful that Emerson would have chosen this subject for himself, though he was already interested in Indian literature and religion, and was familiar with a variety of sources.

As a boy Waldo had visited India Wharf in Boston and seen the great stores of products imported from the Orient. All his life he had heard of the work of American and British missionaries in India. Then, too, his father had published articles on India in *The Monthly Anthology,* which he had recently read, as well as other discussions in *The North American Review.* Aunt Mary was also writing him about "a remarkable Hindoo Reformer," Rammohun Roy. Most important of all were the translations of Hindu classics by Sir William Jones, which Emerson had been reading in the Harvard Library, especially the *Laws of Menu* and the *Bhagavad-Gita.*

A work which Emerson found especially useful was Robert Southey's epic poem *The Curse of Kehama,* provided with information-packed notes. The influence of Southey's poem on Emerson is evident in his use of proper names, allusions, imagery, and even in versification and alliterative diction. Southey's attitudes also helped shape Emerson's. He believed that the colonial administration of Great Britain was rescuing India from her hideous superstitions, such as the immolation of widows at the funerals of their husbands, the voluntary sacrifices of human lives in the path of the juggernaut at the annual festival of Butt-Jattra, and the despair of the lowest caste because they were regarded as unclean and untouchable.[51]

British and American missionaries believed, of course, that they were converting the Indians from their horrible idolatry to the rational humanitarianism of Christianity. Though Emerson regarded some aspects of the doctrine of transmigration and the Hindus' efforts to obtain divine aid by prayer, ritual, and sacrifice of animal and human lives as tragically misguided, he hoped India would recover her glorious ancient civilization and become an independent nation like the American Republic. This idea, which was distinctly American and not British, he expressed in such lines as:

> Dishonored India clanks her sullen chain,
> And wails her desolation to the main.
>
>   .   .   .   .
>
> Alas! thy wreath is sear, thy banners stained,
> Thy faith perverted, & thy shrines profaned.
> The cormorant sits lonely in thy walls,
> The bittern shrieks to Ruin's echoing halls,
> Robbed of its ancient pride, thy brow appears
> Sad with the sorrows of unnumbered years.[52]

Emerson envisioned the rescue of India by the "maids of empire," personifications of Liberty and Freedom, which had rescued the United States from the tyranny of Great Britain. By this trite and naive solution the young poet did not mean that the United States would use material force to free the Indians and restore their ancient heritage, but that a revolutionary spirit of freedom was sweeping the world—a tide in history which would reach India.

Though this poem was stronger in patriotic and humanitarian feeling than in poetic expression, it enabled its moody author to play a role before an appreciative audience. He wanted his Aunt Mary to hear his performance. At first she pretended indifference, but on April 7 Waldo wrote her that his mother wanted her to come, and if she wished her "bashful nephew to do well & claim the ground his own vanity aims to reach, you must encourage him with your presence on Tuesday, 24th April."[53] He warned her not to ask for Waldo the Poet, but for Emerson the Senior. She came, and was still in Boston on August 29, when he graduated.

Class exercises and the announcement of prizewinners took place in

July. Emerson had once more submitted an essay for the Bowdoin Prize, entitled "Dissertation on the Present State of Ethical Philosophy."[54] The subject, of course, was related to his previous Bowdoin essay on "The Character of Socrates," his poem on "Indian Superstition," and his studies with Professor Frisbie. He attempted to trace the history of ethical thought from the Greeks, through the Christian Fathers and the seventeenth-century thinkers of Europe, to the Cambridge Platonist Ralph Cudworth and Dr. Price, author of Waldo's textbook. Again he won a second prize of twenty dollars.

All of Emerson's college honors were partial disappointments. He was selected class poet only after six other boys had declined. But he accepted, and read his "Valedictory Poem" on July 17. The poem itself could hardly be called distinguished, as a quatrain in his Journal (unpunctuated) shows:

Here in the halls of fate we proudly stand
Youth's holy fires by Hopes broad pinion fanned
And while we wait what destiny betides
Gaze on the forms which fairy fancy guides[55]

The long-anticipated commencement was also a time of disappointment. Waldo Emerson had not been elected to Phi Beta Kappa because when the standings were posted he stood thirtieth in a class of fifty-nine. Consequently he was not given a prominent "part" in the commencement program, but as consolation was assigned to a "Conference on the Character of John Knox, William Penn, and John Wesley" with two other seniors. To his Aunt Sarah Bradford Ripley (Uncle Samuel's wife) he wrote on August 22: "Commencement is a week from today, on the 29th—I shall not have a dinner and have not asked any body—for a conference is a stupid thing."[56] But he added, "if you think of coming we shall be very happy to see you; Mother and Aunt and a host of brothers will be there. My room is No. 9 Hollis."

On commencement day one of the boys scheduled for the "conference" failed to appear, and Waldo himself, in his disgust, had not memorized his sentences and had to be prompted several times. He felt that it was a miserable ending for his college career. President Kirkland was disappointed in him, too, and told him that he could not understand how the author of

the Bowdoin essay could be such a poor student of Locke, Paley, and Butler, which he had attempted to teach him. Next day William Cullen
Bryant, who was at the height of his fame as a poet, gave the Phi Beta
Kappa oration. Though it was open to the public, Waldo apparently did
not hear it. The future did not seem promising. He still hoped for an
ushership (instructorship) in the Boston Public Latin School, but would
fail in that ambition also because of his mediocre record at Harvard.

CHAPTER IV

The Dupe of Hope

Thus far the dupe of hope . . .[1]

I

When Waldo Emerson failed to secure an ushership in the Boston Public Latin School after his graduation from Harvard, his brother William employed him as his assistant in the girls' school which he was conducting in his mother's rented house on Federal Street in Boston. Waldo accepted the position with reluctance. In spite of his success in his uncle's school in Waltham, he was not fond of teaching; besides, he feared he could not live up to his brother's expectations. As he recalled many years later in an informal talk to his former students, William's "mind was method; his constitution was order; and, though quiet and amiable, the tap of his pencil, you well remember, could easily enforce a silence and attention which the spasmodic activity of other teachers cannot often command."[2]

What most intimidated Waldo, however, was its being a girls' school attended by daughters of some of the leading families in the city, confident young women scarcely less mature than himself. In his recollections this was the condition still most vivid in his memory:

> I was nineteen; had grown up without sisters, and, in my solitary and secluded way of living, had no acquaintance with girls. I still recall my terrors at entering the school; my timidities at French, the infirmities of my cheek, and my occasional admiration of some of my pupils . . . and the vexation of spirit when the will of the pupils was a little too strong for the will of the teacher. . . .[3]

Waldo complained to his Aunt Mary, "the fates have condemned me to school-keeping," and referred to the beginning of the term as his "fatal Gehenna."[4] She reproved him for thinking of teaching as degrading (she had once been a teacher herself), though she admitted that she thought the male intelligence superior. Moreover, she saw no reason why teaching, as a temporary necessity until Waldo could afford to attend a theological school, should prevent his "courting the Muse." To the latter consolation, he quipped, "Will the Nine be shamed by the company of their sex?"[5]

This jesting about the sex of the Muse betrayed a deeper source of Waldo's dissatisfaction: he longed above all else to make a name for himself as a poet. This ambition far outweighed his desire to become a minister, though he may not have been entirely aware of the fact. His aunt probably sensed the complacency of his ministerial ambition when she sternly reminded him of his duty to a "holier Muse," to which he replied that if he was in "the very jaws of peril," he needed the shield of her Cassandra insight. But this was flattery, for he often did not take her advice. She objected, for example, to his reading the metaphysical arguments for the existence of God by Samuel Clarke, the famous chaplain to Queen Anne, and he continued reading Clarke. He did not take seriously, either, her saying that "like Cicero . . . your poetry will not be valued because your prose is so much better."[6]

Waldo's discouragement undermined his self-confidence, but his vanity also caused him to look for a scapegoat. On February 26, 1822, he confessed in his Journal: "I have not much cause, I sometimes think, to wish my Alma Mater well, personally; I was not often highly flattered by success, and was every day mortified by my own ill fate or ill conduct"[7]—the "or" shows that he was too honest to throw all the blame on Harvard. Yet his return one day to the Harvard Yard gave him "a crowd of pleasant thoughts," as he revisited familiar places and recalled his few partial triumphs. One reason for the change in mood was seeing again a boy, whose name he disguised in his Journal, an "ignotum amicum" (Martin Gay?), and a girl whom he knew slightly but would like to know better. One of his difficulties was that he had no intimate friends except his brothers, and he could only fantasize in secret about girls, accompanied, probably, by urges to masturbate. In his Journal he recorded and then heavily canceled: "I have a nasty appetite which I will not gratify."[8] Feelings of guilt over this appetite, which every moral authority he knew said was a sin, doubt-less contributed to his somber mood.

On May 7 Emerson took stock of his situation. A year before, in his chamber in Hollis Hall, he had felt "flushed & proud" of his position as class poet and eagerly anticipated reading his poem at the exhibition. Now he was a miserable schoolteacher, without even the satisfaction of believ-ing that he performed his duties well—"a disappointed spirit brooding over the fall of his castles in the air." He would soon be nineteen years old, which he counted "a miserable thing." And if his accomplishments were minuscule, the history of his heart was worse—almost a total blank. "I have not the kind affections of a pigeon."[9]

Of course this severe judgment of Waldo Emerson on himself must be largely discounted—or at least modified. He was not so much selfish as unsocial, and this in turn was the result of his introversion, lack of confi-dence, and inability to take the initiative in meeting young people of his own age—what he had called "cheek." His affections needed only exercise, and his constant self-analysis was not healthy. On May 14 he was planning to take a walking tour with William at the end of the school term, but he worried that he might not enjoy it, though he certainly looked forward to the temporary relief from the schoolroom mortifications. However, the vacation with William was not a disappointment. They walked to North-borough, about twenty miles from Boston, and boarded at a farmhouse beside a pond large enough for rowing and fishing. Waldo relaxed and added several pounds to the one hundred and forty-four which he had weighed in May. On his return to Boston early in July, he began an ambi-tious essay on religion in the Middle Ages, which *The Christian Disciple* printed in its November–December 1822 issue (actually published in Jan-uary 1823). This was Emerson's first publication (never collected).[10]

II

Emerson's second year of teaching in the girls' school was less of an emo-tional strain than the first. Perhaps writing his essay on religion in the Middle Ages also helped him forget himself and stop his neurotic brood-ing. He now began to think of his preparation for the ministry, though he had no idea when he could attend a theological school. For the present he and William must support their mother and younger brothers.

Waldo had grown up in a liberal religious atmosphere. His father's First Church in Boston had been Arminian for two generations. At the time of William Emerson's death in 1811 he was known as a Unitarian. (The American Unitarian Association would not be formed until fourteen years later, but the term had been used in Europe since the sixteenth century, and Unitarian missionaries had been active in England for many years.) Two of the Reverend William Emerson's predecessors in the First Church, John Clarke and Charles Chauncy, for whom he had named two of his sons, had published the doctrine of universal salvation, to the alarm of the Congregational churches in New England.[11]

In *The Salvation of All Men* (London, 1784) Chauncy said that both the Bible and "natural religion" reveal God to be infinitely benevolent, wise, and powerful.[12] Mankind possessed virtues as well as sinful tendencies, and by a change of heart any man could obtain God's pardon. Chauncy did not entirely deny original sin, but thought it remediable by men's own efforts. This was what the Dutch theologian Arminius had taught in the sixteenth century, and Charles and John Wesley in the eighteenth. Reward or punishment, Chauncy said, would be in proportion to men's deserts, in this life or hereafter, and was for the purpose of reformation; thus, even damnation might not be eternal.

The course Emerson had taken in natural religion at Harvard had also emphasized "divine benevolence," which the New England Arminians attempted to demonstrate *a posteriori,* from God's visible works, rather than *a priori,* by metaphysical reasoning from "first cause." Though natural religion resembled deism, its adherents did not regard God as an engineer detached from his cosmic machine, but as a beneficent power constantly animating all parts of nature. Thus, their social philosophy was humanitarian, and they eagerly accepted scientific discoveries. They tolerated new theories on the origin of the world which contradicted the naive story in the first book of the Bible. Here was the origin of Emerson's later doctrines of "compensation," "polarity," and the animating influx of divine energy (the "Over-Soul"). Arminian theology was, in fact, a "supernatural naturalism," which Emerson never outgrew, though he later rejected specific interpretations of it.

In addition to having studied natural religion, Emerson had also attended and read the annual Dudleian lectures, endowed by a former chief justice of Massachusetts, Paul Dudley, for public discussions of "natural" and "revealed" religion. Waldo thought that the most brilliant sermon he had ever heard was the Dudleian lecture on "The Evidence of Revealed Religion" by William Ellery Channing, delivered at Harvard on March 14, 1821.[13] He was also deeply impressed two years later by Dr. Channing's sermon, in the Federal Street Church in Boston, called "Discourse upon Revelation." Himself a supernatural naturalist, Channing argued that nature alone was not sufficient revelation, and that "God's word" was "the final expounder of his works . . . as much a part of the order of things as any other event." In most respects the most liberal minister of his day, Channing was a conservative on "revelation."

Miracles recorded in the Bible had long been a problem for the Harvard rationalists. As early as 1744 Charles Chauncy had admitted that "It was necessary the Christian Revelation should be *approved of GOD, by Signs, and Wonders, and Miracles, done in the midst of the People.*"[14] But as an opponent of the "enthusiasm" of the Great Awakening of that time, he added, "there is no Need of the like *extraordinary* Influence of the DIVINE SPIRIT, *now* that Christianity has received its Confirmation and been establisht, in the World, as a Religion coming from GOD." One reason the supernatural rationalists vigorously defended miracles was to distinguish themselves from the deists, often called atheists. But also the belief in the miracles of the Bible had become an emotional issue. In 1821 Dr. Channing preached that "Christianity is not only confirmed by miracles, but it is itself, in its very essence, a miraculous religion."

On the Atonement, however, certainly the greatest miracle in the Christian religion, Channing stood firmly with the most liberal Arminians. These were better known after the controversy around 1815 as Unitarians, meaning that they believed in "one God" instead of "the three Gods" of the Trinitarians. In a sermon preached in 1815, Channing declared: "Christians have been inclined to believe that Christ lived and died to influence the mind of God, rather than the mind of man,—to make God favorable to us, rather than to make us obedient to God."[15] He found no authorization in Scripture for the doctrine of "an angry God," and he also thought it a degrading idea that God needed to be persuaded to forget His wrath. The Scriptures teach that "holiness, or excellence of character, is a vastly greater blessing than pardon or forgiveness." Holiness "is God himself dwelling in the human heart. It is heaven enjoyed on earth . . . and

Jesus Christ can perform no ministry more noble than the recovering of a sinful mind to a heavenly state."

By the time Emerson entered college the heated controversy between the Trinitarians and the Unitarians had begun to cool, but Dr. Channing continued to give it a tone of sweet reasonableness. This frail man with the light-brown hair, slight build, quick gestures, and melodious voice had replaced the famous orator Edward Everett as Emerson's hero. To the Trinitarians' accusation that the Unitarians were heretics, Channing replied calmly that "the state of the heart and affections is the great point by which a Christian is to be judged."[16]

In May 1820 at the Berry Street Conference in Boston, Dr. Channing had announced that the purpose of the meeting of liberal ministers was not to agree upon a specific theological doctrine but to share opinions, to encourage each other, and to defend their right of religious freedom.[17] By force of the character and personality almost miraculously emanating from his frail body, Dr. Channing personified this spirit of tolerance in the Unitarian churches of Massachusetts. It was not surprising that this lovable man should hold a lofty view of human nature: "We have not merely capacities of attaining just ideas of God; there is a foundation in our nature for feeling and loving, as well as discerning, his character."[18]

III

In May 1822, Dr. Channing sailed for Europe on a fourteen-month vacation, but in his absence, as Waldo Emerson wrestled with such theological problems as the nature of God, the necessity of evil, and the origin of man's "moral sense," Channing's influence continued in the answers the young man wrote in his Journal. Of course Emerson was also reading Samuel Clarke and other writers on natural religion, in spite of Aunt Mary's disapproval, but the Channing altruism shines through like a golden thread in a tapestry. Where did he get the idea of God's perfection? Waldo Emerson, the spiritual heir of John Clarke, Charles Chauncy, and William Ellery Channing, answered: ". . . the intelligence who formed our minds adjusted them in such manner as to admit suitable notions of himself from the exhibition of his works, or from the consciousness of our own existence."[19]

Among the "suitable notions of himself," this Divine Intelligence had planted in the human mind a "moral sense," so firmly rooted in human nature "that we feel it to be implied in consciousness."[20] To Emerson, "sovereign necessity which commands every mind to abide by one mode of conduct, & to reject another" operated intuitively, instantaneously, without recourse to rational analysis. "Upon the foundation of my *moral sense,* I ground my faith in the immortality of the soul. . . ."[21] Thus, by the beginning of 1823 Waldo Emerson had found the keystone to his evolving personal theology, and it owed more to Dr. Channing's supernatural naturalism than to the rationalism he had been taught in Harvard College.

In fact, Emerson had already the previous November recorded a conviction which would later develop into his "Transcendentalism," namely that the "Moral Sense . . . coextensive and coeval with Mind . . . derives its existence from the eternal character of the Deity. . . ."[22] This "universal feeling that approves or abhors actions" could not come from "matter" (nature), "which is altogether unmoved by it . . . but from a Mind, of which it is the essence. That Mind is God." Reading Plato, the English Neoplatonists, and Coleridge and Carlyle (the interpreters and adapters of German "Transcendentalism") would only confirm this early conviction of Emerson's that an omnipotent Mind thus acted upon and through man's finite mind.

Yet in spite of this conviction, Emerson was still plagued by doubts and uncertainties over the arguments for "the benevolence of God." During much of December 1822 he had tried to find answers to nagging doubts. He could not accept his Aunt Mary's contention that there were some providential mysteries which the human mind could not, and perhaps should not, understand. He could not believe in the goodness of a God who "would open to our view terrific doubts, which, our ray of reason was insufficient to satisfy."[23]

God had obviously not distributed *mind* equally, though He held all men equally responsible for their conduct—this trace of Calvinism remained in Waldo's conscience. Tentatively he explored an answer outside his "moral sense": perhaps God had distributed His wisdom through a community of unequal minds who depended "much and constantly upon each other," that they might understand and perform their responsibilities. "We learn so little of ourselves in our span of earthly existence, that we are altogether unable to discover the nature and limits of this common connection of finite minds."[24] But whatever the "connection," education was necessary. Possibly Emerson intended to exempt his intuitive "moral sense" from this necessity, but the drift of his conjecture seemed to be away from supernatural naturalism back to the rationalism of natural theology. In finding a justification for the existence of evil, Emerson also fell back upon the rationalist's conception of "a harmonious whole" in which opposites balance or compensate each other.

Though Channing's young acolyte completely rejected the Calvinistic view of heaven and hell, he felt the need to believe in some kind of immortality, and it was characteristic of him to think of it in terms of mind or intellect. God, he speculated, might preserve those "intelligent beings" (minds?) who had proved their right to continued existence, and "deny the gift of eternity to those whose guilt has forfeited the promises, and in stern mercy may annihilate the mind when he stops the warm current of human life." Emerson carefully labels this an "opinion," and adds that every man's dream of heaven is different, "and is coloured by the character and tone of feeling most natural to his mind."[25] Thus, he reverses the doctrine that God created man in His image to man creates God in his image.

Emerson also regarded prayer in a new light. The idea that "Omnipotence could be chained down by sacrifice and entreaty"[26] seemed like a pagan superstition to him. He liked Milton's attitude in *Paradise Lost* (XI, 307–313):

> And, if by prayer
> Incessant I could hope to change the will
> Of Him who all things can, I would not cease
> To weary Him with my assiduous cries;
> But prayer against his absolute decree
> No more avails than breath against the wind,
> Blown stifling back on him that breathes it forth.

Emerson was not opposed to prayer, only to the superstitious use of it for petty or selfish ends. As a mode of intercourse between a finite mind and the Supreme Mind, prayer was highly important. Though the world could not be reformed by "prayers & penances," the mind could be protected against the gross appetites of the body by communication with God through prayer. To Emerson, "salvation of the soul" consisted in maintaining "the balance that Nature fixed in our compound frame." Perhaps he was remembering Juvenal: "Your prayer must be that you may have a sound mind in a sound body" (*Orandum est ut sit mens sana in corpore sano—Satires,* X, 356).

IV

As he neared his twentieth birthday, Waldo wondered how nearly ready he was for the "manly robe." On March 25, 1823, he confided in his Journal:

> From childhood the names of the great have ever resounded in my ear. And it is impossible that I should be indifferent to the rank which I must take in the innumerable assembly of men, or that I should shut my eyes upon the huge interval which separates me from the minds which I am wont to venerate. Every young man is prone to be misled by the suggestions of his own ill founded ambition which he mistakes for the promptings of a secret Genius, and thence dreams of an unrivalled greatness.[27]

Maybe he had misled himself, but Emerson did privately feel these possibilities lying dormant inside him, and both the assumption of his family that the Emerson boys were "born to greatness" and his New England conscience urged him to bestir himself. The Puritan belief that sloth is sin had survived all the Arminian and Unitarian reforms. "It is slothful sensual indulgence," Waldo wrote in his Journal, "which most forcibly impedes the natural greatness of his mind," and when "a man has overleaped this, God has set no bounds to his progress." This doctrine was strongly reinforced by a motto he encountered frequently in the *Works of Francis Bacon,* his favorite reading at this time: *Faber quisque fortunae suae* ("Every man is the architect of his own fortune"). Here we find already full-blown Emerson's later doctrine of "Self-Reliance," which spoke "life and courage" to his soul. "Mistrust no more your ability, the rivalry of others, or the final event. . . . Habits of labour are paths to Heaven."[28]

A month later, still somber, Emerson mused over the opportunities for a young man in America. He believed, as he had been taught, that of all nations his was most "separated from the contaminations which infect all other civilized lands," and he was still a Boston Federalist (though the name was changing to "National Republican"): ". . . the vast rapidity with which the desarts [*sic*] & forests of the interior of this country are peopled have led patriots to fear lest the nation grow *too fast* for its virtue & its peace." The western "pioneers," later to be romanticized even by Emerson himself, he believed in 1823 to be commonly "the offscouring of civilized society who have been led to embark in these enterprises by the consciousness of ruined fortunes or ruined character or perchance a desire for that greater license which belongs to a new & unsettled community."[29]

Like John Quincy Adams, who would win the presidency over Andrew Jackson and Henry Clay the following year, Emerson feared that these western lands, instead of being held as a national treasure to be used prudently and lawfully, would be pillaged by "an accursed tribe of barbarous robbers." Such a "calamity," Emerson thought, threatened to subvert God's plan for America, which He had intended to be an example to the world. A year earlier Waldo had written a classmate: "Will it not be dreadful to discover that this experiment made by America, to ascertain if men can govern themselves—does not succeed?"[30]

Young Emerson's outburst of moral indignation at the prospect of selfish and wicked men settling the western lands with "ignorant and licentious people" was certainly in part a response to the fears of the leading citizens of New England, from merchants and bankers to the Unitarian ministers; but it was also an indication of his smug moral nature at this time. For several weeks he filled pages of his Journal with his thoughts on men's *moral obligations* to God. The tone of these meditations is deeply earnest, and at times almost Puritan. Emerson had, indeed, been reading Jonathan Edwards, and the influence of his Aunt Mary is also apparent. He becomes almost as impassioned as Edwards or his aunt on the sovereignty of God:

> First, then, you are not your own, but belong to another by the right of Creation . . . God animates a clod with life in a corner of his dominions . . . he breathes into it life . . . which was not; having come from himself, it is a part of himself . . . and the intimate unconditional sovereignty which God holds over this being implies the most unreserved submission to his will on the part of the creature.[31]

Yet in spite of these neo-Puritan sentiments, Emerson is still Arminian. Unlike Edwards, who regarded men as "worms crawling in the clod," he believes that "God has wrought man in a perfect mould, quickened him with exquisite senses and lastly inspired him with intelligence." This intelligence gives man the "key to the Universe," which he is free to use for good or ill. His innate "natural sense" should prevent the latter, but often it does not—hence Emerson's "appeal[s] to your hearts."[32] And he also appeals to the imagination of his envisioned audience. Yet once again his words are reminiscent of Edwards's diary when he proclaims that God "has spoken also in thunder to your fears & warned you of wrath to come."[33] God having proclaimed His will to man both through His "sacred books" and through the phenomenon of nature, "No voice on earth, no accents of man ever called such awful images out of the abyss as they have invoked to strike transgression with salutary dread."

Then, ambivalently, Emerson returns in his experimental sermon to the fold of Dr. Channing, the New Testament prophet. Christ, whether human or divine, "passed his life in publishing the character of God."[34] Thereafter, men could no longer stand in ignorance of their "moral obligations."

This "treatise," as Emerson calls it finally, was finished on a Sunday evening in May, probably the eighteenth; for the following Sunday, which he dated May 25, he added a cheerful conclusion in which he acknowledged that "Our constitution would be equally defective if we could never doff the cowl and crown ourselves with the rose & vineleaves; if this dark shadow [of responsibility for our sins] which eclipses & embitters our days could never give place to gleams of light."[35]

This date is particularly interesting, for it was Emerson's twentieth birthday, and his first full day in a new home. The day before, his mother had moved her family from Federal Street in Boston to a small farmhouse in Roxbury, which Cabot describes as "a woodland district . . . some four miles from Boston as it then was, but now [1887] within the city limits . . . Here they hired a farm-house on Canterbury Lane.—also called Dark Lane, or, in irony, Light Lane, from the gloom of overshadowing woods; or sometimes Featherbed Lane, from the rough pebbles of the road. . . ." The soil was too poor and rocky for successful farming, but it was, to quote Cabot again, "a picturesque region of rocks, hills, and woods, with very few habitations."[36] It must have been at its most attractive stage at the time the Emersons moved there.

In his Journal Emerson failed to mention another experience which occurred at the end of his first week in Lower Canterbury. On May 31 he and William joined their father's church in Boston. In signing the "Declaration of Faith" the brothers publicly professed, as their mother had done when she joined the First Church, belief in "the only living and true God"; in "the Lord Jesus Christ . . . sanctified of the Father, and sent into the world, that he might 'redeem us from all iniquity' "; and "in that gospel, which was ratified by the death and resurrection of its author. . . ." The final paragraph pledged them to "live in Christian love . . . waiting in joyful hope for an eternal happy intercourse in the heavenly world."[37]

Several phrases in this declaration sound surprisingly Trinitarian for a Unitarian church, but the pastor himself, the Reverend Nathaniel Frothingham, William Emerson's immediate successor, did not believe in a narrow and literal interpretation. Not until 1835, according to Perry Miller, did he mention the word *Unitarian* in his pulpit, "explaining that hitherto, in the ethos he had created at the First Church, explicit avowal had been unnecessary: 'We silently assumed the ground, or rather found ourselves standing upon it . . . We have made more account of the religious sentiment than of theological opinions.'"[38]

The Reverend Frothingham was a man of imposing dignity, rigid decorum, and solid scholarship in Greek, Latin, and German. Through his translations many Bostonians first learned of Herder, Uhland, Rückert, and other recent German poets. He married a wealthy wife, daughter of Peter Chardon Brooks and sister-in-law of Edward Everett and Charles Francis Adams. Later he would be shocked by some of Emerson's supposed heresies, but Emerson would always respect him. In 1837, on receiving a letter from Frothingham, Emerson wrote in his Journal: "The sight of that man's handwriting is parnassian. Nothing vulgar is connected with his name but on the contrary every remembrance of wit & learning & contempt of cant."[39] Yet in spite of his imposing appearance and impressive learning, Frothingham was not inspiring, and when Dr. Channing returned to his church in August, Waldo listened to his sermons instead of those of his own pastor.

That Waldo Emerson, son of a minister and intending to become one himself, should wait until he was twenty to join the Church was not as unusual as one might think today. Ever since Puritan times in New England, when one had to give evidence of being one of "God's visible saints" before being permitted to become a Church member, joining the Church had been a very solemn occasion. Children were baptized as soon as possible after birth, but were expected to grow to maturity before formally joining the Church. The two years of teaching in William's school had indeed matured Waldo, and his recent journalizing on his "moral obligations to God" had prepared him to take this expected step.

V

In June, Emerson wrote one of his Harvard classmates: ". . . I am living in the country . . . 'O fortunate nimium'! As of yore, my brother, & I teach, aye teach teach in town, in the morning, & then scamper out as fast as our cosset horse will bring us to snuff the winds & cross the wild blossoms & branches—of the green fields."[40] The horse, of course, was their own "shanks' mare."

Waldo's Aunt Mary, "alone among women" and "an idolater of Nature . . . was anxious that her nephew might hold high & reverential notions regarding it as the temple where God & the mind are to be studied & adored . . ." But he had to confess that he had not found nature half so poetical or visionary as he had been led to expect: "In short I found that I had only transported into the new place my entire personal identity, & was grievously disappointed." But he admitted that after being cured of his "air-castles" he had found that his mind and body breathed more freely and that "parti-coloured Nature makes a man love his eyes." He recorded in his Journal that "many a sultry afternoon" that first summer in Canterbury, "I left my Latin & my English to go with my gun & see the rabbits & squirrels & robins in the woods."[41] He does not say whether he discharged his gun at a rabbit or squirrel, but it is interesting that he carried a gun into the woods, instead of a book of poems or a notebook.

In August, instead of attending the Harvard commencement, Waldo took a walking trip through the Connecticut Valley as far as Northampton and Amherst. He found that he could easily walk twenty miles a day. On Monday evening, August 25, he sat in Bartlett's Inn at Amherst, ninety miles from home, visualizing his family: William, "chiefest of men calling the young satraps to order from the elbow chair & secretly meditating golden schemes in an iron age"; Edward, "the young lion of the tribe, (to change the metaphor) now resting & musing on his honorable

Oars [pun on arse]"; Robert Bulkeley, "my loud-voiced & spare-built friend, loving duty better, oh abundantly better than pudding"; and Charles, "the medalled youth anxious Driver & Director of the whole establishment; Peace to his Bones."[42] These humorous characterizations were so accurate as to be almost prescient: William was contemplating an ill-advised trip to Germany to study theology; Edward's devouring ambition to excel would destroy his health; and Charles, no less ambitious than Edward, was torn by self-destructive anxiety. "Peace to his Bones" was intended as irony, but was unknowingly prophetic.

Waldo returned home by stagecoach, refreshed by his outing, and resigned to taking charge of the girls' school while his elder brother studied theology at the University of Göttingen, a plan heartily encouraged by Professors Everett and Ticknor, and perhaps by Dr. Frothingham. Dr. Channing sensibly advised William to prepare for the New England ministry at Harvard, but he was outargued by the German-worshipers. Edward was wildly enthusiastic about William's plan. He proposed to teach in Roxbury during his winter vacation, and then after his graduation from Harvard the following summer he would combine teaching and studying law until William's return. Thus assured of financial support for the family during his absence, William spent the autumn making arrangements. After several delays, he finally sailed from Boston in a small brig on December 5, 1823.[43]

Most of the girls in the Emerson school enrolled again after the August vacation, and to all appearances it ran as smoothly under Waldo's direction as under William's. But he still found little satisfaction in teaching, and continued to have periods of depression. He found time, however, for reading, and in his Journal mentions Edwards, Priestley, Belsham, and Hume on "necessity"; on the other side, Clarke, Stewart, and Thomas Reid. David Hume's *Philosophical Essays* caused him to lament to Aunt Mary on October 16, 1823: "I ramble among doubts to which my reason offers no solution."[44] Knowing himself incapable of refuting by logic the skepticism of Hume, he simply asserted, in his own characteristic way: ". . . there is an impulse to do good continually urging us, an eternal illumination upon virtuous deeds that attracts the beholder. His heart applauds; it is his hands that fail."

A few days before Christmas, Waldo's melancholy gave way to defiance: "I say to the Universe, Mighty one! thou art not my mother; Return to chaos, if thou wilt, I shall still exist. I live. If I owe my being, it is to a destiny greater than thine. Star by Star, world by world, system by system shall be crushed,—but I shall live."[45] Though Emerson's moods continued to fluctuate between despair—at times almost physical nausea for the world—and spiritual exhilaration, he became steadily more ascetic and Idealistic in the philosophical sense (supremacy of mind over matter). He approved Archibald Alison's theory in *Essays on the Nature and Principles of Taste* that "the beauty of the object [is] in the mind of the beholder." His last entry in his Journal for 1823 was these verses (first stanza omitted):

> I am not poor, but I am proud
> Of one inalienable right
> Above the envy of the crowd—
> Thought's holy light.
>
> Better it is than gems or gold
> And oh it cannot die,
> But thought will glow when the Sun grows cold
> And mix with Deity.[46]

VI

Waldo's pleasure in escaping from the boredom of his classroom in Boston to the rural retreat in Roxbury encouraged him to romanticize his new home. At the end of February 1824, he copied into his Journal a rough version of "Goodbye, Proud World":

> Goodbye, proud world, I'm going home
> Thou'rt not my friend & I'm not thine[47]

In this mood he began to think more seriously of his professional plans. On April 18 he recorded in his Journal: "In a month I shall be *legally* a man. And I deliberately dedicate my time, my talents, & my hopes to the Church."[48] He asked Dr. Channing what books he ought to be reading, and Channing lent him Jeremy Taylor's *Holy Living* and *Holy Dying* and Hannah More's *Practical Piety*. These were light fare for a young man who had been reading Hume, but perhaps Dr. Channing thought he did not have time for more intellectual theology. It is also questionable that

Waldo needed encouragement at this time in *otherworldliness*. Recently he had written in his Journal:

Shall I embroil my short life with a vain desire of perpetuating its memory when I am dead & gone in this dirty planet? I complain daily of my world, that it is false, disappointing, imperfect, & uncomfortable, & reason would that I should get thro' it as silently & hastily as I can & especially avoiding to tie any hopes or fears to it. I make it my best boast that I am the citizen of a far country far removed from the low influences of earth & sea, of time & change; that my highly destined nature spurns its present abode & aspires after a mode of existence & a fellowship of beings which shall eclipse & efface the gaudy glory of this. When my body shall be in the clods my triumphant soul, glad of any deliverance, will think no more of it or its habitation ...[49]

This passage might have been written by Waldo's Aunt Mary. Like her, too, he made concessions to "this dirty planet" and went on planning how best to live on it. For him this meant preparing for the ministry, and calculating his chances of success. "I cannot dissemble," he admitted, "that my abilities are below my ambition." His "reasoning faculty" was weak, but he had a strong imagination, and "the preaching most in vogue at the present day depends chiefly on imagination for success, and asks those accomplishments which I believe are most within my grasp." Dr. Channing's Dudleian lecture on "The Evidences of Revealed Religion" was a model of "the highest species of reasoning upon divine subjects," using "moral imagination" instead of logic.

Yet Emerson knew he had serious defects of character. He still believed himself deficient in "common *sympathies*" and afflicted by "a levity of the understanding." Apparently what he meant by these phrases was impatience with the banalities of the average conversation and intolerance of the petty vanities of ordinary human nature. Because of his impatience and self-consciousness he was ill at ease with people, and sometimes laughed or snickered at embarrassing moments. He criticized harshly, and when he praised he often overdid it. These defects of character—today we would probably say personality—would disqualify him for the practice of law or medicine. "But in Divinity I hope to thrive." To his credit he listed "a formality of manner and speech" inherited from his father, and "from him or his patriotic parent a passionate love for the strains of eloquence." He yearned for Cicero's *"Aliquid immensum infinitumque"* ("something great and immeasurable"), and "What we ardently love we learn to imitate."[50]

To make up for his deficiencies, Emerson resolved to train himself by diligence and self-discipline. He would eat sparingly, overcome his tendency to waste time, guard his speech, and try to compensate for lacking a warm heart. "And I judge that if I devote my nights & days *in form,* to the service of God and the War against sin—I shall soon be prepared to do the same *in substance. . . .* My trust is that my profession shall be my regeneration of mind, manners, inward & outward estate. . . ."[51] Or at least it would be a starting point: he would put on eloquence and goodness like a robe. This is a remarkably revealing confession. Emerson's resolve to play the role of an ideal minister is a confession that he must *force* himself to be what he knows he is not—though he uses different words. He certainly did realize that being a clergyman would not come easily or naturally to him. Instead of suspecting that his profession might be uncongenial to his nature, he regarded his deficiencies as simply weaknesses, or immaturity of character which he might outgrow.[52]

If he judged his future prospects by his experiences in teaching, Emerson had to admit that his chances of success were not bright, but he pleaded, "I never expected success in my present employment." Moreover, he had not chosen it; it was forced upon him by circumstances. He could say, "My scholars are carefully instructed, my money is faithfully earned, but . . . the duties were never congenial with my disposition." Though he realized that he might continue to be "the dupe of hope," he believed he had freely chosen the clerical profession; so he would hope. However, throughout the spring of 1824 he continued to feel that he was drifting, and he obtained small satisfaction from his reading. Metaphysics taught him only what he already knew, arranging his knowledge but not augmenting it. He called both metaphysics and ethics "outside sciences": "They give me no insight into the nature & design of my being . . ."[53]

VII

A few days before his twenty-first birthday Waldo wrote William, "I have made some embryo motions in my divinity studies & shall be glad of any useful hints from the Paradise of Dictionaries & Critics."[54] At that time his knowledge of the German critics of the Bible was vague, though William had written that he was attending the lectures of Professor Johann Gottfried Eichhorn, the originator of the study of the Bible on historical principles.⁵⁵ Eichhorn assumed that the supernatural phenomena related in the Bible were fanciful reports of men who lived at a time when everyone believed in magic. He did not think that a sane religion or rational ethics could be based on books permeated by superstition. He was also the first to point out that the Gospels were compiled by later writers from documents no longer available for verification. Rational minds, he concluded, could not regard either the Old Testament or the New as sacred.

In a letter to a friend, William Emerson described Professor Eichhorn as a "venerable old man of 75, lithe, polite, below common stature—wears old-fashioned light gray coat, buckled shoes, his white hair combed back from his forehead, child-like simplicity, speaks clearly and distinctly, without the slightest attempt at oratory—colloquial, friendly, but somewhat dramatizes by using questions and answers. Studies and writes as diligently as in his youth." These were exactly the qualities of personality and character to impress this serious-minded Harvard graduate.

For all his Unitarian liberalism, William Emerson was not prepared for Herr Doktor Professor Eichhorn's iconoclastic ideas, but by August 8 he had to confess, "My mind seems to have undergone a revolution which surprises me." Dr. Channing knew something of the German "higher criticism" when he advised William to study theology at Harvard, evidently fearing the intellectual revolution which he did experience. But William did not dare write his family what he was being taught, or its effects on him.

In his first letters, however, William did not need to conceal anything because he soon discovered that he did not know enough German to follow the professor's lectures. He did confess that his first reactions to the German university were painful and disillusioning. Student life shocked him, with its dueling, heavy drinking, and frivolity; and the majestic aloofness of most of the faculty discouraged him. But within a few weeks he could understand at least the gist of the lectures, and even met some members of the faculty. His opinion of Göttingen improved, and he began urging Waldo to join him. At first Waldo replied that he would "come to fairy-land as soon," but he was thinking mainly of the financial difficulty. Later he was tempted, though he wrote William that he hated the idea of studying German and Hebrew. Discussing the subject by correspondence was awkward because the letters took weeks and even months to cross the Atlantic, and William might have a different argument before Waldo had answered a previous one.

Late in June 1824, after two months at Göttingen, William asked that either Edward or Waldo try to secure a Harvard M.A. diploma for him, which he would need for admission as a Ph.D. candidate. At that time the only requirement for the M.A. at Harvard was that the candidate had graduated at least two years previously, had a sound moral reputation, and would pay five dollars for the diploma. "The Germans are so title mad," William wrote, "that it would much increase their respect for me, but I am personally, I believe, wholly indifferent about it."[56] This request did not arrive until after the Harvard commencement of 1824.

General Lafayette created great excitement by attending commencement and sitting on the platform. Of course for the Emerson family the chief attraction was Edward's oration on "The Advancement of the Age." He had won the honor by standing first in his class by a wide margin. The authorities had asked him to praise "the benefactors of the University," and part of the time he seemed to speak directly to the distinguished guest. Everyone, not least his brother Waldo, thought the performance was brilliant—though years later, on reading the manuscript, he realized that it had been only a good schoolboy oration.[57]

After graduating from Harvard in such glory, Edward was "smitten to the bowels with ambition," Waldo wrote William a few weeks later, and was already counting "the tedious hours of his own captivity & others w'd probably be impatient for him if he were not." William, of course, understood that Edward's captivity was the school for boys in Roxbury. He would also soon begin studying law in Daniel Webster's office in Boston. He could not afford to attend the Harvard Law School, but everyone recognized that it was a signal honor to be trained by the great Daniel Webster. Actually, most lawyers at that time trained in law offices instead of in formal law schools.

As for Waldo himself, "I must not be left in the lurch, nor will my dilapidated academy let me if I would." In earlier letters he had complained that the school for girls which William had started was meeting stiff competition and losing students. But, perhaps realizing that he sounded as if he were reproaching William for studying in Germany, he added: "Thus far I have not been at all inconvenienced by your demands," nor had the family had to retrench because of them. "You shall have all the overplus of family expenditure only the less you have the longer it will last you." In their ambitions the three brothers were beginning to jostle each other just a bit; yet no crisis seemed near in Waldo's letter of September 12, 1824.[58]

Meanwhile William was completing his first term at Göttingen. On September 15 he wrote his mother: "Yesterday Eichhorn finished his lectures, and tomorrow evening, with knapsack on back, I set off on a fortnight excursion—possibly as far as the capital of Saxony."[59] He did get as far as Dresden, after he had detoured to Weimar with the hope of meeting Goethe, then in his seventy-fifth year. On October 10 William could report that he had actually visited the great poet. "He hardly ever admits a stranger, since he is so plagued with requests of that kind; but the words—'of Boston, N. America'—which I wrote on my card, served as a passport." Goethe was kind and friendly, and during the half hour William spent with him, he managed to tell the poet that his theological ideas had changed since he had come to Germany and that he was worried about returning to New England to preach doctrines he no longer believed. Goethe advised him to be practical, to keep his doubts to himself, and his parishioners would be none the worse for the harmless deception. Of course William left this part of the interview out of his letters to his mother, and his family had no idea that he was battling with his conscience.

Weeks before William's family received his letter about his visit to Goethe, Waldo had decided to revolt against his servitude to schoolteaching. Edward encouraged him to stop and begin his study of theology at Harvard. For the present Edward would continue teaching, studying law at the same time. He could earn seven hundred to eight hundred dollars a year, and by borrowing a thousand dollars on Mrs. Emerson's Haskins inheritance, the family could manage. William had estimated his expenses at four hundred a year, and Waldo suggested that he would have to borrow half of that. But he did not mean to discourage William in his plans; in fact, he thought William ought by all means to see Italy before his return.[60] William believed he could complete the requirements for the Ph.D. degree—not rigorous in those days—by the following June. But before that time came he had decided that the degree was not worth the required sixty-dollar fee. In the autumn of 1824 Waldo considered borrowing money himself to study at Göttingen,[61] but settled on the Harvard

Divinity School, in which he planned to enroll for the second semester.

Of course Waldo confided to his Aunt Mary his plans to study theology at Harvard, and at the same time wrote without reserve his doubts about a number of conventional doctrines. "I am blind, I fear," he confessed in one letter, "to the truth of a theology which I can't but respect for the eloquence it begets, and for the heroic life of its modern, and the heroic death of its ancient, defenders."[62] It was bad enough, she thought, to admire Christianity only for its aesthetics or heroic history, but worse heresy was to follow: "that the administration of eternity is fickle, that the God of revelation hath seen cause to repent and botch up the ordinances of the God of Nature, I hold it not irreverent but impious to assume." Dr. Channing saw no conflict between the "God of revelation" and the "God of Nature," and he would perhaps have agreed that "Paley's deity and Calvin's deity are plainly two beings."

This talk about two Deities was most alarming, and then, in a letter which has not survived, Waldo made some remark about the Holy Ghost which set her wild. "He talks of the Holy Ghost. God of Mercy what a subject!" To raise any doubt about the Holy Ghost was the worst heresy yet. He should not go to Cambridge. "True they use the name *Christo,*" but she thought the Divinity School was a very feeble ornamental arch in the temple of Christianity.[63]

Miss Emerson still hoped, however, that for her nephew "This deep & high theology will prevail & German madness be cured." She had heard of the German "higher criticism" even before her other nephew went to Göttingen, though how much is uncertain. Now she also regretted "the time of illusion" when "it seemed best to tell children how good they were." Whether she blamed herself for laxity during her nephews' childhood, or blamed their father, she was hitting at the "easy theology" of the liberal Unitarians. But the "time of illusion & childhood is past," she reminded Waldo, "& you will find mysteries in man which baffle genius. . . . May the God of your fathers bless you beyond your progenitors to the utmost bounds of your undying existence."[64]

Waldo Emerson dutifully copied his aunt's letter into his Journal, and went on making his plans to prepare himself at Cambridge for ordination in a Unitarian church.

CHAPTER V

House of Pain

He has seen but half the universe who never has
been shown the house of pain.[1]

I

Waldo Emerson closed his school in Boston on December 31, 1824, and
rested at home in Roxbury for nearly six weeks, pretending to read theology in preparation for enrolling in the Harvard Divinity School. On January 4, 1825, he sat down before his Journal to take stock of his situation:
"My unpleasing boyhood is past . . . and this day a moment of indolence
engendered in me phantasies & feelings that struggled to find vent in
rhyme."[2] The thought of leaving Roxbury made him sad, though he was
doing so to perform a "sterner errand":

> Days that come dancing on fraught with delights,
> Dash our blown hopes as they limp heavily by,
> But I the bantling of a country Muse,
> Abandon all those toys with speed to obey
> The King whose meek ambassador I go.[3]

Two weeks later, in a more exuberant mood, Waldo wrote William:
"You are I doubt not suitably shocked at the innovations & rumors of innovations which by this time have thunderstruck you."[4] William had indeed been thunderstruck by Waldo's precipitous actions and had written
him a week earlier that he thought in giving up his school he was reck-
lessly endangering the family's livelihood. "Had I dreamed of such a revo-

lution when at home, I should as soon have gone to Greenland as to Göttingen." But of course it was now too late to protest, so he could only "rejoice that you are rushing to jail in such good spirits."

In his January letter to William, Waldo gave an optimistic report on the family income which, when William finally received it some weeks later, considerably allayed his fears. The Haskins heirs had invested the estate in a hotel, which was expected to yield Ruth Emerson two hundred dollars a year. Waldo himself had deposited five hundred and eighteen dollars in the bank at interest. If necessary they could mortgage his mother's share in the hotel for a thousand. And meanwhile Edward would continue teaching. He, more than anyone else, had encouraged Waldo to begin his theological studies at Harvard without further delay.

Edward thought Waldo was too prone to trust in Providence and to dally instead of seizing every opportunity to achieve his goal. When on February 6 newspapers erroneously reported that Henry Clay had been killed in a duel, Waldo quoted in his Journal a sentence he had heard George Bancroft, Boston minister and historian of the United States, pronounce in a sermon: "Man is but the poor organ thro' which the breath of Him is blown."[5] Two days later Waldo learned that the "story of the duel was false." Clay lived, in fact, to throw the presidential election to John Quincy Adams by his vote in the House of Representatives after the failure of any of the three candidates to get a clear majority in the Electoral College. Men, it seemed, caused events to take place.

On his last evening in Canterbury Lane, February 8, Waldo wrote in his Journal, "I go to my College Chamber tomorrow a little changed for the better or worse since I left it in 1821." His "Cardinal vice" was still "intellectual dissipation—sinfully strolling from book to book." He had resolved two months earlier to read a chapter of the Greek Testament every morning before breakfast, and had also drawn up a list of other books to read in philosophy, psychology, science, and ethics. He had dipped into James Mackintosh, John Playfair, Dugald Stewart, and a few others, but he had read nothing systematically.[6] However, he had paid his debts and banked over two thousand dollars. He could return to Cambridge with a feeling of financial independence.

Waldo was in Divinity Hall at Harvard when the news of John Quincy Adams's election was received. He and Edward decided to celebrate it by visiting John Adams, the second President, now confined, in feebleness and pride, in his Quincy home. The Emerson brothers had known him all their lives, for he was a member of their father's church in Boston. "The old President sat in a large stuffed arm chair, dressed in a blue coat, black small-clothes, white stockings. And a cotton cap covered his bald head. . . . We told him he must let us come & join our Congratulations to those of the nation on the happiness of his house."[7] He *was* happy, he said, and astonished that he had lived to hear of the event—he would be ninety the following October. He thought his son had more "political sense" than any man he had ever known. But he never expected to see him again: ". . . Mr. Adams will not come to Quincy but to my funeral. It would be a great satisfaction to me to see him but I don't wish him to come on my account."

Edward and Waldo spent an hour with the old man, listening to him reminisce about his life at Harvard, about the preaching of George Whitefield and Jonathan Sewall, and his favorable opinions of Cooper's novels. Near the end of the visit, "The old gentleman exclaimed with great vehemence 'I would to God there were more ambition in the country, ambition of that laudable kind to excel.' "

Probably Emerson began his residence in the newly completed Divinity Hall, north of the Harvard Yard, on February 9, though he did not register until two days later, when he was admitted to the "middle class."[8] The advanced standing meant less than the words suggest, for the Divinity School did not at that time grant degrees, and the studies consisted mostly of supervised reading rather than of a definite curriculum.[9] The reading was under the personal direction of President Kirkland; Henry Ware, the Hollis Professor of Divinity; and Andrews Norton, the Dexter Lecturer of Biblical Literature. Professor Norton, whom unfriendly critics called the "Unitarian Pope," was regarded as the "dean" of the school, though possibly more because of his aggressive character than as a result of delegated authority. In fact, except for the Law and Medical schools, postgraduate education at Harvard had scarcely begun, and consisted mostly of residence in or near the university, with access to lectures, use of the library, and advice from the faculty.

Actually, because of ill health, Emerson spent only a few weeks in 1825 in the Harvard Divinity School. First he suffered from a lame hip, and a month later from trouble with his eyes. James Elliot Cabot thought the trouble with the hip came from Waldo's rooming on the lower floor of the northeast corner of the building, which was cold and damp.[10] Though painful, the "rheumatism" of the hip did not incapacitate Waldo for reading, but in an autobiographical note dated March 1825, perhaps written later, he recorded: "lost the use of my eye for study." Here he says one eye, but in another notation, probably written still later: "Being out of health, and my eyes refusing to read, I went to Newton, to my Uncle Ladd's farm, to try the experiment of hard work for the benefit of my health."

What was wrong with Emerson's eyes is a matter for conjecture. But in the spring Dr. Edward Reynolds in Boston successfully operated on one eye, and on the other in late summer or early autumn.[11] Since the operations completely restored Emerson's use of his eyes, it seems unlikely that the "affection" (Cabot's word) was either an *infection* or a psychosomatic symptom. But the condition was severe enough to stop Emerson from journalizing or writing letters for nearly a year. Naturally the interruption in his studies discouraged him and caused his ambition to sputter like an oil lamp with an untrimmed wick.

II

In April Mrs. Emerson moved to Cambridge, into a rented house a couple of blocks west of the Harvard Yard.[12] Waldo doubtless aided her out of his savings, but Edward, still teaching in Roxbury, was the only member of the family with a steady income. However, Edward's restlessness, of which Waldo had warned William several months earlier, developed into alarming symptoms of serious illness. His physician told him that his lungs were already damaged by tuberculosis, and advised the sovereign remedy of the time, a trip to Europe, preferably to the southern region. This may sound like a superstitious remedy, but at least it would give Edward a needed respite from his too-steady application to teaching and studying law. His Uncle Samuel Ripley offered to finance the trip, thus enabling Edward to close his school at the end of August and sail for Europe on October 23, five days after William's return from Germany.[13]

Before William's arrival and Edward's departure, Waldo had begun teaching thirty or forty boys in a Classical School (probably modeled on the Boston Public Latin School) at Chelmsford, a village about ten miles from Concord. Chelmsford was a peaceful rural community, whose farmers, as Waldo recalled later, "were all orthodox, Calvinists, mighty in the Scriptures"; they believed that "life was a preparation and 'probation,' to use their word. They read no romances, but with the pulpit on one hand and poverty and labour on another, they had a third training in the town meeting."[14]

That autumn in Chelmsford, Waldo began to recover the use of his eyes, and the improvement continued. Meanwhile the troubles of the Emerson family began to multiply. Bulkeley had become so emotionally disturbed that the family taking care of him in Roxbury could no longer manage him, and his mother felt that she could not, either; consequently, Waldo took his younger brother with him to Chelmsford, where he employed someone to look after him. In Waldo's words in a letter to William, "Bulkeley is perfectly deranged & has been ever since I have been here."[15]

For Waldo the great shock of these troubled times, however, came soon after William returned to Boston on October 18. During a very stormy crossing of the Atlantic, when William several times thought his small ship was going down, he decided that he could not take Goethe's advice.[16] Realizing what his decision would mean to his family, he rushed down to Chelmsford to discuss it with Waldo before telling his mother and Edward. There is no record of the conversation, but every indication is that Waldo was sympathetic, and that he agreed William must find another profession. This would be a great disappointment to his mother, who had counted on his following in the footsteps of his father and grandfather. William also felt guilty at not being able to contribute to the support of the family during this difficult time. He could, of course, teach again, and we may be sure that he and Waldo discussed that possibility, but teaching was a precarious way to earn a living, and William wanted a more reliable profession. He evidently found comfort in Waldo's understanding, and returned to Cambridge to tell his mother of the change in his plans.

During William's visit Waldo would also have been sure to discuss his own problems at Chelmsford. The community liked him, and he had one especially promising student, Peter Hunt. But the enrollment had dropped to twenty, and Waldo felt that he could not afford to stay, especially since Edward's recent patrons were begging him to reopen the school in Roxbury. They said he should be able to earn as much as two thousand dollars a year there. No decision was reached while William was in Chelmsford, but in December Waldo asked his advice by letter, and then responded to

William's reply: "In obedience to your letter I am about to close my school here & to migrate to your latitudes [of Cambridge–Boston]."[17] He had given notice that he would close the school on December 31, 1825. Bulkeley would have to be left, but arrangements could be made for him.

A week later Waldo wrote again to inquire whether William might be willing to take the Chelmsford school for a few weeks while the School Committee searched for another master . He did not urge William to accept, and wrote only because he had been asked to do so. However, William would have only eighteen students because two were going with Waldo to Roxbury. Waldo said he would "keep school" through Saturday, at which time he expected his brother Charles and "Chas. Wain" to transport him and the two students and their baggage to Roxbury.[18]

It is likely that either Waldo's brother William or his Uncle Ralph Haskins, who lived in Roxbury, had already found quarters for the school before the new teacher arrived. Immediately after New Year's, 1826, Waldo opened his school on the first floor of Octagon Hall, so called for its shape, but known also as the Norfolk Bank Building. With its square tower and high Gothic windows it was a pretentious setting for an elementary school.[19] Most of Edward's former students attended, including two Haskins cousins. Waldo boarded with a second cousin, David Greene. Thus surrounded by friends and relatives, he should have found the new position pleasant, but he was still worried about the delays in his preparation for the ministry. He wrote nothing in his Journal about his school, but much about his theological and literary ideas and ambitions.

On March 16 Waldo wrote in his Journal: "My external condition in life may to many seem comfortable[,] to some enviable but I think that few men ever suffered more genuine misery [footnote: in degree not in amount] than I have suffered."[20] His frequent praise of poverty suggests that physical privation had not caused this extreme misery, and his recent afflictions of eyes and hip were not that severe. The pain, therefore, was mental, and largely self-inflicted. On March 27 he lamented: "My years are passing away. Infirmities are already stealing on me that may be the deadly enemies that are to dissolve me to dirt and little is yet done to establish my consideration among my contemporaries & less to get a memory when I am gone."[21]

Several times in the past Waldo had complained of an unhappy childhood, and he now repeats: "My recollections of early life are not very pleasant. I find or *imagine in it* [italics supplied] a meanness[,] a character of unfounded pride cleaving to certain passages which might come to many ears that death has not yet shut. I would have the echoes of a good name come to the same ears to remove such imputation." He gives no clue to the identity of these persons. They might have been his Step-grandfather Ripley, his mother, possibly his brothers, or even the childhood school-mates with whom he had quarreled. Yet however trivial his youthful sins, real or imagined, his psyche was deeply disturbed. This could have been partly the result of the return of the "rheumatism" in his hip, but whether the mental state was cause or effect, who can say? At any rate, the lame hip had returned, and was painful enough to make him close his school in Roxbury on March 28, after it had been operating only three months. However, it should be remembered that three-month terms of school were not unusual at that time.

The twenty-eighth was a Tuesday, and this fact suggests that Waldo may have terminated his school suddenly, a conjecture strengthened by a note he wrote from Cambridge on March 30 to the librarian of Harvard, saying, "I am confined by a lameness to my chamber," and asking that his privilege of borrowing books be extended. On that day Charles drew out two books in his name.[22] A week later Waldo wrote his Aunt Mary: "My eyes are well comparatively, my limbs are diseased with rheumatism."[23] But the news from Edward in southern Europe was encouraging; he "writes that he mends daily." No mention is made of William. What was he doing? It was quite unlike him to remain idle, and if not employed, why did he not take over Waldo's school in Roxbury?

In Aunt Mary's last letter to Waldo she had expressed anxiety about Charles, and in a postscript to his April 6 letter to her, Waldo asked why she was worried. Charles was first in his class at Harvard, loved letters, and loved goodness. What Waldo did not know was that Charles had written her: "I see none whom my vanity acknowledges as more intelligent than myself, but at home where they surely ought to know best, why they think but little of me."[24] Doubtless he was disadvantaged in being the youngest son, but it was also difficult for him to impress William and Edward with his college honors because they had already made similar records. Waldo, of course, had not, but he underrated his youngest brother because he compared him unfavorably, and perhaps unfairly, with Edward. Charles, Waldo continued in his postscript, "will be eloquent, &

will *write* but comes not up to the force & nobleness of the transatlantic boy—certainly to my cherished image of the same." Apparently Charles had some justification in complaining of being unappreciated at home. Waldo did not know that Charles, too, was highly susceptible to tuberculosis—may, in fact, already have had some early symptoms. Before long he would in his turn join the "house of pain," and contribute one more problem to the troubled Emerson family.

Waldo was not so absorbed in his own miseries that he forgot his responsibilities as a breadwinner for the family. Within a few days after his leaving Roxbury, his mother moved into a house she had rented from Professor Levi Hedge on Winthrop Square, west of the Harvard Yard.[25] It had a large room which Waldo could use for still another private school, and he opened it without delay. That he could obtain pupils so readily shows the excellent reputation the schoolteaching Emerson brothers must have enjoyed. Possibly William assisted in recruiting students. Waldo's lameness was no great handicap in this schoolroom right in his mother's home, and there he doggedly taught a group of boys throughout the spring and summer of 1826. One of his students was Richard Henry Dana Jr., who was both astonished and pleased by Emerson's mild discipline. When *Two Years Before the Mast* was published some years later, Waldo remarked of the author to William, "He was my scholar once, but he never learned this of me, more's the pity."

III

The coincidental deaths of John Adams and Thomas Jefferson on July 4, 1826, set Waldo Emerson and his Aunt Mary to ruminating on the hand of Providence in human affairs. Until near the end of their lives Adams and Jefferson had been bitter enemies, but they had finally exchanged letters of reconciliation. That the second and third Presidents of the United States should both die on Independence Day seemed providential to many Americans. Waldo wrote, with more than his usual prolixity: "God in these eminent instances of these our latter days departs from the ancient inviolable sternness of an unrespecting providence to harmonize the order of nature with the moral exigencies of humanity."[26]

Waldo was inclined to agree with his aunt that this historic coincidence portended a new epoch for the nation, and against this background of wonders he was also making his own fateful decisions: "In the wind of these great events I am to assume my office, the meek ambassador of the Highest." Yet the thought of finally becoming God's ambassador did not excite him, and he begged Aunt Mary to "awaken a sympathetic activity in [my] torpid faculties." His hope was that with some stimulation he could overcome his torpor. Miss Emerson realized that he was flattering her, and she loved it, but he was sincere in appealing for help.

On August 1 Waldo wrote Aunt Mary: "In the fall, I propose to be *approbated,* to have the privilege, tho' not at present the purpose, of preaching but at intervals."[27] Then this curious statement: "I do not now find in me any objections to this step." The words convey reluctance—certainly lack of enthusiasm—and the following sentences are equally revealing: "'Tis a queer life, and the only humour proper to it seems quiet astonishment. Others laugh, weep, sell, or proselyte. I admire." Henry Adams, seventy-five years later, would strike the same pose of ironic amusement in his autobiography, though his ironic mood (Emerson's "humour") would really express his bitterness and resentment over his powerlessness. He, the grandson and great-grandson of Presidents and son of a candidate for the vice-presidency, pretended to be amused at the trick fate had played on him. Waldo Emerson was on the threshold of the profession of *his* distinguished ministerial ancestors. Perhaps his sardonic "humour" expressed his feeling of deprived spiritual power.

Shortly before the Harvard commencement on August 30, at which Charles "received one of the two first Boylston prizes in elocution,"[28] William left for New York to study law in a firm on Wall Street. To support himself he would have to tutor on the side, write newspaper articles about Germany, and live with extreme frugality. Edward, after his return from Europe in October, would resume his apprenticeship in Daniel Webster's office in Boston. Thus Waldo was still the chief means of support for his mother, Charles, and Bulkeley. Consequently he continued teaching in Cambridge while trying to prepare for his "approbation." He had recovered from his lameness and could visit faculty members of the Divinity School for advice and direction in his reading.

Soon after William's departure, Waldo wrote him about a little book— hardly more than a pamphlet—published in Boston. This work was *Observations on the Growth of the Mind,* by Sampson Reed. Waldo called it "one of the best books I ever saw."[29] His enthusiasm grew, and two weeks later he added: "in my poor judgment the best thing since Plato of Plato's kind, for novelty & wealth of truth."[30]

The author of this unusual book had graduated in William's class, but had received an M.A. degree and given an oration at the time of Waldo's graduation in 1821.[31] His "Oration on Genius" had so impressed William that he had asked Waldo to borrow the manuscript with permission to copy it. Thus Sampson Reed's ideas were already known to both Waldo and William Emerson. Reed's conversion to the doctrines of Emanuel Swedenborg convinced him while in college that he could never become a Unitarian clergyman, as he had intended.

Various religious sects have looked forward to the "Second Coming" of Jesus Christ, but Swedenborg claimed to have witnessed the second advent in 1757 and received at first hand instructions in the new dispensation, or the "New Church." The New Church was not an institution but a body of spiritual teachings. Swedenborg's followers did establish a Church, with a creed, a ritual, and a formal organization, but that was not his intention. The basic doctrine of the New Church was the coexistence of a spiritual world and a material world duplicating each other in every detail; thus, for every physical fact there was a corresponding spiritual fact. This was called the doctrine of "correspondence," with obvious resemblances to the two realms in Plato's philosophy.

Sampson Reed became a member of the Boston New Jerusalem Church, and later used income from his profitable wholesale pharmaceutical firm to pay for the publication of tracts, a magazine, and translations of Swedenborg's works. Emerson read some of these, but most of his knowledge of Swedenborg's teachings came from Reed's oration and his book, neither of which mentioned the name of Swedenborg or the New Church. Many who heard the oration probably associated his theory with the ideas of Wordsworth, in whose poetry Reed found states of mind similar to Swedenborg's. Therefore, Emerson in his enthusiastic response to Reed was not embracing a visionary cult or an esoteric theology. Yet what he got from Reed was more than some general parallels to aspects of English Romanticism.

For example, though Emerson would later study the "organic theory" of art elaborated by Coleridge, Reed had already impressed him by the Swedenborgian version in his college oration. "Every man has a form of mind peculiar to himself," Reed declared.[32] "The mind of the infant contains within itself the first rudiments of all that will be hereafter, and needs nothing but expansion; as the leaves and branches and fruit of a tree are said to exist in the seed from which it springs. . . ."

The Platonic doctrine of preexistence of the soul and Wordsworth's "intimations of immortality" fused in Reed's interpretation of Swedenborg: "The arts have been taken from nature by human invention; and, as the mind returns to God, they are in a measure swallowed up in the source from which they came." Or again: "The mind, as it wanders from heaven, moulds the arts into its own form, and covers its nakedness . . . but it is only when the heart is purified from every selfish and worldly passion, that they are created in real beauty; for in their origin they are divine." All Christian ministers preached against selfishness, but Reed added an appealing spiritual aesthetics: "It is only necessary that the heart be purified, to have science like poetry in its spontaneous growth."

Reed anticipated Emerson by seventeen years in his attack on the "dead church," though without the repercussions of Emerson's "Divinity School Address": "It needs no uncommon eye to see, that the finger of death has rested on the church." By "church" he meant all Christian churches except the New Church, though he did not take time to explain this in his oration. What he did say was ambiguous enough to be accepted by his piety-conscious audience.

In *Observations on the Growth of the Mind* Reed extended the hints he had given in his college oration—again without naming Swedenborg.[33] By "growth" he meant the unfolding of the mind's original, innate potential. "The laws of the mind are in themselves as fixed and perfect as the laws of matter; but they are laws from which we have wandered." [8] There was a time when the human mind was in perfect harmony, [48] but "the society of earth is no longer the society of heaven." [54] Even the lower orders of creation have "suffered a change in consequence of that in the condition of man. . . ." [56] Nevertheless, God still speaks to the human mind through the language of things [45]: the purpose of the natural world is "to draw forth and mature the latent energies of the soul." [36]

The spirit of God is as necessary to the development of the mind as the sun is to the growth of vegetables; or, to use another "correspondence," God acts on mind as gravitation on matter. [24] The reservoir of knowledge is seated in the "affections," [22] and what is loved is remembered. The mind of man, by acknowledging its dependence on Divine Mind and adoring the world which is "the mirror of Him who made it," can extend consciousness [77] and return to the original harmony. "Syllogistic reasoning is passing away," [69] giving place to imagination, which is God's creative power acting through the human mind. This doctrine leads to distinctions between "understanding" and "reason":

> Reason is partly natural and partly an acquired power. The understanding is the eye with simply the power of discerning the light; but reason is the eye whose powers have been enlarged by exercise and experience. . . . In the progress of moral improvement no power of the mind, or rather no mode of exercising the understanding, undergoes a more thorough .and decisive change than this. It is like the change from chaos to creation . . . reason should therefore come to revelation in the spirit of prayer, and not in that of judgment. . . . [71]

Reed's interpretation of *understanding* and *reason* are not so clearly differentiated as in Kant's use of these terms. Basically, in his view, understanding deals with things in a practical way; reason, with origins and abstractions which bring order to the chaos of experience.

IV

These ideas would bear fruit a decade later in Emerson's *Nature,* but they were of little practical value to him in the autumn of 1826 as he prepared desperately to be examined for a license to preach. On September 23, 1826, he wrote in his Journal:

> Health, action, happiness. How they ebb from me! Poor Sisyphus saw his stone stop once at least when Orpheus chaunted. I must roll mine up & up & up how high a hill. . . . It would give me very great pleasure to be well. It is mournful the expectation of ceasing to be an object of hope that we may become objects of compassion, and then go gloomily to nothing in the eye of the world before we have had one opportunity of turning to the sun what we know is our best side.[34]

To William, six days later, Waldo wrote:

> Among my other scarecrows to fill the gaps of conversation [in this letter], are my lung complaints. You must know in my vehement desire to preach I have recently taken into my bosom certain terrors not for my hip

which does valiantly, nor my eyes which deserve commendation, but for my lungs without whose aid I cannot speak, and which scare me & thro me scare our poor mother's sympathies with strictures [chest plasters] & jenesaisquoisities. But we must not cry before we are hurt, and any sufferings of this sort are so few & small that tho' they may fill a paragraph of my letter such has got to be my desire to call out sympathy they may not give you or me any farther distress.[35]

This last sentence, added to calm William's alarm, is so at odds with the preceding sentence that it hardly makes sense. Yet in spite of his almost frantic worries, Ralph Waldo Emerson met with the Middlesex Association of Unitarian Ministers on October 10, 1826, and was "approbated" (licensed) to preach. Five days later he preached his first sermon at Waltham, in his Uncle Samuel Ripley's church, on the text "Pray without ceasing" (1 Thessalonians 5:17).[36] This text had been suggested to him the previous summer by an uneducated Methodist hired man on Uncle William Ladd's farm in Newton. While they were pitching hay, the hired man, named Tarbox, remarked that men were always praying, for a *wish* is a prayer, and men shape their lives by their wishes. This so impressed Waldo Emerson that he chose the subject for his first sermon, in which he concluded, "We must beware, then, what we wish." Waldo's mother, his Aunt Mary, and other aunts and uncles came to hear and praise him for his first effort, but he was pleased most by the remark of a farmer: "Young man, you'll never preach a better sermon than that."

Edward did not reach home in time to hear Waldo's first sermon. He landed in New York instead of Boston, stopped to visit William, and did not reach Cambridge until October 19.[37] He seemed to be in better health, but he alarmed his mother and brothers with his report that William was starving himself. Waldo wrote his older brother: "Will you please eat some dinner tomorrow. Edward has struck us all with sincere alarm by his account of your excessive abstemiousness. . . . So please, pray, do overcome the Stoic to be an Animal."[38] But Waldo's news of himself was alarming, too: "For me, I have resigned my understanding into the hands of my doctors Moody & Bliss. & Warren[.] I give up my school this week. I journey next I know not where. I am not sick nor very well."[39]

Waldo's description of his latest affliction is curious: "in my vehement desire to preach I have . . . taken into my bosom certain terrors . . .

for my lungs." Exactly what was wrong with his lungs to terrify his "bosom"? All his biographers have assumed that he had tuberculosis, which had caused Edward to flee to Europe. Now Waldo was on the point of flight from the Massachusetts weather because of a "constriction" in his lungs—or at least one lung. He wrote William that he had "no symptoms that any physician extant can recognize or understand. I have my maladies all to myself." This does sound psychosomatic. Though tuberculosis of the lungs would continue to be a difficult disease to treat until the discovery of antibiotics in the twentieth century, physicians in New England had had a great deal of experience in diagnosing it, and Waldo Emerson had consulted the best in Boston.

Everyone agreed that the newly approbated young minister must avoid spending the coming winter in Massachusetts. Waldo himself accepted this decision at the end of October, after he had repeated his "Pray Without Ceasing" sermon in the pulpit his father had occupied, before many friends of the Emerson family, including seventeen of the girls he had taught.[40] All assured him of his success. The pain in his chest could hardly have been caused by his fear of failing in the pulpit; but it persisted, and this fact really frightened him. For the present he could not preach, and he must seek a mild climate in which to recuperate. His doctors recommended Charleston, South Carolina, and the ever-generous uncle, Samuel Ripley, advanced him seventy dollars and a letter of credit on a Charleston bank.[41]

Dr. Ezra Ripley had recently (November 2) lost his sister Sarah, who had been his housekeeper. He invited Ruth Emerson to keep house for him in Concord during Waldo's absence, and this solved the immediate problem of his mother's support, for Edward could board in Boston, and Bulkeley was still in Chelmsford. Relieved that his mother would not be in need during his absence, Waldo left Boston on November 25, two days after Thanksgiving, on board the *Clematis,* a commodious ship with twenty-five sails, bound for Charleston.[42]

After a few days of seasickness, Waldo adjusted to the motion of the ship. On Sunday, December 3, he wrote in his Journal:

> 'Tis a nine days' wonder to me, this voyage of mine. Here I have been rolling thro' the weary leagues of salt water, musing much on myself and on men with some new but incoherent thinking.... After a

day or two I found I could live as comfortably in this tent tossed on the ocean, as if it were pitched on the mountains ashore.[43]

The *Clematis* usually made the trip from Boston to Charleston in eleven days, but this trip took twelve. Finally on December 7 Waldo landed and found a boarding place with a Mrs. Fisher on East Bay Street at six dollars a week. The trip had been "the most extraordinary event" he had ever experienced, and Charleston was like a foreign country to him. To combat loneliness he wrote in his Journal, started new sermons which he did not finish, and wrote letters to his family and friends. His classmate Mellish Motte lived in Charleston and promptly introduced him to the Library Society. Samuel Gilman, a tutor at Harvard when Waldo was a freshman, and now pastor of the Unitarian church in Charleston, also befriended the young minister without a church.

What most impressed Emerson in Charleston was the cordiality of the people, and in his Journal he speculated on the influence of the climate. Manners, he decided, "belong more to the body than the soul, & so come under the influence of the sun."[44] Here everyone was more polite and ceremonious than in Boston. Even the black slaves greeted each other with courteous formality on the street, while balancing a burden on their heads. "There is a grace & perfection too about these courtesies which could not be imitated by a northern laborer were he designed to be extremely civil. Indeed I have never seen an awkward Carolinian."

But the sun was not as warm as Carolina manners. Two weeks after his arrival Waldo confessed to William that his health had not improved. "My chest is a prey to certain oppressions & pangs, chiefly by night, which are very tolerable in themselves, but not very agreeable in their auspices to such an alarmist as I." The new year greeted him with a "bitter cold eye." On January 4 he recorded: "A new year has found me perchance no more fit to live & no more fit to die than the last."[45] Three weeks later he wrote William that the cold was scaring him out of Charleston. He planned to "take passage for St. Augustine, where I am promised the most balmy air in the world."[46] A little earlier he had considered going to the West Indies, and his Uncle Samuel had written immediately that he would pay the extra expenses, but it was to St. Augustine that he sailed on January 10, 1827.

Waldo was still desperately hoping to be able to return home in April or

May. William, now better able to support himself by private tutoring and a salary of three dollars a week in his law office, wanted Waldo to become a candidate for pastor of the Second Unitarian Church in New York City. The position had been offered to Henry Ware Jr., pastor of the Second Church in Boston, but he was not interested. Waldo did not like New York and replied, "I had rather be a doorkeeper at home than bishop to aliens, tho' I confess it mends the matter that there is such a huge fraction of Yankee blood in New York."[47]

At first Emerson found less to admire in St. Augustine than in Charleston. This oldest town in North America, founded by Spaniards, had belonged to the United States for only six years. The inhabitants reminded Waldo of the barnacles exposed on the rocks at low tide. "The entertainments of the place are two," he wrote Charles, "billiards & the sea beach; but those whose cloth abhors the billiards—why theirs is the sea beach."[48] The climate was almost ideal, the thermometer never going higher than seventy-two in the daytime or lower than sixty-five at night. On January 29 Waldo wrote William: "The air & sky of this ancient fortified dilapidated sandbank of a town are delicious. I am therefore very decidedly relieved from my stricture which seemed to hold its tenure from Boreas. . . ."[49]

Yet St. Augustine was a "queer place." Its eleven or twelve hundred inhabitants included invalids like himself, public officers, and Spaniards, whom Waldo called "Minorcans." No one seemed to work, and oranges grew without cultivation. "The Americans live on their offices. The Spaniards keep billiard tables, or, if not, they send their negroes to the mud[bank] to bring oysters, or to the shore to bring fish, & the rest of the time fiddle, masque, & dance." Waldo himself strolled on the beach, sometimes sailed a boat, but mostly sat, read, and thought of sermons which he might never deliver. He also wrote homesick poems. One, entitled "St. Augustine," contained these lines:

> An hour of busy noise
> And I was made a quiet citizen
> Pacing a chamber in a Spanish street.
> The exile's bread is salt his heart is sad
> And happy is the eye that never saw
> The smoke ascending from a stranger's fire[50]

In a small notebook Emerson kept a "Mem. for Journal St. Augustine" in which he jotted down observations on this old town, full of ruins and chimneyless houses. The houses of the Spaniards and Yankees had cellars, filled with stagnant water. "Why? Because there are cellars in Madrid and Boston." The two cemeteries, one Catholic and the other Protestant, were once enclosed by wooden fences, but the Protestant fence had been burned "by these idle people for firewood." The Catholic fence had blown down, "but not a stick or board has been removed,—and they rot undisturbed such is the superstition of the thieves." Emerson watched two Spaniards "entering this enclosure, and observed that they both took off their hats in reverence to what is holy ground."

Irish immigrants had not yet come to Boston in great numbers, and Emerson was not acquainted with the Catholic liturgy. On February 25 he attended mass in the St. Augustine Catholic church and noted: "The mass is in Latin & the sermon in English & the audience who are Spaniards understand neither. The services have been recently interrupted by the imprisonment of the worthy father for debt in the Castle of St. Marks."[51] In another note written next day, Emerson admitted he had been "scandalized" by the private conversation of the priest, and added that the cathedral was "full of great coarse toys."[52]

Of the people, he observed: "The Minorcans are very much afraid of the Indians."[53] Their houses were built like forts, with apertures through which a musket could be fired. When he asked, "But what are you afraid of? Don't you know Gen Jackson conquered all the Indians?" they replied, "Yes, but Gen Jackson no here now." "But his son is, for you know the Indians call col. Gadsden his son." "Ay, Ay, but they Indians, for all that." But Emerson also made less amusing observations in St. Augustine:

> I saw by the city gates two iron frames in the shape of a mummy with iron rings on the head. They were cases in which the Spanish governor had hung criminals upon a gibbet. There is a little iron loop on one side by the breast in which a loaf of bread & a vessel of water were contained. Thus provided the wretch was hung up by suspending the ring over his head to a tree & left to starve to death. They were lately dug up full of bones.[54]

There were contemporary cruelties in St. Augustine, too. One day Emerson attended a meeting of the Bible Society and heard in a courtyard nearby the voice of an auctioneer selling slaves:

One ear therefore heard the glad tidings of great joy whilst the other was regaled with "Going gentlemen, Going!" And almost without changing positions we might aid in sending the scriptures into Africa or bid for "four children without the mother who had been kidnapped therefrom."

V

The beginnings of sermons which Emerson wrote in Charleston and continued in St. Augustine give clues to his state of mind at the time. In Charleston on January 6 he started "to sketch out the form of a sermon . . . upon the events of the Crucifixion."[55] The conventional rhetoric of this young Unitarian minister is surprising. He envisions Christ's eyes resting "on you, my friends," bidding you to "take up the cross and follow him," rid of "the tremendous load of moral depravity by which the head of humanity has been so long borne down to earth." Now, "He sits at the right hand of God. You can enter into a sublime sympathy with him . . . that blood was shed for the healing of the nations."

Nine days later in St. Augustine, Emerson was still meditating on the need for the Atonement. "My friends we are sinful men. We can copy from our own memories the fatal history of the progress of sin."[56] These thoughts led the brooding young man back to his own "many prejudices which I well remember to have influenced my conduct when a child, which I now despise & ridicule." But then he begins to wonder whether God does indeed see all, hear every word he utters, read every thought of his brain, and bring into judgment "every significant passage of my life. . . ."[57] One doubt leads to another until Emerson begins to challenge the whole structure of religious faith—the existence of God, life after death, and "the conditions on which my salvation is suspended." The believer claims strong "historical and internal" evidence, but "now it must be admitted I am not certain that any of these things are true. The nature of God may be different from what is represented. I never beheld him, I do not know that he exists." However, he decides he will embrace faith in God as an experiment, and "guard against evil consequences resulting to others by the vigilance with which I conceal it [doubt]." William had rejected the hypocrisy suggested to him by Goethe, but at the moment Waldo feels like concealing his thoughts. But then, he was not even sure of his doubts, and may have suspected that they were temporary.

Two weeks later Waldo Emerson had arrived at a firm answer to the "shallow philosophy"[58] that a man can sin in secret and "cover transgressions with an impenetrable cloak." The man who says, "I have sinned; but I live; I am in health; I shall not sin again; and how am I the worse & no man shall know it," is deluded. The "laws of the moral universe" are inexorable, and violations of them are punished, not after death but instantaneously. God "secured the execution of his everlasting laws by committing to every moral being the supervision of its own character, by making every moral being the unrelenting inexorable punisher of its own delinquency."

This doctrine would become one of Emerson's most profound convictions, the pivotal tenet in his philosophy of "compensation." But it was no palliative for a guilty conscience. If anything, it was even more severe than the punishments of a vindictive God, but it did allow for free will, making each man responsible for his own salvation or damnation. It meant "self-reliance" all the way.

When two days later (Sunday, February 4) Emerson began a sermon on the theme of "man is always dying,"[59] he was not returning to morbid Puritanism, but was attempting to state—with echoes of Jeremy Taylor and Hannah More—his doctrine of *immediate reward or punishment* in a manner to affect his imagined parishioners: "We are the changing inhabitants of a changing world. . . . The ground on which we stand is passing away under our feet. Decay, decay is written on every leaf of the forest, on every mountain, on every monument of art."

Here Emerson's rhetoric is reminiscent of Jonathan Edwards, but he does not continue to a Calvinistic conclusion. In fact, he stops with "you will soon stand at the gates . . . of the tomb," and notes: "Continued on p. 73."[60] But when we turn to page 73 in his manuscript, he is excited about having met a "consistent atheist."[61] Evidently he had intended to continue the sermon but had lost interest. Yet there may be a connection between this unfinished sermon on dying and Emerson's meeting Achille Murat, a real, live atheist. The text of the sermon was to have been Psalm 112: "He shall not be afraid of evil tidings; his heart is fixed trusting in the Lord."[62]

Napoléon Achille Murat was the nephew, on his mother's side, of Napoleon Bonaparte, and was the elder son of Marshal Joachim Murat, Napoleon's distinguished cavalry leader and King of Naples by the Emperor's appointment.[63] When Napoleon escaped from Elba, his old marshal joined him and shared with him the defeat of 1815, after which Murat was captured and executed. Both of his sons emigrated to the United States, though the second, Lucien Charles, returned to France and later won recognition there. Achille married a distant relative of George Washington's and settled on a plantation near Tallahassee, Florida. His Uncle Joseph Bonaparte bought a plantation near Bordentown, New Jersey, and Achille was on his way there when he and Emerson boarded the sloop *William* on March 28 and shared the same cabin.

On April 7 Waldo wrote William Emerson from Charleston about his meeting Murat on the voyage from St. Augustine to Charleston.[64] Usually the sloop made the trip in two days, but fifty miles from St. Augustine a storm blew the ship off course, and then it was becalmed for a week, so that the twenty-five passengers aboard did not reach Charleston until nine days after leaving port, with food running low. During these extra days Emerson was so exhilarated by his talks with Murat that he did not mind the delay.

A painting of Napoléon Achille Murat hanging in the Tallahassee Public Library shows a glowingly handsome young man (he was only two years older than Emerson), clean-shaven, with dark, wavy hair, a high forehead, regular features, and alert, expressive eyes. He is fashionably dressed in broadcloth coat and starched shirt with high wing-collar tips showing above his silk stock. It is easy to imagine that he was a vivacious and brilliant talker, and such Waldo Emerson found him to be: "a philosopher, a scholar, a man of the world very sceptical but very candid & an ardent lover of truth. I blessed my stars for my fine companion & we talked incessantly." That they talked much of religious beliefs is evident from Emerson's comments in his letters and his Journal.

A few hours after landing in Charleston, Emerson wrote in his Journal: "A new event is added to the quiet history of my life."[65] He had "connected" himself by friendship to a man who loved truth as ardently as he did, but who professed to disbelieve in the existence of the soul and in immortality. Emerson had never met an atheist before, and he was profoundly impressed, all the more because he found Murat such an attractive personality. Instead of feeling that his own faith had been shaken, he had an exultant conviction that it had been tested and found to be sound. In this pleasant frame of mind, he experienced what might be called an epiphany. On the evening of April 17, while he waited in Charleston for a ship to carry him to Baltimore, meditating on "the glory of the world" and the mind's "own glory," he acknowledged that his new friend was "at home" in both these realms, whereas he had hitherto regarded them as incompatible. At this point his mind was flooded by a pleasurable assurance which made him feel ecstatic:

The night is fine; the stars shed down their severe influences upon me and I feel a joy in my solitude that the merriment of vulgar society can never communicate. There is a pleasure in the thought that the particular tone of my mind at this moment may be new in the Universe; that the emotions of this hour may be peculiar & unexampled in the whole eternity of moral being. I lead a new life. I occupy new ground in the world of spirits, untenanted before. I commence a career of thought & action which is expanding before me into a distant & dazzling infinity. Strange thoughts start up like angels in my way & beckon me onward. I doubt not I tread on the highway that leads to the Divinity.[66]

These thoughts gave him deep contentment. And why not? He felt sure that "God is here," and that his attractive friend was blind to Him. Yet Emerson began to wonder if it mattered whether "this Being be acknowledged or denied." Would morality be affected? His friend seemed to be an admirably moral person, in spite of his professed atheism. Emerson did not have a definite answer, but he certainly had a new tolerance for nonbelievers. The following September, Murat would write him from his uncle's home in Bordentown that he had been affected by his discussion on the sloop, and would suggest that they debate their views by letter. Murat proposed to write a monograph on "Truth,"[67] but events prevented his doing so. (Shortly after writing Emerson from Bordentown, Murat returned to Europe, and briefly commanded a cavalry regiment in Belgium, then sought asylum in England, where he befriended the exiled Louis Napoleon. Finally he returned with his wife to his Florida plantation, where he died in 1847. Some of these events Emerson would not know until years after.)

When Waldo wrote his Aunt Mary on April 10, 1827, from Charleston, "I fancy myself wiser for the excursion," he certainly had Murat in mind.[68] But confidence was also returning to him with the improvement in his health. He felt well enough to preach in Charleston on the fifteenth, and he hoped to preach after he reached Baltimore. But when he arrived there on Saturday, April 28, he found wintry weather, and he was forced to stay indoors. Writing from Alexandria, Virginia, on May 3, where he was visiting his Ladd cousins, he complained in a letter to his Uncle Samuel Ripley, "as soon as I come, so do the snow storms."

Two weeks later Emerson wrote Aunt Mary that on Sunday, May 13, he had preached without pain or inconvenience.[69] Thus encouraged, he visited his childhood friend and schoolmate William Henry Furness, pastor of the Unitarian church in Philadelphia.[70] He felt well enough to go sightseeing and to visit the Academy of Art, the Philosophical Society, and Independence Hall. Around June 1 he proceeded to New York, where he and William had much to talk about. But he must hasten on to Boston, for his brother Edward had written him that the First Church wanted him to preach for several weeks in the absence of its pastor, the Reverend Nathaniel Frothingham, who was vacationing in Europe.[71] By mid-June all danger of frost in Boston was long past, and Waldo Emerson could look forward to a warm welcome in his father's church.

CHAPTER VI

The Ordained Heart

Great Nature hath ordained the heart to
love . . .[1]

I

The benefits of Waldo Emerson's winter in the South were apparent in his
enjoyment of the boat trip from New York to Boston. He had become so
used to traveling by sea during the past month that he still had his "sea
legs," and was amused that a fellow passenger, the great Daniel Webster,
was "tremendously sick off Pt. Judith [Rhode Island] in our steam boat
passage," he wrote William from Boston on June 24, 1827.[2]

Waldo was writing from the home of his cousin George B. Emerson
after preaching his fourth sermon from the pulpit his father had occupied
in the First Church. "It is now the ev^g of the Second Sunday y^t I have of-
ficiated all day at Chauncy Place," meaning he had preached both at the
morning and afternoon services. At the end of the second of his "all-day"
preaching, however, he felt exhausted—and he had probably used up his
small hoard of prepared sermons, though he did not mention this difficulty. "I am all clay, no iron," he lamented to William. He had told the
First Church committee he could not preach the following Sunday, and he
was even meditating "total abdication of the profession on the score of
health." But how could he earn a living? He might turn author, but his
Muse seemed "unwilling." "Yet am I no whit the worse in appearance I
believe than when in N.Y. but the lungs in their spitful lobes sing Sexton & Sorrow whenever I only ask them to shout a sermon for me."

Although Waldo had engaged a room in Divinity Hall at Harvard to be occupied later,[3] during the summer of 1827 he spent most of each week with his mother and step-grandfather in Concord. Every sunny day he roamed the hills and fields familiar to him since childhood and associated in his memory with the history of the Emerson family. In June the river, in which he had fished as a child, overflowed its shallow banks, and then subsided into the normal slow-flowing stream. Later in the summer he picked wild berries along its marshy banks. These old haunts, the nearby battlefield, and the rustic bridge where the American Revolution had begun, had changed scarcely at all since he first knew them:

> These are the same, but I am not the same,
> But wiser than I was, and wise enough
> Not to regret the changes, tho they cost
> Me many a sigh. Oh, call not nature dumb;
> These trees and stones are audible to me,
> These idle flowers, that tremble in the wind,
> I understand their faery syllables,
> And all their sad significance.[4]

The Manse built by his grandfather was large enough to accommodate Dr. Ripley, Ruth Emerson, Waldo, Charles during his vacation from Harvad, Edward on his weekend visits from Boston, and William if he could come in August; but the rooms were small and the whole family lived in intimate contact. Sometimes at night Waldo wrote letters at the library table with his mother sitting opposite and Charles at his elbow.

Through the summer Waldo kept William informed of family affairs. Charles seemed to be "swimming on his easy tides . . . a pleasing stripling, & locuplete of friends."[5] Perhaps, as usual, his habitual good manners, which had won social success for him in college, deceived Waldo into thinking him facile and shallow, though sure to succeed in life. But Edward was cause for real anxiety. He did not appear to be well, and he seemed indifferent about his work, quite unlike the ambitious boy he had been in college. However, Daniel Webster was satisfied with his progress and was planning to take him to Washington in the autumn to instruct the Webster children, while Edward continued the study of law where it was being made.

Mrs. Ruth Emerson had some cause for worry about each of her sons.

Earlier in the summer Bulkeley had made her anxious when he went "rambling" for two weeks, as far as Mount Vernon, New Hampshire, where, Waldo reported to William, "he carried a paper proposing to teach a singing school & succeeded in getting 15 or 16 subscribers, ere the wise men of Gotham found him out." He was taken back to Chelmsford, where he had been boarding, but his mother still felt uneasy about him.

Charles gave an oration at the Harvard exhibition on July 16, and in a joint letter to William (Charles acting as scribe) Waldo playfully reported its success: "It was a sculptured form (elegant leg) in classic costume, from whose lips the muses poured their inspiration, (the very hand [Charles's] blushes scarlet) the form itself passive to the influence ... The nations counted it a triumph, the Romans a defeat."[6] Considering Waldo's real opinion of Charles's easily won honors, the high-flown eulogy was not exactly a compliment.

At commencement on August 29, Edward also gave an oration on the occasion of his receiving the Harvard honorary M.A. degree. His subject was "The Importance of Efforts and Institutions for the Diffusion of Knowledge."[7] To William, Waldo praised both the matter and the manner of delivery, though he qualified the latter by saying Edward spoke too slowly and deliberately, without sufficient excitement: "... people were pleased & called it the finest of orations &c &c—no lack of praise—but ... they should have been electrified." Perhaps Waldo expected too much, but it is probable also that the state of Edward's health affected his performance. In a postscript Waldo suggested to William: "You will say to Edward if you say anything that you have heard from Waldo of his success for, I have heard today that 'it was the perfection of speaking' & he looks sad under the suspicion that it was not."

As the summer continued, Waldo's own health improved, "mended with the weather," as he expressed it to William on August 31, "heat being my best medicine." Dr. Frothingham had returned "in excellent health and spirits" and resumed his pastoral duties. But meanwhile Waldo was receiving invitations from various places and would be able to continue earning his usual fee of ten dollars every Sunday:

I am going to preach at Northampton, in the service of the Unitarian Assoc., for Mr. Hall, a few weeks, whilst he goes into the adjoining towns to missionize[.] His church is a small one, & I shall be able to preach all day I suppose without inconvenience. Afterward I am at liberty to do the same for Mr Willard of Deerfield & send him on the same errand. But that shall be as health & circumstances may be. Meantime be pleased to rejoice, that I have in my trunk eleven entire sermons all which I have preached at First Ch[urch].[8]

While industriously increasing his stock of sermons—which he always read, never memorizing them or trusting himself to speak extempora-neously—Waldo Emerson continued to examine his own religious con-victions. He characterized himself as a "Seeker," doubtless having in mind the seventeenth-century English sect which cultivated an open mind on all theological questions. "Confused with the irreconcilabilia of the moral world," he confessed to William, "I am & shall be I hope a great many years of the sect of Seekers." But his frankest confessions were usually made to his Aunt Mary, for in spite of her more rigid theology, she was fond of argument and enjoyed denouncing her nephew's latitudinarian-ism. She was the person, therefore, to whom he confided his philosophy of self-reliance in preaching:

When I attended church on the other half of a Sunday & the image in the pulpit was all of clay & not tuneable metal I said to myself, that if men would avoid that general language & general manner . . . every man would be interesting. . . . But whatever properties a man of narrowed intellect feels to be peculiar, he studiously hides; he is ashamed or afraid of himself; and all his communications to men are unskilful plagiarisms from the common stock of tho't & knowledge & he is, of course, flat & tiresome. We shall become wiser with age, that is with ages.[9]

This condemnation of the mediocre pastor methodically performing his duties in the pulpit may at the time have sounded only like the protest of an impatient young man against boredom, but a percipient observer would have been justified in predicting an uncertain career for him in his chosen profession. Even in the ultraliberal Unitarian Church, people sat complacently in their rented pews on Sunday to hear soothing words of comfort. The familiar theological clichés and ecclesiastical tone of voice were restful, and in a vague way "uplifting." But here was a young man who demanded that the preacher examine everything he said and say nothing he did not honestly, even passionately, believe in, and say it not according to tradition, in well-worn patterns of rhetoric and intonation, but in his own way, even eccentrically, if that was more characteristically his own. Sooner or later this young man with a mind of *his own* would lose patience with every inherited creed, ritual, and ecclesiastical hierarchy, and demand such complete honesty in every word and deed that no religious institution could satisfy him—or maybe even tolerate him. Aunt Mary was already a little apprehensive on this score, for she was more aware of her nephew's potential heresy than anyone else.

There were also other intimations of the direction in which Emerson's mind and conscience were headed. His rereading Hume's essays, and perhaps his talks with William about Professor Eichhorn's "higher criticism" of the Bible, had made him skeptical of the historical reliability of the New Testament accounts of the life and death of Jesus. Regretting that his eyes did not permit him to "be learned," he nevertheless confided to his Aunt Mary: "I am curious to know what the Scriptures do in very deed say about that exalted person who died on Calvary, but I do think it at this distance of time & in the confusion of langu[ages] to be a work of weighing of phrases & hunting in dictiona[ries]." He could not agree with his aunt that Jesus had died to save a "fallen world." It was now Waldo's firm conviction that "A portion of truth bright & sublime lives in every moment to every min[d.] It is enough for safety tho' not for education." To translate this cryptic sentence, every person has sufficient intuitive knowledge of good and evil to guide his moral conduct (that is, "save his soul"), but this intuition does not extend to other branches of practical knowledge: one still needs to be "educated" in mathematics, languages, history, science, and so on.

During the autumn of 1827 Emerson moved from town to town in Massachusetts, "supplying" the pulpits of small Unitarian churches. On October 7 he wrote Dr. Ezra Ripley that he had led a "roving life since I left your hospitable roof."[10] He had expected to supply the pulpit in Northampton for four weeks, and then that at Deerfield or Greenfield for another four, thus gaining leisure to increase his stock of sermons, and perhaps also to benefit from the healthy mountain air of these places. But he had shifted around so frequently to half a dozen churches that he had had little time either for rest or for the study needed to write more sermons. And now Mr. Henry Ware Jr., pastor of the Second Church in Boston, had asked him to supply Mr. Orville Dewey's pulpit in New Bedford, the famous whaling harbor, for three weeks in November, "which I consented to do, much against my will, for I wanted to go to Concord for a little time." He still hoped to visit his mother and Dr. Ripley for a day or two on his way to New Bedford, but being an itinerant preacher was "not a little unfavourable to my purposes of study."

In December, however, Emerson was able to return to Cambridge and begin his delayed residence in Divinity Hall. Here he was befriended by Frederic Henry Hedge, a brilliant young man two years his junior, who had studied in Germany before entering Harvard; after graduating he had enrolled in the Harvard Divinity School. The two men were later to be closely associated in the American Transcendental movement, but Hedge remembered that during Emerson's year's residence in Divinity Hall no one was greatly impressed by his ability:

> There was no presage then, that I remember, of his future greatness. His promise seemed faint in comparison with the wondrous brilliancy of his younger brother, Edward Bliss Emerson, whose immense expectation was doomed never to be fulfilled. A still younger brother, Charles Chauncy, had also won admiration from contemporary youths; while Waldo had as yet given no proof of what was in him. He developed slowly; yet there was notable in him then, at the age of twenty-five, a refinement of thought and a selectness in the use of language which gave promise of an interesting preacher to cultivated hearers. He never jested; a certain reserve in his manner restrained the jesting propensity and any license of speech in others. . . . He was slow in his movements, as in his speech. He never through eagerness interrupted any speaker with whom he conversed, however prepossessed with a contrary opinion. And no one, I think, ever saw him run. In ethics he held very positive opinions. Here his native independence of thought was manifest. "Owe no conformity to custom," he said, "against your private judgment." "Have no regard to the influence of your example, but act always from the simplest motive."[11]

That the appearance of this reserved, serious-minded, slow-moving young man, with no propensity for jest, was deceiving, Dr. Hedge later became fully aware, and even at the time of Emerson's residence in Divinity Hall his family and a few intimate friends knew that he had a sense of humor and an attractive personality which his self-consciousness concealed. His great strength was hidden in his character and his complete dedication of his mind and talents to the moral life. In a more sophisticated age it is difficult to appreciate the importance of such uncompromising purpose in the life of an artist, but it was what would later make Emerson the daring thinker and great influence on his generation which he was.

Emerson's early sermons also concealed and at the same time betrayed his innate moral power. One of the best examples is a sermon "On Showing Piety at Home,"[12] which he first preached—or read, in his quiet manner—in the First Church of Boston on August 12, 1827, and then repeated in various New England churches during the following months. It was his favorite sermon, then and later. Using as his text 1 Timothy 5:4, "Let them first learn to show piety at home," he began: "It is a very common mistake to regard the eminence of the actors in our estimate of virtue . . . Hence it happens that we ourselves desire conspicuous occasions for the exhibition of our moral principles." However, "the main part of life is made up of small incidents and petty occurrences." The test of virtue is how a man lives in these daily experiences—"domestic piety," Emerson called it; how a man acts at the end of a tiresome day when he returns home and gives up all attempts to impress people, to appear better than he is:

> He takes off his goodness like a cumbersome garment and grows silent and splenetic. He has got rid of the prepossessing elegance of his address, that buoyant alacrity in the offices of politeness that won your praise. He is intemperate at his table; he is a sluggard in his bed; he is slothful and useless in his chair; he is sour or false in conversation. He breaks the commandments because he is at home. A strange reason surely for license and vice! Will the curtains of his windows shroud him from the Omniscient Eye? When we need the stimulus of a great occasion and many observers to excite our virtue, what is it in effect but to say that we fear man more than God and respect men more than we respect ourselves?[13]

If the virtues advocated here are domestic and commonplace, so are the vices: impoliteness, intemperance, sloth, untruthfulness—and not simply prevarication, but "sour or false . . . in conversation." To this strict integrity Emerson adds consideration for the feelings of other people. His emphasis on these small virtues, which he insists are not petty but of major significance, is almost a throwback to Puritan morality. And perhaps it was, for he asks rhetorically, "Will the curtains of his windows shroud him [the sinner] from the Omniscient Eye?"

One must never relax moral vigilance for a single moment, or, to emphasize the positive, "It is a beautiful but monitory thought that not an hour of our waking time after we have learned to distinguish good and evil ... but may be signalized by a virtuous action ..." Perhaps realizing the near impossibility of such constant and intense vigilance, Emerson suggests concentrating on one "well spent hour"—reminiscent of his mother's customary period of prayer and meditation every morning after breakfast: "One well spent hour is the proper seed of heaven and eternity." Let us, then, "aim to spend *one single hour* of every day without spot or blemish, without an error even in thought [Puritan again: to think a carnal sin is to be guilty of it] and give ourselves with our might to the performance."[14] The reward, says Emerson, will be "the resplendent home of all the good," for he still believes in a "Heaven," but also on earth, in the love of brothers, sisters, parents, and friends, and no less in one's own daily happiness.

II

The Reverend Waldo Emerson read his sermon on domestic piety the ninth time on December 23, 1827, at Concord, New Hampshire, where he had gone to preach three Sundays to a newly organized Unitarian congregation meeting temporarily in the Court House. One would like to think that a pretty sixteen-year-old girl named Ellen Tucker—the minister's future wife—was in the audience, but he recorded in letters and in an "Autobiographical MS" that he first met her the day after he preached his Christmas sermon on "The Nativity."[15]

With some reluctance Emerson had accepted the invitation to preach three Sundays at Concord, during the Christmas and New Year's period of 1827–28. "New Concord," as he called the town, was only about sixty miles north of "Old Concord," and a daily stagecoach (via Boston) connected the two, but it was still a tiresome, chilly journey in midwinter. Two days after agreeing to the New Hampshire invitation, Emerson received a similar one from nearby Brighton, and this made him regret still more that he must make the trip. Expecting to be bored and lonely, he "stocked" his trunk with books. On the last day of December he wrote

William that he was "comfortably lodged & provided for, but New Concord is a bitter cold place & cannot in any respect, in my judgment compare with the Old." Most of the thirty-five hundred inhabitants of the town lived on an unusually wide street a mile long, beside which stood the modest but imposing state capitol, the governor's house, a prison, and other state buildings.

The Unitarian Society, recently organized under the leadership of the Kent family, was planning to build a church, and was eager to increase its membership. Colonel William A. Kent was one of the town's most prominent citizens, a retired businessman, former state treasurer, who had entertained President Monroe and General Lafayette in his home during their visits to Concord. Daniel Webster was also a frequent guest. Colonel Kent had been married twice, and his large family consisted of his children by his first wife and those of his second wife, Margaret Tucker, whose first husband, a Boston merchant, had left her and her children considerable wealth.[16]

One of Colonel Kent's sons, Edward, had been a classmate of Waldo Emerson's at Harvard, and had praised the young minister to his family. Two of the colonel's own children lived with him, as well as Margaret and Ellen Tucker. Because of her fragile health, Ellen probably had not attended the Christmas service. She was in the early stages of tuberculosis of the lungs, that terrible scourge of New England in the early nineteenth century, which also afflicted her mother, her sister Margaret, and a stepbrother.

Everyone said Ellen Tucker was very beautiful, in spite of her pallor and lack of stamina. But she made only a mildly pleasant impression on Waldo Emerson on his first acquaintance with her—unless a mysterious undated confession in his Journal for this period indicated a reluctant interest: "I ought to apprise the reader that I am a bachelor & to the best of my belief have never been in love."[17]

Not only had Waldo Emerson never been in love; he had never even had a friendship with a woman who was not as old as his Aunt Mary or Sarah Bradford Ripley, his Uncle Samuel's awesomely intellectual wife. When he sentimentalized about an ideal friend, as he frequently did, he thought of a male friend. From New Concord he wrote Charles on New Year's, 1828, in acknowledgment of his brother's essay on "Friendship" in the January *Harvard Register:*

I would give more than I now own to find a convenient acquaintance such as I have read of & heard of & thought of times without number that would answer anyhow to the fabulous descriptions of a friend—yours for instance in the Register . . . Here in the snows, and at Cambridge in the chambers [of Divinity Hall,] I want him. A thousand smart things I have to say which born in silence die in silence for lack of his ear.[18]

Much as Waldo loved his brothers, they could not fulfill this need, because their education and way of life were too similar to his own. Even as he wrote this letter to Charles in a boardinghouse, awkwardly supporting the sheet of paper on his knee, "with a stranger by my side," he felt the pinch of this deficiency in his life. "My quarrel is with the race which will not give me what I want, either in the shape of man or woman." Evidently he had as yet no intimation that he had met such a friend in the "shape" of a young woman. However, his social life in Concord was just beginning. Next day he was to join a sleighing party to the Shaker community at Canterbury, about ten miles north of Concord. Maybe, he joked, he would join the Shakers: "Among the earliest institutions to be invented, if I read the stars right, is a protestant monastery, a place of elegant seclusion where melancholy gentlemen & ladies may go to spend the advanced season of single life in drinking milk, walking the woods & reading the Bible & the poets."

One of Emerson's favorite books since his youth was Bacon's *Essays,* and it is not unlikely that he had brought a copy to New Hampshire. At any rate, he was still in a Baconian frame of mind regarding friendship, love, and marriage. He agreed with Lord Bacon that it is a "miserable solitude to want true friends; without which the world is but a wilderness," and he often echoed Bacon in enumerating his need for a friend to share his emotions, give him advice, allow him to clarify his thoughts "by explaining them to a friend," and, in short, *be another self.*[19]

The previous year Emerson had confessed in his Journal (May 18, 1826): ". . . the friends that occupy my thoughts are not men but certain phantoms clothed in the form and face and apparel of men by whom they were suggested and to whom they bear a resemblance."[20] Phantoms of men, not women, we notice; phantoms compounded of ideas gleaned from Waldo's voluminous reading and the companionship of his brothers. *Love* still meant to him primarily the affection of male friends. Puritanical

Boston had taught him to be wary of sexual love, and Bacon's cynicism reinforced the lesson: "great spirits and great business do keep out this weak passion . . . For there was never proud man thought so absurdly well of himself as the lover doth of the person loved; and therefore it was well said, *That it is impossible to love and to be wise.*"[21]

Of course Lord Bacon admitted the necessity of "nuptial love" for the sake of procreation. But in another essay, "Of Marriage and Single Life," he proclaimed: "He that hath wife and children hath given hostages to fortune, which are impediments to great enterprises . . . Certainly the best works, and of greatest merit for the public, have proceeded from the unmarried or childless men; which both in affection and means have married the public." Emerson was too much of a Protestant to feel that he was married to his Church, and he felt no inclination to give "hostages to fortune."

III

At the end of three weeks in New Concord, Waldo was glad to return by stagecoach to Boston, and thence to his room in Divinity Hall at Harvard.[22] There on February 8 he wrote William he was busily engaged in writing sermons, but still apprehensive about his health: "I am living cautiously, yes treading on eggs to strengthen my constitution. It is a long battle this of mine betwixt life & death & tis wholly uncertain to whom the game belongs. So I never write when I can walk or especially when I can laugh."[23]

Occasionally Charles visited Waldo in Divinity Hall, and seemed to his hypochondriacal brother to be "the same honey catcher of pleasure, favor, & honour that he hath been & without paying for it like Edward with life & limb." In truth, Charles was paying a higher price than Waldo understood at the time, and so was Edward. "Edward lasts so well maugre these unutterable murderous diseases of which he talks that I think his chance is good to last long; quite as good as mine." In spite of his afflictions, however, Edward labored manfully in Boston at his legal studies, while Charles read Plato and Aristophanes in Greek and continued to impress the Harvard faculty. Waldo had begun reading Plato, too, but in Thomas Taylor's awkward translation, for he could read Greek only with laborious effort.

At the beginning of April, Waldo took up temporary residence with his mother in the Old Manse in Concord, partly because he would preach for several Sundays at nearby Lexington, and partly because Dr. Ripley, who had never been out of New England, had decided to assist at an ordination in Baltimore late in the month and to visit the Emerson in-laws in Alexandria, Virginia, and Mount Vernon.[24]

While Waldo was staying at the Old Manse, William alarmed his mother, in one of his infrequent letters from his garret in New York, by admitting that he had been ill. Waldo chided him for forgetting "that all the Emersons overdo themselves," and advised his brother to imitate him. He had been "lounging on a system for these many months writing something less than a sermon a month" and then resting after "such unparalleled exertions."[25] At the slightest twinge in his chest, he had sought out someone in Divinity Hall to divert his mind. "Especially do I court laughing persons; and after a merry or only a gossiping hour where the talk has been mere soap bubbles I have lost all sense of the mouse in my chest." It was no joke that Waldo had been seriously cultivating his childhood streak of "levity" as physical and psychic therapy. And it was beginning to work. But he could not persuade his career-haunted brothers to try it, especially the intensely ambitious Edward.

One of Waldo's fellow theological students who obliged him with diversion was George Burnap. On February 14 Waldo had recorded in his Journal:

> Burnap was very witty tonight. He said there was one man who had the queerest reputation—Dr. [Isaac] Watts—such a mixture of heathenism & scholastic learning & Calvinism & love & despair & mullygrubs—he was the funniest old cock in the theological walk; that that old Betty should be one of the three legs that support the Trinity & that the Church should go chanting his hymns for centuries mistaking the effusions of belly ache for the inspirations of David—was the greatest phenomenon. Then that he should write a treatise on Logic, & then one on the Improvement of the mind! Then, that his sun should set clear after being foggy all day! . . .[26]

Such irreverent interludes of merriment, however, are infrequent in Emerson's Journals. More often he is worried about the fogginess of his own mind and soul. "Did the morning sun find us awake? did we snatch with an angel's eagerness every moment for the mind that could be won from the care of life & health?" His conscience was still oppressed by inherited Puritanism, which at times conflicted with his emerging intellectual and moral independence. Thus in Divinity Hall he prepared a sermon for the annual day of "Fasting, Humiliation, and Prayer"[27] at the spring equinox, a somber tradition corresponding to the Jewish Day of Atonement, Yom Kippur, brought to the New World by the Puritan colonists and still observed in New England in Emerson's day. "When our fathers shook off the dust of the old world from their feet," Emerson asks in his fasting sermon, "did they shake off all its pollutions?" Like the Puritan ministers, Emerson replies that man has not changed since God cast him out of the Garden of Eden; "he has not lost one passion nor parted with one frailty." One of the events that is said to have shaken many people's belief in Divine Providence, as interpreted by the Calvinists, was the horrendous Lisbon earthquake in 1755, yet Emerson can still declare in this sermon: "I see no reason why the awful calamities of Lisbon should not be punishments & monitions. I see no superstition in such a regard. I bow to this hint, this expression of Omnipotence."

In another sermon, on Romans 8:14 ("For as many as are led by the Spirit of God, they are the sons of God"), he declares that "our happiness depends more on what we think of ourselves than on what others think of us." But he was not defending pride, for he goes on to say, "Give yourself no manner of anxiety about events, about the consequence of actions. They are really of no importance to us. They have another Director, controller, guide. The whole object of the Universe to us is the formation of Character."[28] With this lofty view of eternity, to quote another sermon in a preliminary stage of composition, "the events of this life cease to appear important." But "The principle which induced you when a boy to brave the displeasure of your Companions for truth's sake and when a man to cleave to your opinions tho' your bread or your life was the forfeit, shall ennoble you & endear you to the Deity in that far distant & awful hour."[29]

The time would come when this "principle" would indeed endanger Emerson's bread, and almost his life, but by that time he would believe in a "Day of Judgment" quite different from the one alluded to here. There were other contradictions which had not yet been resolved. In a Journal notation added several weeks later, Emerson felt consoled by the thought that every generous impulse which guided him as a child made him akin to "an archangel performing his awful duties." By such obedience, "I exchange the rags of my nature for a portion of the majesty of my maker. I am backed by Divine strength . . . I lean on [interpolated: "the Universe"] Omnipotence." But realizing the danger of this thought, Emerson hastily warns, "Do not suffer yourself to entertain this overweening conceit."[30]

Perhaps Emerson's reversion to a kind of Neo-Calvinism can be better understood in view of what was happening to him in the spring and summer of 1828. At the end of April he was still in Concord, at the Old Manse, but planning to return to Concord, New Hampshire, for six weeks, beginning late in May. The newly formed Unitarian congregation in New Hampshire was plainly interested in him as its prospective minister, but he had already turned down three other invitations to churches seeking a pastor, and had clearly indicated to the "New Concord" group that he did not feel strong enough to consider a permanent position anywhere. Nevertheless, when he started to Boston to catch the stagecoach for the trip, he had good reason to feel satisfaction in the prospect. He had gained strength, and Edward had finally agreed to take a vacation from his legal studies, reporting that he was "*healthier* & happier than ever in my life."[31] But this euphoria was deceptive. Even as Waldo preached on Sunday, May 25, Edward was seized by "fainting fits" in Concord, where he had gone to rest during Waldo's absence. Charles wrote Waldo to return as soon as possible, which he did.

A week later (June 2) Waldo wrote William from the Manse: "Edward is a great deal better. We were all thoroughly scared . . . He had fainting fits, a delirium, and had been affected strangely in his mind for a fortnight." One of his mental delusions was that at the time he stopped reading law he was completely cured of his tuberculosis of the lungs. Dr. James Jackson told the Emerson family that this was not true, though he blamed Edward's too-intense application to study as the main cause of his nervous collapse.

Waldo felt so encouraged by Edward's improvement that he returned to Concord, New Hampshire, for another two weeks. But on June 30 he wrote William from Divinity Hall in Cambridge: "We are born to trouble."[32] His mother had written him that Edward was ill again, "in a state of violent derangement," requiring restraint. She thought he would have to be committed to the hospital in Charlestown for the insane. Waldo hastened to Concord.[33] On July 2 he hired a closed carriage and, with the assistance of Dr. Josiah Bartlett and Edward Jarvis, William's Harvard classmate, carried Edward to McLean's Asylum. The superintendent, Dr. Rufus Wyman, did not want to accept Edward because he thought it would look bad for the family, but Waldo insisted that they could not manage him at home. His mother could not stand the strain any longer.

In the afternoon Waldo returned to Concord by way of Waltham, where he picked up his Aunt Sarah Bradford Ripley, who had offered to stay with his mother until she recovered from exhaustion. Waldo thought all she needed was rest, but he almost feared to hope for Edward—though "God can do all things." In the haste to get Edward settled in the asylum, Dr. Bartlett "gave his name as surety," though Waldo intended to assume this obligation. Bulkeley had been in the asylum for several weeks, but was now better. While there, Waldo learned that Dr. Frothingham, his father's successor in the First Church, had been secretly paying Bulkeley's expenses. Waldo took Bulkeley back to Chelmsford to stay with the same kind family which had kept him while Waldo taught there.

These errands accomplished, Waldo returned to Divinity Hall and described Edward's condition to William:

He has been now for one week thoroughly deranged & a great deal of the time violent so as to make it necessary to have two men in the room all the time. Concord people were very kind. . . . His frenzy took all forms; sometimes he was very gay & bantered every body, & then it was only necessary to humour him & walk the room with him. Afterward would come on a peevish or angry state & he would throw down every thing in the room & throw his clothes &c out of the window; then perhaps on being restrained wd. follow a paroxysm of perfect frenzy & he wd. roll & twist on the floor with his eyes shut for half an hour.—But whats the need of relating this—there he lay—Edward the admired learned eloquent thriving boy—a maniac. Poor Charles dismayed at these tidings asks what good it is to be [a] scholar? Edward did not sleep—that is—hardly ever . . .[34]

Edward already had many debts, totaling around seven hundred dollars, and Waldo still had unpaid debts of his own. Fortunately, he wrote William, "Charles' debts end [with his graduation from Harvard in August] & now if God is merciful to him, he will be in a condition to help us." Charles had just won the first prize for his Bowdoin dissertation, but under the circumstances Waldo regarded this as "a kind of mockery."[35] To this distinction Charles would soon add two more, the honor of delivering the valedictory oration to his class on July 15, and a commencement oration on August 27.

Of course Waldo heard the commencement oration, and was disappointed in it because he thought Charles took his audience too much for granted, as if he believed it had come to hear him and not he to stir it. Charles also had barely failed to win first place in his class standing, but his always critical brother thought this might do him good, "push him out of his enchanted circle"[36] and make him feel he must struggle like other people. Whatever the justification of this severe judgment, whether unconscious jealousy or Puritan ethic, it contradicted the advice Waldo had been giving Edward and William—and himself—to take it easy and float with the tide. But Waldo had never really understood Charles's need for encouragement.

IV

At the beginning of July, Waldo Emerson received some good news, though at the time he felt little joy in it. Dr. Henry Ware Jr., pastor of the Second Church in Boston, was gravely ill.[37] Waldo was saddened by this report, and not greatly cheered by having been invited by the Standing Committee to substitute for Dr. Ware until his recovery. Waldo knew that there was a strong possibility that the engagement could be permanent, and he still was not ready to assume that responsibility. However, he agreed to preach for four Sabbaths for sixty dollars, the income particularly welcome just then. Actually he continued to preach more or less regularly in the Second Church until the end of November, when he withdrew because he felt that his occupying the pulpit prevented the congregation from hearing other candidates who might suit it better than he. No urging could change this scruple. He might be unsure of his own ability, but when his conscience spoke he obeyed it without hesitation.

Edward's collapse, which Waldo considered a manifestation of the "constitutional calamity" of his family, made the youthful minister more introspective than ever; yet he did not feel himself liable "to the same evil," he recorded in his Journal on July 10:

I have so much mixture of *silliness* in my intellectual frame that I think Providence has tempered me against this. My brother lived & acted &

spoke with preternatural energy. My own manner is sluggish; my speech sometimes flippant, sometimes embarrassed & ragged; my actions (if I may say so) are of a passive kind. Edward had always great power of face. I have none. I laugh; I blush; I look ill tempered; against my will & against my interest. But all this imperfection as it appears to me is a caput mortuum, is a ballast—as things go—is a defence.[38]

Emerson's providential nature protected him in two ways, both of which we have seen before in his life, but they now assume new importance. The first of these was his fondness for strolling—that is, walking in the fields, for much of his reading had also been intellectual strolling:

I deliberately shut up my books in a cloudy July noon, put on my old clothes & old hat & slink away to the whortleberry bushes & slip with the greatest satisfaction into a little cowpath where I am sure I can defy observation. This point gained, I solace myself for hours with picking blue berries & other trash of the woods far from fame behind the birch trees. I seldom enjoy hours as I do these. I remember them in winter. I expect them in spring. I do not know a creature that I think has the same humour or would think it respectable. Yet the friend, the Anteros, whom I seek through the world, now in cities—now in wildernesses—now at sea—will know the delight of sauntering with the melancholy Jacques.

The other means of salvation was Emerson's manner of making his old ideas—and future doctrines—of self-reliance and compensation work together. A trial sermon which he finally completed and preached in November began: "It is an important fact that a man carries about with him his own favour or disgrace."[39] Emerson did not mean *fate* in the Greek sense, or Calvinistic predestination, though he did believe that character is fate and that every man bears the seeds of his own destruction. "Do not you see that every misfortune is misconduct; that every honour is desert; that every effort is an insolence of your own? . . . You carry your fortune in your own hand."[40]

Therefore, "The great business of life is to learn *ourselves*." Reading history, studying science, acquiring skill in a profession are useless unless they end in self-knowledge. No other text would ever mean more to Ralph Waldo Emerson than Luke 17:21: "The Kingdom of God is within you." The obvious teaching from this is that the "powerful Spirit" within each person "may be trained into an angel or deformed into a fiend," and

Emerson certainly embraced this interpretation. But he was also evolving an original moral philosophy of greater psychological subtlety and of profound significance for his own life: "If you stammer in your talk or are cloudy, why then it is because your purpose is not pure. If the plan you explain is high-minded[,] generous on your part[,] why then the reason you stammer is because you tell it to get credit for your magnanimity[.]"

Although this doctrine toughened Emerson's moral fiber, and gave him the strength and confidence to overcome his inherited weaknesses, it gave him no holidays from his responsibilities. Not only God but also his own psyche required his absolute *purity of purpose* at all times. This was indeed as stern a doctrine to live with as the Calvinistic absolute sovereignty of God, but Emerson's providential "levity" and fondness for strolling prevented the tension from growing unbearable. Yet there was a tension, which resulted in what came to be his notorious paradoxical duality, not yet fully developed.

Waldo Emerson would never at the time have admitted even to himself that sex had anything to do with this tension between duty and self-preservation, or if the thought ever crossed his mind, he felt ashamed and guilty. And of course he would use high-minded words. "It is hard to yoke love & wisdom," he wrote in his Journal sometime in November or December 1828.[41] This sounds more like the worldly cynicism of Lord Bacon than Plutarch, whom he was reading at the time. He was rereading one of his favorite books, Plutarch's *Morals,* and was especially interested in the symposium "Of Love," in which he found "the ancient theory"—though he labels it "a sweet falsehood"—that "Beauty is the flower of Virtue."[42] This symposium explored almost every aspect of love imaginable: homosexuality, heterosexuality, lust, conjugal love (which Plutarch praises), and various degrees of "spiritual" love. But Emerson cogitates the subject with wariness: "Experience looks grave . . . when the radiant eye peeps out upon him, and he stands half-convinced . . ."

The tempting eye could have belonged to no other woman than Ellen Tucker, the beautiful girl with the consumptive pallor whom he had met the previous December, when she was only sixteen. So far as is known, he had not communicated with her by letter since then. But she reminded him that at twenty-four (he was now twenty-five) he had "never been in love."[43] That his casual meetings with her during his few weeks of preaching in her church in May and June had made him conscious of his susceptibility to her attractions is evident in other sentences of the same Journal entry quoted above: If thrown "into circumstances favorable to the sentiment of love[,]" he suspected his "reason would stand on a perilous unsteady footing." He distrusted his own judgment and feared to gamble:

> The terms of intercourse in society are singularly unpropitious to the virtuous curiosity of young men with regard to the inner qualities of a beautiful woman. They may only see the outside of the house they want to buy. The chance is very greatly against her possessing those virtues & general principles which they most value.[44]

However, he did trust "the moral harmony of human nature" and "the fact that the deportment of a beautiful woman in the presence of her admirer never offends point blank against the great laws whose violation would severely shock him." What "laws"? Modesty, playing the game of coquetry with such guarded decorum that a proper young man such as the Reverend Waldo Emerson could pretend that the attractive young woman was not trying to ensnare him with the lure of sex. Of course Emerson was not so innocent as to be unaware of the necessity—even desirability—of the sexual appetite, but it must be refined and held in check by other emotions. Plutarch had taught him the difference between Venus and the "God of Love":

> For indeed the great and wonderful work of generation is properly the work of Venus, where Love is only an assistant when present with Venus; but his absence renders the act altogether irksome, dishonorable, harsh, and ungrateful. For the conjunction of man and woman without true affection, like hunger and thirst, terminates with satiety, and produces nothing truly noble or commendable; but when the Goddess by means of Love puts away all loathsome glut of pleasure, she perpetuates delight by a continual supply of friendship and harmony of temper. Therefore Parmenides asserts Love to be the most ancient of all the works of Venus . . .[45]

More important still, Plutarch taught Emerson that sexual love could be a ladder to spiritual love of the highest order:

> This love, entering through the body, becomes a guide to lead the soul from the world below to truth and the fields of truth, where full, pure, deceitless beauty dwells . . . a generous and modest lover . . . lighting upon

the beauty of a visible body, and making use of it as a kind of organ of the memory, he embraces and loves, and by conversation [that is, sexual intercourse] augmenting his joy and satisfaction still more and more inflames his understanding. But neither do these lovers conversing with bodies rest satisfied in this world with a desire and admiration of this same light . . .[46]

After reading such a beautiful doctrine of love, Waldo Emerson was already prepared, however unwittingly, to fall in love with Ellen Louisa Tucker when he left Boston, accompanied by his brother Edward, on December 6, 1828, for Concord, New Hampshire. Edward had finally recovered his sanity and seemed to be gaining strength each day, but Waldo thought a couple of weeks in New Hampshire would be good for him. In the uncertain state of his own emotions, perhaps Waldo also felt he might need the companionship of the brother with whom he had always been closest since childhood. Of course, as it turned out, Edward was left much to himself, but the New Hampshire legislature was in session and he could amuse himself by attending the sessions as a spectator.

One small piece of evidence that Emerson did not suddenly and unexpectedly fall in love with Ellen is that before leaving Boston he had purchased a sentimental anthology in ornate binding, known at that time as a "gift book," entitled *Forget Me Not,* which he inscribed "for ELT."[47] But Ellen was as ready for his affection as he was for hers, and the courtship progressed so rapidly that on December 17 she promised to marry him,[48] a few days before he had to return in order to keep his promise to preach in Waltham for his Uncle Samuel Ripley on Christmas Day. The day before Christmas, Waldo wrote William from Divinity Hall:

I have the happiness to inform you that I have been now for one week engaged to Ellen Louisa Tucker a young lady who if you will trust my account is the fairest and best of her kind. Not to drive you to scepticism by any extravagances, I will tell you a simple story. She is the youngest daughter of the late Beza Tucker a merchant of Boston of whose children you may remember William Sewall was guardian. When we were at Roxbury they lived in the Sumner house on the Dedham turnpike. The mother has been now three or four years the wife of Col W. A. Kent of Concord, N.H. It is now just a year since I became acquainted with Ellen at that house—but I thought I had got over my blushes & wishes when now I determined to go into that dangerous neighborhood again on Edward's account. But the presumptuous man was overthrown by the eye &

the ear & surrendered at discretion. He is now as happy as it is safe in life
to be in the affection of the lady & the approbation of the friends. She is 17
years old, & very beautiful by universal consent. Her feelings are exceedingly delicate & noble—and I only want you to see her. Edward is very
highly gratified . . .

A miniature portrait of Ellen Tucker painted a few months later shows a
pale girl with a wide forehead and pointed chin (making a heart-shaped
face), with large, dark eyes, cupid lips, long, shapely nose, and curly black
hair arranged in a low pompadour style. Her notably small waist, evidently
tightly corseted, makes her appear rather surprisingly full-breasted for a
delicate seventeen-year-old girl. Edward testified that he thought the portrait "nearly perfect," though Charles, the enthusiast, later declared, on
first meeting his future sister-in-law, that it did not do her justice. Charles
was also impressed by her "unstudied dignity."[49] Probably, because of her
strong character as well as her precarious health, she was somewhat intellectually and morally precocious. She had already had several suitors, but
no one to compare in charm and gift of language to this young Unitarian
pastor. Being quite religious herself, she would of course have been more
susceptible to a devout minister.

Already deeply in debt and without an assured income, Emerson felt it
his duty to give Ellen a frank appraisal of his "prospects," but she impatiently told him she did not wish to hear about them. The reply indicated
both her idealism and her innocence, though in fact she had an income of
her own from her father's estate and felt independent. As for her health,
she had a premonition that she might not live long, but neither she nor
her family was aware how short her life would be. She had "raised blood"
some months earlier, and had frequent spells of exhaustion which necessitated her resting in bed. Both her father and her brother had died from
tuberculosis of the lungs, and her sister Margaret had also been coughing
up blood—and her mother as well.[50] Yet none of her family seemed un-
duly alarmed—perhaps the symptoms were so familiar that they had lost
some of their terror. Emerson himself was well aware of the danger, but he
had survived his illness two years before and seemed in a fair way to recover entirely. He hoped that by the most devoted care and the science of
the best physicians in Boston he could save the life of this precious girl.
This ambition, in fact, was undoubtedly one of her attractions for him.

Waldo's worshipful love for Ellen turned him to prayer. Four days after his engagement he prayed: "Will my Father in heaven regard us with kindness, and as he hath, as we trust, made us for each other, will he be pleased to strengthen & purify & prosper & eternize our affection!"[51] On January 17, 1829, he wrote in his Journal: "She has the purity & confiding religion of an angel. Are the words common? the words are true. Will God forgive me my sins & aid me to deserve this gift of his mercy." Thus, in six nerve-racking months Emerson's devotions had progressed from a desperate plea to God to "rescue & restore" Edward to sanity, to a tremulously happy prayer to God to "eternize" his shared love with the angelic girl who had promised to marry him.

CHAPTER VII

The New Eye of the Priest

It is the office of the priest ... to see the creation with a new eye....[1]

I

Waldo Emerson's engagement to Ellen Tucker affected him like a religious conversion, which actually it was. His whole world seemed suddenly flooded with God's benevolence. He had no doubt whatever that his finding Ellen was providential, and that her love for him was a holy blessing. Then, as if in confirmation of the divine origin of this blessing, the Second Church in Boston, where he had substituted for the ailing pastor, gave him a "call" which would enable him to support a wife and at the same time start him on the professional career which he had been postponing for two years, afraid to trust his health—really, afraid to trust himself.

On January 17, 1829, at his desk in Divinity Hall in Cambridge, he recorded his thoughts in his Journal:

My history has had its important days within a brief period. Whilst I enjoy the luxury of an unmeasured affection for an object so deserving of it all & who requites it all,—I am called by an ancient & respectable church to become its pastor. I recognize in these events, accompanied as they are by so many additional occasions of joy in the condition of my family, I recognize, with acute sensibility, the hand of my heavenly Father. This happiness awakens in me a certain awe: I know my imperfections: I know my ill-deserts; & the bounty of God makes me feel my own sinfulness the more. I throw myself with humble gratitude upon his goodness. I feel my total dependance. O God direct & guard & bless me, & those, & especially *her,* in whom I am blessed.—[2]

The official invitation of the Second Church to Emerson had been voted only a week earlier (January 11),[3] but he had probably been informally approached some days before, and his first reaction had been a feeling of awe mingled with gratitude and fear, "an apprehension of reverse always arising from success."[4] On January 6 he confessed in a letter to his Aunt Mary:

> You know—none can know better—on what straitened lines we have all walked up to manhood. In poverty and many troubles the seeds of our prosperity were sown. . . . Now all these troubles appeared a fair counterbalance to the flatteries of fortune. I lean always to that ancient superstition (if it is such, though drawn from a wise survey of human affairs) which taught men to beware of unmixed prosperity, for Nemesis keeps watch to overthrow the high.[5]

The "unmixed prosperity" included not only Emerson's engagement and the means of supporting his future wife, but also his brothers' improved health and prospects of success in their careers. Waldo spelled out the happy situation for his aunt: "William has begun to live by the law. Edward has recovered his reason and his health. Bulkeley was never more comfortable in his life. Charles is prospering in all ways." His own health was no longer cause for concern, and he could not wish for better professional prospects. Perhaps, he wrote Aunt Mary, "The way to be safe is to be thankful," to give the credit to God and not himself. His aunt had always predicted his success, "and now, when it seems to be coming, I chuse to direct to you this letter which I enter as a sort of protest against my Ahriman [Persian Prince of Darkness], that, if I am called, after the way of my race, to pay a fatal tax for my good, I may appeal to the sentiment of collected anticipation with which I saw the tide turn and the winds blow softly from the favouring west."

There were, indeed, deeper reasons than superstition for Emerson's uneasiness. He may have been unaware that the health of Edward and Charles was more precarious than surface appearance indicated. But he was certainly aware that Ellen's life was menaced. And it was scarcely two weeks before she "raised blood" again. This happened in Boston on January 19, for Ellen and her family had moved to the city early in the month to be near Waldo, further augmenting his happiness—and uneasiness.[6]

Waldo had also himself unwittingly contributed to Ellen's relapse. His mother had not yet met her, and he was eager to exhibit his jewel. Consequently, soon after Ellen reached Boston, Waldo took her to Concord, and of course was delighted that his mother and step-grandfather adored her on sight. But the young couple returned to Boston in the rain, and the exposure and exertion stirred up "that dangerous complaint," as Waldo termed it in a letter to William on January 28. He called himself "one of her nurses most unskilful but most interested & am writing my letter in her chamber." By this time, "Beauty has got better & so I am better . . ."[7]

But Waldo was still so concerned for Ellen's safety that he had not yet accepted the "call at the Old North," thinking that the doctors might tell Ellen she "ought to go away" to a milder climate. In that case Waldo would accompany her and reject the enticing offer of the Second Church. To Charles he expressed the premonition that "she is too lovely to live long"; yet, even if she should die next day, "it would still have been a rich blessing to have been permitted to have loved her." He felt that no sacrifice would be too great to prolong this blessing, and his only worry was how to accomplish it.

In this mood Emerson sought the advice of Dr. James Jackson, whom he believed to be the best physician in Boston. Dr. Jackson told him that he did not believe Ellen's disease was so far advanced that it could not be cured with sufficient care and attention, and he saw no reason for her to leave Boston.[8] Thus reassured, Waldo decided to accept the invitation of the Second Church to the office of junior pastor.

In his acceptance letter of January 30, 1829, Emerson admitted his reluctance and qualms of conscience:

If my own feelings could have been consulted, I should have desired to postpone, at least, for several months, my entrance into this solemn office. I do not now approach it with any sanguine confidence in my abilities, or in my prospects. I come to you in weakness, and not in strength. In a short life, I have yet had abundant experience of the uncertainty of human hopes. I have learned the lesson of my utter dependency; and it is in a devout reliance upon other strength than my own, in a humble trust on God to sustain me, that I put forth my hand to his great work.[9]

However, Emerson wanted the Proprietors to know that he understood his duties and would "shun no labour" to *fulfill* them. He felt encouraged by the overwhelming vote of the pewholders for his appointment, and diplomatically expressed "the hope of enjoying the counsel and aid of the distinguished servant of God who has so long laboured among you." Dr. Henry Ware Jr. would continue to receive his salary of eighteen hundred dollars a year as the senior pastor while he took a leave for his health, but it was expected that he would resign in a few months to accept a professorship in the Harvard Divinity School. Until then, Emerson's salary would be twelve hundred dollars.

On February 3 Waldo wrote William: "Ellen is mending slowly & I am very much encouraged about her."[10] He could now turn his thoughts to his ordination, which was set for Wednesday, March 11. As the time drew near, he sentimentalized to William about leaving room No. 14 in Divinity Hall.[11] He sounded like a bachelor on the eve of his wedding, and indeed his ordination would be closely related in his mind to his wedding, though that must be postponed until Ellen was stronger.

The ordination was conducted by friends and relatives in a manner that could hardly have been friendlier or more encouraging. Ellen was still too weak to attend, but her mother was present. Of course Waldo's own mother was a proud spectator, and his brothers Edward and Charles—William could not leave his law practice in New York. Venerable Grandfather Ripley gave the "charge," as he had at Waldo's father's ordination in 1792; generous Uncle Samuel Ripley (who had financed Waldo's health-seeking trip to Florida) preached the ordination sermon; the Reverend Nathaniel Frothingham, William Emerson's successor at the First Church, gave the right hand of fellowship; the Reverend Francis Parkman, minister of the New North Church, gave the ordaining prayer.

Other visiting ministers also spoke. One of them was the Reverend Ezra Stiles Gannett, who had graduated from Harvard the year before Emerson. He declared with acerbity perhaps sharpened by experience, "If I must choose between the condition of a slave in Algiers, & the servitude of a clergyman, who dares not speak lest he sh^d startle a prejudice, give me the former."[12] The purpose of this vehement statement was to advise Emerson's parishioners to give him free rein in carrying out his duties according to his own conscience. Presumably this advice was provoked by the Reverend Gannett's own professional observations and not by prescient understanding of Emerson's future relations with his congregation. Yet the advice was prophetic, fortuitous or not, and it ominously foreshadowed one of the perils of Emerson's pastorate.

At the end of the ordination ceremonies the audience dined at four long tables in nearby Hancock School. Then Waldo's mother left the banquet to take tea with her future daughter-in-law and give her a full account of the happy events. Except for the absence of Ellen, Aunt Mary, and William, the new junior pastor of the Second Church could take deep satisfaction in the day's proceedings.

II

The Second Church was indeed, as Emerson called it in his Journal, "venerable," having been founded in 1650 and presided over for more than a century by the two great Puritan divines Increase Mather and his son Cotton.[13] But the present building on Hanover Street near the corner of Richmond, a three-story brick structure with a square tower surmounted by a pointed spire, was not even on the site of the original church, a wooden building on Clark Street, which British soldiers tore down in the winter of 1775 and used for fuel.[14]

After the Revolution the Second Church united with the New Brick Church on Hanover, but retained its name. Some people still called it "Old North," but it was not the "Old North Church" celebrated by Longfellow in his fanciful poem on the midnight ride of Paul Revere. That was another "Old North" (there were several), or Christ Church, the second Anglican church in Boston (now Unitarian), where the Reverend Francis Parkman preached.

The North End had never entirely recovered from the British occupation. Middle-class people still lived there in 1829, including several wealthy merchants and shippers, but it had become unfashionable. As early as 1822, members of Christ Church complained that "the young gentlemen who have married wives in other parts of the town have found it difficult to persuade them to become so ungenteel as to attend worship in the North End."

Clipper and packet ships anchored at the wharves a few blocks to the east of the Second Church, but saloons and brothels also flourished in this region and contributed to the social decline of the North End. The most notorious brothel was "the Beehive," on Ann, a short street running from the harbor to Richmond, which intersected Hanover near the Second Church. The police frequently raided the Beehive, and respectable citizens joked about "the nymphs of Ann Street." One memorable raid took place on July 22, 1825, when spectators saw "old marm Cooper scudding through School alley under full sail at a rate that would have done credit to a privateersman." Ann Street acquired such a bad reputation that some years later it was renamed North.

The Second Church did not, therefore, compare in social prestige with the First Church, where Emerson's father had preached, but it was still a desirable parish. During his twelve-year pastorship Dr. Ware had increased the membership to nearly a hundred, and there was no lack of candidates for the position Emerson had accepted. One of these was Dr. Charles Follen, professor of German at Harvard, who had married one of the Cabots of Boston.[15] The salary was more than adequate for the period.

During his substitute preaching for Dr. Ware, Emerson had made many friends, as the vote of the pewholders for his appointment indicated (seventy-six out of seventy-nine—the three negative votes were cast by one person who held three pews and wanted Dr. Follen). One of Emerson's most loyal friends was Abel Adams, a merchant at Central Wharf, who became treasurer of the Second Church in 1829. Until his marriage Emerson boarded with Mr. Adams on Chardon Street.[16]

Of course Emerson would not have been considered for the position of Dr. Ware's assistant (and successor) if Dr. Ware himself had not favored the appointment. A few months later the senior pastor would be somewhat alarmed by rumors that his young colleague neglected the authority of Scripture in his sermons, but Emerson's relations with him were friendly, in spite of differences in personality. Fourteen years later Emerson described Dr. Ware's paradoxical character in his Journal. Though outwardly frigid, he was "a volcano covered with snow." He did not display "enthusiasm," yet drove himself without mercy and was impatient with the American Unitarian Association for its timidity and lack of enterprise.

All his talent was available & he was a good example of the proverb no doubt a hundred times applied to him of "a free steed driven to death." He ought to have been dead ten years ago, but hard work had kept him alive. In the post mortem examination his lungs were found healed over &

sound & his disorder was in the brain. A very slight & puny frame he had, & the impression of size was derived from his head. Then he was dressed with heroical plainness. I think him well entitled to the dangerous style of Professor of Pulpit eloqu[enc]e[,] none but W. E. Channing so well & he had ten times the business valour of Channing. This was a soldier that flung himself into all risks at all hours, not a solemn martyr kept to be burned once & make the flames proud. In calm hours & friendly company, his face expanded into broad simple sunshine; and I thought le bon Henri a pumpkin-sweeting [a variety of sweet apple].[17]

Such a hardworking minister was not easy for Emerson to follow, but less difficult in preaching than in the other pastoral duties. Naturally diffident and uncomfortable in the presence of strangers, Emerson especially disliked the custom of visitation. But he kept to a rigorous schedule. After preaching twice on Sunday, March 22, marrying a couple, baptizing a baby, and assisting in administering the Lord's Supper, he wrote Grandfather Ripley:

I have been exceedingly busy the last week in making my introductory visits in the parish. It is a new labour & I feel it in every bone of my body. I have made somewhat more than fifty pastoral visits and am yet but in the ends & frontiers of my society. . . . I fear nothing now except the preparation of sermons. The prospect of one each week, for an indefinite time to come is almost terrifick.[18]

Charles wrote William on April 12:

He visits his people without any other guide or introduction, than his own knowledge of the street wherein they live. And thus he has sometimes made long calls, kindly & affectionate on families who had no other claim to his attention, than that of bearing the same name with his parishioners.[19]

Of course, preaching was no novelty for Emerson, for he had delivered twenty-six sermons (that was the extent of his hoard of manuscripts) nearly two hundred times, some of them more than once in the Second Church. If pressed for time he could repeat more, and actually did reuse twenty-two of the twenty-six. Once a month he could also exchange pulpits with some minister in the region, and this did not require a new sermon. But to keep up his reputation in his own church, he must write new sermons appropriate for his congregation.

Emerson liked to write; it was the *necessity* of being prepared each Sunday that kept him uneasy. Each morning he usually read or wrote for four hours, then made professional calls in the afternoon. This schedule did not leave as much time as he wished to spend with Ellen, who boarded in the vicinity, but he sacrificed his personal pleasure for duty. However, his will was not as strong as his sense of duty, and he often procrastinated. "I sit Friday night and note the first thought that arises," he confessed in his Journal. "Presently, another, presently five or six—of all these I take the *mean,* as the subject for Saturday's sermon."[20] *Saturday* because on that day he must write a rough draft of his sermon, often getting up early Sunday morning to make a readable copy. But probably many of the sermons he dated Saturday were actually finished that day. When he planned to repeat an old sermon, he often, though not always, revised it—noting the fact on the manuscript. On some of his manuscripts he also recorded the time he had consumed in a practice reading of it. In the early sermons the average time was thirty-five minutes, but in later sermons he might consume fifty minutes. If he could have spoken extempore, or even from notes, he might have saved himself much labor, but he never knew exactly what he wanted to say until he could see it on paper. The right words somehow came to him in the act of writing, an experience which affected his theory of consciousness as God-directed.

The traditional order of the church service made Emerson feel cramped and uncomfortable, with the invariable opening prayer, the reading of Scripture, singing of the first hymn, then the sermon, followed by another prayer, another hymn, and the formal benediction. Though he had no ear for music and rather disliked it, he enjoyed selecting the hymns, for he had decided favorites, choosing them for the words and sentiment. But praying in public, which was extempore in most Protestant churches, was painful. In writing his sermons he could weigh and select his words until they satisfied him, but in praying in public he could not pause for thought. The necessity of avoiding awkward pauses sometimes made him say what he did not entirely believe, or fall back upon clichés, and insincerity was to him a cardinal sin.

But with the sermon manuscript before him, Emerson could enunciate the words with confidence. Once he had begun reading in the rich baritone voice he had inherited from his father, supported by the semicircular mahogany arms of the desk of the pulpit, occasionally glancing down at the friendly upturned faces, he felt a deeply satisfying pleasure in his performance. Charles thought he became more eloquent each Sunday. Sometimes he would suddenly boom out a sentence for emphasis, and he could see the nodding heads come to attention. Why had they come to church at all? He knew that many of his congregation had come less to hear him, or, more important, to engage in genuine worship, than to be seen, to be sociable, or simply out of habit. He took his own dedication so seriously that he worried about the motives of less dedicated church members. Religion was not to him a matter of creed, ritual, or conformity to traditional thought or conduct, but an intensely felt experience of his relation to God.

III

In his first sermon after his ordination, "The Christian Ministry," in two parts, delivered at the morning and evening services on March 15, Emerson attempted to define his duties as minister and those of his parishioners to their church and their pastor. After an eloquent little oration on the Apostle Paul's declaration to the Romans on "the power of God unto salvation" before Paul's departure for Rome and martyrdom, Emerson turned to the practical aspects of his own duties to the Second Church. Under "public ministrations" he included prayer and preaching. Prayer, he said, was the "fruit of a frame of mind . . . to be sought in the affections and not in the intellect."[21] Prayer could "soothe and refresh and edify the soul as no other exercise can." However, the minister makes good prayers for his congregation "not so much by efforts . . . as by leading a good life." Then will he be able "to call his Father by names which he will acknowledge and in tones and sentiments that shall find their echo in every pious heart."

In prayer the Christian minister "is only the voice of the congregation, he merely utters the petitions which all feel." (In a few months Emerson would grow away from this doctrine.) But in preaching "he undertakes to instruct the congregation, [though] himself an erring man, to deal out to his brethren the laws of the Almighty, to carry the conviction of duty home to their hearts, to encourage the faint hearted, to persuade the reluctant, to melt the obdurate, and to shake the sinner."

Some of these words almost echo the convictions of the early Puritan ministers of the Second Church, such as Cotton Mather, who confidently regarded himself as God's spokesman. Even the apologetic phrase "himself an erring man" is reminiscent of the Calvinists' "original sin" doctrine, which as a Unitarian Emerson emphatically rejected. Perhaps he let his subject and the occasion influence him in his choice of words. Nearly a year later in his Journal he complained that in preaching, "Topics are the masters of the preacher. He cannot often write in the way he deems best & most level with life. He is obliged to humour his mind in the choice & the development of his subject."[22] (By "humour" he meant, probably, not penetrating sufficiently beneath surface consciousness to his own "soul" or conscience.)

In preliminary notes for this sermon, Emerson thought of the Christian minister as "a man who is separated from men in all the rough courses where defilement can hardly be escaped; & who mixes with men only for purposes that make himself & them better . . ."[23] But he did not mean these words in quite the arrogant or seclusive sense they imply. He was by nature aloof, but not conceited or antisocial. What he meant (as his notes make clear) was that the minister must keep himself "aloof from the storm of passion, from political hatred, from the jealousy & intrigue of gain, from the contracting influence of low company & little arts." In other words, the minister must exemplify in his own moral life the ideal he preaches. In Part I, Emerson says that "every man [not just the minister] who gives himself up wholly to a just sentiment which he lives to inculcate, will be eloquent." Walt Whitman, Emerson's disciple, later wanted to make his own life a poem. Emerson set the example by wanting to make his life a sermon.

In 1829 this was a more radical doctrine for the pulpit than it might appear to be, as becomes apparent when Emerson goes on to criticize contemporary preaching and to set forth his own intentions:

Men imagine that the end and use of preaching is to expound a text and to unfold the divisions and subdivisions of meaning of *Grace,* of *Justification,* of *Atonement,* of *Sanctification,* and are permitted to forget that Christianity is an infinite and universal law which touches all action, all passion, all rational being; that it is the revelation of a Deity whose being the soul cannot reject without denying itself; ... yes, religion is the *home of the mind,* from which man may wander, but he wanders unhappy, and bewails at every new departure his inability to return.

Though scorning the theological terms mentioned here, Emerson's statement contains far-reaching metaphysical assumptions which we shall examine later (several times). In the context of this sermon, we may recapitulate simply: religion is a state of mind, a *feeling* of one's relation to God, with no authority except one's own deepest intuitive convictions. Intending to exhibit this kind of religion in his sermons, Emerson warns his audience that he will not be "afraid of innovation" and "new forms of address." Some may find "the want of sanctity in my style, and the want of solemnity in my illustrations." But Jesus himself spoke in parables of "low and familiar" things: ". . . let me ask, if he addressed himself to the men of this age and of this country, [would he not] appeal with equal frequency to those arts and objects by which we are surrounded, to the printing press and the loom, to the phenomena of steam and of gas, to the magnificence of towns, to free institutions, and a petulant and vain nation?"[24]

What Emerson meant, of course, was that religion was not something experienced only by Hebrew prophets or Christ's Apostles centuries ago and embalmed in the antique language of the Bible, but a way of life to be lived now. As the spokesman for such a view Emerson also imposed the highest possible demands upon himself:

It may be easily inferred that my views of my duty as a Christian teacher impose on me the necessity of giving to my own mind the highest cultivation, and that of every kind my manner of life will permit. *It imperiously demands the critical knowledge of the Christian Scriptures, which are to be considered the direct voice of the most High—the reason of God speaking to the reason of man.* But does it less demand the contemplation of his benevolence and his might in his [God's] works? It demands a discipline of the intellect, but more than all it demands a training of the affections. Whatever else can be shared this is essential. Any defects can be excused but the defect of a pure heart and a good life.

No doubt Emerson inserted and emphasized the importance of the Scriptures for those in his church who had reported to Dr. Ware that he neglected the Holy Word, but he wanted also to stress his belief that God still spoke to men both through the Bible and through his visible creation. And the last thing he wanted, Emerson told his congregation, was for them to depart from the church whispering praises of his pulpit manner, his language, his voice, or his musical periods. He wanted to stir their minds and emotions so deeply that they would remember his sermon and be permanently influenced by it.

In Part II of "The Christian Minister," Emerson amplified the leading idea in Part I: "the minister should be a man of feeling, or I fear he will vainly endeavour to excite movements in other souls that have no archetypes in his own."[25] He could "easily conceive a perfection in the performance of a minister's duties which far exceeds the low limit" of his powers. But he hoped to "see with emotion" the afflictions of his parishioners and see "by his own experience how it can be made to redound to your good . . ."

Here we have a variation on the Puritan doctrine of Providence, which taught that every affliction or happiness was God's specific punishment or reward. With Emerson, however, human effort could *make* it "redound to your good," and he hoped as a minister to assist each member of his church in turning every experience to good use. To do this he must know intimately the lives of his parishioners, who in turn must give him their friendship and trust. In this ideal he doubtless remembered those boyhood buggy rides with his Grandfather Ripley through Concord, and perhaps he had not yet realized that he did not have Dr. Ripley's gregarious sympathy.

Then, coming to the duties of the church members to himself, Emerson asked them to accept him in the same spirit of friendship and confidence he extended to them, making allowances for his mistakes and inexperience. They should not expect him suddenly to rival their former, incomparable pastor. He needed time to grow in his new office. Fortunately, Dr. Ware's "prayers and his hopes shall be blended with ours." With such backing, "I enter on my duties with all good hope, but without levity and without presumption."

Emerson said he stood upon "holy ground," where the walls of this ancient temple echo "the voices of the elder saints and holy fathers of the New England church." Perhaps the young minister was letting himself be carried away by the emotions of the occasion, or straining too obviously to flatter Dr. Ware and the Second Church, but he did sincerely intend to mount "to glory" with his pastoral charges, "by faith, by obedience, by prayer, and by love." Above all, by love.

However, Emerson was as little evangelical as doctrinaire, and the subjects of his sermons continued to be on personal salvation (cultivating one's inner spiritual resources) and ordinary conduct which could be directed toward self-improvement and helping others—not very exciting subjects. The nature of his sermons during his early months as pastor is clearly indicated by his titles: "The Best Part of Life Is Unseen," "Religion Is Doing One's Duty," "The Love of Virtue Is Innate," "Man Is Improvable," and so on. Later Emerson wrote in his Journal: "Preaching is only an exposition of our human nature . . ."[26] In preaching "original sin" the Calvinist had also thought he was exposing human nature, but Emerson never forgot that his view was personal and subjective: "I do not affect or pretend to instruct . . . it is God working in you that instructs both you & me. I only tell how I have striven & climbed, & what I have seen, that you may compare it with your own observations of the same Object."[27]

The young pastor tried to keep individual members of his congregation in mind as he wrote his sermons. "Take care, take care," he reminded himself, "that your sermon is not a recitation; that it is a sermon to Mrs. A. and Mr. B. and Mr. C."[28] Arthur C. McGiffert Jr., editor of a selection of Emerson's sermons, thinks that the individuals in his audience must have recognized themselves in the "anonymous references to varieties of human condition and experience." In one of his sermons Emerson declared: "I see the disappointed man in whose hands every prospect fails; I see the lonely and unhappy women; I see age left childless and the invalid of many years." Sometimes he made up dialogue for these people, thus, as McGiffert says, "dramatizing his hearers to themselves." To what extent Emerson succeeded we do not know, but he tried hard enough to make the members of his church feel that he understood and sympathized with them. Of course this was not easy for such an introspective and reserved young man as the Reverend Waldo Emerson, with his own emotional problems and deep sense of responsibility to his delicate fiancée, his dependent mother, and his struggling brothers. They all believed absolutely in the importance of his ministry and supported him in every way they knew how; yet family and church did compete for his time and strength.

IV

For the first half of 1829 Emerson almost stopped keeping a Journal. After his ordination he was too busy with professional duties and serving on local committees to have time for study or private meditation. He had also been elected to the School Committee, and his cooperation was sought— and expected—for all manner of community charity projects. Then in the spring he was appointed chaplain of the Massachusetts State Senate, though this was more an honor than a demanding task.

Besides seeing Ellen daily, Emerson had other distractions. His Uncle Ralph Haskins failed in business and had to stop the regular payments to Mrs. Emerson from her father's estate.[29] She was, of course, still house-keeper for Dr. Ezra Ripley in the Old Manse, and not in special need of money, but her only income was cut off. Then, Waldo wrote William, "Charles is looking to me for support when he gives up his School, as he may possibly after 6 months." Edward was not yet ready to practice law, and William was barely supporting himself. "I am sorry I am no richer at this time," Waldo declared to William, "having abundant use for two or three hundred dollars more than I have got." However, on July 1 his salary would be increased from twelve hundred to eighteen hundred dollars a year, and he hoped "to grow easier in my worldly condition."

Ellen, meanwhile, had grown stronger, and at the end of April she returned with her family to Concord, New Hampshire. Now almost daily Waldo wrote, and heard from her nearly as often. His letters have not survived, but hers have, and several poems which he wrote to or about her. In a rough version of one he declared:

> And do I waste my time
> Scribbling of love to my beautiful queen
> And is it idle to talk in prose and rhyme
> Of one who at midnight & morning's prime
> In daylight is fancied, in visions seen?[30]

Frequently he also refreshed his vision of her by opening the morocco case holding the miniature recently painted by Sarah Goodrich. Miss Goodrich had also made a miniature of him, and Ellen said she often "read in it," though she found it a poor substitute for the live original.[31] There are so many evidences of the depth of Emerson's feelings for Ellen that we need not doubt his thoughts were often on her during the busy day and she was the subject of his dreams at night. The temporary separation was painful to both of them, but probably more to her because she had so many tedious hours to fill with longing for his presence.

The Kents visited friends at several places before reaching home. At Worcester, Massachusetts, on May 1 Ellen wrote Waldo: "It never occurred to me that I should be so really and almost sinfully impatient to see you before I had been absent 3 or 4 days . . ."[32] She consoled herself by "building fairy castles for next summer and I place myself as their mistress . . ." She may have been alluding only to Waldo's visiting her in New Hampshire, though she also hoped to become his bride as soon as she was stronger. His "love letters" made her feel, she said, that she was one of the most favored of women. She also declared ambiguously, "I know each day that . . . [to] love as I do now brings me more gratefully near to Heaven and ennobles me to a higher purer worship—"[33] Perhaps this was only an exalted way of trying to describe the intensity of her emotions, but from the beginning of their betrothal she and Waldo had thought of their love as ordained and a preparation—even a pathway—to an immortal life.

As with all young lovers, Ellen and Waldo invented pet names for each other which an outsider would find silly. He called her "Queen" and "Ellinelli." She in turn called him "King," to match his "Queen," but often also "Grampa," for to her, at seventeen, he seemed immensely more mature at twenty-six. She was, indeed, hardly more than a child, and perhaps because of her delicate health was overprotected and coddled by her whole family. They had gone to Boston in January to look after her in the proximity of her adored minister. She appreciated and depended upon the physical and emotional support of her mother, her stepfather, and her older sisters, Margaret and Paulina.

Ellen poured out her adoration so prodigiously in her letters that Waldo apparently feared his ardor was less than hers, but she replied on May 12: "if he [my friend] merits love I'm sure I care not if he gives me but a pint[.] I shall give him an ocean . . ."[34] This was hyperbole similar to Emily Dickinson's, later, in her love letters, and Ellen was confident that Waldo loved her as much as she loved him. Her only doubts were regarding her lease on life. She prefaced her plans for the future with "if I live . . . ," and this was another reason for her fantasizing on the immortality of their love.

Mr. Kent had added a room to the house for Ellen. "I did not ask," she wrote Waldo, "but they read in my eye—I had more to be alone for than they—"; that is, with her love thoughts.[35] Ellen's piano was also moved from the parlor to an adjoining room (the one occupied by Waldo on his visits) so that she could play it whenever she felt like it. She was extremely fond of music and regretted that Waldo was not. One window of her room overlooked the garden, which she thought especially beautiful in moonlight. Early in the morning she liked to take a walk to the wooded place she and Waldo had named "Paradise." Her frequent allusions to this spot imply that Waldo had proposed to her there—or at least whispered for the first time that he loved her. That had been in winter, but the words "melted its icy coldness and now they live on the summer air . . . When you come up we'll say them to each other and it will be an evergreen spot on the face of the earth—"[36]

With a little prompting from Ellen, the Reverend Moses Thomas, "New Concord's" Unitarian minister, invited the Reverend Emerson to occupy his pulpit for two Sundays in June, and the Kents prepared the spare room for him. "Oh Waldo," Ellen begged, "do not cruelly disappoint Mr Thomas—come if it lies in your will . . ."[37] Of course it did, and Waldo did not "disappoint" Ellen! He came in time to preach on Sunday, June 21, and repeated the performance the following Sunday. He probably brought with him the sermon on "Summer" which he had read in Boston the previous Sunday. "My brethren," Emerson declared, "all nature is a book on which one lesson is written . . . the omnipresence of God—the presence of a love that is tender and boundless."[38] The minister's own overflowing human love doubtless found an outlet in his lyrical sermon on the beauties of nature by which God speaks to the soul of man. Furthermore, "There is nothing in external nature but is an emblem, a hieroglyphic of something in us." Seven years later, Emerson would elaborate this conceit in his first book (*Nature,* 1836).

It is not certain, however, that Ellen heard this so carefully prepared sermon, for the excitement of seeing Waldo caused her to suffer another hemorrhage of the lungs, and all their plans for the future were thrown into uncertainty again. Whether the relapse began with Waldo's arrival or developed during his ten-day visit is uncertain, but the situation of the previous January was repeated. Ellen was confined to her bed, and was still discouragingly weak when he departed, and for some days afterward.

On July 3 Ellen was too feeble to write a whole letter, and Paulina wrote Waldo for her. Though unable to go outdoors, "she has every day since you left trudged as far as your room as if she there expected to see your *ghost-ship* or some relic of your departed self."[39] A day or two later Ellen wrote: "Waldo the parting prayer murmured over my pillow is sweetly recieving [*sic*] its answer—God is with me and I feel he is making me well—"[40] Yet she alludes to the "Bermuda plan," and tries to reconcile herself to indefinite waiting for their marriage: "We have heaven and earth before us in which to live and love each other . . ." Perhaps Waldo was less reconciled, for, as if replying to his latest letter, she begs him, "Be a good boy—let our paths if decreed be miles apart" on earth, for "we [will] meet and taste heavens joy together . . ."

Dr. Jackson advised Waldo not to visit Ellen until she had fully recovered. Perhaps there was also a question of whether she should marry at all, for Ellen writes of her mother's impending visit to Dr. Jackson—whom she liked to refer to impishly as "Betty Jackson"—to see if he could be "coaxed out of his determination."[41] She thought, "Mother *must* see him—you are an awkward person (excuse me) to employ in such matters . . ."

Mrs. Kent herself became ill and had to delay her trip to Boston, but Ellen did not want her to go away "till I am firm." It was apparently difficult for Waldo to understand how he, the tenderest of lovers, could be a threat to her health, and Ellen tried to explain. If she did not love him so much, his appearance would be no danger, "but you never watched the union of drops [of water] so as I have if you do not know that at the instant of meeting there is a universal jar—a thrill—remember and watch your window when the sky weeps."[42] Should she live to be a hundred, "and had been seperated [*sic*] from you a month after living with you all my days there would be a chance of frighting the soul from the old shell when we met—by its tremour of joy perhaps . . ." But she continued to imagine and plan not only for his coming but also for her return with him to Boston—or a warmer climate, though she hoped it would be Boston— and tried to prepare her family for the move. Neither she nor they could bear the thought of a separation, even for marriage to the man they all adored. For Papa it would be a sacrifice, for he liked the climate and his friends in New Hampshire, but "Mother *will* go and if Mother goes—Father comes in a matter of course—"[43]

As Ellen's strength returned, she went horseback riding every fair day, gradually increasing the distance. By the end of July she was covering nine miles a day, and when August arrived she exulted that she was "getting well—getting well" and thinking of going to Boston "for good."[44] But first, Waldo could now visit her, and he did not delay, arriving on August 6.[45]

Next day, Waldo and Ellen set out in a chaise for an excursion in the White Mountains.[46] Mrs. Kent followed in a covered carriage in which Ellen could take refuge in case of rain or illness, but that did not prove necessary during the whole ten-day outing. It was almost like a trial honeymoon. Both were in nearly a delirium of ecstasy, to judge by their joint letters and Waldo's accounts. They visited the Shaker colony at Canterbury, where one of the Sisters preached to them the "beauty of virginity," but Waldo replied that they "were yoked together by Heaven to provoke each other to good works so long as we lived."[47] They drove as far as Conway and Bartlett, and returned by way of Hanover, covering in all over two hundred miles on the hard-packed, rocky roads. Both Ellen and Waldo thought the journey and fresh air were good for her.

Waldo returned to Boston on August 19, having been away from his congregation longer than he had intended—"but the absence was a duty of impossible omission," he wrote William. Next day, Ellen wrote "Dearest Waldo," using the superlative for the first time, "We have tried a short journey together and like [it] so well that we think of taking a *longer*—"

The only jarring note during this blissful visit was caused by Waldo's making a suggestion of some kind regarding Ellen's will—possibly merely suggesting that she ought to have one. The details are impossible to recover from the ambiguous references in Ellen's letters. (Waldo's letters to her, as remarked earlier, have not survived.) She called it "the ugly subject," and was reluctant to have her mother write Pliny Cutler, the executor of her father's estate. On August 25 she called "that plan which has been convulsing the wise heads" dull and laughable.[48] "Mother never seemed to like it—and would only do it to please *you*—glad am I that you being a babe in such things will resign them to more experienced noddles and I thank you—"

In her next letter Ellen referred to "the ugly *insurance* business" (emphasis hers), and said that if it were mentioned to Mr. Cutler, "He would think you were doubting *yourself* and would be justified in doubting too—"[49] Nevertheless, on August 30 she reported to Waldo that a letter had been written to the lawyer. But her stepfather "the disbeliever told Margaret that he was confident we should not live together this winter—"[50] Almost any conjecture we might make on this mysterious debate would be unfavorable to Emerson, though possibly all he had done was to urge Ellen to make a will. If so, it was sound advice, though we might wish the lover had been less prudent. What is certain is that Waldo had said nothing that diminished Ellen's infatuation with him, or her confidence in the approaching marriage.

In Ellen's same August 30 letter she wondered what he was doing at the moment and declared, "it pleases me often to think that we must chance to wake and sleep at the same time—"[51] By September 4 Mr. Kent had replied to Waldo's dutiful request to marry his stepdaughter, and Ellen was trying to envision her new "dear, warm, faithful *home*," but warned, "I may be a mere nothing for a year to come—a being of perfect dependance—not fit to perform the every day offices of love and friendship for any of my friends . . ." But she did not "repine" or "blame" herself, for she knew Waldo understood.

On September 7 Waldo returned to Concord, New Hampshire, for another excursion with Ellen, this time to Merrimack, Worcester, and Springfield, where he preached "all day" on Sunday, then back to Worcester and Concord.[52] As before, the lovers traveled in the open chaise, with Mrs. Kent and Margaret following in the carriage. Waldo had sprained his knee before leaving Boston, and the weather for part of the time was "funerally cold," yet the second outing was also a great success. From Springfield, Waldo wrote Charles: ". . . we botanize & criticize & poetize & memorize & prize & grow wise we hope . . ."[53] Waldo forgot his self-conscious dignity and giggled and capped silly rhymes with Ellen. They were like a couple of children suddenly released from school.

On September 18 Waldo returned to Boston, with Ellen's instructions to arrange boarding accommodations for all of her family at Mrs. Hannah

Keating's on Chardon Street, near Waldo's friend Abel Adams. Waldo engaged the rooms and returned once more to Concord, New Hampshire, but this time for the wedding, which was held quietly in the Kent home on September 30, with Reverend Thomas performing the ceremony.

The only member of Waldo's family able to attend was Charles, who complained a few days later in a letter to William: "3 whole days in that big house full of women, sat I, putting all the time a sober face on the fool's errand I went to do, while W. & the fair Ellen were whispering honied words above stairs, & I was turned over to the compulsory attentions of the stranger folk. These lovers are blind—purblind these lovers be—I forgive them freely."[54] Of course he did, but he would continue to feel, during the remaining months of Ellen's life, that he must compete for Waldo's attention. Waldo, in fact, was too absorbed in Ellen to be aware that he was neglecting Charles or anyone else.

Perhaps the two excursions had so well prepared Ellen for the actual marriage that she was able to bear the excitement of the occasion without any ill effects. On October 21 Waldo could write William, "she has been very well ever since she has been in town," where the newlyweds came after a brief honeymoon, if any—no information has survived. Boarding relieved Ellen of domestic cares. Since Waldo's salary was now augmented by her own income, they bought two carriages and she was free to ride out by herself whenever he was too busy to accompany her.

The knee Waldo sprained before his wedding had now become inflamed and painful. After returning to Boston he found he could not stand in the pulpit and had to read his sermon while sitting in a chair. As late as December 1 he wrote William: "My old knee is about the same. I am still a prisoner of chairs and chaises. Tonight I have received the visit of the quack doctor Hewitt, having quitted Drs Warren & Ware."[55] Simon C. Hewett (not -*itt*) called himself a "surgeon bone setter." A week later Waldo wrote again to William that he was "walking about with great firmness, thanks to Dr. Hewett—who cured me in two hours"[56]—presumably by manipulation rather than with ointments or drugs.

As the end of 1829 approached, Waldo Emerson had no serious worries. He thought Charles was now settling down to the study of law, but he could not understand why Edward had gone to New York with the hope of practicing there instead of accepting an offer from Mr. Samuel Hoar in Concord to become his junior partner.[57] Waldo had never understood why

William preferred New York to Boston. But he offered to help support Edward in that strange city if he needed help until he could get established. However, Waldo wanted his brothers to understand that his marriage had not made him wealthy. "I have a fancy that if you shd examine my income & outlay since my marriage you wd say I was poorer not richer, therefor. But richer I surely am by all Ellen, if she bro't no penny."[58] He now walked miles every day to strengthen his knee, and on sunny days rode out in his carriage with Ellen. He had never been so happy.

CHAPTER VIII

The Heavenly Stair

Another round, a higher,
Ye shall climb on the heavenly stair . . .[1]

I

Although Emerson did not write his poem on "Initial, Daemonic and Celestial Love" until nearly two decades later, its origin went back to his courtship and marriage to Ellen Tucker. From the beginning of their engagement both regarded their earthly love as a means of climbing to spiritual love:

Thou must mount for love;
Into vision where all form
In one only form dissolves . . .

In the poem Cupid instigates "initial love," arousing the amorous senses, "And touching all things with his rose."

There is no mask but he will wear;
He invented oaths to swear;
He paints, he carves, he chants, he prays,
And holds all stars in his embrace.

This god certainly taught Ellen and Waldo oaths with which to swear their undying devotion, flowery imagery for their love poems, prayers for the welfare of each other, and made them long for a "stricter privacy" in which they, "being two, shall still be one." In their married life they experienced "Daemonic," or sexual, love, though the maid's "lotus wine" had been snitched by the poet from the table of Plato's "Banquet":

> The maid, abolishing the past,
> With lotus wine obliterates
> Dear memory's stone-incarved traits,
> And, by herself, supplants alone
> Friends year by year more inly known.
> When her calm eyes opened bright,
> All else grew foreign in their light.
> It was ever the self-same tale,
> The first experience will not fail;
> Only two in the garden walked,
> And with snake and seraph talked.

Waldo Emerson did indeed walk in the "garden" with Ellen, and experienced the remorse of this poem after he lost her, but while she lived they talked more with the seraph than with the snake. Their married life, so far as can be determined, was blissfully harmonious, though the husband's happiness was recurrently marred by panic fear each time Ellen's lips were stained by her life's blood. Thus the few months of his first marriage were both the happiest and the most miserable of his entire life.

But this was also a period of rapid and profound spiritual and intellectual growth for Emerson; not because the girl-wife taught or indoctrinated him in any way, but because she thawed his emotions and expanded his human sympathies. Then after he had lost her, his desperate struggle to find the means of living without her strengthened his reliance upon himself and liberated his mind from the stereotypes of his education and Church.

Before meeting Ellen Tucker, Emerson had complained, as we have seen in previous chapters, of his own "coldness," and in afteryears this conviction returned to him. But his letters to his brothers about Ellen before his marriage, the poems he wrote to her, and the references to her in his Journals, leave no doubt that she stirred his emotions as no one else ever had—or would again. Charles, who came frequently from Cambridge to Chardon Street, found Waldo so absorbed in his domestic life that he could spare little time for his lonely younger brother. In a letter to Edward and William in New York, Charles complained:

> I wonder if everybody is lost to their brothers & all ties of blood & sympathy, the moment they are settled & married? I suppose I quarrel with what is a necessary state of things. . . . I mean not to murmur at any neglect—not a bit—I mean just what I say—to wonder whether t'is [*sic*] the invariable effect of business & marriage to make one independent of, & therefore indifferent to old relationships & intimacies.[2]

Charles was perhaps a little jealous, as he had been at Waldo's wedding, but he was also an acute observer, and his testimony anticipated Waldo's poem in which the "maid" supplants "Friends year by year more inly known."

Some students of Emerson have wondered, considering Ellen's frequent invalidism, whether the marriage was ever consummated. All the information we have is that they lived in physical intimacy, evidently shared the same bed, and scorned the Shaker Sister's advocacy of chastity. That Waldo was at all times considerate of Ellen's delicate health may be taken for granted, but there were weeks, even months, when both she and he believed her lungs had healed. Though most of her poems and some of her letters reveal a foreboding sense of early death (perhaps influenced to some extent by the melancholy poems then in vogue), Waldo could imagine a long life together, as in this poem which he copied into his "Blotting Books" on February 26, 1830:

> And, Ellen, when the graybeard years
> Have brought us to life's Evening hour,
> And all the crowded Past appears
> A tiny scene of sun & shower,
>
> Then, if I read the page aright
> Where Hope, the soothsayer, reads our lot,
> Thyself shalt own the page was bright,
> Well that we loved, wo had we not; . . .[3]

During the autumn and early winter of 1829 Mrs. Waldo Emerson seemed to gain strength. To Aunt Mary Emerson she wrote in December, apologizing for not having written earlier: "*Exercise—Exercise* is the command and I strictly obedient to all such . . ."[4] Consequently, "unless I can write walking or riding, must burden my friends with sleepy words or cease all intellectual exercise . . ." The regimen of exercise and fresh air had doubtless been recommended by Dr. Jackson, but Waldo himself believed in it almost fanatically. Yet, ironically, rest and protection from cold winds might have saved Ellen Emerson's life.

After Aunt Mary came to know Ellen personally, she was sympathetic and tolerant, though few people had found her to be either. Knowing how highly Waldo valued his eccentric aunt's approval, Ellen had written her in January 1829 from Boston, and Miss Emerson had replied: "As soon as I read your character—lovely Louisa [no one else used Ellen's middle name] I could do nothing but commend you to God—and pray that you might be a lasting blessing to him it is your favored lot to attach."[5] Then she urged the future bride not to "Lean on him for resources—but urge him on to aid in the work of moral improvement which is going on for Heaven. Be yourself a ministering angel to him and society." Of course Ellen herself would have liked nothing better than to be such a person, if only she had the strength.

Ellen was not offended by Aunt Mary's brusque advice, and was most curious to meet her. "I have heard from many tongues of Aunt Mary . . . yet have at every mention of you made some alteration in my ideal Aunt Mary and now as I write a thousand differing forms of you keep crossing my brain—" In words almost as incoherent as Aunt Mary's cryptic messages she called herself "no common object for sympathy." Perhaps she meant she did not want to be the object of sympathy, for she added: "and the more as my days go by—and now the deepest and most impressive are *far far* from reaching that chord which is trembling with its own impatience to be heard and touched into expression . . ." This seems to be an apology for lack of accomplishments, and she hints at her melancholy fate: "Rosy hours perchance *all* may experience—a *rosy life* falls to few—"

Ellen Emerson did not suffer any alarming relapse of health in the winter of 1830, though in January and February some familiar symptoms began to reappear, and Waldo decided in March to take her to milder Philadelphia. By stagecoach they traveled to Hartford, where Waldo stopped to fill preaching engagements and to introduce Ellen to Aunt Mary, who had come briefly to rest in nearby Weathersfield in the home of a minister.

"I like her better than I dreamt," the unpredictable aunt wrote her nephew Charles on March 15, "but not near so handsome—genius and loveliness are enough."[6]

The Emersons and Margaret Tucker continued by stage to New Haven, covering the thirty-four miles in eight hours and arriving by six p.m. They had expected to catch a night boat to New York, but were told that no boat would leave before Wednesday morning. "When we had made up our minds to this loss of a day," Waldo wrote Abel Adams from New Haven on Tuesday, "what was our chagrin to learn at 10 minutes before 8 o'c. that a boat wd. sail at 8' in the ev.[8] & we all unpacked, both in our baggage & purposes."[7] Perhaps that was just as well, because the trip to Hartford had tired Ellen. She did "walk abroad 3 times" that day, yet was "not so well" as Waldo could wish.

Wednesday morning the party of three boarded the steamboat at six a.m., expecting to arrive in New York by four that afternoon. Since the route was through Long Island Sound, partly protected from the roughest waves of the Atlantic Ocean, no difficulties were expected. But a few hours after they left New Haven a gale came up from the southwest and the boat had to anchor off Norwalk until next morning. After they finally reached New York, Waldo wrote Charles:

> There we lay pouting & snuffing the insufferable mephitis of the cabin, & hearing the rain patter & looking at each other grimly, forty stout passengers, (though fortunately only two besides E. & M. in the ladies cabin) & lastly sleeping or trying to sleep in an air that wd doubtless have put out a lamp on the floor. But morning came, the wind abated, & the steam chimney began once more to puff. The clouds broke, & we were repaid for our troubles by a noble passage up the Sound—fine sun[,] mild air, swift vessels, beautiful shores, noble seats—& through all—got to this long London town [New York]—to the American Hotel at 2 o'clock yesterday.[8]

It is hardly surprising that Ellen was "quite weak" on Friday, though she insisted on going to Philadelphia next day as planned. Waldo had chosen what he thought was the best means of reaching New York from New Haven, yet he could not help blaming himself for the bad luck. "You may imagine I bit my lip with mortification," he confessed in his letter to Charles, "to find I had got the queen into this bad navigable box." However, "She bore it well—all but the impossibility of sleep." On Saturday they would take another boat to Philadelphia, but this time by "inland instead of outland" waters, meaning the Raritan River. Waldo now expected that he would not be able to leave Ellen as soon as he had planned, for she was again troubled by her "red wheezers" and "fulness in the head."[9] Consequently he asked Charles to see that his pulpit was sup- plied until he could return.

After a brief stop at the U.S. Hotel in Philadelphia, the Emersons found "good accommodations" at a Miss McElroy's on the corner of Chestnut and Eleventh streets. Besides the Reverend William Henry Furness, Waldo's Latin School classmate, he had other friends in the Quaker City, and all extended the most cordial hospitality. With these kind people and Ellen's sister Margaret, Waldo felt that his wife was in good hands and would not want for companionship in his absence. Yet he would not leave her until "the evil symptoms" abated, he wrote William on the twentieth.

On Thursday, March 25, Waldo wrote Charles: "As to Ellen, she is pretty well but I would rather see her a grain more robust before I go away." At this point she herself took up the letter and wrote: "Really!—I have given him leave yea have urged his going away *now*—for he is every whit as much out of his element as at *Concord, N. H.*—and (oh tell it not) not a text has he expounded not a skeleton of a sarmint has he formed not a sonnet has he perpetrated since he turned his back *B ward* . . ."[10]

Next day in a long letter to Aunt Mary, Waldo himself admitted, "I am getting to be sadly impatient of my life here, which has petty engagements which tear time into slivers, and are singularly unfavorable to anything like intellectual progress."[11] But he thought he would be "recreated" if "not enriched" when he got back to his familiar armchair. Perhaps it was really his study rather than the pulpit which he most sorely missed. And of course he had always been bored with small talk and mere sociability. But on April 1 from New York he could report to Aunt Mary: "I have boldly left Ellen in Philad. ramparted round with troops of friends. She seems better, & there is a good physician, and *there is a good Physician.* I shall be in Boston tomorrow . . ." Possibly the emphasis on Ellen's Philadelphia phy- sician reflected some dissatisfaction with "Betty" Jackson, but Waldo gave no further clue.

Before leaving Philadelphia, Emerson preached in Mr. Furness's church on March 28. Ellen called it his "Golden rule" sermon, and reported to

Aunt Mary with obvious pleasure that she had also heard the second sermon that day, preached by "a stranger."[12] She liked the simple beauty and
"chaste taste" of this Unitarian church, though her description, in her
acute awareness of being in Philadelphia, made it sound rather more
Quakerish than Unitarian.

Ellen said that "though his absence will be a thorn to me," she did not
regret Waldo's leaving her on Wednesday, for "the ladies parlour or chamber is no place to dust your mind and regulate your soul and his sermons
would not weigh so well as if they were born in his own study." But she
would rejoin Waldo in May, and she trusted the "elasticity of the bands
which bind us" to stretch the three hundred intervening miles. She also
assured Aunt Mary that she was eager to see her again, with "tenfold desire
greater" than before the meeting in Hartford. She urged her not to "keep
your wings always in motion for flight when you come to see us," which
she hoped would be in Boston soon after the exile's return.

Early in April, Ellen's mother joined her and Margaret, and she seems to
have been less lonely than Waldo by himself in Boston. In a letter to Edward she asks if he and William still "rise at 6 & walk as usual."[13] If they
called at her boardinghouse in Philadelphia at that hour, they would find
her and Margaret "long gone out and bound either for the banks of the
Schuylkill or Delaware," though they did not find much natural beauty in
the region. The few wild flowers looked "as if Dame Quaker rather than
Dame Nature had arranged them ..." She had been to the Museum and
found she did not admire Benjamin West's famous painting of "Christ
Rejected." It had "too many charcoal strokes," and the artist had failed to
portray "the uncommon expression of the face of Jesus ..." Perhaps she
was opinionated, but she did not sound bored.

II

Because of his delayed return to Boston, Emerson was unable to commem-
orate the first anniversary of his ministry at the Second Church on the
Sunday nearest the date, which would have been March 14. But three days
after his return on April 1, he delivered "The Ministry: A Year's Retrospect."[14] If Ellen was correct that he had not written even a "skeleton of a
sarmint" in Philadelphia, then he must have written this one hurriedly on
Saturday. Haste, fatigue, and possibly the realization that he had neglected

his congregation, however unintentionally, may have influenced his tone of dissatisfaction with himself and his parishioners. It was not the sermon of a happy minister.

As in his first sermon after his ordination, Emerson considered again "the obligations that arise to you and to me out of the pastoral relation." He freely admitted he had not fulfilled the "sanguine hopes" with which he had begun his ministry a year before. "I confess I am oppressed with doubt and sorrow, and if I stopped with this view, I should despond." But he found comfort in Saint Paul's phrase "the foolishness of preaching," which in Emerson's words is only "one voice in the choir of the world." The spirit of Christ speaks to men through their daily experiences and the events of the day more loudly than in sermons from the pulpit.

The implication of this downgrading of preaching may not have been obvious to Emerson's congregation, but he was telling them that every creed, doctrine, and theological opinion is finite, fallible, and of less importance than their own experience of "God's Providence." Exactly the doctrine for which the Puritans tried Anne Hutchinson in the seventeenth century. So, the Reverend Emerson was not discouraged by his own insignificant failures: "If I have neglected my duties I shall leave it in silence."

He could not remain silent, however, over one failure of his congregation: "The difference in the attendance on church in the two parts of the same day you are aware is often very great." More concisely, many had been staying away from the second service, and he doubted that family responsibilities had kept them at home. He begged them not to let this negligence become a habit, for "it will grow fast to an alarming laxity and libertinism." Here he spoke in the commanding tones of the early ministers of the Second Church, rather than in his usual voice of gentle persuasion. His failure to attract a full house twice a day may have pricked his self-esteem, perhaps unconsciously.

Emerson's most eloquent self-defense, however, concerned another shortcoming which he was acutely aware of, but unwilling (or unable) to remedy. "The activity which is the duty of a Christian minister in the discharge of his office, is of two kinds, preacher and pastor, and often in some measure incompatible."[15] He evidently knew of dissatisfaction with his pastoral performance, especially for his spending more time in his study than in visiting the members of his church.

The minister "attempts with no better spiritual light than his brethren enjoy, to study the Scriptures and to explain God's laws . . ." Probably he realized that he was speaking to church members who thought his theological training and the traditions of the Unitarian Church had already supplied him with the essential answers, and that all he had to do was to explain them and exhort his hearers to obedience. It was subtly becoming apparent that in Emerson's mind nothing was settled. The *truth* must be sought by constant mental effort and attending in "silence and solitude" to what passed from intuition to consciousness in his own mind. He might have told his congregation that "conscience" is a cognate of "consciousness." He did tell them that "the laws of thought are not accommodated to a time-schedule." Then he defended "the character" of his exhortations. He did not preach against gross sins, such as murder and adultery, because he believed his hearers were more susceptible to little, insidious sins: against temperance, charity, love of neighbor, and love of God. This had long been a favorite notion of his, as we have seen. Consequently:

> I shall count it no reproach if I am reminded that my subjects have little variety. I count it the great object of my life to explore the nature of God. For this I would read and think and converse and act and suffer, and if I shall succeed in enlarging in any degree your conceptions of the divine nature and government or confirming your convictions I shall praise him that he has permitted me to be so honored an instrument in his hand.

Even before he entered the ministry, Emerson's "great object" had been to explore "the nature of God." But was he now in the right place to make that exploration? Possibly he had not yet asked himself that question, but he was becoming increasingly impatient with the time his pastoral cares took away from progress in his *higher* duties. Anecdotes were already circulating about his ineptitude in consoling the sick and eulogizing the departed. Once, a Baptist minister in a neighboring church invited him to assist at a funeral and remarked afterward that he did not "make his best impression" on such an occasion. His successor at the Second Church would tell of his visiting a hero of the American Revolution on his deathbed and showing so much hesitation and embarrassment that the old man said sternly, "Young man, if you don't know your business, you had better go home."[16] And that was exactly where he wanted to be: in his own study, praying, thinking, and writing.

During April and May, however, Emerson's thoughts were frequently not on his duties as pastor of the Second Church, but on his recuperating wife in Philadelphia. He spent a considerable amount of his time in writing poems to and about her. On May 11 he apologized to William for neglecting to write him, "but I have been sonneteering now ever since March opened—and—when you are married—"[17] Actually his poems were not sonnets but spontaneous lyrics for Ellen. In one poem, addressed to "thou sweet daughter of God, my angel wife," he complained, "I am alone. Sad is my solitude." He asked in these impromptu verses:

> Why dost thou leave me thus in the great stranger world
> Without one sign or token, one remembrancer
> Sent o'er the weary lands that sunder us
> To say I greet thee with a beating heart.
> *Does* thy heart beat with mine? does thy blue eye
> Ever look northward with desire, O do thy prayers
> Remember me when thou hallowest thy maker's name,
> Remember him
> Who never failed to grace his orison
> With thy dear name, believes it acceptable
> And prays, that he may pray for thee—[18]

This does not sound like rhetorical compliments, but real anxiety that he may not be constantly in her thoughts, as she is in his. Perhaps she had only been a little negligent in writing him as often as she had before their marriage, and he wanted news of her every day. Actually, not a single letter of hers to him during this period has survived, though she must have written some. In April (no day given) she wrote Edward: "I send these letters to you because it is not quite so important whether very soon or a little later they reach B—"[19] What letters are not specified, but they were probably carried by someone going to New York—mail service between cities was expensive and not always dependable. Her final comment to Edward was "Heard yesterday from Waldo—well but lonely—"

Ellen sometimes teased Waldo, and it may have been at this time that she asserted her independence in this charming little poem:

When we're angels in heaven
Dont raving mad be
If without notice given
I stay out to tea.

For what e'er sister angel
My presence may honour
I think you may as well
Place dependance upon her.

I shan't keep a carriage
My wings will be strong
And our earthly marriage
Will be vain as a song.

I therefore shall use them
As I may see fit
And tea out and dine out
Nor mind you a bit.[20]

It was in quite a different mood that Waldo wrote "To E. T. E. at Philadelphia," expressing his sentiments in the voice of spring flowers, ending with this stanza:

'O come, then, quickly come!
We are budding, we are blowing;
And the wind that we perfume
Sings a tune that's worth the knowing.'[21]

In preparation for Ellen's return, Waldo rented the "old Aspinwall house" in Brookline, which Uncle Ralph Haskins had lived in "one summer long ago," and about the middle of May his mother took possession of it. She would be housekeeper while Ellen continued to convalesce. Waldo wrote William that the house had "a parlor & 3 chambers one for Mother one for wife [and husband] and one for you when you will come & welcome."[22] He did not say whether the house was furnished, but probably it was.

On Tuesday, May 18, Waldo Emerson left Boston for a quick trip to Philadelphia. The exact day of his return with Ellen is not certain, but it was in time for Election Day, May 26. On May 27 Waldo wrote William that they had made "the shortest passage ever made through the Sound, fourteen hours and fifty-three minutes from New York to Providence"— they carefully avoided New Haven. Almost immediately they plunged into "the burdensome bustle" of Election Week, with sermons, political ceremonies, and numerous social activities. Charles was a guest in Brookline, and all enjoyed the festive week. Apparently Ellen suffered no ill effects from the excitement. But Waldo discovered the inconvenience of "traveling four miles out & home daily."

The retreat in Brookline also had another disadvantage: Waldo had not been able to bring his library from Boston, though one wonders how much mental effort would have been possible after his wearisome trips to and from the city in the midsummer heat. Nevertheless, he felt guilty over the time he wasted without his books and resolved that in the autumn he would "methodize" his days.[23] It was easier, he knew, to make resolutions than to keep them, "but God grant me persistency enough, so soon as I leave Brookline & come to my books to do as I intend."

In July Emerson recorded his weight as 157 pounds, which meant that in spite of heat and travel he had gained weight—perhaps because he had worried less during the first half of the summer. But in August Ellen was again coughing up blood. Charles in a brief letter to William on August 11 said "it casts trouble & anxiety over her husband's prospects. They will probably go off this Fall to Southern latitudes."[24] Three days later he wrote again: "Poor Waldo feels the disappointment strongly, & seems now to make up his mind that he must break or untie all bonds that fasten him here, & go off in search of kinder elements. For my part, I doubt whether there is any climate that will save Ellen."

However, Ellen rallied, and on the last day of August felt strong enough for a trip, by easy stages, to her old home in Concord, New Hampshire. Waldo accompanied her as far as Lexington, Massachusetts, then returned to his duties in Boston. In a letter to William on September 6, in which he told of Ellen's trip to New Hampshire, Waldo added: "She mends fast. We ponder many plans, but she inclines after all to stay at home this winter. Dr. Jackson leans to that opinion."[25]

After a month in New Hampshire Ellen came back, not to Brookline but to Boston. She and Waldo had decided to rent the house on Chardon Street in which they had boarded before going to Brookline. With the assistance of Waldo's mother they would be able to keep house, as planned the previous spring.[26] In a letter to a cousin dated simply "Autumn," Ellen described her domestic felicity:

> Here sit I in my own little domicile & *realize* that I am Mrs Emerson to the full for Betsy & Nancy and Martin must have their daily & nightly tasks allotted—and Mr such a one with his wife are in town and they must come to tea tomorrow—no cake—bless me how many eggs? how much sugar? and there are those brasses and the spare chamber bed must be attended—only imagine the careless, one eyed skittish Ellen Tucker in this situation & send her a little fairy Order to tap with her wand upon the household duds and ease me of my woe—Do I alarm you? Verily I am happier than it often falleth to the lot of mortals to be and am thrice happy to be able to offer you chamber—3 if so many you choose to occupy and the hearty welcome of 3 united hearts namely R W & E T & Mother [Emerson]—come if you set your face Boston ward directly to Chardon St for we keep the same house that last winter we borrowed . . .[27]

Unfortunately, this interlude of happiness was soon marred by illness in the family: first of Bulkeley, who had to return to the asylum in Charlestown from the place in the country where he had been boarding; then of Edward, whose health had collapsed in New York; and Charles's symptoms were also becoming cause for worry. Then Ellen's own health and her mother's were still constant cause for uneasiness.

In November William wrote from New York that Edward had decided his only chance for recovery was to go to Puerto Rico for the winter. On November 29 Waldo urged William "to bundle him up warm, & send him here immediately—for Mother and Ellen to nurse him. He can here be effectually taken care of."[28] But if he must go south, why not to Magnolia, Florida? There he could be near Waldo's friend Achille Murat. Waldo thought Santa Cruz (St. Croix) would be very expensive and uncomfortable because of the humidity.

Edward, however, stuck to his plan to sail without delay to Santa Cruz. His mother wanted to rush to New York, but worried for fear she would arrive too late to see him, so she waited impatiently for more news. Finally, not having heard anything more from William, she started out on Thursday, December 9, but was detained two days at Newport because the ocean was too rough for the steamboat to venture out. As a consequence, she arrived in New York on Sunday morning, half an hour after Edward's ship had sailed. She tried to find consolation in the fact that he had "a fine wind to set out with," and in William's assurance that he would be well taken care of on the trip.[29]

On December 16 Waldo wrote Grandfather Ripley: "Mother returned this day very safely & tho disappointed yet in some degree comforted by seeing William & Dr Perkins [presumably Edward's New York physician] & learning that Edward improved for a few days previous to embarking for St Cruz."[30] In the same letter Waldo said, "Ellen & I went to Waltham to find Aunt Mary, & bro't her with us to Boston. She means to spend a week with us." After her departure Ellen wrote Edward:

> Aunt Mary has appeared in our home an instant but the whole was like a dream—She seems not of the earthly nor altogether of the heavenly—to be wondered at and in some sort admired—She has gone with Charles to Concord where she means if it seemeth her good after a trial to pass the coming winter—[31]

Around this time in an undated letter to her Aunt Hubbard, Ellen reported that "Paulina went off very unexpectedly [she failed to explain that her sister had married Captain Joshua Nash] and since her departure I have been very unwell myself and Mother has been suffering from the great enemy of our family . . . she has raised some blood and looks pale & thin[.]" Ellen felt extremely anxious about her: "I cannot tell you how anxious—But her spirits are very good and every fair day she rides out—& seems delighted that she is with her children."

On Christmas Eve, Ellen wrote Edward again (though she had not yet received a letter from him since his arrival in Puerto Rico), telling him he had escaped a cruel winter in Boston: "thermometer at 6, snow, wind, long icicles blue noses and sad looking invalids . . ."[32] She envied his "timely retreat," and suggested half-seriously that he "pick out a pretty spot for Waldo & wife to live," for "in spite of 2d church and blk gown Bostonians" she still indulged in "such golden dreams." She thought she would prefer the quick death of "scorpions" there to the "cold winds and changes here," which bring "a slow, uncertain death or an ill-spent life . . ."

By "ill-spent" she meant the condition which she described to Aunt Mary on January 12: "I am as stupid and unlovely as when you were here.

Waldo has gone to preach and Mother to hear and I am left to pout it out or perchance to find relief in some magical leaf of poetry or musick note or thread of thought . . . it is in vain to attempt to tell how dry & arid my soul is . . ."[33] Evidently her mother's health was better than her own. Ellen had read Waldo's sermon on "Self and Others," and said it had made her own "views of benevolence—or motives for benevolence" clearer. In his sermon Waldo declared, "The fear of death is unworthy of a man."[34] The remedy he recommended was "Go and see the death of one who spends the last breath in devoted serving of others and you see the ruins of human nature clothed with beauty and all the meanness of death taken away."

Was the minister preaching to his wife, or trying to quiet his own fears, or loftily generalizing? He knew that Ellen was again in danger, though he probably did not realize just how seriously—nor did she. She knew only that she did not have the strength to "serve" anyone, and felt useless and depressed. Even Waldo said "the new year's eve was indeed a failure." Then, speaking her own sentiments, "the year went out—but its wing was hardly heard it fluttered and fluttered and crept at last—"[35] That was exactly how she felt in January 1831.

III

Some of Emerson's ideas about God and religion at the time of his first marriage might lead one to think he was more orthodox than he actually was. With Ellen he had a childlike faith in the eternal life of the soul, expecting after his death to become an angel in heaven. He and Ellen would recognize each other and continue their happy association, though there would be "no sex" there, "in thought, in knowledge, in virtue; and the kingdom of Heaven is the kingdom of these."[36] This heavenly life sounds rather like a mental existence, perhaps almost a nirvana. In his Journal he quoted Ellen as wondering "Whether . . . the Spirits in heaven look onward to their immortality as we on earth, or are absorbed in the present moment."[37]

Indeed, Emerson's Idealism, in the philosophical sense, was steadily growing during these years, encouraged by his reading of Coleridge's *Aids to Reflection* and *The Friend,* and he was also influenced by his secondhand knowledge of the Eleatic school of philosophy, such as of Parmenides, who taught that by thought alone men arrive at knowledge of being:

thought is being, and God is not anthropomorphic. Since his college days Emerson had believed God to be an all-embracing Mind, and that the human consciousness is only a minute fragment of the Divine "Reason" (Emerson used the word before he had read Coleridge). From James Marsh's edition of *Aids to Reflection* he copied "*Quantum sumus, scimus*" ("We are what we know").[38] Coleridge followed this aphorism with: "That which we find within ourselves, which is more than ourselves, and yet the ground of whatever is good and permanent therein, is the substance and life of all other knowledge." Increasingly, to Emerson, life was consciousness, and he sought constantly to deepen and enrich it. This made him at times seem strongly "otherworldly," as when he declared, "How ridiculous that the follies of the world should vex you."[39]

Emerson had valued intuition, as we have seen, before reading Coleridge, but the English philosopher-poet confirmed his belief in it as a cardinal point of his religious philosophy. He had already preached that "it is God working in you that instructs both you & me." For this "inner voice" of divine origin he used various terms, but most often "soul"— later the Transcendental "Reason." Most conversation, he observed in his Journal, comes "from the floating parlance of the time & not from the soul."[40]

In this theory he seemed at times to anticipate later theories of the "subconscious." Dr. William Ellery Channing told him of a Frenchman (no name given) "who had written that there were two souls in the human body," one "which never suspended its action, & had the care of what we call the involuntary motions . . ." This soul "knew a good deal of Natural magic, Antipathies, instincts, divination & the like," or in later psychoanalytic terminology, neuroses, hysteria, amnesia, delusions, and so on.

The other was "the vulgar waking practical soul," or ordinary consciousness. Emerson believed this theory had a "glimpse of truth" in it. The Frenchman's theory sounds rather like Freud's later concept of the unconscious, but Emerson himself leaned toward a theory of the "other soul" as the origin of truth-laden intuitions, healthy instincts, the eternal Reason speaking to human reason. Of course his thought had to rise to consciousness before he could act upon it, for otherwise even his thinking would be nothing but instinctive reflexes, and Emerson was not a determinist.

At times Emerson almost seemed to anticipate William James in his theory that the unconscious might be the doorway to God. At least Emerson believed that he could arrive at "truth" not from listening to the opinions of society but from some deeper level of the "soul," which spoke from a "tender conscience" and total sincerity (that is, he must ignore public opinion). This truth was more felt than thought out, and prayer could help clear the channel of communication.

Here we begin to approach one of the great paradoxes in Emerson's ideas: his *self-reliance* versus his *God-reliance.* To say, as some critics have, that his self-reliance is simply God-reliance deprives him of his profound belief in free will. In his Journal Emerson proposed a subtle escape from the determinism of God-reliance; although God is omnipotent, His actions are not foreordained:

> The government of God is not on a plan—that would be Destiny; it is extempore. The history of the universe is a game of which the object to be gained is the greatest good of the whole, and is attained by a long series of independent *moves.* The omniscient Eye makes each new move from a survey of all the present state of the game. Hence the efficiency of *Prayer.* God determines from all the facts—& my earnest desires make one of the facts.—[41]

Emerson's notion that his desires may become "one of the facts" on which God acts curiously anticipates William James's unfinished universe in which God needs help, even finite human help: "We and God have business with each other . . ."[42] But unlike James, who reasoned on the basis of a "Pluralistic Universe," Emerson cited for proof this subjective phenomenon:

> Every man by God's arrangements whilst he ministers & receives influence from all others is absolutely imperially free. When I look at the rainbow I find myself the centre of its arch. But so are you; & so is the man that sees it a mile from both of us. So also the globe is round, & every man therefore stands on the top.—King George, & the Chimney sweep no less.[43]

But is it a fact or an illusion that every man "stands on the top"? It is, as stated above, a psychological or subjective phenomenon. Yet in the realms of the mind, and the influence of thought on action, it may have far-reaching consequences. Aunt Mary had written Emerson: "The greater God is, the greater we are."[44] Emerson took this to mean that a man enlarges his own life by enlarging his concept of God. Thus, "Every man makes his own religion, his own God, his own charity; takes none of these from the Bible or his neighbour, entire."[45] Furthermore, "Creeds grow from the structure of the creature," and structures vary with individuals:

> Every man has his own voice, manner, eloquence, & just as much his own sort of love & grief & imagination & action. Let him scorn to imitate any being, let him scorn to be a secondary man, let him fully trust his own share of God's goodness, that correctly used it will lead him on to perfection which has no type yet in the Universe save only in the Divine Mind.[46]

"Then it seems to be true that the more exclusively idiosyncratic ["individual" deleted] a man is, the more . . . infinite." In listening to his "own reason" he does not become more selfish, but falls back "on truth itself & God. For it is when a man does not listen to himself but to others, that he is depraved & misled." This is the basis of Emerson's "self-reliance" doctrine and his ever-increasing personal independence. He made a distinction, however, between "moral" and "intellectual" truth.[47] After an intellectual truth such as Newton's law of gravity has been discovered, it must be accepted as final. But moral truths are more subjective, though Emerson added that if a person "perceives the whole expediency [usefulness?] and authority of a moral law he will keep it."

Emerson appears to have contradicted himself when he wrote in his Journal on December 10, 1830, that "The moral sentiment of a multitude when undisturbed is I believe more correct than of an individual."[48] But he qualified the statement by *"when undisturbed,"* evidently meaning that multitudes can also "listen" to the dictates of their souls if not prevented or corrupted by external (social, authoritarian, and so on) pressures. The following day he added: "Internal evidence outweighs all other to the inner man."

In making notes for a sermon on "Miracles" (preached on January 23 and 30, 1831), Emerson wrote that even if the New Testament had perished and "its teachings remained" (presumably in the conscience of Christian people), he would have the same faith in the spirituality of the Apostles. Controversy over miracles, as remarked in an earlier chapter, nearly split the Unitarian Church. Emerson intended to defend the authenticity of the miracles recorded in the New Testament, but some of his argument sounds rather sophistical. For example, Christianity is "incompatible with imposture & therefore its miracles are real."[49] And he also extends the meaning of the word: everything "we see & do is a continual miracle. The facts observed[,] the Springs concealed . . . All things are full of God." He quoted with approval Sampson Reed's statement that "The miraculous is the measure of our alienation from him [God]"—[50] meaning, perhaps, that if one is not alienated, one does not make distinctions between the natural and the phenomenal event, both of which exist through God's power.

As Christmas approached, Emerson concentrated his thoughts on the meaning of Christianity. "Now Jesus has made it apparent," he recorded in his Journal on December 21, "that the end of all things is the soul, that God is preparing the soul for himself, & designs that it should be tempted, and resist, & triumph . . ."[51] The title for his sermon on December 5 was "Trust Yourself," identifying *self* with *soul*. "That which is made for an immortal life must be of an infinite nature."[52] Therefore, the soul should be reverently respected: "it is a house of God, and the voice of the eternal inhabitant may always be heard within it." He ended his sermon by advocating an asceticism reminiscent of primitive Christianity:

> Let us leave this immoderate regard to meats and drinks, to dress and pleasure and to unfounded praise, and let us go alone and converse with ourselves, and the word of God in us. What that bids us do let us do with unshaken firmness and what it bids us forbear, let us forbear. Let us love and respect each other as those who can assist us in understanding ourselves and let us hear the distinct voice of Scripture which has taught us to forsake the world and its vanities and deceptions, and seek God who is to be worshipped in our hearts.

The title of Emerson's New Year's sermon (preached December 31, 1830) was "How Old Art Thou?"[53]—meaning, How ready are you for death and immortality? He paraphrased Sir Thomas Browne's "The world is but a large urn." And, "The soul escapes to God affrighted by the decays of the universe." Death is a *new birth.* "In the spiritual world only can we live. In this world we die daily." But the passage of the soul from the physical to the spiritual world is *"a passage from death unto life"* (Emerson's italics). The burden of the whole sermon is the overcoming of the fear of death, and preparing for "our birth and adoption into that world, of which God is the everlasting light, where is no age but immortal youth and no change but from glory to glory."

Whether or not Emerson realized the timeliness of his December and January sermons for the approaching agonistic drama of his wife—and there are some indications that he did not—they nevertheless created in his home an atmosphere of supreme spirituality and resignation to God's will during the last weeks of her life. For whatever reason, the minister's religious emotions had been deeply stirred and his imagination stimulated, for he composed six new sermons in January, almost a record for him. The fact that his imagery was often stereotyped indicated only how completely he accepted the Christian teachings on death and immortality. He spoke almost as a man mesmerized by his visions of heavenly reward.

                                    IV

In one of her later poems, probably written in the winter of 1831, Ellen Emerson expressed her premonition of imminent death:

> I am the grave's, its seal is set upon me
> It's [*sic*] chalky white & startling vermeil red
> I am the grave's with death cold hand it warns me
> My home is never here & my weak ease
> I'm warned to leave.—[54]

Every member of her family knew of this premonition, but at the beginning of 1831 Ellen was not noticeably worse. In spite of the December snowstorms, she still rode out in her carriage almost every day, under the mistaken opinion of Dr. Jackson and her husband that the fresh air would be healing for her lungs. Obviously, exactly the opposite was true. On January 13 her lungs began to bleed again, at first slightly, but her cough increased and with it the bleeding. Still, as her mother-in-law wrote Edward, "The air was so reviving to her that notwithstanding the wintry cold she continued to ride almost every day."[55]

On January 16 the snow was so deep that Waldo had to cancel his morning service. The weather continued to be cold and blustery, and by the twenty-fourth Ellen was having to skip her daily outings. In a letter to Edward, Waldo said she was quite ill, and two days later: "Ellen has been more weak & sick since [the twenty-fourth], but gets out to ride a little way yesterday & day before." If she could continue to do this "with impunity, I shall hope the reestablishment of her health but we have come to the prefixing of *if* to all our plans."[56]

On the last day of January, Waldo wrote William:

My poor Ellen has been sadly sick &, we flatter ourselves, is a little better. Nurse is rubbing her cold hands this moment to quicken her circulations. (I write in her chamber) Soon, please God, we hope to pass by your house in our jou[rney] southwards. Yet perhaps February & its snow must melt away first before we can have strength or roads.[57]

During the next week she rallied and relapsed. Dr. Jackson made daily calls. But on Wednesday, February 2, she went out riding in the morning and again in the afternoon. Charles felt encouraged, but when he returned to Chardon Street on Saturday he found her "sadly altered & her husband & mother [Ruth Emerson] without any hope of her recovery." Ellen herself was convinced she would not last many days, but hoped to live long enough to hear of Edward's safe arrival in St. Croix. She talked calmly of death, and later, as her mother-in-law wrote Edward, "in her intervals of suffering" she spoke in "short ejaculations" to thank her friends for their kindness and God for his mercy.[58]

On Sunday she breathed with great difficulty, and Waldo scarcely left her bedside. He had arranged for Dr. Follen to preach for him in the morning and Mr. Frothingham in the afternoon. Charles wrote William that Waldo was "as one over whom the waters have gone."[59] To ease her pain Dr. Jackson gave her opiates, which caused her to doze, but at intervals she woke up fully conscious. Sunday evening Charles wrote Aunt Mary:

She spoke this afternoon very sweetly of her readiness to die, [said] that she told you she should not probably live through the winter—tho' she did not know that she should have been called so soon. She saw no reason why her friends should be distressed—it was better she should go first, & prepare the way. She asked Waldo if he had strength, to read her a few verses of scripture, and he read a portion of the XIV chapter of John ["In my Father's house are many mansions"]—Waldo is bowed down under the affliction. Yet he says tis like seeing an angel go to heaven.[60]

Meanwhile, Ellen's parents and sisters had been summoned, and she was surrounded by her dearest friends and relatives. Dr. Ripley came on Monday and prayed with her. Charles, who had to return to Cambridge, bade her farewell, and she asked him to "cheer up Waldo when she was gone, not to let him think too much of her." Charles thought she looked like a saint and declared in the spirit of Waldo's sermon on dying, "The House of Mourning for such sufferers, is better than the House of feasting."[61] In fact, the serenity, unwavering faith, and selflessness of Ellen Emerson in her final hours so buoyed up the spirits of her whole family that the shock of her actual death was a delayed reaction.

Two hours after her last breath, Waldo Emerson, still in a state of euphoria, wrote his Aunt Mary:

My angel is gone to heaven this morning & I am alone in the world & strangely happy. Her lungs shall no more be torn nor her head scalded by her blood nor her whole life suffer from the warfare between the force & delicacy of her soul & the weakness of her frame. I said this morn & I do not know but it is true that I have never known a person in the world in whose separate existence as a soul I could so readily & fully believe & she is present with me now beaming joyfully upon me, in her deliverance & the entireness of her love for your poor nephew. I see it plainly that things & duties will look coarse & vulgar enough to me when I find the romance of her presence (& romance is a beggarly word) withdrawn from them all. But now the fulness of joy occasioned by things said by her in the last week & by this eternal deliverance is in my heart. . . .

But the past days the most eventful of my life are all a dim confusion & now the pall is drawn over them, yet do they shine brilliantly in my spiritual world. Say, dear Aunt, if I am not rich in her memory?[62]

In the secular twentieth century, Emerson's strange "happiness" may seem like a morbid perversion—one is reminded of Poe's infatuation with the death of beautiful ladies—but it should be understood in the context of the religious faith Emerson had been expressing for several months in his sermons and private Journal. Also, he had grown up with this reaction to death. His mother had "rejoiced" in the death of her first son, John

Clarke, and of her sister. Furthermore, Ellen had died in such a way as to make her extremely religious husband feel it was a kind of final spiritual consummation of their marriage. Like Dante's Beatrice, she had led him up to a landing on the stairway to heaven.

In his Journal Emerson described the remarkable seven-hour drama preceding his wife's exit from the physical world:

> A little after 2 o'clock on Tuesday morn, she said she felt that she was going soon & having asked if Mother, Margaret, & Paulina were all present she wished them to be still & she would pray with them. And truly & sweetly did she pray for herself & for us & infused such comfort into my soul as never entered it before & I trust will never escape out of it. After this she kissed all, & bid her nurses, 'love God'; & then sunk very fast, occasionally recovering her wandering mind. One of the last things she said after much rambling & inarticulate expression was 'I have not forgot the peace & joy.' And at nine o'clock she died. Farewell blessed Spirit who hast made me happy in thy life & in thy death makes me yet happy in thy disembodied state.[63]

Two nights later in his dreams Waldo again hears her breathing and sees her dying. Awake, he thinks he would like to join her in the tomb, but feels his unworthiness. He asks her to pray for him, and he prays *to* her: "Dear Ellen (for that is your name in heaven) shall we not be united even now more & more, as I more steadfastly persist in the love of truth & virtue which you loved?" His mind is an open book to her, and she knows the sins and selfishness he has concealed from her: "help me to be rid of them; suggest good thoughts as you promised me, & show me truth. Not for the world, would I have left you here alone; stay by me & lead me upward."[64]

Two days later, exactly a week after Ellen's death, her distraught husband tried to communicate with her in a poem:

> Once more I call
> Doest thou not hear me Ellen
> Is thy ear deaf to me
> Is thy radiant eye
> Dark that it cannot see

In yonder ground thy limbs are laid
Under the snow
And earth has no spot so dear above
As that below

And there I know the heart is still
And the eye is shut & the ear is dull

But the spirit that dwelt in mine
The spirit wherein mine dwelt
The soul of Ellen the thought divine
From God, that came—for all that felt

Does it not know me now
Does it not share my thought
Is it prisoned from Waldo's prayer
Is its glowing love forgot[65]

Ellen had been buried, at her request, in her father's "tomb" in Roxbury. (Whether this meant a mausoleum, which her prosperous father could have afforded, is not known, for the cemetery was moved many years ago, and apparently all records destroyed.) Every morning Waldo Emerson walked to the Roxbury cemetery and tried to commune with his "saint," but this poem, and many passages in his Journal, reveal his inability to establish the sweet communication.

In another poetic fragment his frustrations have become so unnerving that he exclaims, "Teach me I am forgotten by the dead . . . And I no longer would keep terms with me." He would not "murder, steal, or fornicate," or "break the peace of towns; / But I would bury my ambition[.]" He is so extremely agitated that he becomes almost incoherent and his handwriting is nearly illegible. He begs Ellen to meet him "on the midnight wing of dreams," but she does not come to him even in dreams, and he asks in despair:

Why should I live
The future will repeat the past
Yet cannot give
Again the Vision beautiful too beautiful to last

And o perhaps the welcome stroke
That severs forever this fleshly yoke
Shall restore the vision to the soul
In the great Vision of the Whole.[66]

The only unambiguous statement in these lines is that the poet, Hamletlike, questions life itself. But what are we to make of "The future will repeat the past"? Possibly that he might find someone else to love, though never again the "Vision . . . too beautiful to last." Death, therefore, might be better, absorbing him and his "visions" of love into "the great Vision of the Whole."

On the second Sunday after his wife's death Emerson preached a sermon on "Consolation for the Mourner." Though everyone knew he was the mourner, his theme was that the loss of a loved one is a universal experience. He said frankly, "Let me speak as I feel,"[67] but he meant by this not so much his personal grief as the thoughts which gave him consolation. To read the sermon and not his private Journal and his half-incoherent poems, one would assume that his faith in God's Providence was untroubled, and that he actually had found consolation. But in view of the other personal confessions, this sermon must be read as the religious assurances he was trying to make himself believe. What it clearly conveys is Emerson's *profession* of Christian faith on February 20, 1831.

The minister admits that no man in his circumstances could help grieving, but the grief can be assuaged by accepting the Christian teaching that the soul is separated from the body only that it may enter "into a nearer relation to the Father of Spirits." Fear of the grave can also be removed by observing the manner in which the "pious" die, going "down to the tomb with prayer and praise on their lips, and the thoughts of heaven," even as they are seized by "the convulsions of death." Ellen Emerson had done precisely that, completely fulfilling the predictions of his December and January sermons.

In the second place, the minister says, Christian faith removes dread of the grave because "in the mind of the mourner . . . the dead are present still," giving their sympathy, their prayers, "and whatever aid the spirit out of the body can give to the spirit in the body." He is even more explicit:

The soul that has thought with us, and preferred our interest to its own, and known well what was in our heart, is now only a step removed from us, and we believe, looks back with more than earthly love, mixing the recent knowledge of human wants, with the newness of the revelations now made to it by change of state.

This sympathy between the disembodied and the still-bodied soul becomes a "sublime attraction":

When we have explored our desolate house for what shall never there be seen, we return with an eagerness to the tomb as the only place of healing and peace. It seems to us that willingly—oh yes, joyfully, we would, if permitted, lay down our head also on the same pillow, so that God would restore us to the society we have lost.

But this attraction is also a temptation to be selfish, making a man forget "his place in society." The Christian faith "keeps *Duty, the soul's everlasting object, always uppermost;* . . . a neglect of any of our appointed trusts, a life of inaction, a death of grief, would disqualify us for that very happiness we aim at . . ." Thus, "the best tribute the living can offer to the dead is to be faithful in our place as they were faithful in theirs," keeping up "courage and good hope." By such conduct "the tie may really grow stronger between one on earth and one in heaven."[68]

This was Emerson's firm intention in February 1831, but in subsequent weeks and months he would find great difficulty in doing what he preached. The struggle between faith and experience which failed to support it would bring about vast changes and developments in his theological and moral thinking.

CHAPTER IX

The Law of Compensation

... let my bark head its own way toward the
law of laws, toward the compensation or action
& reaction of the Moral Universe ...[1]

I

Five days after his wife's death, Emerson prayed: "God be merciful to me a
sinner & repair this miserable debility in which her death has left my
soul."[2] He knew that his apathy would in time wear off, though he almost
feared the time when it would, for that would make him feel even more
remote from the beautiful soul in heaven. On April 4 he still felt dazed as
he tried to collect his thoughts for the "Fast Day" sermon he was to deliver three days later:

> The days go by, griefs, & simpers, & sloth, & disappointments. The dead
> do not return, & sometimes we are negligent of their image. Not of yours
> Ellen—I know too well who is gone from me. And here come on the for-
> mal duties which are to be formally discharged, and in our sluggish minds
> no sentiment rises to quicken them, they seem—[unfinished][3]

Though the Puritan custom of observing a day of fasting and prayer was
still an annual ritual in Massachusetts, it had lost much of its original
meaning. In his Journal Emerson called it the "remainder of an ancient
race & like old furniture to be dispensed with." As pastor of a church
founded by the Puritans, and painfully conscious of the loved one he had
lost, he was in the mood to observe the day more devoutly than was customary. "It is well to remember the departed. . . . I will respect this Fast as

a connecting link by which the posterity are bound to the fathers; as a trump through which the voice of the fathers speak." He was thinking, of course, of the seventeenth-century Puritans, not of his own father, who was less a Puritan than himself. In his sermon Emerson would examine the institution and find: "It does not belong to the Pilgrims only. It belongs to a wider country. It belongs to human frailty."[4]

Gradually Emerson was learning to alleviate his grief by finding analogies and themes for sermons. On May 18 he wrote in his Journal: "Went tonight to the Sunday School meeting, but was myself a dumb dog that could not bark."[5] However, back in his study his thoughts flowed easily. One was the use of his great loss: "The mourner reads his loss in every utensil in his house, in every garment, in the face of every friend." But if in heart and soul one truly worships God, "He will see the religious face of every thing." A few days later he reminded himself: "All things take their character from the state of the spectator."[6] In reading Mme. de Staël's *Germany* he had been impressed by her statement that "Almost all the axioms of physics correspond with the maxims of morals." This led Emerson to conclude:

> The universe is pervaded with myriads of secret analogies that tie together its remotest parts as the atmosphere of a summer morn[in]g is filled with innumerable gossamer threads running in every direction but revealed by the beams of the rising sun. So when the soul which in its activity is light begins to throw out its rays, it finds it has been living amidst beauty all unperceived, amidst power with which it has never armed itself, and wisdom, yet was a fool[.][7]

The idea that nature is a "sublime alphabet," which would become the leitmotif five years later of his first book (*Nature*), was connected in Emerson's mind with his "law of laws,"[8] compensation. As we have seen, this concept was not new with him, but it now became a major source of consolation. It had a number of meanings for him, and he would continue to find applications in future years. The physical basis of compensation was the real scientific axiom that for every action there is a proportional reaction, but Emerson extended this Newtonian law into psychology, theology, and personal mythology. Psychologically, for every loss there is a gain, and vice versa. "But will you gain nothing by the loss? Consider it well; there's no cheating in Nature."[9]

What are often called Emerson's "mystical" tendencies had recently been encouraged by his reading of Plotinus (in Thomas Taylor's translation), and he had indexed quotations in his "Blotting Book" under the term "Theoptics," which the editors of the new edition of his Journals translate as " 'visions of God'—with a transcendental perspective of time and of the single soul infused into all phenomena."[10] Thus Emerson could now write in his Journal: "I see plainly that the ends to which I live, are independent of time & place; & neither the hope nor the fear of conscience profess themselves satisfied with the scanty inches of mortal life."[11]

The relationships of these ideas of compensation, nature as God's symbolic language, and the moral basis of physical laws, Emerson would explore later in more detail, but he would never be able to test them by rational analysis. His faith that all existence emanated from a single Soul enabled him to accept them without regard to contradictions. He *felt* them to be true, and he believed that the "God in us worships God."[12] But he had decided that "God cannot be intellectually discerned,"[13] and that "wisdom comes more from the heart than the head."[14] These convictions he had arrived at through meditation in the spirit of prayer:

To reflect is to receive truth immediately from God without any medium. . . . To take on trust certain facts is a dead faith—inoperative. A trust in yourself is the height not of pride but of piety, an unwillingness to learn of any but God himself. . . . You are as one who has a private door that leads him to the King's chamber. You have learned nothing rightly that you have not learned so[.][15]

This kind of self-reliance (or God-reliance) Emerson had been preaching in his church for nearly two years. Now that he was being compensated for Ellen's loss by an increasing sense of independence from worldly rewards, his own thinking became more daring. In June he declared in his Journal:

I suppose it is not wise, not being natural, to belong to any religious party. In the bible you are not directed to be a Unitarian or a Calvinist or an Episcopalian. Now if a man is wise, he will not only not profess himself to be a Unitarian, but he will say to himself I am not a member of that or of any party. I am God's child[,] a disciple of Christ . . . As fast as any man becomes great, that is, thinks, he becomes a new party. . . .

A Sect or Party is an elegant incognito devised to save a man from the vexation of thinking.[16]

In July Emerson tried to versify this thought:

> I write the things that are
>   Not what appears;
> Of things as they are in the eye of God
>   Not in the eye of Man.[17]

If taken literally, this may seem like a most arrogant and dogmatic statement. But Emerson certainly did not mean that he had become so Godlike himself that he could speak, like Moses, for God, but rather that he attempted to interpret the religious life in terms of the spiritual rather than the materialistic ambitions of most men in the society of his day. It was also now and would henceforth be his conviction that all moral improvements must start with a change of heart. He quoted with approval Pestalozzi's statement at the end of the French Revolution "That the amelioration of outward circumstances will be the effect, but never can be the means of mental & moral improvement."[18]

For this reason Emerson was skeptical of charity: unless the inner man is regenerated, no amount of improving his physical conditions will do him any permanent good. To Emerson the remedy was very simple, though he recognized the difficulty of propagating it: all any man has to do to begin his spiritual regeneration is to listen to his own conscience, for "God dwells in thee."

> And thou canst learn the laws of Nature
> Because its author is latent in thy breast.
>
> . . . . .
>
> And since the Soul of things is in thee
> Thou needest nothing out of thee.[19]

Though this doctrine of self-reliance based on his divine promptings had become Emerson's most stubborn personal belief, he was not actually a mystic in the sense of one who hears the voice of God in a trance or some other unnatural state of mind. However, like the classic mystic, he did cultivate a passive receptivity, especially in prayer. Since the beginning of his ministry he had insisted that in prayer one should not ask God for favors but simply invite Him in. Thus, divine truth comes to one in meditation, in reverie, and in prayer.

Emerson was also reading the Neoplatonists, whose views he had found summarized in Victor Cousin's *Introduction to the History of Philosophy* (both in the 1828 French version and in the English translation of 1832).[20] Then he read the Neoplatonists themselves in Taylor's translations. He was also by this time curious about the "Hindu Scriptures," and did a little exploration, but his mystical ideas would always owe more to the Neoplatonists than to any other source (either the Greek philosophers or the English Platonists of the seventeenth century). He read also the pre-Socratic metaphysicians: "Heraclitus grown old complained that all resolved itself into identity. That thought was first his philosophy, & then his melancholy—the life he lived, & the death he died."[21] In some manuscripts dated July 6, Emerson tried to versify Heraclitus' thought:

> There is nothing else but God
> Where e'er I look
> All things hasten back to him
> Light is but his shadow dim.[22]

From Christian theology Emerson had received the doctrines of self-denial as a virtue, the sinfulness of the appetites, and the superiority of moral character over physical possessions. Neoplatonism reinforced his distrust of sensual delights. From Porphyry's *Vita Plotinus* he quoted both in Latin and in Greek: "Plotinus appeared to be affected with a certain shame because his soul was in a body" (Greek version: "he seemed ashamed because he was in a body").[23] Emerson was not really ashamed of his body (or especially proud of it, either), or fanatically ascetic, but he preferred what he regarded as the permanent to the transitory satisfactions:

What are your sources of satisfaction? If they are meats & drinks, dress, gossip, revenge, hope of wealth, they must perish with the body. If they are contemplation, kind affections, admiration of what is admirable, self command, self improvement, then they survive death & will make you as happy then as now.[24]

Doubtless all members of Emerson's church paid lip service to these values and approved of his preaching against sensuality and materialism.

They, too, believed that "The soul rules over matter" and that "the Soul is the kingdom of God[,] the abode of love, of truth, of virtue." But at least some of them did not accept this doctrine to the extent he did. On December 19 he reported in his Journal:

When I talk with the sick they sometimes think I treat death with unbecoming indifference and do not make the case my own, or, if I do, err in my judgment. I do not fear death. I believe those who fear it have borrowed the terrors thro which they see it from vulgar opinion, & not from their own minds. My own mind is the direct revelation which I have from God & far least liable to mistake in telling his will [than] of any revelation.[25]

Later some members of Emerson's church would murmur about their pastor's Quakerish tendencies, and indeed he may have been somewhat influenced by his friends in the church in New Bedford in which he had preached from time to time, beginning in 1827. They were Hicksite Quakers who formed a Unitarian congregation of their own.[26] At any rate, by the beginning of 1832 Emerson's inner voice was beginning to alienate him from institutional religion. On January 10, 1832, he confessed in his Journal:

It is the best part of the man, I sometimes think, that revolts most against his being the minister. His good revolts from official goodness.... The difficulty is that we do not make a world of our own but fall into institutions already made & have to accommodate ourselves to them to be useful at all, & this accommodation is, I say, a loss of so much integrity & of course of so much power.[27]

Though the American Unitarian Association was one of the most liberal of Protestant denominations, it was an institution, and it did have some theological traditions. Moreover, the leading members of the Second Church were prominent merchants, shippers, and professional men in Boston, men more concerned with practical affairs of the world than with abstract ideals, and therefore likely to be satisfied with "official goodness." There is no evidence of real friction between Emerson and his parishioners until the following summer, but a notation made in his Journal on January 30, 1832, indicates that he was dissatisfied with his own performance:

Every man hath his use no doubt and every one makes ever the effort according to the energy of his character to suit his external condition to his inward constitution. If his external condition does not admit of such accommodation he breaks the form of his life, & enters a new one which does. . . . Thus Finney can preach, & so his prayers are short. Parkman can pray, & so his prayers are long. Lowell can visit & so his church service is less. But what shall poor I do who can neither visit nor pray nor preach to my mind [that is, in my own estimation].[28]

Emerson's "inward constitution" was making it increasingly difficult for him to accommodate it to his "external condition" as pastor of the Second Church.

II

On December 2, 1831, Emerson was feeling low and dissatisfied. "The day is sad, the night is careful, the heart is weighed down with leads," he wrote in his Journal; "what shall he do who would belong to the Universe, '& live with living nature a pure rejoicing thing'?"[29] The quotation came from Ellen's poem "The Violet," whose theme was death and resurrection:

> When winter reigned I'd close my eye, but wake with
>   bursting spring
> And live with living Nature, a pure rejoicing thing.[30]

Both the quotation and the comment that followed showed that Emerson was sad because he could not communicate with their author: "O friend, that said these words, are you conscious of this thought & this writer? I would not ask any other consolation than to be assured by one sign that the heart never plays false to itself when in its scope it requires by a necessity the permanence of the soul."

Certainly Emerson could never for a moment doubt the steadfastness of Ellen's heart even in heaven, if it were possible for her to have a human emotion in heaven. His sadness was caused by a deeper doubt. A few days later he mused, "How we came out of silence into this sounding world is the wonder of wonders. All other marvels are less."[31] He was puzzled and frustrated by the impossible barrier between the world of spirit and the world of nature, however much he might theorize about the harmonious relation between soul and body. These doubts were causing a gradual change in his concepts of God and Soul, though he himself may not yet have been fully aware of the extent of the change.

There were also immediate and personal causes of Emerson's mental depression. Both his sister-in-law Margaret and his mother-in-law, whom he called his "living monuments to Ellen," had been ill since August, with temporary periods of improvement followed by relapse, as in Ellen's case. Emerson feared that "a hard winter may bereave me of them both." Then Ellen would be "still farther from my mortal sight"; but he also loved "them both for themselves." At the time he was perhaps more worried about Margaret than about Mrs. Kent, for he wrote Edward: "sad sad it will be [*will*, not *would*] to me to lose my highminded sister . . ."[32]

Margaret and Mrs. Kent lived at 7 Central Court,[33] on the other side of Boston, three miles or more from Chardon Street, but Emerson kept closely in touch with them. Paulina and her husband, Captain Nash, were contesting Ellen's will, but by mutual consent between Emerson and his in-laws the settlement was to be made by the Supreme Court of Massachusetts. Waldo wrote William: "I take no [legal] step without advising with Mr & Mrs Kent and Margaret Tucker."[34] Apparently they sympathized with him.

It was Charles, however, who gave Waldo most concern in the winter of 1831–32. In September he described Charles in a letter to Edward as "in body like a wilted apple," and again in October as "quite unwell."[35] For weeks he had had a bad cough, with other symptoms of a severe cold, and "a great stupor & indisposition to any exertion even so much as to speak. He is pale & weak—all sad signs in a frame so slender." Waldo could see the end of his dream of having the three brothers live together again. (Bulkeley would have to be tended by someone else; he was now back in the asylum at Charlestown, at Waldo's expense.)

William was still struggling in New York, and Waldo had been urging him to return to Boston and form a law partnership with Charles. With William's writing talent and Charles's gift of tongue, "you & he would make a partnership of your opposite excellencies that would turn the whole Suffolk bar out of doors."[36] However, William had begun to earn money and in December he was appointed counselor of the Supreme Court of New York.[37] Now even Waldo admitted that he would be wise to remain in New York City. Moreover, Charles was in no condition to practice law. On October 19 Waldo wrote William that he had slept little the night before for worrying about Charles. "Who would have thot," he lamented, "that Edward & Charles on whom we put so much fond pride shd. be the first to fail whilst Ellen, my rose, is gone."[38] He wrote "fail" instead of "die," but he seemed to expect the worst.

Four days later Waldo thought Charles better as a result of the treatment Dr. John Ware had been giving him, though as described to William it sounds barbaric and of doubtful value: "Blisters & leeches & bleeding have been the means of relieving his pleurisy." His family rejoiced "before God that the boy promises to get well soon, & if we can we will keep him in New England"—instead of letting him join Edward in Puerto Rico. Dr. Jackson "tho't very favorably of his case from the first sight." But so had he of Ellen's case. And Charles's improvement was also illusory. In his weakened condition the doctor's bleeding him would have been sufficient to cause a relapse. His family and physician decided at last that he must avoid another Boston winter; so he sailed on December 7 on the brig *Jasper* with a shipload of mules and arrived in San Juan on December 22. Edward had meanwhile secured employment as bookkeeper and secretary to Mr. Sidney Mason, the U.S. consul in San Juan, and was now self-supporting. Charles, of course, had to receive financial support from his family.

On Christmas Day, 1831, Waldo wrote Edward that Charles had barely escaped the cold in time.[39] Soon after he sailed, the coastal waters froze solid, a month earlier than usual, before ships had brought in sufficient fuel for the winter. As a consequence coal and wood were very scarce and costly. In New York the scarcity of fuel was even more acute than in Boston. But as Waldo wrote, a thaw was beginning—though it would be temporary at that time of year.

Charles Emerson, the introspective and proper Bostonian, experienced severe culture shock on his arrival in San Juan, on the "anniversary of the Pilgrim Landing" in New England, as he was quick to remember. He knew scarcely a word of Spanish, and had undertaken the trip too suddenly to begin studying the language. He wrote William on December 23[40] that when the ship passed El Morro castle and he began to glimpse the city, with its high walls and "black jail-like rows of dwelling houses," his heart sank. Unable to understand the shouted commands in Spanish, he felt he was coming to a desolate community. But as soon as the *Jasper* anchored, Mr. John Mason, "with honest face, & English speech," came for him, said Edward was well, and guided him to a café where Edward was waiting. Charles now began to be "amazed and amused," but still found the noise appalling. It seemed to him that everyone lived in the street, and to judge by the uproar, no one was "afflicted with complaints of the lungs."

The roughly cobbled streets were dirty, yet the odor of citrus blossoms sweetened the air. Social contrasts were notable also. Mr. Sidney Mason lived in baronial style in a building extending from one street to another, with large, high-ceilinged rooms, long passages to a courtyard, and servants lodged in various quarters. But most of the natives lived in severe poverty. The landscape reminded Charles of a Washington Allston painting, "as warm & softly shadowed—smooth waters & dark browed hills." But "This glorious region, these wonders of Nature, preach to a servile & insensible race. They read no lessons of eternal beauty & order, no revelations of God, in the heavens which drop fatness, or the earth which teems with fruits & smiles with love." Waldo must have been reminded of his own first impressions of St. Augustine, Florida, in the winter of 1827—though he had made no attempt to describe them in quite such romantic clichés.

On further acquaintance with San Juan some of Charles's prejudices softened, while others hardened. On January 9, 1832, admitting that he landed with "a dismal idea of the Spaniards," he wrote Waldo that he found himself "in a lively little city, which looked so picturesque & smelt like an orange . . ."[41] And "the inhabitants instead of knives & pistols wore the most peaceable garb in the world, & had a smile and a greeting even for the strangers." But he was offended by the sight of "a garrison of 1200 whiskered soldados, with mortars & twenty-four pounders planted thickly round the ramparts on every side—an irreligious people, in an utter stagnation of all healthy impulses from within or without—in no ways in keeping with the softness [of the air and landscape] . . ." Waldo, of course, took keen interest in Charles's unsophisticated observations, written in response to his older brother's urgent request. But best of all was Charles's assurance that he felt better and hoped before many months to return home, cured. For the moment he was now one less worry for Waldo.

There were, however, other worries for him in the spring of 1832, and his Journal entries indicate that they were personal. An entry dated March 10 begins innocently, "Temperance is an estate. I am richer, the Stoic migh[t] say, by my self command than I am by my income."[42] Then in the second paragraph this confession: "This year I have spent, say $20 in wine & liquors which are drunk up, & the drinkers are the worse." Emerson was never a prohibitionist, and it was not the drinking that bothered his conscience, but the waste of money. He could "have bought a beautiful print" with the twenty dollars, "or have paid a debt that makes me wince this hundred years." What debt of long standing? Most likely the money his Uncle Samuel Ripley lent him to make the trip to Florida for his health in 1827. Four days later Emerson was again thinking of temperance: "Be master of yourself, and for the love of God keep every inch you gain." That he was preaching to himself is indicated by his notation on March 28: "my food per diem weighed 14½ oz."[43] Next day, thirteen ounces, and on April 2, twelve and a half ounces. He was dieting to discipline himself.

The strangest of all revelations, however, is Emerson's entry in his Journal for March 29, 1832: "I visited Ellen's tomb & opened the coffin."[44] That is the complete entry, without the slightest clue to this strange action. It has been suggested that it was only a dream,[45] but we have no reason to make this assumption. Besides, Emerson had not been able to dream of Ellen since February 11, 1831, three days after her death.[46] The terseness of the notation is similar to his brief recording of her death, when he was under terrible emotional strain.

If, as surmised in Chapter VIII, Ellen was buried in her father's mausoleum, the opening of the coffin would have been a little less gruesome than digging it up out of the ground. Yet even so, the act remains so unnatural as to seem almost insane. And it is also unlikely that in that period in Boston the body was embalmed. There is no indication that the coffin needed to be moved, only that it was opened to satisfy some morbid compulsion. It may be significant that Emerson did not mention Ellen again in his Journal until November 1832, when Margaret Tucker died, and he wrote: "Go rejoice with Ellen . . ."[47] But his cousin David Greene Haskins says that he continued his practice, "until his departure for Europe, of regularly walking out in the early morning to visit her grave in Roxbury."[48]

Nearly three months earlier, on January 9, Emerson had recorded having had "Hideous dreams last night and queried today whether they were any more than exaggerations of the sins of the day. We see our own evil affections embodied in frightful physiognomies."[49] Almost two weeks after that, on January 21, he returned to the subject of dreams: "Dreams & beasts are two keys by which we are to find out the secrets of our own nature. All mystics use them. They are like comparative anatomy. They are test objects."[50]

Though Emerson seems to suspect that dreams convey some kind of truth ("They are test objects"), he thinks the world still waits for a satisfactory explanation of them. It is interesting, too, that he links this mystery with animals as keys to human nature. He may have had some pre-Darwinian intuition of the origin of human conduct in that of the "lower animals," but he had had no experience and scant opportunity to test such opinions. His real interest in animals he indicated by a resolve on April 2, 1832: "Write a sermon upon Animals. They are to man in life what fables about them are in ethics."[51] He intended to moralize on "the bee, ant, fox, hedgehog, ermine, swine, roe, woodpecker, pigeon, worm, moth, mite." In writing Sermon 152, "The God of the Living," delivered April 22, 1832, he drew upon René Réaumur's *Mémoires pour Servir à l'Histoire des Insectes* and works on comparative anatomy by the British surgeons John Abernethy and William Hunter. In May he was also reading James Drummond's *Letters to a Young Naturalist.*[52]

Astronomy had also now become one of Emerson's great interests. After reading Sir William Herschel's *Discourse* (printed in *American Library of Useful Knowledge*) the previous December, he had written William that the work was "enough to tempt a man to leave all duties to find out natural science."[53] He hoped someday he could have an observatory, a telescope, and a laboratory. The following May he wondered, "What is there in Paradise Lost to elevate & astonish like Herschel or Somerville?"[54] The contrast between "the magnitude & duration of the things [in astronomy] observed & the animalcule observer" was like "a mere eye sailing about space in an eggshell," stationed on a "little cock-boat of a planet." Every white spot in the sky "is a lump of Suns[,] the roe[,] the milt of light & life[.]" Emerson concluded that "God has opened this knowledge to us to correct our theology & educate the mind."

In his sermon on "Astronomy,"[55] delivered on May 27, Emerson attempted to show how knowledge of astronomy *had* corrected theology, taking as his text Acts 17:24ff.: *"God that made the world and all things therein, seeing what he is Lord of heaven and earth, dwelleth not in temples made with hands; neither is worshipped with men's hands as though he needed anything, seeing he giveth to all life and breath and all things . . ."* Since Paul here affirms that the "God of Nature and the God of the Bible" are the same, Emerson argues that "the records of the divine dealings with men" should be read by "the light of nature." The great controversy over contradictions between science and religion had not yet split Christendom (that would come after Darwin published his *Origin of Species* in 1859), but already in 1832 Emerson had examined the subject and found only useful education in science.

In "Astronomy" Emerson assumed the enlightened position of Professor Eichhorn, whose lectures William Emerson had attended at Göttingen. Possibly William's talks with Waldo were partly responsible, though Waldo's own studies in "natural religion" at Harvard had prepared him to be receptive to the revelations of the modern astronomer. Now he preached that in "the infant religion of all nations" God has been "clothed in human form, and idolatry imputed to him the passions as well as the person of man." That religion, "suffering from the caprices and errors of men," had degraded the concept of God. Ptolemaic astronomy assumed the earth to be the center of the universe, and theologians regarded man as the object of its existence. For many generations they taught that "God from all eternity had foreseen the fall of man and had devised in his councils a method by which man might be saved."

The telescope was fatal to Ptolemaic cosmology, and Copernican astronomy "made the theological *scheme of Redemption* absolutely incredible." The earth was now known to be an insignificant dot in boundless space, into which "We are newcomers into space. Our planet is gray and scarred with wrinkles of immense age, but its inhabitant is a novelty in the cheerful eternity, long ago as bright as now, into which we are born." Many of those other worlds must be inhabited by creatures different from us. "And to suppose that the constitution of the race of yesterday that now plants the fields of this particular planet, should be the pattern for all the orders that people the huge globes in the heaven is too improbable to be entertained." However:

The investigations of the last two hundred years have brought to light the most wonderful proofs of design—beneficent design—operating far and near in atoms and in systems, reaching to such prodigious extent both of time and space, and so perfectly answering their end, that the mind cannot weigh them without ever increasing surprise and delight.

Even deviations in nature's rhythms, as Joseph Louis Lagrange had demonstrated, are cyclical, a deviation in one direction being exactly compensated by a reverse movement. This principle delighted Emerson because it added scientific confirmation to his cherished law of compensation. But in a larger context he was finding new arguments for the theories of Paley and Butler, though he disliked these men. Those eloquent apologists of "design," however, would hardly have agreed with Emerson that "if we carry the New Testament to the inhabitants of other worlds we might need to leave Jewish Christianity and Roman Christianity, Paul and Apollos [*sic*] and Cephas and Luther, and Socinus . . ." Yet, though these might be found too limited and earthbound, Emerson declared that "the moral law, justice and mercy would be at home in every climate and world where life is . . . ," for moral law is in harmony with universal physical law. This harmony Emerson does not attempt to prove but accepts, as he long had, as an obvious truism. "The greatest enlargement that our views of the solar system or of the Creation can attain can never throw the least shade upon the truths, upon moral truth, upon the truths which it was the office of Jesus to unfold." The distinction he seems to be making is between "theological" and "moral" truth.

The divinity of Jesus was still an unsettled question among Unitarians, and Emerson was not a heretic in his Church by accepting him as the greatest of all moral leaders while rejecting him as the literal Son of God. However, not all members of his parish were ready to accept their minister's doctrine that since "The Scriptures were written by human hands" (Professor Eichhorn's "higher criticism"), therefore "God intends by giving us access to this original writing of his hand to correct the human errors that have crept into them [the Scriptures]." Or even if they agreed in principle to this view that nature rather than the Bible is the best source of truth, they could not all agree on which were the specific "human errors." In his enlightenment Emerson had found one "error," on which he must take a personal moral stand. It concerned the interpretation of the authority of

Christ's Last Supper as a Christian institution, and it produced a crisis in his life almost as traumatic as his loss of Ellen—and possibly the final effect of that loss.

III

On June 2, 1832, Emerson wrote in his Journal: "Cold cold. Thermometer Says Temperate. Yet a week of moral excitement."[56] The "moral excitement" was the controversy with his church which he started by declaring that he could no longer administer the communion service (the Lord's Supper) with a clear conscience because he had decided that Christ had not intended it to become a perpetual ritual. He wrote a letter to the Proprietors of the Second Church stating his position and requesting that he be permitted to discontinue this ceremony.

In New England the Lord's Supper had often been the subject of controversy. The early Puritans believed that only members of the Church should take communion, and to become a member of the Church one had to offer evidence that God had chosen him as one of His "saints," predestined to go to heaven. For an "unsaved" person to take communion was believed to be blasphemy. Solomon Stoddard, the grandfather of Jonathan Edwards, had been savagely attacked by Increase Mather for accepting profession of faith and repentance as prerequisites for Church membership and communion. Later the more liberal Congregational churches went even further and said that taking communion could aid in redemption and should therefore be open to everyone.

Emerson's own position had been similar to Stoddard's when he preached a sermon on "A Feast of Remembrance" to the Second Church on September 27, 1829. He said then that it should be extended to "all men who believed in the divine authority of Christianity and not as now, only a small minority. . . . I cannot by straight covenants exclude any man, nor can I take it upon myself to say that any man's sin shall exclude him."[57]

Emerson also said that "our nature shall be progressive," and "So it is with the institutions of religion." Perhaps even more portentous: the Lord's Supper should be "accommodated to every age," and every Christian should see it "coloured by the complexion of his own mind." These assertions might have warned Emerson's congregation that as the "complexion" of his mind changed, he might alter his opinions on the Lord's Supper. By the spring of 1832 he had, in fact, come around to the position of the Quakers, who rejected the ceremony altogether. Emerson would permit it to anyone who found consolation in it, but he felt that it would be hypocritical in him to administer it to worshipers who thought it had divine authority and supernatural efficacy.

Subconsciously Emerson may have been searching for a means of breaking with his church—or provoking it to break with him, thus preserving his own sense of innocence. His dissatisfaction was actually more with the ministry itself than with the Second Church. A year before, he had thought it unwise and unnatural "to belong to any religious party," and the previous January he had written in his Journal that the best part of man revolts against his being the minister.[58] And now on June 2, after confessing his psychosomatic chill, he returns to the January thought, but with more conviction:

> I have sometimes thought that in order to be a good minister it was necessary to leave the ministry. The profession is antiquated. In an altered age, we worship in the dead forms of our forefathers. Were not a Socratic paganism better than an effete superannuated Christianity?[59]

Emerson's letter to the Second Church was referred to a committee for consideration. Two of his best friends, George A. Sampson and his cousin George B. Emerson, were on the committee, and he had confidence in a fair decision, but on June 16 the committee reported that it could not approve his request. At a meeting of the membership of the Second Church five days later, the report of the committee was approved, and Emerson was placed in the position of having either to back down or to resign.[60]

Fortunately for him, at this time church services were suspended for a month so that some needed repairs could be made on the building. This gave him time to consider his course of action. He was sure of his own thoughts on the Lord's Supper, and of his dissatisfaction with the restrictive conventions of the ministry, but he knew how much distress his resignation would cause his mother, brothers, and many in his parish. In considerable anguish he decided to visit his Aunt Mary in Waterford, Maine, and ask her advice. One might think he would know what that would be, but he was still in some ways the child whom she had comforted in his infancy. When hurt, he turned to her, rather than to his mother, though his mother was far more tolerant—and rational, too— than his eccentric aunt.

Waldo invited Charles, who had returned with Edward from Puerto Rico, to accompany him to Waterford. Charles had always been Aunt Mary's favorite, and since his return from San Juan he and Waldo had been closer than ever. The brothers left Boston on June 22 and went straight to Waterford; then after a few days their aunt accompanied them to Fryeburg, near the New Hampshire border, where Waldo was scheduled to preach. After that they separated because Waldo wanted to meditate in solitude in the White Mountains of New Hampshire. His aunt had given him little comfort, for she wanted him to remain in the ministry, following the example of generations of his ancestors and the great Puritan divines of Boston, "the Mathers & Sewalls of that venerable City."[61] It was strange how he sought her advice, calling her his sibyl, and then ignored it.

At Conway, New Hampshire, on July 6 Emerson wrote in his Journal: "Here among the mountains the pinions of thought should be strong and one should see the errors of men from a calmer height of love & wisdom."[62] But his thoughts in the mountains were very similar to his thoughts in Boston. It is significant, too, that he says "see the errors of men," not his own possible errors. In fact, he was not even debating the soundness of his own convictions, only what price he must pay for them. While preparing to preach at Fryeburg, he had asked himself: "What is the message that is given me to communicate next Sunday?" Then answered: "Religion in the mind is not credulity & in the practice is not form. It is a life." Religion, not creed or doctrine, had been "life" to him ever since he began studying theology.

Charles, writing William the same day (July 6) from Conway, expressed Aunt Mary's opinion as well as his own when he declared: ". . . I hope his own mind will be brought to the persuasion that it is his duty to stay where he is & preach & pray as he has done & administer the ordinance as nearly as he conscientiously can, in accordance with the faith & wishes of his pious parishioners—"[63]

On Sunday, July 15, Emerson was still pondering his situation in a summer boardinghouse at Conway, which was operated by Ethan Allen Crawford. An "unsabbathized Sunday," he called it in his Journal. Perhaps he felt guilty for not attending church, and his thoughts were somber. "But the hours pass on—creep or fly—& bear me and my fellows to the decision of questions of duty; to the crises of our fate; and to the solution of this mortal problem."[64] Was he tilting, like Don Quixote, at a windmill? But it was more than a scruple: "I think Jesus did not mean to institute a perpetual celebration." Yet a "commemoration" might be useful, if each person observed it in his own way:

> I know very well that it is a bad sign in a man to be too conscientious, & stick at gnats. The most desperate scoundrels have been the over refiners. Without accommodation society is impracticable. But this ordinance is esteemed the most sacred of religious institutions & I cannot go habitually to an institution which they esteem holiest with indifference & dislike.[65]

Emerson had been reading William Sewall's history of the Quakers, and he greatly admired George Fox, who "told the priests that he was no man-made priest," and preferred to preach outdoors. Fox rejected all rituals of the Established Church, and for his nonconformity was thrown in prison. "They gave him liberty to walk a mile from jail, hoping he would escape. Socrates-like he would not. They offered him bounty if he would serve against [King] Charles. He said his weapons were not carnal."[66] Emerson admired him as, in his college thesis, he had admired Socrates. He would have liked to emulate Fox and Socrates, but some innate discretion held him back, and his body began to rebel against his mental turmoil.

While Emerson wrestled with his conscience in Conway on July 15, his Aunt Mary, who was only about twelve miles away in Fryeburg, was writing him that she was saddened to see him ruin his career; she wished he would return to the truth of his ministerial ancestors.[67] A few days after receiving this letter Waldo left New Hampshire for Boston, still feeling miserable and soon to suffer physical humiliation. On July 24 Charles wrote William: "Waldo has got home—is for this last day or two troubled with a diarrhoea which he is nursing lest a worse thing come upon him." And on August 11 Waldo recorded in his Journal: "A stomach ache will make a man as contemptible as a palsey. Under the diarrhoea have I suffered now one fortnight & weak am as a reed."[68] But he added: "Still the truth is not injured."

Nor was his body quite as injured as he had thought, for in a second paragraph he added: "Before tea I counted not myself worth a brass farthing & now I am filled with thoughts & pleasures and am as strong and infinite as an angel."[69] Of course he saw in this change his compensation principle at work and a moral analogy "that after the ruin the resurrection is sure." Then, after further rumination, he concluded that "The principle of repairs is in us[.]" That was probably true, but for the next four and a half months he would find the repairs hard to make, and would continue to alternate between hope and near-despair as his intestinal pain fluctuated.

Either not understanding the extent of his Aunt Mary's disgust with him or unwilling to accept it, Waldo wrote her on August 19: "I have been shut up almost ever since I returned home with the meanest complaint & though I came home stronger & fatter than for years it has stripped me to bones."[70] Apparently his illness had also caused him to become almost paranoid, for he complained bitterly: "The air is poisoned here to every person who is only slightly imprudent." Aunt Mary must have snorted over "slightly imprudent." Nor could she have been satisfied by his saying, "I remain of the same mind not prepared to eat or drink religiously, tho' it seem a small thing, & seeing no middle way, I apprehend a separation." Could his feeling about *eating and drinking* religiously have affected his alimentation?

But to return to Emerson's impending "separation," he tried to find comfort in the thought that "Ellen is beyond misfortune, & I will not invite any others to penury & disappointment if I am doomed." This understated his situation, too, for not only would his family be disappointed (William could best understand), but his mother, Bulkeley, and to some extent Charles were his dependents. He was also daydreaming when he suggested that he might "go into the country ... & you will come & board with Mother & me," and they would read and discuss Goethe, who interested him just at present, even though William could not take the great man's advice to preach what his parishioners wanted to hear and keep his opinions to himself. Of course if Ellen's estate were ever settled in Waldo's favor, he might be able to live in modest retirement with his mother and his books—but not peacefully with his sharp-tongued aunt.

One favorable piece of news for Emerson's Aunt Mary was that Waldo's three brothers were with him on Chardon Street. William had just returned from Portsmouth, New Hampshire, where he had become engaged to Susan W. Haven,[71] to the delight of his whole family. Edward had come back with Charles from Puerto Rico for a month's vacation. Charles did not intend to return to the West Indies with Edward, and was considering opening a law office in Concord, but he had not yet fully decided.

Waldo had undoubtedly discussed with William his confrontation with the Second Church over the Lord's Supper. Soon after his return from Germany, William had written out his objection to this institution in a letter to his step-grandfather, Dr. Ezra Ripley.[72] Whether or not William's view had influenced Waldo, the brothers were in complete agreement, and William's sympathetic understanding must have encouraged Waldo as he prepared the sermon which he read to the Second Church on September 9.[73]

For his text Emerson chose Romans 14:17: "For the kingdom of God is not meat and drink; but righteousness, and peace, and joy in the Holy Ghost." He began with William's arguments that in the history of the Christian Church the Lord's Supper had been frequently the subject of controversy and never of unanimous agreement. It should also be remembered that Jesus, a Jew, was observing Passover with his Jewish Disciples when he blessed the bread and wine and ate and drank ceremonially with his companions.

Of the four Evangelists who recorded the occasion, only Luke recalled these words: "This do in remembrance of me" (Luke 22:19). Emerson did not doubt that Jesus may have said this, but, mindful of his approaching death, he probably meant to say only that next time his companions observed the Passover, they should recall their last supper together: "It is now a historical covenant of God with the Jewish nation. Hereafter it [the Passover] will remind you of a new covenant sealed with my blood."[74]

As for the words "This is my body ... This is my blood ...," Jesus often spoke in parables, and this was his customary language. When John used the same language (John 6:27–60), he explained "that we might not think his body was to be actually eaten, that he only meant we should live by his commandments." John closed his discourse with these explanatory expressions: "The flesh profiteth nothing; the words that I speak to you, they are spirit and they are life."[75] And Paul's purpose in his Epistle to the Corinthians "is not to enjoin upon his friends to observe the Supper, but to censure their abuse of it ... to chide them for drunkenness."[76]

This was one of Emerson's most closely reasoned and concisely expressed sermons. He could be an able debater when he wanted to be, in spite of his protests that he never argued. But his central theme, after proving to his own satisfaction that the Lord's Supper had no clear authority in the New Testament, was that Christ came into the world to provide a *living* religion to take the place of the empty formalism of the Jewish religion, not to instigate new forms and rituals.

As a Unitarian, Emerson, as we have repeatedly seen, accepted Jesus as the greatest of all teachers, but not as the Son of God. To observe the Lord's Supper would be "to produce confusion in our views of the relation of the soul to God. It is the old objection to the doctrine of the Trinity,—that the true worship was transferred from God to Christ . . ."[77] Thus the observance could be actually pernicious. Emerson was willing to let anyone worship in that way if he wished, but he begged to be excused from doing so himself. "It is my desire, in the office of a Christian minister, to do nothing which I cannot do with my whole heart." However, since it is "the prevailing opinion and feeling in our religious community that it is an indispensable part of the pastoral office to administer this ordinance, I am about to resign into your hands that office which you have confided to me."[78]

On September 18 Charles reported to William, now back in New York:

A week ago Sunday Waldo preached his "opinions" to his people—It was a crowded house—a noble sermon—If the Parish were to be polled probably 3/4 would be for keeping their minister on his own terms—but this will not be done—because certain of the most influential men in the Church & Society adhere to the ordinance, & would be thereby grieved & sent away—So they have chosen a committee which is to confer with Waldo & which will probably after some talk & expression of unfeigned regret, let him go & bid him God speed . . .[79]

Charles understood the situation well, and his predictions came true. The deciding vote was held not by church members in general but by the Society of Proprietors, the men who had bought or rented the pews. They were the wealthiest of the congregation, and also conservative. By "sent away" Charles meant that if they were alienated they would withdraw from the Second Church, thereby weakening it both financially and in social prestige. Practical people did not want that to happen, though the battle was not entirely one-sided.

On September 26 Charles wrote William again: "Waldo is very feeble," but "His people dont like to let him go away from them."[80] Charles now thought they would work out a compromise and keep Waldo. And on October 5 the "parish committee" was still in session. No decision had been reached when Emerson delivered his sermon on "The Genuine Man" on October 21.[81] "The genuine man" might have been Emerson himself, a man "who recognizes his right to examine for himself every opinion, every practice that is received in society and who accepts or rejects it for himself." This sermon probably did the minister's cause little good, but he did not deliver it as a palliative. A week later, October 28, by a vote of 34 to 25, with many staying at home, according to Charles, "rather than vote to lose their minister," the Reverend Waldo Emerson's connection with the Second Church was severed. Then by a vote of 30 to 20 his salary was continued until the end of 1832. Meanwhile the pulpit would be supplied by visiting ministers, to be engaged by the departing pastor.[82]

Three weeks later, Waldo wrote William that "the severing of our strained cord that bound me to the church is a mutual relief." Though he felt sorrowful, he could now "walk firmly toward a peace & a freedom which I plainly see before me albeit afar."[83] But scarcely more than a week later, Charles wrote William: "Waldo is sick again—very much dispirited—& talking of the South, the West Indies & other projects—We may break up & disperse at any moment." The day before (November 26) Charles had written Aunt Mary in even greater alarm: "I never saw him so disheartened." Charles did not like to think he was doomed, but his illness had quenched "the fire and freedom of his hopes and purposes."[84]

By December 10 Waldo had decided to go to Italy. Dr. John Ware had advised a sea voyage, and Emerson had learned that the brig *Jasper* would soon sail to Naples. On impulse he made arrangements to go on the *Jasper*.[85] Charles thought the trip might help him, but he was "loath to have him go." To Aunt Mary he confided, "Foreign skies cannot change him . . ." Like her, Charles had hoped Waldo would be able to work out his problems and continue in the ministry. But:

Now, things seem flying to pieces, and I don't know when they will again be put together and he harnessed in (what I think he requires) the labors of a daily calling. . . . I do not doubt he may write and be a fine thinker, all alone by himself; but I think he needs to be dragged closer to people by

some practical vocation, however it may irk his tastes.... We break up
housekeeping forthwith. Mother goes to board, probably at Newton, with
Aunt Ladd. I shall remain in the city.[86]

Charles was understandably upset by the sudden breaking up of the
Chardon Street home. But his mother took the change calmly and raised
no objections to boarding with her sister Mary, wife of William Ladd, in
Newton, Massachusetts. In Waldo's weakened condition he had to let his
mother arrange for disposing of the furniture by auction, and see that he
had suitable clothes for his trip. He wrote William that his mother and
Mr. Abel Adams were "smoothing the way" for his departure.[87] Probably
Mr. Adams offered to lend him money, but the Second Church made that
unnecessary by paying his salary in full on December 21. Next day he
wrote a farewell letter to his church,[88] which was read the following day
from the pulpit in his absence, for he was too ill to read it himself. The
Standing Committee voted to have three hundred copies printed and "distributed to the Proprietors & Worshippers." Waldo Emerson now had
nothing to do but wait for his ship to sail.

First Church in Boston (Chauncy Place).

Ruth Haskins Emerson (mother).

Grandfather Haskins's house, Boston.

The Old Manse in Concord.

Reverend William Emerson
(father).

Miniature of Emerson, 1844.

Miniature of Ellen Tucker (first wife).

Miniature of William Emerson (brother).

Second Church in Boston (RWE, pastor).

Emerson in clerical garb.

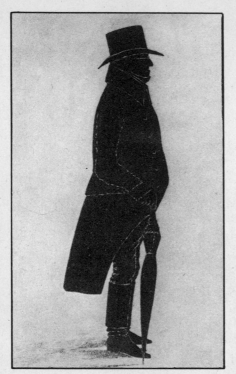

Silhouette of Dr. Ezra Ripley
(step-grandfather).

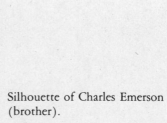

Silhouette of Mary Moody Emerson
(aunt).

Silhouette of Charles Emerson
(brother).

"Standing on the bare ground, — my head bathed by the blithe air, & uplifted into infinite space, — all mean egotism vanishes. I become a transparent Eyeball." Nature, p. 13.

The "transparent eyeball," caricature by Christopher Cranch.

Emerson in lecture costume.

Waldo Emerson (first son).

Lidian (second wife) with son Waldo.

Emerson with Edward (son) and Edith (second daughter).

Emerson home in Concord.

Elizabeth Hoar (Charles's fiancée).

Margaret Fuller Ossoli in Rome.

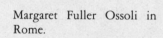

Ellen Tucker Emerson (first daughter) in 1860.

Emerson in 1874.

Emerson's grave in Sleepy Hollow. *On left,* headstone of Lidian (wife); *on right,*
that of Ellen (daughter).

Inscription on rough headstone:

*The passive Master lent his hand
To the vast soul that o'er him planned.*

CHAPTER X

Wayfaring Man

... my lonely wayfaring man ...[1]
—Carlyle

I

"What is *called* practical is not always so but what is felt to be practical is
so," Emerson wrote in his Journal November 14, 1832.[2] In less than a
month he would act upon this sentiment in one of the most crucial decisions of his life, which at the time appeared to be foolhardy. Early in December he had planned to go to the West Indies to spend the winter with
Edward. Although it is difficult in retrospect to see how this might have
solved any of his problems, his family would have approved. But on the
tenth Waldo wrote William that "in a few hours the dream changed into
a purpureal vision of Naples & Italy & that is the rage of yesterday & today
in Chardon St."[3]

Perhaps Emerson's discovery that the brig *Jasper,* in which Edward had
made his first voyage to Puerto Rico with a load of mules, would soon sail
from Boston with a cargo for Malta was responsible for his change of plan.
The *Jasper,* a small merchant brigantine of 236 tons, had very little space
for passengers.[4] At the time Emerson's "purpureal vision" came to him,
the *Jasper* was being loaded with additional freight to supplement the mahogany logs, tobacco, sugar, and coffee which the ship had brought north,
to accumulate a full load. Captain Cornelius Ellis was reluctant to take
Waldo Emerson as a passenger because he did not believe Emerson was
strong enough to survive a six-week voyage on the stormy Atlantic in midwinter. But the captain was persuaded to let him accompany four other

passengers, Mr. and Mrs. S. P. Holbrook, a Miss Holbrook (probably their daughter), and Mr. Samuel Kettell.[5]

When Waldo wrote William on December 10, he expected the brig to sail in a few days and begged his brother either to send hastily or to bring the mattress William had used on his own European trip. William responded by rushing to Boston with the mattress, but the departure of the *Jasper* was delayed so long that he had to return to New York without seeing Waldo off. Finally at nine-thirty on Christmas morning the little ship pulled up anchor and left Boston just ahead of a threatening storm.[6]

The storm caught up with the *Jasper* next morning and she wallowed in rough seas for a week. All five passengers were so seasick that they had to lie in their bunks, and the violent pitching of the ship made sleep almost impossible. The cabin floor was continually wet, clothing was clammy and cold, and the odor of the accumulated filth sloshing around was almost as nauseating as the motion of the creaking ship. Though unable to eat most of the time, Emerson nevertheless suffered pangs of hunger. It hardly mattered that all cooking had to be suspended until the seas were less violent, but the lack of heat intensified the misery.

When the winds finally subsided, Emerson was able to take nourishment, and by January 2 he felt strong enough to make the first entry in his Journal since leaving Boston. His most vivid recollections were of "the ugly sound of water in mine ears, anticipations of going to the bottom, & the treasures of the memory." Unable to read or talk, he "remembered up nearly the whole of Lycidas, clause by clause, here a verse & there a word . . ."

Yet miserable as he had felt during his first week at sea, Emerson's seasickness and enforced fasting may have been the best therapy for his diarrhea. He did not mention this affliction during his entire trip, and within a couple of weeks he had a sailor's appetite and surprising endurance. It is useless to speculate on exactly what cured him. Probably it was the total experience of shock and exhaustion, followed by sound sleep, return of appetite, and relaxed nerves.

The other passengers did not provide much companionship. The two men were anonymous hack writers for Samuel Goodrich's *Peter Parley* books for children and other popular publications. Their interests and Emerson's seldom coincided. Miss Holbrook never once ventured on deck, and Emerson did not mention Mrs. Holbrook in his Journal. But he

talked frequently with Captain Ellis, took a keen interest in the daily latitude and longitude of the ship, and received lessons in the use of the quadrant. He also found that Captain Ellis knew the Bible better than he did:
"He confounded me the other day about the book in the Bible where God
was not mentioned, and last night upon St. Paul's shipwreck."[7] (Answers:
Esther and Acts 27.)

Emerson found unlimited time for quiet meditation. On January 3 he
rose at sunrise and "under the lee of the spencer sheet had a solitary
thoughtful hour." Two days later the breeze was so light that the ship
made only one or two knots an hour, to the displeasure of everyone on
board except Emerson. In the thirty-seven-degree latitude the sun was
warm and he felt delightfully carefree. He took up his Journal but found
he had nothing to record: "I have read little. I have done nothing." But
while he was not consciously doing anything, his mind was at peace with
his body, and nature was restoring his health. He had wisely followed his
sudden impulse to take this trip.

On January 6 Emerson recorded: "Storm, storm; ah we! the sea to us is
but a lasting storm. We have had no fine weather to last an hour." This
was the expression of a feeling, not literal fact, for on January 3 the calm
lasted all day, and actually he had reason to be grateful for the bad weather,
for he added: "Yet I must thank the sea & rough weather for a truckman's
health & stomach,—how connected with celestial gifts." (By "celestial"
he could have meant either meteorological or providential.)

Emerson seldom traveled without books, and he had brought some on
this trip, including an Italian grammar and dictionary and a selection in
Italian from the comedies of Carlo Goldoni. In the latter he failed to find
"a just sentiment or a well contrived scene,"[8] but at least the book gave
him some practice in the language. (Possibly he disliked it because he had
no taste for comedy.) He probably also had brought Byron's poems, or at
least *Childe Harold's Pilgrimage,* which he frequently quoted when he visited a place described in that poem. He may also have brought Goethe's
Italienische Reise, which he read on his way through Italy, though he could
have bought or borrowed a copy in Rome or Florence. However, on a clear
night it was more fun to watch the stars and practice using the quadrant.
"Another voyage would make an astronomer of me," he opined. "How
delicately come out these stars at sea." In spite of the motion, he thought
the ship made "a fine observatory."[9]

To a man not sociable by nature and jealous of his privacy, the cramped living space on the little brig was a constant annoyance. In the third week of his voyage Emerson confided in his Journal: "The inconvenience of living in a cabin is that people become all eye. 'Tis a great part of wellbeing to ignorize a good deal of your fellowman's history & not count his warts nor expect the hour when he shall wash his teeth."[10] The *Jasper* probably had only two cabins, one in the prow for the crew and another in the stern for passengers, both below decks, with curtains providing the only privacy. Life in the rear cabin was also boring, though that was not without its compensations to Emerson: "The sea tosses on the horns of its waves the framework of habits so slight & epicurean as mine & I make the voyage one long holiday which like all holidays is dull."[11]

By January 20 the *Jasper* was in the Strait of Gibraltar, and next day passed the Pillars of Hercules. Presently Emerson could see the Barbary Coast on the lee side. The Sierra Nevada to the north reminded him of New England, "though far higher than any of our snow banks." Finally on February 2 he noted: "Made St Elmore's light at 1 o'clock this morning; lay to in a gale till daylight & then sailed into St Paul's bay."

Immediately everyone on the ship was quarantined for two weeks, "imprisoned for poor dear Europe's health lest it should suffer prejudice from the unclean sands & mountains of America."[12] Emerson seldom sounded so bitter. But at last on February 16 came pratique, followed by the search for lodging.[13] Emerson decided that "It is an advantage to enter Europe at the little end so we shall admire by just degrees from the Maltese architecture up to St. Peter's [in Rome]." His first interest was St. John's Church, "full of marble & mosaic & guilding," but the posted notice advertising indulgences for sale offended him.

On Sunday Emerson was a spectator at mass in St. John's, then at eleven o'clock joined a small English Protestant congregation in "Mr Temple's plain chapel." He enjoyed again hearing "the English bible read, & Watts' psalms sung, & a good sermon." Afterward Mr. Temple invited him to his house. From the terrace on top of the flat roof Emerson could see Mount Etna, a hundred and fifty miles away. Shortly, through the courtesy of the American consul, he received an invitation to a fancy-dress ball in the governor's palace. There he saw some "beautiful faces in the dancing crowd," but of course he remained a spectator. He was more pleased by a visit to the chemical laboratory of Dr. John Davy, brother of the more famous Sir Humphrey.[14]

Five days of sightseeing in Malta were more than enough for the five Americans. By the evening of February 21 they were glad to board a Sicilian brigantine bound for Syracuse, on the east side of Sicily. Emerson was amused by the democratic camaraderie of the fourteen-man crew, who were even more curious about the Americans. It seemed that "the whole interest of master & men was concentrated on us his five passengers. We had hired for $30 the whole cabin, so they put all their heads into the scuttle & companionway to behold all that we did, the which seemed to amuse them mightily." Next morning the mate brought a gazetteer and read aloud the description of Boston while all the crew gathered around and listened. But in spite of the lax discipline, or maybe because of it, the Americans enjoyed the sixteen-hour sail to Syracuse.

William had urged Waldo to visit Sicily, for it was one of the places that had impressed him on his Italian journey in 1825. Consequently, after five days of sightseeing, Waldo wrote his brother from Syracuse, one of the oldest cities in the world. It reeked of antiquity—quite literally—its narrow, foul streets full of refuse and dirty beggars. But its historical associations were exciting. Emerson visited the Temple of Minerva, breakfasted on Hyblaean honey, drank from the Fountain of Arethusa, admired the fields where Proserpine gathered flowers, plucked papyrus on the banks of the Anapus, and visited the catacombs described by Cicero, once the quarry of a great city. This region was once the playground of the Greek and Roman gods and goddesses, though Syracuse was now a shabby place. Yet great wonders remained.

A Capuchin monastery at the *latomia* (marble quarry) seemed so restful that Emerson felt "half Resolved to spend a week or fortnight there," and the friars offered him a room, but he decided to continue traveling with his party. They started out from Syracuse to Catania on mules, but before long Emerson preferred to walk. The women rode in a litter. When they arrived at Catania, they found it a town of lava: "Houses are built, streets paved with [blocks of] lava; it is polished in the altars of the churches. Huge black rocks of it line the shore, & the white surf breaks over them."[15]

Catania itself was full of fine old buildings, many of which Emerson visited. St. Agatha Cathedral was the finest he had yet seen, and the museum was filled with ancient Greek and Roman bronzes, marbles, mosaics, coins, and utensils. He gazed at the ancient baths under the cathedral, and the ruins of a theater in another place. He attended the opera, but decided he had sufficient comedy and tragedy in himself.

Two days in the stagecoach brought Emerson to Messina, where a Sicilian priest and three companions attempted to show him the points of interest in the city. The only difficulty was that they spoke Italian with such a strong Sicilian accent that he could not understand them, or they the Roman Italian he had been studying. They tried to converse in Latin, which Emerson remembered fairly well, but they spoke Latin with the same Sicilian accent.[16] The coachman told them that the American was a *sacerdote* (priest) in his own country (he had learned this in Catania), and then at Emerson's every utterance they exclaimed, " 'che bravo Signore!' so modulated as only Italians can."

By steamboat Emerson traveled from Messina to Palermo,[17] where he visited a few of the four hundred churches and convents. He accepted a lady's invitation to a carriage ride and was rather scandalized that the curtains were closed.[18] As Emerson left her residence, her coachman waylaid him on the stairs and demanded half a dollar, which he paid with annoyance. The Capuchin friars were also beggars, he observed, but he liked them anyway, though he did not enjoy being led once more through another cavern of grinning skeletons, each with a name tag around its neck. At the opera he "could not help pitying the performers in their fillets & shields & togas, . . . their strained & unsuccessful exertions."

He arrived in Naples determined not to be overawed by the name, and his experiences soon confirmed his skepticism. He never succeeded in finding comfortable lodging, and it rained nearly every day. At the Accademia he saw fine paintings by Raphael, Titian, Reni, and Correggio, and statues of Cicero, Aristides, Seneca, and numerous Dianas and Apollos. On March 16 he noted in his Journal:

Last night stayed at home at my black lodgings in the Croce di Malta & read Goethe. This morn sallied out alone & traversed I believe for the seventh time that superb mile of the Villa Reale; then to the tomb of Virgil. But here the effect of every Antiquity is spoiled by the contrast of ridiculous or pitiful circumstances. The boy who guided me was assailed by men, women, & children with all manner of opprobrium. A gang of boys & girls followed me, crying "Signore, C'e un mariolo."[19]

Emerson was disgusted that the silence of Vergil's tomb "must be disturbed with the altercations of these Lilliputians." Presently he met "a company of muleteers who set up a shout of 'lade' & 'mariolo' when they saw my cicerone; so I hastened to get rid of my suspicious companion, & engaged another to conduct me to the Grotto del Cane." The cave was on the shore of beautiful Lake Agnana. Through a crevice in the rock sulfurous fumes filled the grotto, where it was the custom to expose, for a fee, a dog to the vapor until he lost all signs of life, then was revived to repeat the experiment for the next tourist. Emerson refused to pay the fee, thus saving the hapless dog from one fainting.

Naples seemed to Emerson more like "the wards of a hospital." The way people lived was both shocking and ridiculous. Opposite his window on the fourth story of the Crocelle a family lived "with poultry cackling around them all day," and "today I observed a turkey in the chamber across the street stepping about the 2d story. A goat comes up stairs every day to be milked."

On March 22 Emerson wrote his future sister-in-law a homesick letter. Though he had not yet met her, he was already fond of her, and wrote without reserve. He said he had had his pockets picked twice, and mentioned other disagreeable experiences. He thought he was easy to please, "but here in Naples I am lonely & a-'cold & my chamber is dark, & who can go to Vesuvius or Paestum or the Villa of Cicero when the rain pours?"[20] However, he did manage to see Pompeii and Herculaneum, the pleasure grounds two thousand years before of Roman senators and emperors. Time and earthquakes had "made sad work of the palaces," but the natural beauty that charmed the Romans still survived.

Emerson climbed Mount Vesuvius, too. After taking a coach to Resina, he rode "a braying ass who but for his noise was a good beast"[21] to a mile beyond the Hermitage, then continued on foot through the cinders and ash to the rim of the crater. The wind blew smoke and sulfur fumes into his face and often hid his party, but he struggled to the top, where he looked down into the red and yellow pits. He had expected to see "a

chasm opening downward to unknown depths, but it was all closed up."
The following day, Sunday, he rested, except for attending services in the
English Chapel.

II

Early Monday morning, March 25, Emerson left Naples in a coach for
Rome, accompanied by two recent Harvard graduates, Patrick Grant (class
of '28) and James Warren ('32), and a couple of congenial Englishmen.[22]
They traveled all day, passed safely through the Pontine marshes that
night, "molested neither by malaria nor robbers," and arrived in Rome a
little after noon next day. After registering at the best hotel, the Gran
Bretagna, on the Piazza di Spagna, Emerson felt too exhausted to begin
sightseeing that day.

Next morning, rested and eager, he set out at nine o'clock with his new
English friend, a Mr. Kingston. They crossed the Tiber, visited St. Peter's,
the Chambers of Raphael, the Temple of Vesta, the house of Cola di
Rienzi (Byron's "Last of the Romans"), the Forum, and the Colosseum.
At the Vatican many of the statues were familiar to Emerson because he
had studied the plaster casts in the Boston Athenaeum. It did not seem to
him that the originals were better than the copies, but with Raphael's
painting of the *Transfiguration* there was no doubt that it could not be
satisfactorily reproduced. He had expected to be surprised by its "blaze of
beauty," but the "familiar simple homespeaking countenance [of Jesus] I
did not expect."[23]

Many Bostonians were in Rome, some of them young sculptors and
painters. But Emerson found visiting their studios disillusioning. "What
is more pathetic," he wrote in his Journal, "than the studio of a young
artist? Not rags & disease in the street moves you to sadness like the lonely
chamber littered round with sketches & canvass & colourbags."[24] One
morning James Warren and Patrick Grant took him to Bertel Thorvald-
sen's studio. Emerson admired the Danish sculptor's statue of Byron, but
was not otherwise much impressed. Later that day he was exhilarated by
Raphael's *Forrarinia* in the Barberini Palace, Andrea del Sarto's *Madonna*
in the Borghese Palace, and several Titians in the Colonna Palace.

Emerson had arrived in time for Holy Week, which began on March 31
with Palm Sunday. At the Sistine Chapel he watched Pope Gregory XVI,

in scarlet robes and mitre, bless the palm and heard the choir chant the "Passion." The cardinals entered in their purple robes, ermine capes, and red caps. After the Pope was seated, they approached the throne, knelt, and kissed his ring. The ceremony ended with His Holiness, seated in his ornate chair, being lifted up and carried out, "preceded by the long official array & by his chanting choir." This ritualistic performance seemed to Emerson a strange memorial of "the gentle Son of Man who sat upon an ass amidst the rejoicings of his fickle countrymen." It was "millinery & imbecility."

In the afternoon Emerson found more enjoyment in the music at St. Peter's, and still greater that evening at the Chiesa Nuova. But he observed, "Those mutilated wretches [castrated choirboys] sing so well it is painful to hear them." On Wednesday he was greatly affected by hearing the "Miserere" sung in the Sistine Chapel. On Thursday he witnessed the Pope's washing the feet of thirteen pilgrims, one of them from Kentucky. "These forms," he confessed, "strike me more than I expected, & yet how do they fall short of what they should be."[25] Pope Gregory XVI was reported to be learned, able, and pure of character. But "Why should he not leave one moment this formal service of fifty generations & speak out of his own heart?" And on Good Friday Emerson saw "nothing affecting" in the "Mystery of the Tre Ore" (three hours), when "religious processions [paraded] in the streets muffled in black with staves surmounted by death's heads."

Easter morning, April 7, the Pope, wearing a triple crown, said mass in St. Peter's, and at twelve o'clock pronounced benediction from the great window above the principal door. "The troops were all under arms & in uniform in the piazza below, & all Rome & much of England & Germany & France & America was gathered there also."[26] The great bell tolled, drums beat, trumpets sounded, and at a signal the crowd became silent. The Pope read briefly from the book handed him, then stood up, spread his hands, and blessed the people. Everyone knelt; the Pope repeated his gestures (the words were inaudible) and pronounced benediction. "Then sounded drums & trumpets, then rose the people, & every one went his way." Emerson had to admit, "It was a sublime spectacle."

By the following Tuesday, most of the Americans had left Rome, and Emerson began to feel lonely, and to be more aware of his deficiencies in the language. Two still left were the Bridgen sisters from Albany, New

York. Anna said that "so inveterate were her Dutch instincts, that she sees almost no wonder of art in Italy, but she wants to give it a good scrubbing, the Duomo, the Campanella, & the statues."[27] Emerson himself felt Rome to be "ruinous." Flowerpots stood on marble blocks salvaged from broken columns, and fragments of carved and fluted stones were cemented into the walls and foundations of buildings.

As the time drew near for his departure, Emerson remembered that he had promised to purchase a music box with two Beethoven tunes for Mr. Francis Cunningham, whom he had employed to preach in the Second Church after his resignation. He also remembered to look for a small edition of Dante for Mrs. Sarah Bradford Ripley. He found the book but not the music box.

Waldo Emerson was now in the best health he had enjoyed since his boyhood. He awoke every morning eager for new adventures. On April 20 he visited Tivoli with two artists, John Cranch and William Wall, and a young man named Smith.[28] The sun was bright and the fields glowed with spring flowers. They visited the ruined villa of Catullus and the reputed sites of the homes of Horace and his patron, Maecenas. In the Capitoline Museum the *Dying Gladiator* reminded him of Byron's comment "butchered to make a Roman holiday." No one knew how fine a poet Byron was until he had seen the subjects of his verse.

Next day, in the Church of San Pietro in Vincoli Emerson saw another Michelangelo masterpiece, his *Moses,* the embodiment of law. But he did not like "those emblematic horns."[29] Scholars would later point out that the sculptor had been deceived by a mistranslation in the Latin Vulgate of Hebrew *quaran* ("shone") for *queren* ("horned").

III

On April 23 Emerson left Rome by carriage for Florence with five friends: Wall, Cranch, Robert Walsh, and two new friends, Brantz Mayer, a famous lawyer and journalist of Baltimore, and a Father O'Flanagan. On the twenty-eighth they reached Florence, with its clean streets, spacious and well-furnished lodgings, elegant but inexpensive cafés, splendid art galleries—and "No beggars"! Florence had long been the favorite city of artists, including Michelangelo, and its art treasures rivaled, if they did not surpass, those of Rome. In the cathedral was Michelangelo's *David,* and in the Uffizi Gallery the statue that enchanted the world, *Venus de' Medici*.[30] Emerson felt like Childe Harold, "dazzled & drunk with beauty." And he had never seen anything more charming than the shady walks along the banks of the Arno with throngs of sweet-singing birds in the trees. All night, too, the streets echoed with airs of the operas sung by "this musical people."

On May 7 a letter from Charles informed Waldo that on February 28 Mrs. Kent, Ellen's mother, had died in Concord, New Hampshire. Emerson mused again on the partition separating flesh and spirit, and wondered sadly, "Does the heart in that world forget the heart that did beat with it in this?"[31] With an effort he turned his mind back to his physical world and visited Professor Giovanni Battista Amici, who had made a microscope with a power of six thousand diameters. He had filled an order for a telescope for Herschel in London, and one for a microscope for Dr. Edward Jarvis, whom Emerson had known in college. Professor Amici demonstrated for him how to polarize light.

In his senior year at Harvard, Emerson had known a tall, handsome, energetic freshman named Horatio Greenough. He was now living in Florence, and at twenty-eight, two years younger than Emerson, was already famous for his sculptures. In mid-May Emerson met Greenough, perhaps by chance, and was invited to his studio. "His face was so handsome and his person so well formed that he might be pardoned, if, as was alleged, the face of his Medora and the figure of a colossal Achilles in clay, were idealizations of his own."[32] At the time of Emerson's first visit to his studio, Greenough had just received a letter from Secretary of State Edward Livingston commissioning him to do a statue of George Washington for the rotunda of the Capitol, but Congress had not yet appropriated funds for it, and he was worried that it might not. (Eventually it would.)

One of the half-dozen living English writers whom Emerson admired was Walter Savage Landor, the author of *Imaginary Conversations*. Landor was now living in Florence in an ancient villa at San Domenica, on a hillside on the way to the town of Fiesole, with a magnificent view of Florence and the Arno.[33] Greenough obtained an invitation from Landor for Emerson to call on him. The Villa Gherardesca had been built by the historic family Ugolino, immortalized by Dante in his *Divine Comedy*. In May the grounds were fragrant with roses, pomegranates, mimosas, myrtles, olives, and vines of various kinds. Here Landor had lived for several years with his wife and four children, numerous cats and dogs, tame nightingales, and his art collection. He was known for his irascible temper, and it was rumored that in a sudden rage he had thrown his cook out the window. He was built like a prizefighter, or Roman gladiator, and his personality was formidable. But the ruddy-faced man who greeted Emerson, buttoned to the chin in his English broadcloth on a warm day in May, was surprisingly courteous and genial.

Yet conversation was impossible with Landor, for he spouted his dogmatic opinions without pause. He disliked the Scottish writers, including Thomas Carlyle, and praised Robert Southey, his brother-in-law. His favorite painters were Raphael, Perugino, and Giotto. He glorified Lord Chesterfield, belittled Socrates, and was indifferent to science. "Herschel he knew nothing about, not even his name."[34] Emerson was disappointed, though he visited Landor three times.

After leaving Landor's house on his third visit, May 18, Emerson went straight to the Museum of Natural History, as if in reproach of his host's ignorance. The museum had a wax exhibit of the *Plague of Venice,* and wax models of every organ of the human body, which Emerson did not enjoy seeing, for he preferred to be unconscious of his internal organs. Two years past he had liked an anonymous essay in *The Edinburgh Review* called "Characteristics," which he later learned Carlyle had written. It began: "The healthy know not of their health, but only the sick . . . the first condition of complete health, is, that each organ perform its function unconsciously, unheeded . . ."[35]

Hot weather had arrived in Florence, "six or seven blazing hours every day." But the early mornings and the evenings were still pleasant. On May 21 Emerson recorded: "Rose early this morning & went to the Bello Sguardo out of the Roman gate. It was a fine picture this Tuscan morning and all the towers of Florence rose richly out of the smoky light on the broad green plain."[36] He still enjoyed seeing the masterpieces of art in Florence, but almost as much returning to his lodging in the evening to read Goethe's travel books or the histories of Simonde de Sismondi, which he had earlier read in French translation. Manzoni's *I Promessi Sposi* made him rejoice "that a man exists in Italy who can write such a book. I hear from day to day such hideous anecdotes of the depravity of manners, that it is an unexpected delight to meet this elevated & eloquent moralist."

With the coming of hot weather it was time to start north. Emerson left Florence by stage Tuesday morning, May 28, and by June 1 had reached Padua.[37] There he visited the university, in which Galileo had lectured and Dante, Petrarch, and Tasso had studied. From Padua he proceeded with his companions to Venice, arriving late at night at the Gran Bretagna hotel. A narrow bridge connected the hotel with St. Mark's Square; "so out we went under the full moon to see the same," finding it "rich & strange & visionary."[38]

Next day, Emerson admired the bronze horses and the winged lion in St. Mark's, the Bridge of Sighs, the Doge's Palace, the canals, and rode in a gondola to the churches and the Accademia. He was pleased with Titian's *Assumption of the Madonna,* but still preferred the painter's *Transfiguration.* The churches surpassed in splendor those of Florence. He was overwhelmed by the spacious murals of Tintoretto, of Paolo Veronese and his son.

The dark side of Venice could still be seen in the black dungeon which the Austrians had opened to public view when the city was ceded to them by Napoleon in 1797. Lord Byron had visited it and in *Childe Harold* quoted the "sad inscriptions" on the wall. The Austrians still ruled Venice, but Emerson was told that their government was more humane than that of the Venetians themselves before the French invasion of Italy. He declared himself "satisfied" with Venice, but called it "a great oddity—a city of beavers."[39] It smelled always of bilge water, and the necessity of traveling by gondola made the residents unsociable. These strange boats held only one or two passengers, who were usually concealed by canvas shades or Venetian blinds. It seemed like a mean, solitary way of living.

Consequently Emerson was glad to leave Venice on Tuesday, June 4, with his young companions William Wall, Thomas Stewardson, and the Bridgen sisters, with the same "trusty Vetturino who brought us from Florence." After returning to Padua, they turned north and reached Milan on the morning of June 6. Somehow they met Count del Verme, who took them on a guided tour of the city in his private coach.

On Tuesday morning, June 11, the five Americans left Milan in the diligence.[40] They rode for three days and nights, stopping only for meals, crossed the Alps at night by the Simplon Pass, reached Sion at dawn, Montigny by afternoon, and Lausanne before dark. Although it was nearly mid-June, snow still lay on the high mountains, and Emerson was riding on the outside of the stage, having chosen that seat by day. He was thank-

ful to one of the Bridgen sisters for lending him a shawl. But he suffered
no ill effects from the exposure and exhaustion.

In Lausanne the party visited the house where Gibbon wrote his *Decline
and Fall of the Roman Empire.* Then at ten a.m. they boarded a steamboat
and chugged up Lake Leman to Geneva.[41] Emerson's companions insisted
on visiting the château where Voltaire had lived in exile, and he went
along, protesting all the way, but finally admitted, "He did his work as the
bustard & tarantula do theirs." In Geneva he was finally able to buy the
music box he had promised Mr. Cunningham. It cost fifty francs, and
would be delivered in Paris.

IV

At four o'clock on Monday morning the travelers left Geneva by diligence
for Paris. They crossed the Jura Mountains and, after three days and a half
of continuous travel, except for rest stops and changes of horses, they
reached Paris at noon on Thursday, June 20. The journey ended at the
Hôtel Montmorenci on the boulevard Montmartre.[42] At first Emerson
found Paris disappointing. It seemed to him that "in leaving Italy I had
left forever that air of antiquity & history which her towns possess & in
coming hither had come to a loud modern New York of a place." However, he had friends here, including a second cousin, Ralph Emerson, and
Oliver Wendell Holmes, who had come to Paris to study medicine. Impulsively he engaged a pension for a month.

After a few days Emerson discovered that Paris was "the most hospitable
of cities." He had only to show his passport to gain admission to any of
the public institutions. He promptly obtained a schedule of free lectures
and began hearing Joseph Louis Gay-Lussac and Louis Jacques Thénard on
chemistry at the Jardin des Plantes and Théodore Jouffroy on philosophy
at the Sorbonne. One might doubt his ability to comprehend these lectures, but his knowledge of French was sufficient for him to enjoy the theater. He also became a frequenter of public reading rooms. The English
Reading Room on the rue Neuve Augustine received four hundred newspapers in all languages.

On July 4 Emerson and nearly a hundred other Americans attended a
dinner at Lointier's.[43] General Lafayette was the principal speaker and

Emerson exchanged pleasantries with him. One of the Americans was a Lieutenant Levi of the U.S. Navy, a Jacksonian Democrat, who took offense at the unenthusiastic toasts to the President. He asked sarcastically, "Is this a meeting of the Hartford Convention or of citizens of the United States?"[44] For a fact, New England Federalists were in the majority. James Russell jumped to his feet and demanded that the assembly cut off the lieutenant's buttons and eject him from the party. Somehow a riot was avoided, or the challenge to a duel (Lieutenant Levi had already killed his man in one), and Holmes even called it a dull affair. They all ate too many partridges stuffed with truffles and drank too much wine, for which they each paid seven dollars, a large sum for a dinner in 1833.

The Louvre only mildly excited Emerson, but he had memorable experiences in the Musée Nationale d'Histoire Naturelle and the Jardin des Plantes. In several pages of his Journal he described the many kinds of birds, insects preserved in amber, and "the inexhaustible riches of nature," leading him to conclude:

> The Universe is a more amazing puzzle than ever as you glance along this bewildering series of animated forms,—the hazy butterflies, the carved shells, the birds, beasts, fishes, insects, snakes,—& the upheaving principle of life everywhere incipient in the very rock aping organized forms. Not a form so grotesque, so savage, nor so beautiful but it is an expression of some property inherent in man the observer, —an occult relation between the very scorpions and man. I feel the centipede in me—cayman, carp, eagle, & fox. I am moved by strange sympathies, I say continually, "I will be a naturalist."[45]

Perhaps Emerson really enjoyed Paris more than his moral inhibitions would permit him to admit. His friend Holmes took full advantage of his newfound sexual freedom, but Emerson was shocked by it, commenting in his Journal:

> Young men are very fond of Paris, partly, no doubt, because of the perfect freedom—freedom from observation as well as interference,—in which each one walks after the sight of his own eyes; & partly because the extent & variety of objects offers an unceasing entertainment. So long as a man has francs in his pocket he needs consult neither time nor place nor other men's convenience ...[46]

As a discreet observer, Emerson did enjoy the human spectacle. He visited the morgue and a gambling hall (as a spectator), heard revolutionary students condemn the government, and listened to the radical priest Abbé Chatel preach his new religion.[47] In the Champs-Élysées he listened to an orchestra, watched acrobats and dancers performing, and strolled with the crowd around gambling tables, a merry-go-round, and refreshment stands. French churches disappointed him. Even Notre Dame was "mean inside." Paris was expensive, indulgent, and for Emerson alien and uncomfortable.

V

On July 18 Emerson and Francis Alexander, who was returning to America after two years of studying painting in Italy, set out for Boulogne.[48] After twenty rough hours on the English Channel they finally steamed up the Thames Sunday morning to the Tower Stairs. The principal landmarks were so familiar from pictures that Emerson felt as if he were coming home. When the two men disembarked, it was still only seven o'clock and the streets on that quiet Sunday morning were almost deserted. A friend in Paris had recommended lodgings with a Mrs. Fowler at 63 Russell Square; so they engaged a porter to carry their bags and they walked from the Tower to Russell Square, a distance of three or four miles. It was a pleasure to hear English spoken again, and to understand the words of children at play. As they passed St. Paul's a service was in progress, but they paused only long enough to peep in.[49] Three days later Emerson would return and admire this church almost as much as he had Westminster Abbey the previous day. He would soon find that what interested him most in London were the churches, the House of Commons, the British Museum, the Zoological Gardens, the Gallery of Practical Science, and Regent's Park.

The most impressive spectacle Emerson saw in London was the funeral of William Wilberforce, leader in the abolition of the slave trade and other reforms, who died on July 29. He was buried in Westminster Abbey with traditional ceremonies, witnessed by thousands of people and attended by the important officials of Church and State.[50] The one man Emerson was most curious to see was the Duke of Wellington, and he got a good view of him at the funeral.[51]

There were other men in England whom Emerson wanted not just to meet but to know personally. First was Thomas Carlyle, who he had learned was the author of anonymous essays he had been reading for several years; he supposed Carlyle lived in Edinburgh. In Italy Gustave d'Eichthal had said he knew John Stuart Mill, a friend of Carlyle's, and he would ask Mill to write an introduction. Mill received Emerson in India House, and agreed to write, but he was not much impressed by his caller and wrote that Carlyle should be guided by d'Eichthal's letter.[52] Perhaps to compensate, Mill suggested that Emerson call on Dr. John Bowring, Jeremy Bentham's literary executor. Though Emerson had a low opinion of Bentham's philosohy of Utilitarianism, he did call on Dr. Bowring, who lived in the house John Milton had occupied while Latin secretary to Cromwell. Emerson liked the inscription on the garden wall: "Sacred to Milton, The Prince of Poets." To be polite, he also let Dr. Bowring show him Bentham's house and give him a lock of Bentham's hair.

Emerson did not have an introduction to Coleridge, but he knew he lived in Highgate, a northern suburb of London. On the morning of August 5 he went out to Highgate, but he did not know exactly where Coleridge lived.[53] No one seemed to recognize the name, until finally a porter asked "if I meant an elderly gentleman with white hair? 'Yes, the same'— Why he lives with Mr. Gillman. Ah yes that is he. So he showed me the way." Dr. James Gillman had rescued Coleridge from his opium addiction, and now, in his sixty-first year, the poet lived with this kind surgeon. When Emerson called, he "sent up a note to Mr. Coleridge requesting leave to see him. He sent word that he was in bed but if I would call after 12 o'clock he would see me. I named one o'clock."[54]

Promptly at one, Emerson returned and was met by "a short thick old man with bright blue eyes, black suit & a cane, & any thing but what I had imagined, a clear clean face with fine complexion—a great snuff taker which presently soiled his cravat & neat black suit." He asked if Emerson knew Washington Allston, the American painter. Coleridge had known him in Rome and possessed one of his paintings, which he thought Titianesque. Dr. William Ellery Channing had visited him, but "what an unspeakable misfortune to him that he should have turned a Unitarian after all." Coleridge himself had once been a Unitarian, but was now a firm Trinitarian. Emerson confessed that he himself was a Unitarian. "Yes, he said, I suppose so & continued as before."

At last when Coleridge paused for breath, Emerson told him many Unitarians in America who did not subscribe to his theology read his books, but this did not soften the old man's prejudices. *Aids to Reflection* had been edited and published (1829) in the United States by James Marsh, but Coleridge said he had not corresponded with him. He had been ill at the time a copy of Marsh's edition had arrived and had never acknowledged it. Thus the interview went. Emerson had been warned not to stay more than half an hour to avoid tiring the poet, but it was over an hour before he could gracefully withdraw. The interview had been an exhibition rather than a conversation. Coleridge might have been—and perhaps was—reciting paragraphs from his books. All Emerson gained was some satisfaction of his curiosity. "He was old and preoccupied, and could not bend to a new companion and think with him."[55]

VI

On Friday morning, August 9, Emerson left London for Oxford, and then during the next week visited Kenilworth, Warwick, Matlock, Reading Hall, Bakewell, Sheffield, York, Newcastle, and Berwick. He arrived in Edinburgh August 16, and stayed until the twenty-first.[56] He carried a letter of introduction to Dr. Samuel Brown, "the chemical philosopher," but Dr. Brown was busy and asked a young journalist, Alexander Ireland, to show him the places of interest. The Unitarian minister invited him to preach on Sunday, the eighteenth, in the Unitarian chapel.[57]

Ireland was so impressed by the sermon and the speaker that he became Emerson's lifelong friend. He was accustomed to hearing Dr. Thomas Chalmers, professor of theology in the university and a leader of the evangelical branch of the Church of Scotland called the Free Church, who preached with vehement energy and turgid eloquence. Many years later Ireland still recalled that Emerson's "voice was the sweetest, the most winning, and penetrating of any I ever heard." His delivery was calm, dignified, and without the least effect of oratory, and yet with "singular directness and simplicity of manner, free of the least shadow of dogmatic assumption."

Emerson had assumed that in Edinburgh he would have no difficulty in locating Thomas Carlyle, but no one there could tell him where he lived until he thought of asking the secretary of the university, who told him that Carlyle lived in a remote farmhouse at Craigenputtock in Dumfriesshire.[58] Carlyle's father, a stonemason in Dumfries, had sent him to Edinburgh University. After graduating he taught for several years, then returned to the university to study law. But law did not suit him; so he tutored, learned German, traveled in Europe, wrote articles, and made translations. Goethe had been pleased with his translation of *Wilhelm Meister*. The essays Emerson had been reading were written at Craigenputtock rather than in Edinburgh, as he had supposed. After marrying Jane Welsh in 1826, Carlyle had tried unsuccessfully to earn a living in Edinburgh by his writing, and then in 1828 had moved into the house in Dumfries which his wife had inherited. Emerson was surprised that a man who had published a *Life of Schiller* and become the chief interpreter of German literature in English should be so little known.

Dumfries was nearly thirty miles south of Edinburgh, and Emerson decided to see the Highlands before searching out Dumfries in the Lowlands. He was told that in two days he could "see that famous country of Ben Lomond, Loch Katrine, & the rest" by taking a steamboat up the Forth to Stirling.[59] This adventure turned out to be as exhausting as his trip over the Alps. A cold rain kept him in his cabin all the way to Stirling. There he spent so much time seeing Cambuskenneth Abbey and Stirling Castle that he missed the last coach to Callender and had to ride the ten miles after dark in an "open car" (carriage). After seven hours of sound sleep he left next morning at five a.m. for the Trossachs.

"This passage was made in an uncovered car again & the rain fell in torrents & wet me thro' my own coat & my landlord's over that . . ."[60] Then with several others he walked to Loch Katrine. The rain stopped, but the wind was so strong that they gave up trying to row across the lake and walked fourteen soggy miles to a hut at the end of the lake. There they dried their shoes, drank Scotch whisky, and ate oatcakes. After five more miles of walking they came to another hut at Inversaid, where all the natives spoke Gaelic. Here the party of fifteen boarded a steamboat and traveled fifteen miles on it to Ballock, where they took a coach to Dumbarton, then another steamboat up the Clyde to Glasgow.

When Emerson reached his inn in Glasgow, his baggage, sent by another route, had not arrived.[61] The only room left was a cubbyhole in the loft, but he was grateful for any place to rest. By morning his trunk had arrived and he was able to shave and put on a clean shirt. Of special interest to him was the twelfth-century cathedral, now a Presbyterian church, which Sir Walter Scott had used for a scene in *Rob Roy*. Always interested in science, Emerson also visited the Hunterian Museum (both Scottish-born John Hunter and his brother, William, had made important physiological discoveries).

Two days later Emerson reached Dumfries, a hundred miles south of Glasgow, in the Lowlands. He learned that Craigenputtock was in the parish of Dunscore, sixteen miles from Dumfries. On Sunday morning, August 25, he rented a weather-beaten gig and a driver for his eagerly anticipated pilgrimage.[62] Dunscore Road passed by farms that reminded him of parts of New England, though the stone fences were more neatly built than those of Vermont or New Hampshire, and the hedgerows were not found in New England, but the granite boulders and rocky soil were. Many of the hilltops were wooded with oak, elm, spruce, and on the slopes an occasional gnarled hawthorn, limbs twisted by the wind. Fields too rocky to cultivate were covered with heather, rose at this time of year, broken by clumps of yellow gorse, or "furze." A few cattle browsed in green fields watered by crystal-clear brooks. On the hillsides grazed flocks of dirty-gray sheep. The farmhouses were low, built of native stone, neatly whitewashed, and roofed with thatch or slate. Stables and outbuildings usually adjoined the dwellings. Because of frequent rains, the barnyards were often bogs of muck and cowdung.

Finally the gig passed over a hill, descended into a valley, and Carlyle's house in lower Craigenputtock came into sight. It was larger than most of the farmhouses along the road, more like a manor or grange, with massive stone walls and deep-set windows. When Emerson climbed out of the gig, it was twelve o'clock and the Carlyles were eating their midday meal. But with exuberant cordiality they invited him in and insisted that he spend the night. So Emerson dismissed the gig and asked the driver to return for him next morning. His visit was not entirely unexpected, for Carlyle "had heard of my purpose from his friend [probably Mill] who gave me my letter."[63] But all the Carlyles knew about him was that he was an American who admired Thomas's publications, for Emerson's own publications were still only ideas in his head.

Thomas Carlyle was a tall, gaunt man with a craggy brow and a big, deep voice. He laughed easily and talked pungently in a broad Lowland Scottish accent. The two men became friends at once, and that afternoon they walked for miles over the rugged hills, pausing to rest on mossy stones while they continued to exchange experiences and ideas.

The Carlyles had lived for five years in this lonely spot, seven miles from the nearest post office. They had not actually been unhappy here, and Thomas had completed a considerable amount of writing, including *Sartor Resartus* in 1831, which *Fraser's Magazine* would begin to publish by installments in November. Of course Emerson had not heard of this work, but he was already familiar with some of the ideas in it, such as the degeneration of modern society, which only hard work and recovery of religious faith could halt, and that attempts at social reform were only symptoms of the disease.

From the post-Kantian German philosophers Carlyle had acquired the conviction that the material universe is only an emblem of its spiritual foundation. In spite of their disagreement on social reform, both men believed that only a strengthening of individual character could save the nineteenth century from disaster. But Emerson found his congenial host vague or indifferent on specific religious questions. When asked about immortality, Carlyle said he had no opinion. "My own feeling," Emerson wrote Alexander Ireland, "was that I had met with men of less power who had yet greater insight into religious truth." Thus Carlyle, too, proved not to be the "master" Emerson had come to Europe to find, but a stimulating friend nonetheless.

After their long ramble, during which Emerson must have told his new friend about Ellen, and his reason for resigning his pastorate, they returned to an excellent meal prepared by Mrs. Carlyle. Though Jane was often impatient with her dyspeptic husband, she was also proud of him, and took pleasure in this visible proof that his name had reached faraway America. Not robust herself, she was, nevertheless, a conscientious housekeeper, enjoyed riding her lively black pony over the hills, and even found satisfaction in being a dairymaid. But she was also sociable, with a quick mind that scintillated in intellectual society, and she often found life tedious in this barren place. Jane told Emerson she had been eagerly preparing for a trip with Thomas to Weimar, Germany, when a letter from the bookseller reported that the translation of *Wilhelm Meister* had earned too little money to pay for the trip. As consolation Goethe sent her a gold chain, the first of many gifts, which she proudly displayed to her guest.[64]

To Emerson the Carlyles' rustic life seemed enviable, and he expressed the hope that they would not move to noisy, distracting London. But Thomas had begun collecting material for a history of the French Revolution, and he needed books, as well as stimulating minds, which he thought he could find only in London. John Stuart Mill, he said, had the best mind of anyone he knew. He believed Mill had worked himself free of his father's adherence to Bentham's "pig-philosophy."

Next morning Emerson's gig returned and carried him back to Dumfries. He then continued on to Carlisle in England, where in his Journal he described the previous day's experiences as "A white day in my years."[65] And to Carlyle it had also been a memorable experience. In a letter to his mother he told of the visit of the unknown young man from Boston:

> Three little happinesses have befallen us ... [one] was the arrival of a certain young unknown friend, named Emerson, from Boston, in the United States, who turned aside so far from his British, French, and Italian travels to see me here! He had an introduction from Mill and a Frenchman (Baron d'Eichthal's nephew), whom John [Thomas Carlyle's brother] knew in Rome. Of course we could do no other than welcome him; the rather as he seemed to be one of the most lovable creatures in himself we had ever looked on. He stayed till next day with us, and talked and heard talk to his heart's content, and left us all really sad to part with him. Jane says it is the first journey since Noah's Deluge undertaken to Craigenputtock for such a purpose. In any case we had a cheerful day from it, and ought to be thankful.[66]

Two days later at Ambleside Emerson described in his Journal a visit to Wordsworth at Rydal Mount.[67] Wordsworth, in his sixty-third year, was better preserved than Coleridge, but his prejudices had hardened more than his arteries. On Emerson's inquiry, the poet's daughters called him, and a plain-featured, white-haired, elderly man wearing green goggles came in, sat down, and talked with ease and simplicity. He professed friendly feelings for America, but had some very decided opinions about the country. He thought moral culture was lagging in England, and probably even more in the United States. He was not so much worried about American vulgarity of manners, which was perhaps a phase of their "pioneering state of things," as their making "political distinction the end & not the means." When asked what he thought of Carlyle, he said he thought at times he was insane. Goethe's *Wilhelm Meister* was "all manner of fornication." Emerson strongly defended Carlyle and *Wilhelm Meister,* and Wordsworth admitted he had read only the first book, but promised to take another look at it.

However, Wordsworth was not able to read much because of his inflamed eyes. The affliction did not handicap him in composing poems because he carried many, even hundreds, of lines in his head before writing them down. In fact, he had recently been to Staffa and had composed three sonnets on Fingal's Cave. Would Mr. Emerson like to hear them? Thereupon he repeated the sonnets with great animation, and Emerson thought two of them more beautiful than any of Wordsworth's printed sonnets. He said he hoped they would soon be published. Secretly, however, he thought the famous poet looked rather silly as he recited his poems like a schoolboy, but then reconsidered and realized how much he had been honored. When Emerson was ready to leave, Wordsworth insisted on walking with him a mile on the way back to Ambleside, "anon stopping short to impress the word or the verse & finally parted from me with great kindness & returned across the fields."

By coach Emerson proceeded leisurely to Manchester, where he boarded a train for Liverpool. This was another new experience, and he carefully noted that the thirty-two miles were covered in an hour and a half—sometimes in an hour, he was told. The engine left a trail of glowing cinders beside the track, and the hissing steam made bystanders stand back. It was a double-track railroad, and returning cars darted by "like a trout." At Liverpool Emerson talked with Jacob Perkins, formerly of Boston, who had developed steam boilers for the British trains and was now manufacturing steel plates in England.[68]

On August 30, his European trip now ended, Emerson registered at the Star and Garter Hotel in Liverpool to wait for the sailing of the *New York,* on which he had booked passage. The exact day of departure for New York would depend upon the weather. In preparation for the cold and probably wet crossing he purchased a Mackintosh waterproof overcoat. While waiting he also presented his letter of introduction from Henry Ware to James Martineau, brother of the more famous author Harriet, and one of the leading Unitarian ministers in the British Isles. Emerson told him the history of his resigning from the Second Church, and the Reverend Martineau said to himself that his guest would never return to the ministry. On Sunday, September 1, Emerson went to hear James Yates, author of *Vindicating Unitarianism,* and called it "the best sermon I heard in England."[69]

The *New York,* a ship of 516 tons, carrying fourteen cabin passengers and sixteen in the steerage, was finally towed out of the Liverpool harbor by a steam tugboat on the afternoon of September 4. Emerson felt no regret on seeing "the last lump of England receding." It had been a rewarding trip, not least in the recovery of his health, but he was now impatient to return home and make crucial decisions for his future. While still in the Channel, off the coast of Ireland, he wrote in his Journal: "I like my book about nature & wish I knew where & how I ought to live."[70] Charles had written him that the court would likely decide his suit over Ellen's will in his favor, but no money had yet been awarded him. He would have to find some way to support himself while he wrote his "book about nature."

Though on a more comfortable ship than the merchant brig which had brought him over, Emerson had no congenial companions on the *New York* except Captain Hoxie. As usual, he found the captain more entertaining than anyone else aboard. After a few days of seasickness he settled down to making the best of the "long, crooked, rough" ride from Liverpool to New York. "Four meals a day is the usual expedient (& the wretchedness of the expedient will show the extremity of the case) & much wine & porter[;] these are the amusements of wise men in this sad place."[71]

On Friday the thirteenth Emerson recorded: "The sea is to us but a lasting storm. How it blows, how it rocks. My sides are sore with rolling in my berth. We have a torn sail & lost a hencoop & its inmates, but the bulwarks are firm." He felt especially sad for the steerage passengers, old women and children sitting up all night or lying in wet berths. "The poor cow refuses to get up & be milked, & four dogs on board shiver & totter about all day & bark when we ship a sea." On the night of the nineteenth the gale was so fierce that the mate said the firing of an eight-pounder on the deck would not have been heard aloft. Ten days later it was still "storm storm storm." But at the end of the month at sea the weather was clear, balmy, and the sea calm. It was time to begin looking for land. Emerson's last entry in his Journal before reaching Boston was on Friday, October 4.[72]

New York newspapers reported the arrival of the *New York* on October 7.[73] After a brief visit with William, Waldo continued on to Boston. On October 11 he wrote William asking him to present his apologies to Captain Hoxie for not seeing him again before leaving the city, but he had left sooner than he had expected. And would William please also ask the steward of the ship if he had found a copy of *Fraser's Magazine* which he had promised to search for: "It contains a capital print of Coleridge which I should regret losing."[74] After spending a few days with George Sampson in Boston Emerson would join his mother in Newton. His plans for the future were indefinite, except for delivering a lecture in November to the Natural History Society.

CHAPTER XI

Ancestral Fields

Hail to the quiet fields of my fathers! Not
wholly unattended by supernatural friendship &
favor let me come hither.[1]

I

In glowing health and at peace with the world and himself, Emerson confessed in his Journal on December 14, 1833, nearly two months after his
return from Europe: "I please myself with contemplating the felicity of my
present situation. May it last. It seems to me singularly free & it invites me
to every virtue & to great improvement."[2]

To an observer unaware of what was going on in his mind, Emerson
might appear to be drifting, without plan or even ambition. To those who
whispered that he had had a nervous breakdown, his conduct might seem
to confirm the rumors. Emerson himself was well aware that he had not
yet answered the questions of *where* and *how* to live, but he refused to
worry. Instead of a New Year's resolution, he wrote on January 2, 1834:
"The year, the year, but I have no thoughts for time."[3] One reason for his
assurance was that he had a purpose, even if he did not have a plan: "My
own bosom will supply, as surely as God liveth, the direction of my
course."[4] His intuition would guide him, as it had in regaining his health
by suddenly taking a trip to Europe on a small ship in dead winter in face
of an impending storm.

Within a few months, Waldo had been assured by Charles, who looked
after his legal affairs, that he would have an annual income from Ellen's
estate, but neither the amount nor the date of the first payment was yet

certain. He did not build any definite plans on that eventuality, though he did daydream vaguely of retiring to a modest house in the Berkshires with his mother and Edward, if his younger brother could leave the Puerto Rican climate. Edward refused to take this plan seriously, and possibly Waldo did not put much stock in it himself. For the present he rented a room in Boston near Charles, visited his mother in Newton, and waited for his intuition to prompt him.[5]

Emerson thought he had definitely left the Church, but that was not entirely true; he had left only the Second Church in Boston. He was still conscious of the scar on his psyche, though he was not bitter. He gladly accepted an invitation to preach to his old congregation on the second Sunday after his return, and again on December 15. He wrote a hymn for the ordination of his successor, the Reverend Chandler Robbins, which began, "We love the venerable house / Our fathers built to God . . ."[6] He exulted in his freedom from pastoral duties and restrictions, but almost by reflex he felt emotionally attached to places of worship and still experienced a sense of exaltation on entering them.

Standing in the familiar pulpit, Emerson found that he enjoyed preaching as much as ever. And when invitations began to arrive from other churches in Newton, Cambridge, Waltham, and in towns as far away as New Bedford in one direction and Plymouth in another—he gladly accepted. He preached nearly every Sunday, drawing heavily on his hoard of sermons in manuscript. He felt almost as stimulated as a promiscuous lover when he addressed an unfamiliar congregation, and confessed in his Journal: "A new audience, a new Sabbath, affords an opportunity of communicating thought and moral excitement that shall surpass all previous experience . . ."[7]

This delight in being an itinerant preacher was another indication that Emerson was beginning to find a second vocation, as a professional lecturer who must adapt himself to different audiences. Soon after his return to Boston, the Natural History Society invited him to give a lecture, and he responded on November 5 with a discourse on "The Uses of Natural History."[8] Probably Charles, who knew of his brother's growing interest in this subject, and was a member of the society, was largely responsible for the invitation.

Today, in an age of specialization, Emerson's temerity in lecturing on scientific subjects may seem pretentious, but in the decade of the 1830s, scientific education was in the kindergarten stage in the United States. Emerson had read widely on the discoveries and contemporary theories in astronomy, geology, and the morphology of plants and animals. Though by no means a disciplined or systematic student, he had something of interest to tell the members of the Natural History Society, for most of them had not read as extensively in the field as he. Furthermore, all his thinking about science was influenced by theology and Romantic poetry. Thus in his lecture he discussed the uses of physical energy provided to man by God's generosity, the moral significance of natural laws (much influenced by Mme. De Staël), and the aesthetic enjoyment of natural objects (partly derived from Wordsworth). In a note for a later lecture on "The Study of Natural History" Emerson declared: "Natural history by itself has no value; it is like a single sex. But marry it to human history, & it is poetry."[9] By this he meant that the bare natural fact, whether the orbit of a planet or the noise of an insect, became important only when it suggested some analogy in human nature.

Emerson cited the fable of the giant Antaeus, who in wrestling with Hercules was nearly suffocated whenever his feet left the ground but regained his strength every time he touched earth. The fable signified that "Man is the broken giant, and in all his weakness he is invigorated by touching his mother earth, that is, by habits of conversation with nature."[10]

Perhaps Emerson was unaware that in his own fable of man as a "broken giant" he had found a substitute for the fable of "original sin" which he vehemently rejected. Modern man was feeble because in his ignorance of the laws of nature—partly the result, Emerson thought, of Calvinism—he had become alienated from the physical world to which he owed his existence, his health, and the possibility of happiness. "The knowledge of all the facts of all the laws of nature will give man his true place in the system of being."[11] By this statement Emerson intended more than practical improvements in living through the use of natural resources. "Being" had metaphysical implications. Emerson had been deeply impressed by Swedenborg's teaching that "Nature is a language," and that "The visible world . . . is the dial plate of the invisible one."[12] Coleridge had said it more poetically in "The Destiny of Nations: A Vision":

> For all that meets the bodily sense I deem
> Symbolical, one mighty alphabet
> For infant minds.[13]

In this doctrine Emerson had found not only the theme for his gestating book on nature but also the subject for future sermons, lectures, essays, and poems; and new dimensions for his developing apocalyptic idealism: "it may be, [that] all this outward universe shall one day disappear, when its whole sense hath been comprehended and engraved forever in the eternal thoughts of the human mind."[14] Thus he had curiously anticipated the twentieth-century mysticism of the French philosopher-scientist Pierre Teilhard de Chardin.[15]

The success of Emerson's lecture to the Natural History Society led to other invitations to lecture on science in the winter of 1834. On January 6 he gave a Franklin Lecture in Boston on "The Relations of Man to the Globe," on the seventeenth a lecture on "Water" at the Mechanics Institute, and on May 7 an address at the fourth annual meeting of the Natural History Society on "The Naturalist."[16] He had found a secular pulpit for his new (or partly new) message, with all the freedom he needed to develop it in whatever way his thoughts led him.

II

However, Emerson was not yet finished with the pulpit. In mid-November, just when he was beginning to feel like settling down after his return from Europe, he received an urgent plea from the Unitarian church in New Bedford, where he had preached many times since 1827, to substitute for his cousin Orville Dewey, who was ill.[17] The Reverend Dewey was also considering a call to William Emerson's Unitarian church in New York City, and Emerson was assured that the New Bedford congregation was interested in having him for its permanent pastor. He was not sure he wanted the responsibility of another church, but he gladly rushed down to the famous whaling town because he liked his cousin and his parishioners. He would have to miss William's wedding to Susan Haven in Portsmouth, New Hampshire, on December 3, but he wrote his brother that "Charles is the best representative of the family and we will all endorse his commission."[18]

The whaling industry did not especially attract Emerson, if we may judge from his letter to ten-year-old Abby Adams, adopted daughter of his Boston friend Abel Adams. He asked her if she knew where New Bedford was, and explained:

> It is worth knowing, for though it is a small town it has more ships than any other town in the United States except New York & Boston. At least they say so here. All these vessels are employed in chasing the poor whale wherever he swims all round the globe, that they may tear off his warm jacket of blubber & melt it down into oil for your lamp, & steal from him his bone to make stays & parasols for ladies. . . .[19]

Though the tone of this letter was purposely adapted to a ten-year-old mind, it expressed considerably more sympathy for the whale than for the whalers, at a time when most people regarded them as courageous adventurers, risking their lives for the public good. But Emerson himself was sufficiently interested in the romance of whaling to record in his Journal the story a seaman had told him in the coach during one of his trips back to Boston: the story Herman Melville would use nearly twenty years later about "a white whale . . . who rushed upon the boats which attacked him, and crushed the boats to small chips in his jaws . . . A vessel was fitted out at New Bedford . . . to take him."[20]

But Emerson was more interested in the New Bedford Quakers than in stories of white whales. He boarded with a Quaker woman, Mrs. Deborah Brayton,[21] who dutifully used "thee" and "thou" to him and avoided the pagan names of the days of the week and months. At the time of his first preaching in New Bedford in 1827, the Quakers there, as in some other American communities, were fiercely divided over the radical teachings of the Long Island Quaker preacher Elias Hicks.[22] Finally the Hicksites in New Bedford went their own way, and the more orthodox Friends joined the Unitarian Church, which made some concessions to them in the observance of "the sacraments." By 1834 Emerson himself had become more Quaker than Unitarian, and objected to praying in public unless the spirit moved him. This scruple prevented his being offered the pastorship of the New Bedford church, because some of the members did not agree with the Quakers on this subject.

Several years earlier, while serving in this same church as a substitute minister, Emerson had been deeply impressed by the sight of the leading

Quaker in the town, Miss Mary Rotch, quietly leaving the church when the rite of the Last Supper was about to be observed. It is not unlikely that her example influenced him in the controversy which forced him to give up his pastorate of the Second Church. That she thereafter became one of his most cherished friends he testified himself. She reminded him of his Aunt Mary, and to some extent took her place during his aunt's coolness to him after his resignation in Boston. Miss Rotch told him that she had been spiritually disciplined during the years of dissension in New Bedford, "driven inward, driven home, to find an anchor, until she learned to have *no choice,* to acquiesce without understanding the reason when she found an obstruction to any particular course of action."[23]

These discussions with Miss Rotch interested Emerson so much that he recorded them in his Journal. She refused to call her experiences "spiritual direction" from God, or even "an impression or an intimation, or an oracle." It was none of these, yet it was so "simple it could hardly be spoken of." Emerson suggested that "it was not so much any particular power, as, a *healthful state of the mind,* to which she assented cordially." He said, "it must produce a sublime tranquility in view of the future—this assurance of higher direction; and she assented."

Though he seemed to understand Miss Rotch's experiences so perfectly, Emerson was nevertheless somewhat astonished—or at least sufficiently impressed to ask himself in his Journal: "Can you believe, Waldo Emerson, that you may relieve yourself of this perpetual perplexity of choosing? & by putting your ear close to the soul, learn always the true way." He remembered Plutarch's story of Socrates' daemon, which warned him not to take a certain road. His friends laughed at him and took that road, only to meet with an accident. Emerson had once thought the story "anomalous"; now he wondered if it might not actually have happened.[24]

After preaching in New Bedford for a month, Emerson returned to Boston for a few weeks, and then was again in New Bedford from late January 1834 to the end of March. Although it would be an exaggeration to say that under the Quaker influence he attained a *new* consciousness, for a favorite theme in his earlier sermons had been trust in the "inner voice" through which God communicated with men, yet he did unmistakably gain confidence in that voice while in New Bedford and became more uncompromisingly self-reliant.

Back in Boston again, Emerson had leisure to explore his consciousness and keep a record in his Journal. On April 12 he wrote: "We are always on the brink of an ocean of thought into which we do not yet swim."[25] (Later, William James would call this the "fringe" of the "stream-of-consciousness.") Emerson felt that he had unused, even undiscovered, powers of thought which he vaguely sensed. On rare occasions a "truth" dawned upon him with the intensity of an epiphany; sometimes when talking with Aunt Mary or Miss Rotch, or as on that golden day he spent with Carlyle (never in church, he carefully noted), or as on "this delicious day [Sunday, April 13], or whatever celestial fingers touched the divine harp—I woke to a strain of highest melody . . ."[26] Perhaps he was indulging in hyperbole, for ecstasy was rare for him. He was "born tranquil," and not since Ellen's death had he experienced the extremes of grief or happiness. He stalked his revelations with dogged persistence, but they came unexpectedly:

> Set out to study a particular truth. Read upon it. Walk to think upon it. Talk of it. Write about it. The thing will not much manifest itself, at least not much in accommodation to your studying arrangements. The gleams you do get, out they will flash, as likely at dinner, or in the roar of Faneuil Hall, as in your painfullest abstraction.[27]

Although Emerson had only a vague conception of the unconscious, he was actually on the border of discovering its power in his own life—that is, the unconscious of Wordsworth, not Freud's den of vipers. Later in the year he asked himself, "What is the doctrine of *infallible guidance* if *one will abdicate choice,* but striving to act unconsciously, to resume the simplicity of childhood?"[28] Whether childhood is really so wholesomely innocent is beside the point (which might depend upon the child's earliest experiences—and maybe its genes). "Blessed is the child," he declared, "the Unconscious is ever the act of God himself."[29] All his mistakes had been made when he ignored his own intuition and tried "to see the object from another person's point of view"[30]—which is to say, when he tried to adopt the point of view of society, of tradition, or *human authority.* In a rhetorical question he declared: "Could it be made apparent what is really true[,] that the whole future is in the bottom of the heart, that, in proportion as your life is spent within,—in that measure are you invulnerable."[31]

Psychologically, and perhaps subconsciously, Emerson was striving for emotional invulnerability. He had been so deeply hurt by Ellen's death that he was now trying to convince himslf that he was "born tranquil" and was not constituted to suffer keenly. He would continue trying to teach himself this fiction, and his theory of abdicating choice and trusting to the infallible guidance of "Reason," by which the Omnipotent Mind filtered through his unconscious into his active consciousness, was another attempt at self-protection. Nevertheless, the relentless struggle to accept and act upon these notions enabled him to tap a reservoir of creative energy, which in the future would bring him success as a religious and literary thinker.

III

Early in May 1834 Emerson received one-half of his inheritance from Ellen's estate, with the other half to be paid in July. Some of it was in cash, but most of it was in stocks and bonds. On May 31 he wrote Edward that he was now sure of twelve hundred dollars a year, the income from a little over twenty-three thousand dollars.[32] He said again that he was thinking of buying a little place in the Berkshires, where he and his mother could nurse Edward back to health.

Since Emerson had experienced difficulty in living on the eighteen hundred dollars a year he had earned as pastor of the Second Church, this inheritance did not make him feel wealthy, but by supplementing it with fees from lectures and sermons he felt confident that he could pay off his debts and support himself and his mother, pay Bulkeley's board in Chelmsford, and give Edward what assistance he needed. His mother's income from the La Fayette Hotel, in which her inheritance from the Haskins estate had been invested, had declined to less than a hundred dollars a year, and Charles and William were barely self-supporting. Nevertheless, Waldo now had sufficient economic stability to be able to do more or less whatever he wished with his life.

The only immediate change he desired was a pleasant spot where he and his mother could spend the summer, and he found exactly the place he sought in nearby Newton in a farmhouse owned by a Mr. and Mrs. Allen. On May 31 he wrote Edward from the Allens': "Here sit mother & I among the pine trees still almost as we shall lie by & by under them. Here we sit always learning & never coming to the knowledge of." The quietness was broken only by the hum of insects, the chorus of singing birds, and at long intervals in the distance the steam whistle of the trains, which now went as far as Waltham, twice a day to and from Boston.

Nearly every Sunday Emerson preached in Waltham, Fall River, or somewhere else, and no doubt he wished the railroad went there. "Get into the railroad car," he wrote in his Journal, "and the Ideal Philosophy takes place at once. . . . The very permanence of matter seems compromised & oaks, fields, hills, hitherto esteemed symbols of stability do absolutely dance by you." While this happened, he could believe that matter is "phenomenal."[33] He found it a delightful experience, and the convenience pleased him, too. He wrote George Sampson that he and Charles could easily come out to Newton on the train in time for tea, and return next morning. He was eager to show them the delightful walk about two miles from the station through the trees to the Allen farm.

In July Emerson went to Bangor, Maine, to preach for a month. The new Unitarian church was without a minister, and, he wrote Frederic Hedge on July 12, the members "have got beyond the period when a violent Unitarian is wanted." He felt "almost persuaded to sit down on the banks of this pleasant stream [the Penobscot River]," if he could only persuade some of his friends and family to join him.[34] Actually, he did not seriously consider settling down in Maine, though he took keen interest in every aspect of the backwoods life. He rode the steamboat up the river to the sawmills, visited an Indian village at Oldtown, and walked in the virgin forest, where the trees were so tall they shut out the sunlight, preventing the growth of underbrush. One could drive a horse and chaise between the huge trees.

At a Fourth of July celebration Emerson attended, someone alluded to two recent large fires, and a farmer remarked that "the city of Bangor makes no more account of losing 20 houses than his wife would of spilling a nice pan of milk. A man goes out & puts up a frame of a house before breakfast as an ordinary morning's work."[35] The farmer said one of his neighbors was "making a street directly into the woods," apparently expecting a town to spring up like a toadstool. Mr. William Emerson, a merchant in Bangor and probably a distant relative of Waldo's, said the builders got "two dollars for every one they lay out."

In Exeter Emerson visited his Harvard classmate J. B. Hill, now a successful lawyer. "There sat my old classmate in his office with a client,—

himself without coat or vest or neckcloth, unshaved, &, as he said, fat & rusty." Waldo was plainly shocked, but Mr. Hill "kept his countenance wondrously, & talked as of yore." Emerson thought him a "magnanimous man altogether incapable of pettyfogging & stout hearted as of old; a whig in the midst of a town where the tories [Jacksonian Democrats] are 300 to 30."[36]

Those weeks in Maine revealed a way of life hitherto unknown to Emerson, for it was still very nearly a frontier society. But the excursion ended in sadness. George Sampson, one of Emerson's closest friends in Boston, had planned to join him in Bangor and return with him by steamboat, but he became ill in Portland and died there, probably of a heart attack, on July 23.[37] Emerson returned to Boston a week later, and the following Sunday, August 3, conducted a memorial service for his friend in the Second Church.

Not even the rural life in Newton could redeem the summer for Emerson after the loss of his friend. He had accepted an invitation to read a poem at the annual meeting of the Harvard chapter of Phi Beta Kappa on August 28, and he had looked forward to sharing the poem and the delivery with George. Now he had difficulty in finishing the verses, and did not think well enough of the finished poem to collect it in any of his published works. Probably the high point of interest to his audience was an extravagant eulogy of Daniel Webster, "A form which Nature cast in the heroic mould," whose "clarion accents broke,/As if the conscience of the country spoke."[38] At the time, Webster was his absolute ideal of statesman and patriot, but fifteen years later he would be disillusioned over Webster's role in the Compromise of 1850.

As autumn approached, Emerson began to ponder again *where to live*. The arrangement he and his mother had made with the Allens in Newton was only temporary. Dr. Ezra Ripley was without a housekeeper, and he invited Ruth Emerson and Waldo to come live with him in the Manse at Concord. Mrs. Emerson accepted promptly, but Waldo was still, he wrote his step-grandfather on September 1,[39] trying to make up his mind regarding New Bedford—though, as we have anticipated, that decision would be taken out of his hands by some of the orthodox members of the church.[40] On September 20 Waldo wrote again to Dr. Ripley to say he would not become the pastor in New Bedford, "& therefore I return with pleasure to our former prospect of spending the winter at Concord."[41]

At this time Aunt Mary was visiting Waldo and his mother in Newton, and she said she wanted to find a boarding place somewhere in Concord, but no one suggested the Old Manse. The second week in October, Mrs. Emerson accompanied her son to Boston to help him pack his books and a few pieces of furniture, which would be sent to Concord by wagon. Then she went to Concord while he departed for New York, where he had agreed to substitute for several Sundays in the Second Unitarian Church. Waldo had written his brother: "As Mr [Orville] Dewey is waited for & as you will doubtless make permanent arrangements with him I who am no candidate can fitly fill the crevice of the time."[42]

On the day of his arrival in New York, October 18, Emerson received the news that Edward had died in Puerto Rico on October 1. He had caught a cold after getting wet in a rainstorm, which aggravated his chronic cough. A few days later his physician found that his lungs were so badly infected with tuberculosis that death was imminent. On Waldo's first day in New York he wrote in his Journal: "So falls one pile more of hope for this life. I see I am bereaved of a part of myself."[43]

Waldo Emerson had never liked New York City, and this loss of the brother who had been closest to him until his departure for Puerto Rico cast a pall over his visit to William and Susan. He had met his sister-in-law the previous April by accident when she stopped in Boston on her way to Portsmouth, New Hampshire. William had not notified any of his family to expect her, and she had had difficulty in finding overnight lodging. Somehow Charles heard of her plight and alerted Waldo, who took her to his boardinghouse on Franklin Place.[44] He liked her immediately and had looked forward to seeing her again in New York.

During the month Waldo was in the city, he was alarmed and disgusted by the frenzied political campaign raging between the Whigs and the Jacksonian Democrats. Every day his ears were assaulted by the violence of words, noisy demonstrations, and, as the November election drew near, by actual rioting in the streets. Though his sympathies were with the Whigs, he was not pleased by their conduct, either. On October 27 he attended a "Merchants' Meeting at the Exchange," which Mayor Philip Hone had called. Emerson found it humiliating to "see what words are best received & what low animal hope & fear patriotism is."[45]

The mayor boasted that his party had the votes to win, but Emerson thought this a call to "stupid persons who in the absence of all internal strength obey whatever seems the voice of their street, their ward, their town, or whatever domineering strength will be at the trouble of civilly dictating to them." It was a lesson in popular government, and Emerson was morally revolted. On the same evening the Jackson men marched down to Castle Garden, where they feasted, consumed quantities of whisky, according to Whig reports, set off fireworks, and rejoiced over previous victories.

The election was for the governor of the state, several congressmen, and numerous city officials, but in Mr. Hone's opinion it was actually "to decide whether the principles of General Jackson are approved and ratified by the people, and whether Mr. Van Buren is to be his successor . . ." Emerson remained in New York during the voting on November 3, 4, and 5. Wednesday evening, the fifth, Mr. Hone recorded in his Diary: "The election closed this evening. The Governor's votes were canvassed in all the wards except the sixth, and by nine o'clock enough was known to satisfy us . . . that we are beaten,—badly beaten; worse than the least sanguine of us anticipated."[46]

On the day that Mr. Hone admitted defeat, Emerson philosophized in his Journal: "The good cause is always on the defensive . . . Because the unscrupulous can not only avail themselves of innocent means to their ends but all evil ones likewise."[47] He was thinking of the Whigs' charge that the "Tories" after voting legally had then brought in from other wards gangs of "forsworn gallows birds" to vote more than once "to elect the officers that are to hunt, try, imprison, & execute them"—or, by implication, not to do so. Like the Whigs, Emerson regarded the manipulation of the destitute of the city as extremely dangerous, encouraging revolution. "If the wishes of the lowest class that suffer in these long streets should execute themselves [take action?], who can doubt that the city would topple in ruins."[48]

But these observations did not make Emerson a reformer at this time— or a satirist, who is a disillusioned and angry idealist. He was still an idealist, in both the popular and the philosophical sense. He believed that defeat would make the Whigs compensate by trying harder and thus become "irresistible"; they would "redeem America as they once redeemed England . . ." This, of course, was not good prophecy, and revealed Emerson's political naiveté. He was still too concerned with his own inner world to be a reliable judge of the external.

On the last day of October Emerson had recorded: "I believe in the existence of the material world as the expression of the spiritual or real, & so look with a quite comic & condescending interest upon the show of Broadway ... Broadway is Trade & Vanity made flesh."[49] Thus he learned little from his month in New York in the autumn of 1834, and was eager to escape the "comic" political immorality and bad manners he was witnessing.

IV

Early in November Emerson returned from New York to Boston and then took the new train to Concord. "We traversed the 15 miles of railroad in 32 minutes," he boasted in a letter to William.[50] The black ash trees lining the avenue in front of the Old Manse had shed their leaves, and the weather-beaten boards of the austere building were somber in the November light; but as Waldo passed between the tall rough-stone gateposts he felt that he was coming home.

Dr. Ripley was recovering from a severe illness, but he talked of preaching a fortnight thence, though he had not yet been out of his bedroom. Waldo's mother was still feeling sad over Edward's death, but was in good health, and as usual said little about her grief. Aunt Mary was boarding in the village, and had not yet quarreled with anyone—so far as is known. Recently she had suddenly appeared at the Manse in a very shabby chaise which she had borrowed from a man shopping on Main Street. He had reluctantly lent her his gig, after she reminded him "that she was his own townswoman, born within a mile of him." As she drove off he told her not to hurry. Charles had negotiated a lease for her farm in Maine, so that she now had a small but steady income. Later at intervals she would decide that she had been cheated, though she let the legal settlement stand.

Emerson's life at the Manse soon settled into a routine of reading, writing, and daily walks. Since Dr. Ripley now had little use for the study on the second floor, in which thousands of sermons had been written by several generations of clergymen, it was assigned to Waldo. A few years later, after Dr. Ripley's death, Nathaniel and Sophia Hawthorne rented this house, and in *Mosses from an Old Manse* Hawthorne described this study, in which Emerson wrote his lectures and began *Nature*. "When I first saw the room," Hawthorne wrote, "its walls were blackened with the smoke of unnumbered years, and made still blacker by the grim prints of Puritan ministers that hung around." They must still have been there in the winter of 1834–35. Certainly the great willow tree was "that swept against the overhanging eaves [and] attempered the cheery western sunshine," for Emerson mentioned it in his Journal:

> The great willowtree over my roof is the trumpet & accompaniment of the storm & gives due importance to every caprice of the gale and the trees in the avenue announce the same facts with equal din to the front tenants. Hoarse concert: they roar like the rigging of a ship in a tempest.[51]

The study had three windows with small, leaded, old-fashioned panes of glass, two on the west side, through which Waldo could see Dr. Ripley's prized orchard, and beyond, between the limbs of the big willow, catch glimpses of the slow-moving river. At the third window, on the north side, he had a better view of the river and the bridge where the British troops had clashed with the local militia on that April day in 1775. At this very window his grandfather had stood when the shots were fired, scarcely a hundred yards away. These associations were dear to Waldo Emerson, but he valued this room most for its seclusion.

On November 19 it seemed like a special occasion when Dr. Ripley, in his cloak and velvet cap, joined Waldo and his mother for evening prayers in the parlor. Listening to him talk, Waldo decided, "In things within his experience he has the most robust erect common sense."[52] His mind was as clear and vigorous as that of a man of thirty. But outside his limited circle of knowledge his opinions were often puerile, though he spoke with the dignity and assurance of a Jefferson or Franklin. He prayed "as usual with the happiest pertinence. 'We have been variously disciplined; bereaved, but not destitute; sick, but thou hast healed, in degree, our diseases; and when there was but a step between us & death, thou hast said, Live.' " Waldo imagined he was like an Indian Sagamore, "a sage within the limits of his own observation, a child beyond." And he would never forget what his step-grandfather had said to him "after Grandmother's death. 'Well, the bond that united us, is broken, but I hope you and your brothers will not cease to come to this house. You would not like to be excluded, and I shall not like [to] be neglected.' "

However, there were times when Waldo did not feel sympathetic with Dr. Ripley. After living with him for a few weeks he recorded this astonishingly harsh judgment:

A real interest in your fellow creatures is of necessity reciprocal. For want of it how tragic is the solitude of the old man. No prayer[,] no good wish out of the whole world follows him into his sick chamber. It is as frightful a solitude as that which cold produces round the traveller who has lost his way. This comes of management, of cunning, & of vanity. Never held he intercourse with any human being with thorough frankness, man to man but always with that imp-like second thought. And so hath no friend. Yet I forget not his generosity[,] his tenderness to E[llen]. And his faults have not descended to his children. . . .[53]

Except for the comment about the old man's tenderness to Ellen, one might doubt that Emerson was actually characterizing Dr. Ripley. And nearly three weeks later he felt more charitable toward him: "A little above [in this Journal] I referred to one of my characters. It might be added that if he made his forms a straight jacket to others, he wore the same himself all his years & so reanimated for his beholders the order of La Trappe."[54] Possibly as he recuperated he became easier to live with, for Emerson began this entry: "When the sick man came out of doors the stars seemed to shine through his eyes into his heart, & the blessed air that he inhaled seemed to lighten his frame from head to feet."

That Dr. Ripley's conduct was not consistent is indicated by a further remark in Emerson's Journal: "Sage & Savage strive harder in him than in any of my acquaintance, each getting the mastery by turns, and pretty sudden turns." When he prayed, "Save us from the extremity of cold, & violent sudden changes," he could have been praying for his own interior meteorology. His language was always sharp and expressive, as when he declared after the death of one of his parishioners, "It is cruel to separate old people from their wives in this cold weather." Emerson was also amused when he said pleasantly at supper "that his last cup was not potent in any way, neither in sugar, nor cream, nor souchong; it was so equally &

universally defective that he thought it easier to make another, than to mend that."[55] His gestures, too, were memorable; on another occasion Emerson observed that he could not "eat sponge cake without a ramrod."[56]

While residing at the Old Manse, Emerson also recorded some caustic opinions of other persons living in Concord:

How sad how disgusting to see this Neidrig [*niedrig,* "base"] air on the face, a man whose words take hold on the upper world whilst one eye is eternally down cellar so that the best conversation has ever a slight savor of sausages & soapbarrels. Basest when the snout of this influence touches the education of young women & withers the blessed affection & hope of human nature by teaching that marriage is nothing but housekeeping & that Woman's life has no other aim. Even G. was capable of saying 'the worst marriage is better than none.' & S. made a similar stab at the sanity of his daughter.[57]

It seems unlikely that "S." could be Samuel Hoar, the leading lawyer of the county and one of Concord's most respected citizens, who lived in a fine brick house on Main Street. His son was George Frisbie, and his daughter, Elizabeth, to whom Charles Emerson was engaged. The Honorable Samuel Hoar was elected to Congress in December 1834, and Waldo wrote William on the sixteenth: "Perhaps he will want Chas to take his office here." But he hoped Charles would remain in Boston.[58]

Was it possible that Waldo did not sympathize with Charles's engagement to Elizabeth Hoar? He complained in his Journal that as soon as his brother became engaged he began to magnify every trait of his betrothed into a positive virtue: "Talent becomes genius; inoffensiveness, benevolence; wilfulness, character, & even stupidity simplicity. Poor dear human nature; leave magnifying & caricaturing her."[59] She would be more admirable, Waldo thought, if accepted as she actually was, with all her faults and virtues mingled. If this was Charles and Elizabeth he was thinking about, he would soon change his mind and cherish Elizabeth as one of his dearest friends. She was a tall brunette with ordinary features, rather timid, very religious, and intense in her loyalties. In the spring of 1835, after Charles had taken over the law office of his future father-in-law, both he and Elizabeth taught Sunday school in Dr. Ripley's church.

With Charles in Boston and Edward now where no letter could reach him, Waldo Emerson depended mainly upon his own mind for companionship. Riding in his gig to East Sudbury one Sunday in December to preach, he amused himself "with the beauties & terrors of the snow," and observed that "Nature in the woods is very companionable. There, my Reason & my Understanding are sufficient company for each other. I have my glees as well as my glooms, alone."[60] If only God could assure him that "I shall have my dead & my absent again, ... I could be content & cheerful alone for a thousand years." But he could find assurances only through imagining affinities with nature. "The moment we indulge our affections," he mused, "the earth is metamorphosed; all its tragedies & ennuies vanish, all duties even, nothing remains to fill eternity with but two or three persons."

Though all the famous men Emerson had met on his travels in Europe had disappointed him except Carlyle, who was not yet really famous, in books he could find minds that had something to say to him. Of course none of the great authors of the past was perfect, either, but "Out of these fragmentary lobsided [sic] mortals shall the heaven unite Phidias, Demosthenes, Shakspear [sic], Newton, Napoleon, Bacon, and St John in one person."[61] That perfect life was to be the goal of Emerson's own search, not simply in these projected lectures but actually in all his future writings and personal conduct. Probably "there are very few persons at any one time in the world who can address with any effect the higher wants of men." However, "Socrates, St Paul, Antoninus, Luther, Milton have lived for us as much as for their contemporaries if by books or by tradition their life & words come to my ear. . . . We participate in their act by our thorough understanding of it."[62]

For his lecture series on "Biography" Emerson chose Michel Angelo Buonaroti (his spelling), Martin Luther, John Milton, George Fox, and Edmund Burke, to be introduced by a lecture on "Tests of Great Men" (which has been lost). Luther, Fox, and Milton had each *spoken* to him during some crisis in his life, and the others had acquired special meaning for him in one way or another: Michelangelo during his Italian travels as the supreme artist, and Burke over a period of years as an example of intelligent moderation, counterbalancing such revolutionaries as Luther and Fox. On December 18 Emerson wrote in his Journal: "I am writing my Lecture on Michel Angelo clothed with a coat which was made for me in

Florence."[63] This lecture was delivered on February 5, 1835, and the others each following Thursday through March 5.[64]

With Carlyle, Emerson had already begun a stimulating correspondence. Soon after his return from New York he had received a letter from Carlyle, written not from Craigenputtock but 5 Great Cheyne Row in Chelsea, London, where Carlyle had settled in order to have the benefits of big libraries and intellectual companionship.[65] After reading the installments of *Sartor Resartus* in *Fraser's Magazine*, Emerson had thanked the author for his "brave stand . . . for Spiritualism," but admitted dissatisfaction with "the form, which my defective apprehension for a joke makes me not appreciate."[66] He had wondered if "this humor proceeds from a despair of finding a contemporary audience." He detected wisdom in the "grotesque Teutonic apocalyptic strain"[67] of *Sartor,* but could not see why its author should lavish "celestial truths . . . in that spend-thrift style."

Carlyle had replied that he had indeed written in loneliness and despair of an audience. "Poor Teufelsdröckh!—Creature of mischance, miscalculation, and thousand-fold obstruction!"[68] Nevertheless, Carlyle had had the installments of *Sartor* bound and had sent Emerson four sets. On November 20 Emerson wrote Carlyle that his letter had "made a bright light in a solitary and saddened place."[69] He had had time to reread *Sartor* in the "stitched pamphlet," and liked the work so much better that he had now "eaten nearly all my words of objection." He predicted that it would not "lack a present popularity," in spite of having been ignored in England.[70]

Emerson had sent Carlyle a copy of Sampson Reed's little book called *Observations on the Growth of the Mind,* which had at least interested the author of *Sartor* as a literary curiosity. Emerson saw some parallels between Teufelsdröckh's "philosophy of clothes" and the Swedenborgian doctrine of "correspondence," "for they esteem, in common with all the Trismegisti [cabalistic prophets], the Natural World as strictly the symbol or exponent of the Spiritual, and part for part . . ."[71] Emerson himself was contemplating a work on this subject (*Nature*), in which the influence of the "Spiritual Philosophy" of both Reed and Professor Teufelsdröckh would be assimilated.

A few months later (March 12, 1835) Emerson was able to report to Carlyle that "some thirty or more intelligent persons understand and highly appreciate the *Sartor."* One of these was Dr. W. E. Channing, whom Carlyle had met without enthusiasm. "Some friends here," Emerson added, "are very desirous that Mr. Fraser should send out to a book-seller here fifty or a hundred copies of the *Sartor*. So many we want very much; they would be sold at once." He thought these copies would test the feasibility of an American edition. "The lovers of Teufelsdröckh here are sufficiently enthusiastic. I am an icicle to them."[72]

V

For several years, unknown to Emerson, an unusual woman of about his own age (actually eight months his senior) who lived in Plymouth, Massachusetts, had been fascinated by him. She was Lydia Jackson, daughter of the late Charles Jackson, merchant and owner of several merchant ships, and of Lucy Cotton, also deceased, a descendant of the "Pilgrim" John Cotton. In January 1831 she was visiting friends in Boston when by chance she attended Sunday service in the Twelfth Church, on Chambers Street. Instead of Dr. Barrett, an unknown visiting minister was in the pulpit, and she was astonished by the length of his neck. At the end of the sermon she realized that she had been sitting with such rigid attention that she had a cramp in her back.[73]

Then in the spring of 1834 this same man preached in Plymouth, and again Miss Jackson was strangely affected. In the words of her daughter Ellen, to whom she dictated her memoirs: "On the second Sunday mother was so lifted to higher thoughts by the sermon that she hurried out of the church as soon as it was over and home lest anyone should speak to her."[74]

Exactly when Emerson finally met Miss Jackson is not definitely known, but it was probably after he gave a lecture in Plymouth on March 13, 1834. His appearance had been instigated by his friend George Bradford, who two years earlier had taught German to Miss Jackson and a group of her friends. Mr. Bradford probably introduced his former student, a slender, tall woman with a small head, dark brown hair, gray eyes, and a face without noticeable defects yet not beautiful.[75] She carried herself with dignity and an air of aloofness, as if she were thinking of something far away or walking in her sleep. Some people found this trait disconcerting, but others attributed it to her spirituality and deep thoughts. She was a Unitarian, but sympathetic with some of the American writers on Swedenborg, and was herself "mystically" inclined.

Sometime after Miss Jackson finally met Emerson, she had a waking vision one day as she climbed the stairs of the Winslow House, the old Colonial mansion in which she lived—it is still today a showplace in Plymouth. As in a mirror she saw herself dressed as a bride, walking down these stairs with the Reverend Emerson. To quote her daughter's account again:

> It struck her as most shocking, and yet she did not feel to blame, for such a thought had never entered her mind at all. It would have seemed to her a great impropriety to have such ideas. She stopped indignant and said aloud, "I have not deserved this!" and she knew she *was* innocent. So she banished the thought and forgot it.[76]

Emerson returned to Plymouth on January 21, 1835, to give another lecture, probably one of his series on "Biography." He stayed with Captain Russell, whose son Le Baron had visited him in Concord[77] and ridden with him to Waltham, where he was to preach. Le Baron's older sister, Mary, had been Lydia Jackson's companion since childhood. Possibly Emerson's friendship with Miss Jackson had begun some months earlier, but he had not corresponded with her and there is no mention of her in any of his surviving letters or in his Journal until January 23, when he recorded cryptically: "Home again from Plymouth, with most agreeable recollections."[78]

Miss Jackson's memories were evidently "agreeable" also, for on Sunday evening, January 25, she had her second vision of Emerson. She suddenly saw him standing close to her, gazing steadily into her eyes, and then the image vanished. Next afternoon she was lying on the sofa in her parlor when the maid brought a letter to her. The address was in an unknown hand, and when she opened the envelope she read with amazement a proposal of marriage from the man whose specter had twice appeared to her.[79] She felt sure she must have experienced the second vision at the time Emerson wrote the letter, which deserves quotation in full because no part of it has ever been published (Professor Rusk, the editor of Emerson's *Letters,* did not know of its existence); also the wording is extremely revealing of the writer's peculiar state of mind:

Concord 24 January 1835

To Miss Lydia Jackson.
    I obey my highest impulses in declaring to you the feeling of deep and tender respect with which you have inspired me. I am rejoiced in my Reason as

well as in my Understanding by finding an earnest and noble mind whose presence quickens in mine all that is good and shames and repels from me my own weakness. Can I resist the impulse to beseech you to love me? The strict limits of the intercourse I have enjoyed, have certainly not permitted the manifestation of that tenderness which is the first sentiment in the common kindness between man and woman. But I am not less in love, after a new and higher way. I have immense desire that you should love me, and that I might live with you alway. My own assurance of the truth and fitness of the alliance—the union I desire, is so perfect, that it will not admit the thought of hesitation—never of refusal on your part. I could scratch out the word ["refusal"?]. I am persuaded that I address one so in love with what I love, so conscious with me of the everlasting principles, and seeking the presence of the common Father through means so like, that no remoteness of condition could much separate us, and that an affection founded on such a basis, cannot alter.

I will not embarrass this expression of my heart and mind with any second considerations. I am not therefore blind to them. They touch the past and the future—our friends as well as ourselves, [period changed to comma; B to &] even the Departed. But I see clearly how your consent shall resolve them all.

And think it not strange, as you will not, that I write rather than speak. In the gravest acts of my life I more willingly trust my pen than my tongue. It is as true. And yet had I been master of my time at this moment, I should bring my letter in my own hand. But I had no leave to wait a day after my mind was made up. Say to me therefore anything but no. Demand any time for conversation, for consideration, and I will come to Plymouth with a joyful heart. And so God bless you, dear and blessed Maiden, and incline you to love your true friend,

Ralph Waldo Emerson.[80]

The fact that Emerson had not previously corresponded with Miss Jackson, or even intimated his thinking of her as a future wife, indicates that he made his decision suddenly on a characteristic impulse. It is also obvious to an objective reader that he pleads to be loved but is wary of saying he loves Miss Jackson. Even when he attempts to do so, he is oblique and says he loves "after a new and higher way."

The "second considerations" were evidently arguments against the marriage, concerned even with the "Departed" (capitalized). Probably Miss Jackson knew he was a widower, but this was perhaps her first intimation that his "first love" affected a second. This was the secret of his inability to love another woman as he had once loved Ellen—as his second wife would discover in future years. The other secondary considerations would have been mainly financial: his mother depended upon him for support; he had taken on the responsibility of paying the debts Edward had incurred in Puerto Rico; and he was paying the board of his mentally defective brother, though the sum was not large enough to be much of a burden.

On the positive side, Emerson believed that intellectually and spiritually he and Lydia had much in common: their religion, interest in the philosophy of "Reason" and "Understanding" which they had encountered in Sampson Reed and Coleridge, and belief in direct communication with a Divine Mind. Their sympathy for the Quakers and the Swedenborgians probably made them think they were more alike in their nonconformity to Unitarianism than they actually were. He was doubtless impressed also that Lydia read German and spoke French and Italian. The latter languages she had acquired, with her sister, Lucy, at a private school in Jamaica Plains, near Boston. She had also taken dancing lessons from a French master and acquired a graceful walk.

The unhappiness of Miss Jackson's childhood Emerson would learn on further acquaintance.[81] Both her father and mother had died in her sixteenth year, after prolonged illnesses which depressed the spirits of their three children (four had died in infancy), Lucy, Lydia, and Charles Thomas. The cause of Mr. Jackson's illness is not known, but his wife suffered from tuberculosis of the lungs for ten years. The three children sustained each other to an extent, but Lucy made an unfortunate marriage, was deserted by her husband and left with two children to support. From her father's estate Lydia had an income of six hundred dollars a year, which she felt duty-bound to turn over to her sister. Emerson assured her that he had no objection. (Later she would learn that she was being cheated by a dishonest cousin who managed her funds.)

Miss Jackson herself was not strong, and suffered frequently from dyspepsia. To counteract her poor health she took strenuous measures. She believed in the current fad of hydropathy and took cold baths the year round. She also slept with her windows open in all weathers, fasted when she had dyspepsia, and tried to toughen her body by sleeping four hours a night, as she had read that Napoleon did. Perhaps Emerson hoped to modify some of these practices. Open windows in New England winters must have alarmed a man who was "born cold."

Miss Jackson's letters to Emerson have not survived (probably destroyed by her in one of her black moods), but it appears that she did not delay in sending him an encouraging reply, for five days after his proposal of marriage was received he was in Plymouth for the "conversation" he had invited. This was satisfactory to both of them, and Emerson liked its "quietness," he wrote after his return to Concord, addressing her as his "Queen" and as "Lidian." He did not like "Lydia," possibly because after her marriage New Englanders would supply a "linking *r*" between the two vowels and call her "Lydia-remerson"[82]—though there may have been a more esoteric reason.

Anyway, Emerson wrote on February 1 that he was delighted with his "domesticated position" and the "good understanding that grew all the time." He realized that he "went & came without one vehement word—or one passionate sign."[83] Did he even kiss her? "In this was nothing of design," he assured her, but felt "a sort of grandeur" in their "modulated expression of love." Denying that he was "a metaphysical lover," he admitted being pleased that "between us the most permanent ties should be the first formed & thereon should grow whatever others human nature will." It would seem that he was satisfied with a domestic tie, though hoped emotional ones might grow out of it, in an unobtrusive way. This suspicion is confirmed in a letter to William on February 5 announcing his engagement "in a very different feeling from that with which I entered my first connection. This is a very sober joy."[84]

The engagement settled, the next question was where they should live. Lidian preferred her familiar Plymouth, and of course the Winslow mansion. She loved the old town, most of her friends lived there, and she had a garden and a flock of chickens. She was especially proud of her old-fashioned roses and Dutch tulips. But Waldo did not like Plymouth, which he thought had aristocratic airs, and he felt that he was being spied on when he visited Miss Jackson.

Since Emerson had no permanent position to tie him down to one place, Lidian thought he could just as well settle in historic Plymouth— even older than Concord. Of course Concord was historic, too, but in a different way, and Emerson felt that his cultural and emotional roots went deep in the fields of his ancestors. By chance he had been born in Boston, but that didn't count. He was attached to the river, the ponds, and especially the woods around Concord. "I must win you to love it," he wrote

Lidian. "I am born a poet, of a low class without doubt yet a poet. That is my nature & vocation. My singing be sure is very 'husky,' & is for the most part in prose."[85] Yet he was a poet in the sense of "a perceiver & dear lover of the harmonies that are in the soul & in matter." He might find them in a hundred towns, but "Plymouth I fear is not one. Plymouth is streets; I live in the wide champaign." In another letter (February 13) he said that to be deprived of Concord would cripple him in "some important resources."[86] So Lidian gave in and Waldo would not have to sacrifice his ancestral and sylvan "resources." It was the beginning of Lidian's taking second place, though Waldo did not mean to be selfish.

Emerson's lectures on "Biography" also entailed further sacrifices in writing and visiting Lidian. He could not spare the time to return to Plymouth until they were over. However, Miss Jackson bridged the gap by visiting friends in Boston. Accompanied by her friend since childhood, Mary Russell, she stayed in the home of Mrs. Elizabeth Bliss, who would later become the second wife of the historian George Bancroft.

At Mrs. Bliss's the ebullient Elizabeth Peabody met Miss Jackson at tea on February 24, and described the meeting in a letter to her sister Mary. When she arrived, Miss Jackson was upstairs writing a letter to Waldo, who was in Concord trying to finish his lecture on George Fox, scheduled for delivery in Boston two days thence. "By and bye she descended—she looks very *refined* but neither beautiful or elegant—and very frail—&c. as if her mind wore out her body—she was *unaffected* but *peculiar.*" Miss Peabody had just finished reading Carlyle's letter to Emerson, which his friends were passing around. "She sat down by me—and we had a beautiful talk about a variety of most intellectual & spiritual things." She seemed to have "inexhaustible originality," and Miss Peabody stayed until ten o'clock.[87]

On March 4 Emerson asked in a letter to Lidian what she had done with his Plymouth sermon. He did not want it passed around like Carlyle's letter, for he intended to use it again; just "keep it out of sight."[88] He had the same attitude toward his lectures and disliked to have them reported fully in newspapers, which diminished their reusability. He was unable to accept Mrs. Bliss's invitation to her house in Boston because he had to lecture at Waltham Saturday evening, March 7, and then preach there twice next day. In the same letter he requested, "please never write my name with that prefix *Rev.* Have I not told you, dear Lidian, that I meet much more reverence than I know what to do with?" Charles and his most intimate friends, "as if by consent," though he had never asked them, "write me simple Mr—" He also wanted her to call him "Waldo," but she would never be able to do so, and would continue all her married life to address him as "Mr. Emerson."

He wanted Lidian to meet his family and had invited her to Concord.[89] He wrote that he would arrive in Boston Tuesday evening with his horse and chaise, though he might be late, and in that case would not see her until Wednesday morning at nine o'clock. According to plan, on Wednesday Lidian went with him to the Old Manse, where Waldo's family received her graciously. Lidian's daughter says in the reminiscence that she liked Grandma (Ruth Emerson), Aunt Lizzy (Elizabeth Hoar), and Uncle Charles, who had now settled in Concord and announced his engagement.

Charles had already met Lidian in Boston, and had written William: "The lady is a sort of Sybil for wisdom—She is not beautiful anywise that I know, so [if?] you look at the outside alone. Mother is pleased, & everybody."[90] On the visit to Concord, she stayed over the weekend, probably accompanied Waldo to Waltham on Sunday to hear him preach again, and returned home the following week. Emerson preached at Waltham every Sunday in March, but went to Plymouth for a sermon on April 5, thus combining business and pleasure, as he had done at Concord, New Hampshire.

Aunt Mary, for some reason, seems not to have been satisfied when she met Lidian during her visit to Concord, and at some time during the spring or summer she made a trip to Plymouth to see Waldo's fiancée again. The story of that strange encounter has survived only in Ellen Emerson's version of her mother's experiences.[91] Apparently Lidian and her sister, Lucy, were expecting Miss Emerson, and had prepared roast beef for dinner. But soon after her arrival the unpredictable Miss Emerson remarked that fish must be plentiful in Plymouth and said she regarded fish as a great luxury.

Lucy rushed out to procure a large, choice fish, then cooked it with care. But when it was offered to her at the table, Miss Emerson declined, saying she "never tasted fish." Miss Jackson thought that her guest could not resist the "glorious opportunity" of making her feel uncomfortable. Whether Waldo was coming to Plymouth for his April 5 sermon, or at another time heard of the visit and went to the rescue, he is reported to have arrived in his gig and taken his aunt home. As told to Ellen by her mother, Miss Emerson argued furiously on the long drive against the engagement. "I cannot bear to lose my nephews," she is later reported as saying, "and I did the same when Charles was engaged to Elizabeth. I tried to cure him of his caring for her." But having failed in both cases, she gave in and expressed her approval.

Now that the engagement had survived Aunt Mary's meddling, the only remaining problem was where to live in Concord. A suitable house was not easy to find, and it would take too much time to build one. Lidian was discouraged by Waldo's difficulties and opened her Bible at random, as the Puritans had done, for an answer. It opened at the text "Furthermore I tell thee that the Lord will make thee an house" (1 Chronicles 17:10). Actually the house was already built, and in July Emerson acquired title to the "Coolidge house" beside the Lexington Road, on the outskirts of Concord. Though not brand new, it was only about six years old and soundly constructed, but needed landscaping. Waldo paid thirty-five hundred dollars for it, and expected to spend five hundred more on remodeling.[92] He wanted Charles and Elizabeth to live with him, and accommodations would have to be made for them.

Meanwhile, Emerson had been invited to deliver the main address at the two-hundredth anniversary of the settling of Concord on September 12, 1635.[93] Elaborate plans were being made for the celebration, and the historical address was to be the showpiece of the program, which the governor and other notables were expected to attend. Emerson felt his responsibility, and knew also that he would have to do a great deal of research; so he asked Lidian to put the wedding off until two days after his address, or September 14. That would also allow time for getting the house ready for their occupancy.[94]

CHAPTER XII

Stars over Concord

The stars & celestial awning that overhang our simple Concord walks & discourses are as brave as those that were visible to Coleridge as he talked or Dryden or Jonson & Shakspear [*sic*] or Chaucer & Petrarch & Boccac[c]io when they met.[1]

I

The summer of 1835 was one of the busiest Waldo Emerson could remember. On August 5 he recorded in his Journal: "Our summer, Charles says, is a galloping consumption and the hectic rises as the year approaches its end."[2] Emerson's brain was buzzing with ideas, projects, arrangements for his approaching marriage, and anxiety lest he not have his address for the Second Centennial Anniversary of Concord ready to deliver on September 12.

On August 20 Emerson took time out from his many activities to deliver a lecture in Boston to the American Institute of Instruction on "The Best Mode of Inspiring a Correct Taste in English Literature." He assured his audience that he had no confidence in pedagogical "inventions and contrivances," though more inexpensive editions of the best authors were needed. His main advice was to teach students to read the great writers, such as Chaucer, Spenser, Shakespeare, and Milton, to the neglect of the lesser. The lecture was well received, but its contents suffered from its hasty preparation.

The Concord address, however, was a distinct triumph.[3] At ten-thirty in the morning of September 12, five hundred schoolchildren gathered on both sides of the Common, which lay between the Town Hall to the east and Shepherd's Hotel on the west side. The Meeting House was a short distance south of the Common. At eleven o'clock, to the beat of martial music, the Concord Light Infantry and the Artillery led the procession of distinguished guests and local dignitaries to the church. The governor had not come, but Lieutenant Governor Samuel Armstrong was present, with the Honorable Edward Everett, the Honorable Stephen Phillips of Salem, Philip Hone of New York City, R. C. Winthrop, direct descendant of the first governor of Massachusetts, and Alden Bradford, descendant of the second governor. Charles Emerson was one of the marshals. The old Meeting House had never been so crowded since its construction in 1812. The floor had been reinforced to prevent a possible collapse. Dr. Ripley, now in his eighty-fifth year, occupied the pulpit and gave the invocation. Ten veterans of the fight at the North Bridge on April 19, 1775, sat in the front row, four of them residents of Concord: Abel Davis, Thaddeus Blood, Tilly Buttrick, and John Hosmer.

When the Centennial Committee selected Waldo Emerson for the principal speaker, many people in Concord thought it had made a mistake in not choosing Charles, the rising young lawyer, who had won fame at Harvard for his oratory. However, Waldo fully justified the judgment of the committee. He did not attempt an oration, such as his brother or Edward Everett might have given, but, as he called it, an "Historical Discourse."[4] He traced the origin and development of the "first island town" in New England from 1635, selecting the most memorable and instructive episodes for critical comment, which he gave respectfully but with surprising frankness, without exaggeration or flattery. Concord was still a rural town, and "the agricultural life favors the permanence of families." The names of most of the original settlers were represented in his audience, "and the family is in many cases represented, when the name is not." He himself was an example. "If the name Bulkeley is wanting, the honor you have done me this day, in making me your organ, testifies your persevering kindness to his blood."[5]

Emerson did not exalt the original settlers as either heroes or saints. Though men of courage, and usually of integrity, they were not without faults, as could be seen in examining the records of their town meetings. There "the great secret of political science was uncovered, and the problem solved, how to give every individual his fair weight in the government, without any disorder from numbers."[6] A law passed in 1641 gave everyone, without exception, the right to speak his mind at a town meeting, and in the records Emerson found not a single complaint that anyone had been denied this right. Good counsel did not prevail without challenge, though in the process men learned their capacity for self-government, and the result was usually civic contentment.

Unlike some neighboring towns, Concord had never had witch trials, whipping of Quakers, or other persecutions for heresy; yet it did have one black spot in its early history.[7] When the first settlers arrived at Musketaquid, they found friendly Indians, from whom they purchased six square miles of land—though the price paid, as in most bargaining between the whites and Indians in those days, was ridiculous. John Eliot, who learned to preach to the Indians in their own language, converted a large group of them, and they became known as "Eliot's praying Indians." They asked and were granted permission to reside near Concord village, and remained good neighbors for half a century. But during the Indian uprisings known as King Philip's War some people in neighboring towns became hysterical and demanded the expulsion or extermination of all Indians in the region. No Indians attacked Concord, and the "praying Indians" begged to remain. Indignantly Emerson declared: "It is the misfortune of Concord to have permitted a disgraceful outrage upon the friendly Indians settled within its limits, in February, 1676, which ended in their forcible expulsion from the town."[8]

For his town's participation in the American Revolution, however, Emerson had nothing but praise. The Provincial Congress, which met in Concord under the presidency of John Hancock in 1774, "was composed of the foremost patriots, and adopted those efficient measures whose progress and issue belong to the history of the nation."[9] Of course Emerson was proud of his Grandfather William Emerson's role in opposing British tyranny, and of the farmers who made their historic stand at the bridge in 1775. And since then, "For the most part, the town has deserved the name it wears."[10] Those soiled and musty records testify to this fact. "The old town clerks did not spell very correctly, but they contrive to make pretty intelligible the will of a free and just community."[11]

Two days later Charles wrote William that Waldo's discourse lasted an hour and forty-five minutes, "which none but the children I think found too long."[12] The town authorities asked permission to print the address, and early in November Charles was able to send William a copy.

II

Sunday afternoon Waldo drove in his chaise to Boston, where he spent the night with friends before starting out early next morning for Plymouth. The stableman in Concord had attached bright yellow reins to the horse's bridle, but Waldo had them changed in Boston to sober black ones.[13] It was raining steadily and was not a pleasant day for a forty-mile drive. In Plymouth superstitious Lidian wondered if the weather was a bad omen, but she forgot her worries when her future spouse arrived at four o'clock.[14]

The wedding ceremony was scheduled for seven-thirty, with the Reverend Dr. Kendall officiating before a small group of Lidian's relatives and friends, and one mutual friend, Professor George Bradford, whom Emerson had chosen for his best man. Lidian's sense of time was notoriously deficient, and she sat in the parlor talking until the minister arrived. Then she rushed upstairs to dress, but took so long that Emerson became impatient and finally started up the steps to ask when she would be ready, only to meet her on the landing. Thus it happened that they descended the stairs together to be married, exactly as in her vision before her engagement.

Meanwhile the weather had cleared and the sun was setting behind golden clouds. Lidian was sure this was a favorable omen. She felt radiant in her wedding gown, with her high tortoiseshell comb in the twist of hair at the back of her head. Someone had given her the shell and in a moment of extravagance she had had it carved. Because her head was small she fluffed her brown tresses out with false curls. For the wedding she did not wear a veil or carry flowers. After exchanging nuptial vows, the bride and bridegroom dined in the Winslow mansion, where they also spent their wedding night.

No honeymoon had been planned, and next day Waldo drove his bride directly to Concord, where his mother and Charles had prepared to receive them in their new home. Ruth Emerson would live with her son and daughter-in-law and had contributed what furniture she still possessed, as well as her maid, but the house would be furnished mainly from Lidian's home in Plymouth. She had also brought her most prized Holland bulbs and some old-fashioned rosebushes which her family had cherished. Her chickens, too, were being transported from Plymouth.

Though Lidian had seen her new home, she was probably a little apprehensive, but she found it strikingly similar to the Winslow mansion, resplendent in its new coat of white paint and green wooden shutters.[15] The floor plan was so nearly the same that she might have found her way from room to room in the dark. The main body of the house was square, with four large chambers on both the first and second floors, each a corner room, with windows on two sides. The front door opened into a foyer, from which a door on the right led to Waldo's study and one on the left to the parlor. The stairway was broad to the first landing, then branched off on both sides to stairs leading to bedrooms. On the southwest corner of the house an ell, half the width of the main house, provided a kitchen and servant quarters for the cook and housemaid. Waldo intended within a few months to raise the roof of the ell and build an apartment for Charles and Elizabeth Hoar.

The Emersons' new home stood beside the Cambridge Turnpike, about half a mile from the center of town.[16] A short distance east of the Turnpike the Lexington Road angled toward it and the two highways converged before reaching the Common. Both were heavily traveled by farmers carrying produce to Boston, and by stagecoaches going in both directions. The traffic left something to be desired in privacy, and the location itself was not very attractive, though convenient to public transportation. On the other side of the Lexington Road there was also an elementary school, but Emerson liked to hear the voices of the children at play.

Emerson's two acres of land extended on the west down to the Mill Brook (so named because it supplied water for the grist mill on Main Street), beyond which stood the red-brick poorhouse on a dirt road to Walden Pond. Sometimes when the windows were open he could hear the screams of some poor demented woman in the red house. Lush grass in the meadow would provide good grazing for the cow in spring and summer. The barn, a short distance beyond the ell, had a stall for the horse, another for the cow, a harness room, shelter for the chaise, and a shed in which the chickens would have to roost, for the outbuildings did not include a hen house.[17]

At the time he bought the house Emerson wrote William: "It is a mean place & cannot be fine until trees & flowers give it a character of its own. But we shall crowd so many books & papers, & if possible, wise friends, into it that it shall have so much wit as it can carry."[18] His hospitality began even before the unpacking had been completed. A day or so after the newlyweds arrived from Plymouth, Mr. and Mrs. Benjamin Rodman, Waldo's Quaker friends from New Bedford, dropped in for a visit, and he promptly invited them to spend the night. Lidian was aghast, but she managed somehow to unpack the furniture for the guest room and get it ready for the Rodmans while her thoughtless husband entertained his guests. Fortunately for her, Waldo's mother had considerately decided to make a long visit to William and Susan in New York, at 104 Fourth Street, before settling into her room on the second floor. Charles for the present remained at the Manse, though he frequently dined with Waldo and Lidian. Lidian had liked him since their first acquaintance, and Waldo was now sure that Charles had the best mind and character of any man he knew.

The Emerson household soon had an established routine.[19] A little before breakfast at seven, Mrs. Emerson called the servants to the dining room to hear her husband read a short passage of Scripture and give an impromptu prayer. After breakfast she gave instructions to the cook for dinner, and Waldo on his way to the post office stopped at the grocery and butcher shops to leave orders. Dinner was served promptly at one o'clock, after which letters were written to catch the three-o'clock mail to Boston. Then Lidian took a nap, followed by a walk with her husband—at least in the autumn of 1835; later he walked alone or with male friends.

Waldo did not preach during October and neglected his Journal. These were the "honeymoon" weeks, during which he was a very attentive husband. Lidian was so happy that she wrote her sister to come and witness the marvelous life she was leading. "Little did they know Waldo Emerson," she exclaimed, "who believed he could be content to pass through life without domestic happiness. [No clue as to who believed this.] He was formed for it as perhaps few are. And not only to enjoy but to impart, all the warmer charities of social and domestic life."[20] In a few weeks Mrs. Lucy Brown did, in fact, come, to stay until the following May. After Waldo's mother returned from New York, Lucy boarded with Mrs. John Thoreau.

The Emersons' only problem of any consequence during this autumn was financial, and that was not acute. After earnest consultations they decided that by cautious spending they could just manage to stay solvent, though Waldo would need to do more lecturing and for the present continue preaching. He said he would wear his old clothes as long as he could, and she said she would mend them. William also needed money for his real-estate ventures on Staten Island; Waldo had none to lend, but he offered to sell or borrow on his Boston Mill Dam stock, inherited from Ellen, and an arrangement was worked out.

On November 1 Emerson began preaching in East Lexington—East Village, it was called.[21] He declined to accept the pastorate but agreed to preach or secure a substitute every Sunday on a temporary basis. It was a liberal congregation, recently organized, and he need not worry about expressing unorthodox opinions. Once after reading a sentence in an old sermon, he looked up and said nonchalantly, "I no longer believe that." Lidian usually rode with him in the chaise to East Lexington.

III

Visitors to the Emerson home soon began arriving with increasing frequency—friends, mostly, but also reformers, bores, and later freaks of various kinds. On October 10 Emerson recorded: "This morning Mr. May [Reverend Samuel May of Brooklyn, Connecticut] and Mr. George Thompson [the English abolitionist] breakfasted with me. I bade them defend their cause as a thing too sacred to be polluted with any personal feelings."[22] Probably he meant personal ambitions, for he suspected that some of the abolitionists were seeking notoriety. He believed in their professed purpose, but declined to be "used" in any organized movement.

Aunt Mary is said to have arranged for Mr. Thompson to have breakfast with her nephew.[23] The abolitionist movement was growing in Massachusetts, as well as corresponding opposition, some of it violent. Miss Emerson, Mrs. Thoreau, and several other Concord women were energetically organizing an Anti-Slavery Society in the town, and they warmly welcomed the English reformer. Dr. Ripley was sympathetic and let the Englishman speak in his church. Charles announced his support of abolition, and Waldo felt hard-pressed to defend his passive role.

During these troubled times Miss Harriet Martineau, whom Emerson had met in Glasgow in 1833, was touring the United States to gather material for a book on American society. She had not come especially to propagandize against slavery, but she was a candid person and could not suppress her indignation at the inhuman institution. As a consequence, threats were made on her life nearly everywhere she went, but she refused to be intimidated. Boston gave her as violent a reception as Virginia, and she was not safe even in Cambridge, where Emerson had visited her in August, a few weeks before his wedding, though his only comment in his Journal was that she was "a pleasant unpretentious lady,"[24] to whom he had enjoyed talking in spite of having to speak into her ear trumpet. In the autumn, when she was forced to flee Boston, he gave her brief sanctuary in his home in Concord. The following January he expressed in his Journal his indignation over "this foolish charging of Miss Martineau with ingratitude for differing in opinion from her southern friends."[25] The charge was that she had betrayed their hospitality by attacking their institution of slavery.

In her *Autobiography* Miss Martineau expressed her gratitude to Charles and Waldo Emerson:

At the time of the hubbub against me in Boston, Charles Emerson stood alone in a large company in defence of the right of free thought and speech, and declared that he had rather see Boston in ashes than that I, or anybody, should be debarred in any way from perfect free speech. His brother Waldo invited me to be his guest, in the midst of my unpopularity, and, during my visit, told me his course about this matter of slavery. He did not see that there was any particular thing for him to do in it then: but when, in coaches or steamboats or any where else, he saw people of colour ill-used, or heard bad doctrines or sentiment propounded, he did what he could and said what he thought.[26]

In spite of her own more active course, Miss Martineau respected Emerson's position and praised him highly in her *Retrospect of Western Travel* (1838): "Great things are expected for him; and great things, it seems, he can not but do if he have life and health to prosecute his course."[27] Having struggled in two separate periods of his life to regain his health, having lost Ellen and Edward to tuberculosis, and with Charles not strong, Waldo Emerson was determined not to let anything sap his strength or consume the time he needed for the work he felt he could do—was created to do. Perhaps no one understood his motives better, or sympathized more with him, than Miss Martineau.

Probably at this time Lidian also understood Waldo's need for self-protection, but certainly his Aunt Mary did not. Since his early manhood she had been increasingly at odds with him over religion, and now she was hot for antislavery activities and could not tolerate his aloofness. One day in February at his dinner table she became so violently abusive that she felt ashamed of herself.[28] But instead of apologizing, which was a psychological impossibility for her, she announced that she would never again enter his house, not as long as she lived—on second thought, not afterward, either, even for her funeral, if her wishes were obeyed.

But she did not swear never to write again, and on March 31, 1836, she wrote Waldo that she had been confiding in Sarah Bradford Ripley about "my separation from your house."[29] She said "she should no more think of a promise made in heat than if she had said she would kill me." But for Miss Emerson her angry declaration was binding, and she begged Waldo, "never trifle" with it. Probably Lidian had returned taunt for taunt, for Aunt Mary added, "If I could leave a message in this letter to Lydia I would say that I believe we shall then [on examination] find I did nothing to deserve complaint in her house—except two or three jokes for w'h I grieve." She thought her "known character" ought to bring forgiveness for her lapse. "However it is true the more I'm understood the less tolerated—& the prophecy I made in your youth that you would like me better is not fulfilled." She was never more pathetic in her conflict of pride and love, complicated by her inability to understand her nephew: "I don't know that I should forgive myself for protracting a connection after losing you in the chaos of modern speculation—I knew not on what ground you did anything—nor where to find your principles—they were an enigma."

Of all Emerson's guests in his new home, an eccentric schoolteacher in Boston became his favorite, a friend who immediately understood him and was understood in turn.[30] He was Bronson Alcott, a stocky man of medium height, with huge sloping forehead and shaggy eyebrows that might remind an anthropologist of a Stone Age savage, but the kind, gentle man was the most complete Platonic idealist of his time—at least in America. He had grown up on a poor hillside Connecticut farm, peddled housewares in the Carolinas in his youth, and had become a schoolteacher because he loved children and had new theories about how to teach them. By good luck he had gained access to libraries, in which he discovered that the idealistic philosophy of Plato, the seventeenth-century Cambridge (England) Neoplatonists, and Coleridge constituted his natural intellectual element. It was as if his soul had awakened to a former existence.

When Emerson visited his school in Boston in the summer of 1835, the two men were immediately attracted to each other.[31]

On October 17, accompanied by George Bradford, Alcott arrived in Concord to spend the weekend. Emerson's earlier impression was confirmed. After his guests left, he wrote in his Journal of Alcott: "a wise man, simple, superior to display, & drops the best things as quietly as the least. Every man, he said, is a Revelation, & ought to write his Record."[32] But not necessarily a book. Alcott was trying to write his in his school in Boston.

With the help of Miss Elizabeth Peabody and the encouragement of Dr. William Ellery Channing and some other liberal people in Boston, Alcott had opened his Temple School in the Masonic Temple the previous year, and at the time he visited Emerson it seemed to be prospering. He had furnished the classroom with pictures and statues, comfortable chairs which the children could pull into a circle for one of the famous conversations with the master, and had provided a carefully selected library, all at his own expense. Miss Peabody taught the conventional subjects, leaving him free to conduct the conversations.

Bronson Alcott took quite literally the Platonic idea of preexistence of the soul, as expressed in Wordsworth's "Ode":

> . . . trailing clouds of glory do we come
> From God, who is our home:
> Heaven lies about us in our infancy!

Before the clouds had faded entirely from his pupils' minds, perhaps they could describe the vanishing reflections, or at least give some clue to their existence. "All truth is within," Alcott taught. "My business is to lead you to find it in your own Souls."[33] Emerson had also preached the inwardness of eternal truth to his congregation in the Second Church. Alcott had heard him as early as 1828, and thought him the best preacher in Boston, but he had made no attempt to meet him personally, and Emerson did not at that time know of his existence.

Alcott would begin a conversation with his children by remarking, "You all appear to think, that you have something within you godlike, spiritual, like Jesus, though not so much. And what is this?" In a chorus the children would reply, "Spirit, conscience." And another child would add, "Conscience is God within us." Although Alcott thought he was being completely objective and neutral, of course unwittingly he had conditioned them to think as he did. Some of the children did give astonishing answers, especially precocious six-year-old Josiah Quincy, as Emerson observed when he visited the school.[34]

In addition to helping Alcott with the instruction, Miss Peabody was also writing *Record of a School, Exemplifying the General Principles of Spiritual Culture,* which she published at her own expense at the end of the first year of the school. Emerson read it with "great delight." In his Journal he noted: "It aims all the time to show the symbolical character of all things." He had no doubt that, as Miss Peabody alleged, "the children take the thought with delight."[35]

But not everyone was so unqualifiedly pleased with the *Record.* Even Dr. Channing wrote Miss Peabody: "I want light as to the degree to which the mind of the child should be turned inward." He feared too much introspection and self-analysis. "The soul is somewhat jealous of being watched, and it is no small part of wisdom to know when to leave it to its impulses and when to restrain it."[36] Alcott might have done well to listen to this tactful criticism, which undoubtedly Miss Peabody passed on to him, but of course he was incapable of understanding it, believing as he did in the all-importance of the spiritual life. Whether or not the *Record* aided or injured the reputation of the school, it did no serious damage to it. But Miss Peabody was also recording Alcott's conversations on the Gospels with the children, and some of their answers contained seeds of destruction. However, it would not be published until the following winter (1836–37).

Meanwhile Emerson was reading Alcott's remarkable diary observations of his own children, begun at the birth of his first child, Anna, in 1831, and continued for Louisa May (born 1832) and Elizabeth (1835). As Emerson remarked in his Journal, the problem Alcott was always trying to solve was "Whence is the World? The point at which he prefers to begin is the Mystery of the Birth of a child."[37] He called his manuscript "Psyche, Or the Breath of Childhood." Emerson agreed to read this voluminous document and advise the author whether it was publishable. After several months of agonizing perusal, he finally had to tell Alcott that it was not, because too much "a book *of one idea,*" lacking variety, needing compression, "and even sometimes pedantic from the wilfulness ... with which every thing is forced into the author's favorite aspects & forms of expression."[38] Naturally Alcott was disappointed, but he respected his friend's judgment, and Emerson's frankness did not affect their friendship. In the following months, in fact, it would prove of inestimable benefit to both men.

IV

On October 7 Emerson wrote Carlyle that he would "never again sit six weeks of this short human life over a letter of yours without answering it."[39] This was a reference to Carlyle's letter of June 27, 1835, in which he encouraged Emerson to think that he might yield to the invitation to come to America and try supporting himself as a lecturer, though not until the following year. Only the day before, Emerson had received Carlyle's letter of May 12, sent with four bound copies of the installments of *Sartor Resartus* published in *Fraser's Magazine:* "By a strange oversight [they] have been lying weeks, probably months, in the Custom-House."

In the long-delayed letter Carlyle had also told of his "great mischance . . . the saddest, I think, of the kind called Accidents I ever had to front."[40] After completing the first volume of his *French Revolution* he had lent the manuscript to a friend to read and criticize. But the cleaning maid mistook it for waste paper and burned it. When the "friend" came to report the accident he was so pale and shaken that Carlyle "could not complain," for the "poor man seemed as if he would have shot himself . . ." Emerson replied, "I could cry at the disaster that has befallen you . . . My brother Charles says the only thing the friend could do on such an occasion was to shoot himself, and wishes to know if he have done so."[41] Carlyle had not explained that the friend was John Stuart Mill, and that he had carelessly left the manuscript in his mistress's lodging, where it was destroyed— though perhaps Mill had not told Carlyle the place.

Carlyle's misfortune made Emerson more eager than ever to extend his hospitality to him: "I have not had so much leisure yet but that the fact of having ample space to spread my books and blotting paper is still gratifying. So know now that your rooms in America wait for you, and that my wife is making ready a closet for Mrs. Carlyle."

In the May letter Carlyle had complained that British politicians seemed intent on wrecking the country. Emerson replied that the prospect was not much brighter in his own land:

A man plunges into politics to make his fortune, and only cares that the world should last his days. We have had in different parts of the country mobs and moblike legislation, and even moblike judicature, which have betrayed an almost godless state of society; so that I begin to think even here it behoves every man to quit his dependency on society as much as he can, as he would learn to go without crutches that will soon be plucked away from him, and settle with himself the principles he can stand upon, happen what may. There is reading, and public lecturing too, in this country, that I could recommend as medicine to any gentleman who finds the love of life too strong in him.[42]

It was lecturing that Emerson hoped to be his own salvation, both for sanity and solvency. And now after enjoying a few weeks of leisure with Lidian in their new home, he must buckle down to work. He had agreed to give ten lectures in Boston on the general topic of "English Literature" before The Society for the Diffusion of Useful Knowledge, beginning November 5 in the Masonic Temple.[43] But he did not intend, as he explained in his introductory lecture, to give a history (or what colleges would later call a "survey course"). His Journal for October does not indicate that he did much reading in preparation. Indeed, one might assume that he merely read Thomas Wharton's *History of English Poetry* and reviewed Chaucer, Shakspear (his preferred spelling), Bacon (he could depend mainly on his memory for Bacon), Ben Jonson, Robert Herrick, George Herbert, Henry Wotton, Milton, and some favorite "ethical writers."

None of these lectures is of particular importance in Emerson's biography except his "Introduction," in which he explained his theory of literature; what it is and how it shows man's relations to his world; and it was also a dress rehearsal for *Nature*. Literature he defines as "the recorded thinking of man." What is important is not events, deeds, even experiences, but *ideas*: "The Ideas in every man's mind make him what he is. His whole action and endeavor in the world is to utter and give external shape to those thoughts."[44] A man spends his whole life "in efforts to create outside of him a state of things conformed to his inward thoughts."

The crucial question is: What is the relation between a man's "outside" world and his thoughts? Thus Emerson must begin with a theory of knowledge, which leads to theories of language, metaphor, symbol, image, and so on. Locke, Hume, Berkeley, and finally Kant had all attempted to solve the problem of how external reality can be experienced through the mind, for consciousness never gets out of itself. Kant at this time was hardly more than a rumor to Emerson (if he was ever more than that), but Waldo had studied the British epistemologists, rejected Locke in college, worked himself free of Hume's skepticism, and settled confidently on Berkeley's idealism (or something similar); yet the material world was no less *real* to him, and he was fond of Montaigne and his own sensuous enjoyment of nature:

> Everywhere we find man surrounded by the same company, that is, by what he calls Nature. He dwells with the multitude of his fellows; or alone in the misty fields; wet by the rains, pinched by the frost, cheered by the heat. Over him are the sun and moon; at his feet is the sea; around him are the mountains: the atmosphere embraces him in its soft arms. The stars shine on him with pleasing light; beasts, fire, water, stones, and corn serve him. By continually dealing with these mute and brute natures he learns to make them more useful. Many of the great objects of nature, he is so weak he cannot use, nor explore. But in their friendly company, the little stranger finds himself, every day, more at home, and more skilful.[45]

The only way Bishop Berkeley could find to explain the seeming consistency in man's subjective experience of the world outside his own mind was to assume that everything exists in and by the action of God's mind. At times Emerson felt this way (as, to anticipate, in *Nature* when he speaks of the "noble doubt" that nature outwardly exists), but he was actually not greatly interested in metaphysics. He had always assumed, with his Puritan ancestors, that there is an invisible and a visible world, both created and controlled by God. The natural world might exist only in the mind of God and still be *real* to Him; so why be concerned? What interested Emerson was the *moral purpose* of the external world. Why had God needed it? And how did it function in the divine plan?

Emerson thought he found an answer in reading Elizabeth Peabody's translation (still in manuscript) of G. Oegger's *The True Messiah*, a French work scarcely known today.[46] Through *language*, Oegger taught, objects minister to the mind.[47] While they might yield sensual gratification without being symbolized in words, language makes them vehicles of thought. "All language," Emerson declared in his lecture on "English Literature," "is a naming of invisible and spiritual things from visible things. . . .The use of the outer creation is to give us language for the beings and changes of the inward creation."[48]

For proof Emerson turns (with Oegger) to etymology. "Every word which is used to express a moral or intellectual fact, if traced to its root, is found to be borrowed from some corporeal or animal fact." Examples: *right* means *straight, wrong* means *twisted; transgression, crossing a line; supercilious, raising of the eyebrow;* and so on. Of course, the origin of many words has been lost, but Emerson hypothecates that every one started from man's using a physical detail (or "fact") to stand for a thought. Before one can express a thought or idea, he must find a symbol in nature, which he then names, thus using another layer of symbolism. Oegger says, "And but for these emblems furnished by Nature herself, the moral and metaphysical world would have remained entirely buried in the eternal abyss."

At this point Emerson also draws upon Swedenborg (by way of Sampson Reed), perhaps reinforced by reading *Sartor Resartus:* "It is not words only that are emblematic: it is things which are emblematic. Every fact in outward nature answers to some state of the mind and that state of the mind can only be described by presenting that natural fact as a picture." Notice how metaphors symbolize abstractions: "a fierce man is a lion; a brave man is a rock; a learned man is a torch." This is a prehistoric tendency: "As we go back in history, language becomes more picturesque, until its infancy, when it is all poetry . . . The eldest remains of the ancient nations are poems and fables."[49] This observation leads Emerson to remark that "Good writing and brilliant discourse are perpetual allegories." Here there are also echoes of Wordsworth's theory in his Preface to *Lyrical Ballads,* for Emerson finds piquancy in the metaphors of "a strong natural farmer or backwoodsman," as well as the folksy humor of Jack Downing. He can now refine his definition of *literature:*

> Now, man standing on the point betwixt spirit and matter and native of both elements, only knows in general that one re-presents the other; that the world is the mirror of the soul; and that it is his office to show this beautiful relation, to utter the oracles of the mind in appropriate images from nature. And *this is literature* [italics supplied]. In a limited sense, Literature, so far as it is pictures of thought, and excluding records of facts, is, the clothing of things of the mind in the things of matter.[50]

By "records of facts" Emerson meant science and history, though history also, he believed, shows a "still higher harmony of *events with Nature*"—a theory he would explore further in *Nature*. He sees literature and history as similar in function, the former giving *"voice to the whole of spiritual nature* as events and ages unfold it," while the latter records "in words the whole life of the world."[51] God unfolds His cosmic plan in world events, and both written history and imaginative literature record and interpret it.

Thus Emerson's theory of literature and history turns out to be theological, and also what is usually called "mystical": "The relation between thought and the world . . . is not fancied by some poet, but stands in the will of God, and so is free to be known by all men." He who does perceive it is a poet, or a philosopher—or even a historian. Emerson does not specifically explain why only a few become poets, but he implies that it is because the majority of men are too bound by custom to look at the world from an absolute, impersonal point of view. "Custom presents every thing as immoveably fixed. But the first effort of thought is to lift things from their feet and make all objects of sense appear fluent." We remember Emerson's saying that seeing the landscape from a moving train refuted materialism and made everything seem ideal. Now he mentions the excitement of looking at the shore from a ship or from a balloon (he had to imagine the latter). It is not only that this unfamiliar point of observation makes all things seem to flow into a whole, but, equally important, the observer feels detached from them.

The detachment is essential, and helps to explain why Emerson tried so hard to hold himself independent of society. "To break the chains of custom, to see everything as it *absolutely exists* [italics supplied], and so to clothe every thing ordinary and even sordid with beauty is the aim of the Thinker."[52] This was Emerson's personal goal. The "poetic vision" is "a state of mind" which one can attain by freeing himself from the despotism of his senses so that he can see the *truth* behind the images of things. He becomes a channel "through which streamlets from the infinite abyss of thought pass into the knowledge and use of men . . ." Borrowing a metaphor from the seventeenth-century British Neoplatonist Henry More, he says, "a river of thoughts is always running out of the invisible world into the mind of man."[53] Men who are receptive are poets; the more receptive, the more the poet.

None of the lectures that followed was so original and illuminating as Emerson's introduction. In interpreting Anglo-Saxon and Celtic poetry, and Chaucer, too, he relied too heavily on Thomas Wharton's *History of English Poetry,* not a reliable authority, and said nothing original. Even Shakespeare, whom he had read since childhood, he generalized as poet and philosopher, the "channel" of Divine Reason. He ranked Lord Bacon lower than Shakespeare because Bacon presented the objects of nature "under the agency of the Understanding." Shakespeare's mind was "coextensive with nature," whereas Bacon inventoried it. However, Bacon deserved praise for neglecting no phenomena, even "Natural Magic."[54]

Emerson was offended by the "barbarity of manners and depravity of morals" in the late Elizabethan and Jacobean dramas, but was not squeamish about Herrick's erotic imagery. He showed that the Muse "can tread with firm and elastic step in sordid places and take no more pollution than the sun-beam which shines alike on the carrion and the violet."[55] But Byron's moral faults caused him to waste his great poetic gifts. In fact, the only modern poet who satisfied Emerson was Coleridge, who had taught him to distinguish between reason and understanding, fancy and imagination, and the nature of poetry. Coleridge, in fact, inspired Emerson's closing exhortation: "Nature stretcheth out her arms to embrace man, only let his thoughts be of equal grandeur ... A virtuous man is in keeping with the works of Nature and makes the central figure in the visible sphere."[56]

V

After delivering his tenth lecture in Boston on "English Literature" on January 14, 1836, Emerson repeated them for several months in Salem, Cambridge, and Lowell. It was a severe winter, and the travel and exposure weakened him. On March 22 he recorded wearily in his Journal: "It is now four months that we have had uninterrupted sleighing in Concord; and today it snows fast."[57] He also had many cares and responsibilities. He was trying to remodel his house in preparation for Charles's marriage in the autumn. Lidian was pregnant and suffered more than ever from her chronic dyspepsia, making it difficult for her to convey his frequent instructions to the carpenters. He did not know that he was "hog reeve" for the village until someone's pig got loose and its owner called for his services. This appointment was a traditional initiation for all newly married men.[58] On top of all these responsibilities, he was elected a member of the School Board and was frequently consulted about school matters.

Emerson's greatest worry, however, was the health of his brother Charles.[59] The severe winter had sapped Charles's strength, and he seemed unable to throw off a cold which had left him with a racking cough. Though he now had a law office in Concord, he still pleaded cases in the Boston courts. From Salem, where Waldo was lecturing, he wrote Lidian on Tuesday, April 19, about his concern for Charles. He hoped he could persuade Charles to suspend his law practice and visit William in milder New York. By Thursday morning he was so anxious that he made a hasty voyage to Boston, a twenty-five-mile trip each way, to see for himself how ill his brother was. That afternoon, back in Salem, he wrote Lidian that he found Charles "too feeble to go alone [to New York]. I have therefore returned this P.M. to Salem, & there obtained liberty to postpone the rest of my lectures." He intended next day to start out with Charles on the train to Worcester, and as soon as his strength permitted they would proceed by stage to New Haven, where they would take a boat to New York. Waldo apologized to Lidian for leaving her alone "at this time when so many things are to be considered & done."[60]

Saturday was a "raw chill day," but after a rest in Springfield the brothers continued their journey. "I fear," Waldo wrote Lidian, "I shall not feel any love of my fatherland until Charles's cough is relieved." However, it did seem a little better, and Dr. Jackson (the same doctor who had given hope about Ellen's condition, though he may have known she was doomed) thought that Charles had only a "catarrh." In Springfield Waldo wrote William to announce their coming: "I can ill spare the time for this journey though I am to see you but I could worse spare Charles. So tell Mother we must get him well instantly & give my love to Susan & to my nephew whom I hope shortly to see."[61]

After spending a night in New York, Waldo rushed back to Concord. Lidian had written to New York to tell him that Dr. Ripley's assistant, the Reverend Hersy Goodwin, was ill, and Waldo was requested to preach in his place on Sunday. He was also asked to substitute for Goodwin at the "teachers' meeting." Probably Emerson declined the latter request, for on Monday he returned to Salem in time to give his second lecture. From

Salem next day he wrote William of still another misfortune: Bulkeley was so deranged he had had to be confined once more in the McLean Asylum in Charlestown.[62]

On Wednesday Emerson received a letter from William saying that Charles was worse and should be taken farther south. Next day Waldo wrote this news to Lidian and told her he felt he must return to New York as quickly as possible. But he could not leave Salem immediately because the Reverend Upham was ill and he had promised to preach for him on Sunday. He would leave for Boston immediately after the sermon in order to be able to start for New York Monday morning; consequently he could not go to Concord. He hoped she might wait for him in Boston at the home of her brother, Dr. Charles Jackson, but if she could not he would not complain.[63]

In Boston Emerson found a letter from William reporting that Charles's health was declining so rapidly that he could not live much longer. Waldo then decided to return to Concord and invite Elizabeth Hoar to accompany him, but about the time they left Concord Charles died in New York. Wednesday morning Waldo wrote Lidian: "Charles died Monday afternoon instantly after returning from a ride with Mother—fainted & did not recover—Elizabeth sits with his body and is soothed by the repose of his face. The funeral is this afternoon [May 11]. And this is all I have to say with my love to you." As we have seen before, Emerson was always spare of words when deeply moved.

Since it was not practical at that time to bring Charles's body back to Concord, it was placed in the tomb of a Mr. Griswold, friend of Susan's. Before it could be moved, someone removed the nameplate on the casket and destroyed the identification, so that Charles's remains never were returned to Concord.

After the funeral Waldo wrote Lidian their plans for returning. They would take the boat to New Haven Thursday afternoon, bringing Waldo's mother with them. She, like Elizabeth, was bearing her sorrow with stoic calm, as she always had. Waldo wondered whether he would find Lidian waiting for him in Boston, or at home preparing to receive them on Saturday. He must have known that she would be apprehensive about having her mother-in-law live with her. He said it was unimportant whether she greeted them in Boston or Concord, "Only I wish Mother to sit down as gently & wontedly in her chamber in your house, as if she had never been in any other."[64] However, this message did not reach Lidian until after her mother-in-law's arrival, having failed to catch the steamboat mail Waldo intended. "I was sorry," he wrote William, "for it was written to apprise her of Mother's return so that she might dismiss her friend [and housemaid] Miss Bartlett, who is a stranger to Mother. It is of small importance only as it mortifies Miss B. to be still here."[65] Apparently, relations with Waldo's mother could be prickly.

Possibly, in his letter to Lidian, Waldo was trying tactfully to keep her from feeling displaced in domestic authority; but his tone also rather intimated that she should be willing to share *her* house with *his* mother. That there would be some friction was almost inevitable, though Mother Emerson appears to have kept to her room and tried to avoid upsetting Lidian's domestic routine, and in turn her own privacy was respected. Writing many years later in a personal account of her mother's life, Ellen Emerson called the relationship an armed truce, scrupulously observed by both sides.

Lidian had been almost as fond of Charles as she was of Waldo, and she liked Elizabeth so much that she began treating her like an adopted daughter. On her return from New York Elizabeth spent one night with her mother and then took up temporary residence with the Emersons. Her presence gave mutual consolation. In writing Lidian from William's home, Waldo had confessed another reason from the one he had given before his marriage for his wanting to settle in Concord, though apparently it was not new to Lidian, for he said, "as you know, because he was there . . ." Now Waldo felt "not only unfastened there and adrift but a sort of shame at living at all." He warned his wife that she "must be content henceforth with only a piece of your husband; for the best of his strength lay in the soul with which he must now no more on earth take counsel. How much I saw through his eyes."

The truth of this statement can be partly verified by reading Emerson's Journal for the previous few months. He had often quoted Charles and tested his own ideas on his brother's judgment. During the last weeks of their life together in Concord they read one of Plato's dialogues and Sophocles' *Electra* in Greek, or rather, as Waldo confessed in a letter to Miss Martineau, "more properly, [he read] *to* me . . ."[66] But it was Charles's companionship, his presence and understanding, that Waldo missed most. In his early manhood he had speculated on the theme of *friendship,* which he could not separate from *love,* and now he realized that he had had "a brother and friend in one."[67]

In going through Charles's papers with Elizabeth, Waldo was surprised to find that, for all his brother's scorn of keeping a journal, he had made diary notations on loose sheets of paper. In reading these pages and the letters he had written Elizabeth, Waldo discovered a side of Charles he had not known, a "nocturnal side ... melancholy, penitential, self-accusing." If he had been more attentive and sensitive, he would have been aware of this side of his brother long before. While walking with him the previous November, Charles had called life "an *amabilis insania,*" and said he saw no reason "why the world should not burn up tonight. The play had been over, some time."[68] Did he mean himself or mankind? This remark may have startled Waldo at the time, but it evidently did not enlighten him. Now, however, the full extent of Charles's despair became known to him.

Charles's private thoughts also raised some doubt as to whether he really wanted to live and marry Elizabeth in September. Waldo did not express this suspicion in his own Journal, but he did note that "He could not bear to think that he should degenerate into a householder & lead the base life"[69]—a thought Waldo had likewise recorded of himself before his second marriage. Charles had asked Elizabeth:

> What is it we seek each in the other?—to enter into a community of being, giving & receiving the freedom of each other's immortal part. If the cares & endearments of earthly marriage cause us to lose sight of this its highest end, & dull in us the perception of this its purest happiness, let us go mourning, let us live alone on the mountains, & bewail our virginity.[70]

In one of her letters, written the previous year, Elizabeth had expressed an exalted anticipation of her marriage:

> You ask if I miss you? I do not know that I miss you because you are in Concord, or in Lincoln. I miss you always so far as anything within us or without us removes [us] from one another. Yes, I miss you, dearest, as I miss the summer whilst it has not yet come, the flower that has not yet opened, the morning that has not yet fully dawned on my waiting eyes; I miss you as I miss the great Future for which I hope, the virtue I have not yet domesticated, the happiness I have not yet deserved.

Waldo Emerson could understand such longing for supernal beauty and happiness. Some of Elizabeth's premonitions resembled Ellen's when she doubted that earthly marriage was possible for her. These feelings may, to some extent, have been reflections of the sentimental culture of the 1830s, but they were unmistakably characteristic of the women who attracted the Emerson brothers. One is reminded of the similar psychology of John Keats when he wrote of the "unravished bride" on the Grecian urn: "Bold Lover, never, never canst thou kiss, / Though winning near the goal—yet, do not grieve: / She cannot fade, though thou hast not thy bliss, / For ever wilt thou love, and she be fair!"

Some such consolation as this enabled Elizabeth Hoar to bear her loss, which now seemed immortalized in her never-to-be-consummated marriage. She would never marry, would take deep satisfaction in being "Aunt Lizzie" to the Emerson children, and Waldo would find in her friendship a constant bittersweet reminder of the remarkable brother he had once had. Keats had written his poem while he was physically doomed by the same disease which had afflicted Ellen and Charles, and his aesthetic theory of sublimated anticipation found confirmation in the experience of both Waldo Emerson and his unmarried "sister-in-law."

CHAPTER XIII

Waking the Giant

The generic soul in each individual is a giant
overcome with sleep . . .

—Emerson

Sometimes I wake from the slumber of the
body to return to myself . . .[1]

—Plotinus

I

"I find myself slowly, after this helpless morning," Emerson confessed in his Journal on May 19, 1836.[2] It was like waking up from a numbing slumber. Normal feeling began to return, and familiar objects to become substantial again. He remembered forgotten states of mind, some of them forgotten before Charles's death, like "the native mountains whose tops reappear after we have traversed many a mile of weary region from home."

In this new mood Emerson turned his thoughts to living persons who in the past had enriched his life: Peter Hunt, his former student; Tarbox, the farmhand who had given him the theme for his first sermon; Mary Rotch, the Quaker in New Bedford; Sampson Reed, the Swedenborgian; and Bronson Alcott, his Platonist friend. "They are to me what the Wanderer in the Excursion is to the poet. And Wordsworth's total value is of this kind. They are described in the lines at the end of the 'Yarrow Revisited.' " (Emerson had in mind these lines: "Dear to the common sunshine, / And dearer still, as now I feel, / To memory's shadowy moonshine!") He would not forget them, or Charles, in "dream-light," but he was now ready to live in sunshine again. At the bottom of the page he wrote: "Here end my extracts from the letters of my brother Charles."

He had hoped to publish a collection of Charles's writings, but when later in the summer his brother's friends lined up a publisher for the book, Waldo was embarrassed, because, as he wrote William, "I do not think

Charles has left any bulk of papers that are now fit to publish: nor would he thank me for so doing."[3] However, a few years later he would decide to publish a few selections in *The Dial*.[4]

Of course, Emerson could not overcome his grief by willpower, but his effort was aided by his usual revulsion against suffering. His own instincts, as in the past, came to his rescue. On June 7 he wrote in his Journal that he had received many letters from friends who had loved Charles, adding, "I know not why it is, but a letter is scarcely welcome to me. I expect to be lacerated by it & if I come safe to the end of it, I feel like one escaped."[5]

Emerson's most successful escape was, as the Romantic poets had taught him, in the "healing influence of nature." He continued his solitary walks in the woods, now especially around Walden Pond. "What learned I this morning in the woods[,] the oracular woods?" he asked himself on June 14.[6] He could sympathize with the pagans who worshiped nymphs and nature deities. A few days later he declared, "I love the wood god. I love the mighty PAN."

Though it is difficult to imagine Emerson's worshiping the Greek god of fertility, it is easy to understand his mood. He had always enjoyed his strolls in the fields and forests, and now he *spiritualized* them more than ever. On June 21 he recorded:

> Yesterday I walked in the storm. And truly in the fields I am not alone or unacknowledged. They nod to me & I to them. The waving of the boughs of trees in a storm is new to me & old. It takes me by surprise & yet is not unknown. Its effect is like that of a higher thought or a better emotion coming over me when I deemed I was thinking justly or doing right. We distrust & deny inwardly our own sympathy with nature. . . .[7]

In the woods Emerson felt detached from his pain and grief. In this state of mind the idea that "Nature is the projection of God . . . the expositor of the Divine Mind" seemed no longer an idea, a mere abstraction, but a reality. He felt exhilarated, at times almost ecstatic. In fact, since the emotion carried intellectual conviction, he was a mystic, not of the extreme visionary type, but like Wordsworth at Tintern Abbey. However, he was at the same time as strongly influenced by his reading of the Neoplatonists and Coleridge as by his own emotional experiences. Coleridge, for example, in his *Aids to Reflection,* had convinced him that "every object rightly seen unlocks a new faculty of the Soul," which he interpreted to mean, "a part of the domain of Consciousness; before it was unconscious truth, now is available Knowledge."[8]

To appreciate the importance of this doctrine to Emerson, we need to trace in rough outline his concept of *soul*. He had grown up with the Christian belief in the dualism of body and soul; that the physical body dies but the soul lives eternally in heaven or hell. Though the soul was said to be immaterial, it was nearly always envisioned as an apparitional likeness of the human body. By early manhood Emerson doubted heaven and hell as places; yet at the time of Ellen's death he still, as we have seen, hoped to join her in the spirit world, and thought they would be able to recognize each other. He had tried to communicate with her "soul" by prayer and mental telepathy, but without success. At times he thought of her as his guardian angel, who could somehow watch over him and insinuate into his consciousness beneficent impulses, even ideas.

But gradually, as Emerson recovered his mental equilibrium, his concept of the life of the soul gave way—or expanded—to a more general and abstract belief in a universal soul, or spirit, permeating and giving life to the whole cosmos. Emotionally, like Wordsworth, in the world of nature he experienced "A presence that disturbs me with the joy / Of elevated thoughts; a sense sublime / Of something far more deeply interfused . . ."

At times during this period Emerson seemed to use "soul" to mean conscience, but he extended his concept of soul as he became a more deeply confirmed philosophical Idealist. He was attracted by the Platonic theory that everything exists in a Universal Mind or Soul, and that the world of nature is only a reflection or weaker copy of the forms or "ideas" in the One Mind. Thus the laws of nature are really the laws of spirit.

In addition to soul's meaning mind or consciousness, at times Emerson seemed to specialize it to mean a reservoir of psychic energy which the human mind could tap, or draw upon, though it seldom did:

> The generic soul in each individual is a giant overcome with sleep which locks up almost all his senses, & only leaves him a little superficial animation. Once in an age at hearing some deeper voice, he lifts his iron lids, & his eyes straight pierce through all appearances, & his tongue tells what shall be in the latest times: then is he obeyed like a God, but quickly the lids fall, & sleep returns.[9]

Henceforth Emerson's greatest ambition in lecturing and writing would be to awaken this sleeping giant. Like Alcott, he became almost a man of one idea—and of the same idea as Alcott's.

On June 22 Emerson recorded that "Mr Alcott has been here with his Olympian dreams. He is a world-builder."[10] Alcott was no world-builder in any ordinary sense, but a visionary Olympian certainly. "Ever more he toils to solve the problem, Whence is the world?" His solution was Neo-platonic, and Emerson understood him because he, too, had been reading Plotinus, who taught that there were levels of existence transcending the world of sense. Plotinus argued that the world of sense (or nature) depended for its existence upon superior realities, which gave it unity and a rational structure.[11]

In the realm of "soul" Plotinus distinguished a World Soul and individual souls. Individual souls aspired to reunion with the One from which they came, but they were hindered by the downward pull of the material world. The individual soul could rise to this union only by turning inward, away from the world of sense, appetite, and human ambitions. Though Plotinus did not ignore social responsibilities in the material world, his doctrines, like those of all mystics, encouraged withdrawal and asceticism. Though Emerson had by now rejected Christian dogma, which denounced sensualism and advocated self-denial, during his youth he had been so thoroughly oriented in the dualism of flesh and spirit, with a bias against the flesh, that he almost by reflex distrusted the appetites of his own body.

Neoplatonism also provided Emerson with a substitute for "original sin." Scorning the "fall of Adam" as bad myth, he nevertheless accepted the Plotinian "fall," and found in it a central theme for his lay preaching. Suddenly in his Journal, after regretting that "We distrust . . . our own sympathy with nature," he produces this startling passage:

Man is the dwarf of himself[.] Is it not true that spirit in us is dwarfed by clay? that once Man was permeated & dissolved by spirit? He filled Nature with his overflowing currents. Out from him sprang the sun & moon[,] from man the sun[,] from woman the moon. The laws of his mind[,] the periods of his deeds externized themselves into day & night[,] into the year & seasons. But having made for himself this vast shell, the waters retired, he no longer fills its veins & veinlets, he is shrunk into a drop. He sees it still fits him but fits him colossaly [*sic*]. He adores timidly his own work. Say rather once it fitted him[;] now it corresponds to him from far & on high. Yet now he starts occasionally in his slumber & wonders at himself & his house & muses strangely at the resemblance between him & it. If now he have power . . . he sees that it is unconscious power; power superior to his will; or Instinct[.][12]

Emerson may have been, as some critics have thought, quoting his friend Alcott, but he was also adapting, whether directly from Neoplatonism or indirectly through his "Olympian" friend, the doctrine of Proclus that out of man sprang the sun and moon, and a passage in Plotinus's *Enneads:*

Each soul should first remember that it was she who by an infusion of the spirit of life produced all the animals on earth, in the air, and in the sea as well as the divine stars, the sun, and the immense heaven [sky]. It was she that introduced order into the heaven and produces its regular revolutions. She does all that, while yet remaining distinct from the things to whom she communicates form, movement, and life. She is necessarily far superior to them. While they are born or die in the measure that she imparts to them or withdraws from them their life, she herself exists eternally because she remains identical with herself. To understand how life is imparted to the universe and to each individual, the soul must rise to the contemplation of the great soul, the world soul.[13]

There are many ambiguities in this soul doctrine, especially in the soul's limitations, or forgetfulness: like the human mind it *rises* or *falls* by resisting or succumbing to physical attractions. "Our soul," says Plotinus, "is of the same kind as the world soul which animates the deities." Yet to attain equal rank with the world soul, the individual soul needs to be stripped of "all the things that have infested her" in order to restore her "pristine purity." Who does the stripping if not the mind of the body she inhabits?—or mind infected by the body. Though Plotinus does not say this, he does say, "Since the soul is such a divine and precious thing, be assured that you will be able to reach the divinity with the help of such a power and begin your ascent." Here "you" is not the soul, but the person Plotinus addresses. It seems, therefore, that "you" can help your soul in her (and your) redemption.

But how can man help himself outgrow his dwarfhood, his present *ruined* condition; or, to change the metaphor, *recover* his "unconscious power"? Emerson's answer owes more to Coleridge than to Plotinus: "Now [at the present time] all man's power over nature is by the understanding; as by manure, steam, the economic use of the wind & water & needle, coal, filling teeth with gold; making wooden legs . . ."[14] In his earlier lecture on science Emerson had shown that he was not opposed to such uses of nature; yet they recover man's lost world "an inch at a time," not by "a resumption of power by vaulting at once into his seat." What is wanted is "an instantaneous in-streaming causing power." This can be obtained by the use of Reason—that part, or faculty, of the human mind most Godlike. But as examples of this *vaulting* Emerson can think only of "Animal Magnetism" and the miracles of such enthusiasts as Prince Alexander Hohenlohe (German practitioner of prayer cure), the Shakers, and the Swedenborgians—all sometimes scorned by Emerson in his more rational moods. However, he also mentions achieving "a principle in Revolutions" and "abolition of the Slave Trade." In these social reforms Reason has been discovered. Reason also favors philosophical Idealism:

> It is essential to a true theory of nature & man, that it should contain somewhat progressive, should ascribe freedom to the will, or benevolent designs to the Deity. And the effect of the ideal theory truly seen is this; Nature is not stable but fluid. Spirit alters, moulds, makes it. The immobility or bruteness of nature is the absence of spirit; to pure spirit it is fluid, it is volatile, it is obedient. Believe that the world exists for you. For you is the phenomenon perfect & what we are, that only we see. All that Adam had, all that Caesar could, you have & can do. Adam called it the earth, Caesar called life Rome; you perhaps call it a cob[b]ler's trade, yet line for line & point for point, you have the whole circle. As fast as your spirit quits its earth, disagreeable appearances, prisons, spiders, snakes, pests, madhouses, vanish; they are temporary & shall be no more seen. . . .[15]

To common sense this thought power may seem like irresponsible lunacy, and in *Nature* Emerson may seem to desert rationality when he says, "Build therefore your own world."[16] But he is speaking metaphorically and not literally. And when he predicts a "Second Coming," or millennium, he envisions a moral utopia which he thinks attainable if Reason could rule men's lives: "This kingdom of man over nature which shall not come with observation, a dominion such as now is beyond his dream of God, he shall enter without more wonder than the blind man feels who is gradually restored to perfect sight."[17]

One comment may be ventured on this apocalyptic prophecy. In spite of the marvels of twentieth-century science, it still seems doubtful that the empirical method alone can provide a "heaven on earth." So far it seems only to have increased prisons, madhouses, diseases caused by industrial pollution, and other evils. Emerson may have been right that a "Spiritual" view could lead to a more fruitful comprehension of man's place in nature, and wiser use of natural resources. His "Ideal Theory," therefore, pleads not for escape from material realities into a visionary world, but for moral reform. Chateaubriand and others, he noted, have seen in the beauties of nature a display of God's imagination. "Yet see how far man is at discord with nature[,] for you cannot at the same time admire the prospect, & sympathize with Wyman & Tuttle [farmers in Concord] who are digging in the field."[18] In other words, no matter how much one sentimentalizes over the landscape, he is not in harmony with nature unless his empathy extends to the toiling men who are in the landscape also and a part of nature.

II

The book in Emerson's head which gave him pleasure to contemplate while he sailed back to America in September 1833 remained only a tantalizing ambition for nearly three years, though from time to time he worked around the edges of it. Two months after his return, in his lecture on "The Uses of Natural History," he declared that in his judgment the "greatest office of natural science . . . [is] to explain man to himself."[19] But he admitted that "there yet remain questions of the highest interest which are unsolved," and he himself had to wait for knowledge and to discover how to present it before writing his book. His intention was clear, but the means still cloudy. In another lecture the following January, he pointed out the preparations God had made for man before the globe was fit for his habitation.[20] That there was an intelligent purpose and design in nature he had never doubted since studying natural religion at Harvard. In still another lecture in January 1833 he declared that natural history has no value unless related to human history.

In March 1835 Emerson thought he would like to write a book resembling William Howitt's *Seasons,* containing the "Natural History of the woods around my shifting camp for every month in the year."[21] Henry Thoreau would write a book of this sort a few years later, but Emerson had never camped in the woods; he was merely fantasizing. What he really wanted to write was a book "on spiritual things,"[22] and by June he was referring to it as "a book of Essays chiefly upon Natural Ethics."[23] In January 1836 he began his Introduction, exhorting his readers to stop building sepulchers for their fathers and "behold the Universe as new and feel that we have a stake [in it] as much as our predecessors." In May he was still trying to outline the book. Then he began to break the logjam.

On June 24 he was revising the last paragraph of his last chapter, stressing that a "true theory of man ... should contain something progressive."[24] Four days later he wrote William: "My little book is nearly done."[25] In bulk it would not exceed Sampson Reed's *Growth of the Mind* (forty-four pages; though Emerson's book actually more than doubled that number). "My design is to follow it by and by with another essay, 'Spirit'; and the two shall make a decent volume." He apparently realized that he had not satisfactorily explained the relation of spirit and matter, or mind and body. After he had nearly completed his revision he confided to William, "There is, as always, one crack in it not easy to be soldered, or welded, but if this week I should be left alone after the probate affair [probate of Charles's will] I may finish it."[26]

During the summer Emerson arranged with James Munroe and Company in Boston to print a thousand copies for a little over a hundred dollars. He did not expect to make any profit on the first edition and told William that "if it attain to a second edition the success should be profit enow."[27] The book was advertised for sale on September 9, and Emerson began sending copies to his friends. To Carlyle he wrote on September 17: "I send you a little book I have just now published, as an entering wedge, I hope, for something more worthy and significant. This is only a naming of topics on which I would gladly speak and gladlier hear."[28]

Nature was a small volume (12*mo*) of ninety-five pages, bound in brown cloth.[29] The title page did not bear the name of the author, but carried this epigraph: "Nature is but an image or imitation of wisdom, the last thing of the soul; nature being a thing which doth only do, but not know. PLO-TINUS." The Contents listed eight chapters after the Introduction: "Na-ture," "Commodity," "Beauty," "Language," "Discipline," "Idealism," "Spirit," and "Prospects." The Introduction explained:

> Philosophically considered, the universe is composed of Nature and the Soul. Strictly speaking, therefore, all that is separate from us, all which Philosophy distinguishes as the NOT ME, that is, both nature and art, all other men and my own body, must be ranked under the name, NATURE. In enumerating the values of nature and casting up their sum, I shall use the word in both senses;—in its common and in its philosophical import. In inquiries so general as our present one, the inaccuracy is not material; no confusion of thought will occur. *Nature,* in the common sense, refers to essences unchanged by man; space, the air, the river, the leaf. . . .[30]

What Emerson called "chapters" are really only divisions of his subject such as he had used in his sermons. Each would be developed more fully in future addresses, essays, and books; hence, feeling the inadequacy of the treatment, he referred to them apologetically as "only a naming of topics."[31] Nevertheless, his scheme was based on a strategy—or two strate-gies: one, illustrating the relation of matter to spirit by tracing a hierarchy in the uses of nature; and, at the same time, enabling the reader to partici-pate in the unfolding of the author's thought, *feeling* it as well as follow-ing the argument. To do this, Emerson used the language not of philosophy but of poetry. The anonymous critic was right who called the little book a "prose poem."[32] This subtle method also illustrates the spiral evolution which Emerson saw as the natural process, in which all living things are climbing a ladder to the divine. In the second edition (1849) he would discard the epigraph for these verses inspired by Plotinus:

> A subtle chain of countless rings
> The next unto the farthest brings;
> The eye reads omens where it goes,
> And speaks all languages the rose;
> And, striving to be man, the worm
> Mounts through all the spires of form.[33]

In Chapter I, Emerson demonstrates "the integrity of impression made by manifold natural objects," when one's inward and outward senses are truly adjusted to each other. The process is dialectical, just as negative and positive poles in the magnet produce an electrical current (though Emerson used this analogy later). To the poetic mind this "intercourse with heaven and earth, becomes part of his daily food." He feels a "wild delight" in the presence of nature.

This wild delight resembles what is often called a "mystical experience":

Crossing a bare common, in snow puddles, at twilight, under a clouded sky, without having in my thoughts any occurrence of special good fortune, I have enjoyed a perfect exhilaration. Almost I fear to think how glad I am . . . Standing on the bare ground,—my head bathed by the blithe air, and uplifted into infinite space,—all mean egotism vanishes. I become a transparent eye-ball. I am nothing. I see all. The currents of the Universal Being circulate through me; I am part or particle of God. The name of the nearest friend sounds then foreign and accidental. To be brothers, to be acquaintances,—master or servant, is then a trifle and a disturbance. I am the lover of uncontained and immortal beauty. . . .[34]

This description has all the essentials of William James's famous definition of the "mystical experience" in *Varieties of Religious Experience* (XVI): the sudden compelling exhilaration; the shrinking and, paradoxically, at the same time expanding of the ego—"nothing," yet "particle of God"; the vanishing of worldly distinctions and attractions; and the vision of "immortal beauty" (for some mystics it is love, for others compassion, or wisdom).

As early as Latin School, Emerson had written a theme on astronomy after looking at the stars one night while crossing the Boston Common, then an open expanse.[35] Perhaps he remembered that early experience when he recalled on December 8, 1834: "I do not cross the common without a wild poetic delight notwithstanding the prose of my demeanour."[36] The following March 19: "Standing on the bare ground with my head bathed by the blithe air, & uplifted into the infinite space, I become happy in my universal relations."[37] Doubtless the emotion was genuine, giving Emerson the sensation of being elevated above the everyday concerns of life; and each time he redescribed his "occult" experience he improved the language and rhetoric, until he produced the marvelous poetic-prose description in *Nature.*

One critic[38] has ridiculed the "eye-ball" metaphor, and any unsympathetic reader can easily turn it to satire, as Christopher Cranch did in his caricatures.[39] Hyperbole is common in mystical writings. Emerson used extravagant imagery not only to describe the ineffable but also deliberately to shock and impress. As a "transparent eye-ball" he *sees* inwardly and outwardly simultaneously, and becomes a passive conductor of the "currents of the Universal Being." (James also says passivity is one of the characteristics of the mystical experience.[40])

In the next four chapters Emerson explains the uses of nature. As a Commodity, "Nature, in its ministry to man, is not only the material, but is also the process and the result."[41] On the lowest level, nature supplies man's physical needs, but on a higher level it gives him sensations which teach him the meaning of beauty, which has more than one face: "Truth, and goodness, and beauty, are but different faces of the same All."[42]

Things are also emblematic of the Spirit or Soul that creates and sustains them. In "Language" Emerson elaborates the theory which he had borrowed from Oegger. This is the longest chapter in *Nature,* and Emerson needed to write it to aid his own self-development. The argument is now too familiar to need detailed exposition: natural objects are but symbols of archetypes preexisting in the mind of God, "and are what they are by virtue of preceding affections in the world of spirit. . . . The visible creation is the terminus or the circumference of the invisible world."[43] It is also part of the divine plan for man that nature should discipline his "understanding in intellectual truths." Properly disciplined, the understanding becomes "the Hand of the mind,"[44] able to manipulate things for spiritual purposes.

Nature pardons no mistakes; her "dice are always loaded."[45] Against her winning numbers man gambles at his peril, but by trusting in nature he can assure his own success. "The exercise of the Will or the lesson of power is taught in every event."[46] Sensible objects also "conform to the premonitions of Reason and reflect the conscience."

The major *premonition* is the unity of all creation, "Unity in Variety." Here, in addition to the Neoplatonic influence, Emerson is also indebted to Goethe's transformation theory in *The Metamorphosis of Plants.*[47] The German poet's observations of plants convinced him that the *Urpflanze* was a leaf: "When leaves divide, or rather when they advance from their original state to diversity, they are striving toward greater perfection, in the sense that each leaf has the intention of becoming a branch, and each branch a tree."[48] In this process Goethe saw the "godhead" at work. He also used the Kantian terms, which Emerson had learned earlier from Coleridge: ". . . reason in its [the plant's] strivings toward the divine, is concerned with growth and life, whereas understanding is concerned with putting to use what has already developed and grown torpid."[49] Though there are some differences between Goethe's and Emerson's expression of this theory, both see universal *likeness* in nature caused by the pulsing life of the "universal Spirit."

However, in the ending of his chapter on "Discipline" Emerson is more Plotinian than Goethean. He thinks the human form is the highest organization in nature, and all others only degradations of it. This doctrine goes back to the Plotinian myth of man's creating all the animals of the world out of himself, mentioned above. Emerson now finds a personal application for his theory of man's divine origin: sometimes God gives one a friend who is "a standard of excellence." When this happens, and the friend's character has been "converted in the mind into solid and sweet wisdom,—it is a sign to us that his office is closing, and he is commonly withdrawn from our sight in a short time."[50] Emerson was no doubt thinking of his late brother Charles. But what has this to do with the argument of *Nature?* Only that in Emerson's opinion nothing finite can be perfect, and as it nears perfection it becomes *spiritual* to the vanishing point of its materiality.

This thought provides a transition to "Idealism." Emerson admits his "utter impotence to test the authority of the report of my senses," but anticipates the Pragmatism of William James in this simple solution: "Whether nature enjoy a substantial existence without, or is only in the apocalypse of the mind, it is alike useful and alike venerable to me. Be it what it may, it is ideal to me, so long as I cannot try the accuracy of my senses."[51] The senses have "a sort of instinctive belief in the absolute existence of nature."[52] This is the "Common Sense" view of the Scottish philosophers, once Emerson's favorites, such as Dugald Stewart, Thomas Brown, and the rhetoricians Lord Kames and Hugh Blair. But "The presence of Reason mars this faith," making "outlines and surfaces become transparent," so that causes and spirits are seen through them, and "Nature is made to conspire with spirit to emancipate us."[53] Rephrasing his theory of language and poetry given in the lecture on "English Literature," he epigrammatizes: "The sensual man conforms thoughts to things; the poet conforms things to his thoughts,"[54] which is to say objects become transformed in the passion of the poet.

Here is the very core of Emerson's "Transcendentalism." Fastening his attention upon "immortal necessary uncreated natures"—that is, upon ideas—in "their beautiful and majestic presence" he feels that his outward life "is a dream and a shade."[55] Nature is now only "an appendix to the soul." By his imagination (though Emerson would prefer the word *Reason*) he ascends to "the thoughts of the Supreme Being." However, he loves the material world too much to fling stones at his beautiful mother. Unlike some of the Neoplatonists ("Plotinus was ashamed of his body"[56] because it was not spirit), Emerson does not want to escape from the material world into a completely spiritual one. It is better, he says, to look upon external beauty as Michelangelo did, as "the frail and weary weed, in which God dresses the soul, which he has called into time."[57]

An important advantage "in the ideal theory over the common faith" (that is, naive confidence in the report of the senses) is that "it presents the world in precisely that view which is most desirable to the mind." The mind sees the world as phenomenal, which virtue subordinates to the mind.[58] "Idealism sees the world in God." This statement proves that Emerson was not, as he was already being accused of being, a pantheist, who sees *God in the world.* From the ideal view, the mind (Emerson writes "soul") does not concern itself with the trivia of the Christian disputes over miracles, persons (was Jesus divine?), or "the niceties of [higher] criticism."[59] It is sufficient to look upon the visible world as "one vast picture, which God paints on the instant eternity, for the contemplation of the soul."

The next chapter, on "Spirit," may at first seem superfluous, for it continues the argument that "the noblest ministry of nature is to stand as the apparition of God." However, pure Idealism does not satisfy Emerson, because "It leaves God out of me."[60] The mind is also a part of nature, and "many truths arise to us out of the recesses of consciousness."[61] The Supreme Being, therefore, "does not build up nature around us, but puts it forth through us, as the life of the tree puts forth new branches and leaves

through the pores of the old." This process gives man access to the mind
of the Creator, and makes him a collaborator:

> The world proceeds from the same spirit as the body of man. It is a re-
> moter and inferior incarnation of God, a projection of God in the uncon-
> scious. But it differs from the body in one important respect. It is not, like
> that, now subjected to the human will. Its serene order is inviolable by us.
> It is therefore, to us, the present expositor of the divine mind. . . .[62]

Elsewhere Emerson would suggest that the unconscious is the doorway
to God.[63] How the unconscious affects human productions he had discussed in his lecture on "Art." Since college he had been reading the
seventeenth-century Neoplatonist Ralph Cudworth,[64] who thought the
soul derived energy from an unconscious source, which tied the soul to
the body. Emerson does not carry this thought further in *Nature,* but proceeds instead to consider human degeneration as the result of the "discord
. . . between man and nature." But his proof that we "are as much strangers in nature, as we are aliens from God" sounds more apocalyptic than
philosophical: "We do not understand the notes of birds. The fox and the
deer run away from us . . . We do not know the uses of more than a few
plants . . . ," and so on.[65]

The ideal concord implied in this indictment of *fallen man* reminds one
of the allegorical "Peaceable Kingdom" painted by the "primitive"
American artist Edward Hicks to illustrate Isaiah's prophecy (Isaiah 11:6)
of the restoration of Israel, when "The wolf also shall dwell with the lamb,
and the leopard shall lie down with the kid . . ." Indeed, in his final chapter Emerson also has his "Orphic poet," as we have seen, prophesy such a
"Second Coming," when man ceases to work upon nature with his understanding alone and learns to use his Reason. But Emerson ends "Spirit"
with an ambiguous poet who "finds something ridiculous in his delight,
until he is out of the sight of men." Is this because man has degenerated
so much? Or does this poet (not the "certain poet") not realize that man
is a part of nature? Or is there a conflict between enjoyment and exploita-
tion of nature? Whatever Emerson's intended meaning, this ending for
the chapter on "Spirit" is unsatisfactory.

The final chapter, on "Prospects," recapitulates the "relation between
things and thoughts" and the artist's copying the "invisible archetype" in
his images of material objects. The "certain poet" who sang that "The

foundations of man are not in matter, but in spirit" could have been, as remarked earlier of the Journal passage, himself or Bronson Alcott, or Plotinus, who taught this doctrine to both. But whatever Emerson's source, the important question is: How can puny man mend his world and unite himself again with his spiritual source? This question Emerson would continue trying to answer for years to come.

Soon after *Nature* was published it began to receive both praise and blame. Bronson Alcott called it "a gem throughout."[66] Samuel Osgood rejoiced that "a poetry of Nature, truly Christian is springing up amongst us."[67] Carlyle's calling it "the Foundation and Ground-plan"[68] on which Emerson could build his future thinking and writing was a true prophecy. The British Swedenborgian Jonathan Bayley thought that if the author was not a member of the New Church, he had read Swedenborg; his mind was imbued with the Swedenborgian truths.[69] But Francis Bowen, professor of philosophy at Harvard, found it confused, illogical, and lacking in sound principles.[70] He did not object to Idealism as a philosophy, but to the substitution of intuition and whim for systematic investigation in the search for truth. The Transcendentalists, he said, "profess to look not only beyond facts, but without the aid of facts, to principles."[71] No sympathy could be expected from a man who regarded Franklin as a better model than Plato for American "philosophical character."

The identity of the author of *Nature* was soon discovered in Boston, but the content apparently baffled more readers than it informed. Margaret Fuller wrote Emerson on September 21 that she heard "much conversation about it that amuses me."[72] But whether favorably or unfavorably, it was correctly regarded as a manifesto. Emerson himself, however, was not satisfied with his little book, and called it a mere "multiplication table" when a friend complained that it lacked connection. Actually *Nature* is deficient in conventional transitions, but has its own structural and stylistic coherence. The flowing images and details imply rather than state explicitly, and have a logic of their own.

Emerson thought well enough of his first book to give away about seventy-five copies, and he was pleased to learn a month after publication (though the report was exaggerated) that five hundred copies had been sold.[73] Considering the kind of book it was, this was not failure. But he did not revise or reprint the book until 1849, after he had published other books which filled out the topics named in *Nature*.

III

While finishing *Nature* Emerson finally became personally acquainted with Margaret Fuller, a remarkable young woman seven years his junior, whom Miss Martineau had praised while she was his guest the previous winter. In fact, he had met her casually at Mrs. Eliza Rotch Farrar's in Cambridge. Miss Fuller was born in Cambridgeport, the civic center of Cambridge, where her father, Timothy Fuller, was a lawyer. He was a better scholar than lawyer, however, and finally retired to a farm near Groton. There he had recently died, leaving a wife and five children with scanty means of support.[74]

Margaret's father had been disappointed that his firstborn was not a boy and had compensated by educating her himself, teaching her Latin at the age of six, and Greek soon after. She had a quick and retentive memory and had learned languages and mathematics easily. Before meeting Emerson she had taught herself Italian and German. Now, at twenty-six, she was perhaps the most learned woman in New England, with the exception of Emerson's aunt Mrs. Sarah Bradford Ripley. Her arrogance, caustic wit, and impatience with slower minds had made her more detested than loved. Yet while living in Cambridge before moving to Groton she had acquired a loyal band of friends who praised her extravagantly. Among these were Emerson's friends Dr. Frederic Hedge and James Freeman Clarke, later to become a Unitarian clergyman in Louisville, Kentucky.

After months of effort, some of Miss Fuller's friends maneuvered an invitation for her to visit the Emersons in Concord during July 1836. Fifteen years later Emerson still vividly remembered his first half hour with her. She was blond, with a fair complexion, a large nose, and, on first impression, an unattractive personality. "Her extreme plainness,—a trick of incessantly opening and shutting her eyelids,—the nasal tone of her voice,—all repelled," he recalled, "and I said to myself, we shall never get far."[75] However, he soon found himself both attracted and shocked by her banter. He was especially impressed by her extensive knowledge of European literature, but he thought she was "too much interested in personal history; and her talk was a comedy in which dramatic justice was done to every body's foibles." She made him laugh in spite of his disapproval, and he felt guilty and a little vexed as a consequence. Nevertheless, Margaret Fuller had determined to make Waldo Emerson her friend, and she won a partial victory on her first visit—by flattery, drollery, shrewd judgments, and overpowering enthusiasm. He almost forgot her plainness, but found talking with her exhausting.

Margaret also made a conquest of Lidian, and was soon on a first-name basis with her, as was her custom. Mrs. Emerson invited her back for a three-week visit.[76] This time Emerson confided in his Journal that she was "a very accomplished & very intelligent person." But next day he mused, "How rarely can a female mind be impersonal," or free of egotism. Sarah Bradford Ripley could be, but not M.F., "with all her superiority."[77] She left to teach in Alcott's school in Boston, replacing Elizabeth Peabody, to whom Emerson wrote in November: "we all here shared your respect for Miss Fuller's gifts & character."[78]

In mid-September Miss Fuller was extremely vexed that her minister in Groton, the Reverend Charles Robinson, had invited Emerson to preach for him at a time when she was in Boston. To console her, Emerson wrote on September 20: "Why cannot you & your friend Miss [Anna] Barker ride up hither & spend a day in our green fens on your way to Groton, if you go thither, or by way of retreat from Boston, if you do not. Lidian thinks it would cure her, as poppy & oatmeal work too slowly."[79] Lidian had not answered her letter because "she is ill, & cannot; but she loves you very much." Margaret replied: "Mrs. Emerson does not love me more than I love her; but I am not sure how successful our visit might have ministered to her well-being."[80] The regimen of oatmeal sounds like Lidian's own remedy for her indigestion, but it is likely that a physician had prescribed the opium ("poppy"), a palliative used indiscriminately at the time. A month later Emerson wrote Margaret again: "My wife remains most of the time in her chamber but is stronger than when you saw her. Her friend Miss Russell from Plymouth is here & a great medicine for her."[81]

Lidian's illness did not curtail the hospitality of her home, or her husband's social activities. He attended the Harvard commencement at the end of August, returned to Cambridge on September 8 for a bicentenary celebration of the college, and a week later, while Lidian was still "quite ill with dyspepsia," entertained Dr. Hedge at home.[82] Hedge had suggested forming a discussion club, and on the nineteenth the second meeting of what would come to be known as the "Transcendental Club" met at George Ripley's house in Boston. Seven men were present; besides Emerson, Hedge, and Ripley, there were Convers Francis, Bronson Alcott, James F.

Clarke, and Orestes Brownson. Except for Alcott, all were or had been Unitarian ministers.

The group dispatched a letter to Carlyle, who they hoped would come to America and join them.[83] They also planned to invite other like-minded men to join, such as Dr. W. E. Channing and Dr. James Walker, then editor of *The Christian Examiner,* later to become president of Harvard. Emerson lamented the poverty of the arts and the low aesthetic taste of the nation: "What shall nourish the sense of beauty now?" he asked. "It was requested that this be the subject of discussion at the next meeting & I should open the debate."[84] This assignment caused him to spend considerable time musing in his Journal on why "there is no genius in the Arts in this country." Washington Allston was only "a beautiful draughtsman," and Horatio Greenough's main interest was to please "prosperous gentlemen & ladies," impervious to "the Universal Yankee nation roaring in the Capitol." In airing these views at the second meeting of the group at Alcott's house in Boston on October 3, Emerson began to germinate the theme of his "American Scholar" address of the following year.

Meanwhile he was finding it difficult to protect what he called his "self-union," the hours he needed for meditation and writing down his ideas. Lidian did not make demands on his time, for her two servants and Mary Russell took care of her needs; and though Bulkeley had had to be returned to the asylum in Charlestown, Waldo had only to pay his bills, with tardy help from William. But he was besieged by people stretching out their mendicant arms to him, people with whom he had little sympathy or common cause. They marred "his days with their follies & then with their tacit reproaches, so that his fair ideal of domestic life & serene household gods he cannot realize ..."[85] (This complaint Emerson recorded in the third person.) Most of the time he did find solid satisfaction in his country home beside the busy Turnpike, but he never knew, when the stage stopped at his gate, whether it would discharge a friend or another nuisance.

On September 29, the day before the anniversary of his marriage to Ellen Tucker, Emerson wrote in his Journal: "I am glad of a day when I know what I am to do in it." But on the anniversary of his first marriage he could think only of "Ellen, Ellen, Ellen," as he doodled her name on his page, and made no further entry that day.[86] This did not mean that he was unhappy in his present marriage, though he did feel that "the frivolous external fancying" had faded out of it. He had convinced himself that he did not regret the ebb of "inclination." It was enough that his marriage rested on mutual respect and confidence. But when Lidian gave birth to a son at eleven o'clock on the night of October 30, his complacent philosophy gave way to ecstatic joy, though not so much for a recovered lover as in a madonna to worship who would give him pride in his paternity.

Next day in his Journal Emerson declared, "Now am I Pygmalion."[87] But he had to admit that "The stimulated curiosity of the father sees the graces & instincts which exist, indeed, in every babe," yet notices only in his own. Actually, "I see nothing in it of mine; I am no conscious party to any feature, any function, any perfection I behold in it. I seem to be merely a brute occasion of its being & nowise attaining to the dignity even of a second cause no more than I taught it to suck the breast."

Of course he quickly became attached to his son and felt him to be a part of himself, but his first response was astonishment to see Lidian so happy. Her maternal joy was a revelation to him. Before the child was two days old she declared that every day it presented a new aspect, "as the face of the sky is different every hour, so that we never get tired" of looking at it. The "happy patronizing look of the mother," as if she were a "high reposing Providence," made "a perfect group," reminding the father of famous paintings he had seen in the Italian museums.[88] For months he would continue to marvel at Lidian, the "maternal woman." Neither he nor she could carry a tune, but he found music in her "earnest talk to the baby" and her "shouts of love."[89] Her health improved, too. On November 13 he wrote Elizabeth Peabody: "Lidian does not go down stairs quite yet, but she is much better than she has been for months past."[90]

Emerson's family and friends thought he should name his son Charles, but he insisted on Waldo. "I call him so," he wrote William, "because it is his natural name; then because it is an old family name; & lastly because it is a convenient & somewhat rare name." Charles had not liked his name because it was not patronymic. Perhaps the main reason "Waldo" was *natural* was that it had enabled the baby's father to escape his Haskins first name and acquire an identity of his own. Nearly two years earlier William had named his son for himself, and the fathers now delighted in exchanging news of their "Willie" and "Wallie."

In January, Waldo Sr. wrote: "Wallie is the most thrifty of babies: he can suck cry laugh coo warble & jump. I shall keep you advised of your nephew's progress in the arts of life. His kiss to his cousin." In March Willie and Wallie caught cold, and their fathers exchanged anxious messages. On April 8 Emerson prayed in his Journal: "Ah! my darling boy, so lately received out of heaven leave me not now! Please God, this sweet symbol of love & wisdom may be spared to rejoice, teach, & accompany me."[91] All his plans for the future included his son. In the autumn he had spent a day "scrambling in the wood" to find "six hemlock trees to plant in my yard which may grow whilst my boy is sleeping."

His son's future also made him cautious in lending his brother money for his real-estate investments. Because of the current economic depression William had difficulty in getting his mortgages renewed, and he frequently appealed to Waldo for help. Waldo was always sympathetic, and completely trusted his brother's honesty, but he felt that he must protect his family. His Boston bankers advised him not to become involved in William's speculations, but he could not resist William's appeals. On December 16, 1836, for example, he wrote: "The terms are punctual payment of interest of [on] $2900. at 6 per cent. It is my living & I depend on this income 1 April & 1 October. And for the sake of wife & child I should ask the landed security you offer."[92]

By early May both Willie and Wallie had recovered from their colds, and Willie, "conscious of his seniority," according to his uncle, visited his Concord cousin. This seemed to be an appropriate time to have Willie baptized. His Grandmother Emerson dressed him in Charles's christening dress, and his Great-(step)grandfather Ripley performed the ceremony. Not long after Waldo's birth Dr. Ripley had asked to examine the prodigious baby. He gently turned him on his stomach, pulled up his gown, and stared earnestly at his back. "Is anything wrong?" asked his anxious mother. "I was just looking for the wings," replied the venerable minister, who had not lost his sense of humor.[93]

IV

For his new course of lectures, to be given in the winter of 1836–37, Emerson had decided on the general topic of philosophy of history. He realized, of course, that he was no historian, and to pretend to have a philosophy of the subject made him feel apologetic in writing William of his plans on October 23: ". . . so much lecturing & now a little printing [*Na-*

ture] has bronzed me & I am become dogmatic; and I mean to insist that whatsoever elements of humanity have been the subjects of my studies, constitute the indisputable core of Modern History!"[94] Though written in jest, this was actually a very accurate statement, for in the new lectures he would attempt to make more coherent and lucid the very ideas he had treated in *Nature,* which he had mulled over for years in his Journals and public lectures.

The new series would be given in the Masonic Temple in Boston (and some lectures repeated in surrounding towns), but not under the auspices of any organization. Both to ensure his freedom of choice in subject matter and, he hoped, to yield him more cash return, he would hire the hall, write his own advertising, and sell tickets through a Boston bookstore. Admission would be two dollars for the series of twelve lectures, to be given on successive Thursday evenings, beginning on December 8, 1836, and closing on March 2, 1837. As usual, he would give many free tickets to friends. The twelve lectures would be on "Philosophy of History (Introduction)," "Humanity of Science," "Art," "Literature," "Politics," "Religion," "Society," "Trades and Professions," "Manners," "Ethics," "The Present Age," and "The Individual." All might have been given the title of the sixth, "Religion."

In his introductory lecture Emerson rejected the usual conception of history, which was nothing but a chronology of mankind's external deeds: wars, conquests, dynasties, crimes, revolutions, and so on. "True History," he insisted, had not yet been written. It should include man's *internal* life, his thoughts, feelings, and ideals: "The true History . . . will traverse the whole scale of the human faculties . . ."[95] It might be objected that Emerson was really not interested in *history,* but in the future fulfillment of man's potential. (It is significant that Friedrich Nietzsche would become one of Emerson's major disciples.) On the uselessness of history: "The ancients are dead, but for us the earth is new today and heaven is raining influences. Let us unfetter ourselves of our historical associations and find a pure standard in the idea of man."[96]

The "idea of man" was Emerson's real subject, not what men have been or are today, with all their defects, but "Universal Man" before he lost his "original and majestic proportions." Each man's mind has access to the Universal Mind, or Reason, and "What Plato has thought he may think . . . What has at any time befallen any man, he may understand."[97] This teaching can be easily misunderstood in two ways: Emerson, unlike Rousseau, did not think that man was perfect before society degraded him. What "a certain poet" sang in *Nature* (VIII) was that once "Man" was "permeated and dissolved by spirit," but after being born into the world of the senses he lost his "original and majestic proportions." In other words, in the actual history of man on earth, he never has been "universal," but, as Emerson had preached for some years, by the aid of Reason he may become so.

The second difficulty is in understanding Emerson's paradox of individualism: "the mind is one and . . . nature is its correlative."[98] Everything that exists or has happened relates to the individual, whose actions make history. Yet Emerson complains that the fault of history as it has been written is that it is concerned only with a few individuals, "an Alaric or a Bourbon, with fighters or lawmakers but it does not satisfy the great ideal we contain or which contains us."[99] Thus, "The Philosophy of Modern History is man's relation to Religion, Law, Nature, Art, Literature."

In *Nature* Emerson had tried to show that the phenomena of nature are the creation of a Mind similar to the human mind, only infinitely more powerful. Thus in his second lecture, on the "Humanity of Science," he argues that "There is in Nature a parallel unity, which corresponds to this unity in the mind, and makes it available. . . . Not only man puts things in a row, but things belong in a row."[100] Because of this parallel unity, man with his feeble mental faculties can measure his world and even the solar system: "Because a straw shows how the stream runs, and the wind blows; because as falls the apple, so falls the moon . . . because in short the wide universe is made up of a few elements and a few laws; perhaps of one element and one law."

From similar observations Emerson deduces that "Nature hates cripples and monomaniacs," and seeks to eliminate them; thus he anticipated Darwin's "survival of the fittest" theory. He was also impressed by Pieter Camper's examples of transformation in comparative anatomy. In studying the gradations of change in skeletal formations one can see how the arm became a wing or a flipper, or vice versa, paralleling Goethe's metamorphosis of plants. There are also striking similarities in the laws of reflection of light, heat, and sound; and those of magnetism and electricity are identical. Newton, Hooke, Boscovich, and Davy conjectured that "the forms of natural bodies depend upon different arrangements of the same particles of matter ..." A central unity "pervades nature from the deep centre to the unknown circumference." Behind all the processes of nature there is life, which Emerson equated with spirit, and which is ever ameliorating. Nature destroys to rebuild and improve. This is his theory of evolution, and the basis of his "Humanity" of science.

"Man's wit is secondary to nature's wit. He applies himself to nature to copy her method, to imbibe her wisdom."[101] The art of medicine, as Dr. Oliver Wendell Holmes also observed,[102] is to aid nature in the healing process; not man's medicine but nature restores health. In fact, man's unconscious mental process is that same mind of nature at work. "And there is a conviction in the mind that some such impulse is constant, that if the Solar System is good art and architecture, the same achievement is in our brain also, if only we can be kept in height of health, and hindered from any interference with out great instincts."[103] This statement anticipates Emerson's third lecture, on "Art."

"The conscious utterance of thought," he says, "by speech or action, to any end, is Art." But his distinction between conscious and unconscious creation is subtle. "Relative to themselves, the bee, the bird, the beaver, have no art, for what they do, they do instinctively; but relatively to the Supreme Being, they have."[104] Emerson agrees with Plato (by way of Cudworth) that "Those things which are said to be done by Nature, are indeed done by Divine Art." He states as a "law" that "The universal soul is the alone creator of the useful and the beautiful; therefore to make anything useful or beautiful, the individual must be submitted to the universal mind."[105] As an analogy, "we do few things by muscular force, but we place ourselves in such attitudes as to bring the force of gravity, that is the weight of the planet, to bear upon the spade or the axe we wield." Emerson then asks: "Who is the artist?"; and answers: "The universal soul is the alone creator."[106]

Precisely how the individual artist can become "an organ through which the universal mind acts" Emerson has difficulty in explaining, but he does give a clue—again by analogy. The Gothic cathedrals, for example, "were built, when the builder and the priest and the people were overpowered by their faith. Love and fear laid every stone." Whereas in "this country, at this time, other interests than religion and patriotism are predominant, and the arts, the daughters of enthusiasm, do not flourish."[107]

Emerson's theory of artistic creation is completely Platonic, so that creation is really re-creation or recovery of an archetype. "The first time you hear [great poetry], it sounds rather as if copied out of some invisible tablet in the Eternal mind, than as if arbitrarily composed by the poet. The feeling of all great poets has accorded with this. They found the verse, not made it."[108] Consequently, the poet is a mediator between God, or pure Mind, and finite minds. However, the form of each literary work is determined by society ("the state of mankind" around the poet), and the author must consciously exert his utmost effort; no great work is an improvisation.[109]

Emerson comes very near in his lecture on "Literature" to locating Reason in the human unconscious. He argues that literature makes conscious the unconscious life: "Whoever separates for us a truth from our unconscious reason, and makes it an object of consciousness, draws . . . a fact out of our life and makes it an opinion . . ."[110] However, the literary presentation of the fact (or truth) gives it a significance which the reader feels to transcend his own human condition, raising it above his cares and fears, making it seem "impersonal and immortal."

The twelfth lecture, on "The Individual," may be taken as the coda to the series. The age, says Emerson, "is the era of increased political and moral power of individuals," though it has often not been wisely used. In fact, "Society never advances." Civilized man has lost as much as he has gained. He has "built a coach but has lost the use of his feet . . . And it may be a question whether machinery does not encumber." Institutions, too, have become mechanical. Christianity has entrenched itself in "establishments," thereby losing vigor and "wild virtue." Today, "what is more rare in Christendom than a Christian?"[111]

This skepticism had driven Emerson out of Unitarianism, and was driving him out of all churches. Yet he believed that Christianity could be the salvation of society if only people would live it and not by habit mouth creeds and inherited clichés. "Cunningly does the world evermore with its thousandfold beauties and qualities tempt forth the spirit in man and challenge the faculties to unfold and play." The "Age of Reflection" imposes a new duty upon the cultivated mind of the time. Let him not read history as oracle, but as embodying "that nature which he has." Then, "Let him read history actively not passively. Let him esteem his own life [as] the text and this the commentary."[112]

On March 4, two days after finishing his series of lectures in Boston,

Emerson thanked Providence for having "given me perfect health & smoothed the way unto the end."[113] He estimated that attendance had averaged 350 persons. After paying expenses, he had $350 left, which he considered to be a good return for his efforts. Considering the fact that the economic depression had grown worse and that a considerable number of other lecturers had competed for the Boston audience, Emerson had a right to feel satisfied.

Added to his other sources of revenue, Emerson now had, he wrote William on April 3, 1837, "a large income, this year, but I seem to be no dollar the better. Yet Lidian thinks she is very shrewd, and I think as well of me. Economy is a science & must be devoutly studied, if you would know it."[114]

CHAPTER XIV

Uriel's Voice of Scorn

. . . . out of good of evil born,
Came Uriel's voice of cherub scorn . . .[1]

I

In the spring of 1837 Emerson was alarmed by the "Loud cracks in the social edifice." After a hard winter, April was cold, "men [were] breaking who ought not to break; banks [were] bullied into the bolstering of desperate speculations; all the news papers [were] a chorus of owls."[2] They reported "Tobacco, cotton, teas, indigo, & timber all at tremendous discount & the end not yet." Thousands of laborers were being thrown out of work, and "these," Emerson observed, "make a formidable mob to break open banks & rob the rich . . ." In New Orleans incendiaries had burned the Exchange, and in New York hordes of depositors had made runs on the banks. On May 14 all banks in New York and Boston suspended payments in specie.[3]

Emerson was not immediately affected, though a few months later his ten shares of stock in the Commerical Bank of Boston would become valueless; and of course dividends, when paid at all, were reduced. However, in July Emerson received additional certificates of stock as the last installment of his first wife's estate. The lawyer who had handled the case hoped he would not turn them over to his speculating brother, and Abel Adams expressed similar views.[4] The deepening of the depression had naturally made it increasingly difficult for William to protect his investments in real estate. Waldo still believed in his judgment, but he admitted, "I do not like so well the new relation of debtor & creditor as the old one of

brother . . ." Most annoying of all, William did not keep him fully informed: "You write to a scholar floundering for the first time in a quag-
mire of business with all the dwarf brevity of a broker, as if it were enough
to such a one to know a sum & date & he could foresee & transpierce all
the rest."[5] Though still willing to do what he could to help, Waldo had
found that "a little business spoils a great deal of time for the Muses."

On May 20 Emerson wondered in his Journal: "Is the world sick? Bankruptcy in England & America: Tardy rainy season; snow in France; plague
in Asia & Africa; these are the morning's news[.]"[6] Even nature seemed to
be out of order. Certainly society was: "Young men have no hope. Adults
stand like daylaborers idle in the streets. . . . The present generation is
bankrupt of principles & hope, as of property." Yet, "The black times have
a great scientific value . . . I learn geology the morning after an earthquake." What he had learned, however, was confirmation of what he had
been preaching for a decade:

> The world has failed. The pretended teachers who have scoffed at the
> Idealist, have failed utterly. The very adulation they offer to the name of
> Christ, the epithets with which they encumber his name, the ragged half
> screaming bass with which they deepen the sentences of sermons on pu-
> rity, martyrdom, & spiritual life, do preach their hollowness & recoil upon
> them. They lash themselves with their satire.[7]

To add more gloom to this grim spring, the greatest Idealist Emerson
knew was being hounded out of his school in Boston. The whispering
campaign against Bronson Alcott which had started in 1835 with the
publication of Elizabeth Peabody's *Record of a School* became a torrent of
abuse when Alcott himself published the *Conversations on the Gospels in Mr.
Alcott's School* (1836–37), which Miss Peabody had transcribed and then
begged him not to publish. She especially feared the effect of such passages
as little Josiah Quincy's saying that babies were the result of "the naughtiness of other people." Actually Alcott seldom mentioned physiological
details, and then in such a "spiritual" way as this:

> You have seen the rose opening from the seed with the assistance of the
> atmosphere. This is the birth of the rose. It typifies the bringing forth of
> the spirit by pain and labor and patience . . . And a mother suffers when
> she has a child. When she is going to have a child she gives up her body to

God, and he works upon it in a mysterious way and, with her aid, brings forth the child's Spirit in a little Body of its own; and when it has come she is blissful.[8]

Miss Peabody suggested that if Mr. Alcott must publish the *Conversations,* all references to birth, circumcision (the children had encountered the term in the Bible), and sex should be placed in an appendix—which, of course, would only call attention to them. Alcott accepted this suggestion, but he was adamant about publishing. Consequently, he went into debt between seven and eight hundred dollars to print the two volumes, the first in December 1836, and the second, transcribed by Margaret Fuller, in February 1837.

An editorial in the Boston *Courier* was typical of the reception of these volumes: ". . . the *Conversations on the Gospels* is a more indecent and obscene book (we say nothing about its absurdity) than any other we ever saw exposed for sale on a bookseller's counter."[9] Emerson tried to reply, but the editor delayed printing his letter. The Unitarian *Christian Register* did print some kind words, and Orestes Brownson published a lengthy sympathetic critique in *The Boston Quarterly Review.* But these sane voices were drowned out by vituperation from the pulpit, most newspapers, and the street. "I hate to have all the little dogs barking at you," Emerson wrote Alcott on March 24, "for you have something better to do than to attend to them . . ."[10]

There was not very much that Emerson himself could do except try to encourage and cheer Alcott up, though he did make a generous contribution to his printing bill. In mid-May he also invited Alcott to spend a few days with him in Concord, where he discussed further a suggestion he had already made that possibly Alcott should give up teaching and try to reform education through his writing.[11] Even if he had to do manual labor to support his family, that would be preferable, Emerson thought, to exposing himself to the perils and insults he was experiencing in Boston. With some disappointment Alcott commented in his Journal: "He values my professional labours somewhat lower than most of my friends. Herein, I think, he errs; while as a writer he over-estimates my ability."[12] In view of Emerson's own despair over Alcott's unpublished manuscript "Psyche," his advice does seem strange. Though Alcott found Emerson more sympathetic than anyone else he knew, for which he was deeply grateful, he became a little disillusioned after his three-day visit. "His sympathies are all intellectual," Alcott complained in his Journal. With some bitterness he added: "He is an eye more than a heart, an intellect more than a soul."[13]

For his part, Emerson was delighted with Alcott's visit, and wrote Margaret Fuller, who had not yet been able to recognize Alcott's merits, that "he has more of the godlike than any man I have ever seen and his presence rebukes & threatens & raises. He *is* a teacher." But then he added a comment that partly confirmed Alcott's private impression: "I shall dismiss for the future all anxiety about his success. If he cannot make intelligent men feel the presence of a superior nature the worse for them . . ."[14] However, to the man struggling to support his family, his friend's lofty confidence seemed ironical.

When the number of his students dropped to ten, Alcott moved his school to the basement of the Masonic Temple, sold most of the school furniture and his library, then collapsed with one of the few illnesses of his life. His future looked grim indeed. His friend George Ripley had told him that most of the Boston clergy were against him because they thought he encroached upon their theological prerogatives; teachers opposed him because his pedagogical methods were a reproach to them; and it was obvious that "respectable" people hated him for disturbing their complacency.[15]

Outside of Boston, Alcott did have some admirers, besides Waldo Emerson. One was Hiram Fuller (no relation of Margaret's), who had raised funds to start an ambitious and innovative school in Providence, Rhode Island, on Greene Street. He had recently hired Miss Fuller to teach for a thousand dollars a year, a salary that Alcott could never have afforded. Mr. Fuller wanted Alcott to give the principal address at the dedication of the Greene Street School on June 10. Probably Alcott was too ill to prepare and deliver the address, but aside from this consideration he feared that in his present unpopular situation his attendance might do the new school more harm than good; so he recommended Emerson.

Emerson himself was not well, and he tried to decline the invitation, but found that through some misunderstanding he had been announced as the speaker. Fortunately he did not need much preparation to say what was most on his mind at the time, which was that the failures of society showed the glaring defects of the methods of education then in use: "The disease of which the world lies sick, is, the inaction of the higher faculties of man . . ."[16] Men were valued for the goods they could produce, or the money they could accumulate, not for their manhood. As a consequence:

> A desperate conservatism clings with both hands to every dead form in the schools, in the state, in the church. A timid political tithe-paying and churchgoing zeal takes the place of religion. That utter unbelief which is afraid of change, afraid of thought, supervenes. The literature feels it. It is factious or it is imitative or it is low and economical. No new work of the human mind of a commanding sort, no creation has for many years appeared.[17]

Though the address was largely an improvisation, it turned out to be a trial run for Emerson's more famous Phi Beta Kappa speech at the end of the summer (which he had not yet been invited to give). The Providence address is also of some importance as a symptom of the extreme impatience Emerson felt with the moribund institutions in the summer of 1837. But his trip to Providence caused a return of his recent illness. On June 16 he wrote Margaret Fuller, who had remained in Providence: "I have been ailing since I came home with a slight but somewhat increased inflammation on the lungs . . ."[18]

Dr. Jackson "aus-cultated" Emerson and assured him he had no cause for worry, but he did worry and wrote William he might "need to make a long journey or voyage" to recover his health. However, after a few days among his garden peas and strawberry vines, he felt well enough to undertake a visit to Plymouth with Lidian and his son. Thus it happened that he was not in Concord on July 4 when his "Concord Hymn" was sung at a celebration of the unveiling of the monument erected on the spot where "the embattled farmers stood/ And fired the shot heard round the world."[19] It would become his most famous poem, but he had composed it only to fulfill a promise to the Monument Committee.

In Plymouth the Emerson family was warmly entertained by George Bradford, the Russells, and Lidian's many other friends, but on the way back Waldo Jr. caught cold and gave his parents some anxiety, though in Concord he soon recovered. Emerson now felt so contented, working in his garden, watering his fruit trees, picking green peas, gathering vine-ripened strawberries, and relaxing in the sun, that like Caesar in Shakespeare's *Julius Caesar,* as Waldo expressed it in a letter to Margaret Fuller, he "would fain be well if there were anything for a man to do."[20]

II

Emerson did not have to wait long for something to do. On June 22 Cornelius Felton, professor of Greek at Harvard, wrote him an invitation to give the annual Phi Beta Kappa address on August 31.[21] It was traditionally scheduled for the day following commencement, always held on the last Wednesday in August. Professor Felton said frankly that the Reverend Dr. Wainwright (possibly Jonathan Mayhew Wainwright, later bishop of New York) had been invited and had declined only a few days before. A vainer person might have refused to be second choice. Emerson had not been even second choice for class poet, and he was only an honorary member of Phi Beta Kappa. So he accepted the invitation graciously and with sincere pleasure. On July 29 he wrote in his Journal: "If the Allwise would give me light, I should write for the Cambridge men a theory of the Scholar's office."[22]

Actually, this topic was an almost inevitable choice. As Bliss Perry has remarked, Emerson's subject had been "a conventional theme of Phi Beta Kappa orations ever since he was a boy."[23] Emerson knew, therefore, what his audience would expect of him, and he would give it to them, but from his own mind and in his own language. To judge by his Journal and correspondence, he did not have to struggle in writing the oration. He continued reading his favorite authors, and drew upon them to some extent, but for the most part his electrifying sentences came out of his own experience and deep convictions.

On the morning of August 31 Waldo and Lidian Emerson drove to Cambridge in their own buggy. The day before, an unexpected rain had settled the dust, and it was a pleasant ride in the clear air and warm sunshine.[24] Phi Beta Kappa day at Harvard was not quite so much like a country fair as commencement the previous day, when brass bands played and the militia paraded before the governor and other dignitaries, while peddlers sold ginger beer on the street and taverns nearby did an even brisker business in harder beverages. But Phi Beta Kappa day was also observed with pomp and traditional ceremony.

Promptly at noon the academic procession formed at University Hall, inside the Yard, then marched through the west gate and across the street to the First Parish Church, keeping step to the band music. The church was an undistinguished wooden structure, painted white, like hundreds of others in New England. Though this building was only three years old, it stood on the exact spot of the original log church in which Anne Hutchinson had been examined for heresy by a synod that August two hundred years before. (Her sentence of exile was pronounced several months later in Boston by the General Court.)

Seated on the platform with President Josiah Quincy and other guests of honor, Emerson could see famous faces in the audience, "the most distinguished," says Professor Perry, with obvious partisan pride, "that could then be gathered in America." Among the Fellows of the Harvard Corporation present were two of the most admired lawyers in New England, Joseph Story and Lemuel Shaw. Judge Shaw had boarded with Emerson's mother in Boston in 1815, and had been so impressed by a juvenile poem on "Liberty" written by Waldo (then called Ralph) that he had kept the manuscript, and later gave it to the Harvard Library.[25]

Perry conjectures that possibly three of the most renowed overseers of the college, John Quincy Adams, Daniel Webster, and Dr. W. E. Channing, were absent, "since the Phi Beta Kappa orator is only a stickit-minister from Concord, author of an anonymous, unintelligible and unsold book on 'Nature'!" ("Unsold" was based on a misconception, but J. Q. Adams *had* called it "unintelligible.") Probably the older members of the faculty, remembering Emerson's mediocre academic record, did not expect a distinguished performance, though two from the Divinity School were kindly disposed toward him, the two Henry Wares, Sr. and Jr.

Over two hundred members of the Harvard chapter of Phi Beta Kappa were present, including both student and alumni (honorary) members. Many undergraduates had also remained at the college for this special occasion. These and local residents filled the church to overflowing. Some even stood outside the open windows, hoping to hear if not see. One young man in the audience, who had received his diploma the day before, was Richard Henry Dana, once Emerson's pupil in Cambridge. He had dropped out of college to make the trip about which he would soon write his *Two Years Before the Mast*. Another young man who had graduated the previous day, and whom one might have expected to be present, was Henry Thoreau, Emerson's neighbor and a recent acquaintance, but there is no evidence that he was there. His closest friends said that after the graduating exercises he had simply disappeared. It is not positively known, either, whether the half-mad tutor in Greek, Jones Very, was present; Emerson would not know him until several months later.

A feisty junior who attended was James Russell Lowell, no great admirer of Emerson at the time, though he would later remember this day as "an event without any parallel in our literary annals." Emerson expected the young people to understand him better than the older, but it was friends nearer his own age who most appreciated his message that day: Bronson Alcott, Frederic Hedge, Margaret Fuller, and Elizabeth Hoar. He would see all of them on the morrow when the "Hedge Club" met at his house.[26]

After a prayer by a Reverend Rogers of Boston, Emerson was introduced and he advanced to the speaker's desk. In his clear, resonant voice, which reminded some in the audience of his father's, he began: "I greet you on the commencement of our literary year. Our anniversary is one of hope, and, perhaps, not enough of labor."[27] Then, a few sentences later, "Our day of dependence, our long apprenticeship to the learning of other lands, draws to a close."

Dr. Oliver Wendell Holmes (Harvard '29) took this declaration to be the main point of the oration, which he called "our intellectual Declaration of Independence."[28] It was that, to be sure; yet Emerson was not simply making another plea for literary nationalism. He went much further and demanded independence from all literatures of the past, from all traditions that had become embalmed in piety and passed for respectable opinion instead of honest thinking. He knew that when an organism stops growing, it dies, and is then useful only to fertilize other organisms. He believed that institutions, books, and ideas also have organic life cycles; yet in churches, schools, colleges, society, politics, even economy, he beheld the worship of dead forms. When the "sacredness which attaches to the act of creation—the act of thought" is transferred to the record, it is worshiped and becomes a tyrant.[29]

By scholar, Emerson meant "Man Thinking"—not a specialist in some field of knowledge, but any man using his God-given mind: "The one thing in the world, of value, is the active soul"—that is, mind.[30] The three chief influences in the education of the scholar, he said, are nature, books, and action. The real subject of his address was the proper use of these. The right use of books is to "inspire"—that is, stimulate. "Books are for the scholar's idle times," or when "intervals of darkness come," and their rays are needed to make the dawn return. But "One must be an inventor to read well. . . . There is then creative reading as well as creative writing."[31]

Practical men, so called, sneer at the scholar as a recluse, a valetudinarian, unfit for physical action, but he learns truth only by action, by experiencing it. "Colleges and books only copy the language which the field and the work-yard made."[32]

The scholar has duties, too, but Emerson did not enumerate familiar moral platitudes. The scholar's first duty, he pointed out, is integrity to his own mind, which, as Emerson had always preached, is but an extension of the Divine Mind. The scholar must resist the "popular cry" of this or that "great decorum, some fetish of a government, some ephemeral trade, or war, or man," and hold to his own convictions. "As the world was plastic and fluid in the hands of God, so it is ever to so much of his attributes as we bring to it."[33]

Emerson believed, as we have seen in *Nature,* that man had been dehumanized, had been wronged and had wronged himself: "men in the world of to-day are bugs, are spawn, and are called 'the mass' and the 'herd.' "[34] Yet he saw "auspicious signs" of change "through poetry and art, through philosophy and science, through church and state." The "low" and the "common" had been explored and poetized (he doubtless had Wordsworth in mind, especially): "The literature of the poor, the feelings of the child, the philosophy of the street, the meaning of the household life, and the topics of the times." This was a "great stride" and would bring "new vigor" to both literature and philosophy.

> Give me insight into to-day, and you may have the antique and future worlds. What would we really know the meaning of? The meal in the firkin; the milk in the pan; the ballad in the street; the news of the boat; the glance of the eye; the form and the gait of the body; . . . let me see every trifle bristling with the polarity that ranges it instantly on an eternal law; and the shop, the plow, and the ledger referred to the like cause by which light undulates and poets sing; . . . one design unites and animates the farthest pinnacle and the lowest trench.[35]

Emerson praised Swedenborg for having interpreted the "lower parts of nature" exhibited in insanity, in beasts, and "unclean and fearful things."[36]

He called this "the connection between nature and the affections of the soul." In modern terminology, "lower parts of nature" meant sexual aberrations, neuroses, delusions, and perhaps the whole range of diseases. Most of his hearers would have been profoundly shocked if they had fully understood the implications of his defense of Swedenborg. But the interesting point is that he foresaw the need for the "psychologists of the soul" long before they appeared: Charcot, William James, Freud, Adler, and Jung.

However, Emerson was less concerned with the underside of nature than with the "unsearched might of man": ". . . if the single man plant himself indomitably on his instincts and there abide, the huge world will come round to him." Resoundingly he concluded: "We will walk on our own feet; we will work with our own hands; we will speak our own minds." He still had little hope for reform by political parties, societies, or altruistic cooperation; only faith in the indomitable will of individual men and women who feel themselves "inspired by the Divine Soul which also inspires all men."[37]

Emerson spoke for exactly an hour and fifteen minutes—the Reverend John Pierce, minister of a Congregational church in Watertown, had timed him. After a benediction, the Phi Beta Kappa members then returned to the Yard for dinner in University Hall. Charles Warren, of Plymouth, offered this toast: "Mr. President, I suppose you all know where the orator came from; and I suppose all know what he said. I give you—The Spirit of Concord—*it makes us all of one mind.*" Probably no irony was intended, but as Bliss Perry observes, "Far from making them all of one mind, the man from Concord had sowed discord—and Emerson, at least, knew it."[38]

Friends demanded that Emerson publish his oration, and he readily agreed to do so. James Munroe and Company promptly published an edition of five hundred copies, and it sold out in less than a month.[39] Emerson then corrected the text for a new edition. But meanwhile he sent Carlyle a copy of the first, and received laudatory thanks: "My friend! you know not what you have done for me . . . lo, out of the West comes a clear utterance, clearly recognizable as a *man's* voice, and I *have* a kinsman and brother."[40] He said he could have "*wept* to read that speech; the clear high melody of it went tingling through my heart . . ." Jane Carlyle declared that nothing like it had been heard since Schiller died.

III

On September 13, 1837, Emerson wrote Carlyle to thank him for his *French Revolution* and apologize for not having written since March 31: "Between many visits received, and some literary haranguing done, I have read two volumes and half of the third . . ."[41] The work suited exactly the theory he had expounded recently in his "American Scholar" address and earlier in his lecture on "History": "You have broken away from all books, and written a mind. It is a brave experiment, and the success is great. We have men in your story and not names merely . . ." Yet he must confess that he did "doubt sometimes whether I have the historic men." In other words, Carlyle's imagination was stronger than his history, and his style was "Gothically efflorescent." Still, it was "a wonderful book, which will last a very long time."

Emerson also reported to Carlyle that the American edition of *Sartor,* published at Emerson's risk, had sold 1,166 copies. On November 2 he wrote again to say that he had arranged with an American bookseller to print the *French Revolution,* making haste to get it out before it could be pirated from the British edition. Emerson himself would sell as many copies as he could by subscription, giving Carlyle the total net profit.

In his September letter to Carlyle, Emerson also wrote: "I called together a little club a week ago, who spent a day with me—counting fifteen souls,—each one of whom warmly loves you."[42] This group, later to be known as the "Transcendental Club," had met in Emerson's home the day after his Phi Beta Kappa address, and it numbered seventeen "souls" instead of fifteen, counting Emerson himself and three women who attended for the first time: Elizabeth Hoar, Sarah Bradford Ripley, and Margaret Fuller. Since there was no formal membership, any woman who was interested would have been welcomed, but it is difficult to think of any other women in the region except Elizabeth Peabody or Sarah Clarke who would not have been bored beyond endurance by the conversation of this group of ministers, divinity students, ex-ministers, and schoolteachers (Alcott, George Bradford, and Margaret Fuller, who was still teaching in Providence).

It was a group of "like minded" men and women, or as Emerson sometimes thought, "unlike," for they enjoyed arguing, and the main thing they agreed upon was that nothing was settled or too sacred to be questioned. The only rule the club had (unwritten) was that no one should be invited who might be embarrassed by discussion of new or unpopular ideas. In theology perhaps no one was quite as liberal as Emerson, but they did not find his views obnoxious, and they all praised *Nature.* Some of them read German, and they all admired Goethe, another reason for their liking Carlyle. Several of this group also attended meetings of the Aesthetic Club, which met a few days later in Newton in the home of James and Sarah Clarke.

In his November 2 letter to Carlyle, Emerson also confided: "I find myself so much . . . freer on the platform of the lecture-room than in the pulpit, that I shall not much more use the last; and do now only in a little country chapel at the request of simple men to whom I sustain no other relation than that of preacher."[43] The "little country chapel" referred to the small congregation in East Lexington, where Emerson had preached nearly every Sunday since settling in Concord. His relations with this group were still excellent, but he wanted to give his full attention to his public lectures. He did not definitely resign his position until the following February, and even then retained responsibility for finding someone to fill the pulpit each Sunday.[44]

Emerson began his busy lecture season in Lowell, where he repeated his series on "The Philosophy of History" during October. On December 6 he began his new series in Boston on "Human Culture," again acting as his own manager. These were even more successful than his Boston series the previous year, the audience increasing each week until at the end he was speaking to about five hundred people.[45] Emerson's spreading reputation and his increasing skill in public speaking were perhaps mainly responsible for his growing audience, but his subject was also of special interest to New Englanders. The rapid spread of the Lyceum movement testified to the interest of Americans everywhere in educational lectures, and New Englanders especially were eager to improve their minds. Lectures on "culture" were sure to attract them, though perhaps few would have agreed on the meaning of the term. In his introductory lecture Emerson defined his term:

> Culture in the high sense does not consist in polishing and varnishing, but in so presenting the attractions of nature that the slumbering attributes of man may burst their sleep and rush into day. The effect of Culture on the

man will not be like the trimming and turfing of gardens, but the educating the eye to the true harmony of the unshorn landscape, with horrid thickets, wide morasses, bald mountains, and the balance of land and sea.[46]

This was a definition which George Bancroft might have accepted for his *History of the United States* (Emerson had read the first volume and had been annoyed by its Jacksonian point of view). But in a city still largely and unconsciously Puritan, many people were unprepared to accept Emerson's assertion that "the unfolding of his nature, is the chief end of man. A divine impulse at the core of his being impels him to this." However, Emerson had preached faith in this "divine impulse" ever since his ordination in Boston. He had modified some of his beliefs since then, but not this one. In his letter to Carlyle he had called the lecture platform his "new pulpit," and that was literally true. His purpose in this series was to give his listeners confidence in their ability to solve all problems—with the aid of nature, and their own nature first of all.

The following nine lectures were ingenious in explaining what could be done by men and women in the use of their natural faculties. In "Doctrine of the Hands" he tried to show that "A man in the view of political economy is a pair of hands, a useful engine quite able to subdue the earth, to plant and build it over."[47] *Hands* is a metaphor for *work:* the need for "proper work," and the almost infinite possibilities of what can be achieved by effort. This lecture also contained radical teachings of social reform: ". . . you may [that is, should] do nothing to get money which is not worth the doing in its own account."[48] And "Society, however proud or polished, . . . is barbarous until every industrious man can get his living in it without dishonest compliances."[49]

In "The Head," Emerson presented his "Culture as Intellect." Teaching, as he always had, that "pure intellect is God," he had nothing new to say about Reason and Understanding, but his metaphysics anticipated later psychology. True intellectual growth is spontaneous, and the human mind should be permitted to unfold without impediments, for "God comes in by a private door into every individual: thoughts enter by passages which the individual never left open." Consequently, "Our spontaneous action is always the best."[50]

"The dark walls of your mind are scrawled all over with facts, with

thoughts. Bring a lanthorn and read the inscriptions."[51] Forgotten memories of childhood may contain valuable information (or revelations) for
the adult mind:

> It is long ere we discover how rich we are. ... But our wiser years still
> run back to the before despised recollections of childhood and always we
> are fishing up some wonderful article out of that pond, until by and by we
> begin to suspect that the biography of the one foolish person we know, is
> in reality nothing less than a miniature paraphrase of the hundred volumes
> of the Universal History.[52]

Here Emerson anticipates Jung rather than Freud, for he does not view
the unconscious as a pool of slimy horrors but as the repository of wonderful things. The "paraphrase ... of Universal History" sounds very
much like Jung's collective unconscious. But Emerson did not carry this
theory beyond a general reverence for the "silent stream ever flowing in
from above ..."[53] ("Above" also distances Emerson from Freud's
"below.") His practical rules for encouraging the flow are: (1) solitude—
"sit alone" and listen to your spontaneous thoughts; (2) "keep a journal"
to record "the visits of Truth to your mind."

In "The Eye and the Ear" Emerson expounded his Platonic aesthetics.
These organs "furnish us with the external elements of our idea of
Beauty," but the *idea* is internal: "all form is the effect of character ... all
outward harmony depends on interior harmony ..." With Edmund
Spenser he believed that "the Soul makes the body."[54] Therefore, "The
great artist does not aim at imitation," as in Aristotelian aesthetics. "He
seeks not nature but the ideal which nature herself strives after ..."[55]

In "The Heart," symbolizing "the powers of affection," Emerson examined social relations. "The Heart is ... a community of nature which really
does bind all men into a consciousness of one brotherhood." Though the
heart truly regards all men as its neighbor, "in the actual state of society it
presently finds abundant obstacle to the indulgence of sympathy."[56] In
marriage and friendship the heart limits its "diffusive nature" to one.
Later, on closer analysis, Emerson would find limitations to the indulgence
of the affections even in marriage; and he had always said that, with the
exception of his first wife, no living person could become the completely
ideal friend.

The three most popular lectures in this series seem to have been "Heart," "Heroism," and "Holiness." One evidence of this is that these were the ones friends most often wanted to borrow for private reading, and Emerson was generous in sharing the manuscript, his only fair copy. Sometimes he had difficulty in recovering a particular manuscript in time to use it for his next lecture engagement. According to an eyewitness, Emerson startled his Boston audience by declaring, near the end of his lecture on "Heroism," "It is but the other day, that the brave Lovejoy gave his breast to the bullets of the mob, for the rights of free speech and opinion, and died when it was better not to live."[57] (On November 7, 1837, a proslavery mob in Alton, Illinois, killed the Reverend Elijah P. Lovejoy for trying to start an abolitionist newspaper.) Abolition was almost as unpopular in Boston as in southern Illinois, and George Bradford said that some of Emerson's friends "felt the sort of cold shoulder [shudder?] which ran through the audience at the calm braving of the current opinion."[58]

In this speech Emerson also referred to a personal observation of less dramatic heroism: "The fair girl, who repels interference by a decided and proud choice of influences, so careless of pleasing, so wilful and lofty, inspires every beholder with somewhat of her own nobleness."[59] This girl has been identified as Caroline Sturgis, a friend of Margaret Fuller's, whom Emerson had met two years earlier. Eleanor Tilton says: "Part of Miss Sturgis' charm for Emerson was that, the daughter of the wealthy William Sturgis, Boston's ideal man of business, she scorned society and its expectations and rejected the style of life her wealth and her father's position entitled her to; that, at least, was part of Emerson's view of her."[60] This vivacious brunette of eighteen also happened to be very attractive and articulate. Friends said she looked like a Gypsy, and she was thought to be talented as a painter and as a poet. Emerson had also begun to lend her his manuscripts, and an intimate friendship was beginning.

The lecture in the series which stirred up most discussion was that on "Holiness," given in Boston on January 31, 1838. Emerson admitted that holiness was less attractive than heroism, less dramatic, often concealing the courageous willpower which heroism exhibits for anyone to see. Yet relying on the divinity within one's self also demands unwavering integrity and persistence, and the curbing of every selfish impulse. "I am constrained in every moment to own a higher origin for events than the will I call mine."[61] Most Christians, and all Calvinists, would have agreed to this statement.

But then Emerson restated his radical faith in the "moral sentiment," which comes in sudden flashes of light—or epiphanies. His confidence in these private revelations made him as antinomian as Anne Hutchinson, and listening only to the voice of God in one's own conscience was still a challenge to "all the accents of other men's devotion. Their prayers even are hurtful to him, until he has made his own. The sentiment is instantly vitiated, if it is not primary,—if it is not my own, but, instead, is imported into me from another soul."[62]

On February 7 in his concluding lecture in Boston, called "General Views," Emerson declared: "What we know is but a point to what we do not know. . . . We dwell on the surface of nature . . . Under every cause, another cause."[63] Men scarcely knew enough to ask the right questions. Only by recognizing this ignorance could they begin to awaken from the deep sleep of their higher faculties. Such a view of human knowledge was not only a challenge but a reproach to persons who esteemed themselves scholars.

By the time Emerson began repeating these lectures in Cambridge, which he did immediately after giving his last in Boston, rumors of his dangerous thinking had preceded him. The Cambridge audience included Harvard faculty members, divinity students, and graduates of the college—an elite audience. They were interested, alert, and skeptical. Henry Bokum, a law student, came late for the introductory lecture, and asked to borrow the manuscript. William Dexter Wilson asked to borrow the one on "The Head." Ellis Gray Loring, a young Boston lawyer, gave a dinner for Emerson on the day of his lecture on "The Head," the guests including Caroline Sturgis and the Reverend Convers Francis.[64]

After hearing "Holiness," Loring recorded in his Journal that Reverend Francis had given him a reassuring interpretation of Emerson's theory of the Deity, but next day in a conversation with the author himself (which may have taken place in President Josiah Quincy's house in the Harvard Yard), Loring found that Francis was wrong. Emerson "did not conceive the Deity as personal in the sense of his being a will"; and he called the Bible "fabulous" unless one had a personal revelation to confirm its truth. Even John Dwight, Emerson's successor in East Lexington, was disturbed by his friend's impersonal God, defined as "the ideal part of man's nature." This seemed to Dwight "like making a divinity of 'The Spirit of the Age' or 'The Genius of our Institutions.' " Professor Tilton comments: "It can scarcely be said that Harvard was unprepared for the Divinity School Address."[65]

IV

Throughout the winter and spring of 1837–38 Emerson repeated his lectures on "Culture" several times, in Concord, Framingham, Roxbury, and single lectures in Acton and East Lexington. He was in such demand that he had to decline some invitations. When snow came, he traveled in his sleigh, and occasionally Lidian accompanied him. During the Boston series she heard the introductory lectures, then wrote her sister, Lucy: "We have established it as a regular custom in the family that on Thursday evegs Mr E reads the lecture of the evening before to Elizabeth [Hoar] & myself."[66] When Elizabeth's brothers Edward and Rockwood were in town, Lidian invited them, too, also Henry Thoreau, "for his having walked to Boston to hear the Introductory." Emerson had given him a complimentary ticket for the series, but attending the private performances was less strenuous.

On February 14 Lidian left the two Waldos and her house in charge of her three maids (her mother-in-law was spending the winter in New York with William and Susan) and started out in a snowstorm for Plymouth. Waldo had expected to meet her in Boston, where he had stabled his horse while he went to Framingham by train to lecture, but his train was late in getting back to Boston and he missed seeing her off. Two days later he wrote her from Concord:

> I came home last night bringing Rockwood H. with me in my sleigh and arrived safe at 10 o'clock and have not today either cold, fever, or rheumatism.... We made up a fire, found the boy fast asleep dreaming of mamma—Mercy (well deserving her name) got me coffee & pie & left me to the same & my new Boston books, & I did not get to bed till nearly one.[67]

He hoped Lidian would be very happy in Plymouth, write long letters, which she usually did not, and "entirely leave behind you that same Dominican Chest with its flagellant contents." (Saint Dominic was reputed to have flagellated himself.) Waldo often teased his wife about her self-torturing conscience. In one of his letters to Carlyle he called her "an incarnation of Christianity." She was his "Asia" because she "keeps my philosophy from Antinomianism."[68] Though their views on religion had not yet created a barrier between them, Waldo's jokes revealed his awareness of their growing differences. On February 19 he wrote Lidian that the day before he had asked the Lexington church committee to relieve him of his "charge," and he wondered: "But does not the eastern Lidian my Palestine mourn to see the froward man cutting the last threads that bind him to that prized gown & band the symbols black & white of old & distant Judah?"[69]

Lidian Emerson did her best to share her husband's theological convictions and compunctions. He had quoted her in December in his Journal as saying "it is wicked to go to church Sundays."[70] But she probably felt wicked for saying that on a sympathetic impulse. Calvinism was so ingrained in her conscience that she could never fully liberate her mind from it. Waldo had an innate capacity for growth toward intellectual freedom, and asserting his independence gave him the kind of satisfaction the Quakers experienced in following the guidance of their "inner light." Though he never felt guilty for his opinions, he was haunted by memories of his failures, quite possibly imaginary, in his personal relations. On March 4 he recorded in his Journal:

> Last night a remembering & remembering talk with Lidian. I went back to the first smile of Ellen on the door stone at Concord [New Hampshire]. I went back to all that delicious relation to feel as ever how many shades, how much reproach. Strange is it that I can go back to no part of youth[,] no past relation without shrinking & shrinking. Not Ellen, not Edward, not Charles. Infinite compunctions embitter each of those dear names & all who surround them . . . I console myself with the thought that if Ellen, if Edward, if Charles could have read my entire heart they should have seen nothing but rectitude of purpose & generosity conquering the superficial coldness & prudence. But I ask now why was not I made like all these beatified mates of mine *superficially* generous & noble as well as *internally* so. . . . [Inserted] This is the thorn in the flesh.[71]

This confession reveals as much about Lidian as about Emerson himself, and both revelations are keys to their characters. Lidian listened with the patience of a Griselda and with genuine sympathy to her husband's "delicious relations" with his first wife, though his emotional memories must have made her realize that she could never affect him so poignantly. And these confessions to his second wife revealed either Emerson's callousness toward her feelings or his psychological blindness resulting from deep-seated inhibitions. What did Lidian "read" in *his* heart? Did he never have any twinges of conscience about his conduct to her? His Journals give no evidence of it.

Emerson's introspective nature also protected him against the oppressive moral and intellectual influence of his friends, the Church, society, and made him extremely impatient with dull and tradition-bound ministers. They seemed to him like "permanent embryos which receive all their nourishment through the umbilical cord & never arrived at a conscious and independent existence."[72] Dr. Ripley's assistant sometimes tempted him to declare he would never go to church again. Sincere, decorous, and impersonal, the Reverend Barzillai Frost's sermons "had no one word intimating that ever he had laughed or wept, was married or enamoured, had been cheated, or voted for, or chagrined."

During the spring of 1838 Emerson's irritation with preachers became painfully acute. On May 26 he confessed: "Nettled again & nervous (as much as sometimes by flatulency or piddling things) by the wretched Sunday's preaching of Mr H. [in Cambridge]." In the woods "God was manifest as he surely was not in the sermon."[73] Though this statement reflected the "romantic" taste of the period, it was also another indication of the pleasure Emerson found in escaping from people, social demands, and the pressures of "seem" (pretending). But he liked to share his sylvan walks with someone who felt as he did. Lidian in the letter to her sister quoted above said that "Mr E" had taken to Henry Thoreau "with great interest & thinks him uncommon in mind & character." She also indicated that it was quite unusual for "Mr E" to invite anyone to accompany him on his cherished walks.

Exactly when Emerson first met Thoreau the biographers of both men have not been able to determine. The previous summer Emerson had written to the president of Harvard, at Dr. Ripley's request, recommending that Thoreau be given a grant to help him settle his college expenses before his graduation.[74] Since the Thoreaus lived almost in the center of town, Emerson could scarcely have avoided knowing Henry. In

December he knew him well enough, as we have seen, to give him tickets to his lectures. By February the two men were becoming intimate friends, so far as intimacy was possible between two such individualists.

Henry David Thoreau (he had reversed his given names), now in his twentieth year, was of slight build, though lithe and wiry, several inches shorter than Emerson, with a large nose, gray eyes, and dark, slightly curly hair. His unprepossessing appearance and his brusque manner made it difficult for him to win friends. People thought him prickly. He was not morose or bitter, but affected a lofty disdain for the world. At Harvard he had made a better academic record than Emerson had, though he had not tried to do as well as he might, for he was contemptuous of academic competition. Yet he could read Latin, Greek, German, and French with more than adequate facility, and was excellent in mathematics. He had acquired a taste for writing under Professor Edward T. Channing. But he did not begin keeping a journal until Emerson suggested it.[75]

Soon after Thoreau's graduation from Harvard, the School Committee in Concord employed him to teach in its public school near the village square. But he taught only two weeks. At the end of the second week a member of the School Committee visited his classroom and severely criticized him for not whipping his students. How could they learn without being birched! Thoreau then feruled several boys and girls at random and resigned.

Unable to find another position that school year, Thoreau aided his father in making pencils, an industry John Thoreau carried on in the family residence. But making pencils did not occupy all his time, and he was able to take frequent walks with his eminent neighbor. Emerson's Journal testifies to the pleasure he found in this young man's society. For example, February 17:

My good friend Henry Thoreau made this else solitary afternoon sunny with his simplicity & clear perception. How comic is simplicity in this doubledealing quacking world. Every thing that boy says makes merry with society though nothing can be graver than his meaning. I told him he should write out the history of his College life as Carlyle has his tutoring. We agreed that the seeing the stars through a telescope would be worth all the Astronomical lectures. Then he described Mr Quimby's electrical lecture here & the experiment of the shock & added that "College Corporations are very blind to the fact that that twinge in the elbow is worth all the lecturing."[76]

Emerson's own critical state of mind enabled him to relish Henry's satire. Often it was waspish, but Emerson also felt strong indignation for the follies that Henry detested. He agreed completely that astronomy could not be taught effectively without a telescope, or electricity without experimental apparatus. Thoreau was not yet the accomplished naturalist his later Journals reveal, but he was a keen observer, and in his presence nature became more concrete and real to the author of the prose-poem called *Nature,* a work Thoreau knew almost by heart. He was the "forest seer" described by Emerson a few months later in "Woodnotes":

> A minstrel of the natural year,
> Foreteller of the vernal ides[77]

V

During the spring of 1838 Emerson also became acquainted with Jones Very, mentioned above. Very was a tutor in Greek who talked earnestly to his Harvard students about the state of their souls and published devotional sonnets in his hometown newspaper, the Salem *Observer.* Miss Elizabeth Peabody, who had recently returned to her family on Charter Street in Salem, first met him when Nathaniel Hawthorne, engaged to her sister Sophia, brought him on one of his calls. She immediately decided that he was a genius and arranged for him to read his essay on "Epic Poetry" to the Salem Lyceum. Then she wrote Emerson that he ought to meet so remarkable a young man.[78]

Early one April morning Very set out to walk the twenty-odd miles to Concord, carrying his essay and a copy of *Nature* to be autographed. Emerson was greatly impressed by Very's spirituality and complete subjection of his will to the will of God, which he believed to be guiding him in his every word and action. This was the sort of life Emerson had preached in many a sermon and lecture. The intensity of Very's religious "enthusiasm" did not especially alarm him, though he had never seen anything like it and marveled.

Very's essay on "Epic Poetry" made good sense to Emerson, and betrayed no mental aberrations. Somewhat indebted to German Romantic theory—perhaps indirectly—it brilliantly stated the theory that the Homeric epic manifested "that stage of society when men's physical existence assumed an importance in the mind like that of our [belief in] immortality . . ." In Homer the conflict is all external. But "as the mind expands and the moral power is developed [in later ages], the mightiest conflicts are born within . . ."[79] Christianity made "the individual mind the great object of regard, the center of eternal interest . . . transferring the scene of action from the outward world to the world within . . ." This was a theory sure to appeal to Emerson, and he urged Very to publish the essay.

After Very's visit, Emerson made a quick trip to New York to bring his mother back to Concord. At home again, he felt renewed confidence in the prospects of the nation. On April 19 he wrote in his Journal:

I have been to New York & seen [William Cullen] Bryant & [Orville] Dewey, & at home seen young Jones Very, & two youthful philosophers who came here from Cambridge, Edward Washburn & Renouf, & who told me fine hopeful things of their mates in the senior class. And now young [Frederic] Eustis has been here & tells me of more aspiring and heroical young men, & I begin to conceive hopes of the Republic. Then is this disaster of Cherokees brought to me by a sad friend to blacken my days & nights. I can do nothing. Why shriek? Why strike ineffectual blows?[80]

The Cherokee Indians affair was one of the first injustices to test Emerson's determination to leave reform to others while he did his work. In 1835 a few Indians, without the consent of their tribe (or "nation"), signed a treaty with the United States government, giving away the Cherokee lands in Georgia for a promised reservation beyond the Mississippi River. Recently, President Van Buren had ordered the U.S. Army to use force in moving the Cherokees off their ancestral grounds. After attending a protest meeting in the Unitarian church in Concord on April 22, Emerson wrote a public letter to the President, but hated himself for doing so. In nearly two thousand words of moral outrage Emerson displayed a mastery of invective, sarcasm, and satire one would hardly have expected of him:

It now appears that the government of the United States choose to hold the Cherokees to this sham treaty . . . and the American President and the

Cabinet, the Senate and the House of Representatives, neither hear these men [a Cherokee delegation] nor see them; and are contracting to put this active nation into carts and boats, and to drag them over mountains and rivers to a wilderness at a vast distance beyond the Mississippi. . . .

In the name of God, sir, we ask you if this be so . . . does this government think that the people of the United States are become savage and mad? From their mind are the sentiments of love and a good nature wiped clean out? The soul of men, the justice, the mercy that is the heart's heart in all men, from Maine to Georgia, does abhor this business.[81]

Emerson mailed this letter not directly to the President but to Massachusetts Congressman John Reed, who arranged for its publication in *The National Intelligencer,* where it appeared on May 14, and other papers reprinted it. Having fulfilled his promise to write the protest, Emerson felt that he had done all he could—and actually both the President and the land-greedy politicians were deaf to all humanitarian pleas. Books are still being published about the Cherokees' "trail of tears," in which hundreds of the Indians, especially women and children, died.

However, Emerson's detesting himself for his futile attempt to advance a cause he passionately believed in revealed a deep conflict in his psyche. Several months earlier he had confessed in his Journal that "When a zealot comes to me & represents the importance of this Temperance Reform my hands drop—I have no excuse—I honor him with shame at my own inaction."[82] It was the same with all other "reformers and philanthropers." "None of these causes are foreigners to me. My Universal Nature is thus marked. These accusations are part of me too. They are not for nothing." This shame was another manifestation of that peculiarity of his character which inhibited his outwardly expressing the secret love which he felt for his dearest friends and relatives. He also objected to the professional reformers because they seemed to find pleasure in courting martyrdom, "and nothing is so dog-cheap as martyrdom." They reminded him of the sophomore who exclaimed during a college rebellion, "Come, Bowers! let us go join these noble fellows."[83]

Yet when abstract principles of moral and intellectual honesty were endangered, Emerson found his response welling up inside him spontaneously. That had happened in writing his "American Scholar" address. And in March he was willing to address the American Peace Society in Boston on "War," without regrets afterward. George Willis Cooke writes:

He said that war could not be avoided in savage times, for religion leads to it. It does actually forward the culture of men, but is a temporary and preparatory state. . . . It is the subject of all history, has been the principal employment of the most conspicuous men, the delight of half the world. . . . Yet war goes with coarse forms of life, and is a juvenile and temporary state. "Not only the moral sentiment, but trade, learning, and whatever makes intercourse, conspire to put it down."[84]

Emerson was eager to talk to young people, his only hope for real reform. He had recorded on April 1 that "The Divinity School youths wished to talk with me concerning theism. I went rather heavy hearted for I always find that my views chill or shock people at the first opening. But the conversation went well & I came away cheered."[85] It went so well, in fact, that the seniors of the school invited him to address them in the Divinity School chapel on the evening of their graduation, July 15. Of course he accepted. He now had an excuse to write his discourse on the clergy.

The invitation came entirely from the students, numbering no more than half a dozen, and was in no way sponsored by the faculty. It could even be said that it was a private talk, so small was the audience, which included only the small faculty and a few invited friends of the students and the speaker.[86] Among those present were: the Reverend Andrews Norton, former professor of Biblical literature, who had retired to write a definitive work on *The Evidences of the Genuineness of the Gospels;* the Reverend Henry Ware Jr., professor of divinity, whom Emerson had assisted in the Second Church; the Reverend Henry Ware Sr., Hollis Professor of Divinity, who had "approbated" Emerson to preach; Dean John G. Palfrey; and possibly Dr. W. E. Channing. Emerson's personal friends included George Ripley, Frederic Hedge, James Freeman Clarke, Elizabeth Peabody, and Theodore Parker, minister of a church in West Roxbury.[87]

But Emerson did not give this little group an informal talk. He had composed a polished discourse on the decline of the Unitarian clergy and how it might be redeemed by stronger faith in the life of the soul. Theologically, it contained little that Dr. Channing, long regarded as the chief spokesman of New England Unitarianism, had not said in 1819 in his ordination sermon for Jared Sparks in Baltimore: that "the creation is a birth and shining forth of the Divine Mind"; that "We see God around us because He dwells within us"; that "God's infinity has its image in the soul"; and that "through the soul, much more than through the universe, we arrive at this conception of the Deity . . ."[88] It may seem surprising that scarcely twenty years later Emerson's reassertion of these ideas should create a sensation at Harvard. But there are several explanations. Officially, Harvard was nondenominational, but in actuality the Divinity School was the stronghold of New England Unitarianism. Except for eastern Massachusetts, most of the churches of the state were still Congregationalist, in which a modified Calvinism still survived.[89]

Unitarians still rejected the Trinity, but many could not give up belief in the divinity of Christ, or in the New Testament account of miracles. Furthermore, all institutions tend to guard their own power, and complete individual freedom of conscience challenged the authority of the clergy, as it had done in Anne Hutchinson's day. Professor Norton, especially, thought that the "higher criticism" had undermined belief in the sacredness of the Bible. He also thought it very unfortunate that German philosophy had elevated the heart (emotions) over the head (intellect). Professor Henry Ware Jr. likewise feared that doubt of the literal truth of the miracles undermined the authority of Christianity.

Not only did Emerson challenge the convictions of the Nortons and the Wares, he accused the Unitarian clergy in general of incompetence and stupidity: "now the priest's Sabbath has lost the splendor of nature; it is unlovely; we are glad when it is done; we can make, we do make, even sitting in our pews, a far better, holier, sweeter [Sabbath] for ourselves."[90] Why this "famine" in the churches and bereavement of consolation? Because the ministers have preached a secondary, not a primary, faith—not a faith based on personal experience of one's own "indwelling Supreme Spirit." When this happens, then "miracles, prophecy, poetry, the ideal life, the holy life, exist as ancient history merely . . ."

> Jesus Christ belonged to the true race of prophets. . . . He saw that God incarnates himself in man, and evermore goes forth anew to take possession of his World. . . . He spoke of miracles; for he felt that man's life was a miracle, and all that man doth, and he knew that this daily miracle shines as the character ascends. But the word Miracle, as pronounced by Christian churches, gives a false impression; it is Monster. It is not one with the blowing clover and the falling rain.
>
> . . . it is still true, that tradition characterizes the preaching of this country; that it comes out of the memory, and not out of the soul . . . historical Christianity destroys the power of preaching, by withdrawing it from the

exploration of the moral nature of man . . . It is the office of a true teacher
to show us that God is, not was; that He speaketh, not spake.[91]

What is needed is not new rites and forms. "Rather let the breath of new
life be breathed by you through the forms already existing."
Three weeks later Emerson wrote Carlyle:

I have written and read a kind of sermon to the Senior Class of the Cambridge Theological School a fortnight ago; and an address to the Literary
Societies of Dartmouth College; for though I hate American plenilo-
quence, I cannot easily say *no* to young men who bid me speak also. And
both these are now in press. The first I hear is very offensive. I will now try
to hold my tongue until next winter.[92]

CHAPTER XV

Vanishing Gods

> It would indeed give a certain household joy to
> quit this lofty seeking[,] this spiritual astron-
> omy ... & come down into warm sympathies
> with you [my friends], but then I know well I
> shall mourn always the vanishing of my Mighty
> Gods.[1]

I

"Spent the night at Mr. Emerson's," Dr. Convers Francis, the Unitarian minister at Watertown and faithful attendant of the "Hedge's Club," wrote in his diary early in September 1838. "When we were alone he talked of his discourse at the Divinity School, and of the obloquy it had drawn upon him. He is perfectly quiet amid the storm." This was the way he appeared to all his friends. Dr. Francis voiced objections to some of Emerson's statements in his address, and received such patient and good-natured replies that he concluded: "He is a true godful man; though in his love for the ideal he disregards too much the actual."[2]

Emerson's early biographers all said that he remained undisturbed by the tempest he had stirred up (Carlyle called it a "washbowl storm"),[3] and to most observers he appeared so. But his Journal shows that he was deeply hurt, though defiant, and in the long run the controversy only stiffened his determination to speak his mind without any regard for the consequences. However, it was several weeks before he realized the extent of the opposition to him. When he left Concord on Saturday, July 21, for Hanover, where he was scheduled to address the literary societies of Dartmouth College the following Tuesday at commencement time, he knew only that he had displeased some members of the Divinity School faculty.

The address at Dartmouth on "Literary Ethics" could be called a lower-keyed companion of the "Divinity School Address,"[4] but criticizing contemporary American intellectual life was safer than telling Unitarian clergy to their faces that they were preaching a dead theology. America, Emerson told the Dartmouth students, had so far failed to achieve anything of significance in art, literature, or thought. The cause, as he had expressed it more forcefully in his "Divinity School Address," was diffidence, fear of innovation, too much respect for authority, custom, and inherited opinion. Intellectual activity was not yet respected by the nation because no one had yet made it vital and important. "Make yourself necessary to the world, and mankind will give you bread, and if not store of it, yet such as shall not take away your property in all man's possessions, in all men's affections, in art, in nature, and in hope."[5]

On his return from Dartmouth, Emerson found a letter from his former colleague, the Reverend Henry Ware Jr., waiting for him. It was dated July 15 and expressed the author's second thoughts after having told Emerson while entertaining him in Cambridge that he assented to the main ideas expressed in the address. On reflection Ware had decided that "their prevalence would tend to overthrow the authority and influence of Christianity."[6] He still rejoiced "in the lofty ideas and beautiful images of spiritual life" which Emerson had so beautifully expressed, but felt he must frankly state his strong reservations.

"What you say," Emerson replied on July 28, "is just what I might expect from your truth & charity combined with your known opinions." He confessed he "could not but feel pain in saying some things in that place & presence where I supposed they might meet dissent [in his rough draft he deleted "offend"]—the dissent, I may say, of dear friends & benefactors of mine." Yet his own conviction was that he had said exactly what he believed, and now he could only add: "These things look so to me; to you otherwise: let us say out our uttermost word, & let the all prevailing Truth, as it surely will, judge between us."[7]

Dr. Ware hoped Emerson would at least revise his address before publishing it, and Emerson promised "to revise with greater care." The senior class in the Divinity School had first planned to publish the address, then backed off and suggested only printing it in a limited edition, but Emerson decided to publish it, and also "Literary Ethics." His half-uncle, the Reverend Samuel Ripley, heard a rumor of this plan, and said emphatically that he hoped Waldo would not carry it out. He did not want to see him classed with the notorious atheists Abner Kneeland and Tom Paine. But after it was published (advertised in *The Christian Examiner* on August 25), Samuel Ripley announced to his congregation that he still supported the author entirely. With the exception of Aunt Mary, other members of Emerson's family were just as loyal. William wrote that he, his wife, and his father-in-law were in "no way shocked at your heresies." Of course Aunt Mary was, and William tried to assure her that Waldo was as religious as Luther and Calvin.[8]

In delivering his address Emerson had left out a passage in his manuscript (now lost) in which, in the words of George Willis Cooke, he cautioned "against looking on the past with contempt, and against setting up their own souls as higher standards of truth than that of Jesus!"[9] Miss Elizabeth Peabody urged him to restore the passage in his printed version, but Emerson said, "No: these gentlemen have committed themselves against what I did read . . ." Cooke regretted this decision because the omitted words would have shown "that he appreciated the historic side of religion, and the social nature of worship." Possibly, but he also offended by saying that the defect of historical Christianity was the "noxious exaggeration about the *person* of Jesus."

On September 23 Dr. Ware preached a sermon on "The Personality of God," which he had printed and sent to Emerson with a letter in which he asked what arguments Emerson held that "the soul knows no persons."[10] In his famous reply on October 8 Emerson pleaded, there is "no scholar less willing or less able to be polemic. I could not give account of myself if challenged."[11] All he could do was tell what he thought. However, the controversy would not die down, and the following July Professor Andrews Norton attacked Emerson in his own address to the alumni of the Divinity School called "The Latest Form of Infidelity." Norton accused Emerson of following "the celebrated atheist Spinoza, and while claiming to be Christian, denies Christianity in a denial of its miracles."[12]

Norton mentioned the "German thought," from which he supposed the American "Transcendentalists" had borrowed their philosophy. In newspapers and sermons George Ripley, Orestes Brownson, James Freeman Clarke, and Theodore Parker defended Emerson—and American Transcendentalism (the name was beginning to stick)—but the popular view was that Emerson was a dangerous man, and he would not be invited back to Harvard for many years.

As the outcry continued, Emerson began to fear it might affect his ability to supplement his income with more public lectures. On September 26 he wrote William that he might not be able to lend him any more money for a while. He had planned to lecture again in Boston during the winter, but "perhaps the people scared by the newspapers will not come & pay for my paper & pens. In that case, I should not be able to meet my expenses for October to April & lend anything."[13] That he was seriously worried is corroborated in his letter to Carlyle on October 17. For months he had been strongly urging Carlyle to visit him and lecture in Boston and other American cities, but now this plan might be in danger:

> ... I think you must postpone, for the present, the satisfaction of your friendship and your curiosity. At this moment I would not have you here, on any account. The publication of my *Address to the Divinity College* (copies of which I sent you) has been the occasion of an outcry in all our leading local newspapers against my "infidelity, pantheism, and atheism." The writers warn all and sundry against me, and against whatever is supposed to be related to my connection of opinion &c., against Transcendentalism, Goethe, and *Carlyle.* I am heartily sorry to see this last aspect of the storm in our washbowl. For, as Carlyle is nowise guilty, and has unpopularities of his own, I do not wish to embroil him in my parish differences.[14]

Carlyle had been included in the sinister Emersonian influences not only because he was a translator and interpreter of German literature and philosophy but also because Emerson had sponsored the publication of his books—at the time his *Miscellanies* was being printed. Emerson especially regretted the inclusion of Carlyle's name in the attacks on him because he was "getting to be a great favorite with us all here." He was glad, therefore, as he never thought he would be, that Carlyle had not yet decided to come. "Let us wait a little until this foolish clamor be overblown." He did not doubt that that day would come, but "it seems very clear to me that, if I live, my neighbors must look for a great many more shocks, and perhaps harder to bear."[15]

Emerson's greatest fear was that both the blame and the praise would draw him "out of equilibrium,— putting me for a time in a false position to people, & disallowing the spontaneous sentiments . . . Therefore I hate to be conspicuous for blame or praise. It spoils thought." Actually, he found it easier to bear criticism than praise. When he was defended in a newspaper, he felt "as one that lies unprotected before his enemies."[16] He felt comforted and was deeply impressed by Lidian's advice one night: "In the gossip and excitement of the hour, be as one blind & deaf to it. Know it not. Do as if nothing had befallen." He wrote in his Journal: "Blessed be the wife!"[17]

Yet, a week later, Emerson admitted: "I am sensitive as a leaf to impressions from abroad." He claimed that "under this night's beautiful heaven I have forgotten that ever I was *reviewed.*" But he added: "A man thinks it of importance what the great sheet or pamphlet of today proclaims of him to all the reading town; and if he sees graceful compliments, he relishes his dinner; & if he sees threatening paragraphs & odious nicknames, it becomes a solemn depressing fact & sables his whole thoughts until bedtime."[18]

It was not easy to follow Lidian's advice, but Emerson tried to console himself with the thought that if he himself learned nothing useful from an attack on him, then it was shallow and would "die like flies in an hour." When Professor Andrews Norton denounced him in the Boston *Daily Advertiser,* beseeching "the dear people to whip that naughty heretic," Emerson called him in his Journal a coward who had no faith in God. "A believer, a mind whose faith is consciousness, is never disturbed because other persons do not yet see the fact which he sees."[19] Emerson believed that he himself was only destroying "idolatrous propositions" which stood in the way of complete trust in God, yet he reminded himself that he should "never fall into the vulgar mistake of dreaming that I am persecuted whenever I am contradicted."[20]

In actual fact, Emerson was tolerant of disagreement. As one example, during the past summer he had befriended young James Russell Lowell during his "rustication" from Harvard, only to be rewarded by harsh satire on himself and Transcendentalism in the young man's class poem. Lowell had been exiled from Cambridge for having celebrated his election to class poet by appearing inebriated in chapel. As punishment he was suspended and forbidden to read his poem at commencement; nevertheless, he had his poem printed and sent Emerson a copy, accompanied by a letter in which he complained that friends had accused him of having betrayed Emerson's hospitality.[21] He said he had only exercised his right to speak his honest opinion, and he had frankly not liked the "Divinity School Address." Emerson thanked him for the copy of the poem. "I love the spirit of your letter . . . ," he wrote, and invited him to stop at his house next time he came to Concord. "Not withstanding the strictures on the Address, I shall venture to send you a copy of my Dartmouth Oration, wh. I hope you will like better."[22] In a few years Lowell would be one of Emerson's most ardent admirers.

II

In his address to the Divinity School seniors Emerson had declared, "The man on whom the soul descends, through whom the soul speaks, alone can teach." In the autumn of 1839 he witnessed a testing of this doctrine. Early in the new term at Harvard, Jones Very, tutor in Greek, startled his class by crying out, "Flee to the mountains, for the end of all things is at hand."[23] The religious ecstasy which Emerson had observed when Very visited him in the summer had increased to such an extent that the college authorities feared he was insane and asked him to withdraw from the faculty. He returned to Salem, where he accused the ministers of being spiritually dead and lacking genuine faith in Christ. It was as if he had taken Emerson too literally and magnified his condemnation of the moribund clergy. Not only did Very advocate, as Emerson did, submission of one's will to God's direction; he believed that he had so completely done so that, when he spoke or wrote, the words were not his own. Emerson's wanting the "soul" to speak through him was an ideal of spiritual faith, perhaps actually a figure of speech, certainly not the delusion that he was an Old Testament prophet.

But Very, believing in the most literal sense that his every action and utterance was God-inspired, embarrassed and annoyed the citizens of Salem. Some of them strongly urged his mother to commit him to an insane asylum. This she would not do, but she did agree to his voluntarily entering the McLean hospital in Charlestown, where Emerson's brother Edward had spent a few weeks and Bulkeley was again a patient. On September 17, 1838, Very went to Charlestown and placed himself under the care of Dr. Bell.[24] But before leaving home he sent Emerson his essay on "Shakespeare," and in the asylum he revised his other essays on "Hamlet" and "Epic Poetry." In a note accompanying "Shakespeare" he explained: "I am glad at last to be able to transmit what has been told to me of

Shakespeare—'tis but the faint echo of that which speaks to you now. . . .
You hear not mine own words, but the teachings of the Holy Ghost."[25]
On September 29 Emerson wrote Margaret Fuller:

Ha[ve] you heard of the calamity of poor Very, the tutor at Cambridge?
He is at the Charlestown Asylum & his case tho't a very unpromising one.
A fortnight ago tomorrow—I received from him his Dissertation on
Shakspeare. The letter accompanying it betrayed the state of his mind; but
the Essay is a noble production: not consecutive, filled with one thought;
but that so deep & true & illustrated so happily & even grandly, that I ac-
count it an addition to our really scanty stock of adequate criticism on
Shakspear. Such a mind cannot [that is, must not] be lost.[26]

After Very had spent a month in the asylum, the authorities decided
that he was sane and dismissed him. His extreme excitement had subsided,
but his convictions remained the same. He felt no resentment, because in
addition to completing the revision of his two critical studies, he had also
written numerous sonnets during his confinement. For the remainder of
his life he would live in Salem under the devoted care and protection of
his mother and sisters. He would preach occasionally in Unitarian
churches and continue writing his devotional poems, which interested
Emerson and a few others of his school of thought. A week after returning
home, Very again visited Emerson, who recorded in his Journal:

26 October. Jones Very came hither two days since & gave occasion to
many thoughts on his peculiar state of mind & his relation to society. His
position accuses society as much as society names it false & morbid. &
much of his discourse concerning society, the church, & the college was
perfectly just.[27]

These observations led Emerson to add: "Entertain every thought[,]
every character that goes by with the hospitality of your soul." It was in
this spirit that he entertained Jones Very and learned what he could from
his "peculiar state of mind." But what he learned only confirmed some of
his own convictions, as when he wrote in his Journal on October 29: "We
are wiser, I see well, than we know. If we will not interfere with our
thought but will act entire or see how the thing stands in God, we know
the particular thing & every thing & every man."[28]

Although Emerson believed as strongly as Very in the "boundless resources of the soul," he was not as indifferent to human ties, and he deceived himself, as we have seen before and shall again, in believing he was incapable of suffering. Moreover, his subordinating his human will to the dictates of his "soul" did not affect his character and personality as devastatingly as it did Very's. Bronson Alcott, a keener psychologist than Emerson, recognized that Very's fanatical beliefs had almost literally made him dead to the world. On January 29, 1839, Alcott spent the night with him in the home of a friend in Lynn, and recorded these observations:

> He is a remarkable phenomenon. He affects me as a spectre. His looks, tones, words, are all sepulchral. He is a voice from the tombs. He speaks as having once lived in the world amidst men and things, but of being now in the Spirit: time and space are not, save in memory. This idea modifies all his thoughts and expressions, and the thoughts and expressions of others also. . . . We slept in the same apartment, and had much conversation after we returned to our chamber.[29]

Most people found it hard to understand Very's conversation, but Alcott, a dedicated Idealist himself, had no difficulty in translating Very's thoughts into his own vocabulary. "His speech is Oriental. By putting modern life into Eastern images, speech becomes possible with him." But Alcott thought he was physically dying by retreating from his senses, and might well soon decease. "Nature to him is as a charnel house, and the voices of men, echoes of the dead who haunt its dark chambers."

For all his sympathy with Very, Emerson still lived intensely in the world of his senses, and only his sense of humor enabled him to tolerate Very's eccentricities. "J. Very," he observed in his Journal the day Very departed, "charmed us all by telling us he hated us all."[30] Emerson himself had been the chief target of Very's criticism. "He thinks me covetous in my hold of truth, of seeing truth separate, & of receiving or taking it instead of merely obeying."[31] Emerson had replied that his thought and conduct were constitutional, and Very seemed to agree; nevertheless, "the spirit" continued to say to him that his host was "not right."

During Very's visit Emerson came to regard the violence of his language as superficial, and not evidence of insanity. In fact, he wrote Elizabeth Peabody on Tuesday October 30, the day after he had carried Very as far as Waltham on his way to Cambridge: "I wish the whole world were as mad as he . . . he is profoundly sane, & as soon as his thoughts subside from their present excited to a more natural state, I think he will make all men sensible of it." But even if his aberrations persisted, they would not "alter the value of the truth & illumination he communicates."[32]

In making these comments Emerson was thinking especially of Very's conversation, but he was also strongly impressed by his sonnets and the three prose essays. He was not yet sure he fully understood the essay on Shakespeare, but he suspected the dramatist had now another critic to stand with Coleridge and Goethe. The essays were not uniformly related to the religious excitement which had resulted in Very's separation from Harvard. "Epic Poetry" had won the Bowdoin Prize in 1833, and Very had revised it since, but without destroying his original delight in Homer's world of the senses, "a mirror of this outward world."[33] Yet as Very had become more intensely concerned with the internal world, he had sought to solve the puzzle of how Shakespeare, plainly "no saint," could be a great literary genius. Though the theory he evolved owed much to his own "inward" experience, it also was indebted more than he realized to German Romanticism, such as expressed by the Schlegel brothers, August and Friedrich. The Germans first propounded the theory of an "original" or "natural" genius, a person whose ideas come to him without effort, almost unconsciously, so that he writes not as he would but as he must.

Christianity, Very wrote, shifted the center of interest in literature from the external to internal conflict, to the struggle of the will to control the springs of action. A desire for action was the ruling impulse of Shakespeare's mind, but his sense of existence was natural, instinctive, "bearing the will along with it; presenting the mind as phenomenal and unconscious, and almost as much a passive instrument as the material world."[34] Thus Shakespeare simply presented people as they were, without moral judgments on them, though their conduct might cause them to suffer retribution. "We cannot say of him that he conformed to God's will; but that the Divine Will in its ordinary operations moved his mind as it does the material world."[35]

Shakespeare's "simple pleasure of existence . . . made him more than commonly liable to the fear of death . . . From the wrestling of his own soul with the great enemy come that depth and mystery which startle us in Hamlet."[36] These theories interested Emerson so much that he began rereading Shakespeare, and especially *Hamlet*.

A week after Very departed, Lidian, as Waldo expressed it in a letter to Margaret Fuller, broke out into "wild hospitality."[37] At a social gathering Emerson was as out of place as Very, though never as deliberately rude. Incapable of small talk, he was exasperated by banalities. In his Journal he complained: "in an evening party you have no variety of persons, but only one person. For, say what you will, to whom you will,—they shall all render one & the same answer, without thought, without heart,—a conversation of the lips. So is a soirée a heap of lies; false itself it makes falsehoods."[38] He might chuckle at a family joke, but social banter did not amuse him. Once when he visited Orville Dewey in New Bedford, his friend was in a frolicsome mood. Getting up from the supper table, Dewey said, " 'Come let us have some fun,' & went about to tickle his wife and his two sisters. I grew grave, &, do what I could, I felt that I looked like one appointed to be hanged."[39]

On the whole, however, Emerson was fundamentally different from Jones Very. He was probably thinking of his recent guest when he wrote a few weeks after his visit: "One of the tests of sanity is repose. I demand of a great spirit [that is, a spiritual person] entire self command. He must be free and detached, & take the world up into him & not suggest the idea of a restless soul bestridden alway by an invisible rider. He must not be feverish, but free."[40]

III

On November 6, 1838, Waldo wrote William: "I am busy preparing myself for a course of Lectures on Human Life which I have advertised for the first Wednesday of December & the ten following Wednesdays."[41] He felt so doubtful of having a good audience that he expected to give away a large number of tickets "that I may not have labored wholly in vain." He anticipated that on January 1 he would need William's payment due the previous October but held over by mutual agreement. In spite of these worries, many visitors, and a lecture in Portsmouth (where William's brother-in-law, George Haven, read Sir Thomas Browne to him), his first lecture on "Human Life" was ready for delivery in the Tremont Temple in Boston on December 5.

Emerson called his introductory lecture "Doctrine of the Soul,"[42] and it was the embryo of the great essay on "The Over-Soul," which would become the keystone of his philosophy. The word *soul* had connotations for him and his audience which it does not have for twentieth-century readers. But to understand his basic message in these lectures it is not necessary to analyze all his metaphysical and metapsychological assumptions. In fact, his frequent ambiguity suggests that the term had no precise meaning for him. But his main intention was not ambiguous: he wanted to convince his audience that man has almost unlimited possibilities for a better life than history records, though a few individuals, such as Homer, Chaucer, Spenser, Shakespeare, and Milton, have given glimpses of human achievements on a very high scale.

Plato's myth of the charioteer trying to drive two ill-matched horses suggests Emerson's conception of man's equivocal situation, "passing through what a scale of powers and merits from reptile sympathies with the earth to enthusiasm and ecstasy!"[43] The good horse is the soul, and the bad one, man's sensuous nature. Like Freud's unconscious, the soul can no more be observed by conscious effort than man can escape from his brain to observe the external world which his senses report to him. It must be taken on faith or intuition (or Kant's "categorical imperative"). Man is related "by his form to the whole world, and by his soul to the whole universe, with [physical] faculties buried in time and space, but animated by a soul that dwells out of time and space":

> ... the Soul in man ... is not an organ but which animates and exercises all the organs; which is not a function like the power of memory, of calculation, of comparison,—but which uses these as hands and feet; which is not a faculty but a Light, which is not the Intellect or the Will but the master of the Intellect and the Will—the vast background of our being in which they lie, an immensity not possessed and that cannot be possessed.[44]

A seminal influence on this theory was the teachings of Socrates, the subject, it will be recalled, of one of Emerson's college dissertations. It is interesting, therefore, that Samuel Stumpf's definition of Socrates' concept of the soul bears a striking resemblance to Emerson's: "For him [Socrates] the soul was not any particular faculty, nor was it any special kind of substance, but was rather the capacity for intelligence and character; it was man's conscious personality. . . . Socrates identified the soul with the normal powers of intelligence and character instead of as some ghostly substance."[45] This same historian says further of Socrates' teaching, "One takes best care of his soul when he understands the difference between fact and fancy and builds his thought upon a knowledge of what human life is really like." If there is a difference between Emerson's doctrine and Socrates', Emerson placed greater emphasis on what human life *could be* rather than *is*.

In the past, Emerson says, man failed to fulfill his human potential, innate but undeveloped, because he permitted aged customs, ceremonies, and institutions to encumber him instead of following the impulses of his soul for change, growth, and creativity. But "A new spirit characterises the men and works of this age. . . . the ancients observed the fact; we observe its effect upon the mind."[46] Timid people saw in this increased introversion and speculation a threat to cherished values, but to Emerson they evidenced an unfolding of higher faculties in human nature. Wordsworth, almost alone among his contemporaries, heard this "music of humanity," but imperfectly expressed it, Emerson thought.

Of course this "self-analyzing temper" had its "foolish and canting side," though Emerson regarded this as a minor risk. More important, "We know better than we do."[47] Truth lies already in each mind, and needs only to be discovered, revealed, or somehow brought into consciousness. Stumpf points out that this was precisely the objective of Socrates' famous dialectic.

At times Emerson seems almost to anticipate later theories of the unconscious, or "depth psychology." In his lecture on "The Head" he had declared that "God comes in by a private door" never consciously left open, and in the same lecture:

> Always our thinking is an observing. Into us flows the stream evermore of thought from we know not whence. We do not determine what we will think; we only open our senses, clear away as we can all obstruction from the facts, and let God think through us. Then we carry away in the ineffaceable memory the result, and all men and all the ages confirm it. It is called Truth.[48]

This is very similar to William James's "stream-of-consciousness,"[49] which originates in some depth of the mind not accessible to observation (except by introspection). Of course, James was describing the phenomenon of consciousness; Emerson, the emergence of "Truth" in the consciousness. The relationship of the unconscious and consciousness is still a mystery. Even Freud said the unconscious belonged to metapsychology. Therefore, substituting modern terms for Emerson's "soul" does not make it less ineffable.

In the second lecture in this series, "Home," Emerson attempted to domesticate the soul. "The instinct of the mind requires ever some permanent thing—permanent as itself—to be its outward object; to be its home . . ."[50] This implies a necessary relation between nature (the objective world) and the subjective world of the soul. And in his third lecture, "The School," he says, "the sense of being . . . is not diverse from things," but in things "we only see the secondary or modified effects of the one Soul."[51]

The most lyrical of these lectures was on "Love," by which the soul exhibits its nature through affection. This "great enchantment of life, which, like a certain divine rage and enthusiasm, seizes on man at one period, and works a revolution in his soul and body . . . The power of Love is indeed the great poem of nature."[52] This dualism of nature and soul is seen in the phenomenon of sex in organic matter and polarity in inorganic.

Emerson describes the ecstasy of love from his memories of Ellen, but when he theorizes that the rapture of love becomes, in the order of human experience, complacent domestic felicity, he confesses his life with his second wife. "Thus even Love which is the deification of persons must become more impersonal every day."[53] He concludes from these observations that, as a consequence of seeing beauty in one person, the lover comes to see beauty in all souls, thus ascending ever toward the highest beauty, to the love and knowledge of God, by steps on the ladder of created souls. The state of perfection is reached when husband and wife "attain a regard from which everything personal is at last utterly excluded"; it is then "perfect, spiritual, self-sufficing, eternal."[54]

This doctrine probably appealed to Elizabeth Hoar, who had sublimated her lost lover, Charles Emerson, and possibly also to another high-minded maiden lady, Elizabeth Peabody, to whom Emerson gave the manuscript. But it annoyed Margaret Fuller and Caroline Sturgis, who would argue the subject with him during the summer of 1840. One would like to know what Lidian thought of it.

Passing from affection to intellect, Emerson defined "Genius" as the intellect's "spontaneous perception and exhibition of truth."[55] Here he agreed with Jones Very and the "original genius" theories of the Germans. "Not by any conscious imitation of particular forms are the grand strokes of the painter executed, but by repairing to the fountainhead of all forms in his mind."[56] He quotes the *Rime di Michelangelo Buonarroti il Vecchio:* "I know not if it be the reflected light of its author which the soul perceives, or if from the memory, or from the mind . . . or if in the soul, yet beams and glows a bright ray of its preexistence . . ."[57]

Only a few geniuses make full use of the "divine energy" available to all men. They may have a greater portion of it than ordinary men, but most men do not make use of the portion they have, and this moral and intellectual inertia increases with age. Before young men succumb to this inertia, they are often dissatisfied and agitate for change. He was sympathetic with "impatient youth," and his young friend Henry Thoreau in particular, who insisted on living spontaneously and defying restrictions on his freedom. Emerson had observed that most protesters grow weary in time and compromise as they mature, but he said that if one could continue "to bow the knee to no Baal . . . but to keep erect, the head which was given him, erect against the physical and metaphysical turns of the universe; then he has immortal youth." Let a man follow his own "law," and all men will become his allies.[58]

In none of these lectures did Emerson reveal himself more than in "Tragedy" and "Comedy."[59] His theory of tragedy owed nothing to the dramas of Sophocles and Aeschylus, in which the protagonist is led by fate into a course of action ending in his own destruction. The Greek conviction that some evils in the world are irremediable was beyond Emerson's imagination. He did believe with Shakespeare that character is fate, but he thought a man could shape his own character. If he had read Aristotle's treatise, it had made little impression on him; his "catharsis" for *fear* and *pity* was entirely his own.

To Emerson the word *tragedy* meant pain, physical or mental. Its essence was not any particular evil, such as "famine, fever, siege, onslaught, mutilation, palsy, the rack, madness, and loss of friends," but terror—the power of the imagination to "dislocate things orderly and cheerful, and show them in startling disarray. . . . Ungrounded fears, suspicions, half knowledge, and mistakes darken the brow and chill the heart of man." Some people, he said, are temperamentally disposed to crave pain, and "no prosperity can soothe their ragged and dishevelled desolation."[60]

But suppose the fears are well grounded in sordid fact? Emerson had an answer, and it might have come straight out of Marcus Aurelius (not a favorite author, though a familiar one): "The attitude that befits a man is composure. He should not commit his tranquility to things, but keep as much as possible the reins in his own hands, rarely giving way to extreme emotion of joy or grief."[61] He did not mean a "superficial tranquility, a front of marble masking a boiling and passionate soul," but that all suffering is external, physical, and hence inconsequential. A man at ease with his own soul is impervious to tragedy: "The soul will not grieve; the soul sits behind there in a serene peace . . ."[62]

Nature also provides compensations for every loss, strengthening the will and dulling the pain in course of time and forgetfulness. Moreover, it is unnatural to exaggerate pain in others. "Tragedy is in the eye of the observer, and not in the heart of the sufferer."[63] He had Lidian in mind[64] when he declared:

A tender American girl doubts of Divine Providence whilst she reads the horrors of the middle passage [ships carrying captive Africans to the American slave market]. And they are bad enough. But to such as she these crucifixions do not come. They come to the obtuse and barbarous to whom they are not horrid, but only a little worse than the old sufferings. They exchange a cannibal war for the stench of the hold. They have gratifications which would be none to the civilized girl.[65]

In Emerson's defense it should be said that his statement was made in ignorance of the real life of Africans, and later his own sympathies were deeply stirred when he had more knowledge of the subject. But here he deserves to be revealed for his obtuseness because his Stoic theory excluded vicarious suffering. Lidian did not grieve for herself, but for tortured human beings; it did not matter who or where they were. For Emerson, believing himself incapable of sustained grief, convinced that physical pain in general could be borne by moral fortitude, and that discontent was due to a deficiency of "virtue," *tragedy* had little meaning.

Emerson said he lectured on "Comedy" with reluctance, because he was conscious of his deficiency in this field.[66] But there was no need for him to apologize, for a strong sense of the comic was as much his element as tragedy was not. His childhood propensity for "levity" had saved him, as we have seen, from the tragic fate of his younger brothers. And even though he believed that neither nature nor the soul ever jested, he nevertheless had a keen sense of the ludicrous in human conduct.

Furthermore, Emerson had developed a theory of laughter which harmonized with his philosophy of the soul. He called his theory "halfness": when a man's conduct is only a fraction of his pretensions, he provokes laughter.[67] The substance of a joke is a lie, for all sham and insincerity is falsehood. And the joke can work in many ways, from exposing intended deception in others to revealing to one's own self the failure to attain an ideal, or to act on what one knows to be true. Laughter is an effective weapon against hypocrisy and superstition in institutions or individuals; against "halfness" in the spirituality of the Church, corruption in the State, pedantry in scholarship, or artificiality in manners.

Emerson's humor in his addresses and lectures had not been conspicuous, though his intention had been to expose "halfness" and advocate wholeness. Now he says in "Comedy" that "when patriotism merges itself in parties" the "moral sentiment" is forgotten.[68] Politicians judge every issue by the number of votes they can win or lose. All these subjects were capable of comic treatment, but he used only an occasional hyperbole. However, he would begin exploring the effects of the humorous metaphor in reworking his lectures into his first volume of *Essays*. He had already learned to emphasize his thought by such emphatic, and sometimes exaggerated, language that he at times created the effect of satire, whose main function is to expose "halfness." He would "as lief be a sinner," he says in "Duty," "as guilty of the odious religion that watches the food you eat and . . . the orbit of the pitcher at table: that shuts the mouth hard at any remark it cannot twist or wrench into a sermon; and preaches as long as itself and its hearer is awake."[69]

In discussing "Demonology" (the field today of parapsychology) Emerson displayed the same respect for *wholeness*. Anyone who regards his soul theories as only varieties of "mysticism" might expect him to be more sympathetic with efforts to find "truth" in dreams, omens, coincidences, luck, fortune-telling, magic, and so on, "which are supposed to indicate the presence of some foreign, unacknowledged element in nature that produces exceptions to, if not violation of, the ordinary laws."[70] But such expectations seemed to him as superstitious as beliefs in demons; there were no exceptions to nature's laws, though they might not be fully understood.

Emerson did admit, however, a special interest in dreams, which needed further investigation. They seemed to be phantoms of his own imagination, "but they act like mutineers,—and fire on their commander."[71] In studying his own dreams he found sometimes the maturation of knowledge which he had not possessed in his waking state. But he concluded that what he learned most of all was shades of his own character. "The soul contains in itself the event that shall presently befal it,—for the event is only the actualizing of its thoughts." This was only another way of saying "a man's fortune is in his character. As in dreams, so in the scarcely less fluid events of the world, every man sees himself in colossal, without knowing that it is himself he sees."[72]

"Animal Magnetism" (essentially what would later be called hypnotism) seemed to Emerson to be "the phenomena of Disease, . . . of so fuliginous, nocturnal, and typhoid a character, as to repel rather than invite."[73] He admitted that perhaps it ought to be impartially explored, but so far "the inquiry is pursued on low principles." A few years later in his *Blithedale Romance* Hawthorne would show how low the level was. Demonology, therefore, is "the shadow of Theology," containing only a small fraction of truth, if any.

IV

Emerson had planned to give two more lectures in this series, in which he would show "the Limitation of human activity by the laws of the world" (a preliminary look at Determinism), but he suddenly ended with "Demonology" on February 20, 1839. He had caught a "pest of a cold," he wrote Margaret Fuller on the fifteenth, and had difficulty preparing and delivering his last lecture. He had had to postpone his January 2 lecture on "Genius" for a week "on account of my unaccountable vigils now for four or five nights, which destroy all power of concentration by day."[74]

Lidian's health was always precarious during a pregnancy, and she was now in the ninth month of carrying her second child. Usually women servants or friends attended her during her illnesses, so that her husband must have been more than ordinarily alarmed to take on these vigils himself. Margaret Fuller, having been informed by friends that Mrs. Emerson was not seriously ill, taunted Waldo for postponing a lecture because of "a lost night's rest." She had heard, she claimed, that afterward he "rode to Waltham, walked five miles, sawed wood, & by use of these mild remedies" had regained his health.[75]

Lidian's ordeal and Waldo's vigils came to an end at eight o'clock on Sunday morning, February 24, when she gave birth to a daughter. Her father thought she looked like her brother Waldo, "as he used to; only prettier and whiter—with more and darker hair."[76] Lidian immediately named the baby for Waldo's first wife, and he was transported with pleasure. In his Journal he wrote: "Lidian, who magnanimously makes my gods her gods, calls the babe Ellen. I can hardly ask more for thee my babe, than that name implies. Be that vision & remain with us, & after us."[77]

Mrs. Emerson had prepared for the birth of her second child by having the house put in immaculate condition. Then immediately after the delivery, which took place as if scheduled at eight o'clock, she ordered a gala breakfast for the household. Mrs. Thoreau, Henry's mother, had served as midwife and had spent the night with Lidian. After breakfast Waldo wrote a note to Elizabeth Hoar, asking her to come as soon as she could to supervise the household until Lidian could resume her duties. Of course "Sister" Elizabeth came gladly.

Emerson had mixed feelings about his wife's housekeeping. He liked order and punctuality up to a point, but he once said to Ellen in later years, "Your Mammy has no sense of measure."[78] He thought Lidian fanatical in her zeal for perfection. She had a mania for straightening things: a chair at a wrong angle, table silver not properly spaced, a picture slightly out of line, or a rug uneven with the floorboards. Emerson surmised in his Journal that no one had perfectly solved the problem of housekeeping: "Unroof any house & you must find there confusion. Order is too precious & divine a thing to dwell with such fools & sinners as we all are. See how in families where there is both substance & taste, at what expense any favorite punctuality is maintained." He doubted that any house was really kept with perfect balance between order and personal "accomplishments & growth."[79]

That the Irish women the Emersons hired for maids and cooks thought Mrs. Emerson too demanding might be expected. One Sunday in church Emerson wondered what the preacher would think if he could know what each of his listeners was hoping to hear in his sermon, including Lidian: "Here is my wife who has come to church in hope of being soothed & strengthened after being wounded by the sharp tongue of a slut in her house."[80]

The spring of 1839 was another of Emerson's recurring seasons of self-analysis and dissatisfaction with what he found. The birth of his daughter had little if anything to do with it, though increasing demands on his time, including visitors to see her, intensified his discontent. There was no one cause, though several contributing ones. His lectures in Boston had earned almost as much money as those of previous seasons, but he had terminated them short of his plan, and did not feel satisfied with his performance. There did not seem to be the usual demand for repeating them in other towns, though he did give seven of the eight in Concord during the spring. He did not write more lectures, and worked only a little on his anticipated book of essays. He was always happiest when he was being creative, and he was not in a creative mood.

One of the subjects Emerson was contemplating for his collection of essays was friendship, but his thoughts vacillated. "How can I hope for a friend," he asked himself in his Journal on May 28, "who have never been one[?]"[81] In June both Jones Very and Caroline Sturgis visited the Emersons at the same time, though Caroline came earlier. Emerson was editing a little volume of Very's poems and essays, which he had volunteered to get published. But "editing" Very was difficult because he objected to any correction of the words "told" to him by the Spirit. Emerson expressed surprise that the Spirit could not spell better, but the sarcasm was lost on his saintly friend. Also he was losing sympathy with Very's withdrawal. "The lie is in the detachment," he complained in his Journal, "and when he is in the room with other persons, speech stops as if there were a corpse in the apartment."[82]

On June 17 Emerson wrote Elizabeth Peabody: "I cannot persuade Mr. Very to remain with me another day. He says he is not permitted, & no assurances that his retirement shall be secured, are of any avail." But "He gives me pleasure, & much relief after all I had heard concerning him."[83] In spite of Very's noncooperation, Emerson succeeded in getting the *Poems and Essays* published by Little and Brown of Boston in the autumn of 1839.

Caroline Sturgis was a more congenial guest. Emerson especially enjoyed walking to Walden Pond with her, but they were not yet in complete rapport. Then the day that she and Very departed, he was visited by his cousin George Emerson and a Reverend William Adam, a Baptist missionary to India.[84] Someone was always coming or going, until it seemed at times that the whole world was in conspiracy to invade his privacy.[85] He wanted to be hospitable, but he did not want his house to become a confectioner's shop, a playground for children, a hospital for the sick, or "a house of convenience to harbor anyone." On the Fourth of July he felt like preaching "the doctrine of hatred" even to his own family: "I hate father & mother & wife & brother when my muse calls me & I say to these relatives that if they wish my love they must respect my hatred. I would write on the lintels of the doorpost, Whim. Expect me not to show cause why I see or why I shun company."[86] On another occasion he asked himself, "Why should they call me good natured? I too like puss have a retractile claw."[87]

These venomous moods had two causes: vexation over interruption of his meditation, and a sense of guilt for his unsociability. "Most of the persons whom I see in my house I see across a gulf. I cannot go to them nor they come to me." He tried to console himself with the thought that his frigidity made his solitude dearer and "the impersonal God is shed abroad in my heart more richly," as a result of "the porcupine impossibility of contact with men."[88] Yet on October 21 he recorded happily that Alcott and Margaret Fuller "came hither yesterday and departed this morning. Very friendly influences these, each & both. Cold as I am, they are *almost dear*" (italics supplied). He had also enjoyed Margaret's "chronicle of sweet romance, of love & nobleness which have inspired the beautiful & brave."[89]

The "romance" referred to the courtship of Anna Barker by Samuel Gray Ward. Emerson had recently become acquainted with Ward and was eager to meet his fiancée. Ward was a handsome young man with long, curly brown hair and even features. He was several years younger than Emerson and the son of a wealthy Boston banker. At Harvard he had roomed in the home of Professor John Farrar, whose wife was Margaret Fuller's most intimate friend. There Emerson met him after his extensive travels in Europe.

Miss Barker was a celebrated beauty from New Orleans, who had lived abroad and seemed to her Cambridge friends to be an authority on Italian art. Ward planned to take his bride to a country estate in Lenox, though in a few years he would accept his father's position as head of the Boston branch of the great international banking firm of Baring Brothers. In this position he would one day arrange for the purchase of Alaska from Russia by the United States.

Though Ward only played at collecting and studying art, Emerson thought him the most polished, gifted, and knowledgeable authority on art he knew. Ward had collected huge portfolios of prints of famous artworks and he shared them with his friends. When Emerson finally met Miss Barker on October 6 in Margaret's rented house in Jamaica Plains, he recorded his impressions: "A new person is to me ever a great event and few days of my life are so illustrated & cheered as were these two in which I enjoyed the frank & generous confidence of a being so lovely, so fortunate, & so remote from my own experiences."[90] Apparently the glowing, warm-blooded Anna could thaw him out of his social torpor.

For friends at a distance Emerson could also feel strong, comforting emotions, especially for Thomas Carlyle. Already he realized that their attitudes toward society were different, but these were not yet a barrier to their friendly communication. At considerable sacrifice of time and effort Emerson had arranged for the publication in America of all Carlyle's writings, himself advancing the money for paper, printing, binding, and promotion. Because of these advances he was financially hard-pressed in the summer of 1839, but he would eventually recover his investment after turning over to Carlyle every cent of profit. By February he had sent him seven hundred and fifty dollars, with promises of nearly two thousand more.

In June, Carlyle wrote Emerson: "thanks to you . . . I am for the present no longer poor . . . Not for these twelve years, never since I had a house to maintain with money, have I had as much money in my possession as even now."[91] He planned to buy a saddle horse and name it Yankee. Not only had Emerson helped him financially, but Carlyle reported that his success in America had encouraged Fraser to undertake British editions of his works.

One way in which Carlyle repaid Emerson was by keeping him informed of his unseen friends in England. One was a poet and critic, John Sterling, near Emerson's own age. He was a curate in the Church of England, though dissatisfied with its conservatism. Emerson first heard of him in Carlyle's letter of December 8, 1837. "This John Sterling," Carlyle wrote, "has fallen overhead in love with a certain Waldo Emerson."[92] He saw the little azure-covered *Nature* lying on Carlyle's table, borrowed it, and "took it to his heart." News of his conquest thrilled Emerson, and he began reading the anonymous contributions in British magazines which Carlyle identified as Sterling's. They began a correspondence, but unfortunately Sterling was already dying of tuberculosis and did not live until Emerson's next visit to England.

Sterling was not the only admirer of Emerson reported by Carlyle. Among the others was a young Tory member of Parliament, Richard Monckton Milnes, who was preparing an article on Emerson for *The Westminster Review*. Carlyle described him as "A most bland-smiling semi-quizzical, affectionate, high-bred, Italianized little man, who has long olive-blond hair, a dimple, next to no chin, and flings his arm round your neck when he addresses you in public society!"[93] He was also to become the greatest collector of pornography in England,[94] a fact which would not ingratiate him with Emerson.

Another British admirer, Miss Harriet Martineau, had embarrassed and annoyed Emerson in her account in *Retrospect of Western Travel* of a visit to his home. "Meaning to do me a signal kindness," he wrote Carlyle, "she does me a great annoyance,—to take away from me my privacy and thrust me before my time (if ever there be a time) into the arena of the gladiators to be stared at. I was ashamed to read and am ashamed to remember."[95] He was not unappreciative of his friends. On Sunday morning, December 8, he recorded: "I woke this morning with devout thanksgiving for my friends, the old and new. I think no man in the planet has a circle more noble. They have come to me unsought: the great God gave them to me."[96]

One of these friends was the volatile Caroline Sturgis, and another was Henry Thoreau. Already Emerson's affection for him warped his critical judgment. On August 1 he had written in his Journal: "Last night came to me a beautiful poem from Henry Thoreau, 'Sympathy.' The purest strain & the loftiest, I think, that has yet pealed from this unpoetic American forest."[97] This is an interesting poem, but scarcely that good. Possibly Emerson did not fully understand it, because it was a love poem to a boy of twelve, brother of the girl with whom Henry thought he was in love. It was so "transcendental" in its lofty idealism that the psychology was obscured by the language—a phenomenon Emerson himself would soon exhibit in some letters to Caroline.

One of the traits Emerson most admired in Thoreau was his uncompromising independence: "My brave Henry here who is content to live now, & feels no shame in not studying any profession, for he does not postpone his life but lives already . . ."[98] In his own way Henry was a reformer, but he wanted to begin, as did Emerson, with his own life. Most reformers wanted to reform only one thing, such as money (Edward Palmer), diet (Dr. Sylvester Graham), or labor by requiring everyone to work. Emerson commented satirically: "What a mountain of chagrins, inconveniences, diseases, & sins would sink into the sea with the uprise of this one doctrine of Labor. Domestic hired service would go over the dam. Slavery would fall into the Pit. Dyspepsia would die out. Morning [social] Calls would end."[99]

Emerson was in a sarcastic mood because the previous Sunday (June 23) he had attended a meeting in Concord of the Auxiliary Society to the American Unitarian Association, which, as he phrased it, had "proposed to form a very large Society to devise & execute means for propping in some secure & permanent manner this planet."[100] His sympathies were with the "flippant orator" who remarked at the meeting "that the World could stand without linch pins & that even if you should cut all the ropes & knock away the whole underpinning, it would swing & poise perfectly for the poise was in the globe itself. But this is Transcendentalism."

It was a relief to escape for a two-week vacation in the White Mountains with George Bradford. There it seemed that nature was ashamed of man, though not of the giant profile on a mountainside in Franconia Notch. Later, Emerson's description of this rock in the shape of a human face is said to have given Hawthorne the germ for his story "The Great Stone Face."[101]

After his return Emerson attended a meeting in Concord of the Middlesex County Education Association. One of the speakers was Horace Mann, but he was "full of the modern gloomy view of our democratical institutions,"[102] and Emerson did not enjoy it, though he himself complained that "We are shut up in schools & college recitation rooms for ten or fifteen years & come out at last with a bellyful of words & do not know a thing." What things? Such as his young friends John and Henry Thoreau were learning in building a boat, making a tent, and going "up the river Merrimack to live by their wits on the fish of the stream & the berries of the wood." This example was half-satirical, but Emerson did seriously believe that the education of his day was not teaching young people how to live in their environments. It is significant also that in this grumbling protest Emerson favors an "education in things." He respected the farmer, he said, because he was "a realist & not a dictionary."

This is only one of many indications of Emerson's growing weariness with abstractions and his increasing desire to face directly the realities of his contemporary world, even if it meant joining some of the reformers. The tension between Emerson's idealism and realism created paradoxes in his attitudes toward his friends:

> ... though I prize my friends I cannot afford to talk with them and study their visions lest I lose my own. It would indeed give a certain household joy to quit this lofty seeking[,] this spiritual astronomy ... & come down into warm sympathies with you [my friends], but then I know well I shall mourn always the vanishing of my Mighty Gods.[103]

So he would have to continue "this evanescent intercourse. ... We will meet as though we met not, & part as though we parted not."

CHAPTER XVI

Hodiernal Facts

... go straight into life ... to the hodiurnal
[*sic*] facts ...[1]

I

In the summer of 1839 Emerson learned that even a Platonic Idealist can be affected by the stock market. At the beginning of the year it seemed that the nation had recovered from the economic depression of 1837, but six months later this illusion was dispelled. On August 17, 1839, Waldo was grateful to William for a check for one hundred and twenty-five dollars in partial payment on a note because "I had exhausted if not my credit yet certainly my estimate of my credit."[2] He had recently borrowed money to pay the printers of Carlyle's books, and his bank stock did not pay an expected dividend. To make matters worse, his Concord taxes had been raised, and Bulkeley's expenses in the Charlestown asylum had also increased. He hoped in October "to get such payments from the booksellers as to float again" the Carlyle project. But meanwhile, "I see plainly I shall have no choice about lecturing again next winter; I must do it." He had planned to skip one lecture season while he finished getting his book of essays ready for publication. Now the essays would have to wait.

Before the autumn foliage had reached its peak of red and golden brilliance Emerson's enthusiasm for lecturing had returned. He realized anew the advantages of the Lyceum platform: "Here is a pulpit that makes other pulpits tame ..." Here he could "lay himself out utterly, large, enormous, prodigal, on the subject of the hour."[3] What was "the subject of the hour"? "A question which well deserves examination now is the Dangers of Commerce. This invasion of Nature by Trade with its Money, its Credit, its Steam, its Railroad, threatens to upset the balance of man, & establish a new Universal Monarchy more tyrannical than Babylon or Rome."[4] A couple of weeks later he had broadened the question: "Shall I not explore for the subject of my new lectures the character, resources, & tendencies of the Present Age?"[5]

The question was rhetorical, for Emerson had already decided upon this topic, which would enable him to "include what speculations I may have to offer on all my favorite topics." But he must not repeat himself. He had already written in his Journal: "For the five last years I have read each winter a new course of lectures in Boston, and each was my creed & confession of faith. Each told all I thought of the past, the present, & the future. Once more I must renew my work and I think only once in the same form . . ."[6] Though each succeeding lecture had not always been in a new "form," Emerson had nevertheless grown steadily in his lectures, both as a thinker and as an artist, as he had previously grown in his sermons. They were his intellectual autobiography.

Emerson had another reason for feeling good about his return to the lecture platform: Margaret Fuller "writes me that she waits for the Lectures[,] seeing well after much intercourse that the best of me is there."[7] He himself believed that to be true. A fellow townsman had remarked that he "always seemed to be on stilts" when he met his neighbors on the street, and Emerson understood the criticism, though he did not know how to get off the stilts—except on the rostrum. He found pleasure, therefore, in planning to give the best of himself once more to his Lyceum audiences.

Emerson gave the first of his ten lectures on "The Present Age" at the Masonic Temple in Boston on December 4, and continued them each succeeding Wednesday evening, with the exception of Christmas, through February 12, 1840. In preparing the lectures he approached his subject with an open mind, trying not to prejudice any aspect of the age. "All my hope of insight," he wrote in his Journal, "& of successful reporting lies in my consciousness of fidelity & the abdication of all will in the matter."[8] He would not try "to persuade the Vast Ocean of the Time to convert itself into a mill stream" to turn his own wheel, or, to change the figure, "to corrupt if it were possible the incorruptible Wind." Becoming a reporter of experience, letting the details lead the way, was for Emerson a new and exciting way to write lectures. Since he wrote each one only a few days before delivery, it was like acting in a drama without knowing the denouement, and no one was more curious than he to know how it would end.

Every event and condition in Emerson's contemporary world combined to constitute the age, and out of this tangle he must select and try to characterize the "soul." One thing was certain: out of the debris of the past, human ingenuity creates new configurations. Viewing the process, Emerson observed two parties: "The party of the Past and the party of the Future. . . . the movement Party or . . . the Establishment."[9] The conflict of these two parties had split every Church, Papal and Protestant, Calvinist old and new, Quakers likewise, and in politics created Whig and Democrat. Even Constantinople was divided on the wearing of coats, "and the Sultan learns to sit in a chair."

The party of the future believes "the nation exists for the individual." Its adherents "are fanatics in freedom. They hate tolls, taxes, turnpikes, banks, hierarchies, yes, almost laws. They have a neck of unspeakable tenderness." In politics Emerson was still a Whig, a party so much of the past that it would soon cease to exist, but his sympathies were more with the party of the future. By some of his definitions, Andrew Jackson belonged to this party, yet Emerson detested him and his followers. Obviously, his loyalties were divided. The party of the past was more respectful of religious sentiment, parental authority, and patriotism. Though the old Puritans were superstitious, he felt nostalgic for the time when "every day had its saint; every unusual occurrence its supernatural ties."[10] He had no desire to restore Puritanism, but some of its values were worth preserving. The Puritans respected learning; the present generation did not. "Self-made men" liked to declare in public speeches how little they owed to Latin schools and colleges. Emerson disliked to see government "administered for the protection of trade," and law "interpreted and executed on the same principle." Whether this statement condemned Democrats more than Whigs is doubtful. The Democrats were in power, but the Whigs were "protectionist." Actually, he was not enamored of either party.

Emerson also saw much in his age to admire. In spite of the declining religious sentiment, he welcomed the transition from his ancestors' worship, "which enshrined the law in a private and personal history to a worship which recognizes the true eternity of the law . . . The next age will behold God in the ethical laws, and will regard natural history, private fortunes, and politics not for themselves, as we have done, but as illustrations of those laws . . ."[11] But critics of Emerson's "Divinity School Address" would hardly have approved his description of this future religion: "we have found out the mythical character of Christianity, and are every where adopting a new manner of speech in regard to it. Philosophical expressions are supplanting the technical [theological] ones of the last century and men adopt everyday forms of speech which a few years ago they would have repudiated with heat."[12] Revelation had been degraded to fortune-telling. Religion was shifting emphasis from life after death to a more abundant life in this world. Those former expectations of immortality Emerson called "low curiosity." Jesus did not promise immortality; it was his Disciples who did. Emerson was glad to see religion losing interest in miracles, except the miracle of "the sun and moon and the man who walks under them." Science was revealing a physical world as remarkable as the supernatural one of the Old Testament. For Emerson the greatest miracle of all remained: the Godhead or Over-Soul (he is beginning to use this term) dwells in every man.

This shift of interest to the world of everyday experience was leading to needed reform "of domestic, social, civil, literary, and ecclesiastical institutions." Emerson was still impatient with the professional reformers, whose programs were partial or even trivial, as in changing habits of drinking, eating, or dressing. Reform must be total, a reform of "Character . . . the true Theocracy." Yet the spirit of reform presaged a better life on earth for all people. Religion does not "tend now to a cultus but to a human life . . . Let us learn to lead a man's life."[13]

II

At the end of his course of lectures in Boston, Emerson felt let down and depressed. He had hoped to "agitate men, being agitated myself,"[14] but not once had he felt the elation which produces eloquence. Yet his audiences had averaged four hundred (though he had given away more than three hundred free passes), and he knew he ought to be satisfied. If only he had had the "constitutional vigor" to spend sixty instead of twenty-one hours on the preparation of each lecture, maybe "I should hate myself less."[15]

But if Emerson did not feel "agitated" himself in giving these lectures, some of his listeners did. Theodore Parker, an ultraliberal Unitarian minister in West Roxbury, wrote Dr. Convers Francis that the introductory lecture was splendid, *"Democratic-locofoco* throughout."[16] Since Emerson had a low opinion of the Democratic party, he certainly did not intend to be a *"locofoco,"* the nickname of a radical sect of Democrats. George Bancroft, the historian of America and at that time collector of customs of the port of Boston, "was in ecstasies,—he was rapt beyond vision at the *locofocoism* of the lecture." If he will only join *"us,"* Bancroft wrote, "we will give him three thousand listeners" in the Bay State (a Democratic club) instead of the small audience he had. Emerson would not have been pleased, either, to hear that a "Whig-looking gentleman" who heard him "said he could only account for his delivering such a lecture on the supposition that he wished to get a place in the Custom-House under George Bancroft."

Regardless of how Emerson's lectures were interpreted, they were rumored to be lively and provocative. Consequently, other audiences wanted to hear them, and he was invited to repeat parts of "The Present Age" and other lectures in Salem, Concord, New York, and Providence, through March, April, and May. These drew so many people in New York and Providence that the Lyceum organizations made money on them because he spoke for a fixed fee, and more tickets were sold than anyone had expected. In New York, in fact, more tickets were sold for his lectures than for all the other speakers that season, combined.[17]

In Providence, Emerson wrote his mother on March 28 that he was absolutely lionized. "I am reckoned here a Transcendentalist, and what that beast is, all persons in Providence have a great appetite to know ..."[18] Young people, especially, flocked to hear him, and to ask "when the Lecture is coming upon the Great Subject? In vain I disclaim all knowledge of that sect of Lidian's ..." (This was evidently a family joke.) People in Providence seemed to believe that Transcendentalism was a new religion, and waited for the "New Light." But Emerson had no new religion, at least in a sectarian sense, though his ideas were certainly not those taught at Baptist Brown University.

One of Margaret Fuller's Providence friends, Charles King Newcomb, an intensely religious young man, slender, dark, and nervous, listened to Emerson's lectures like the disciple he was, though he was still going through a period of spiritual turmoil. Later in the summer Margaret wrote

Waldo that Newcomb was visiting her and was "wretchedly ill. I think he may die, and perhaps it would be well, for I doubt if he has strength to rise above his doubts and fears." She was thankful that she had a tougher and more resolute intellect, for "No sharp pain can debilitate like this vacillation of mind."[18a] But Emerson knew that better than she did, and was perhaps more sympathetic than she. Newcomb would become one of his most cherished correspondents.

In all his lectures, Emerson wrote in his Journal, "I have taught one doctrine, namely, the infinitude of the private man."[19] That idea "the people accept readily enough, & even with loud commendation," but the moment he called it religion, "they are shocked . . ." What many wanted, perhaps, was some new argument for old beliefs. But not all. Edward Palmer, for example, wanted to abolish Christianity and start over again with a completely new religion.[20] Of course, he also wanted to reform the economy by abolishing money, though he was not averse, Emerson observed, to accepting hospitality at his host's expense.

There was also a group of mystics on Cape Cod who had earned the title of "Come-outers" because they liked to assemble in front of a church on Sunday during worship and yell, "Come out!" Actually their faith was not dissimilar to Emerson's antinomianism, for it was simply the belief that the only source of divine truth was what each man heard God speak to him through his own conscience. But their uncouth tactics set them apart from Waldo Emerson. As Odell Shepard says in his biography of Bronson Alcott, "they sometimes entered the church and trampled across the cushions before the pulpit in the midst of the sermon, by way of homiletic criticism."[21]

A more numerous group of contemporary religious fanatics was led by William Miller of Pittsfield, founder of the Second Adventist sect. In 1831 he became convinced from his study of the Bible that the Second Coming of Christ and the end of the world would take place in 1843. In 1840 he and his followers were diligently preparing for that apocalyptic event. In midsummer they and the Come-outers, with whom they had nothing in common except proselyting zeal, held a joint convention in Groton. Though Emerson did not attend, several of his friends did: George Ripley, still pastor of Purchase Street Church in Boston but soon to resign to start an experimental community; Theodore Parker, the "athlete of scholars," omnivorous reader of books in twenty languages, and in trouble with "Establishment" Unitarians for his heterodoxy; and Christopher Cranch, recently returned from Cincinnati, where he had been a Unitarian missionary.

On a fine day in August they walked the twenty miles from Boston to Concord, spent the night with Emerson, and next day walked the remaining twenty-five miles to Groton to attend the convention. Bronson Alcott, a resident of Concord since April 1, joined them. Among the rough-clad farmers and "common folk" was Joseph Palmer, who had been persecuted and prosecuted in Fitchburg for wearing a beard at a time when beards were not in fashion. Alcott admired Palmer's blunt speech and uncompromising defense of his personal freedom. The Boston friends were amused by the wild oratory of these impassioned men, especially Cranch, who had drawn several caricatures interpreting literally some of Emerson's more extravagant rhetoric; he refused to let his admiration suppress his sense of humor. As Shepard says, Alcott and his friends experienced a "sudden and delightful liberation in hearing simple-minded men speak out . . . precisely those heresies about Church and Priest and Sabbath which had long been yeasting in their own minds."[22]

When Ripley, Parker, and Cranch returned to Boston, they got busy organizing a convention of their own, to be held in the Chardon Street Chapel for the Friends of Universal Reform. Emerson attended the Chardon Street Convention, held in November, and two more during the following year.[23] The first session discussed the Sabbath, the second the Church, and the third the Ministry, not in the literary manner of Emerson before the Harvard Divinity School, but with no holds barred by a boisterous, unrestrained, and at times disorderly crowd. At the first session an attempt was made to eject bearded Joseph Palmer, but Alcott defended him and he was permitted to stay and speak his piece. Alcott himself made speeches on every issue, and was stimulated by the exuberance of the mob. Emerson quietly observed and took notes. Later he described the convention in *The Dial.*[24] Invitations had been widely publicized, and the sessions drew hundreds of people from all parts of New England and the Middle Atlantic States:

> . . . men of every shade of opinion from the straitest orthodoxy to the wildest heresy, and many persons whose church was a church of one member only. A great variety of dialect and of costume was noticed; a great deal

of confusion, eccentricity and freak appeared, as well as of zeal and enthusiasm. If the assembly was disorderly, it was picturesque. Madmen, madwomen, men with beards, Dunkers, Muggletonians, Come-outers, Groaners, Agrarians, Seventh-day Baptists, Quakers, Abolitionists, Calvinists, Unitarians, and Philosophers,—all came successively to the top, and seized their moment, if not their hour, wherein to chide, or pray, or preach, or protest.

Unlike the Groton convention, some "intellectual and cultivated persons" attended and participated, though outnumbered by the uneducated, whose passions made up for their deficiencies. Women were also present and some made speeches. In fact, the woman's rights movement in America might almost be said to have started in the Chardon Street Chapel. Emerson found many of the speeches wearisome, but he was glad to see Bronson Alcott, his "tedious archangel,"[25] have a chance to air his ideas. And on the whole he rejoiced at seeing and hearing sincere men and women defending their personal convictions with absolute freedom, "even amidst opposition and ridicule." True to his own principles, Emerson admired "a man whose mind is made up to obey the great inward Commander."[26]

III

On May 29, 1840, Emerson wrote in his first letter to his unseen British admirer John Sterling: "I am a worshipper of Friendship, and cannot find any other good equal to it. As soon as any man pronounces the words which approve him a master I make no haste[;] he is holy . . ."[27] This was partly Emerson's graceful way of apologizing for his tardiness in acknowledging Sterling's letter to him, for he completed the sentence: " . . . let me be holy, also; our relations are eternal; why should we count days and weeks?" But however "holy," Sterling was not perfect. Emerson expressed warm admiration for Sterling's critical articles and poetry. Some of the poems pleased Emerson immensely, though he did not "set an equal value on all the pieces." To soften this partially negative verdict, he added that he himself hoped someday to attain the "splendid dialect" of poetry, though "up to this day I have only had disappointment in my attempts."

When Emerson prepared a collection of his own essays for the press, the one on "Friendship" gave him the most pleasure, the most difficulty, and provoked the most arguments among his friends. He had given a lecture on "Love" in the "Human Life" series (1838–39) and he used it in his *Essays* (1841) with only minor emendations. But he had not given a whole lecture on friendship, though he had discussed the topic in "Society" (1836–37), in "The Heart" (1837–38), and in "Private Life" (1839–40). For the new essay he drew upon passages and entries in his Journals, but added sentences, tropes, and expanded interpretations. His objective was twofold: artistic mastery and approval by his friends; and it happened that just at this time his relations with several of them were entering a new phase. Indeed, three of them might be called "new" friends, though one, Caroline Sturgis, he had known for three or four years. Samuel Gray Ward and his fiancée, Anna Barker, he had known for a much shorter time.

In exchange for the portfolios of great works of art in engraved reproductions lent him by Ward, Emerson let him read his manuscripts. Ward had also heard several of Emerson's more important lectures, and had been greatly impressed by them. The two men were strongly attracted to each other, and when the younger offered his friendship, the older man eagerly responded. At the beginning of 1840, before he had begun his final revision of "Friendship," Emerson wrote Ward: "This is to me the most attractive of all topics, and, I doubt not, whenever I get your full confession of faith, we shall be at one on the matter."[28] But such a confession must await the development of their affections: "Because the subject is so high and sacred, we cannot walk straight up to it; we must saunter if we would find the secret." It was natural, therefore, that a few months later Emerson wanted Ward's opinion on his essay, and for two reasons: literary criticism and the hope that his ideas on this subject would draw them closer together. Ward responded in a way that cemented their mutual regard, and they now addressed each other as "brother."

With his young women friends, Caroline Sturgis, Margaret Fuller, and Anna Barker, Emerson's friendship was more complicated, especially with Caroline and Margaret. Caroline visited the Emersons for a week in June, and Emerson wrote Margaret that her visit had "been a great satisfaction"; they were "beginning to be acquainted," though it might be a couple of centuries before they became "the best of friends."[29] As his later letters to Caroline would show, he was emotionally excited by this restless, attractive, exuberant young woman of twenty, doubtless more than he realized. She made it harder for him to resist by playing the role of daughter to a father confessor. But he soon discovered that she desired a stronger emotional relationship—ambiguous except for its intensity—than the Concord recluse could give. He tried to satisfy her and at the same time keep their emotions safely under control by agreeing to call her "sister" and encouraging her to call him "brother"—he preferred a fraternal to a paternal role. On August 16(?) he wrote her:

> You & I should only be friends on imperial terms. We are both too proud to be fond & too true to feign[.] But I dare not engage my peace so far as to make you necessary to me as I can easily see any establishment of habitual intercourse would do, when the first news I may hear is that you have found in some heaven foreign to me your mate, & my beautiful castle is exploded to shivers. Then I take the other part & say, Shall I not trust this chosen child . . .[30]

This letter was prompted by a talk Emerson had had with Margaret Fuller two days earlier while he was driving her back to Jamaica Plain at the end of her week's visit to the Emersons. She "taxed me on both your parts with a certain inhospitality of soul inasmuch as you were both willing to be my friends in the full & sacred sense & I remained apart[,] critical, & after many interviews still a stranger. I count & weigh, but do not love." This charge saddened him. He was aware of his "imperfect intercourse," but it was certainly not because of any "deficiency of my affections." He would be glad to spend the remainder of his life in her society, and if she would come and live near him, she could confide in him any time and he would be as "true a brother to you as ever blood made."

A few days later Emerson wrote Caroline again: "I hate everything frugal and cowardly in friendship." But he added: "When we fear the withdrawal of love from ourselves by the new relations which our companions must form, it is mere infidelity." Whether this referred to Caroline's fear of losing Anna Barker's "love" after Anna's marriage to Sam Ward is not certain, though he might have had in mind Caroline's finding a better friend in marriage, for he adds: " . . . and you shall not give me so great a joy as by finding for yourself a love which shall make mine show cold and feeble—which certainly is not cold or feeble . . ."[31]

That Caroline Sturgis had actually fallen in love with Emerson is improbable, but he took pains to warn her against the possibility. It appears, however, that Margaret Fuller was in love with him. Since her childhood she had felt deprived of sufficient affection. The education her father had given her had set her apart from her sex. She realized early that she was not physically attractive, and had resolved to compensate by superior intellectual attainments. But she did not find those sufficiently satisfying and sought emotional attachments, first with her girl schoolmates, then with Mrs. Eliza Rotch Farrar, and later with bright young men she met in Cambridge. One of the latter was a divinity student, James Freeman Clarke, with whom she corresponded after he began his ministry in Louisville, Kentucky, but his personal criticisms of her showed the limits of that friendship. Another correspondent was William Henry Channing, the nephew of the great Dr. William Ellery Channing, but closeness with him did not develop, either.

A love affair between Samuel Gray Ward and Margaret Fuller does not seem probable, either; he the handsome, debonair son of a wealthy banker, undoubtedly desired by many women. But he did appreciate intellect and talent, and sometime between 1835 and 1839 he led Margaret to think theirs was no "ordinary attachment." Early in September 1839 she accused him: "You love me no more—How did you [that is, you *did*] pray me to draw near to you!"[32] He had called her his "best" and "dearest friend," but she felt he was drawing away from her and losing interest in her friends and activities. "You say you love me as ever, forever," and she would try to believe it, she wrote. The fact that he called her "Mother" might suggest that his "love" was not of a sexual nature, but her maternal reply showed how normally and strongly feminine her instincts were:

> You have given me the sacred name of Mother, and I will be as indulgent, as tender, as delicate (if possible) in my vigilance, as if I had borne you beneath my heart instead of in it. But oh, it is waiting like the Mother beside the sepulchre for the resurrection, for all I loved in you is at present dead and buried, only a light from the tomb shines now and then in your eyes.

It seems probable that Ward's engagement to Anna Barker was a great shock to Margaret Fuller, though she wanted to count Anna as one of her friends, too. In an undated letter that appears to have been written a few months before Ward's marriage, Margaret confessed that he had caused her to realize that she "really was capable of attachment, though it never seemed so till the hour of separation."[33] She felt that they had not been "friends as men are friends to one another, or as brother and sister. There was, also, that pleasure, which may, perhaps, be termed conjugal . . ." Still, she insisted that her "only grief" over the "cessation of our confidential intercourse" was that he had deliberately ended it himself. In spite of this, she longed to "honor" him and be "honored" in return. "Now we will have free and noble thoughts of one another, and all that is best of our friendship shall remain."

Margaret showed no resentment of Anna Barker and was eager to introduce her to Emerson. In an autobiographical manuscript she recalled an older woman, probably Mrs. Farrar, whom she had "loved . . . for a time with as much passion as I was then strong enough to feel." She remembered especially one night "when she leaned on me . . . [and] we both felt such a strange mystic thrill . . ."[34] Recalling the intimacy between Mme. Récamier and Mme. de Staël, she wrote: "It is so true that a woman may be in love with a woman and a man with a man." Apparently at one time she had loved Caroline Sturgis in this passionate way, but could write her in the early part of 1840: "I build on our friendship now with trust, for I think it is redeemed from 'the search after Eros.' "[35] In his *Memoir* of Margaret, Emerson would refer to her friendship with women as "not unmingled with passion, and had passages of romantic sacrifice and of ecstatic fusion, which I have heard with the ear, but could not trust my profane pen to report."[36]

In July and August, while Emerson was trying to give his essay on "Friendship" its permanent form, his friendship with Margaret reached a crisis. Though she surprised him by charging him with "inhospitality of soul" toward her and Caroline, he knew something of her jangled emotions as a result of Ward's engagement. On August 29 he promised: "I shall never go quite back to my old arctic habits . . ." Then, perhaps as an example to her, he added: "Ward I shall not lose." He advised her: " . . . *you* must be generous beyond even the strain of heroism to bear your part in this scene & resign without a sigh two Friends [Anna and Sam?];—you whose heart unceasingly demands all, & is a sea that hates an ebb."[37] But by September 26 he had been pushed so hard by Margaret's insatiable demands for more passion in their "friendship" that he wrote in his Journal, with obvious distaste and puzzlement, an imaginary speech to her:

You would have me love you. What shall I love? Your body? The sup-position disgusts you. What you have thought & said? Well, whilst you were thinking & saying them, but not now. I see no possibility of loving any thing but what now is, & is becoming; your courage, your enterprize, your budding affection, your opening thought, your prayer, I can love,—but what else?[38]

This was the tone he was taking with her in his letters, and probably in conversation. She replied that she only wanted recognition of the depth of her feeling. When her "soul, in its childish agony of prayer, stretched out its arms to you as a father,—did you not see what was meant by the crying for the moon . . . ?" He was not certain what she was crying for, but he knew he had no moons to give. By October 24 he had had enough, and wrote bluntly that "Up to this hour our relation has been progressive," but she asked for "sympathies" he did not have. Why not be satisfied with what they did have? "See you not that I cannot spare you?" Then, "Let us live as we have always done . . ."[39] He did not like trying to explain him-self, and warned: "Do not expect it of me again for a long time." She knew better than to push him any further, and their relationship returned to a status pleasing to him, if not, secretly, to her.

The marriage of Anna to Ward on October 3 did not cause new ten-sions in Emerson's relations with his young friends, but the impression the New Orleans beauty made on him gives revealing insights into his charac-ter. For some reason Caroline did not attend the wedding, and two days after that event Emerson wrote her:

Last Saturday afternoon I saw Sam & Anna wedded.—Anna's miracle next to the *amount* of her life, seems to be the intimacy of her approach to us. The moment she fastens her eyes on you, her unique gentleness unbars all doors and with such easy & frolic sway she advances & advances on you with that one look, that no brother or sister or father or mother of lifelong acquaintance, ever seemed to arrive quite so near as this now first seen maiden. It is almost incredible to me—when I spoke with her the other night—that I have never seen this child but three times—or four, is it? I should think I had lived with her in the house of eternity. . . .[40]

The effect Anna had on Emerson sounds like what in the twentieth century is called "sex appeal," a charm she radiated as naturally as the rose its perfume. The interesting thing is Emerson's susceptibility to it. Margaret Fuller did not have it; Caroline probably had it to a lesser degree, but he was on guard against her youthful seductions. However, even in Emerson's exuberant descriptions of Anna's "miracle," there is a hint of his Platonism in his metaphor "house of eternity." This could mean, of course, simply that he felt he had known her *always*. But in view of his otherworldly ideals in his essay on "Friendship," the phrase deserves a closer look.

As in his theory of love, Emerson's theory of friendship was Platonic, resembling Poe's theory of beauty in "The Poetic Principle": "the ancient writers ... said, that the soul of man, embodied here on earth, went roaming up and down in quest of that other world of its own out of which it came into this ..." Therefore, says Emerson, "love, which is the deification of persons, must become more impersonal every day."[41]

After lyrical descriptions of the joys and blessings of friendship, and pointing out that "very seldom can its satisfaction be realized," Emerson declares: "The condition which high friendship demands is ability to do without it.... Leave this touching and clawing. Let him be to me a spirit.... To my friend I write a letter, and from him I receive a letter. That seems to you a little. It suffices me. Friends, such as we desire, are dreams and fables."[42] This is the crux. The dream was not only more perfect, like ideas in Plato's "heaven," but actually more satisfying than the reality.

This conception of friendship was both too lofty and too meagre for emotionally starved Margaret Fuller. Later she wrote to William Henry Channing: "The more I think of it, the more deeply do I feel the imperfection of your view of friendship, which is the same Waldo E. takes.... It is very noble, but not enough for our manifold nature."[43] Even the saintly Elizabeth Hoar told Emerson, after discussing this subject, that she did not wish her friend to visit but to live with her. And Caroline Sturgis pointedly rebuked Emerson in a letter dated November 9, 1840: "With all your faith in Man, you have but little faith in men." Evidently alluding to a recent encounter, she confessed: "The higher we rose in conversation, the sadder I felt." But possibly Emerson deceived himself in his flights of Idealism, for he obviously did care greatly what Caroline, Margaret, and several other friends thought of him—and he wanted them to care.

IV

For two years the members of the "Hedge's Club"[44] had been discussing the need for a magazine to publish their ideas, not so much an organ to publicize what had come to be called American Transcendentalism (for no one could say just what that was) as a forum for the most interesting views of the time. Having such a magazine appealed to Emerson, but he was determined not to be saddled with the editorship.

On October 16, 1839, Emerson wrote Margaret Fuller: "I should heartily greet any such Journal as would fitly print these Journals of yours, & will gladly contribute of my own ink to fill it up. But unless Mr Ripley would like to undertake it himself, or unless you would, I see not that we are nearer to such an issue than we have been these two years past."[45] Reluctantly, Margaret accepted the assignment, and George Ripley agreed to act as business manager. Weeks and Jordan in Boston contracted to publish it without subsidy. The editor was promised a salary of two hundred dollars a year, but as it turned out there were no profits and she collected no salary. To support herself she resumed her "Conversations" to ladies in Boston, beginning the new series on "Classical Mythology" on November 6 at Elizabeth Peabody's bookshop, with forty subscribers, one of whom was Lidian Emerson.[46]

Emerson did not spare himself in aiding Margaret in soliciting contributors to *The Dial*. Alcott had suggested the name, hoping that the magazine would measure the progress of thought. Several members of the club promised contributions but were slow to deliver. Hedge announced he did not want to be associated with the project, for fear of being called an atheist (Emerson's experience at the Divinity School had shaken him up), though he soon relented.[47] Emerson wanted the pages opened to Alcott and to the young friends of whom he expected great things: Henry Thoreau, first of all, and then Caroline Sturgis, William Ellery Channing the younger, and several others. Throughout the winter of 1839–40 he and Margaret furiously exchanged, discussed, and evaluated manuscripts obtained for consideration—"Dialing," he called this correspondence—but he let her make the final decisions. This was fortunate because she was a stricter judge of literary quality; he was too eager to encourage young talent.

Emerson did not want *The Dial* shaped for any particular public in existence, but to create a public of its own. In April, after Margaret had planned the first number, he began thinking that the magazine ought to have a department of foreign "intelligence." But Margaret had enough to do to get the first number printed, with no time to change plans.[48] To fill up the 136 pages agreed upon, she wrote "A Short Essay on Critics" and a critical review of an exhibition of Washington Allston's paintings. Emerson wrote an editorial introduction explaining the purpose of *The Dial,* if it could be called a purpose: "If our Journal share the impulses of the time, it cannot now prescribe its own course. . . . Let it be one cheerful rational voice amidst the din of mourners and polemic[ist]s."[49] He had also promised a long essay called "Thoughts on Modern Literature," but by the time he finally completed it, Margaret had enough copy at the printer's to fill the July issue.

The Emerson family was well represented, however, by an extract from Charles Emerson's papers on Homer, Shakespeare, and Edmund Burke; Edward Emerson's "The Last Farewell," a poem on his last sight of the Boston harbor as he sailed to Puerto Rico and his death; and Ellen Tucker Emerson's lyric, "Life scatters oil . . ." If the poetry was slight in quantity and quality, some of the prose compensated for it, such as George Ripley's twenty-four-page review of *Charles Elwood* by Orestes Brownson, the most formidable contemporary American critic of the Christian Church. Brownson believed that the Church had neglected the teachings of Christ in ignoring temporal problems. The difference between him and Emerson was that he was far more sociological. Theodore Parker had also contributed an impressive treatise on "The Divine Presence in Nature and in the Soul." Except for his more prosaic style, this might have been taken for Emerson's essay. Most of the contributions were unsigned, or identified only by a single letter. An exception was "Orphic Sayings," by A. Bronson Alcott, a ponderous collection of aphorisms.

Among the better poems (though far from first-rate) were Christopher Cranch's "To the Aurora Borealis" and Thoreau's elegy "Sympathy": "Lately, alas, I knew a gentle boy . . ." Margaret included these poems and Thoreau's essay on "Aulus Persius Flaccus" to please Emerson. In August, George Ripley and Theodore Parker visited Emerson in Concord and discussed the July *Dial.* Parker recorded in his Journal: "E. expressed to me his admiration of Thoreau, & his foolish article *'Aulus Persius Flaccus'* in the Dial. He said it was full of life. But alas the life is Emerson's, not

Thoreau's." Emerson excused Thoreau by saying he was "but a boy."[50] Parker hoped he would write more for newspapers and less for *The Dial*.

Emerson wrote Carlyle: "Our community begin to stand in some terror of Transcendentalism, and the *Dial,* poor little thing, whose first number contains scarce anything considerable or even visible, is just now honored by attacks from almost every newspaper and magazine. . . ."[51] But Emerson was not discouraged. In fact, he thought it a positive gain to irritate Boston newspaper editors. It would have been encouraging to have had Carlyle's approval, but he found *The Dial "too* ethereal, speculative, theoretic." Sarah Clarke also had something like this in mind when she remarked that "the spirit of many of the pieces was lonely."[52]

By the end of July, Emerson himself was dissatisfied with *The Dial,* and he wrote in his Journal:

> And now I think our Dial ought not to be a mere literary journal but that the times demand of us all a more earnest aim. It ought to contain the best advice on the topics of Government, Temperance, Abolition, Trade, & Domestic Life. It might well add to such compositions such poetry & sentiment as now will constitute its best merit. Yet it ought to go straight into life with the devoted wisdom of the best men & women in the land. It should—should it not?—be a degree nearer to the hodiurnal[*sic*] facts than my writings are? I wish to write pure mathematics, and not a culinary almanac of application of science to the arts.[53]

It was becoming difficult to ignore "hodiurnal facts" in the summer and autumn of 1840. One reason was the great clamor being created by the Whigs and the Democrats in the presidential campaign. In the election of 1836 Martin Van Buren had succeeded Andrew Jackson, and later he continued most of Jackson's policies. He opposed federal internal improvements, and refused to repeal Jackson's "Specie Circular," which required that public lands be paid for in silver or gold to discourage speculators. He also wanted to establish a national treasury, independent of private banks.

In 1840, to oppose Van Buren, the Whigs nominated General William Henry Harrison, who had won a minor victory over some Indians at the Battle of Tippecanoe. The Whigs never did get around to adopting a party platform, letting their "hero" run on his personal popularity and as a symbol of opposition to the Jacksonians. A Democratic newspaper in Baltimore made the mistake of calling Harrison a "log-cabin, hard-cider" candidate, meaning a frontiersman without any qualifications for the presidency. The Whigs seized upon this image and made the log cabin and the cider jug symbols for banners and "banjo-pickin' " songs. The Whig candidate for Vice-President was John Tyler, who opposed the annexation of Texas; so the slogan "Tippecanoe and Tyler Too" became a familiar refrain at every Whig meeting. Still another symbol was a large red-white-and-blue ball, which the Whig enthusiasts pushed from town to town, to show how they would roll over the Democrats.

The Middlesex County Whigs celebrated July 4 in Concord with a spectacle.[54] The Lowell delegation arrived with an enormous log cabin on wheels, one hundred and fifty persons inside, drawn by twenty-three horses. At the head of the parade, men pushed the ubiquitous red-white-and-blue ball all the way from West Cambridge to Concord. Emerson called the ball, twelve or thirteen feet in diameter, "the most imposing part of this Harrison celebration of the Fourth in Concord as in Baltimore . . ." After speeches at the Court House, a dinner was held at the battleground in a circus tent in the midst of birch trees.

Though Emerson's sympathies were with the Whigs, he was offended by the political oratory of both parties. In September he wrote in his Journal: "The Whigs meet in numerous conventions & each palpitating heart swells with the cheap sublime of magnitude & number."[55] The louder the applause for a given delegation, the greater it was admired. Numbers only counted, but with Emerson "a majority of one" (to anticipate Henry Thoreau's slogan) was sufficient. "It is only as a man detaches himself from all support & stands alone, that I see him to be strong and to prevail. He is weaker by every recruit to his banner. Is not a man better than a town?" Yet he was interested in the outcome of the election—in which, finally, numbers counted—thus revealing his ideal detachment to be overstated and more rhetorical than real. It was by symbols of log cabins and hard cider and not honest "issues" that the Whigs won the election in 1840. After Harrison had been inaugurated and had died in office, Emerson recorded his thought that "General Harrison was neither Whig nor Tory [Whigs accused Van Buren of trying to establish a dynasty, and called his party Tory], but the Indignation President; and, what was not at all surprising in this puny generation, he could not stand the excitement of seventeen millions of people but died of the Presidency in one month."[56]

V

The second number of *The Dial* (October 1840) was considerably superior to the first, not only in poetry, as Emerson wished, but also in substantial prose. If any of his Providence seekers of a "new" religion read the October number, they found several discussions of ideas central to the group now called American Transcendentalists, but less in Emerson's contributions than in those of Christopher Cranch, George Ripley, and Theodore Parker. Cranch wrote a review, with copious quotations, of A. Wylie's *Sectarianism Is Heresy*. Wylie argued for redefining and liberalizing the concept of sectarianism. Cranch would abolish sectarianism altogether; Christianity should not be a theology "but a Holy Life." In "A Lesson for the Day," Parker distinguished "The Christianity of Christ" from that practiced by the Church and by society. He found the Christianity of the Church "a very poor thing," and that of society "bitter in the mouth and poison in the blood."[57] Worst of all, the Church taught Christianity not for this world but for a supernatural one. Parker wanted to find the kingdom of heaven on earth "and enjoy it now."

In a "Letter to a Theological Student" George Ripley almost summarized Emerson's experience with the Unitarian Church, though essentially it was Ripley's, too—and he also would soon resign his pastorate. Even liberal churches and divinity schools, Ripley declared, wanted conformity, complacency, and lip service to religion instead of honest convictions and deep religious experiences.

Ripley also reviewed two books on religion, *The Works* of Dr. William Ellery Channing and Edward Palmer's *A Letter to Those Who Think*. Channing's major contribution had been to show the need of great social changes and a spiritual revolution in Christianity, "of a new bond between man and man, of a new sense of the relation between man and his Creator." Palmer "would have man disencumber himself of creeds and forms, or dependence upon the experiences of others, but go forth freely and spontaneously, in accordance with the promptings of his own moral nature."

No deliberate effort had been made by Emerson or Margaret Fuller to make the October *Dial* a Transcendental number, but of course they had solicited contributions from men whose ideas they shared, and it was inevitable that they should express these views. Emerson's own two essays, "Thoughts on Modern Literature" and "New Poetry," and his poem

"Woodnotes," were less obviously Transcendental than the essays discussed above. He said in "Thoughts on Modern Literature" that "The highest class of books are those which express the moral element; the next, works of imagination; and the next, works of science;—all dealing in realities;—what ought to be, what is, and what appears." In the present age, "The very child in the nursery prattles mysticism, and doubts and philosophizes."[58] Probably Emerson had been reading Schiller's distinction between naive and sentimental poetry, though he uses the terms "subjective" and "objective." Two of the greatest influences on modern literature, he says, have been Wordsworth, whose success has "been not his own, but that of the idea which he shared with his coevals, and which he has rarely succeeded in adequately expressing"; and Goethe, who said to himself, "There are poets enough of the Ideal; let me paint the Actual . . ."

VI

In spite of his general dislike of meddling reformers, Emerson was becoming increasingly dissatisfied with his own domestic life and frequently meditated self-reform. Lidian's housekeeping was conscientious, but he felt that he was not making the best use of his talents and resources. The previous spring (May 17, 1840) he had complained in his Journal that living had got to be so ponderous that his poor spirit could no longer drag "this unnecessary baggage-train."[59] It seemed time to "cut the traces" and make a new start. "The bird & the fox can get their food & house without degradation, without domestic servants, & without lies, and why not we?" A few days later the "Hedge," or "Transcendental Club" met in the home of the Reverend Cyrus Bartol in Boston and discussed the need for social changes. Next day (May 28) Emerson summarized in his Journal the tone of the discussion: "The facts which loomed so large in the fogs of yesterday,—property, climate, breeding, personal beauty, & the like have strangely changed their proportions[;] all that we reckoned settled shakes now & rattles and literatures, cities, climates, religions leave their foundations & dance before our eyes."[60]

One of the talkers was a Methodist minister, Edward Thompson Taylor, better known as "Father" Taylor (and in Melville's *Moby-Dick* as "Father Mapple"). He was not a regular attendant of the club, but had been invited and earnestly spoke his thoughts. He was pastor of the Seamen's

Bethel on Ann Street. Many people believed that Father Taylor, with his love and wisdom, rescued more men and women from degradation than any other minister in Boston. Emerson wrote in his Journal: "This hard-featured, scarred, & wrinkled Methodist whose face is a system of cordage becomes whilst he talks a gentle[,] a lovely creature."

Seeing and hearing Father Taylor, a man so successful in rescuing shipwrecked character, increased Emerson's remorse over his own real or fancied ineffectiveness. Five months later he was still smarting from self-reproach. "I have been writing with some pains Essays on various matters as a sort of apology to my country for my apparent idleness."[61] Then he began defending himself against some unnamed "you" who accused him, though "you" may have been himself:

> You think it is because I have an income which exempts me from your day-labor, that I waste, (as you call it,) my time in sungazing & stargazing. You do not know me. If my debts, as they threaten, should consume what money I have, I should live just as I do now: I should eat worse food & wear a coarser coat and should wonder [muse?] in a potato patch instead of in the wood—but it is I & not my Twelve Hundred dollars a year, that love God.

Emerson was further tested on October 16 when George and Sophia Ripley, Margaret Fuller, and Bronson Alcott visited him to discuss Ripley's plan for an experiment in communal living. Since the seventeenth century many such experiments had been tried in America, first by German Pietists, then from 1825 to 1828 by the Scottish socialist Robert Owen and his followers in New Harmony, Indiana, and in New England the Shaker community still flourished. The usual plan was to establish a group of families (or celibates, in the case of the Shakers) on a farm, share the labor, live on the products of their efforts, and depend upon each other for all their social and intellectual needs. Ripley's plans were still tentative, but he knew of a farm of about two hundred acres near Roxbury which he could buy, and he was seeking ten investors to share in his utopian dream.

Ripley had brought his wife and two friends to help him "sell" his proposal. Bronson and Margaret had no money to invest, but Emerson did. "I wished to be convinced," Emerson reported in his Journal, "to be thawed, to be made nobly mad by the kindlings before my eye of a new dawn of human piety."[62] But Ripley used the wrong arguments, "arithmetic and comfort," a refuge against poverty, an easy life with a minimum of physical effort. If he had stressed hardship and sacrifice, he might have made a better impression. "It was not," in Emerson's words, "the cave of persecution[,] which is the palace of spiritual power, but only a room in the Astor House hired for the Transcendentalists." Moreover, to Emerson it seemed like removing from his present prison to a larger one. "I wish to break all prisons. I have not yet conquered my own house. It irks and repents me." It would be dodging the problem he was determined to solve, and he would not hide his "impotency in the thick of a crowd." More important, to join the community would contradict his theory of self-reliance, and his deep conviction "that a man is stronger than a city, that his solitude is more prevalent & beneficent than the concert of crowds."[63]

Ripley did not want the big fish to get off the hook, for Emerson could be a great asset to the community in many ways besides buying shares. On November 9 he wrote a long letter elaborating his plans.[64] He wanted "to insure a more natural union between intellectual and manual labor than now exists; to combine the thinker and the worker." He proposed to operate a farm to provide subsistence for the participating families, and a high-quality school or college for the education of the children and the cultural benefit of the adults.

Ripley had located a beautiful estate exactly right for these purposes, bordered by Newton, West Roxbury, and Dedham. He said he could purchase the estate and put up buildings for ten families for thirty thousand dollars. He needed ten thousand in cash and subscriptions for the remainder. If the money were raised promptly, construction could begin in time for three or four families to take possession by April 1, 1841.

This letter made an appeal that Emerson found hard to reject. He wrote William on December 2: "We are absorbed here at home in discussions of George Ripley's Community."[65] He admitted he was tempted because "I am very discontented with many of my present ways & bent on mending them; but not as favorably disposed to his Community of 10 or 12 families as to a more private reform." Yet in the community he could learn farm work under skillful direction, have means and opportunities for literary labor, and earn (according to the plan) five percent on his capital investment. Ripley expected to take boarding students for the school at a profit to the community. Emerson and Alcott had been discussing setting up a special college, with limited courses and students, in Concord; thus, Ripley's school was one of his attractions.

However, Emerson's decision was about as inevitable as Margaret Fuller's failure to seduce him. On December 15, 1840, he wrote Ripley that he had decided, "very slowly & I may almost say penitentially," not to join in the enterprise.[66] He said the community would not be good for him, and he might not be good for it, for he had little skill in conversing with people. The community could not provide anything that he could not better provide for himself. He lived "in an agreeable neighborhood, in a town which I have many reasons to love . . ." Here were his friends and kindred. Besides, "My own health & habits & those of my wife & my mother are not of the robustness which should give any pledge of enterprise & ability in reform." Yet he did like the plan for "a concentration of scholars in one place," and perhaps "as the school emerges to more distinct consideration out of the Farm, I shall yet find it attractive."

This decision left Emerson with feelings of guilt. He reproached himself for allowing "the old circumstances of mother, wife, children, and brother to overpower my wish to right myself with absolute Nature; and I also consent to hang, a parasite, with all the parasites on this rotten system of property."[67] If this mood had continued, Emerson would soon have reached an emotional crisis of serious dimensions. However, he was not a Tolstoy—not even a George Ripley. He would continue to compromise in little ways with the "old circumstances," though some of his lectures the following year would take new turns as a result of his growing social consciousness.

One of the problems that nagged his conscience was the plight of the Alcott family. Emerson had encouraged Bronson to move to Concord the previous April, and try to support his family by manual labor. Though Alcott had worked hard, his family was in constant need. On December 21 Emerson wrote William that he had decided, with Lidian's consent, that "next April we shall make an attempt to find house room for Mr Alcott & his family under our roof; for the wants of the man are extreme as his merits are extraordinary."[68] He was also "quite intent on trying the experiment of manual labor to some considerable extent & of abolishing or ameliorating the domestic service in my household." Human nature defeated these resolutions, for neither Emerson's wife nor his mother was willing to do without servants.

However, Lidian consented to "adopt the country practice of having but one table in the house."[69] When she explained this new practice in the kitchen, Louisa, the housemaid, agreed to eat with the family, but Lydia, the cook, objected. Next morning, she flatly refused to leave what she regarded as her place in the kitchen, and Louisa chose to stay with her. "With our other project," Waldo reported to William, "we are like to have the same fortune, as Mrs Alcott is as much decided not to come as her husband is willing to come." She knew that innocent Emerson did not foresee the consequences of his idealistic generosity—friction between herself and Lidian.

PART TWO

CHAPTER XVII

Idealism in 1842

What is popularly called Transcendentalism among us, is Idealism; Idealism as it appears in 1842.[1]

I

"I begin the year by sending my little book of Essays to the press," Emerson recorded in his Journal on January 1, 1841.[2] He was not satisfied with his "imperfect chapters," as he called the individual essays, but he hoped to make improvements in the proofs. Eleven days later he wrote Margaret Fuller that his proofs had begun to arrive, and "I am but a hen with one chicken."[3] His publisher was James Munroe and Company, in Boston, publisher of *Nature* and his two most famous addresses, "The American Scholar" and "An Address . . . in Divinity College." A modern author would envy the simplicity of Emerson's publishing arrangements: no waiting for the editors to pass judgment on his manuscript, no copy-editing or elaborate designing of the book, and no delay while the printer found an open date in his schedule. Today this whole process may take a year or longer. In less than three months Emerson's *Essays* was printed and ready for distribution.

The volume contained twelve essays on "History," "Self-Reliance," "Compensation," "Spiritual Laws," "Love," "Friendship," "Prudence," "Heroism," "The Over-Soul," "Circles," "Intellect," and "Art." The subjects sound like versions of his lectures during the previous several years, except for "Over-Soul," which is a new term, and that impression is correct. The ideas are familiar, but the treatment is new, for the most part. Large segments of lectures and choice sentences from Emerson's Journals will be found in the *Essays,* sometimes without revision but more often trimmed, polished, and refined until they glow with a brilliance found nowhere else in Emerson's writings, past or future. The essay was his natural medium of expression, and he stamped this art form with his inimitable originality. He made it sound spontaneous, personal, with unexpected surprises in paradox, wit, and language.

Several of Emerson's favorite authors had been masters of the essay: first of all Plutarch, whose *Morals* he had read and reread since his youth;[4] then Bacon's *Essays,* a perennial favorite; but above all, Montaigne's *Essays.* Later, in *Representative Men,* Emerson described his first acquaintance with the masterpiece of this sixteenth-century French nobleman, Michel Eyquem de Montaigne (1533–92):

> A single odd volume of Cotton's translation of the Essays remained to me from my father's library, when a boy. It lay long neglected, until, after many years, when I was newly escaped from college, I read the book, and procured the remaining volumes. I remember the delight and wonder in which I lived with it. It seemed to me as if I had myself written the book, in some former life, so sincerely it spoke to my thought and experience.[5]

Emerson did not imitate any of these three great essayists, though influences of each can be found in his own compositions: Plutarch's use of allegory, myth, and anecdote to inculcate moral wisdom; the compact epigrams of Bacon in Emerson's pithy, terse sentences; and the pervading spirit of Montaigne. James Russell Lowell hit the mark exactly in *A Fable for Critics* when he called Emerson "A Plotinus-Montaigne, where the Egyptian's gold mist / And the Gascon's shrewd wit cheek-by-jowl coexist . . ."

Montaigne was more of a skeptic than Emerson, but his skepticism resembled Emerson's suspension of judgment while he looked at both sides of a subject. He found men often irrational, but thought that reason in nature taught them how to bring order and control into their lives. As Blanchard Bates says in his Introduction to an American edition of Montaigne's *Essays:*

> . . . Montaigne found that Nature's trail was no longer clear. Men had blurred the trail of Nature with artificial tracks. Philosophers had drawn so

many arbitrary lines that complete confusion existed. The first task was to reassemble Nature. In the case of man it was to reunite body and soul; their functions were interdependent and could be understood only if the two parts were joined. . . . Experience was Montaigne's main discipline.[6]

Experience was also Montaigne's laboratory. By writing down his own thoughts with absolute fidelity, he believed he could acquire knowledge not only of himself but of the self, because he assumed that all men led similar subjective lives, which was also Emerson's assumption. Therefore he cultivated a style that would convey the movements of his own thoughts, considerably short of a stream-of-consciousness style, yet enriched by intuitions from his subconscious. He valued experience more than books, though he also read widely and collected illuminating thoughts and brilliant sayings from literature, with which he spiced his writings, as did Emerson. But the life he revealed was his own. In "Of Repentance" he declared: "Here my book and I go hand in hand and at the same pace. . . . who touches the one, touches the other." Emerson had this in mind when he wrote of Montaigne:

> The sincerity and marrow of the man reaches to his sentences. I know not anywhere the book that seems less written. It is the language of conversation transferred to a book. Cut these words, and they would bleed; they are vascular and alive. One has the same pleasure in it that he feels in listening to the necessary speech of men about their work, when any unusual circumstance gives momentary importance to the dialogue. For blacksmiths and teamsters do not trip in their speech; it is the shower of bullets.[7]

Emerson might have been writing about himself. To hear the talk of teamsters he had only to stand at his own front gate, and he enjoyed hearing their banter to each other as they drove past or stopped to pick up a package he was sending to Boston. It was the flavor and spontaneity of their speech which he most enjoyed. His idea of good writing was the same as Thoreau's (and Emerson may well have said it first): it was conversation folded many times thick. In the process of composition the repetitions and inanities and expendable words got squeezed out, leaving the vigor and pungency of colloquial language. Hemingway, in a statement which became famous, said that Mark Twain was the first American to write the American language.[8] In fiction that is probably true, but in non-fiction prose Emerson had already captured the rhythms, vocabulary, and inventiveness of American speech. In this, too, his practice followed his theories.

In "History," the first essay in Emerson's 1841 volume, he establishes the personal basis of his book. One mind is common to all men, and what they have experienced and thought, he also can feel and think. "If the whole of history is in one man, it is all to be explained from individual experience."[9] This assumption rests on the metaphysical doctrine found in all Emerson's writings, that the private mind is attached by an invisible umbilical cord to a Universal Mind. Hence his insistence on the value of personal experience: what the mind "does not see, what it does not live, it will not know."

Emerson believed in a kind of "recapitulation theory" in the stages of individual mental development. Why, he asks, do all men find the stories of Homer, or the domestic life of the Athenians and Spartans four or five centuries later, so fascinating? Because "every man passes personally through a Grecian period." This may be as dubious as historical fact as his belief that "The Greeks are not reflective . . . They combine the energy of manhood with the engaging unconsciousness of childhood."[10] But it illustrates his subjective interpretation of history, and harmonizes with his conviction that *God is, not was*. Thus history became for him autobiography. "How easily these old worships of Moses, of Zoroaster, of Menu, of Socrates, domesticate themselves in the mind. I cannot find any antiquity in them. They are mine as much as theirs."[11]

It was remarked above that Montaigne wanted to reintegrate the body and soul, or man and nature. In "History" Emerson says that man is "the correlative of nature. His power consists in the multitude of his affinities, in the fact that his life is intertwined with the whole chain of organic and inorganic being."[12] This is a concept supported by modern scientists—see the Introduction to this biography. Its literary significance in these essays is that the idea pervades the images and metaphors which gave the essays their vividness and pungency:

A man is a bundle of relations, a knot of roots, whose flower and fruitage is the world. His faculties refer to natures out of him and predict the world he is to inhabit, as the fins of the fish foreshow that water exists, or the wings of an eagle in the egg presupposes air. He cannot live without a world. . . . Columbus needs a planet to shape his course upon. Newton and Laplace need myriads of age and thick-strewn celestial areas.[13]

Yet finally Emerson says that "the path of science and of letters is not the way into nature," but "an influx of the ever new, ever sanative conscience" is. It is the unsophisticated mind ("The idiot, the Indian, the child and unschooled farmer's boy") which stands "nearer to the light by which nature is to be read."[14] This anti-intellectual notion gave Emerson a sympathy with the concrete externals of nature which determined his language and syntax.

The next essay, "Self-Reliance," is perhaps the most brilliant display of Emerson's literary strategy in all his essays. This was the essay that would be most often quoted in future years—and often misinterpreted as simply *believe in yourself and you can overcome any obstacle*, overlooking the context of Emerson's self-reliance in "God-reliance." However, "Self-Reliance" is so strongly assertive that this caution is easily ignored. The essay is a twenty-one-gun salute to self-reliance. The compact sentences, with almost no connective words or phrases, march always straight ahead with vigor and emphasis. The reader can almost hear the sentences being shouted. The style, fully as much as the subject matter, has made this one of Emerson's most popular essays. Everyone knows such sentences as:

> To believe your own thought, to believe that what is true for you in your own private heart is true for all men,—that is genius. [This is one of the more complicated sentences, but it ends with the crack of a whip.][15]

> Trust thyself: every heart vibrates to that iron string.[16]

> Whoso would be a man, must be a nonconformist.[17]

> I would write on the lintels of the door-post, *Whim.* I hope it is somewhat better than whim at last, but we cannot spend the day in explanation.[18]

> A foolish consistency is the hobgoblin of little minds, adored by little statesmen and philosophers and divines.[19]

> An institution is the lengthened shadow of one man . . .[20]

> Our reading is mendicant and sycophantic.[21]

As men's prayers are a disease of the will, so are their creeds a disease of the intellect.[22]

Travelling is a fool's paradise.[23]

Critics continue to accuse Emerson of incoherence, but here, characteristically, in "Self-Reliance" every statement emphasizes the exhortation to be true to one's own God-given conscience. "In this pleasing contrite wood-life which God allows me, let me record day by day my honest thought without prospect or retrospect, and, I cannot doubt, it will be found symmetrical . . ."[24]

The main thought in each of Emerson's essays, as previously in his sermons and lectures, is simple and explicit, but he illustrates with such an abundance of examples that an inattentive reader may lose the key to the thought. Here is an example:

There will be an agreement in whatever variety of actions, so they be each honest and natural in their hour. For of one will, the actions will be harmonious, however unlike they seem. These varieties are lost sight of at a little distance, at a little height of thought. One tendency unites them all. The voyage of the best [sailing] ship is a zigzag line of a hundred tacks. See the line from a sufficient distance, and it straightens itself to the average tendency. Your genuine action will explain itself and will explain your other genuine actions. Your conformity explains nothing. . . .[25]

Emerson's first compositions were sermons (if we except his private diaries), and he continued to preach in his essays the same moral ideals of honesty, originality (imitation was to him dishonest), courage, and the rejection of all ready-made formulas. He was not opposed to creeds, churches, prayers, institutions, or property, but to lazy, superstitious, cowardly reliance on them. The main difference between one of Emerson's earlier sermons, or a later published speech, and one of his essays is one of degree in concentration. In his best essays the thought has the heat of the rays of the sun focused through a magnifying lens—the style being the lens. He also keeps the reader interested by his almost endless ingenuity, his (and Emily Dickinson's) "stairway of surprise." In "Compensation," a favorite theme since Emerson's boyhood, he merely illustrates the law of polarity (every action causes a reaction) in nature, transferred to the realms of psychology and ethics, but his insatiable imagination supplies such a variety of illustrations and applications that the thought seems more complicated than it actually is. Emerson wrote as an artist, not as a philosopher.

II

Emerson's *Essays,* First Series, can be read with enjoyment for their superb art and infectious enthusiasm. But the core of his thought is still certain Neoplatonic ideas which he had entertained for several years, and the essays are not fully intelligible unless these ideas are recognized. The Neoplatonic background of *Nature* was explained in Chapter XIII,[26] but a brief summary may be useful here. Plotinus taught that from the One all things flow, or emanate. The first emanation from the One is Mind (*nous*), or Universal Intelligence, which provides a rational foundation for the world. A World Soul emanates from the One, and from the World Soul, the human soul. Below the World Soul lies the realm of nature, existing in time but reflecting the eternal ideas of the One. Both the World Soul and the human soul are eternal, but habitation in a physical body is a "fall." The soul gives the body vitality, sensitivity, and the power of being rational. It survives the death of the body and either transmigrates to other bodies or rejoins the World Soul. Matter is the final and lowest emanation.[27]

Somewhat illogically, Plotinus holds the human soul responsible for its acts, though all events are determined. Evil is the failure of the soul to maintain rational control over the senses and the degrading tendency of matter. Evil is, therefore, negative, the absence of control and order. Salvation lies in climbing the ladder of knowledge to a union with the One, attained when the self surrenders all egotism and is no longer conscious of separation from God. Plotinus also taught, as did Plato, that love refines and purifies the soul. Saint Augustine approved Plotinus's explanation of evil and his teaching of salvation by the stairway of love. In fact, he said that Plotinus would have had only to "change a few words" to become a Christian.[28] Neoplatonism, therefore, was not anti-Christian, but a rational approach to ideals held by Christians, the main reason for its appeal to Emerson.

Emerson's key Neoplatonic essay is "The Over-Soul," and it is supplemented by "Intellect," "Spiritual Laws," and "Circles." The exuberance of "The Over-Soul" was mentioned above as a stylistic characteristic. But why was the author so excited? Because he was writing about the ecstasy which Plotinus attributed to union with the One. Had Emerson actually experienced such a state of mind and emotions, or had he only imagined it to illustrate his theory of the "Soul"? This is a question difficult to answer precisely, because the only evidence is the essay itself. Oliver Wendell Holmes says in his biography of Emerson: " 'The Over-Soul' might almost be called the Over-*flow* of a spiritual imagination. We cannot help thinking of the 'pious, virtuous, God-intoxicated' Spinoza."[29]

In the first paragraph of "The Over-Soul" Emerson says: "Our faith comes in moments; our vice is habitual. Yet there is a depth in those brief moments which constrains us to ascribe more reality to them than to all other experiences."[30] That he had experienced such "moments" seems evident in his writing about them, and most of all in the residual faith they left him in passing. This was a mystery he did not pretend to understand, and could only indicate in poetic metaphors: "Man is a stream whose source is hidden. Our being is descending into us from we know not whence." And:

> As with events, so it is with thoughts. When I watch that flowing river, which, out of regions I see not, pours for a season its streams into me, I see that I am a pensioner; not a cause but a surprised spectator of this ethereal water; that I desire and look up and put myself in the attitude of reception, but from some alien energy the visions come.[31]

Here "visions" could mean no more than "thoughts," but the best thoughts come in epiphanies, sudden illuminations, producing rapture, when "the Maker of all things and all persons stands behind us and casts his dread omniscience through us over things."[32] The *mystical experience,* to use William James's term, reveals wisdom, and causes psychological changes in the person as dramatic as metamorphosis in zoology. But the revelation is of eternal truths, not low, sensual facts.

"The same Omniscience flows into the intellect and makes what we call genius. Much of the wisdom of the world is not wisdom, and the most illuminated class of men are no doubt superior to literary fame, and are not writers."[33] Yet the greatest writers have received from this source the "wisdom of humanity." Psychic "energy" comes to them "as insight . . . serenity and grandeur." All mystics agree that the union of the soul with God is ineffable, and Emerson says: "The simplest person who in his integrity worships God, becomes God; yet for ever and ever the influx of this better and universal self is new and unsearchable."[34] It takes place in solitude: "The soul gives itself, alone, original and pure, to the Lonely, Original, and Pure . . ."[35] The receiver of this divine energy now sees the whole world as a "perennial miracle," all history is "sacred," and he no longer lives a "spotted life of shreds and patches." He will cease from all base and frivolous conduct, be content with his time and place, and "calmly front the morrow in the negligency of that trust which carries God with it."[36]

In the essay called "Intellect," the term means not the product of the individual mind but the Universal Intellect (or *nous*) working through the human mind or soul. Intellect is void of affections; it "goes out of the individual, floats over its own personality, and regards it as a fact and not as *I* and *mine.*" Without higher aid, the mind sees all things in nature as predetermined, or "formed and bound: The intellect pierces the form, overleaps the wall, detects intrinsic likeness between remote things and reduces all things into a few principles."[37]

As the essay continues, Emerson calls these "few principles" *laws*. One is that the growth of the intellect is spontaneous; no man can predict when God will visit him, but he can leave the door open. It follows, therefore, that spontaneous action is always best. Another law is "undulation": "So now you must labor with your brains, and now you must forbear your activity and see what the great Soul showeth."[38] While the brain is quiescent, the constructive intellect can make use of the receptive intellect, and fish up from the well of memory wonderful articles.

On the one hand, this theory seems to anticipate Carl Jung's "racial memory"; on the other hand, it suggests Freudian "depth" psychology, which makes use of experience recovered from the unconscious. Emerson's interpretation is hardly psychoanalytic, but he does believe that dreams may provide "access to primary truth." He had discussed this subject in the lecture on "Demonology," from which Erich Fromm quoted a long passage in *The Forgotten Language,* with the comment that Emerson recognized more "clearly than anyone had recognized before him the connection between character and dream."[39] The special point of Emerson's essay on "Intellect" is that "the truth was in us, before it was reflected to us from natural objects."

It is no wonder that Nietzsche adored these essays, carried them with him when he traveled, and annotated his copy.[40] In "Self-Reliance" Emerson quotes Zoroaster, and Nietzsche's Zarathustra is a variant spelling. In fact, Nietzsche's *Übermensch* was probably derived from Emerson's "Over-Soul"; and "Self-Reliance" was the Over-Man's creed. "Circles" also is in the spirit of the prophet Zarathustra preaching his message of transcending the ordinary human life and discovering one's divine potentialities. The circle is a metaphor for the expanding life of man radiating from the soul at the center.

The remaining essays in the First Series contain more warmed-over thoughts than the works previously discussed. In "Love" and "Friendship" Emerson had nothing of significance to say that he had not already uttered in his lectures on these subjects. "Prudence" also advocates abstract virtues, but it is made interesting by shrewd distinctions between "higher" and "lower" kinds of prudential conduct. "The spurious prudence, making the senses final, is the god of sots and cowards, and is the subject of all comedy. It is nature's joke, and therefore literature's. The true prudence limits this sensualism by admitting the knowledge of an internal and real [spiritual] world."[41] Both "Prudence" and "Heroism" were lectures in the "Human Life" series, and were printed in *Essays* with scarcely any revision. They nicely balance each other. Heroism is a "wild courage" and a "military attitude of the soul," but prudence in the best sense is also courageous. "The hero is a mind of such balance that no disturbances can shake his will, but pleasantly and as it were merrily he advances to his own music . . ."[42] Nothing could be more characteristic of Emerson than his admiration for the stoic but cheerful hero, or his satirical scorn for the unheroic man:

When the spirit is not master of the world, then it is its dupe. Yet the little man takes the great hoax so innocently, works in it so headlong and believing, is born red, and dies gray, arranging his toilet, attending on his own health, laying traps for sweet food and strong wine, setting his heart on a horse or a rifle, made happy with a little gossip or a little praise, that the great soul cannot choose but laugh at such earnest nonsense.[43]

"Art," the final essay in the volume, begins: "Because the soul is progressive, it never quite repeats itself, but in every act attempts the production of a new and fairer whole."[44] Though this was also a reworked lecture, it appropriately ends the *Essays,* First Series, with a progressive—even prophetic—look at art in nineteenth-century America. To begin with, Emerson rejects the Greek and Roman aesthetic ideal of *imitation.* The artist abridges, selects, and interprets. "In a portrait he must inscribe the character and not the features ..." He detaches from the confusing world of surface appearances a fragment which symbolizes and magnifies the inner truth. The work of art *represents* not the physical object but its hidden essence, "the aspiring original within."

Emerson condemns "an effeminate, prudent, sickly beauty," which was the American aesthetic taste of the time. The escapists "reject life as prosaic and create a death which they call poetic."[45] Though he admired the great art of Europe, he said modern art could not "reiterate its miracles in the old arts; it is its instinct to find beauty and holiness in new and necessary facts, in the field and road-side, in the shop and mill." Even a spiritual use could be made of machinery and industrial life. "When the errands are noble and adequate, a steamboat bridging the Atlantic between Old and New England and arriving at its ports with the punctuality of a planet, is a step of man into harmony with nature."[46]

Critical reception of Emerson's *Essays* divided along ideological—or perhaps more accurately, theological—lines.[47] Calvinists detested them, as they also did Spinoza, whom they regarded as an atheist. Emerson's friends and the so-called Transcendentalists hailed them with joy, but more privately than publicly. A critic in *The Princeton Review* (October 1841), defender of Calvinist orthodoxy, thought such essays could be written as rapidly as a man could move his pen, apparently without thinking at all. In the Unitarian *Christian Examiner* (May 1841), a moderately liberal but Harvard-dominated publication, Cornelius Felton, professor of classics, admired the dazzling prose but found the thought often extravagant and resurrecting "ancient errors" which the author had mistaken for truth. He strongly objected to Emerson's doctrine of obeying his instinctual impulses, which Felton said would destroy society and reduce civilization to chaos.

Carlyle professed delight with Emerson's *Essays* and impulsively wrote a preface for an English edition to be published by Fraser,[48] but apparently he did not understand their Neoplatonic background. He advised British readers not to trouble themselves with the author's "notions and half-notions of a metaphysic, Theosophic kind." What delighted him in these essays was "the soliloquy of a true soul, alone under the stars, in this day." He had to admit that the utterance was abrupt, fitful, and not yet fully expressed. Yet these essays brought a breath of fresh air from that green country New England, from her mountains, rivers, mills, and farms. Obviously Carlyle had not read Emerson with much comprehension, and he romanticized the autobiographical element because he liked the man.

Carlyle's preface probably helped to call Emerson's *Essays* to the attention of British readers, but the first reviews paid little attention to his cautions and advice.[49] The *inspirational* value of the *Essays* quickly won a large audience for Emerson, so that when he returned to Great Britain in 1848 to lecture, he was already well known. By that time his *Essays* had been pirated in cheap editions, which sold well, to the profit of his reputation but not of his bank account.

In 1845 Edgar Quinet published his lectures on *Christianity and the French Revolution* in Paris, with a chapter on Emerson, whom he praised as "the most ideal writer of our times," contradicting the European belief that all North Americans were materialists. "On the virgin soil of the new world behold the footsteps of a man, and a man who is moving toward the future by the same road that we are going."[50]

In Paris also the prominent critic Philarète Chasles called attention to Emerson's *Essays,* and the Polish poet Adam Mickiewicz praised them in a lecture at the Sorbonne. Daniel Stern (pseudonym of the Comtesse d'Agoult) heard of the *Essays* through Chasles and Mickiewicz and promptly ordered a copy from London. In her review published in *La Revue Indépendente,* July 29, 1846, the countess declared:

There is no difficulty in following him [Emerson], for we breathe a salubrious atmosphere in his work. Nothing offends, not even the discords, because all is resolved and harmonized in the sentiment of a superior truth. The eccentricities do not shock us; they are not affected eccentricities, but natural, as unsought for, as homogeneous to the mind of Emerson, as certain graceful freaks of vegetation.[51]

It appears, therefore, that Emerson's *Essays* were more enthusiastically accepted in Europe than in his own country until some years later. Their full impact on Victorian England was also still in the making. But these early admirers showed that Emerson had created a work of international importance in 1841.

III

After the publication of his *Essays* Emerson felt at loose ends. He had forgone his usual winter lecture series and had no pressing duty, though he kept reminding himself that he ought to begin collecting his thoughts for the lecture which he had promised months before to give at Waterville College in Maine (later Colby College) on August 11, 1841. Once he asked himself, Why not "write for the young men at Waterville a history of our present literary & philosophical crisis, a portrait of the parties[,] & read the augury of the coming hours?"[52] In England ethics and philosophy were dead; Coleridge was ignored. In the United States the increase in population enabled trade to expand and a few men to get rich. Everyone was excited over the country's progress; yet, in Emerson's estimation, "We are a puny & feeble folk." Nowhere could he see any "great men," in Europe or America. And men of supposed intellect cowardly accepted "the false scale of the populace." How such a jeremiad would have been accepted in Maine is problematical, but Emerson made no effort to write such a lecture (though he had already partly done that in his lectures on "The Present Age"). Instead, while the sleet beat on his study windows, he continued reading his favorite authors, Heraclitus, Plato, Plotinus, Proclus, and felt he was present "at the sowing of the seed of the world."[53]

Three months later Emerson was still reading "with joy" the life of Pythagoras by Iamblichus—of course in Taylor's translation. "Especially I admire the patience & longanimity [his own coinage] of the probation of the novice."[54] Every detail of the Pythagorean's life was severely regulated and restricted, his diet, conversation, periods of silence, study, and meditation—an ascetic discipline predating Christianity by several centuries. Perhaps, Emerson mused, the Roman Church was right to require celibacy of its clergy. In fact it would be good for literary men. In spite of all he had said about manual labor, he now felt that household chores untuned and disqualified him for writing. Also he had a strong religious desire to purify and spiritualize his own body. He wished that his hands, his body, his person, might not "descend" to mix with common clay, but that he might "flow down forever [as] a sea of benefit into races of individuals."[55]

This exalted passion to keep the stream of divine energy in him pure did not make Emerson contemptuous of common people; quite the contrary. "I frequently find the best part of my ride in the Concord coach from my house to Winthrop Place to be in Prince street, Charter street, Ann street, & the like places in the North end of Boston."[56] There men and women engaged in hard work took no notice of their "dishabille," their undignified postures, or their language. They were completely natural and unrestrained, and wonderful subjects for a painter. He wished he could paint them himself, but only a genius could translate "the circumstance in the street into oils & colors." Such power of expression is the "gift of God."

These moods led Emerson's thoughts to his Aunt Mary, and he spent all afternoon of May 3 rereading her letters. They convinced him anew that she was a "Genius always new, subtle, frolicsome, musical, unpredictable . . . her wit is the wild horse of the desart [*sic*] who snuffs the sirocco & scours the palm-grove without having learned his paces in the Stadium or at Tattersall's [a London horse auction]."[57]

But as he continued reading, Emerson became more serious and began thinking of his debt to his aunt's religion, which in his youth "still dwelt like a sabbath peace in the country population of New England." It "taught privation, self-denial & sorrow." Remembering, he felt suddenly that his life was "frivolous & public," and he wished he could retire to some Mount Athos "in the depths of New Hampshire or Maine." Thus the fascination of the Pythagorean disciples for him had its roots in his Aunt Mary's Calvinism. He would never entirely outgrow her hatred of "the poor, low, thin, unprofitable, unpoetical Humanitarians," whom she regarded as "the devastators of the Church & robbers of the soul."[58] She had hoped that the Emerson boys would grow up to purify the old faith of its narrowness and errors, but Waldo would find a purer faith in a religion older than Christianity itself.

Emerson's Neoplatonism, however, was diluted or enriched—perhaps some of both—by his daily walks to Walden Pond and other interesting places around Concord. This pleasure was increased by the coming of Henry Thoreau to live with him toward the end of April. Because of ill health, Henry's brother John had decided to withdraw from the private school they were teaching, and Henry did not feel equal to running the school by himself. When the term ended April 1, Henry was without regular employment, except for occasionally helping his father manufacture pencils.

Emerson saw advantages to both Henry and himself in offering him room and board in exchange for a few hours a day of working in the garden or doing household chores, and Henry gladly accepted. Emerson was awkward with tools and Henry was adept. He enjoyed repairing a broken chair or adjusting a stove damper, and he was an expert horticulturalist. The whole family was delighted to have Henry occupy the little room (later made into a bathroom) at the head of the stairs. Lidian had always liked Henry, and Waldo Jr. and Ellen were charmed by the little games he played with them and his patience in answering their questions about birds, flowers, and stars. Even the maids were fond of "Mr. Thura."[59]

In June 1841, Emerson's Journal had a merrier note, and it was not entirely because of the pleasant weather. On June 6 he recorded his discontent with his home beside the dusty road, "with its sills & cellar almost in the water of the meadow."[60] Then he went out into the morning sunshine, or at night into the tender shadows, and both the sun and the moon transformed the "street of hucksters & taverns" into a Palmyra. But much of his happiness was due to the fact that "the good river god has taken the form of my valiant Henry Thoreau here & introduced me to the riches of his shadowy starlit moonlit stream, a lovely new world lying as close & yet as unknown to this vulgar trite one of streets and shops as death to life or poetry to prose." Rowing on Walden Pond or the river at night was a new experience to him. At sunset Henry's oar dipped into the enchanting liquid and radiated glowing waves of reds, purples, and yellows.

At this time Emerson was giving his final touches to "Woodnotes," part II, which Miss Fuller would publish in the October number of *The Dial*. In the poem the white pine, Emerson's favorite tree, sings the song "Which knits the world in music," while "Nature beats in perfect tune":

> Enough for thee the primal mind
> That flows in streams, that breathes in wind:
> Leave all thy pedant lore apart;
> God hid the whole world in thy heart.[61]

This poem shows how useless it is to try to define or classify Emerson's theism. His "God" is both the Deity of the Old Testament and the "eternal Pan" of Greek myth who hatches the world out of "an egg of stone" and then takes every protean (or pantheistic?) shape in nature: "Of gem, and air, of plants, and worms," while "I, that to-day am a pine / Yesterday was a bundle of grass." Whether God, Pan, or Over-Soul, "He hides in pure transparency . . ."

On June 4 Emerson wrote Caroline Sturgis: "Mary Russell is here & Henry Thoreau, not to mention occasional fanatical flights of birds—of croaking or prophesying song. . . . I have quite deserted my books, & do hoe corn & wheel a wheelbarrow whole days together."[62] Mary Russell, Lidian's Plymouth friend, had set up an improvised school in the barn, where she instructed Waldo Jr., Ellen, and the Alcott children.

Only Lidian, three months pregnant, was not enjoying the summer, but early in June, Elizabeth Hoar announced that she was taking her to Staten Island, which she promptly did. Both women enjoyed the trip and the visit with the William Emerson family. On Monday the fourteenth Waldo wrote Lidian: "The children have both been well and have lived out of doors all the daylight hours . . ." The old church, where Dr. Ezra Ripley was still officially the senior pastor, was scheduled to be torn down to make way for a new building. On Sunday, June 13, Waldo's Uncle Samuel Ripley preached the last sermon in the historical church. Waldo knew that Lidian would find it "droll" that Henry Thoreau was the only member of the household to hear the sermon. Caroline Sturgis was there, and that afternoon Henry was going to take her boating. Waldo had enjoyed her visit, but would be willing to see her leave next day so he could finish his "Waldenic poem" ("Woodnotes"), which he had promised Margaret Fuller for *The Dial.*

July arrived, Lidian and Elizabeth returned, and Emerson had not written a single sentence of his Waterville College address. In desperation he decided to isolate himself for two weeks at Nantasket Beach, on the thin peninsula in Massachusetts Bay extending from Hull to Nantasket. He took with him Plato's *Phaedrus, Meno, The Banquet,* Taylor's translations of Proclus, Ocellus Lucanus, and the Pythagorean *Fragments.* He hoped to find in these books some inkling of an idea for his lecture, but there were distractions even at Nantasket Beach. Among other friendly vacationers were James Russell Lowell and his fiancée, Maria White. Most enticing of all were the beach and the ocean. For many years Emerson had been vacationing in the mountains. His Journals do not mention his having swum in the ocean since his childhood. From his retreat he wrote Lidian, "I read Plato, I swim and be it known unto you, I did verily catch with hook & line yesterday morning two haddocks, a cod, a flounder, and a pollock & a perch."[63]

In the same letter Emerson said the sea reminded him of his sailing to Malta and brought back his Mediterranean experiences, "which are the most that I know of the Ocean; for the sea is the same in the summer all the world over." In a letter to Margaret Fuller he recalled his childhood experiences of hiding from his father's "voice in the garden" summoning him to an enforced swimming lesson. "I am here," he continued, "making a sort of peace offering to the god of waters against whom, ever since my childhood—imprisoned in streets & hindered from the fields & woods—I have kept a sort of grudge." Now he found the sea and the beach receiving him "with a sort of paternal love." The phrase is interesting: had he finally forgiven his father? It would be pleasant to think so, but nine years later he would write the letter quoted at the beginning of this biography, revealing hostility in his forty-seventh year.

Emerson's vacation at Nantasket Beach was a great success as a vacation, but the last week in July he returned home, after meeting Lidian in Plymouth, without having composed any part of his lecture. In Concord he wrote William on July 27 that he had found he "could write out of no inkstand but my own."[64] At the beach he had made a rambling outline while reading Plato and the Neoplatonists, and they were determining the direction of his thoughts—not, of course, for the first time.

Emerson called his lecture "The Method of Nature," but his concept of "nature" was derived from the same Neoplatonists who had so largely shaped his thought in his essays on "The Over-Soul," "Intellect," "Spiritual Laws," and "Circles." It is doubtful, however, that a single copy of his *Essays* had yet reached Waterville College. His main theme was: "In the divine order, intellect is primary; nature, secondary; it is the memory of the mind. That which once existed in intellect as pure law, has now taken body as Nature."[65] He recommends studying "the mind in nature, because we cannot steadily gaze on it in mind"—the first *mind* meaning the Divine Mind, or the Soul emanating through the physical world of nature. When he speaks of "the natural history of the soul," therefore, his paradox must be interpreted Neoplatonically. He does not want, he says, to present man as an abstraction, "an air-fed, unimpassioned, impossible ghost.... And yet one who conceives the true order of nature, and beholds the visible as proceeding from the invisible, cannot state his thought without seeming to those who study the physical laws to do them some injustice."[66] This was Emerson's dilemma, to find language to show how much he valued the man of flesh and blood while insisting on his complete dependence on spirit.

The "method of nature" was difficult to verbalize because "That rushing stream will not stop to be observed." In "The Over-Soul" Emerson had used the same metaphor: "Man is a stream whose source is hidden." In this lecture he says: "nature descends always from above." This process gives *life* to animal and vegetable forms, but the word (*life*) cannot be defined: "the physiologist concedes that no chemistry, no mechanics, can account for the facts, but a mysterious principle of life must be assumed, which *not only inhabits the organ but makes the organ*" (italics supplied).[67]

Here Emerson's Neoplatonism is becoming modified by contemporary science—of astronomy, geology, chemistry, and Goethe's biology. The "tendency" of nature is growth: "All is nascent, infant." He says "tendency" instead of "law," but it pervades the cosmos:

We can point nowhere to anything final; but tendency appears on all hands: planet, system, constellation, total nature is growing like a field of maize in July; is becoming somewhat else; is in rapid metamorphosis. The embryo does not more strive to be man, than yonder burr of light we call a nebula tends to be a ring, a comet, a globe, the parent of new stars.[68]

Nature is not concerned with the single creature but with the survival of the whole tree of life, and it produces with prodigality so that a sufficient number of individuals shall reproduce their kind. Conscious beings have "that redundancy or excess of life ... we call *ecstasy.*" This passionate desire for life is universal in nature.

These scientific ideas Emerson blends with his own modified Neoplatonism. The ultimate achievement of nature is the world of man. He was created to perform a function in nature, that of consciousness: "If only he *sees,* the world will be visible enough." He was born "to deliver the thought of his heart from the universe to the universe; to do an office which nature could not forgo . . ."[69]

"I conceive a man as always spoken to from behind, and unable to turn his head and see the speaker." If he listens "with insatiate ears, richer and greater wisdom is taught him . . . His health and greatness consists in his being the channel through which heaven flows to earth . . . [and] an ecstatical state takes place in him."[70] This is Emerson's familiar theory of genius, "inspiration," and the existence of "great men." All men have access to this ecstasy, but only a few are able to abandon their wills to the Supreme Will radiating through nature. Though Emerson's Deity was no longer an anthropomorphic God, nature taught him "the lesson of an intimate deity" which made him happy. "The doctrine of this Supreme Presence is a cry of joy and exultation." Emerson thought it sufficient to enjoy this life without worrying about immortality:

> I cannot tell if these wonderful qualities which house to-day in this mortal frame shall ever re-assemble in equal activity in a similar frame, or whether they have before had a natural history like that of this body you see before you; but this one thing I know, that these qualities did not now begin to exist, cannot be sick with my sickness, nor buried in the grave; but that they circulate through the Universe: before the world was, they were.[71]

If Emerson had preached happiness through faith in God, his audience might have understood him, but his language was not familiar to his hearers. And had they taken in what he was saying, they would have found two heresies: God appeared both in nature (pantheism was generally regarded as atheism) and in man. But Emerson's audience simply did not understand his address, and he returned home with a feeling of disappointment, though he believed he had given a good performance. He promptly printed the address and sent a copy to Carlyle, who thought it "the best *written*" of all Emerson's addresses he had read, but added, "I do desiderate some *correction* of these beautiful *abstracta.*" Possibly this advice made an impression on Emerson, for within a few months he would begin to withdraw from the rarefied heights of mystical abstractions and draw nearer to his contemporary world; though more likely he was ready to change directions.

IV

On September 4, 1841, Emerson wrote his brother William: "I hope I shall one day write something better than those poor cramp arid 'Essays' which I almost hate the sight of."[72] Though he was pleased at Carlyle's news that his book was being well received in England in spite of its "lapidary" style (Emerson's own term), he now aspired to a different style on the lecture platform, and eventually in print. His stock in the City Bank (inherited from his first wife) had again failed to pay a dividend. This had decided him to give another series of lectures in Boston in the winter of 1841–42 and, as usual, the prospect excited him. He wrote Carlyle on October 30 that he was "haunted with grave dreams of what might be accomplished in the lecture-room ... I imagine an eloquence of infinite variety,—rich as conversation can be, with anecdote, joke, tragedy, epics and pindarics, argument and confession."[73] He wished he could speak extempore, as Carlyle did, but he did not dare try.

"There are two directions in which souls move," Emerson wrote in an undated entry in his Journal, probably in October 1841. One was the passive "worship of ideas"; the other the active exercise of a practical talent, leading to "usefulness, comfort, society, low power of all sorts. The other is solitary, grand, secular."[74] He could choose either way. Many of his essays had shown his preference for the grand and solitary way, but now he desired to try the other road, though he still admired the "secular," in its rarer sense of long-range time. He adored Elizabeth Hoar, whose "holiness is substantive."[75] Lidian also has been observed to be inclined to the "grand" way, but possibly we have misjudged her, for Emerson records this startling observation: "Queenie (who has a gift to curse & swear,) will every now & then in spite of all manners & christianity rip out on Saints, reformers, & Divine Providence with the most edifying zeal."[76]

Buffon said that "Style is the man," but the lapidary style was only one expression of Emerson's many-faceted character, the facet which wrote for the gods. He needed someone "who shall take me off my feet, and make me forget or overcome those sudden frigidities" to which he was prone. Henry Thoreau was the rare friend who could do that, though Emerson told him "that his freedom is in the form, but he does not disclose new matter. I am very familiar with all his thoughts,—they are my own quite originally drest."[77]

With Margaret Fuller he could correspond more freely than he could talk with her. She was his houseguest again early in October, and once more he was undergoing those "strange, cold-warm, attractive-repelling conversations."[78] She was worried about her sister Ellen's engagement to Ellery Channing, whom she regarded as talented but impractical and a poor prospect for a husband. She wanted Emerson to sympathize with her worries. This may have intensified his frigidities, but she, in her highly wrought emotional state, was also half making love to him again, and he knew neither how to interpret her words nor how to reply to them. In frustration she would wander into his library when he was absent and fondle his books. She wrote notes to him, and he wrote replies, with Waldo Jr. acting as messenger. ". . . there is nothing I wish more than to be able to live with you without disturbing you,"[79] she wrote, but she knew both conditions were impossible. Caroline Sturgis had called these ill-matched lovers "the rock and the wave." Margaret had this in mind when she confessed, "The genial flow of my desire may be checked for the moment, but it cannot for long."

Probably Margaret accompanied Emerson on October 13 to Boston, where he attended the first-night performance of the Austrian ballerina Fanny Elssler. In Italy he had not been favorably impressed by ballet, but he was completely charmed by the "wisdom" of Fanny Elssler's feet: "such surpassing grace must rest on some occult foundations of inward harmony."[80] He attributed her popularity to her exhibiting freedom to audiences "pinched & restrained by the decorum of city life."

While in Boston, Emerson also saw Daniel Webster on the street, "black as a thunder cloud & care worn. . . . The canker worms have crawled to the topmost bough of the wild elm & swing down from that."[81] The imagery reflects Emerson's sudden interest in the daguerreotype. On this same Boston trip he may have sat for his own daguerreotype, for several days later he described in minute detail how it felt to sit immovable for several minutes while the camera formed his image on glass. This new art was creating a sensation throughout the country, and Emerson was as fascinated as everyone else. It even began to influence his own art. "Tis certain," he remarked in his Journal, "that the Daguerrotype [*sic*] is the true Republican style of painting. The Artist stands aside & lets you paint yourself."[82] A few days earlier he had wondered, "And why not draw for these times a portrait gallery? . . . A camera! A camera! cries the Century, that is the only toy."[83] Yes, why not in his lectures on "The Times" give accurately observed pictures of contemporary people in their characteristic poses and activities? He did not try to carry out this idea systematically, but it did influence him in striving for a simpler, more natural and colloquial style in the lectures he was writing. Of course, portraiture was not entirely new for him. Recently in describing the death of Dr. Ezra Ripley (September 21) he had dwelt especially in his Journal on the Indian "beauty" of the corpse. Waldo Jr. was probably reflecting his father's attitude when he asked, after walking round and round the body lying on the couch, "Why don't they keep him for a statue?"[84]

V

Emerson read the eight lectures in "The Times" series at the Masonic Temple in Boston between December 2, 1841, and January 20, 1842. The most interesting of the surviving texts are "The Conservative" (second in the series) and "The Transcendentalist" (fourth), both published in *The Dial* and in the first volume of his collected *Works*. Critics have pointed out that Emerson liked to look at both sides of every question, and that he wrote "The Conservative" to balance "Man the Reformer," delivered the previous winter. Although he did habitually weigh the negative and positive sides of a subject, he says in this lecture that the "conservative always has the worst of the argument, is always apologizing, pleading a necessity, pleading that to change would be to deteriorate, . . . whilst innovation is always in the right, triumphant, attacking, and sure of final success."[85] The conservative accuses the reformer of legislating for man not as he is but as he ought to be. The idealist replies: "The conservative assumes sickness as a necessity, and his social frame is a hospital . . ."[86] With sparkling wit and telling irony Emerson plays almost every imaginable variation on the controversy. As one reads the lecture today, it seems to parody the slogans and "positions" of recent political campaigns. Though Emerson's sympathies are obviously anti-Establishment, he admits the need for both factions: "Each exposes the abuses of the other, but in a true society, in a true man, both must combine."[87]

"The Transcendentalist" is important not only for what it says about Emerson's philosophy but also for showing just how he accepted the term which had been applied to his thought without his choosing it. On the few previous occasions when he mentioned the word, he had not taken it seriously, but in 1841–42 he was stuck with it. He begins his lecture by saying it is a misnomer; there is no "Transcendentalist *party*" and no "pure Transcendentalist."[88] Moreover, the *"new views"* are not new, "but the very oldest of thoughts cast into the mould of these new times"—just how old we have already seen; and "What is popularly called Transcendentalism among us, is Idealism; Idealism as it appears in 1842."[89] The two sects of thinkers are the Materialists and the Idealists: those who believe all reality to be composed of physical matter, existing independently of an observing mind; and those who believe that reality is mental or spiritual, existing either in individual minds or in a Supreme Mind. While studying epistemology at Harvard, Emerson had been most impressed by the Idealistic philosophy of Bishop Berkeley. Since then his own Idealistic tendencies had been strengthened by reading Plato, the Neoplatonists, and Coleridge.

Materialism, Emerson says, is founded on experience (Empiricism); Idealism, on consciousness. "The senses give us representations of things, but what are the things themselves, they cannot tell." Locke had limited all knowledge to the report of the senses, but Emerson, in agreement with Hume, says, "it is always our own thought that we perceive,"[90] not the thing itself. Since we are trapped in our own consciousness, Hume argued, no real knowledge of the external world is possible.

Emerson was drawn to Idealism for a number of reasons: he had grown up with the Christian doctrine that the sensual appetites are either sinful or a temptation to sin. Even the Christian confidence in the efficacy of prayer was based on the conviction that the human mind could communicate with God and receive answers—divine wisdom. Then the Neoplatonists had taught him that all *being* emanates from *spirit*. Thus he is now a confirmed "idealist [who] takes his departure from his consciousness, and reckons the world an appearance." He conceives the "facts you call the world as flowing perpetually outward from an invisible, unsounded centre in himself, centre alike of him and of them," so that to him all things have "a subjective or relative existence, relative to that aforesaid Unknown Center of him."[91] In other words, the world takes the shape of the mind perceiving it. Thus, says Emerson, the Transcendentalist "believes in miracle, in the perpetual openness of the human mind to new influx of light and power; he believes in inspiration, and in ecstasy."[92]

The term *Transcendental* was borrowed from the philosophy of Immanuel Kant, but Emerson's debt to Kant was slight and indirect (through

Coleridge and Carlyle, who had reinterpreted Kant in their own way). An anonymous English translation of Kant's *Critique of Pure Reason* was published in 1838; Emerson bought a copy and examined it enough to mark a few passages.[93] His friend Hedge had also published an article on Coleridge and the Transcendentalism of Kant, Fichte, and Schelling in *The Christian Examiner* in March 1833, but it was so general that Emerson could have learned little about Kant from that article. In his lecture Emerson refers to Kant's "imperative forms, which did not come from experience," but he interpreted these as experienced intuitively; hence, "whatever belongs to the class of intuitive thought is popularly called at the present day *Transcendental*."[94]

But Emerson did not understand Kant. By saying that ideas of the self, the cosmos, and God transcended experience, Kant did not mean that they could be produced by intuition, but by pure reason only. The human mind can never have direct knowledge of them, though to satisfy the need for belief it is necessary to presume their existence and act as if they were real. Kant declared that "there is a great difference between something given to my reason as an *object absolutely,* or merely as an *object in the idea*."[95] Emerson made no such distinction. But he also mentions Jacobi and Fichte, and these post-Kantians did hold theories of knowledge similar to his own. Jacobi thought that *truth* could be known by faith and intuition; Fichte, that the conscious ego is the starting point of knowledge of the world; God the absolute ego knows all things, and the individual human ego can arrive at knowledge of God by idealistic reasoning. However, if Transcendentalism is understood in Emerson's terms, it does not matter whether it is more Fichtean or Plotinian than Kantian. It was his Idealism in 1842.

It should not be overlooked that over half of Emerson's address is concerned not so much with defining Transcendentalism as with describing and defending a group of idealistic young nonconformists whom he calls "these seething brains, these admirable radicals, these unsocial worshippers, these talkers who talk the sun and moon away . . ."[96] The description is mildly satirical, but he believes that "this heresy cannot pass away without leaving its [beneficial] mark." Some of these "radicals" have found society falling so far short of their ideals that they have tried to withdraw—"dropouts" of the 1840s; the number of parallels with similar disaffected youth of the 1960s is astonishing. Emerson finds among these young people "many promising youths, and never a finished man!" Nevertheless, "By their unconcealed dissatisfaction they expose our poverty and the insignificance of man to man. . . . and what if they eat clouds, and drink wind, they have not been without service to the race of man."[97] Did he have specific persons in mind? They may have been an abstraction, individualized to dramatize his points in his new style of lecturing, though some of his friends did at least partly resemble these hypercritical idealists, friends such as Henry Thoreau, Stearns Wheeler (who lived alone in a cabin before Thoreau did), Charles Newcomb, Ellery Channing (the poet), and even Caroline Sturgis.

Emerson does not set forth these young people as models of Transcendentalism, but as "novices," unequal in their proficiency. What he honors is their dedication to a more ideal life: "Their heart is the ark in which the fire is concealed which shall burn in a broader and universal flame."[98] They speak "for thoughts and principle not marketable" in contemporary America, though less perishable, in Emerson's estimation, than the mechanical and material progress so greatly admired by the majority. By attempting to "reorganize themselves in nature," they may set examples more useful to their fellowmen than material achievements.

CHAPTER XVIII

Saturnalia of Faith

Transcendentalism is the Saturnalia of faith. It
is faith run mad.[1]

I

Emerson's second daughter was born under circumstances similar to those
of his own birth. On Monday evening, November 22, 1841, he returned
home from a business trip to Boston to find that Lidian had given birth to
a daughter at five o'clock that afternoon. Though hardly as ecstatic as he
had been at the time of the birth of Waldo Jr., or even of Ellen, Emerson
immediately wrote the good news to Lidian's sister, Lucy, to William and
Susan, and to Margaret Fuller. Next day he sent a note to Elizabeth Hoar
to come "see the little Lidian."[2] But Lidian refused to give the baby her
own name, and after considerable argument the child was named Edith.

Whether Aunt Mary was in Concord at the time of Edith's birth is not
quite certain, though she may have been. About two weeks earlier Waldo
and his mother had driven to Newburyport and brought her back, but she
could not force herself to break her vow of never again entering the
Emerson house, and stayed at the hotel. However, she remained only a
"fortnight," and may not have waited until the baby's arrival. Elizabeth
Hoar looked after her in Concord until she took flight again. Emerson
himself was busy preparing the first lecture in the new series, "The
Times," which would start December 2, in Boston.[3]

After delivering his eighth and last lecture in the series on January 20,
1842, Emerson returned home Saturday evening to find Henry Thoreau ill
with alarming symptons of lockjaw, the disease which had killed his

brother John a week earlier. "You may judge we were all alarmed," Waldo wrote William, "& I not the least who have the highest hopes of this youth."[4] Next morning Henry seemed to be recovering, his symptoms of lockjaw having been psychological, or "sympathetic."

But the following Monday, Waldo Jr. was stricken with scarlet fever and died at eight-fifteen Thursday evening, January 27. Ellen was mildly affected by the disease, but the baby escaped. Next day Waldo Sr. wrote his Aunt Mary, now back in Maine, that his "darling & and world's wonderful child, for never in my own or another family have I seen any thing comparable, has fled out of my house like a dream." Of course to his aunt he must try to find some consolation, but he could only say lamely that his son had not lived to be degraded by the world. Actually, he could find no consolation. To Margaret Fuller he wrote that he doubted he could ever love anything again; and to Caroline Sturgis, "On Sunday I carried him to see the new church & organ. & on Sunday we shall lay his sweet body in the ground."[5] Waldo Jr. was buried in Dr. Ezra Ripley's tomb, on the hill to the east, overlooking the town, though later the coffin would be moved to Emerson's own cemetery plot in Sleepy Hollow.

Sheer exhaustion finally enabled Emerson to fall asleep on the night of his son's death, but he slept only a short time: "I woke at 3 o'clock & every cock in every barnyard was shrilling, with the most unnecessary noise."[6] Country people have a superstition that cockcrowing in the middle of the night is an evil omen, probably signifying death. Emerson did not allude to this superstition, but he did feel that everything in nature was awry. "The sun went up in the morning sky with all his light, but the landscape was dishonored by this loss. For this boy in whose remembrance I have slept & awakened so oft, decorated for me the morning sun, & the evening sky" no more. His lively curiosity had touched every detail of the household and his father's daily life. He had carried armfuls of wood for his grandmother's stove, and brought hammer, pincers, or file for his father's use. The microscope, the magnet, the globe in Emerson's study reminded him of his son. Outside, the sandpile, the barn, the meadow were places where he had played. Other friends and members of the family had their own associations. Henry Thoreau had made whistles, toy boats, and popguns for the blue-eyed boy. His Grandmother Emerson had taught him to read and spell, which he did surprisingly well, though only five. Margaret Fuller and Caroline Sturgis had loved him, too, and thought him almost preternaturally bright. Everyone had noticed his remarkable gift of observation and expression. His father remembered his asking "If the strings of the harp open when he touches them."[7] Once it thundered while he was blowing his whistle, and he said, "My music makes the thunder dance."

A week after his great loss, Emerson lamented to Caroline: "Alas! I chiefly grieve that I cannot grieve; that this fact takes no more deep hold than other facts, is as dreamlike as they; a lambent flame that will not burn playing on the surface of my river."[8] This was the same delusion he had expressed after his first wife's death and again after Charles's. Actually his sense of loss was so great that his emotions were numbed by it. He felt that somehow Providence or nature had made a huge mistake. "Dear Boy," he continued to Caroline, "too precious & unique a creation to be huddled aside into the waste & prodigality of things."[9]

Perhaps to save space for more recollections, Emerson put aside the Journal (lettered "J") he was using at the time of little Waldo's death, and did not return to it until the end of April. About that time he began composing his "Threnody." When finished, it would be one of the great elegies in the English language. It began:

> The South-wind brings
> Life, sunshine and desire,
> And on every mount and meadow
> Breathes aromatic fire;
> But over the dead he has no power,
> The lost, the lost, he cannot restore;
> And, looking over the hills, I mourn
> The darling who shall not return.[10]

The season itself seemed cruel in reminding him that the birches bud, but never his "budding man." Every object the boy ever touched, or that suggested association with him, was still unbearably painful. Was there no angel, or divine power, "Could stoop to heal that only child . . . ?" All signs and portents seemed to say,

> This child should ills of ages stay,
> By wondrous tongue, and guided pen,
> Bring the flown Muses back to men.

Perhaps "not he but Nature ailed, / The world and not the infant failed." This was not the trite protest echoed from the literature of elegies, that he was *too good to live*. It was black despair, as devastating as Emerson had ever experienced, except perhaps when his angelic Ellen died.

> The eager fate which carried thee
> Took the larger part of me:
> For this losing is true dying;
> This is lordly man's down-lying,
> This his slow but sure reclining,
> Star by star his world resigning

Threnodies, or elegies (there is essentially no difference in English verse), conventionally pass through the outpouring of personal grief to some kind of consolation in religion or philosophy, but in the spring of 1842 Emerson was unable to find one ray of hope—not even, as with the death of his first wife, the hope of meeting his son in a future world of spirit. This threnody was not a literary exercise, such as Milton practiced in "Lycidas" or Shelley in "Adonais." Emerson was writing his poem out of almost unbearable pain, and the emotion was so devastating that he could not finish the poem. He must lay it aside until his anguish began to subside—if that should ever come to pass.

Ellen, two years younger than little Waldo, was pathetic in her bewildering sensations. For days after the funeral she would go from one window to another, unable to believe that her brother was not lurking outside somewhere in the shadows or behind a tree. One day she asked her grandmother whether God couldn't stay alone with the angels a little while and let Waldo come down to play with her.[11] At mealtimes she wondered if God was not then feeding Waldo. These anecdotes, never forgotten by Ellen, reveal the difference between the faith in heaven taught her by her grandmother and mother and her father's impersonal theism.[12] In Boston a few months later Emerson was talking with Sampson Reed, who replied to something he said, "It is not so in your experience, but is so in the other world." "Other world?" exclaimed Emerson, "there is no other world; here or nowhere is the whole fact; all the Universe over, there is but one thing,—this old double Creator-creature, mind-matter, right-wrong."[13]

II

Emerson's lectures in Boston had yielded him a disappointing income: about $320, or only $49 for each performance, compared with $57 in a better year. Probably the deepening financial depression was the cause, but all that Emerson knew was that he was $200 short of his actual needs. There seemed nothing to do but extend his itinerary. The previous year Providence had received him enthusiastically; so he would try that city again, and friends arranged for him to give five lectures at short intervals between February 10 and 17. But first he stopped in Boston to try to raise funds to enable Bronson Alcott to take a trip to England. Alcott's poverty was more acute than ever, and he was so discouraged that Emerson worried about him. The report of his teaching methods had reached England, and even attracted some disciples there, who had named a school for him. A way must be found to enable him to visit his British friends. Several wealthy men Emerson consulted in Boston refused to help. They had various excuses, but the truth was that they had no sympathy for Alcott.

Because of his failure in his friend's behalf, on top of his continued grief, Emerson himself was in low spirits when he reached Providence; and there he found his audiences pitifully small. After his first lecture he wrote Lidian, begging her to send him news of herself and the two babies. He regretted not being able to come home for the weekend. A week later he was almost beside himself because he had still received no word from her. He wrote petulantly, asking if she thought he didn't care about her, the children, and his mother: "Well is this to punish my philosophy?"[14] Possibly he asked the question half in jest, but it revealed an awareness of the widening chasm between them.

Because his lectures in Providence were a financial failure, Waldo wrote Lidian: "I see no help but that I should go to New York, yet I have not yet mustered energy enough to resolve to do so & write to William." He must come home first, "if only to know if all those dumb friends are safe alive." However, his trip had not been entirely useless, for a friend of Alcott's, Thomas David, had made a very liberal contribution to "the Alcott-Voyage-fund."

Soon after returning to Concord, Emerson wrote William that he wanted to give his lectures on "The Times" in New York. William immediately made arrangements for him to lecture at the Library Society, and friendly editors began announcing the coming event. When he arrived in

New York on Saturday morning, February 26, Emerson found that his first lecture was not scheduled until March 3; so he accompanied his brother to Staten Island for the weekend. Monday morning he returned to the city by the Staten Island Ferry to dine with Horace Greeley, editor of *The Tribune,* and Albert Brisbane, his assistant and a proselyting expositor of the philosophy of Charles Fourier, the French utopian socialist, with whom Brisbane had studied. They dined at a vegetarian "Graham Boarding House," where Greeley quizzed Emerson about Transcendentalism and Brisbane tried to convert him to Fourierism.

In a letter to Margaret Fuller, Emerson described Greeley as "a young man [actually thirty-one] with white soft hair from New Hampshire, mother of men, of sanguine temper & liberal mind, no scholar but such a one as journals & newspapers make."[15] He had founded *The Tribune* only the previous year, and was making it pay by embracing new causes with crusading zeal. Brisbane, two years older than Greeley and more polished in manners, had recently returned from Europe, and Greeley had promptly employed him to publicize the gospel of Fourierism. He liked Brisbane's dynamic personality. As Emerson shrewdly observed to Margaret, Greeley listened to new ideas "with the indispensable New York condition that they can be made available [to newspaper readers]; likes the thought but must keep the power."

Neither Greeley nor Brisbane was Emerson's kind of man, and he felt embarrassed by their assumption that they belonged to his school of thought. Greeley "declares himself a Transcendentalist, is a unitarian, a defender of miracles, &c[.] I saw my fate in a moment & that I should never content him." Brisbane wanted to know how the Transcendentalists "establish the immortality of the soul." It was useless for Emerson to protest that he was not a Transcendentalist: "For me was nothing but disclaimers & still disclaimers." He might have told them to wait for his lecture on Transcendentalism, though that would hardly have stopped their questions. In his letter to Margaret he called them "these kindly but too determinate persons."

As Brisbane expanded his vision of a perfect society based on Fourier's plan, it seemed to Emerson sublimely mechanical, a Ptolemaic system of cycles and epicycles—or phalanxes and phalansteries—supposed to turn every landscape into a blooming Garden of Eden. The arithmetic was exact and complete. Each phalanx should contain 1,680 men and women, including at least one expert in every trade and each branch of science. To prevent "accidents of omissions," make the number 2,000 inhabitants, on 6,000 acres of land. Everything would be organized and "scientific," from horticulture to the nurture of infants.[16]

Yet, paradoxically, Fourier taught that all the ills of society had been caused by the suppression of the emotions. Let everyone give free expression to his affections, including sexual ("free love"), choose work congenial to him, and a happy and productive society would be the result. Children would be cared for in a communal nursery. Each phalanx would be completely socialistic, and no one need save for the future; all one's needs would be taken care of, from the cradle to the grave. Wryly Emerson commented in his Journal: "Mr. Brisbane does not doubt that in the Reign of Attractive Industry all men will speak in blank verse."

To Emerson it seemed that Fourier regarded men as *things,* to be manipulated, molded, polished, or, to change the figure, as vegetables to be developed by sufficient manure, moisture, and sunlight. All basic decisions had been made by the prophet Fourier; members of the phalanx had only to follow a plan already formulated and "to be carried by force of preaching & [obedient] votes into rigid execution." Fourier could not conceive that different minds had their own models of perfection. "Mr. Brisbane seems as one who should laboriously arrange a heap of shavings of steel *by hand* in the direction of their magnetic poles instead of thrusting a needle into the heap, and instantaneously they are magnets."[17]

On March 2, Emerson moved into the Globe Hotel on Broadway, and next day read the first of his six lectures at the Library Society. Greeley printed full reports of all the lectures, and the brash twenty-three-year-old editor of *The Aurora,* Walter Whitman, reported them in his own personal way. This is how he reported the lecture on "The Poet":

The Transcendentalist had a very full house on Saturday evening. There were a few beautiful maids—but more ugly women, mostly blue stockings; several interesting young men with Byron collars, doctors, and parsons; Grahamites and abolitionists; sage editors, a few of whom were taking notes; and all the other species of literati. Greeley was in ecstasies whenever any thing particularly good was said, which seemed to be once in about five minutes—he would flounce about like a fish out of water, or a tickled girl—look around, to see those behind him and at his side; all of which plainly told to those both far and near, that he knew a thing or two more about these matters than other men.

The lecture was on the "Poetry of the Times." He said that the first man who called another an ass was a poet. Because the business of the poet is expression—the giving utterance to the emotions and sentiments of the soul; and metaphors. But it would do the lecturer great injustice to attempt anything like a sketch of his ideas. Suffice it to say, the lecture was one of the richest and most beautiful compositions, both for its matter and style, we have ever heard anywhere, at any time.[18]

Emerson also declared in this lecture that "All things are symbols. We say of man that he is grass . . ." Thirteen years later Whitman (now plain Walt) would call his revolutionary first volume of poems *Leaves of Grass*. Possibly Emerson's "symbol" had germinated in his subconsciousness. That he had been influenced by Emerson all critics agree. In one of his reviews of these lectures he tried to compare Emerson's "Transcendentalism" with Kant's philosophy. After hearing the last lecture he declared (March 15), "We should not be surprised if he made a good many converts in Gotham." The editor may not have suspected at the time that he would be one of the converts.

Of all the people Emerson met in New York, he declared Henry James, father of the future novelist (not yet born) of the same name, to be "the best apple on the tree thus far."[19] James had inherited a comfortable fortune from his Albany father and was using it to devote his life to studying and writing about theology, especially Swedenborg's. The loss of a leg in his youth had incapacitated him for an active life, but his wealth gave him the independence to follow his own whims. He had also been attracted recently to Fourier, and this interest had brought him into friendly relations with Greeley and Brisbane, one of whom probably introduced Emerson to him.

Mr. James had moved into his own house on Washington Place, on the east side of Washington Square, after the birth of his first son, William. There Emerson visited him between lectures. Mr. James proudly took him upstairs to show him his two-month-old son, unaware at the time that not quite two months had elapsed since his guest had lost his own son. Concealing his private emotions, Emerson gave his blessing to the future "Pragmatist." The family tradition that Emerson blessed William may indeed, in future years, have influenced his philosophical thinking.[20]

The New York response to Emerson's lectures was encouraging to him. His audience, he wrote Lidian on March 11, increased with each lecture. He was constantly being visited at his hotel or invited out to dinner. The popular novelist Catharine Maria Sedgwick invited him to tea, and among her guests was William Cullen Bryant, no longer an active poet but editor of the influential *New York Post*. Emerson also visited Mrs. Rebecca Black,[21] who had been highly recommended to him for her remarkable religious experiences, but he found her only "a very good woman with much light in her *heart,* but no equal light in her mind." He soon tired of anyone who could not arouse him with a thought.[22] James, Greeley, and Brisbane had thoughts aplenty, but he soon wearied of them, too—or maybe it was only New York and his desire to return home to his family, which he did in mid-March. His lectures had netted him the two hundred dollars he needed for his bills, and he hoped now to relax for a few weeks.

III

Emerson had scarcely arrived home before he received a letter from Margaret Fuller that shattered his hopes of rest. On March 17 she wrote that she did not feel able to continue editing *The Dial,* both for health and for economic reasons. She had suffered frequent headaches and spells of nervous prostration before taking charge of *The Dial,* and her editorial problems had aggravated them. There was no prospect of her being paid the two hundred dollars a year she had been promised; consequently, she needed to use her time and energy in earning money for her support.

Emerson readily agreed to a "rotation of martyrdom" and decided to become the martyr himself rather than ask Parker or Hedge to edit *The Dial.* He believed that if the magazine could be given more public appeal, it might at least pay for the printing. His first task was to secure more contributors. Margaret had often had to draw copiously from her own writings to fill the pages.

For the July issue Emerson accepted seven poems from Ellery Channing, Jones Very, and Caroline Sturgis, though only Very's had real literary merit. Thoreau contributed a review of a survey of zoological and botanical life of the state, commissioned by the legislature, which he called "Natural History of Massachusetts." The survey was dry reading, but in his review Thoreau began to develop the style which would win him posthumous fame. Albert Brisbane's long essay on "Fourier and Socialism" had considerable public interest.[23] Emerson printed his own introductory lecture on "The Times," an appropriate companion piece to Brisbane's essay, and four poems. For some strange reason he also included a mawkish allegorical story by Charles Newcomb called "Dolon." On a visit in May, Newcomb had questioned Lidian about Waldo Jr.'s appearance and had then used him for his tragic hero. One might think that these details would have been too painful for Emerson to bear, but instead they made him tolerant of Newcomb's literary limitations. Except for "Dolon," the July *Dial* was one of the better numbers.

Emerson's summer was not entirely taken up by his editorial struggles with *The Dial*. He had time to entertain friends, and early in July he acquired some interesting new neighbors, Sophia and Nathaniel Hawthorne. Sophia Peabody, Elizabeth's sister, had waited so long to marry Nathaniel that she was willing to live anywhere with him, and when the Ripley heirs decided to rent the Manse after Dr. Ripley's death, she was delighted. Nathaniel had invested a thousand dollars of his savings in Brook Farm, hoping to make a home for his wife there, but he had decided that the plan would not work, and then had great difficulty in recovering his investment. But the rent on the Manse was only fifty dollars a year, and he could have full use of the garden and orchard. He had inspected the place in June and decided to rent it. Since July was too late to plant a garden, Thoreau had spaded the ground in the spring and planted it with a variety of vegetables for the new tenants. He also sold Hawthorne a boat and taught him to row and fish. They quickly became great friends.

Emerson did his best to show Hawthorne his friendly intentions, but they were temperamentally so different that they could never become intimate. In September they took a two-day walking trip to Harvard, the little village where Emerson's father had held his first church, and next day continued across the Nashua River to a Shaker community. After returning to his study, Emerson filled pages in his Journal with recollections,[24] but when Hawthorne tried to describe the walk in his Notebook, he could remember only that Emerson had argued theology with one of the Shakers.[25]

Emerson had frequently urged Margaret Fuller to settle in Concord, and he had even inquired about houses for rent, but she had decided to stay in

Boston. Of course she was a frequent visitor in Concord, and in September she came for two weeks. It was during this visit that she discovered the pain she unintentionally caused Lidian. When she arrived Lidian was confined to her bedroom with a "slow fever," and Margaret did not visit her for three days, thinking that she would prefer not to be disturbed. But finally she decided she must see her hostess—with the results recorded in Margaret's Diary:

When I *did* go in, she burst into tears, at sight of me, but laid the blame on her nerves, having taken opium &c. I felt embarrassed, & did not know whether I ought to stay or go. Presently she said something which made me suppose she thought W. passed the evenings in talking with me, & a painful feeling flashed across me, such as I have not had, all has seemed so perfectly understood between us. I said that I was with Ellery or H[enry] T[horeau] both of the evgs & that W. was writing in the study.[26]

Margaret decided that she had witnessed "a mere sick moment of L's," but at dinner a few days later she found herself involved in another, even more embarrassing situation. Lidian asked her if she would take a walk with her after dinner, and Margaret said that unfortunately she was engaged "to walk with Mr. E. but—(I was going to say, I will walk with you first.) when L. burst into tears." Everyone at the table stared at his plate, and "Waldo looked on the ground, but soft & serene as ever."

Quickly Margaret said, "My dear Lidian, certainly I will go with you." "No! she said. I do not want you to make any sacrifice, but I do feel perfectly desolate and forlorn, and I thought if I got out the fresh air would do me good . . ." Finally Lidian agreed to walk with Margaret, but insisted that they return early so she could keep her promise to Waldo. During the walk Lidian unburdened her thoughts: ". . . she has a lurking hope that Waldo's character will alter, and that he will be capable of an intimate union," but Margaret thought to herself "that it will never be more perfect between them." She had supposed that Lidian was happy to have her in the house "solely for Waldo's sake, and my own, and she is," yet apparently Margaret's presence reminded Lidian of her own failures.

These experiences with Lidian Emerson led Margaret Fuller to record the kinds of thoughts which would soon compel her to write her epoch-making *Woman in the Nineteenth Century:*

I suppose the whole amount of the feeling is that women cant bear to be left out of the question. And they dont see the whole truth about one like me ... But when Waldo's wife, and the mother of that child that is gone thinks me the most privileged of women, & that E[lizabeth] H[oar] was happy because her love was snatched away for a life long separation, & thus she can know none but ideal love: it does seem a little too insulting at first blush.—And yet they are not altogether wrong.[27]

While at the Emersons', Margaret had another disturbing experience. In spite of Margaret's objections, her sister had married Ellery Channing in Cincinnati the previous September. They now wanted to live in Concord, and Ellery had come with Margaret to look for a house, leaving Ellen to follow from Boston in a few days. Before Ellen arrived, Ellery showed Margaret a letter from Caroline Sturgis urging him to visit her at Naushon. He told Margaret that "when I am once united to E[llen] again, I shall never be separated from her," but he would like to see Caroline, with whom he had once been in love, just one more time. Margaret urged him to go, but when Ellen arrived before his return, everyone was upset: Ellen not to find Ellery there, Margaret unwilling to admit where he was, and the Emersons to see Margaret so agitated. That night Margaret lay awake, thinking over these tangled affairs, and came to the same conclusion she had before:

If I were Waldo's wife, or Ellery's wife, I should acquiesce in all these relations, since they needed them. I should expect the same feeling from my husband, & I should think it little in him not to have it. I felt I should never repent of advising Ellery to go whatsoever happened. Well, he came back next day, and All's Well that Ends Well. ... Mama [Emerson's mother] & Lidian sympathized with me almost with tears. Waldo looked radiant, & H[enry] T[horeau] as if his tribe had won a victory. Well it was a pretty play, since it turned out no tragedy at last. Ellery told Ellen at once how it was, and she took it just as she ought.[28]

Margaret tried to interest Sophia Hawthorne in renting rooms in the Manse to Ellery and Ellen, but when Sophia asked her husband, he said no, absolutely not. He liked Ellery personally, and especially enjoyed going boating with him and Henry Thoreau, but he wanted no one else in his honeymoon paradise. However, the Channings were able to rent the red cottage on Lexington Turnpike, on the edge of Concord. Emerson was delighted. When Alcott returned, they would have the nucleus of a literary colony. To Charles Newcomb, who had joined Brook Farm, Emerson had written: "Those of us who do not believe in Communities, believe in neighborhoods & that the kingdom of heaven may consist of such."[29]

IV

While lecturing in Providence, only two weeks after his son's death, Emerson wrote Bronson Alcott: "It seems to me . . . you might spend the summer in England and get back to America in the autumn for a sum not exceeding four or five hundred dollars. It will give me great pleasure to be responsible to you for that amount, and to more, if I shall be able, and more is necessary."[30] He knew that Alcott was extremely depressed over his failures, for even his attempt to support his family in Concord by physical labor had not succeeded, and only the generosity of his wife's relatives and discreet gifts by Emerson kept them from starvation.

At the time of Alcott's greatest difficulties in Boston, he had received a letter from a man in England named James Pierrepont Greaves, who wrote that a school at Ham Common, in Surrey, ten miles from London, had been named for him. Ever since then, that message had seemed like a mirage of water to a man perishing from thirst. Harriet Martineau had given Greaves copies of Alcott's *Record of a School* and *Conversations on the Gospels* soon after her return from America, and Greaves had been so impressed by them that he named his own experimental school Alcott House. For several years Alcott's ideas and methods had been guiding that school. Greaves had hoped to visit his prophet in America, but ill health prevented; so he invited Alcott to visit him. Unfortunately he died on March 11, 1842, four weeks after Emerson had offered to finance Alcott's trip.

Greaves had been a prosperous merchant in London until the Napoleonic Wars ruined his business. He then turned to educational reform and lived with Pestalozzi in Switzerland for four years. After quarreling with Pestalozzi, he taught English in the Universities of Basel and Tübingen for several years, then returned to England and founded the Infant School Society. He was a vegetarian, a firm believer in the therapeutic value of cold water (taken internally and externally), and preached a doctrine of "Pure Birth." A pure birth was one in which the parents had cohabited spiritually, without carnal desire: "Let Birth be surrendered to the Spirit and the result shall be blessed."[31] Greaves himself was celibate, and he had been extremely upset when two of his teachers, Charles Lane and Henry Wright, married. Both marriages ended disastrously, though Lane still supported a son. Lane became Greaves's most rigidly devout disciple; Wright, principal of Alcott House, was loyal but not fanatical.

Alcott sailed from Boston on May 8 and reached London on June 6. A cabman drove him from London Bridge to a coffeehouse near St. Paul's. After refreshments, he inspected the famous church and thought it "Overwrought with ornament" and a symbol of the hardening of the Apostles' sublime inspirations into dogma and ritual. Nothing in London impressed him favorably. When he entered Westminster Abbey, prayers were being chanted, but to him it was all pantomime and show, with "no worship in it." Everywhere he beheld elegance and magnificence: "All is solid, substantial, for comfort and use," he wrote in his Journal, "but all is for the Body."[32] Emerson had given him an introduction to Carlyle, but without waiting to present it, Alcott fled to Ham Common. There he was received as a founding father of Alcott House; was flattered, consulted, and shown evidence of his theories in practice. He had never been so happy.

Knowing that Emerson was waiting to hear of his meeting Carlyle, Alcott returned to London on June 25 and visited Carlyle in Chelsea for an hour. Emerson had written privately to Carlyle: "You may love him, or hate him, or apathetically pass by him, as your genius shall dictate; only I entreat this, that you do not let him go quite out of your reach until you are sure you have seen him and know for certain the nature of the man."[33] If Carlyle did not immediately perceive "the nature of the man," Alcott sized up his host without hesitation. " 'Twas a dark hour with him," he wrote in his Journal. "His wit was sombre as it was pitiless; his merriment had madness in it; his humor tragical even to tears. . . . His conversation was cynical, trivial, and gave no pleasure."[34] Nevertheless, each man tried to be polite to the other in honor of Emerson.

Carlyle invited Alcott to return as his houseguest, and on July 5 Alcott recorded: "I passed the night at Carlyle's, but we sped no better than at first." Alcott's vegetarianism made him decline the meat dishes set before him. For compensation and as a special treat, Carlyle sent out for some

choice strawberries for his guest's breakfast, but when Alcott dumped
them into his mashed potatoes, so that the juices "fraternized," the sight
so nauseated the dyspeptic Carlyle that he had to leave the table.[35] After a
third visit Alcott wrote his wife on August 2, "*we quarrelled outright,* and I
shall not see him again."[36]

Of course in writing to Emerson, Carlyle tried to find something favorable to say of his friend's protégé, but he could not conceal what he really
thought of Bronson Alcott:

> He is a genial, innocent, simple-hearted man . . . The good Alcott: with
> his long, lean face and figure, with his gray worn temples and mild radiant
> eyes; all bent on saving the world by a return to acorns and the golden age;
> he comes before one like a kind of venerable Don Quixote, whom nobody
> can even laugh at without loving![37]

Carlyle had just published *Past and Present,* in which he displayed his
strong preference for medieval feudalism over modern society. Then a few
strong men ruled and the peasants worked. Carlyle's gospel of salvation
was *work.* He admitted that contemporary social and economic conditions
were bad, but he had no faith in reform—or at least in reformers. Alcott,
of course, had no use for the past—or much knowledge of it—and believed that radical reforms could solve every social problem. It is not surprising that the two men antagonized each other.

What especially angered Carlyle was the particular reformers who gathered at Alcott House to debate socialism, communism, Fourierism, spiritualism, vegetarianism, and almost every other "ism" ever heard of. Some of
those who attended were John Abraham Heraud, poet, editor, dramatist,
and general failure; James E. Smith, mystic and editor of Robert Owen's
Crisis; Richard Henry Horne, epic poet and friend of Mrs. Browning's; Dr.
Henry Mansel, future dean of St. Paul's; Newton Crosland, author of
Transcendental Vagaries; and John Goodwyn Barmby, editor of a penny
magazine called the *Promethean or Communitarian Apostle.* Emerson called
Barmby "A radical poet, with too little fear of grammar . . . and with as
little fear of the Church or of the State."[38] Everyone believed that the
working men and women were ready for revolt, and it was thought that
the explosion might happen any day. Their expectations had alarmed the
Establishment.

In the company of the visionaries at Alcott House, Bronson Alcott and his utopian dreams soared higher and higher. In fact, his common sense so forsook him that for the next year and a half he would live in a state of euphoria. Lane had already been thinking of emigrating to America, and by July both he and Wright were planning to return with Alcott. When Emerson heard of the plan, he wrote Alcott a letter to read to these men, warning them that they should not trust his friend's practical judgment.[39] Alcott showed them the letter, but their judgment was no better than his and they refused to take Emerson's message seriously. They made plans to sail in September, Lane taking his nine-year-old son with him. On August 16 Alcott wrote his wife: ". . . I have just passed the winter of my discontent . . . But now cometh the spring and summer of Hope . . ."[40]

Carlyle's impatience with Alcott finally gave way to alarum. On March 11, 1843, he wrote Emerson:

> By the bye, it were as well if you kept rather a strict outlook on Alcott and his English *Tail*,—I mean so far as we here have any business with it. Bottomless imbeciles ought not to be seen in company with Ralph Waldo Emerson, who has already *men* listening to him on this side of the water. The "Tail" has an individual or two of that genus,—and the rest is mainly yet undecided. For example, I knew old [Greaves] myself; and can testify, if you will believe me, that few greater blockheads . . . broke the world's bread in his day. Have a care of such! I say always to myself,—and to you, which you forgive me.[41]

Before receiving this letter from Carlyle, Emerson had experienced a drama of hopeful expectations and rising doubts in his sympathy for Bronson Alcott, who had returned on October 21, 1842, with his English friends. He brought some fifty volumes in several languages (which he could not read), bought in London with funds given him in England, and Lane brought his private thousand-volume library consisting mostly of books on mysticism and philosophy.[42]

Wright had little money, but Lane, recent editor of the successful journal *London Mercantile Price-Current*, had sufficient means to buy and equip a small farm for their experiment. During the winter of 1843, Mrs. Alcott would help them look for a farm, if they could find the right one for sale Meanwhile, Lane had enforced a monastic asceticism on the family: a cold bath in the morning, even if the ice had to be broken in the basin, and a diet mainly of unleavened bread, water, and fruit—no molasses, milk, or butter. Lane tutored the four Alcott girls while their father sawed and chopped wood, drew water from the well, and baked bread. Wright wearied of Lane's tyranny and left, eventually returning to England, and Mrs. Alcott found the emotional strain so great that she had to spend the Christmas holidays with friends in Boston. But she returned after New Year's to help with the continuing search for a farm.

V

Soon after the arrival of Alcott and the English reformers in Concord, Emerson began the busiest lecture schedule he had yet undertaken. His financial situation had not improved and his expenses had increased. Even *The Dial* was an added economic burden because the subscriptions did not cover the printing bills, which he paid out of his own pocket. He was not yet ready to let this magazine die, and he began trying to make it more relevant to the times. From England, Alcott had bombarded him with pamphlets, reports, plans written by his new friends, and summaries of conferences held that summer in Alcott House. Emerson printed extracts from some of these in the October *Dial,* introduced by his essay on "English Reformers." Though sympathetic with their intentions, he had not lost his critical judgment and said frankly: "These papers have many sins to answer for. There is an abundance of superficialness, of pedantry, of inflation, and want of thought. It seems as if these sanguine schemers rushed to the press with every notion that danced before their brain . . ."[43]

Nevertheless, Emerson wanted them to have a fair hearing, perhaps mainly because they were Alcott's friends. Finding that Mr. Lane had a ready pen, he was invited to contribute an essay on James Pierrepont Greaves (Carlyle's "blockhead"). The article was too long for the October *Dial* and had to be continued in the January number. Lane also wrote an essay on Cromwell, one of the heroes of his school of reform.

In "Hollis Street Council" Theodore Parker examined a controversy nearer home. A Boston minister named John Pierpont had aroused such furious opposition from the officials of his church that a Unitarian "council" had been assembled to examine the charges against him. Most of these, Parker found, disguised the real cause of this quarrel: "The 'peculiar circumstances' of his parish was Rum-selling, Rum-making, Rum-drinking. The head and front of his offending, we honestly believe, is this, the crime of preaching against the actual sins of his own parish."[44] Of course Parker thought the minister had the right to condemn whatever he thought sinful, but admitted that his effectiveness depended upon the confidence of his congregation. Parker recommended, therefore, that all members of the Reverend Pierpont's church take a vote whether to retain him. This was not a question to be settled by an "ecclesiastical council."

The October *Dial* had more variety than any previous number. Margaret Fuller had contributed a long, learned article on "Romaic and Rhine Ballads," Thoreau eight poems, Cranch and Channing one each, and Emerson himself the long poem called "Saadi," after a Persian poet who greatly interested him. He also included his lecture on "The Conservative," which helped to balance "English Reformers."

To give Alcott and his English friends a chance to discuss their plans with men who might be able to make suggestions, Emerson invited George Ripley, Orestes Brownson, Theodore Parker, and a few others to meet them at his house on November 10. Brownson and Parker declined, but Emerson wrote Hedge that "Hawthorne, [Robert?] Bartlett, George Ripley & all Brook Farm came in strength." He himself was impressed by Lane's conversational ability, but found Alcott and Wright boring with their continual talk of "A New Solar System & the prospective Education in the Nebulae. All day all night they hold perpetual Parliament."[45]

Emerson complained also in his Journal that he had scarcely exchanged a rational word with Alcott since his return. Alcott seemed to think that some philanthropist ought to give him a farm for his New Eden. This attitude annoyed the self-reliant Emerson. "This fatal fault in the logic of our friends still appears: Their whole doctrine is spiritual, but they always end with saying, Give us much land & money. If I should give them anything, it would be facility & not beneficence." Possibly Emerson even regretted having enabled Alcott to get himself entangled with these British idealists. Soon after his return from London, Emerson had confided to his Journal that "A. is a singular person, a natural Levite . . . But for a founder of a family or institution, I would as soon exert myself to collect money for a madman." He had such persons in mind when he declared, "Transcendentalism is the Saturnalia of faith. It is faith run mad."[46]

Emerson soon learned that behind Mr. Lane's genteel appearance resided the soul of a fanatic. Lane was obsessed with "purity," not only sexual but dietary as well. Vegetables that grew above the ground were "purer" than root vegetables. Fermentation was wicked. Emerson gleefully recorded his wife's reaction to this doctrine:

> Queenie makes herself merry with the Reformers who make unleavened bread and are foes to the death to fermentation. Queenie says God made yeast as well as wheat, & loves fermentation just as dearly as he loves vegetation, that the fermentation develops the saccharine element in the grain, & makes it more palatable & more digestible. But that they wish the "pure wheat" & will die but it shall not ferment. Stop dear nature these incessant advances[,] let me scotch these ever rolling wheels.[47]

Lane began declining invitations to dine at the Emersons' because he disapproved of their depraved eating habits. Though Emerson was by no means a gourmet, he did believe in supplying his family with plenty of wholesome food, and occasionally served wine. Lane thought Emerson's influence on Alcott was not good for him and wanted to buy a farm far enough away to remove him from that influence. This caused more dissension in the Alcott family because Mrs. Alcott liked Concord and she knew Emerson was their greatest benefactor, with the possible exception of her brother, the Reverend Samuel May. The Hallowell farm near Concord could be bought, and Mrs. Alcott liked it. But on May 20, 1843, Lane and Alcott walked the fourteen miles to Harvard to inspect the Wyman farm. It was on a hillside overlooking the Nashua valley, with ninety acres of land, fourteen in woods. Lane bought it for eighteen hundred dollars— he had no need for an outside philanthropist. Returning to Concord, he paid Alcott's debts, amounting to three hundred dollars, and moved the Alcott family to this farm on June 14. They named the place Fruitlands— someone said because it had no fruit on it.[48]

Emerson's son Edward many years later summarized the self-created difficulties of these Fruitlanders:

> The Fruitlands Community was handicapped in getting support from its lean acres by its theories. Cattle must not be enslaved; animal manure

was abhorrent; all cultivation must be done by manpower when time could be spared from contemplation and high discussion; insects must not be murdered. Meat, fish, poultry, milk, cheese, butter, honey, eggs, as food, and wool and feathers as clothing or bedding, were unlawful, because obtained by wrongs done to the animal creation; leavened bread and fermented drinks were poisonous; cane-sugar, molasses, rice, and spice, and cotton for clothing, were products of slave-labor. Such grain and fruits as could be raised without manure, and wild nuts and berries and maple sugar, must furnish the food, and linen the raiment, for these good but over-refining people. Necessity, which knows no law, prevented their carrying these rules quite to extremes.[49]

Compromises with their theories, they hoped, would be temporary. A man was employed to plow the land before planting, teaming an ox and a cow. Also potatoes, carrots, and turnips were planted (Edward Emerson failed to mention that root vegetables were regarded as impure), along with grains and leafy vegetables. But no manure was used, and neighboring farmers could have told them that June was late for "putting in a crop."

When Emerson visited these dreamers in July, they appeared to be serene and happy: "The sun & the evening sky do not look calmer than Alcott & his family at Fruitlands." But "I will not prejudge them successful. They look well in July. We will see them in December."[50] That was a shrewd reservation. Fruitlands did barely last through December, but on January 8, 1844, Lane abandoned it, taking his son with him to the Shaker community across the river.

The failure was the result both of agricultural and of psychological irrationality. The farm might have produced enough food for the winter if it had been cultivated properly, but both Lane and Alcott spent so much time visiting and talking at other experimental communities that they neglected to weed and hoe their own crops. They were away, in fact, when an early frost caused irreparable damage. Mrs. Alcott, with the aid of William Lane, age ten, and her three older daughters, Anna, Louisa, and Elizabeth, thirteen, twelve, and seven respectively, rescued everything she could, but precious food was lost.

Psychological warfare was even more destructive. Lane, the obsessed celibate, tried to separate Alcott from his wife, and created untold bitterness.

For all his temporary madness, Alcott loved above all else his wife and children. But when Lane left, he felt he had failed them, too. He took to his bed and resolved to starve himself to death, but his wife finally persuaded him to live for the love of her and his daughters. When Mrs. Alcott's brother learned of their plight, he found temporary shelter for them in Still River, a small village only a mile away.

This experience gave Bronson Alcott an emotional shock that brought him back to a sense of reality. The following autumn, Emerson and Mrs. Alcott's brother bought in her name the Cogswell place on the Lexington Road, later made famous by Hawthorne as The Wayside. There Alcott proved that he could be an expert gardener and landscaper, though he would never be able to support himself. Emerson's final connection with Fruitlands was to act as collector for Lane from the purchaser of the farm, Joseph Palmer. As late as 1847 he was still forwarding money to Lane in London.[51]

At the time of the Fruitlands debacle Emerson was extremely busy lecturing from Maine to Maryland. Between January 10, 1843, and the following winter he gave more than thirty lectures in Baltimore, Philadelphia, New York, Brooklyn, Newark, Hartford, and Providence, as well as in Concord and nearby towns. He extended his itinerary because he needed the money, but it was not entirely coincidental that he enlarged his circuit at the same time that he made a radical shift in his subjects. Sometimes he read old lectures, but his new series was on New England.

Having finally abandoned his Neoplatonic topics, Emerson was now concentrating on the history, manners, culture, industrial development, and contributions of New England to the rest of the nation. In 1835, in his oration on the second centennial of Concord,[52] he said that the town had been drained by the continual emigration of its youth, and he now reminded the whole country that New England had supplied schoolteachers to the nation. By this time it was also furnishing textiles, shoes, and other products to the whole country, but especially to the South, which had not begun industrial development.

Emerson managed to edit the January 1843 number of *The Dial* before his trips usurped his time. He printed Charles Lane's conclusion of his article on Greaves, Elizabeth Hoar's translation from the German of an article on "Discoveries in the Nubian Pyramids," Thoreau's translation of

Aeschylus' *Prometheus Bound,* Theodore Parker's review of "The Life and Character of Dr. [Charles] Follen" (a German émigré, teacher at Harvard, and pastor of the Lexington church after Emerson resigned his pastorate there). Emerson himself wrote a memorial article on Dr. William Ellery Channing, who had recently died. He also printed poems by W. E. Channing, Caroline Sturgis, and himself, and reviewed seven books. From his lectures on "The Times" he printed "The Transcendentalist." He continued reprinting "Ethical Scriptures" by including a selection from the *Laws of Menu* made by Thoreau.

Traveling made it impossible for Emerson to edit the April *Dial* and Thoreau took over the duties for him, though Emerson had probably already accepted Lane's long review of Alcott's "Works," and Stearns Wheeler had sent him a "Letter from Heidelberg," where Wheeler was then studying. The "Ethical Scriptures" department was continued by Thoreau's selections from "Sayings of Confucius."

In the summer Emerson found time to edit the July *Dial* himself, and he included several notable items. First of all, "The Great Lawsuit" by Margaret Fuller, which was the preliminary version of her *Woman in the Nineteenth Century* (1845), the first major contribution to the feminist movement in America. Many of her arguments are still being repeated today. Her article brought notoriety to *The Dial,* for most readers were scandalized by her "advanced" ideas on the rights of women.

As might be expected, Lane's "Social Tendencies" in the same number was on the moral and economic reforms being undertaken in "association" communities in France, England, and the United States. The ideal, of course, was being attempted at Fruitlands, described in a separate letter published under "Intelligence": "Here we prosecute our effort to initiate a Family in harmony with the primitive instincts of man."[53] When Lane visited Brook Farm he objected to the concentration on agriculture to the neglect of the spiritual life ("Brook Farm," *Dial,* January 1844). The Shaker community near Fruitlands was more to his taste, not because of its economic efficiency but because of its emphasis on asceticism and self-discipline. Mother Ann Lee, the founder of the Shaker community,[54] taught doctrines on sex which Lane approved. While imprisoned in Manchester, England, she had received a "revelation" that complete abstention from sexual intercourse was the only means of salvation. When she established the Shaker settlement in Massachusetts in 1781, both men and women were admitted to it, but sexual indulgence was the one absolute taboo. She taught also that God was bisexual, and her followers came to believe that, though Jesus was His son, she was His female counterpart. Thus Mother Ann Lee anticipated by more than a hundred years the twentieth-century feminist contention "God is a woman."

The October *Dial* (1843), in addition to Lane's contributions and Emerson's "Ode to Beauty," contained a long descriptive review by Theodore Parker of Charles C. Hennell's *An Inquiry Concerning the Origin of Christianity* (London, 1841), which must have made some readers exclaim that they had known all along that *The Dial* was atheistic. Actually, Hennell was more "liberal" than Parker himself, though he was becoming more obnoxious to the New England Unitarian Establishment every day. Hennell traced the growth of the messianic idea among the Jews, its romantic form after their escape from captivity, the influence of the Essenes (John the Baptist was an "enthusiastic" Essene), and the myths that grew up about the Crucifixion and Resurrection. Hennell thought that Joseph removed the body from the tomb and hid it to avoid persecution for his connection with Jesus. Paul preached the "Second Coming," borrowing from the older myths about Osiris, Adonis, and Hercules. Then "Christianity formed an alliance with Platonism of the Alexandrian school," with new interpretations of the person of Jesus. "Plato had spoken of the Logos, the divine wisdom or intelligence. The Platonic Jews personified it as a divine emanation." Thus Jesus of Nazareth advanced from carpenter's son, to prophet of Galilee, to king of Israel, to the Logos or "Incarnate Representative of the Deity," to identification with God Himself.

None of this was new to Emerson. In fact, this summary shows how closely his theism had paralleled—if not at times anticipated—the most advanced European theories on Christianity. Both as a minister and as a public lecturer he had preached an equivalent of Hennell's learned conclusion: "Neither Moses nor Samuel, Isaiah, nor Zechariah, nor Jesus, nor Paul, nor John can speak more of God than [people] themselves have learned from the sources which he has placed within the reach of all, nature and man's own mind."[55]

It took no daring on Emerson's part to print Parker's exposition of Hennell's book. Besides having long before worked himself free of traditional beliefs in the history of Christianity, he was now more interested in his immediate world than in the world to come. The newspapers kept everyone aware that this was the year that the Pittsfield prophet, William Miller, had predicted the world would come to an end. With amusement Emerson recorded in his Journal: "I read of an excellent Millerite who gives out that he expects the second advent of the Lord in 1843 but if there is any error in his computation,—he shall look for him until he comes."[56] Now there was faith to match that of the "Transcendentalists"!

CHAPTER XIX

Western Gymnosophist

You Western Gymnosophist! Well, we can afford one man for that too.[1]   —Carlyle

I

However lofty and unrealistic Emerson's philosophical theory of friendship may have been, he never failed to serve his friends in practical ways
whenever he could. In the spring of 1843, while Emerson was lecturing in
New York, Thoreau asked him to keep him in mind if he heard of any
employment for someone of his qualifications. Thoreau hoped he might
find some way of supporting himself while he tried to start a career in
writing. It happened that William Emerson wanted a tutor for his seven-
year-old son, Willie, and he offered Thoreau, a former schoolteacher, room
and board and fifty dollars a year.[2] Emerson thought this employment
would leave Henry spare time to get acquainted with newspapermen in
New York such as Greeley, and publishers such as Putnam and the Harpers. Thoreau agreed to the terms of William Emerson, now a New York
State district judge, and left Concord for Staten Island on May 6 with Mrs.
William Emerson, who was ending a month's visit with Lidian and
Waldo.

Lidian had always like Henry, and he had come to look upon her as an
older sister. They had a bond of sympathy in their delicate sensitivity to
animal life, perhaps intensified by their reading of books on Hindu philosophy in Emerson's library. Ellen in her unpublished biography of her
mother has a story about the chickens which her mother brought from
Plymouth after her marriage. Concord winters were more severe than

those in Plymouth, and Lidian worried about the chickens' having to wade around in the snow and ice, until Henry Thoreau made cowhide boots for them.[3] Ellen claims that some of these chicken boots survived for many years and that she remembered them well. This may have been a family joke, but it indicates the close relations between Lidian and Henry. They would go to considerable lengths to avoid killing even a bug or a caterpillar.

On Staten Island, Henry missed Lidian more than any other friend. He wrote her a long letter on May 22, thanking her for her influence over him during his two years in her house. "You always seemed to look down at me as from some elevation—some of your high humilities—and I was better for having to look up. I felt taxed not to disappoint your expectations . . ."[4] She had confessed to him the "doubts" that troubled her.

One of Thoreau's biographers, Henry Seidel Canby, decided, mainly on the basis of the May 22 letter, that Thoreau was in love with Mrs. Emerson. He thought it significant that she did not reply, and that finally Emerson wrote Henry for both of them. Canby interpreted the joint letter as the Emersons' attempt to cool the young man's ardor. But the circumstances suggest other interpretations. Mrs. Emerson was not well, and did not like writing letters, anyway. Furthermore, Ellen's mother told her an anecdote regarding this letter which shows that she did appreciate it. She remarked to Henry's mother that he had written her "a grateful and affectionate letter" which embarrassed her because "I don't deserve it; he sets me higher than I am." Mrs. Thoreau, never one to be tactful, replied, "Well, Henry was always tolerant." As further evidence of Mrs. Thoreau's irascible disposition Ellen matches this story with another from 1853: From the livery stable Emerson bought a secondhand carriage, called a Rockaway. At an Anti-Slavery Society meeting Mrs. Thoreau asked: " 'Was that *your* Rockaway, Mrs. Emerson?' 'Yes,' mother replied, 'I've set up my carriage.' 'I've often seen Mr. Staples bring the prisoners to court in it,' said Mrs. Thoreau."[5]

On Staten Island, Henry Thoreau was unhappy. He did not like the William Emerson family.[6] The judge and his wife were stiff and formal and seemed to have little sense of humor. Perhaps young Willie reflected his parents' attitude toward Thoreau, for he did not take to his tutor, either, though Henry usually got along well with children. Thoreau was ill for several weeks after his arrival, and was slow in exploring New York.

When he did, he hated the city. Henry James, Emerson's friend, received him graciously, though he wrote Emerson that he found him the most conceited young man he had ever met.[7] Horace Greeley received him kindly also, and offered him some advice; but the Harpers brushed him off. Henry made the rounds of the magazines, *The Democratic Review, The New Mirror,* and *Brother Jonathan,* but they gave him no encouragement.

Emerson had suggested that Thoreau review for *The Dial* a book by a German visionary, J. A. Etzler, called *The Paradise within the Reach of All Men, without Labor, by Powers of Nature and Machinery,* published in London in 1842.[8] Etzler's materialistic dream included everything that both Emerson and Thoreau detested, but Henry thought it would be fun to expose the German's wild pretensions, and if John L. O'Sullivan would publish it in *The Democratic Review,* he would be paid for it, as he would not be by *The Dial.* O'Sullivan first accepted the essay, then objected to Thoreau's unfriendly attitude toward "communities," but reconsidered and printed it in the November *Democratic Review.*

Etzler argued that by the proper use of machines, some of which he claimed to have invented already, mankind could create a veritable paradise within ten years, using the natural powers readily available, including wind, tide, waves, sunshine, and the force of gravity. Mountains could be leveled, floating islands created in the ocean, the interior of the globe explored, and travel made possible from pole to pole. Satirically Thoreau summarized: "We will wash water, and warm fire, and cool ice, and underprop the earth. We will teach birds to fly, and fishes to swim, and ruminants to chew the cud. It is time we had looked into these things."[9]

Thoreau was even more doubtful of the cooperative efforts needed to achieve these marvelous predictions. "It will now be plainly seen," Etzler declared, "that the execution of the proposals is not proper for individuals."[10] This idea Thoreau called "the crying sin of the age, this want of faith in the prevalence of a man." Like Emerson, he believed, "Nothing can be effected but by one man. He who wants help wants everything." Thoreau's faith in his mentor's "self-reliance" was absolute: "We must first succeed alone, that we may enjoy our success together." It was not more physical power that men needed, but the *force* of moral power.

Thoreau's values were not those of Etzler. One need not level a hill for the sake of a beautiful prospect, or create a floating island to make a paradise. These can be found in nature without artificial contrivances. The sun and the stars are but shadows of the "divine light" of God shining into men's souls: "the power of love has been but meanly and sparingly applied, as yet."

Emerson's criticism of Ripley's plans for Brook Farm, and in general his objection to Fourierism, was that they pandered too exclusively to human desires for sensual comfort. However, in 1843 he was not as uncompromisingly opposed to industrialism and material "improvements" as Thoreau was. The construction of the Concord and Fitchburg Railroad had now reached Walden woods, and on August 25 Emerson walked out to make a personal inspection. He recorded in his Journal that it brought a "multitude of picturesque traits into our pastoral scenery."[11] Some forty or fifty men worked with a vigor he marveled at, though he wondered if they were not driven too hard. They received a pittance for wages, and lived in shanties set up in and around the town.

Everyone in Concord was excited about the building of the railroad, some eagerly expecting financial gains, others fearing the inevitable changes in their lives. Emerson himself had mixed emotions about it. To Thoreau he wrote on September 8, "Now the humanity of the town suffers with the poor Irish, who receive but sixty or even fifty cents, for working from dark till dark, with a strain and following up that reminds one of negro-driving." Yet, "what can be done for their relief as long as new applicants for the same labor are coming in every day?"[12] This was the decade of the potato famine in Ireland, and hordes of destitute immigrants were arriving almost daily in New York and Boston.

In November, Thoreau returned to Concord to stay. He lived with his family instead of returning to the Emersons', and helped his father manufacture pencils. He found so many ways to improve the product that in a few years this family enterprise was thriving, and Henry could have gained financial independence if he had not had other ambitions.[13]

II

On February 7, 1844, Emerson gave a new lecture to the Mercantile Library Association in Boston on "The Young American."[14] The lecture responded to the rising tide of enthusiasm for the physical expansion of the nation. "This rage of road building is beneficent for America, where vast distance is so main a consideration in our domestic politics and trade ..."[15] More rapid transportation and communication would "hold the Union staunch," and acquaint the American people with the boundless resources of their own soil.

Only recently had Emerson become land-conscious. When the socialist experimenters wanted him to sell his property and join their communal life, his main reply had been that he had his own private work to do, and he could do it best in his own home. But he had not morally defended the institution of private property. He now does so unabashedly, not only with a new appreciation of his own acres, but with an awareness of the potentialities of *land* itself. "The land is the appointed remedy for whatever is false and fantastic in our culture. The continent we inhabit is to be physic and food for our mind, as well as our body."[16] So far America had no public gardens, like the Boboli in Florence or the Villa Borghese in Rome; no domestic architecture; not even a science of agriculture. "I look on such improvements also as directly tending to endear the land to the inhabitants."

Emerson was not disturbed by the "heterogeneous population crowding on all ships from all corners of the world," flooding "the great gates of North America, Boston, New York, and New Orleans." They would fill up the empty West and help the nation become more catholic and cosmopolitan: "It seems so easy for America to inspire and express the most expansive and humane spirit; new-born, free, healthful, strong, the land of the laborer, of the democrat, of the philanthropist, of the believer, of the saint, she should speak for the human race. It is the country of the Future."[17]

Heretofore Emerson had been critical of trade, and had looked upon "business ethics" as inimical to the public good. He now says, "The history of commerce is the record of . . . [a] beneficent tendency." Trade is "a plant which grows wherever there is peace . . . It is a new agent in the world, and one of great function; it is a very intellectual force."[18] Trade is a bulwark against abuses of government. He even thought trade would abolish slavery, and the sequel would be further social combinations, possibly even "beneficent socialism," which he saw as a "friendly omen" in the communist movements in Europe, in the trade unions in England, and in the Anti–Corn Law League. "In Paris, the blouse, the badge of the operative, has begun to make its appearance in the *salons*."[19] The three "communities" in Massachusetts (apparently he still counted Fruitlands along with

Brook Farm and Hopedale) showed that the commonwealth did not stand against socialistic experiments. Though he did not agree with the philosophy of these communities, he thought they were doing much good in educating their members. He objected to most critics of capitalism, however, because their aim was to make a capitalist of the poor man, not to reform him.

Emerson published this speech in the last issue of *The Dial,* April 1844. In the midst of his busy lecture schedule he wrote Margaret Fuller on February 26 that the prospect of liberation from *The Dial* pleased him immensely.[20] For several months he had known that sooner or later he must stop subsidizing this unprofitable magazine. Aside from the financial burden, he needed to save time to prepare the Second Series of his *Essays* and the first edition of his *Poems;* so Number 4 of Volume 4 would be the end of *The Dial.*

It turned out to be one of the best issues—possibly the best of all. The first article was a short but knowledgeable essay on "Immanuel Kant," by Emerson's new friend (and future editor-biographer) James Elliot Cabot, a student in the Harvard Law School. "Life in the Woods," by Charles Lane, was not autobiography, but an argument that primitive society was in some ways superior to civilized society. Of the poetry, only Emerson's "The Visit" (a protest over time-wasters) and C. T. Brooks's translation of Ferdinand Freiligrath's "The Emigrants" are still readable, though Emerson himself liked Ellery Channing's four lyrics, and presumably Margaret Fuller's cliché-filled "The Twin Lovers." Henry Thoreau was not proud of his "Fragments of Pindar," made at Emerson's insistence. Channing also concluded in this issue his tedious dialogue between a young poet and a painter. Their discussions of nationalism in art had perhaps some contemporary interest.

Emerson's "The Young American" was the solidest prose in the April *Dial.* But Thoreau followed it with a vigorous defense of Nathaniel P. Rogers's *Herald of Freedom,* a weekly publication of the New Hampshire Anti-Slavery Society. Thoreau especially liked Rogers's "indignant and touching satire on the funeral of those public officers who were killed by the explosion on board the Princeton, together with the President's slave . . ." This catastrophe had taken place on February 28, 1844, when the man-of-war *Princeton* sailed down the Potomac to test a new gun expected to fire a two-hundred-pound projectile. The gun exploded, killing

six men, including the Secretary of State, Abel Upshur, and the Secretary
of the Navy, Thomas Gilmer. Thoreau called it "an accident which reminds us how closely slavery is linked with the government of the nation.
The President coming to preside over a nation of *free* men, and the man
who stands *next to him a slave!*" Rogers wrote: "The hearses of [the five
politicians] passed along . . . but the dead slave, who fell in company with
them on the deck of the Princeton, was not there. He was held their equal
by the impartial gun-burst, but not allowed by the *bereaved* nation a share
in the funeral."[21]

Although he had always hated slavery, Emerson was only now beginning to become emotionally involved with the antislavery movement. He
also printed in the April *Dial* a short article by B. P. Hunt, an American
businessman in Haiti, on "Saturday and Sunday Among the Creoles:
A Letter from the West Indies." In visiting the Sunday schools, Mr.
Hunt had compared the black children with the white, and found the
black fully equal in intelligence, ability, and manners to the white
children.

Miss Elizabeth Peabody contributed an essay on "Fourierism." Albert
Brisbane had persuaded the Brook Farmers to reorganize on more strictly
Fourierist principles, and some friends of the community, including
Emerson, were uneasy about the changes—which would within three years
destroy the project. What Miss Peabody feared was a decline of Christianity in the phalanx. "Fourier does homage to Christianity with many
words. But this may be cant." She hoped not.

The American friends of Fourier had held a convention in Boston in
January, at which, according to Emerson's Journal, Alcott had been invited to speak but had declined—he may have been still weak from his
fasting at Fruitlands. Emerson doubted that the delegates at the convention fully appreciated Alcott's contribution to the "community" movement, though he had failed in his own. After the breakup of Fruitlands,
Emerson had recorded: "Very sad indeed it was to see this halfgod driven
to the wall, reproaching men, & hesitating whether he should not reproach the gods."[22] Emerson felt "quite ashamed to have just revised &
printed [in the April *Dial*] the old paper denying the existence of tragedy
[his 1839 lecture on "The Tragic"] when the modern Prometheus was in
the last of his quarrel with the gods."

III

During the spring of 1844 Emerson was frequently occupied with entertaining his friends or doing them favors. George Bradford left Brook Farm and accepted Emerson's invitation to live with him while Bradford set up a private school in Concord. Caroline Sturgis stopped on her way to the Berkshires and asked why he and Lidian did not move to the mountains in the summer. Emerson responded that "to cart all my pots & kettles, kegs & clothespins . . . over the mountains seems not worth while."[23] Besides, he would not be nearer the sun or the stars. Margaret Fuller had returned to Boston after her trip to Michigan, Wisconsin, and Illinois with James and Sarah Clarke the previous summer. She was now fascinated by mesmeric and mindreading demonstrations, but could not get Emerson to attend any of them. He was, however, greatly concerned about the publication of her account of her trip, to be called *Summer on the Lakes,* and negotiated with publishers for her until Little and Brown, in Boston, offered her what seemed a good contract.

Early in June the railroad made several trial runs from Charlestown to Concord, and the official run, carrying passengers and dignitaries from Boston, was made on the morning of June 17. The first train arrived with whistle screeching, bell ringing, and banners waving, to be met at the station by a formal welcoming committee and speeches. That evening Emerson wrote his brother William: "Our railroad opens this day & since sunrise the cars have already traversed the distance between our depot & Charlestown 8 times."[24] Eventually the railroad would go on to Fitchburg—and even, it was hoped, to Montreal—but at present it would operate between Charlestown and Concord, four times a day each way. Until a railroad bridge could be built across the Charles River, a stagecoach would transfer passengers from Brattle Street in Boston to the Charlestown depot near Warren Bridge. A one-way ticket cost fifty cents, "an abatement of one-third on the old stage price," *The Concord Freeman* boasted. The trip was made in about an hour, only a fourth of the time required by stage.[25]

But not everyone in Concord was happy with the coming of the railroad. For weeks the drivers of the stagecoaches and wagons had displayed signs reading "No Monopoly!" and "Free Trade and Teamsters' Rights." Owners of taverns and inns expected to lose business because Concord had been a favorite resting place for teamsters and their horses. Even the merchants feared that housewives would buy their clothes and furnishings in

Boston. The town would indeed become suburban. Yet for those who would lose by the changes there were perhaps as many who would gain. Farmers would have better facilities for marketing their produce, and new industries would spring up. Soon a milk car was added to the train, and many farmers turned to dairying. Growing vegetables and strawberries became more profitable than raising corn and wheat. And some men found new employment. Reuben Rice closed his store and became the station agent; Isaac Day switched from driving a stagecoach to punching tickets.

In the midst of these changes, Emerson's second son was born on July 10. Mrs. Emerson, as with all her pregnancies, had had a difficult time, but soon recovered her health. "Edward we call him, and my wife calls him Edward Waldo," Emerson wrote Carlyle. "And when," he asked, "shall I show you a pretty pasture and wood-lot which I bought last week on the borders of a lake which is the chief ornament of this town, called Walden Pond?"[26]

In a letter to William dated October 4, 1844, Waldo explained his transactions. First he had bought eleven acres for $8.10 an acre, then next day three acres of an adjoining pine grove for $125 to prevent its being cut down; "so am landlord and waterlord of 14 acres, more or less, on the shore of Walden, & can raise my own blackberries."[27] He was also thinking of building a cottage for his sister-in-law Mrs. Lucy Brown near his house; "& the dreaming Alcott is here with Indian dreams that I helped [that is, would help] him to some house & farm in the Spirit Land."

From Staten Island, William objected indignantly to Waldo's giving any more financial assistance to Alcott. William himself had sold his house and bought another. During the interval of moving, before starting a new garden and orchard, he did not need his gardener, whose skill had impressed Thoreau while staying at Judge Emerson's. Thus it came about that James Burke became temporarily Waldo Emerson's gardener, and set out for him roots of roses, honeysuckle, raspberries, grapes, and currants, which William sent him from his abandoned garden.

IV

Until the summer of 1844 Emerson had avoided active participation in the abolition movement, though his sympathies for it were becoming stronger all the time. Two years earlier Thoreau, then in charge of the Concord

Lyceum, had stirred up a noisy controversy by inviting Wendell Phillips, one of the leading abolitionists, to speak. No one in Concord was really in favor of slavery, but outright abolition was an explosive issue and many people wanted to ignore it. Two factions took this attitude: the Democrats, because their party was dominated by Southern slaveholders; and businessmen, who felt that New England textile mills must have Southern cotton, no matter what the cost in human rights. Thus, when the Lyceum invited Phillips to speak again in 1843, the town conservatives were so outraged by his speech that they called a meeting to reply to it.[28] Thoreau informed Phillips of the plan, and he unobtrusively took a back seat until the speakers had finished denouncing him, then rose and replied so effectively that the Lyceum members voted to invite him to give another lecture.

The Anti-Slavery Society women of Concord wanted to observe the tenth anniversary of the emancipation of black slaves in the British West Indies, August 1, 1844, and they invited Emerson to deliver an address. Henry Thoreau's mother was one of the most active Concord women in the movement. Lidian Emerson attended the meetings and was sympathetic with them, but played a passive role. Women of twelve surrounding towns planned to hold an antislavery fair in the county courthouse on August 1, and emotions were rising in both pro- and antislavery factions. Emerson accepted the invitation, perhaps after some prodding by Henry and Lidian, and prepared his address with scholarly care. But where could he deliver it? The conservative Church officials refused permission for him to speak in any of the churches. Hawthorne suggested the spacious grounds of the Old Manse, but a rainstorm on the day of the event washed out that arrangement. Finally Thoreau got permission to use the courthouse auditorium. Then at the proper hour he crossed the street and rang the bell of the First Parish Church to announce the address, after the sexton had refused to do so.

Under these circumstances Emerson delivered his address, "Emancipation in the British West Indies,"[29] to a packed house, and did not disappoint his audience. He had never spoken more clearly or effectively. He did not rant (he never did, of course) or exaggerate, but it is doubtful that either Phillips or William Lloyd Garrison could have stated the moral issues more forcefully. He began with a detailed history of the seventy-year struggle in the British Parliament to get slavery abolished in the West

Indies. First the advocates of abolition publicized the atrocities committed in the islands by the slaveowners, and they included nearly every cruelty imaginable. Then they gathered and exhibited articles of African handicraft to prove that these black people were human and capable of civilization.

Parliament abolished the slave trade in 1807, but emancipation did not come until 1834, and even then it was partial, for the black people were required to work for their former owners as apprentice laborers at specified wages. Complete freedom came only in 1838 after Parliament paid the plantation owners twenty million pounds for the loss of their human property. This tactic worked so well that Emerson thought it could be used to solve America's problem, and would continue to argue for it even after the outbreak of the Civil War. No disorder followed emancipation in the West Indies, and the former slaves were quickly accepted as free citizens. The black man "is now the principal if not the only mechanic in the West Indies; and is, besides, an architect, a physician, a lawyer, a magistrate, an editor, and a valued and increasing political power."[30]

Emerson himself had never had any firsthand experience with black people, and only a few years before this he had believed in their intellectual inferiority, but now he was as thoroughly convinced as Mr. Hull in his "letter" to the April *Dial* that blacks needed only a fair chance to develop minds and character to be equal to the most civilized whites. The great effect of British emancipation in the West Indies, Emerson declared, is: "A man is added to the human family. Not the least affecting part of this history of abolition is the annihilation of the old indecent nonsense about the nature of the negro."[31]

But these Anti-Slavery Society members in Middlesex County had not assembled in Concord merely to praise British reform, and Emerson was prepared to say what they wanted to hear, because in reading the history of the abolition of slavery in the West Indies he had experienced "the most painful comparisons" with New England. At that very time in Charleston, Savannah, and New Orleans, free black men from New England were being taken off Massachusetts ships and "shut up in jails so long as the vessel remained in port, with the stringent addition, that if the shipmaster fails to pay the costs of this official arrest and the board in jail, these citizens are to be sold for slaves, to pay that expense."[32]

Emerson called this a "damnable outrage," and denounced the state for continuing to trust the safety of its seamen to the federal government. Massachusetts congressmen and senators should go before Congress and demand that this practice cease. "As for dangers to the Union, for such demands!—the Union already is at an end when the first citizen of Massachusetts is thus outraged." Yet only "one eloquent old man," John Quincy Adams, former President and now a congressman, defended "the rights of the free, against the usurpation of the slave holder."[33] Actually, Adams had not come out for immediate emancipation, which he regarded as premature, but he consistently defied the efforts of Southern politicians to prevent discussion of slavery in Congress.

At times in the past Emerson had himself been offended by the violent rhetoric of some of the abolitionists, but he now says their cause makes them eloquent. "I will say further that we are indebted mainly to this movement and to the continuers of it, for the popular discussion of every point of practical ethics, and a reference of every question to the absolute standard." By "absolute" he meant, of course, the moral conscience. "Virtuous men" could no longer rely on their elected officials.[34]

Governor George N. Briggs did finally decide to do something about the seizing in Southern ports of black sailors on Massachusetts ships, and, ironically, he appointed Concord's leading lawyer and former congressman, Samuel Hoar, as commissioner to investigate. Probably Hoar was selected because he was a known conservative and might be regarded as an impartial investigator. Certainly he took his appointment with utmost conscientiousness. He had friends in Charleston and did not anticipate violence; otherwise he would not have taken his daughter Elizabeth with him. When they stepped ashore Thursday morning, November 28, the air was fragrant of bougainvilleas, and Elizabeth was eager to see the city, but first her father had to write a note to Governor James Hammond explaining his mission.

While waiting for the governor's reply, Mr. Hoar and his daughter spent a delightful weekend in Charleston; but Monday evening the sheriff, the mayor, and the aldermen of the city called at their hotel to inform Mr. Hoar that the governor regarded his mission as an insult to South Carolina, and that the legislature had that day voted his immediate expulsion. Mr. Hoar insisted that he could not be intimidated and would not leave. Next morning the hotel manager begged him to leave before a mob which had assembled set fire to the hotel. Realizing that he must retreat or be killed—probably Elizabeth, too—he saw nothing to be gained by choosing martyrdom.

On his way home Mr. Hoar stopped in Washington to talk with the Massachusetts congressmen and senators, and in Boston with Governor Briggs. Then in Concord he reported his experiences at a town meeting called for this purpose. Everyone was incensed at South Carolina. But some people, including Ellery Channing, who was now in New York working on Greeley's *Tribune,* wondered if the squire's conduct had been heroic. When Channing expressed this opinion in a letter to Emerson, the latter replied in a letter printed in *The New-York Daily Tribune* on December 20, 1844. He wrote Ward: "Mr. Hoar has just come home from Carolina, and gave me this morning a narrative of his visit. He has behaved admirably well, I judge."[35] An old friend of his had tried to persuade him to flee to his friend's plantation Monday night, but Mr. Hoar told him "he had rather his broken skull should be carried to Massachusetts by somebody else than to carry it home safe himself, whilst his duty required him to remain." He confessed to Emerson that "he regretted a little afterwards [saying this], as it might sound a little vapouring." When it became obvious that the mob intended to carry him to his ship by force, "he got into the coach himself, not thinking it proper to be dragged."[36] This dignity Emerson appreciated.

In his Journal Emerson revealed that Mr. Hoar's experience had dispelled one illusion: "Massachusetts was dishonoured before; but she was credulous in the protection of the Constitution & either did not believe or affected not to believe that she was dishonoured. Now all doubt on that subject is removed . . ."[37] Some Boston merchants would try to "salve the matter over, but they cannot hereafter receive Southern gentlemen at their tables, without a consciousness of shame." Emerson overestimated a Boston merchant's conscience.

V

In October 1844, James Munroe and Company, in Boston, published Emerson's *Essays,* Second Series. The book contains eleven essays, beginning with one of his best, "The Poet," followed by "Experience," almost as good and of special biographical interest. Those that follow are minor in comparison, but clear, direct, and lively in style. Just as "The Over-Soul" and "Spiritual Laws" conveyed the Neoplatonic basis of Emerson's ideas in the First Series, "Nature" contains the philosophical assumptions of the Second Series: namely, "Nature is the incarnation of a thought [in the mind of God] and turns to a thought again [at the death of the body] as ice becomes water and gas. The world is mind precipitated . . ."[38] But except for "Nature," these 1844 essays can be read with pleasure without giving particular attention to the Neoplatonism, as Carlyle had advised the British audience to do in reading the *Essays* of 1841.

"The Poet" was the culmination of Emerson's thinking on the nature and function of the poet. He had given a lecture on the subject in Boston in December 1841, and repeated it in New York the following March, but he had not been able to finish the essay in time to include it in his 1841 edition. Since 1838 he had also been working on a poem on this subject, which he would never complete or publish, though his son appended it to the edition of his *Poems* in *Complete Works* (Volume IX, 1904). In this unfinished poem the poet is "Born and nourished in miracles,"[39] and like a Greek god's his conduct is superhuman:

> A Brother of the world, his song
> Sounded like a tempest strong
> Which tore from oaks their branches broad,
> And stars from the ecliptic road.
> Times wore he as his clothing-weeds,
> He sowed the sun and moon for seeds.

Emerson's concept of the ideal poet may have been influenced at this time by two German books on Persian poetry by Joseph von Hammer: a *History* (*Geschichte der schönen Redekünste Persiens,* Vienna, 1818) and a translation of Persian poems into German (*Der Diwan von Mohammed Schemseddin Hafis,*[40] Stuttgart and Tübingen, 1812–13).

Emerson's idea of the inspired poet switches back and forth in the unfinished poem between an elemental cosmic observer,

> I snuff the breath of my morning afar,
> I see the pale lustres condense to a star: . . .

and an intoxicated poet like Hafiz (later it will be the more sober Sa'di),

> One who having nectar drank
> Into blissful orgies sank; . . .

Perhaps Emerson never finished this poem because he was acutely aware of his own limitations:

> He, foolish child,
> A facile, reckless, wandering will,
>
> .   .   .   .   .
>
> Timid, self-pleasing, sensitive,
> With Gods, with fools, content to live;
> Bended to fops who bent to him;
> Surface with surfaces did swim.

In the essay on "The Poet" Emerson attempts to do the same thing for poetics that he had hoped to do for religion in his "Divinity School Address"—that is, to make poetry a matter of experience and not theory, especially theory based on authority. He complains that "men seem to have lost the perception of the instant dependence of form upon the soul." This "instant dependence" is the Neoplatonic doctrine of Edmund Spenser in "An Hymne in Honour of Beautie," which Emerson quotes:

> For, of the soul, the body form doth take,
> For soul is form, and doth the body make.

Second-rate poets "write poems from the fancy, at safe distance from their own experience." Every sensual fact conveys hidden truth, which it is the function of the poet to discover and reveal, or *express*. (In Neoplatonism *truth* and *beauty* are synonymous.) "The man is only half himself, the other half is his expression." The only whole man is the poet, because he has the gift of expression; he, therefore, is "representative": "He stands among partial men for the complete man, and apprises us not of his wealth, but of the common wealth."[41] The "truth" he expresses is not an answer to the riddle of a sphinx, or a didactic message, but an awareness of the presence of nature: "Too feeble fall the impressions of nature on us to make us artists. Every touch should thrill. Every man should be so much

an artist that he could report in conversation what had befallen him. . . .
The poet is the person in whom these powers are in balance."

In articulating the thought or stimulus which agitates him, the poet resigns himself to his mood. Thus his expression is "organic" (a term borrowed from Coleridge) and takes the shape "which things themselves take
when liberated": "For it is not metres, but a metre-making argument that
makes a poem,—a thought so passionate and alive that like the spirit of a
plant or an animal it has an architecture of its own, and adorns nature
with a new thing. The thought and the form are equal in the order of
time, but in the order of genesis the thought is prior to the form."[42]

The poet is the *sayer,* the *namer.* He expresses the eternal beauty which
nature symbolizes. "For poetry was all written before time was," and the
poet hears "those primal warblings. . . . The men of more delicate ear write
down these cadences more faithfully, and these transcripts, though imperfect, become the songs of the nations." Both words and deeds are modes of
the divine energy. "Words are also actions, and actions are a kind of
words."[43]

This theory of words is the same as Emerson's doctrine of symbols in
Nature (1836). "We are symbols and inhabit symbols; workmen, work
and tools, words and things, birth and death, all are emblems"[44] because
"The Universe is the externization of the soul." We regard material objects as self-existent, but they "are the retinue of that Being we have." Science keeps abreast of contemporary religion and metaphysics; "if any
phenomenon remains brute and dark it is because the corresponding faculty in the observer is not yet active."[45] Every man "is so far a poet as to be
susceptible of these enchantments of nature." Hunters, farmers, grooms,
and butchers are poets, "though they express their affection in their choice
of life and not in their choice of words."

"Every word was once a poem," and "Language is fossil poetry."[46]
Emerson is referring to etymology, which reveals that most (perhaps once
all) word roots were originally images of physical objects; "language is
made up of images and tropes." And just as the physical image came to
symbolize thoughts or abstractions, so the world itself "is a temple whose
walls are covered with emblems, pictures and commandments of the
Deity . . ."[47] But the moral implications of these "commandments" must
not be thought of as fixed. That is the fault of what Emerson calls the
"mystic," such as Swedenborg, who "nails a symbol to one sense." Emer-

son objects to these arbitrary interpretations, as he does to religious creeds and theological dogmas. "For all symbols are fluxional; all language is vehicular and transitive, and is good, as ferries and horses are, for conveyance, not as farms and houses are, for homestead."[48] Here, incidentally, is one of the secrets of Emerson's literary appeal: his choosing metaphors of everyday experience to convey his subtle abstractions.

And they are indeed subtle abstractions, what has often been called Emerson's "Transcendentalism." "The path of things is silent," he says, meaning, in the Kantian sense, that what *things are in themselves* can never be known, only their external appearances. The poet resigns "himself to the divine *aura* which breathes through forms."[49] It is not, therefore, with his intellect, or conscious effort, that the poet learns these secrets, but by *abandoning* himself "to the nature of things." Like the enraptured worshiper of God, the poet unlocks "his human doors" and permits "the ethereal tides to roll and circulate through him; then he is caught up into the life of the Universe, his speech is thunder, his thought is law, and his words are universally intelligible as the plants and animals."

The idea that the poet functions only in madness is as old as Plato—who distrusted the poet for that reason. And Emerson, as remarked above, had also recently been reading about the *intoxication* of Persian poets, who spoke wildly, or with " 'the flower of the mind' . . . not with intellect alone but with the intellect inebriated by nectar." The same idea Emerson had found in the Welsh bardic tradition. Bards, he remarks, notoriously love wine, narcotics, and whatever produces "animal exhilaration." Lest he be misunderstood, Emerson adds that "the great calm presence of the Creator, comes not forth to the sorceries of opium or of wine. The sublime vision comes to the pure and simple soul in a clean and chaste body." Emerson means the ecstasy of thought, not a "counterfeit excitement." In fact, "the poet's habit of living should be set on a key so low that the common influences should delight him."[50]

The "transparent eye-ball" experience in *Nature* is usually labeled *mystical,* but in "The Poet" *unconscious* seems a better term for the source of the vision or fantasy which the poet attempts to translate into words:

Doubt not, O poet, but persist, Say, "It is in me, and shall out." Stand there, balked and dumb, stuttering and stammering, hissed and hooted, stand and strive, until at last rage draw out of thee that *dream*-power which every night shows thee is thine own; a power transcending all limit and privacy, and by virtue of which a man is the conductor of the whole river of electricity. . . . Comes he to that power, his genius is no longer exhaustible.[51]

"River of electricity" is a metaphor for what at other times Emerson calls the transcendental Reason, or Logos, or First Cause. What makes him seem so modern in "The Poet" is this stress on the hidden psychic power, which requires some great mind-expanding stimulus to bring it to the surface of consciousness and articulation. With the "old painter" the poet says, "By God it is in me and must go forth of me." Most of the time what comes out is conventional, which is to say, *not his,* but "by and by he says something which is original and beautiful," and he knows it is *his.* "Once having tasted this immortal ichor, he cannot have enough of it, and as an admirable creative power exists in these intellections, it is of the last importance that these things get spoken."[52]

The conditions for being a poet are as difficult as Christ's injunction to the rich man to "sell all thou hast . . . and follow me." Emerson's injunction: "Thou shalt leave the world, and know the muse only." Or again: "Thou shalt lie close hid with nature, and canst not be afforded to the Capitol or the Exchange."[53] But "I look in vain for the poet whom I describe. . . . Time and nature yield us many gifts, but not yet the timely man, the new religion, the reconciler, whom all things await."[54] When he comes, the "ideal" shall be real to him, "and the impressions of the actual world shall fall like summer rain, copious, but not troublesome to [his] invulnerable essences."[55]

VI

Of all Emerson's essays, First or Second Series, "Experience" shows most clearly his own experiences, and how he adjusted to them. His faith in God and nature had been severely tested not only in the death of his first son but by life in general. Disillusionment with the Church, the state and federal government, education, social justice, and even with some personal friends such as Alcott, had necessitated adjustments in his personal philosophy, and in his psychology also. Many times in the past he had lamented his lack of physical vigor, and now he wonders if his birth fell "in some fit of indigence and frugality in nature."[56]

That he could ask this question shows that Emerson was now troubled by the idea of determinism. Indeed, the doubt went even deeper: life seemed like a dream. If not an illusion, at least it was pitifully brief and its purpose a mystery. "We wake [birth] and find ourselves on a stair; there are stairs below us, which we seem to have ascended; there are stairs above us, many a one, which go upward and out of sight." This statement can be interpreted either as the progress of the soul in its many *incarnations* (imprisonments in flesh) or as animal evolution, from primitive organisms to man—and beyond? Actually, both interpretations are possible, and almost surely intended.

Birth is, figuratively, an awakening from sleep, but the drowsiness lingers, and it is only occasionally that one is fully awake, completely conscious. Even grief seems shallow. Emerson says it leaves no scar, but what he really means is that it "can teach me nothing." He wants to penetrate the secret heart of nature and know what it really is. But he is confined in his own half-waking consciousness: "Dream delivers us to dream, and there is no end of illusion." One mood follows another, and each is a different lens through which to see—and distort—life. "Nature and books belong to the eyes that see them." Is there no certainty anywhere? A man's morals, his thoughts, his experiences, depend on his "structure and temperament." This is determinism with a vengeance, which Emerson had never before seriously entertained. "Temperament is the iron wire on which the beads are strung."[57] A "witty physician" (Dr. Gamaliel Bradford) had claimed that a man with a diseased liver became a Calvinist; with a sound liver, a Unitarian. In the view of science, everyone is caught in a trap, with no escape from "the links of the chain of physical necessity."[58]

Of course Emerson could not accept this view, and he insists that a door is still open for free will, or "creative power." But this assertion he bases on nothing except faith, or, in his present state of mind, stubborn hope. "The intellect, seeker of absolute truth, or the heart, lover of absolute good, intervenes for our succor . . ." This is a clear anticipation of William James's "Will to Believe." Logically, James will admit, there is absolutely no escape from "Determinism"; yet the human mind and emotions are not made for this pessimistic philosophy and cannot live in sanity and health with it. Ergo: since a belief in free will is psychologically beneficial, assume it to be true. James admits that the number of human actions which can possibly be free are quite limited, yet even a few keep the iron bands from pinching beyond endurance.

Emerson's adjustment to his situation was similar but not completely parallel to James's. He might not be able to see through his illusions, but in his stream of consciousness he detected what seemed to be a "necessity of a succession of moods or objects." This was a psychological observation of pragmatic value. "Our love of the real draws us to permanence, but health of body consists in circulation, and sanity of mind in variety or facility of association."[59] It is then necessary to be elastic, to take each experience as it comes. "We must set up the strong present tense against all the rumors of wrath, past or to come."[60] (Don't worry about your fated origin or reward in a life after death.)

If the intellect cannot solve the transcendental questions, then be non-intellectual. "Intellectual tasting of life will not supersede muscular activity. If a man should consider the nicety of the passage of a piece of bread down his throat, he would starve."[61] Nature takes care of such problems by instinct and reflex action. "Do not," therefore, "craze yourself with thinking, but go about your business anywhere. Life is not intellectual or critical, but sturdy." By no means has Emerson turned hedonist; he is only advocating taking life on faith and making the best use of each experience. "To fill the hour,—that is happiness; to fill the hour and leave no crevice for a repentance or an approval. We live amid surfaces, and the true art of life is to skate well on them."[62]

Temperamentally, Emerson had always disliked complainers, and at times he still found it difficult to understand his wife's suffering, because she was an habitual complainer. Heredity may have stinted him on physical vigor, but it had given him a sound digestion. "The fine young people despise life, but in me, and such as with me are free of dyspepsia, and to whom a day is a sound and solid good, it is a great excess of politeness to look scornful and to cry for company."[63] He was, either by natural temperament or by his Aunt Mary's ascetic training, a modern Stoic. Unlike the dissatisfied young people, "I begin at the other extreme, expecting nothing, and am always full of thanks for moderate goods." He would dig away in his own garden and not think of tomorrow. "The results of life are uncalculated and uncalculable."[64]

The "illuminations" which he occasionally experienced were discontinuous in his consciousness, coming in "flashes of light in sudden discoveries of ... beauty and repose ... I do not make it; I arrive there, and behold what was there already." In each person consciousness is "a sliding scale, which identifies him now with the First Cause, and now with the flesh of his body."[65] The question is, "at whose command" the action or experience takes place, at the command of God or one's own flesh? "The baffled intellect must still kneel before this cause, which refuses to be named,—ineffable cause ... So, in particulars, our greatness is always in a tendency or direction, not in an action."[66]

"It is very unhappy, but too late to be helped, the discovery we have made that we exist. That discovery is called the Fall of Man."[67] When consciousness is examined, it dwells within itself, and has no way of testing the accuracy of the lenses through which it sees the external world, if there is an external world. Emerson solves this dilemma as Bishop Berkeley solved it: simply accept the fact that all experience is subjective. Nature is a subjective phenomenon: "it is the eye which makes the horizon, and the rounding mind's eye which makes this or that man a type or representative of humanity." Emerson cites Jesus as such a creation, and doubtless many of his readers objected to this example of phenomenalism. However, since all experience is phenomenal, the example is blasphemous only to a dualist, who believes in the separate existence of mind and body.

Emerson feels so isolated in his own subjectivism that he is almost solipsistic. "Two human beings are like globes, which can touch only in a point."[68] Of course the solipsism is not absolute if they can touch at any point. But at what point? He has learned that he "cannot dispose of other people's facts; but I possess such a key to my own as persuades me, against all their denials, that they also have a key of theirs."[69] He explains the "key" only in a parable of a swimmer among drowning men, "who all catch at him, and if he give so much as a leg or a finger they will drown him. They wish to be saved from the mischiefs of their vices, but not from their vices."

We are back with Emerson's self-reliance; every man must save himself. Even God is neutral—though in Emerson's example of Flaxman's drawing of the Eumenides of Aeschylus, the god is mythological; Apollo, "surcharged with his divine destiny," takes no interest in a human destiny. Emerson accepts this condition, and stoically admits that the "lords" of his life are "Illusion, Temperament, Succession, Surface, Surprise, Reality, Subjectiveness." He has little patience with people who insist that the only reality is "an overt or practical effect." For him life wears "a visionary face. Hardest roughest action is visionary also. It is but a choice between soft and turbulent dreams. People disparage knowing and the intellectual life, and urge doing. I am very content with knowing, if only I could know."[70]

If *only I could know.*" He is not quite as reconciled to the doubt as he assumes. "I know that the world I converse with in the city and in the farms, is not the world I *think.*" Someday (after death?), he hopes he will know the difference, but he must content himself to wait. Some people make "manipular attempts to realize the world of thought," but in their experiments they only make themselves ridiculous. Probably he means the séances and mindreading performances which Margaret Fuller tried unsuccessfully to get him to attend. But his patience persists: "Patience and patience, we shall win at the last." The physical, everyday life seems timid, soon forgotten; "but in the solitude to which every man is always returning, he has a sanity and revelations which in his passage into new worlds he will carry with him. . . . there is victory yet for all justice . . ."[71]

None of the other essays in the Second Series has the depth of "The Poet" and "Experience." The others require less concentration to read, and "Gifts" has the ease and charm of an informal essay. Though the author thinks flowers and fruit are always appropriate for a friend, the best gift of all is something one has made with one's own hands or mind. In "Manners," also, Emerson is personal and crotchety. Manners are to facilitate life, get rid of obstructions, and allow a man's energy to manifest itself. Great men are usually too busy to be fashionable: "Fashion is made up of their children . . ."[72] Most of the time he regards fashion as a nuisance, and says, to avoid it, move to a suburb. He prefers "stateliness to an excess of fellowship. . . . Let us not be too acquainted."[73]

In this essay Emerson also gives a clue to the origin of the mysterious "Osman" in his Journals, used as a self-disguise: "The king of Shiraz could not afford to be so bountiful as the poor Osman who dwelt at his gate." But his humanity was so broad and deep that every poor outcast sought him out, though his freedom with the Koran disgusted the dervishes. Emerson also gives more personal meaning to his essay by ending it with an original fable. Jove was so disgusted with the rogues and vixens on earth that he talked of destroying the human race. Minerva replied that the little creatures were ridiculous, especially seen from afar, but "if you called them bad, they would appear so; if you called them good, they would appear so."[74]

In "Nature" Emerson makes some of the same points he had discussed in *Nature* (1836), but he keeps a light touch and his metaphors are less esoteric and often witty. His general topic is the influence of natural objects. We admire in nature what is best in us, but "If there were good men, there would never be this rapture in nature. . . . Man is fallen; nature is erect . . ."[75]

Both science and Neoplatonism combine in Emerson's insistence on the identity of all matter—"one stuff," whether in distant star, nearby tree, or man. "Motion or change and identity or rest are the first and second secrets of nature . . ."[76] The motion is always forward, "a system in transition." Even plants grope toward consciousness. Young men, "having tasted the first drop from the cup of thought, are already dissipated." Maples and ferns are still uncorrupt, "yet no doubt when they come to consciousness they too will curse and swear."[77]

This idea that consciousness is growing and spreading throughout the biological world anticipated Teilhard de Chardin's twentieth-century theory that every molecule has a psyche through which Deity is approaching the Omega Point (*The Phenomenon of Man,* 1955). It is interesting also that Emerson quotes contemporary astronomers on the origin of the universe: "Once heave the ball from the hand, and we can show how all this mighty order grew." Twentieth-century astronomers would call it the "Big Bang."

In "Politics" Emerson argues that society is fluid and can always change the State to suit current needs and wishes. He is in favor of the least government possible, the fewest laws, and limited power. He believes, as in "Character," that "The antidote to this abuse of formal government is the influence of private character, the growth of the Individual."[78] If men were wise enough, no government would be necessary, but "there will always be a government of force where men are selfish." As a consequence of such incidents as Mr. Hoar's being driven out of Charleston, Emerson had little confidence in the federal government, and scarcely more in the cowardly politicians of Massachusetts. This should be borne in mind when we read: "I do not call to mind a single human being who has steadily denied the authority of the laws, on the simple ground of his own moral nature."[79] This was becoming his strongest social and political conviction, that the moral conscience is superior to law and government and should take precedence over statutory laws. In a few years Thoreau would adopt this doctrine as "civil disobedience," which in turn would influence Gandhi's "passive resistance" in the twentieth century.

Any person with such absolute faith in his moral conscience would be a reformer. Emerson had always been a reformer in principle, and he was now passing over from theory to practice. However, his Platonic belief in universals protected him from fanaticism. In "Nominalist and Realist" (those terms of Scholastic philosophy) he points out that every human being has faults and imperfections. We can define the qualities of a perfect lady or gentleman, but no individual has all these qualities. "Great men or men of great gifts you shall easily find, but symmetrical men never. . . . there are no such men as we fable"[80] in Jesus, Pericles, or George Washington.

Human nature causes us to believe every other person "an incurable partialist, and himself a universalist." Perfection should be our ideal, but reality teaches that it is unattainable. Consequently, in "New England Reformers" Emerson ends his essay by cautioning: "Do not be so impatient to set the town right concerning the unfounded pretensions and false reputation of certain men of standing."[81] In spite of appearances, most people mean well, prefer truth to falsehood, and would like to do the right thing. "That which befits us, embosomed in beauty and wonder as we are, is cheerfulness and courage, and the endeavor to realize our aspirations."

Carlyle praised the Second Series of *Essays* and called them "a *sermon* to me."[82] He promptly wrote what he called a preface for Chapman's London edition—though it was doubtful that Chapman could get a British copyright—and Carlyle admitted that his preface was nothing more than a statement that the book had been correctly printed. To Emerson, Carlyle wrote, "I have to object still . . . that we find you a Speaker indeed, but as it were a *Soliloquizer* on the eternal mountain-tops," remote from actual human affairs. "We have terrible need of one man like you down among us! It is cold and vacant up there; nothing paintable but rainbows and emotions; come down, and you shall do life-pictures, passions, facts,—which *transcend* all thought, and leave it stuttering and stammering!"

Emerson replied (December 31, 1844):

... of what you say now and heretofore respecting the remoteness of my writing and thinking from real life, though I hear substantially the same criticism made by my countrymen, I do not know what it means. If I can at any time express the law and the ideal right, that should satisfy me without measuring the divergence from it of the last act of Congress.[83]

In his own country Emerson's 1844 *Essays* was received more enthusiastically than the First Series. *The Democratic Review* praised them for their lofty and commanding point of view—nothing about being lost in the clouds.[84] The reviewer called the earlier collection a book of philosophy, the second the results of the author's speculative reasoning. Dr. Hedge's review in *The Christian Examiner* was no doubt based on attentive reading and honest reactions. His only objection was to Emerson's references to Jesus as mythical or fabulous. Otherwise his admiration for the essays was unbounded: "We dare to predict for them a devotion coetaneous with the language in which they are composed. So long as there are lovers of fine discourse and generous sentiment in the world, they will find their own."

Chapter XX

The Central Man

We shall one day talk with the central man . . .[1]

I

At the time of delivering his "Young American" speech in February 1844, Emerson shared the heady optimism of the national expansionists. There were rumors of trouble between Texas and Mexico over the annexation question, and discussion was heating up between Great Britain and the United States over the Oregon territory between the forty-ninth and fifti-eth parallels. But Emerson was so little alarmed about these problems that he could say in his speech: "To men legislating for the area betwixt the two oceans, betwixt the snows and the tropics, somewhat of the gravity of nature will infuse itself into the code."[2] While other nationalists were calling for a literature to match America's mountains and lakes and prai-ries, Emerson, too, said that "here shall laws and institutions exist on some scale of proportion to the majesty of nature."

Yet a few weeks later in his Journal (the month is uncertain, but it was probably March 1844) Emerson shows a strangely ambivalent attitude to-ward "annexation":

The question of the annexation of Texas is one of those which look very differently to the centuries and to the years. It is very certain that the strong British race which have now overrun so much of this continent, must also overrun that tract, & Mexico & Oregon also, and it will in the course of ages be of small import by what particular occasions & methods it was done. It is a secular question. It is quite necessary & true to our New England character that we should consider the question in its local and temporary bearings, and resist the annexation with tooth & nail.[3]

What Emerson seems to be saying is that, looked at completely objectively and impersonally, the absorption of the whole continent by the British race was inevitable. But New Englanders would not be able to look at it as a "secular question"; their Puritan consciences would compel them to condemn it as immoral. As prophecy, this was an acute observation; Emerson was still able to take the long view. Apparently this double vision was not unique with him. Two years later his friends at Brook Farm displayed the same ambivalence in an editorial in *The Harbinger,* their Fourier journal:

> There can be no doubt of the design being entertained by the leaders and instigators of this infamous business, to extend the "area of freedom" to the shores of California, by robbing Mexico of another large mass of her territory; and the people are prepared to execute it to the letter. In many and most aspects in which this plundering aggression is to be viewed it is monstrously iniquitous, but after all it seems to be completing a more universal design of Providence, of extending the power and intelligence of advanced civilized nations over the whole face of the earth. . . . In this way Providence is operating on a grand scale to accomplish its designs, making use of instrumentalities ignorant of its purposes, and incited to act by motives the very antipode of those which the real end in view might be supposed to be connected with or grow out of.[4]

Evidently blind instinct was in conflict with professed morality. Though these New England idealists bitterly condemned President Polk's policies as wicked, they could not entirely suppress a secret pride at the thought of a United States extending from Atlantic to Pacific. Possibly even their concept of "Providence" was changing in the direction of the scientific Determinism of the second half of the century. Henry Adams would observe later in his *History of the United States during the First Administration of James Madison* that Governor William Henry Harrison's reports to President Jefferson on Indian affairs illustrated "the law accepted by all historians in theory, but adopted by none in practice; which former ages called 'fate,' and metaphysicians called 'necessity,' but which modern science has refined into the 'survival of the fittest.' "[5] In Adams's view, once European settlers, with superior technology, had established a foothold on the North American continent, the extinction of the aboriginal inhabitants was inevitable.

The inconsistency in Emerson's thinking on this subject did not weaken his moral stand on the annexation of Texas, though his sympathy was not with Mexico. The Democratic party had hardened his position in the summer of 1844 at their presidential convention in Baltimore by nominating James K. Polk, who stood for annexing Texas and acquiring "all of Oregon" and California. In the dispute with Great Britain over the boundary in Oregon, the Democrats wanted possession up to 54°40'; so their campaign slogan became "Fifty-four forty or fight." The Whigs nominated Henry Clay, who opposed annexation of Texas. The real issue in regard to Texas was whether the new territory (and later state) would permit the ownership of slaves. The Southern politicians wanted Texas in order to strengthen the political power of the slavocracy. The northeastern states opposed annexation on both moral and political grounds, though they talked more about the moral.

After Polk was elected, Congress passed a resolution for the annexation of Texas even before the new President could be inaugurated. But in the final settlement, the Missouri Compromise of 1820, in which Clay had played a leading part, was maintained. This excluded slavery to 30°36', and thus from Texas. On July 4, 1845, at a convention in Texas, annexation was accepted, though it was generally believed that this act would lead to war with Mexico. President Polk sent troops to the Rio Grande under General Zachary Taylor, with instructions not to provoke an attack but to be prepared for one. The first clash came on April 25, 1846, not without some provocation, and on May 13 Congress declared war.

Emerson was indignant. "New England is subservient," he wrote in his Journal. "The President proclaims war, & those senators who dissent, are not those who know better, but those who can afford to, as Benton & Calhoun."[6] Actually, both Thomas Hart Benton of Missouri and John C. Calhoun of South Carolina voted for the declaration, though they expressed reservations. "Democracy," Emerson continued, "becomes a government of bullies tempered by editors." Most newspapers did support the war, though Horace Greeley, the former New Hampshire boy, opposed it. The most effective opposition came from Emerson's young friend James Russell Lowell in his dialect satire in the *Biglow Papers.*

One effect of the Mexican War on Emerson was to make him cynical. He thought Massachusetts supported it because her textile factories needed Texas cotton. "Cotton thread," he growled, "holds the union together, unites John C. Calhoun & Abbott Lawrence. Patriotism for holidays & summer evenings with music & rockets, but cotton thread is the union."[7] It was not only manufacturers, however, who lacked moral fiber. "The scrupulous & law-abiding became whigs, the unscrupulous & energetic are locofocos. The people are no worse since they invaded Mexico, than they were before, only they have given their will a deed."[8] Presently he includes the Whigs, too, in his disgust: "The whigs cant & the locofocos blaspheme." Then he predicted with bitterness: "The United States will conquer Mexico, but it will be as the man swallows the arsenic, which brings him down in turn. Mexico will poison us."

In Concord animosity between the critics and the patriotic supporters of the war created a tense situation. One evening at the Lyceum, Emerson listened with delight to Parker Pillsbury, who had succeeded Nathaniel Rogers as editor of the abolitionist *Herald of Freedom,* denounce an editorial in *The Concord Freeman* supporting the war. The editor of *The Freeman* was in the audience and listened to Pillsbury's sarcastic attack. To Emerson, Pillsbury was "that very gift from New Hampshire which we have long expected, a tough oak stick of a man not to be silenced or insulted or intimidated by a mob . . . he stands in the New England Assembly a purer bit of New England than any, & flings his sarcasms right & left, sparing no name, or person, or party, or presence."[9] Emerson respected him more than the timid clergy. "What is the Church for? if, whenever there is any moral evil to be grappled with, as Intemperance, or Slavery, or War, there needs to be originated an entirely new instrumentality?"

Emerson felt almost more contempt for the "snivelling opposition" to President Polk than for his "rabble at Washington," though the rabble had the effrontery to see "how much crime the people will bear."[10] Governor Briggs in acquiescing to the Mexican War had "immolated the honor of Massachusetts."[11] Daniel Webster did tell "them how much the war cost, that was his protest, but voted the war, & sends his son to it. They calculated rightly on Mr. Webster." Emerson admired his young friend

Henry Thoreau for going to jail rather than paying his poll tax. "On him they could not calculate." Near the end of July, Thoreau had been arrested for failure to pay his poll tax and had spent a night in the Concord jail, though next morning his aunt paid the tax for him. Actually, his poll tax did not directly support the war, but he was making a gesture of protest against his state's acceptance of the federal policies. Apocryphal stories were later told of Emerson's disapproval, but at the time he sarcastically observed, "The abolitionists denounce the war & give much time to it, but they pay the tax." They "ought to resist & go to prison in multitudes on their known & described disagreements from the state."[12]

Emerson contemptuously called the state "a poor cow," in need of hay for its four stomachs. "Take this handful of clover and welcome. But if you go to hook me when I walk in the fields, then, poor cow, I will cut your throat." Violent language was becoming habitual with him. The abolitionists thought the cow had already hooked them; therefore they ought to cut its throat. Emerson's indignation extended to them, too. "Remove a few specified grievances, & this present commonwealth will suit them." He did not spare himself, either. Speaking to an ambiguous "you" (apparently himself), he continues: "Your objection then to the state of Massachusetts is deceptive. Your true quarrel is with the state of Man."[13]

Refusing to pay "the state tax does not reach the evil so nearly as many other methods within your reach. The state tax does not pay the Mexican War. Your coat, your sugar, your Latin & French & German book, your watch does. Yet these you do not stick at buying." Emerson did not explain how buying books supported the war, but perhaps the principle was that buying imported goods and paying a tariff on them supported the government. Probably he was confessing his own sense of guilt over not taking some positive action. The time would come when he would propose boycotting all goods produced by slave labor, but he had nothing definite to propose in the summer of 1846.

II

In 1845 American was on the move: soldiers marching to the Rio Grande; ships carrying sailors around the Horn to California, in case England, Russia, or some other nation tried to seize the lightly held Mexican ports; hundreds of hardy folk traveling in covered wagons to Oregon by the trail opened three years previously; and John C. Frémont setting out on his third trip to the Rocky Mountains to explore and map the region, and perhaps give assistance if trouble broke out in California.

Emerson's own traveling was confined to short trips in Massachusetts to repeat his lectures of the previous season, except for a "Discourse" delivered at Middlebury College in Vermont on July 23, and repeated at the Connecticut Wesleyan University commencement on August 6.[14] The Methodists had recently decided to educate their ministers and had established a university at Middletown. Emerson had intended to publish his "Discourse," but some of his statements on religion so alarmed President Stephen Olin that he begged Emerson either not to publish it or to change a few sentences which he feared would offend some of his wealthy supporters, and thus hinder the growth of Wesleyan. Emerson agreed not to publish. Now he had learned that the Methodists were as easily offended as the Unitarians at Harvard.

But pleasant things were also happening during the spring and summer of 1845. Ellery Channing returned from New York and once again joined Emerson on his walks. Before leaving the city, he had written Thoreau suggesting that Henry get Emerson's permission to build himself a cabin at Walden Pond, and the idea appealed both to Thoreau and to Emerson.[15] Late in March, Thoreau borrowed an ax from Alcott and began cutting down white pine to use as rafters for his hut. He needed a quiet place where he could write and think. His aunts, sisters, and compulsive-talking mother made it difficult to concentrate at home. He was also fascinated by news of those pioneers streaming westward, dotting the wilderness with their log cabins. Later, in a famous essay on "Walking," he confessed the urge to withdraw always into the wilderness. "I must walk toward Oregon, and not toward Europe."[16] But this was only a symbolic westering. Actually, in going to Walden Pond he walked only two miles from the center of Concord—and eastward toward Boston, at that. He liked to play with the meanings of words. In the book which he would complete at Walden, *A Week on the Concord and Merrimack Rivers,* he would declare: "The frontiers are not east or west, north or south; but wherever a man *fronts* a fact, though that fact be his neighbor . . . Let him build himself a log house with the bark on where he is, *fronting* IT, and wage there an Old French war for seven or seventy years, with Indians and Rangers, or whatever else may come between him and the reality, and save his scalp if he can."[17]

By May, Thoreau was ready to raise the frame of his single-room hut, ten by fifteen feet. He had done all the preliminary work himself, and would finish his hut after the "raising." He liked the rural custom of making a social occasion out of this work; so he invited Emerson, Alcott, Ellery Channing, and several other friends. The latter included a Concord farmer, Edmund Hosmer, whom both he and Emerson liked and admired, and Mr. Hosmer's three sons, John, Edmund, and Andrew. Recently two young men at Brook Farm, George William Curtis (later a distinguished editor) and his brother Burrill, had decided they would rather live near Emerson and Thoreau than near George Ripley, and were now trying to support themselves on a small farm near Concord. They were the other invited guests.

Thoreau took his time in finishing his hut. In fact, it was not finished on July 4 when he moved in. By coincidence, that was the very day when Texas voted annexation to the United States. Though he could hardly have foreseen the exact date of that event, Thoreau knew that Concord patriots would be celebrating the national holiday by parades and speeches supporting the war with Mexico. Thus his taking up residence at Walden on July 4, 1845, was, among other things, an act of defiance and protest.

Other friends of Emerson's were moving around also, coming and going. Ellery Channing brought him news that his young admirer Giles Waldo, a young man he had met in New York, had left to become vice consul at Lahaina in the Sandwich Islands (Hawaii). George Bradford gave up trying to teach a private school in Emerson's barn and began a new school at Roxbury. Sam Ward and other visitors came for brief visits. Emerson wrote to Elizabeth Hoar on June 17: "Caroline S. staid a week into June, and then departed to Woburn. Of her there is always much to say."[18] But there was much that he did not say to Elizabeth. He and Caroline Sturgis had been carrying on a kind of high-minded flirtation for several months. On May 10 he had written: "I wish you were my brother to travel through the world with me. I should go to you, as I do not to Charles K. [Newcomb]."[19] He thought he prized his "friend," presumably Caroline, "with a foolish extravagance, and you only waste good time for me & I for you, if we come near."

Sometime after her visit in June, Caroline considered finding a boarding place in Concord so she could be geographically near Emerson, and on August 23 he wrote her that Lidian had offered "to take you as a boarder herself, if the Hawthornes could not." In making this offer, Lidian was again playing her favorite though painful role of the patient Griselda, for she was worried about the relations between her husband and Caroline. "I told her," Emerson wrote to Caroline, "you had no claims such as she is wont to hear of, & this was a case where each of the parties, herself & yourself & myself should deal very unreservedly by yea & nay."[20] Perhaps he meant that if they were completely frank with each other, they could avoid misunderstandings. At any rate, Lidian was no doubt relieved that Caroline declined her offer, explaining, "Lidian would find me more trouble than she anticipates, for I am always unpunctual & generally invisible at meal-times & so unsocial at all times that I must give pain even to the most generous . . ."[21]

After delivering his address at Wesleyan University, Emerson continued on to New York, to visit his brother on Staten Island and others. One of the others was William Tappan, Ellery Channing's best friend during his sojourn in the city. In 1840, it will be recalled, Emerson had written Caroline that he would be glad to see her find a young man near her own age who could return her "love" better than he could. A letter he wrote to Caroline from Concord on August 17, 1845,[22] soon after his return from New York, conveys the impression that he thought he had found the right man for her, and was doing his best to arouse her interest in him, and his in her—an attempt destined to succeed. After failing to find William Tappan in his father's office, Emerson went to his residence in Brooklyn and then brought him back to the City Hotel in New York. "He appeared to as great advantage as ever," Emerson wrote Caroline, "and surpasses in figure, grace, quiet strength & charm of manners every one whom I see: He says good things and provokes you to say good things, but I fear he dreams away his time & leads but an Indian life."

While dining with Emerson at the City Hotel, Tappan said he fancied he knew what Caroline looked like, though he had never met her. During the meal he asked if a young girl sitting at the other end of the table resembled her, but Emerson said she did not. "Afterwards in some compassion I told him of George Curtis's remark on the 'Roman Girl' in the 'Gift' [that she reminded him of Caroline], to which he lent earnest heed." After dinner Emerson invited William to accompany him to Turtle Bay, on the East River, to meet Margaret Fuller, now living with Mr. and Mrs. Horace Greeley.

Since December 1844 Margaret had been writing three columns a week for *The Tribune* and living with the Greeleys. Greeley had liked her *Summer on the Lake* so well that he employed her to take Albert Brisbane's place after his departure for Brook Farm. During the autumn of 1844, before joining the *Tribune* staff, Margaret had lived with Caroline Sturgis at Fishkill on the Hudson for six weeks while she revised her *Dial* "Great Lawsuit" article for publication as a book; it was finally published as *Woman in the Nineteenth Century* in February 1845, by Greeley and McElrath.

Woman aroused great interest, much of it hostile, but Greeley was delighted with it.[23] Margaret was now a celebrity, known to every literary person in New York, and many abroad, including George Sand, for being the first American author to write a book on women's rights. Her position on *The Tribune* enabled her to continue her attacks on the social and legal barriers to equality for women. Greeley expected her to write two columns of literary criticism and one on social questions each week, but she sometimes used more space for the latter. As a literary critic she was rivaled only by Poe. On social and political subjects she shared the views of Greeley, who gave her all the front-page space she wanted. He called her "the most remarkable and in some respects the greatest woman whom America has yet known."[24] She shocked "respectable women" by interviewing prostitutes and visiting women in prison. After seeing Hopper House, a rehabilitation center for "fallen" women, she wrote James Nathan, a young German émigré whom she had recently met and was falling in love with, "I like them better than most women I meet, because, if any good is left, it is so genuine, and they make no false pretensions nor cling to shadows."[25]

Emerson did not record this interview with Margaret in his Journal, but he undoubtedly found her somewhat changed from the Boston intellectual he had known. As coeditor of *The Dial* she had not been concerned with "leading public opinion," but with stimulating every reader to think for himself. Now as a journalist she wanted to influence the public, and was doing so. She and Emerson agreed, of course, on the wrongs of the Mexican War, the character of "Jimmy" Polk, and the cowardice of Northern politicians, but he may have had some difficulty in understanding her infatuation with New York. She was finding that she had more freedom there than in cold, narrow-minded Boston, though she was fast outgrowing America, too, and would soon need a bigger theater for her personal development. Though Emerson himself was assuming a more active role as social critic and reformer, he still had a low opinion of journalism, and probably felt that it was coarsening Margaret's character. After returning to Concord, he wrote her less often, though this may have been because she was too busy to write him. Yet it was also an indication that their lives were diverging, his toward a major literary career, and hers toward greater participation in world events.

III

For his 1845–46 lecture series Emerson chose for his theme "The Uses of Great Men."[26] He gave the first of his seven lectures at the Odeon in Boston on December 11, 1845, and the last on January 22, 1846. He repeated the series in Concord, beginning December 31, and part or all of these lectures in more than thirty different places during the next two years. It was apparently the most successful series, both financially and in popularity, he had yet given. The great, or as he called them, *representative,* men of these lectures were Plato, Swedenborg, Montaigne, Shakespeare, Napoleon, and Goethe. Between May 1847 and November 1848 these same men were to be the main subjects of his lectures in England, though he would add a few other themes for variety. Then in 1850 he would publish the original seven lectures, after considerable polishing, as *Representative Men.*

Some critics have regarded this book as Emerson's version of Carlyle's *Heroes and Hero-Worship.*[27] But, strictly speaking, the six men were not exactly *heroes* to him, and he did not worship them, though he admired each for one reason or another and found in each something with which he identified—most with Plato, though almost as much with Montaigne. Oliver Wendell Holmes in his biography says that "Emerson holds the mirror up to them at just such an angle that we see his own face as well as that of his hero, unintentionally, unconsciously, no doubt, but by a necessity which he would be the first to recognize."[28] That is a good observation, but before testing it, we should examine the theory which Emerson explained in his introductory lecture.

"The search after the great man," he says, "is the dream of youth and the most serious occupation of manhood."[29] On his trip to Europe in 1832–33 Emerson had hoped to find a teacher of wisdom, but was disappointed, as we have seen, with every "great man" he met except Carlyle, who did become his friend, though not his fountain of wisdom. From the trip Emerson learned that no one could help him except himself; it was his greatest lesson in self-reliance. Now he tells his audience, "Man is endogenous, and education is his unfolding. The aid we have from others is mechanical compared with the discoveries of nature in us."[30] Yet men who inhabit "a higher sphere of thought" (this is Emerson's definition of "great men") can help one discover the truth in himself: "Behmen and Swedenborg saw that things were representative. Men are also representative; first, of things, and secondly, of ideas. . . . Each man is by secret liking connected with some district of nature, whose agent and interpreter he is; as Linnaeus, of plants; Huber, of bees; Fries, of lichens; Van Mons, of pears; Dalton, of atomic forms; Euclid, of lines; Newton, of fluxions."

The truth about nature which each of these men discovered had been waiting throughout the ages for the right man, under favorable circumstances. But the discoverer need not be a scientist (in the usual sense); he can be a "definer and map-maker of the latitudes and longitudes of our condition." He teaches "the qualities of primary nature,—admit[s] us to the constitution of things."[31] Yet admiration for the benefactor can degenerate into idolatry. For this reason Emerson is opposed to hero worship, which leads to intellectual suicide. What is important is the idea and not the man. "When we are exalted by ideas, we do not owe this to Plato, but to the idea, to which also Plato was debtor."[32] Moreover, the truly great man effaces himself in his deed. It is nature's deformities who are conceited. These "worthless and offensive members of society" think themselves ill-used and are astonished at the ingratitude of their contemporaries. There are no unappreciated geniuses, for "Nature never sends a great man into the planet without confiding the secret to another soul."

Nature also rotates her special gifts. A great man is never followed by his duplicate. Furthermore, his greatness consists in a larger portion of qualities common to all: "there are no common men. All men are at last of a size; and true art is only possible on the conviction that every talent has its apotheosis somewhere."[33] In the whole procession of famous men, not one has reached the summit of human possibilities. Each is incomplete, and the human race is needed to make a *complete man.*

Emerson selected his six representative men, not because they were the greatest but because of what each represented: Plato, the philosopher; Swedenborg, the mystic; Montaigne, the skeptic; Shakespeare, the poet; Napoleon, "the man of the world" (note: not military genius); and Goethe, "the writer." If he had selected his favorite philosopher, it should have been Plotinus, to judge by his frequent reading of him and the detectable influence. But in the history of philosophy, Plotinus was a lesser figure, whereas Plato was the fountainhead. Someone has remarked, and many have agreed, that all Western philosophy consists of footnotes to Plato. Emerson says nearly the same thing in his own way: "Out of Plato come all things that are still written and debated among men of thought." And again: "Plato is philosophy, and philosophy, Plato,—at once the glory and the shame of mankind, since neither Saxon nor Roman have availed to add any idea to his categories."[34] The Alexandrians (Neoplatonists), the Christians, and in England the Elizabethans—all built on him. Calvinism borrowed from his *Phaedo.*

Emerson did not attempt to summarize Plato's philosophy, and indeed it is difficult even for a scholar to be sure exactly what Plato thought, because he presented his ideas in dramatic form, and the problem is which character, if any, speaks for him. In college Emerson's favorite philosopher was Socrates, but what Socrates thought is known only through Plato's dramatization of him in the dialogues. Socrates posed as knowing nothing and invited his opponent to teach him, meanwhile driving his victim into a corner by astute questions. This strategy served to bring out all sides of an argument. Though Emerson, a hater of the science of logic, did not himself play the Socratic game, he did learn from Plato's Socrates to think and write dialectically. This may have been his greatest debt to Plato.

Plato also served Emerson as an example of the interdependence of all thought. Plato absorbed the learning of his time, and was in turn absorbed; consequently, Emerson says, "When we are praising Plato, it seems we are praising quotations from Solon and Sophron and Philolaus. Be it so. Every book is a quotation . . ."[35] This matter of quotations fascinated Emerson, not only in the symbolical sense ("every man is a quotation from all his ancestors") but also quite literally. He copied down quotations while reading, and filled many notebooks with them. Not only was he aware of his own indebtedness to thinkers of the past, he also constantly reminded himself that the community of intellect has no boundaries in either finite or infinite time and space: all human minds form a community which exists by the grace of an Infinite Mind.

Though little is known of Plato's life, Emerson accepted the tradition that he had made pilgrimages to the East, and there "imbibed the idea of one Deity, in which all things are absorbed. The unity of Asia and the detail of Europe," or the "real" and the "ideal," which accounts for his "polarity."[36] There was also a polarity in his stylistic delight in illustrating "transcendental distinctions" with homely analogues, expressed in the language of cooks, potters, horse-doctors, butchers, and fishmongers. "Plato keeps the two vases, one of aether and one of pigment, at his side, and invariably uses both." He studied the theories of the physicists, and pronounced natural laws to be secondary to the First Cause (God's ordination). In *Timaeus*, one of Emerson's favorite works, Plato declared: "All things are for the sake of the good, and it is the cause of everything beautiful."[37] This was Emerson's dogma also.

In several personal ways Emerson felt an affinity with Plato. In the political eras of Jackson and Polk, Emerson felt the same impatience with "popular government" which Plato had expressed, precisely because he shared the philosopher's reverence for justice and honor. He felt a kinship in Plato's cool head and warm imagination, and in his "hard-headed humor," which had "a probity as invincible as his logic." But the greatest similarity is in the lack of "system" in their individual philosophies. Plato did attempt a theory of the universe, but "He is charged with having failed to make the transition from ideas to matter."[38] Emerson had confessed the same failure about his first book, *Nature*, and he knew that critics accused him still of dwelling in the clouds. Plato, Emerson admits, failed to explain the enigma of existence, but no one ever had, nor was anyone likely to. Nevertheless, Plato was "a more complete man, who could apply to nature the whole scale of the senses, the understanding and the reason." But what most endeared him to Emerson was his "moral aim": " 'Intellect,' he said, 'is the king of heaven and of earth'; but in Plato, intellect is always moral."[39]

In his essay on "The Poet" Emerson had condemned "the mystic" because he "nails a symbol to one sense."[40] He had in mind Swedenborg, as his lecture on "Swedenborg; or, the Mystic" plainly shows. Swedenborg's visions seemed to Emerson a variety of demonology, which he had severely criticized in an early lecture. He had no use for abnormal psychic phenomena, and he found Swedenborg distinctly unhealthy, a neurotic man at war with himself. Sampson Reed's interpretation of Swedenborg's doctrine of "correspondence" had favorably impressed and influenced Emerson, and he now admits that some of the Swedish mystic's "moral insights" had "corrected popular errors." He also admires Swedenborg's reputed achievements in science, such as his anticipating Kant and Laplace in the nebular hypothesis, predicting the discovery of a seventh planet, and other scientific contributions.

In his fifty-fifth year, Swedenborg turned his back on science after he had one day ascended into heaven and talked with the angels—an experience he declared he repeated many times. Emerson says he "almost justifies his claim to preternatural vision, by strange insights of the structure of the human body and mind."[41] Of the body Swedenborg observed that every organ is made up of many organs of similar structure. Of the mind, he said that in heaven it is forbidden "to stand behind another and look at the back of his head; for then the influx which is from the Lord is disturbed."

In "Conjugal Love" Swedenborg, who never married, wrote that "sex is universal," and that in the "spiritual world the nuptial union is not momentary, but incessant and total ..." The heavenly life as an endless orgasm was too much for Emerson and he called this fantasy "a child's clinging to his toy; an attempt to eternize the fireside and nuptial chamber." He called the vision false, "For God is the bride or bridegroom of the soul. Heaven is not the pairing of two, but the communion of all souls."[42]

Sex in heaven was bad enough, but Emerson objected even more strenuously to Swedenborg's self-inquisition in his war on intellect. Swedenborg called philosophers "vipers, cockatrices, asps, hemorrhoids, presters, and flying serpents; literary men are conjurers and charlatans." Here, Emerson thought, was the seat of Swedenborg's pain; he was paying the penalty for his "introverted faculties." He had fallen into "jealousy of his intellect." The result was "theologic cramp," making him confuse *evil* and *sin*. To Emerson, evil was the absence of good, a deprivation, but "good in the making." He thought, "The less we have to do with our sins the better. No man can afford to waste his moments in compunctions."[43]

Not only did Swedenborg believe in sin; he believed in devils as well. "That pure malignity can exist is the extreme proposition of unbelief." It was unnatural, the "last profanation," outright atheism. "To what painful perversion had Gothic theology arrived, that Swedenborg admitted no conversion for evil spirits!" To Emerson, "the divine effort is never relaxed; the carrion in the sun will convert itself to grass and flowers; and man, though in brothels, or jails, or on gibbets, is on his way to all that is good and true."[44]

Emerson objected not only to Swedenborg's "Gothic theology" but also to his ludicrous vision of heaven. Swedenborg's angels were country parsons attending a Lutheran evangelical picnic, where prizes were given to virtuous peasants. Swedenborg himself "goes up and down the world of men, a modern Rhadamanthus in gold-headed cane and peruke, and with nonchalance and the air of a referee, distributes souls." The real world of warm, passionate people "is to him a grammar of hieroglyphics." How different is Jacob Behmen, who listens awestruck to gentle humanity, and when he declares that " 'in some sort, love is greater than God,' his heart beats so high that the thumping against his leathern coat is audible across the centuries." He is "healthily and beautifully wise, notwithstanding the mystical narrowness and incommunicableness. Swedenborg is disagreeably wise, and with all his accumulated gifts, paralyzes and repels."[45]

From dismal Swedenborg, Emerson turns happily to Montaigne, the wholly human "skeptic," whom he had loved since reading the *Essays* in his youth. Montaigne was a kindred spirit who spoke Emerson's own thought and experience. It was not just in his own doubting moods that Emerson turned to Montaigne, but at all times. What he represented was the basic frankness and honesty which formed the hardpan of Emerson's own character. Montaigne's "biblical plainness coupled with a most uncanonical levity" was Emerson's also, so offensive to Professor Andrews Norton at Harvard and the orthodox everywhere.

Here is an impatience and fastidiousness at color or pretence of any kind. . . . he will indulge himself with a little cursing and swearing; he will talk with sailors and gipsies, use flash and street ballads . . . Whatever you get here shall smack of the earth and of real life, sweet, or smart, or stinging.[46]

Conventional and timid people associate "skepticism" with atheism, but Emerson calls it "the attitude assumed by the student in relation to particulars which society adores, but which he sees to be reverend only in their tendency and spirit."[47] Society resents any suspicion of the existing order. "But the interrogation of custom at all points is an inevitable stage in the growth of every superior mind, and is the evidence of its perception of the flowing power which remains itself in all changes." Such a mind finds itself "equally at odds with the evils of society and with the projects that are offered to relieve them." This was Emerson himself, severe critic of his state and federal government and with reforms of them which stopped with superficial remedies. The wise skeptic knows that "our life in this world is not of quite so easy interpretation as churches and school-books say. He does not wish to take ground against these benevolences," to sneer and vilify them. "But," he says, "there are doubts." To know that one does not know is valuable knowledge. "The dull pray; the geniuses are light mockers." However, Emerson was aware of the danger of "the levity of intellect."[48] His young friend Charles Newcomb, whom he calls "San Carlo," had reached the stage of thinking the lawgivers and saints infected. "They found the ark empty; saw, and would not tell; and tried to choke off their approaching followers, by saying, 'Action, action, my dear fellows, is for you!' "

Emerson compared this type of skepticism to "frost in July," but it was not as serious as "the cloy or satiety of the saints" to certain intellectuals and poets such as Byron and Goethe, which made them "fly for relief to the suspected and reviled Intellect, to the Understanding, the Mephistopheles, to the gymnastics of talent." This "hobgoblin" did not worry Emerson. "I think that the intellect and moral sentiment are unanimous; and that though philosophy extirpates bugbears, yet it supplies the natural checks of vice, and polarity to the soul." The result is greater faith in the natural and moral economy. He had no patience with philosophies of Determinism: "fate is for imbeciles; all is possible to the resolved mind."[49] The words *fate* and *destiny* express the idea that the laws of nature are not friendly to mankind, and of course Emerson believes they are.

In his lecture on "Shakespeare; or, the Poet," Emerson labors his thesis that "no great men are original.... The greatest genius is the most indebted man."[50] In justifying this notion Emerson shows his familiarity with Shakespeare scholarship: the desperate attempts to recover the poet's biography, and the technical studies of his sources. Shakespeare was not even experimental. He found the popular theater ready for him, and he soon became an expert at revising old manuscripts of plots and characters from Plutarch, English chronicles, histories of the "royal Henries," and a "string of doleful tragedies, merry Italian tales and Spanish voyages, which all the London 'prentices know."[51] The popular appeal of his material had already been tested. His mastery was in enlivening and presenting it in a diction and versification that surpassed all previous efforts. Edmund Malone had proven that the text of *Henry VIII* was only partly written by Shakespeare. Emerson says he himself can easily detect Shakespeare's lines because "the thought constructs the tune, so that reading for the sense will bring out the rhythm," whereas the older lines "are constructed on a given tune, and the verse has even a trace of pulpit eloquence."[52]

Instead of the worn-out theory of Shakespeare's "original genius," to which Emerson had been inclined in his earlier lectures, he now believes that this greatest of poets proves "that what is best written or done by genius in the world, was no man's work, but came by wide social labor, when a thousand wrought like one, sharing the same impulse."[53] The English Bible is a wonderful specimen of the strength and music of the English language. "But it was not made by one man, or at one time; but centuries and churches brought it to perfection." The translation of Plutarch "gets its excellence by being translation on translation . . . All the truly idiomatic and national phrases are kept, and all others successively picked out and thrown away."[54]

This assessment of Shakespeare's merit might seem to contradict Emerson's usual stress on individualism and self-reliance, but there are subtleties and paradoxes in his interpretations. In Shakespeare's own day "nobody suspected he was the poet of the human race."[55] He lived in an age of great writers, but those thought greatest have given place to the man regarded as a mere entertainer. His dramatic skill Emerson grants, but thinks he was more important as poet and philosopher. "He was a full man, who liked to talk; a brain exhaling thoughts and images, which, seeking vent, found the drama next at hand." And "what he has to say is of that weight as to withdraw some attention from the vehicle." He was not an "eminent writer," but an inconceivably wise man. "An omnipresent humanity co-ordinates all his faculties." His ability to transfer "the inmost truth of things into music and verse, makes him the type of the poet . . . Things were mirrored in his poetry without loss or blur."[56] (This is almost a reversion to the "original genius," who performed instinctively, almost unconsciously.)

Emerson always admired cheerfulness, and he thought Shakespeare had this "royal trait," as did also Chaucer, Homer, and Sa'di. "He [Shakespeare] loves virtue, not for its obligation but for its grace: he delights in the world, in man, in woman, for the lovely light that sparkles from them." Yet, attractive as Emerson found this trait, he concludes that it made Shakespeare "share the halfness and imperfection of humanity." He rested in the beauty of his creations "and never took the step which seemed inevitable to such genius, namely to explore the virtue which resides in these symbols and imparts this power . . ."[57] In "talent and mental power, the world of men has not his equal to show. But when the question is, to life and its materials and its auxiliaries, how does he profit me? . . . It is but a Twelfth Night, or Midsummer-Night's Dream, or Winter Evening's Tale."[58] How about the great tragedies? Emerson does not mention them. But then, we remember that he did not like tragedy. So he concludes that the world still awaits the Messiah, the true "poet-priest." He did not see that Shakespeare, like Plato, presented moral truth dramatically, not homiletically. There were times when Emerson could not escape his ministerial background.

In his lecture on Napoleon, Emerson also took an ambiguous attitude of admiration and dislike. Napoleon was never a real hero to Emerson, though he admired his energy, his intellectual and executive ability, and his determination. Emerson calls him "the incarnate Democrat," by which he means that Napoleon had the instincts for material success of the middle class.

> Bonaparte was the idol of common men because he had in transcendent degree the qualities and powers of common men. There is a certain satisfaction in coming down to the lowest ground of politics, for we get rid of cant and hypocrisy. Bonaparte wrought, in common with that great class he represented, for power and wealth,—but Bonaparte, specially, without any scruple as to the means. All the sentiments which embarrass men's pursuit of these objects, he set aside.[59]

In calling Napoleon an "incarnate Democrat," Emerson was almost (or, it may be, intentionally) punning on the word, for, as we have frequently seen, he regarded Presidents Jackson and Polk as also without scruples. He certainly had American politics in mind when he explained further:

> ... I said, Bonaparte represents the democrat, or the party of men of business, against the stationary or conservative party. I omitted then to say, what is material to the statement, namely that these two parties differ only as young and old. The democrat is a young conservative; the conservative is an old democrat. The aristocrat is the democrat ripe and gone to seed;—because both parties stand on the one ground of the supreme value of property, which one endeavors to get, and the other to keep. Bonaparte may be said to represent the whole history of this party, its youth and its age; yes, and with poetic justice its fate, in his own.[60]

This interpretation clearly reveals Emerson's own political-social position. He had always favored the Whigs over the Democrats, though he disliked their obsession with property. What was needed in politics, he thought, was *conscience*. Napoleon showed the tragic consequences of the use "of the powers of intellect without conscience." Eventually "Men found that his absorbing egotism was deadly to all other men." He failed because he violated "the nature of things, the eternal law of man and of the world . . . Every experiment by multitudes or by individuals, that has a sensual and selfish aim, will fail. . . . As long as our civilization is essentially one of property, of fences, of exclusiveness, it will be mocked by delusions."[61]

Emerson had been trying to come to terms with Goethe ever since he became acquainted with Carlyle, who admired Goethe supremely. Emerson bought a pocket edition of Goethe's writings, in German, in fifty-five volumes, and laboriously taught himself to read them. Possibly the effort colored his response to Goethe, though he had a natural dislike for any man who enjoyed the world and sensual gratifications with as much gusto as Goethe did. "Writer," Emerson calls him, defining the term as a "secretary, who is to report the doings of the miraculous spirit of life that everywhere throbs and works."[62] He receives the facts into his mind, then selects the eminent and characteristic. This ability Emerson grants Goethe, who seemed to possess the most encyclopedic mind of his time, as scholar, scientist, and philosopher.

I described Bonaparte as a representative of the popular external life and aims of the nineteenth century. Its other half, its poet, is Goethe, a man quite domesticated in the century, breathing its air, enjoying its fruits, impossible at any earlier time, and taking away, by his colossal parts, the reproach of weakness which but for him would lie on the intellectual works of the period.[63]

Emerson never liked the first part of *Faust,* though he thought it a brilliant idea to recreate the Devil in the form of a European gentleman who represented "pure intellect, applied,—as always there is a tendency,—to the service of the senses . . ." Mephistopheles is "the first organic figure that has been added [to literature] for some ages, and which will remain as long as the Prometheus." The second part of *Faust* Emerson called "a philosophy of literature set in poetry," the result of eighty years of wise observation. "This reflective and critical wisdom makes the poem more truly the flower of this time."[64]

In his conversation with Wordsworth in 1833, it will be recalled, Emerson had defended *Wilhelm Meister,* and had even forced the old poet to agree to read it (he had read only the first part) instead of judging the novel by its English reputation. But actually Emerson had some of Wordsworth's moral compunctions himself. Though he joins the admirers who call the novel "the only delineation of modern society," he thinks the conclusion lame and immoral. He prefers George Sand's *Consuelo* as "a truer and more dignified picture." Her hero breathes and works for man, in poverty and extreme sacrifice: "Goethe's hero, on the contrary, has so many weaknesses and impurities and keeps such bad company, that the sober English public, when the book was translated, were disgusted."[65]

Emerson's final quarrel with Goethe is that he believed "a man exists for culture; not for what he can accomplish, but for what can be accomplished in him." This idea dominates *Dichtung und Wahrheit.* The German doctrine that man exists for the State, not the State for man, came later, but Emerson seemed to have a premonition of where Goethe's attitude toward culture could lead. Carlyle thought him the healthiest man of his time, and Emerson grants that he was "entirely at home and happy in his century and the world. None was so fit to live, or more heartily enjoyed the game." But he was incapable of self-surrender to Emerson's beloved "moral sentiment." He was not devoted to "pure truth; but to truth for the sake of culture."[66]

IV

Sometime in the late winter or early spring of 1846, Emerson fantasized in Journal O on "the central man." Afterward he superscribed, *"Walking one day in the fields I met a man."* It might have been a trial line for one of Wallace Stevens's poems, for the "central man" theme, perhaps remembered from Emerson, attracted Stevens. Presumably Emerson was thinking of turning his Journal musing into a parable of the complete, or ideal, man, which he saw only partially exemplified in the "Representative Men" of his lectures. Here is his unrevised Journal entry:

> We shall one day talk with the central man, and see again in the varying play of his features all the features which have characterised our darlings, & stamped themselves in fire on the heart: then, as the discourse rises out of the domestic & personal, & his countenance waxes grave & great, we shall fancy that we talk with Socrates, & behold his countenance: then the discourse changes, & the man, and we see the face & hear the tones of Shakspeare,—the body & the soul of Shakspeare living & speaking with us, only that Shakspeare seems below us. A change again, and the countenance of our companion is youthful and beardless, he talks of form & colour & the riches of design; it is the face of the painter Raffaelle that confronts us with the visage of a girl, & the easy audacity of a creator. In a moment it was Michel Angelo; then Dante; afterwards it was the Saint Jesus, and the immensities of moral truth & power embosomed us. And so it appears that these great secular personalities were only expressions of his [the central man's] face chasing each other like the rack of clouds. Then all will subside, & I find myself alone. I dreamed & did not know my dreams.[67]

A variety of subjective interpretations could be made of this interesting daydream. What did Emerson mean by the last sentence? Probably that the protean character in his "dream" did not exist in any person he knew or had studied in literature or history, though he had glimpsed intimations of him in Socrates, Shakespeare, Raphael, Michelangelo, Dante, and so on. The list could be extended, yet none would be "the central man": "these great secular [even including "Saint Jesus"] personalities were only expressions of his face chasing each other like the rack of clouds." A composite of all these historical persons would fall short of the archetype *Man*. Nowhere did Emerson attempt to describe "the central man," but we may find hints in several of his compositions.

Perhaps the "Orphic poet" in *Nature* (1836) gives the first clue—though still earlier ones might be found in Emerson's sermons. "Man is the dwarf of himself. Once he was permeated and dissolved by spirit."[68] This was the original Man out of whom God created men, in whom, for some mysterious reason, spirit and matter began to grow apart. "At present, man applies to nature but half his force." He is now completely dualistic. "Yet sometimes he starts in his slumber, and wonders at himself and his house, and muses strangely at the resemblance betwixt him and it." *House* is a symbol of his body, or his physical existence, in which he meets the exigencies of his life by use of his *understanding*. Emerson wants to awaken him from his sleep to consciousness of his lost Reason. The final message of *Nature* is:

> Know then that the world exists for you. . . . All that Adam had, all that Caesar could, you have and can do. Adam called his house, heaven and earth; Caesar called his house, Rome; you perhaps call yours, a cobbler's trade; a hundred acres of ploughed land; or a scholar's garret. Yet line for line and point for point your dominion is as great as theirs, though without fine names. Build therefore your own world.[69]

In his lectures on "Representative Men" Emerson was trying to show in them characteristics which could be evaluated and utilized (or avoided, as in some of Swedenborg's and Napoleon's objectionable traits) by his audience in achieving an ideal life. On July 27, 1846, Emerson wrote Elizabeth Hoar, who was visiting friends in New Haven: "We should be no better than parsnips, if we could not still look over our shoulders at the Power that drives us, and escape from private insignificance into a faith in the transcendent significance of our doing & being . . ."[70] He was impatient to show her some poems he had lately written in which he had attempted to make this "escape" through ecstasy-inducing rhythms and tropes. The underlying motif of the poems he wanted to show Elizabeth ("Mithridates," "Merlin," and "Bacchus") was a glimpse of the "power" he attributed to his "central man." After many years of discouraging trial and experimentation, he was beginning to produce verses that satisfied him better than the prose with which he entertained lecture audiences.

CHAPTER XXI

The Gai Science

Poetry is the *gai science.*[1]

I

New England still did not observe Christmas as a holiday in 1846 (gifts were usually exchanged at New Year's), and on this day James Munroe and Company published Emerson's *Poems* (dated 1847), containing fifty-nine poems, printed on 251 small pages (16*mo*), and bound in white boards—a few in cloth. Emerson called it his "little white book."[2] On December 29 *The Boston Courier* reviewed it, calling the book "one of the most peculiar and original volumes of poetry ever published in the United States."[3] This would be the reaction of nearly everyone who read it, from Longfellow and Lowell in America to Carlyle in England. And if "peculiar" meant different, unconventional, they were right. Emerson's poems in no way resembled the productions of the country's most widely read and admired poets: Bryant's *Poems* (1832), Whittier's *Ballads and Anti-Slavery Poems* (1838), Longfellow's *Voices of the Night* (1839), or Poe's *Raven and Other Poems* (1845).

The objections made to Emerson's *Poems* were both literary and religious. Readers accustomed to Poe's syncopated rhythms and rich rhymes, or Longfellow's facile meters and bland diction, were not prepared for Emerson's innovations in rhyme and meter. A few critics also objected to his religious views in his poems as in his prose. In *The Christian Examiner* Cyrus Bartol protested that nowhere in the *Poems* did Emerson recognize the merits of Christianity, or even distinguish between God and man.

Orestes Brownson, recently turned Catholic after experimenting with several other denominations, said emphatically in *The Massachusetts Quarterly Review* that Emerson had written "hymns to the devil."[4] Even Emerson's most intimate friends expressed only lukewarm appreciation of his poetic efforts. Margaret Fuller in her *Papers on Literature and Art* (1846), collected from her critical articles in *The New-York Daily Tribune,* expressed serious reservations:

> R. W. Emerson, in melody, in subtle beauty of thought and expression, takes the highest rank upon this list [of American poets]. But his poems are mostly philosophical, which is not the truest kind of poetry. They want the simple force of nature and passion, and, while they charm the ear and interest the mind, fail to wake far-off echoes in the heart. The imagery wears a symbolical air, and serves rather as illustration, than to delight us by fresh and glowing forms of life.[5]

These words were written before Margaret Fuller had the volume of *Poems* in hand, but she had read most of the contents in *The Dial* or in manuscript. Caroline Sturgis had, of course, also read the poems in manuscript, including, probably, "printer's copy." She wrote Emerson in October 1846:

> I must tell you the simple truth about the poems: at first I could not read them because they had the old words in them, but I remembered that every spring brings the same flowers, every night the same stars, & having thus soothed my feelings I found much pleasure in them as thoughts— perhaps not as poems. Should not a poem be an old thing transmuted into a new one—into something rich & strange: withering leaves suddenly changed into gold as in these October days . . . Your poems are too good not to have been written better than they would be in prose, & yet I take a mischievous delight in seeing how ingeniously they are contrived . . . you should have . . . followed the Muse in longer silence through your pine-vistas & not have written down her words before they were fully uttered.[6]

As usual, not all of Caroline's phrases are coherent—what are "pine-vistas"?—but it is clear that she thought Emerson's verses were carelessly written and inferior to his prose. Perhaps as an apology for her brash criticism, she adds: "I should like to have red hair & eyes like a comet. But redhaired people are always a little too active; they cannot stand still but have to shift from one foot to the other to keep their balance." Whether she herself was such a precariously balanced person or not, her criticism of Waldo's poems does not reveal even a superficial understanding of them, making one wonder whether he had not overrated her intellect. He had a tendency to let his affections enhance his judgment of his friends: he thought, for example, that Ellery Channing was a poet. In fact, when negotiating a contract for publication of his own poems, he had insisted that Munroe also publish an edition of Channing's.

Emerson had arranged for John Chapman in London to publish a British edition of his poems simultaneously with the American. On January 21, 1847, he wrote Carlyle:

Long before this time you ought to have received from John Chapman a copy of *Emerson's Poems,* so called, which he was directed to send you. Poor man, you need not open them. I know all you can say. I printed them, not because I was deceived into a belief that they were poems, but because of the softness or hardness of heart of many friends here who have made it a point to have them circulated. Once having set out to print, I obeyed the solicitations of John Chapman, of an ill-omened street in London [Newgate], to send him the book in manuscript, for the better securing of copyright.[7]

Carlyle replied on March 2 that he had read the *Poems* while visiting friends in Hampshire, with "a real satisfaction and some tone of the Eternal Melodies sounding, afar off, ever and anon, in my ear!" Carlyle was no great admirer of poetry—except Goethe's—and this fact should be borne in mind in evaluating his ambivalent response to Emerson's:

A grand View of the Universe, everywhere the sound (unhappily *far off,* as it were) of a valiant, genuine Human Soul: this, even under rhyme, is a satisfaction worth some struggling for. But indeed you are very perverse; and through this perplexed *un*-diaphanous element, you do not fall on me like radiant summer rainbows, like floods of sunlight, but with thin piercing radiances which affect me like the light of the *stars.* It is so: I wish you would become *concrete,* and write in prose the straightest way; but under any form I must put up with you; that is my lot.[8]

Carlyle said Chapman's edition was "very beautiful," and he predicted that it would readily sell in Great Britain. It would be bought and *studied*. Reviewers would probably not dare to call it "unintelligible moonshine"—perhaps because Emerson already had a reputation in England. Then Carlyle added: "It is my fixed opinion that we are all at sea as to what is called Poetry, Art, &c., in these times; laboring under a dreadful incubus of *Tradition* . . ." Though this statement rather gives away his uncertainty as to whether Emerson's verses are poetry, he is not sympathetic with the "incubus of Tradition," and seems to realize that Emerson's *Poems* should be judged by new criteria. In that he was right.

But why had Emerson pretended to Carlyle that he had printed his poems only to satisfy his friends? Some friends had doubtless importuned him, Elizabeth Hoar especially. But others, as we have seen, had been puzzled by them in manuscript, or when printed in *The Dial*. Habitually modest about his own talents, Emerson felt less confidence in his poems than in his lectures and essays because they had not met with the same comprehension and audience response. Yet he was secretly proud of this volume. Otherwise, why had he sent gift copies to more than one hundred and fifty of his friends and acquaintances, as his Journal records?[9]

Since his childhood, Emerson had wanted to be a poet. When he reached the age of discretion he realized that his juvenile verses had been vastly overpraised by his too easily impressed teachers and relatives. After reading the Romantic poets, he turned his back on the neoclassic tradition, which in his youth had formed his ideas of what poetry should be. Wordsworth taught him to be receptive to intimations of eternal truth and beauty in moments of sudden "illuminations," or heightened sensibility in the presence of nature, symbol of Divine Reason. Recently, his reading the Persian poets, even in a clumsy German translation, which he had laboriously retranslated into English, had led him to associate poetry with music, dance, and intoxication of the senses. On July 6, 1841, he had written in his Journal:

In every week there is some hour when I read my commission in every cipher of nature, and know that I was made for another office, a professor of the Joyous Science, a detector & delineator of occult harmonies & unpublished beauties, a herald of civility, nobility, learning, & wisdom; an af-

firmer of the One Law, yet as one who should affirm it in music or dancing, a priest of the Soul . . .[10]

The following January in a lecture on "Prospects" (in the series on
"The Times") he repeated his words on being a "professor of the Joyous Science," and added: "The effect of every fine natural gift is to exhila-
rate. Can you sing well, dance well, speak, write, blow the flute, or horn,
jump, dive, swim, fell a tree, build a house, paint a picture, whistle, mimic,
ventriloquize, or whatsoever[?]"[11] The gifted person finds pleasure in
creating pleasure. The poet has a wide range of subjects to select from, but
he does best when he produces what most pleases himself. Later, in "Poetry and Imagination," he would elaborate this idea:

> What else is it to be a poet? What are his garland and singing robes?
> What but a sensibility so keen that the scent of an elder-blow, or the
> timber-yard and corporation-works of a nest of pismires is event enough
> for him,—all emblems and personal appeals to him. His wreath and robe is
> to do what he enjoys; emancipation from other men's questions, and glad
> study of his own; escape from the gossip and routine of society, and the
> allowed right and practice of making better. . . .
> Poetry is the *gai science.*[12]

From Emerson, Nietzsche would later pick up this phrase and entitle
one of his rhapsodic books *Die fröhliche Wissenschaft* (*"la gaya scienza"*),
which Walter Kaufmann has translated as *The Gay Science*[13] (an earlier
translation was called *The Joyous Wisdom*). For this book Nietzsche chose
an epigraph from Emerson's essay on "History": *"Dem Dichter und Weisen
sind alle Dinge befreundet und geweiht, alle Erlebnisse nützlich, alle Tage heilig,
alle Menschen göttlich"* ("To the poet, to the philosopher, to the saint, all
things are friendly and sacred, all events profitable, all days holy, all men
are divine"). Emerson associated "the joyous science" with Zoroaster, as a
result of reading an article on "The Oracle of Zoroaster,[14] the Founder of
the Persian Magi" (1835), and Zoroaster (Greek spelling of the Persian
Zarathustra) was a link between him and Nietzsche, in *Ecce Homo* as well
as in *Thus Spake Zarathustra.*[15]

The importance of Emerson's influence on Nietzsche (though the men
were more different than alike) is that it gives a suggestive clue to the na-

ture of Emerson's poetry. "Gay science" comes from the Provençal *gai saber*. Though Nietzsche translated *saber* as *Wissenschaft* (science), he knew that it did not mean the physical sciences, nor does *Wissenschaft* mean "wisdom" in German, as Kaufmann points out. In *Ecce Homo* Nietzsche says that *The Day of Dawn* was "emphatically reminiscent of the Provençal concept of *gaya scienza*—that unity of *singer, knight,* and *free spirit* which distinguishes the wonderful early culture of the Provençals from all equivocal cultures."[16] Emerson, of course, was no troubadour, but he conceived *gai science* to be light-footed, Dionysian, scornful of all rigidities in religion, philosophy, and social custom. Many of his poems compensate for his self-conscious personal reserve. As a poet he had a special gift for laughter, directed at himself or at a pompous antagonist. Though he disliked cachinnations, he reveled in silent laughter. Consequently he evaded—and still does—the solemn reader of his poems. The role of Bacchus was one of the masks he wore as a poet, but it was not a false mask. Behind it he expressed a real though little-known side of his character.

The Bacchus role grew out of the combined influence of what might seem to be two incompatible sources: Neoplatonism and the Persian poets Hafiz and Sa'di, whom Emerson read in a German translation, as mentioned above, but this was before his Waterville address. Proclus he had read at intervals in Taylor's translation. Sometime in the spring of 1843 (the exact month is not indicated) he received a new infusion of enthusiasm for this Neoplatonist, as William Butler Yeats would also a century later:

> I read Proclus for my opium, it excites my imagination to let sail before me the pleasing & grand figures of gods & daemons & demoniacal men[.] . . . By all these & so many "rare & brave words" I am filled with hilarity & spring, my heart dances, my sight is quickened, I behold shining relations between all beings, and am impelled to write and almost to sing. I think one would grow handsome who read Proclus much & well.
>
> But of this inebriation I spoke of, it is an old knowledge that Intellect by its relation to what is prior to Intellect is a god. This is inspiration.[17]

Three years later Emerson bought a copy of Hafiz's *Divan* in Elizabeth Peabody's bookshop in Boston.[18] However, he knew something about Sa'di and Hafiz before then, for in his Journals for 1841–43 he refers several times to these Persian poets, and he was prepared for the *Divan* before buying it. Thus in the months immediately preceding the publication of his *Poems* the spiritual ecstasy of Proclus blended in his imagination with Hafiz's intoxication of the senses. From *The Book of the Cupbearer* he translates (by way of von Hammer) over one hundred and fifty lines, which he printed in his *Poems* as "From the Persian of Hafiz":

> Butler, fetch the ruby wine
> Which with sudden greatness fills us;
>
> .   .   .
>
> Bring to me the liquid fire
> Zoroaster sought in dust:
> To Hafiz, revelling, 'tis allowed
> To pray to Matter and to Fire.[19]
>
> .   .   .
>
> Bring me wine which maketh glad,
>
> .   .   .
>
> That I reason quite expunge,
> And plant banners on the worlds.
>
> .   .   .
>
> Bring wine, that I overspring
> Both worlds at a single leap.[20]

That Emerson took the wine of inspiration to be symbolical is evident in "Bacchus," not a translation but an imitation: "Bring me wine, but wine which never grew / In the belly of the grape." Vicariously Emerson shared Hafiz's sensual abandon and his mocking of the pious Fakirs. He was fascinated by the Persian poet's imagery, dancing rhythms, and diction. This influence would continue, and as late as 1866 Emerson would write in his Journal:

> Hafiz's poetry is marked by nothing more than his habit of playing with all magnitudes, mocking at them. What is the moon or the sun's course or heaven, and the angels, to his darling's mole or eyebrow? Destiny is a scurvy night-thief who plays him or her a bad trick. . . . But I am always struck with the fact that mind delights in measuring itself thus with matter,—with history. A thought, any thought, pressed, followed, opened, dwarfs nature, custom, and all but itself.[21]

In Journal O (1846) Emerson made one of his smoothest translations of Hafiz, which he copied without punctuation and never finished for publication:

> Come let us strew roses
> And pour wine in the cup
> Break up the roof of heaven
> And throw it into new forms .
>
> So soon the army of cares
> Shed the blood of the true
> So will I with the cupbearer
> Shatter the building of woe . . .[22]

J. D. Yohannan points out that Emerson's interest in Persian poetry coincided with "his first significant poetic production. His most characteristic manner, that of a cryptic and often metrically crude expression—giving the effect, in words, of roughly hewn sculpture—is certain to be found in the plainly rendered German versions of Persian poetry by von Hammer."[23] This is an important clue to the "crudity" of Emerson's poems which so puzzled and annoyed his contemporaries.

Of course the Persian influence was assimilated with the Welsh, the Anglo-Saxon, the Classical (Greek and Roman), and English Romanticism. "Merlin," for example, is ostensibly "bardic," but some of the imagery, and certainly the rhythms, might be Persian (via the German translation):

> Great is the art,
> Great be the manners, of the bard,
> He shall not his brain encumber
> With the coil of rhythm and number;
> But, leaving rule and pale forethought,
> He shall aye climb
> For his rhyme,
> 'Pass in, pass in,' the angels say,
> 'In to the upper doors,
> Nor count compartments of the floors,
> But mount to paradise
> By the stairway of surprise.'[24]

II

The earliest poem in date of composition in the 1847 volume is "Good-Bye," written in Roxbury in 1823, while Emerson was unhappily teaching in his brother's school for girls in Boston. Sixteen years later his friend the Reverend James Freeman Clarke, then a Unitarian pastor in Louisville, Kentucky, asked him to contribute a poem to his *Western Messenger,* and Emerson sent this poem, with an apology for its misanthropy, "a shade deeper than belongs to me . . ."[25]

Emerson had written better poems before 1839 which he might have sent. One was "The River,"[26] composed in 1827, soon after his return from Florida. For some reason he never printed this poem, possibly because he realized how much it owed to Wordsworth's "Tintern Abbey," in versification (blank verse) and nature conceits. He had returned to his "father's fields" and "the rock" (Harold Bloom sees the rock as a symbol of faith),[27] "where, yet a simple child," he caught his first fish. The voices of nature spoke to him, and he was soothed by the eloquent speech of the river, the trees, the grass, the sighing wind, all uttering "sounds of 'monishment / And grave parental love." Wordsworth had taught him what to feel.

One reason for Emerson's not including "The River" in his 1847 *Poems* may have been that he had based "Musketaquid" (the Indian name for the Concord River) on his experiences in the Old Manse, the town, and the surrounding fields and hills. Using the same Wordsworthian blank verse, he stressed his contentment with the low-lying village, the sluggish stream, and his own modest wants. The sentiments of "The River" are those of a weary young man resting from his travels; those of "Musketaquid" are of a mature man who respects his yeoman neighbors, men whose brains and character are the local meadows and wooded hills transmuted; while he feels himself to be "a willow of the wilderness, / Loving the wind that bent me."

"Good-Bye," written four years earlier than "The River," shows the influence of Gray, Collins, Goldsmith, and other poets of their period, rather than Wordsworth. The octosyllabic couplets (with rhyming variations in the first stanza) keep step to a monotonous tune, obvious rhymes, and worn epithets: "weary crowds," "driven foam," "Flattery's frowning face," and so on. Yet in spite of the conventional generalizations and personifications, the lines are pithy and buoyant, giving promise of a better poet:

O, when I am safe in my sylvan home,
I tread on the pride of Greece and Rome;
And when I am stretched beneath the pines,
Where the evening star so holy shines,
I laugh at the lore and the pride of man,
At the sophist schools, and the learned clan;
For what are they all, in their high conceit,
When man in the bush with God may meet?

"The Apology" is almost a companion piece to "Good-Bye," though the date of composition is unknown. The apology is:

Think me not unkind and rude
    That I walk alone in grove and glen;
I go to the god of the wood
    To fetch his word to men.

Prosodically, it is smoother than "Good-Bye," and is just as conventionally Romantic: the poet's idleness is not slothfulness, but a harvesting of a "second crop" from the acres of his song. It is not a great poem, but it is a gem of its minor kind.

Emerson had already printed in *The Dial* three of Ellen Tucker's love poems to him. These he included in his 1847 edition with five of his poems to her, which he had also printed in *The Dial*. They show only that Emerson in 1829 was steeped in traditional English love lyrics. Their personal associations for him made him value them beyond their merits.

During the 1830s Emerson wrote only a few poems, mostly short but increasingly personal and introspective lyrics. In "Each and All" he versified in four-stress couplets a childhood experience at the seashore, which he had remembered and recorded in his Journal on May 16, 1834.[28] On the beach he had been so charmed by the shapes and colors of some shells that he carried them home, only to find them grown dry and ugly. From this experience he learned what later as an adult writer he would call "composition": that beauty does not exist in isolation. Both the experience and the diction sound like Robert Frost:

I wiped away the weeds and foam,
I fetched my sea-born treasures home;

But the poor, unsightly, noisome things
Had left their beauty on the shore
With the sun, and the sand, and the wild uproar.

But the poet goes beyond this rational explanation. Like Wordsworth, he had learned to yield himself "to the perfect whole," while overhead "soared the eternal sky, / Full of light and of deity," and he heard again (as if recollected in Wordsworth's "tranquility") "The rolling river, the morning bird," and felt Beauty stealing through his senses. Similarly in "The Rhodora" (1834) Emerson versifies the idea that "Beauty is its own excuse for being." His imagery is still somewhat general (sea winds, solitude, woods, desert), but he is beginning to use more color: purple petals float in black water, in which the red-bird cools his plumage, an anticipation of Amy Lowell's "Imagism."

On May 14, 1837, when the nation was suffering from a devastating economic depression, Emerson wrote in his Journal: "The humblebee & the pine warbler seem to me the proper objects of attention in these disastrous times."[29] Then he proceeded to write a sixty-three-line poem on "The Humble-Bee" (usually called bumblebee), "Epicurean of June / . . . Wiser far than human seer, / Yellow-breeched philosopher!" The humble-bee sees only what is fair, sips the sweet, and sleeps through woe and want when the cold winds of winter arrive. In this whimsical mood Emerson developed a light touch for the philosophical lyric, as Auden and Yeats would do after him. By reducing the natural accents to three and using extra unstressed syllables he could quicken the rhythm and suggest the jerky, darting movement of the humble-bee.

The octosyllabic couplet had now become Emerson's favorite, and seemingly most natural, prosodic medium. He could use it for either reflective or buoyant moods, as Milton had done in "L'Allegro" and "Il Penseroso." It may have been from Milton that he learned to take liberties with this verse form, such as beginning with a headless iamb (omitting the initial unstressed syllable), ending with a feminine rhyme, inserting extra unstressed syllables to quicken the tempo, or using spondees for weight and emphasis. In "The Problem" (dated November 10, 1839) he adroitly pounds home his strong paradoxical convictions by a regular beat, slow and emphatic:

I like a church; I like a cowl;
I love a prophet of the soul;
And on my heart monastic isles
Fall like sweet strains, or pensive smiles;
Yet not for all his faith can see
Would I that cowled churchman be.

The paradox in this poem is not limited to the poet's admiration and aversion for the priestly life; it also extends to his theory of inspiration:

These temples grew as grows the grass;
Art might obey, but not surpass.
The passive Master lent his hand
To the vast soul that o'er him planned;
And the same power that reared the shrine,
Bestrode the tribes that knelt within.
Ever the fiery Pentecost
Girds with one flame the countless host,
Trances the heart through chanting choirs,
And through the priest the mind inspires.

If the Divine Mind inspires the priest, why does the poet find it impossible to wear his robes? Perhaps because he must have his inspiration direct, bypassing temples and intermediaries, even though they may be inspired, too. Emerson had expressed similar ideas, though less personally, in his essays (and lectures) on "Self-Reliance," "The Over-Soul," and "Spiritual Laws."

The same mastery of diction and rhythm enabled Emerson to write that almost flawless occasional poem, "Concord Hymn" (1837). It was sung to the hymn tune of "Old Hundred," and perhaps its firm structure owes much to the familiar hymn meter. However, this poem in which "the embattled farmers . . . fired the shot heard round the world" is hardly typical of Emerson, and may even sound more like Whittier (for example, "Ein Feste Burg Ist Unser Gott"), but it is one poem in which each word seems inevitable and permanent as the letters cut in the marble monument.

Some of Emerson's best poems on nature were written in the early 1840s, such as "Woodnotes" (1840), "The Sphinx" (1841), and "The

Snow-Storm" (1841). In the 1847 *Poems,* "Woodnotes" begins with these
lines:

> For this present, hard
> Is the fortune of the bard,
>   Born out of time;
> All his accomplishment,
> From Nature's utmost treasure spent,
>   Booteth not him.

When he revised this poem for his 1876 *Selections,* Emerson dropped these
lines as too self-pitying and began with "When the pine tosses its cones,"
but in both versions the poem still protests that what the poet knows
"nobody wants"; then it lyrically describes what the poet knows, which is
intimate knowledge of the appearance and actions of nature.

The "forest seer" in section two sounds so much like Thoreau that it is
difficult not to make this interpretation, but Emerson may have been describing an ideal rather than a specific person, as his son reported.[30] In fact,
the naturalist in the heroic couplets of section three, who visits the lumber
camp in Maine, anticipated Thoreau's trip by five years. It is quite possible
that this poem influenced Thoreau to make his first trip to Maine in 1846,
later described in *The Maine Woods.*

In the second part of "Woodnotes" the pine tree sings the thoughts and
sentiments Emerson had expressed in *Nature* and various essays, as well as
in his earlier lectures on science. Here the concept of the creation of the
world is a curious mixture of the account of Creation in Genesis and
nineteenth-century science—almost anticipating the twentieth-century
"Big Bang" theory of the cosmologists. The world slept as an egg of stone
until "God said, 'Throb!'" and gave it motion, which then continued in
ceaseless metamorphosis:

> Halteth never in one shape,
> But forever doth escape,
> Like wave of flame, into new forms
> Of gem, and air, of plants, and worms.
> I, that to-day am a pine,
> Yesterday was a bundle of grass.

This has been called pantheism, but it is a poetic version of Emerson's doctrine of the Godhead or Primal Mind in nature.

In "The Sphinx" (1841) the two-stress lines sound like a ritual chant, almost hypnotic in effect—not inappropriate for the riddle motif. Emerson's model could have been the Anglo-Saxon two-beat strophe or hemistich, or Persian verse, if he was sufficiently well acquainted with it at the time (see section III below). Unlike the Anglo-Saxon, Emerson uses rhyme instead of alliteration in a pattern of three- and two-stress lines. The verses beginning with a stressed syllable emphasize the thought with startling concentration:

> The fáte of the mán-chìld;
>   The méaning of mán;
> Knówn frúit of the unknówn;
>   Dædálian plán;
> Oút of sléeping a wáking,
>   Oút of wáking a sléep;
> Lífe déath ovèrtáking;
>   Deép undernéath déep?[31]

Contemporary readers of this poem were so concerned with its philosophical meaning that they could not appreciate its merry tune and ironical humor. Though as childishly simple as Mother Goose, the tune is also subtle, mocking the cheerful optimism of the poet—Emerson laughing at himself, for the sphinx refutes his "Transcendentalist" answers. As William Sloane Kennedy pointed out, Emerson's sphinx is not the Egyptian sphinx but the riddle-propounding creature in the form of a winged lion with the face of a woman sent by Hera to ravage the Thebans. (Emerson had seen a picture of the stone statue of the Theban sphinx.) She sat by the roadside and demanded that every passing Greek answer her riddle or forfeit his life. Most critics have assumed that the poet in the poem wins by causing the sphinx to rise out of stone and "flower" into the beautiful forms of nature, but Kennedy's interpretation is more plausible:

We are left to infer that, like her prototype, she gobbled the poet sooner or later. For she had reminded him that instead of answering the question-riddle with his reply of *Love at the centre* he was not competent to reply at all, since he was but a part of her (Nature) and so a part of the question-riddle or mystery itself. If he could only see and really know his physical eye, know that it only belonged to the phenomenal, or illusory, world, he would know that a solution obtained by means of its reports could not be of absolute value.[32]

"The Snow-Storm," also published in *The Dial* in 1841, has no thematic link with "The Sphinx," except that it mocks man-made art. Reverting to skillfully handled blank verse, Emerson describes a farmhouse isolated by a snowstorm, so effectively that Whittier would borrow some of the lines as an epigraph for his "Snow-Bound." But the fragile capriciousness of this natural phenomenon distinguishes Emerson's poem from Whittier's domestic drama. In one night the snow *mimics* the stone structures that men require ages to build. This poem need not have had any source except Emerson's delight at nature's freaks and his amusement at human pretensions and limitations.

A few years later Emerson based "Hamatreya" on a passage in Book IV of the *Vishnu Purana* about the folly of princes who "cherish the confidence of ambition when they are but foam upon the wave."[33] (Why Emerson changed the Hindu name Maitreya to Hamatreya is not known.) Though the theme was borrowed from a foreign literature, Emerson found it surprisingly adequate for his Concord neighbors and ancestors. "Minott, Lee [in 1876 changed to Bulkeley, Hunt], Willard, Hosmer, Meriam, Flint," were among the most ancient family names in historic Concord, and pride in ownership was understandably characteristic of them. The irony of the poem is accentuated by the abnormal number of stresses in the first and third lines. Then the Earth-song in a sort of runic tune mimics and taunts the mortal tenants of the "sit-fast acres." The singsong rhythm is perfect for its purpose, and so also is the slower tempo in the coda:

> When I heard the Earth-song
> I was no longer brave;
> My avarice cooled
> Like lust in the chill of the grave.

A year later (1846) Emerson was still in a satirical mood. In "Alphonso of Castille" the king is vexed that nature lets things degenerate, and he asks the gods, whom he addresses as "Seigniors," whether *they* or "Mildew" are in charge of the world. He will give them some good advice. No more famine: "Ply us now with a full diet." Too many people in the world? Simple: "kill nine in ten" and "Stuff their nine brains in one hat . . ."[34] Also make man more durable, as long-lived as the marble statues he erects: "So shall ye have a man of the sphere / Fit to grace the solar year."

In the same vein, "Mithridates" is the song of a man who wants to make himself immune to all kinds of poisons by eating them. He begs to be filled with every hurtful thing in nature:

> I will use the world, and sift it,
> To a thousand humors shift it,
> As you spin a cherry.

In "Guy" we find a man to whom no misfortune ever happens. He has "caught Nature in his snares," without effort or reason; he was simply born lucky. There is no irony in the poem, as in Edwin Arlington Robinson's "Richard Cory," about a man similarly fortunate and envied, who "Went home and put a bullet through his head." Emerson intended a *jeu d'esprit,* nothing more.

In "Uriel" the humor is more purposeful; perhaps it is the most pointed satire Emerson ever wrote. Its framework is an allegory, based on Milton's Arch-Angel in *Paradise Lost,* Book III, of the furor caused by Emerson's "Divinity School Address." The poem could have been written anytime between the summer of 1845 and its publication in the 1847 *Poems,* but the humor is more characteristic of Emerson's mid-1840s years, and the philosophy also.

Milton's Uriel was "The sharpest-sighted Spirit of all in Heav'n," who interpreted God's will to the other angels, including the treacherous Satan.[35] The first stanza of "Uriel" merely sets the scene; the only detail in it of a satirical nature is that Paradise stands for Harvard. Uriel's lapse began when Seyd (Professor Andrews Norton) heard the "young gods" (divinity students) discussing impious theological ideas. Uriel (Emerson), the speaker "with the low tones that decide," had voiced the doctrine that "Line in nature is not found," and that "Evil will bless, and ice will burn." To the "stern old war-gods" (Norton, Henry Ware, and others) this seemed like bending "the balance-beam of Fate" (denial of evil and providential retribution).

The "sad self-knowledge" that fell on Uriel was Emerson's realization that Harvard and leaders in the Unitarian Church had abandoned him. Consequently, Uriel "Withdrew ... into his cloud," and a "forgetting wind" stole over him. Yet Emerson continued his "truth-speaking" through his lectures and writings, and he liked to think that he shamed his "angel" critics: "a blush tinged the upper sky, / And the gods shook, they knew not why."

III

Exactly when Emerson first became acquainted with Persia's other great poet, Sa'di [Musleh Al-Din, Shaikh, 1194–1282 or –92], is not known, but he mentioned Saadi (his spelling) in Journal G in 1841, and published his poem "Saadi" in *The Dial* in 1842. Von Hammer printed some translations of Sa'di in his second volume of Persian poetry, but he did not represent him as fully as he had Hafiz in the first volume. Possibly Emerson already knew one of the earlier translations of *Gulistan,* or *The Rose-Garden.* What is definite is that early in the decade Sa'di became Emerson's favorite poet, and that he used the name as a guise for himself.[36]

Why Sa'di appealed to Emerson is not difficult to understand. *Gulistan,* the most popular of his works in translation, is a humorous miscellany on ethical subjects in rhymed prose. *Bustan* is a long moralizing poem that must have reminded Emerson of his perennial favorite, Plutarch's *Morals.* However, Sa'di's best poetry is said to be in his *ghazals,* a form resembling the English sonnet.[37] (Emerson called one of his imitations "Ghaselle.") One critic says, "As a thinker and moralist, despite his moderate fatalism, Sa'di looks upon the world with humorous sympathy. His moral teachings, although flavoured with mystical idealism, reveal a preference for practical wisdom."[38] This could be a description of Emerson, Lowell's Plotinus-Montaigne-Yankee—though Emerson's fatalism was more subtle than Sa'di's.

The first trait that Emerson shared with Sa'di was a love of solitude:

> God, who gave to him the lyre,
> Of all mortals the desire,
> For all breathing men's behoof,
> Straightly charged him, 'Sit aloof;'

> Many may come,
> But one shall sing;
> Two touch the string,
> The harp is dumb.
> Though there come a million,
> Wise Saadi dwells alone.

Saadi loves the race of men, but he must dwell alone in order to share the wisdom of the gods. The sad-eyed Fakirs preach the decay of the world and say that Allah sends men wormwood to drink.

> And yet it seemeth not to me
> That the high gods love tragedy;
> For Saadi sat in the sun,
> And thanks was his contrition; . . .

What his eyes have seen, Saadi can paint in words. The world swims in ecstasy, and suns "rise and set in Saadi's speech." Seek not the goods of the world, his Muse advises, and "Fortune seeketh thee."

> 'Wish not to fill the isles with eyes
> To fetch thee birds of paradise:
> On thine orchard's edge belong
> All the brags of plume and song; . . .

Allah pours the "flood of truth" through the doors of men, and the beggar "Admits thee to the perfect Mind." He is told not to seek "redeemers" beyond his cottage door. The "blessed gods in service masks" perform household tasks for him. This was not a new thought for Emerson. In *Nature* (Part III) he had quoted George Herbert's poem on "Man": "More servants wait on man / Than he'll take notice of . . . / Man is one world, and hath / Another to attend him."[39] Ideologically, Emerson learned nothing new from Sa'di, but in his poems he found a kindred spirit and his ideal poet, whose prosodic medium satisfied his own desires for expression. It made no difference that Sa'di's god was Allah. Yet one can see why a sectarian like Orestes Brownson—more dogmatic for being a recent convert—might accuse Emerson of writing poems to the Devil.

Emerson's "Ode, Inscribed to W. H. Channing" (manuscript dated June 1846)[40] is closely related to American history and Emerson's attitudes toward events of the time. It begins as an apology for Emerson's unwillingness to join the Reverend William Henry Channing in his abolition activities; the poet cannot leave his "honied thought / For the priest's cant, / Or statesman's rant." Yet he does, because "The angry Muse / Puts confusion in my brain." The Muse will not let him rest comfortably in his aloofness. Heatedly the poet asserts that only a blind worm could behold the United States harrying Mexico and still believe his nation is civilized. And the curse of slavery is not confined to the South; even in Maine the United States marshals ("jackals" in the poem) are hounding escaped slaves.

The most telling satire in the "Ode" is aimed at Daniel Webster, once Emerson's hero and a friend of his family. He had listened to Webster's address on June 17, 1843, at the dedication of the Bunker Hill Monument. The senator had bragged of American superiority in the arts, commerce, and civil and religious liberty.[41] At the time Emerson compared the orator to Polonius, and now three years later he is completely disillusioned by Webster's willingness to tolerate slavery for the sake of preserving the Union, and declares, "The God who made New Hampshire," Webster's native state, "Taunted the lofty land / With little men . . ."

> Virtue palters; Right is hence;
> Freedom praised, but hid;
> Funeral eloquence
> Rattles the coffin-lid.

Webster serves "things" and not people, but "Things are of the snake."

> 'Tis the day of the chattel,
> Web to weave, and corn to grind;
> Things are in the saddle,
> And ride mankind.

Emerson would keep the "law for thing" and the "law for man" discrete, and not have the latter sacrificed to the former. Lands should be cultivated, and ships built, but not at the expense of humanity.

Then, surprisingly, Emerson returns to his Saadi theme: the poet's duty is to serve the Muse; he would not have the senator seek votes from thrushes in the solitudes: "Every one to his chosen work." The "over-god" is at work, anyway, bringing good out of evil, and eventually "the astonished Muse finds thousands at her side." Emerson still has faith in the Divine Destiny which he mentioned in his Journal at the beginning of the Mexican War. But this is not a convincing or satisfactory ending for an otherwise magnificent poem.

Several of Emerson's best poems in the 1847 volume are philosophical treatments of love. All have the rose-scented and -tinted imagery of Sa'di, and similar staccato rhythms, though only one, "Hermione," is an outright imitation. In "Ode to Beauty" the poet is haunted by promises and glimpses of beauty, which forever lead him in pursuit. Finally he pleads,

> Dread Power, but dear! if God thou be,
> Unmake me quite, or give thyself to me!

The theme of "Hermione" is similar: it is the story of the Arab who had forsaken his lonely retreat to become a bridegroom, only to lose his wife through someone's deceit, though whose is not clear. This poem is the "Ode to Beauty" turned into allegory:

> 'River, and rose, and crag, and bird,
> Frost, and sun, and eldest night,
> To me their aid preferred,
> To me their comfort plight;—
> "Courage! we are thine allies,
> And with this hint be wise,—
>
> .   .   .   .   .
>
> She shall find thee, and be found.
> Follow not her flying feet;
> Come to us herself to meet."'

In one of Emerson's most ambitious—though not most successful—poems, "Initial, Daemonic, and Celestial Love," he continues the theme of "Hermione," but in imagery and conceits of Plato's *Banquet*. In one of his lectures on "Plato; or, the Philosopher" (*Representative Men*) Emerson had said that Plato teaches in the *Banquet* "that the love of the sexes is initial, and symbolizes at a distance the passion of the soul for that immense lake of beauty it exists to seek. This faith in the Divinity is never out of [Plato's] mind ... Body cannot teach wisdom;—God only."[42] In Plato's theory, the Daemonic is a plane of life between the human and celestial, or mortal and immortal.

Emerson begins his poem with a beautiful description of Venus searching for her lost son, Cupid, who is a boy no more, wears many disguises, and carries no bow or quiver. In other words, he is not easily recognized, and practices his deceits at will:

> Cupid is a casuist,
> A mystic, and a cabalist,—
> Can your lurking thought surprise,
> And interpret your device.
> He is versed in occult science,
> In magic and clairvoyance; ...

Venus warns all "nymphs" to shun this "arch-hypocrite," who follows "joy, and only joy." What Venus allegorizes is nineteenth-century "Romantic Love." The "Daemonic" is sexual love, the climax of Romantic Love, which begins in idealization and ends in physical ecstasy.

As in the essays on "Love" and "Friendship," Emerson believes with Plato (and Dante) that there is a higher and "purer" love:

> Thou must mount for love;
> Into vision where all form
> In one only form dissolves;
>
> .   .   .   .
>
> Where unlike things are like;
> Where good and ill,
> And joy and moan,
> Melt into one.

In this celestial realm, love is not directed toward individual persons, and no love tokens are exchanged. This love is pure because it has no taint of the physical, and is without limitations: "For he that feeds men serveth few; / He serves all who dares be true."[43] This is the same doctrine which had given pain to Lidian Emerson, Elizabeth Hoar, and Margaret Fuller, making them despair of attaining Waldo's "love."

In Emerson's longest composition in his 1847 *Poems,* "Monadnoc," the mountain bids the bookworm, in true Wordsworthian fashion, to end his sloth and respond to the beckoning Oreads. But the language sounds more like Sa'di:

> Let not unto the stones the Day
> Her lily and rose, her sea and land display.
> Read the celestial sign!

Mount Monadnock, in New Hampshire, near Peterborough, is not one of New England's most spectacular mountains, being only a little over three thousand feet high, but it was one of Emerson's favorites. On May 3, 1845, he climbed it before sunrise, and remained from six to ten a.m., accumulating and recording his impressions in trial lines of verse.[44] None of these was kept in his finished poem, but they show that he began with the mountain as a symbol of a purposeful Creation. He went to Monadnock with the hope that a "thousand minstrels" would wake within him. Consequently, his first responses were the Romantic ones he had carried with him. By literary tradition, human freedom was born in the mountains of the world, and it was to be expected that a fortunate race of men lived in sight of Monadnock; that "Man in these crags a fastness find / To fight pollution of the mind . . ."[45] But when he observed the typical inhabitant of the region, Emerson found:

> He was no eagle, and no earl;—
> Alas! my foundling was a churl,
> With heart of cat and eyes of bug,
> Dull victim of his pipe and mug.[46]

Thus the initial theme of this poem is the freeing of the poet's mind from preconceptions. His first reaction is that if the "squalid peasant" is all that the "proud nursery could breed," then let the mountain sink into the swamp, taking the "highland breed" with it. But then Emerson's usual dialectic begins to work, and he sees that the rude men are well adapted to "fit the bleak and howling waste / For homes of virtue, sense and taste." The mountain speaks its scorn of the summer visitor, who is incapable

of understanding the cosmic processes at work through time and change
in building a mountain and a world:

> ' 'For the world was built in order,
> And the atoms march in tune;
> Rhyme the pipe, and Time the warder,
> Cannot forget the sun, the moon.

When the bard shall come who understands these mysteries, he will
"string Monadnoc like a bead" on the chain of Reason:

> He comes, but not of that race bred
> Who daily climb my specular head.
>
> .   .   .   .   .
>
> And he, poor parasite,
> Cooped in a ship he cannot steer,—
> Who is the captain he knows not,
> Port or pilot trows not,—
> Risk or ruin he must share.

The mountain frightens this parasite half to death with falling rocks,
then lets him escape "into his dapper town, . . . / and forget me if he can."
If Emerson's diction were more precise, and his tone less relaxed, his satire
on the passenger cooped in a ship he cannot steer might have greater force.
But such a satire would have taken anger, which Emerson did not feel.
When the poet speaks, he shows comprehension of the mountain as an
image of

> . . . the stable good
> For which we all our lifetime grope,
> In shifting form the formless mind,
> And though the substance us elude,
> We in thee the shadow find.

To paraphrase, if substantive knowledge evades the finite mind, at least it
can catch a glimpse, a notion ("shadow") of ultimate reality. This Platonic assurance links "Monadnoc" to Emerson's philosophical poems on
love.

IV

John Jay Chapman, a great admirer of Emerson, complained that:

> There is throughout Emerson's poetry, as throughout all of the New
> England poetry [the time is 1899], too much thought, too much argu-
> ment. Some of his verse gives the reader a very curious and subtle
> impression that the lines are a translation. This is because he is closely fol-
> lowing a thesis. Indeed, the lines are a translation. They were thought
> first, and poetry afterwards. Read off his poetry, and you see through the
> scheme of it at once. Read his prose, and you will be put to it to make out
> the connection of ideas. The reason is that in the poetry the sequence is
> intellectual, in the prose the sequence is emotional. It is no mere epigram
> to say that his poetry is governed by the ordinary laws of prose writing,
> and his prose by the laws of poetry.[47]

Chapman is partly right, but not entirely. Emerson's poems are at times
intellectual, abounding in learned allusions, and his syntax is occasionally
so contorted that it has to be deciphered. Yet his "gay science" is not
without its own kind of emotion—or high spirits, reckless abandon, and
intoxication of the senses.

Emerson's obscurities are usually not the result of "mysticism," as Carlyle thought, but of syntactical oddities, such as the lines from "Monadnoc" quoted above:

> Let not unto the stones the Day
> Her lily and rose, her sea and land display.
> Read the celestial sign!

Expanded, and unscrambled: Day (or daylight) should not display the sea
and land, which are as beautiful as the lily and the rose, to stones (people
without aesthetic appreciation). "Read the celestial sign!" is metaphorically, not syntactically, obscure: the viewer should perceive the *eternal
beauty* (with Neoplatonic connotations) of the sea and land. Or to interpret in a Swedenborgian context (and that of the 1836 *Nature*): this
beauty is the *signature* of the Creator.

These puzzles are not frequent in Emerson's 1847 *Poems,* but they do
exist, and not so much because of his inverting subject and predicate for

the sake of a rhyme (though this happens sometimes, too), but more often because he tries to strip his language down to the bare bones. Not infrequently he omits the subject, as in "Cupid is a casuist, / . . . [He] Can your lurking thought surprise, / And interpret your device." Here "device" is a surprising word to find in this context, and it can be regarded either as a bold synonym for "stratagem" or an inexact indication of evasive or deliberately concealed thought. The judgment depends upon one's sympathy with the poet, or lack of it.

Hedge was wrong in an 1880 review in saying that Emerson's poems were improvisations. If, as Yohannan says, Emerson liked to leave his sculpture rough, it was deliberate.[48] His Notebooks and Journals show that he worked hard to achieve his intended effect, and he left a great batch of poems unpublished because they did not seem *finished* to him. Though perhaps he seldom achieved the perfection of his Concord Monument "Hymn," he did often, in satire especially, write words so clear and straightforward that they remain in the memory of the reader forever, as in "Things are in the saddle / And ride mankind." Or in "Fable" the squirrel's reply to the mountain:

> 'If I cannot carry forests on my back,
>   Neither can you crack a nut.'

Some critics of the twentieth century, poets especially, have wondered why Emerson did not, in accordance with his dictum on a "metre-making argument," discard rhyme and meter altogether and write free verse. At times he almost did, and doubtless could have gone further if he had wished. In Greek poetry, Milton's *Samson Agonistes,* and in some of Goethe's lyrics, to mention examples he knew, Emerson had excellent precedents. Some advantages would have been eliminating inversions for the sake of rhyme, those nineteenth-century contractions (*o'er, e'er*), and perhaps many of his archaic words (*behoof* to rhyme with *aloof*). To the modern reader these are annoyances. But Emerson liked rhyme, or an approximation of rhyme, without being a slave to it. If he did not, like Robert Frost, feel that writing poems without rhyme was like playing tennis without a net (and Emerson was no tennis player), he did like to hear some iteration of sound, like the *ping* of the ball hitting the racket. After discovering the Persian poets, his association of poetry with dance and music gave him an added reason for retaining at least a semblance of rhyme.

Probably Emerson's unusual dimeters, trimeters, and a fondness for octosyllabics, have contributed to his lack of popularity. When he sent his "Ode to Beauty" in manuscript to Thoreau, who at the time was staying with William Emerson on Staten Island, Henry wrote:

> . . . I have a good deal of fault to find with your ode to Beauty. The tune is altogether unworthy of the thoughts. You slope too quickly to the rhyme, as if that trick had better be performed as soon as possible or as if you stood over the line with a hatchet and chopped off the verses as they came out—some short and some long. But give us a long reel and we'll cut it up to suit ourselves. It sounds like a parody.[49]

Some passages, it is true, could be "chopped" differently without affecting the thought, such as:

> Ah, what avails it
> To hide or to shun
> Whom the Infinite One
> Hath granted his throne?[50]

This might easily be read as two lines (though then the internal rhyme "shun" would seem obtrusive), but the short line produces an effect Emerson evidently wanted. His short lines are more emphatic. Moreover, they follow the structure of his sentences. He was composing almost by phrases—"phrasal prosody" it would be called in the twentieth century. In "free verse"—and especially in the early French *vers libre*—the rhythmical unit is a grammatical phrase rather than a pattern of metrical feet. Emerson pioneered in breaking the shackles of metrical feet.

This is only one of many ways in which Emerson, in spite of the conventional appearance of his poems, was an innovator. Fortunately he would continue to write poems and to hone his medium after 1847. Some of his best poems would be published twenty years later in *May-Day*.

CHAPTER XXII

England Revisited

The occasion of my second visit to England was
an invitation from some Mechanics' Institutes
in Lancashire and Yorkshire . . .[1]

I

In December 1846 William Lloyd Garrison brought a letter from England
to Emerson from Alexander Ireland, the kind young man who had guided
Waldo around Edinburgh in 1833.[2] Emerson's letter of introduction had
been to the famous chemist Dr. Samuel Brown, but Brown had been busy
and had asked Ireland, a young journalist, to be his substitute host, and
Ireland had found it one of the most memorable experiences of his life. He
thought Emerson's sermon in the Unitarian Chapel on August 18, 1833,
the finest he had ever heard; and now, thirteen years later, he was writing to
invite the former minister to come to England again to give lectures in the
Mechanics' Institutes in Liverpool, Manchester, and other industrial cities.

Since meeting Emerson, Ireland had become part owner and co-manager
of the two newspapers in Manchester, and an active supporter of the Institutes and libraries which the wealthy industrialists had established for the
education of their employees—partly for humanitarian reasons, and partly
to increase their usefulness.[3] These Institutes were similar to the Lyceums
in the United States, though more coordinated and better administered.

Emerson replied to Mr. Ireland that he had opened "many flattering
possibilities that I shall cheerfully entertain."[4] Though Emerson indeed
felt attracted, he hoped to postpone a decision to some future date, but
Ireland was so eager and insistent that finally he agreed to sail for Liverpool in the autumn. Emerson was not fond of traveling, and he dreaded all

the preparations that would be needed before he could leave Lidian and the children for several months. In January 1847 he had bought three more acres of land adjoining his property on the east side, for which he agreed to pay $500 on April 1, though he was not sure where he could get the money. He already owed $450 to the Concord Bank. Part of this he had borrowed to rescue his Aunt Mary from a very foolish transaction in which she would lose some of the farm she had inherited.[5]

Emerson was lecturing steadily (seventeen times between early January and the end of March), but averaging only about $12 a lecture. Fortunately, before the April deadline, William paid him $974 on one of his notes. This eased his problems but did not solve all of them. He had hoped to make a small profit on his *Poems,* and eventually did, but not until the following December, when payment on copies sold exceeded his bills for printing, paper, and binding by $142.62. Of course he might receive another small payment later from his British publisher, but lectures were still his only sure way of earning money, at home or abroad.

The British trip appealed to Emerson partly because he was bored and dissatisfied with his life in the spring of 1847. "We must have society, provocation, a whip for the top," he wrote in his Journal on March 25.[6] He needed something to set him aglow. He had wished for a professorship, but none had been offered, or was likely to be—certainly not at Harvard, where his name was still in a shadow. He even wished for another pulpit, much as he disliked the Church, for "the stimulus of a stated task." Participation in an abolition campaign had been suggested to him by the editor of an abolitionist journal, and he wondered if that might give him the stimulation he needed. Yet, he doubted that "a course of mobs would do me much good." If he could follow his own inclination, he would rather go to Canada: "I should withdraw myself for a time from all domestic & accustomed relations & command an absolute leisure with books—for a time."[7]

Even the newly acquired land was a mixed pleasure. In April he hired two Concord laborers to set out seventy fruit trees (thirty apple and forty pear) on his new property. These gave him pleasant dreams of future harvests—several years thence. But that year, gardening did not seem to be as much fun as in the past. "With brow bent, with firm intent, I go musing in the garden walk. I stoop to pull up a bidens that is choking the corn, and find there are two; close behind it is a third, & I reach out my arm to a fourth; behind that, there are four thousand & one. I am heated & untuned . . ." He wakes up from his "idiot dream of chickweed & redroot, to find that I . . . am a chickweed & pipergrass myself."[8]

A few days later Emerson began to regret having bought the three acres from his neighbor:

In an evil hour I pulled down my fence & added Warren's piece to mine. No land is bad, but land is worse. If a man own land, the land owns him. Now let him leave home, if he dare. Every tree and graft, every hill of melons, every row of corn, every hedge-shrub, all he has done and all he means to do, stand in his way like duns when he so much as turns his back on his house. . . .[9]

This tension between Emerson's feeling of responsibility and his desire for freedom affected his creativity, and he wrote no new lectures, though he did read widely in mythology, ranging from India and Persia to Scandinavia. The thought of lecturing in England whetted his interest in the Norse heritage of the British people, and he read Paul Henri Mallet's *Northern Antiquities* and a translation of *The Younger Edda*.[10]

By early summer Emerson had definitely made up his mind to go to England, and also to visit Paris again before his return. In preparation for Paris he began taking lessons in French conversation from a teacher in Boston, and asked William to send him copies of a French newspaper from New York. He tried again to write some new lectures, but could not sustain interest. Anyway, he could start with the "Representative Men" series and write additional lectures in England if he needed them. He had promised to contribute to *The Massachusetts Quarterly Review,* which Parker and other friends were trying to start, but he could not find time or inclination. During the summer he did find time to speak a good word at every opportunity for Ellery Channing's *Conversations in Rome.* This book was the product of Channing's trip to Italy on funds supplied by Caroline Sturgis and himself. To the needy Alcott trying to live on his garden at Hillside, a short distance down the Lexington Road, Emerson offered fifty dollars to build a summerhouse in his garden. Alcott accepted this assignment as a challenge to his ingenuity, and spent the summer constructing a gazebo with gables, curved rafters, and so many decorations that the neighbors called it a "whirligig."[11]

Margaret Fuller was now in Europe, having sailed from New York the previous summer with a wealthy New York merchant, Marcus Spring, and his wife, Rebecca. She had carried a letter of introduction from Emerson to Carlyle and, surprisingly, she got along well with him. He wrote Emerson: "Margaret is an excellent soul: in real regard with both of us here."[12] And she wrote: "He let me talk, now and then, enough to free my lungs and change my position, so that I did not get tired."[13] He was "not afraid to laugh," she reported pointedly to her inhibited friend. On a second visit Giuseppe Mazzini, in exile from Italy for his revolutionary activities, was present. He was "a dear friend of Mrs. C.," Margaret wrote, but Carlyle called his ideas of social reform "rose-water and imbecilities." Mrs. Carlyle whispered to Margaret, "These are but opinions to Carlyle, but to Mazzini . . . a matter of life and death."[14]

In her *Tribune* articles Miss Fuller described her experiences in England. She met most of the famous authors, and in the company of Harriet Martineau called on Wordsworth at Rydal Mount. In Liverpool she visited the Mechanics Institute, and wrote Emerson that she thought his invitation to lecture to the Institutes came from honorable and enlightened men. She descended into a coal mine at Newcastle, observed "the sooty servitors" tending the blast furnaces in Sheffield, visited a "model prison" in Pentonville, and returned to London to brood over its contrast in luxury and agonizing squalor.[15] She then went to Paris, where she met George Sand, Adam Mickiewicz, and Chopin, who played for her.

Having heard that Mickiewicz, the exiled Polish poet teaching Slavic literature at the Collège de France, had quoted Emerson's *Essays* in his lectures, Margaret sent him a copy of Emerson's *Poems*. He called to thank her and they became friends immediately. Her *Woman in the Nineteenth Century* was already known in Paris, and her essay in *The New-York Daily Tribune* on American poets had been translated and reprinted in a French newspaper. Mickiewicz wrote her after his call: "Your spirit is linked with the *history* of Poland, of France, and is beginning to link itself with the history of America."[16] Margaret wrote Emerson, Elizabeth Hoar, and Caroline Sturgis about meeting Mickiewicz, but did not quote a curious statement in his letter: "You have acquired the right to know and to maintain the rights and obligations, the hopes and the exigencies of virginity. For you the first step of your deliverance and of the deliverance of your sex (of a certain class) is to know, whether you are permitted to remain a virgin."

Margaret did write her American friends about the new sense of freedom she had found in Europe, and defended George Sand's sexual liberty. Emerson wrote her on June 4, 1847 (in a letter to be delivered to her by Dr. Hedge, who was on his way to Greece): "By all means keep the Atlantic between you & us for the present, as you love your eyes." The famine in Ireland "only affects potatoes, the sterility in America continues in the men." Now that she planned to go to Rome, he hoped Rome would keep "its promises to your eyes & mind."[17]

Margaret knew that Italy was verging on revolution, but neither Emerson nor she had any premonition of the shattering experiences in store for her. In fact, by midsummer Emerson's thoughts were almost wholly taken up with his own impending journey. On June 29 J. W. Hudson, head of the Central Committee of the Yorkshire Union of Mechanics Institutes, wrote him: "I can engage for the north and south of England that we should hail with delight the great transatlantic Essayist and our Lecture Halls would be crowded with men who have already learned to love and now only wait to *see* the American poet." On the last day of July Emerson replied: "I have written to Mr Ireland, that I decide to sail for England about the 1 October and that I shall hold myself ready to accept at least part of the several engagements you so liberally offer me."[18]

Emerson was now less worried about leaving his family because Lidian had decided to invite Henry Thoreau to live with them during her husband's absence, and he had readily accepted. The children adored Henry, and Lidian had complete confidence in his ability to assume the responsibility of being man of the house. Thus it came about that Thoreau gave up living in his hut at Walden Pond after exactly two years, two months, and two days. Emerson's mother would live with William and Susan on Staten Island, and Lidian had invited her sister, Lucy Brown, to spend the winter with her.

II

Emerson sailed from Boston on Tuesday, October 5, 1847, on the packet ship *Washington Irving*.[19] A steamship could reach Liverpool in twelve days, while a sailing vessel usually took at least twenty-four, and sometimes longer. But sail was cheaper, and Emerson had traveled that way before. The *Washington Irving* was registered as weighing 750 tons, but Emerson estimated that when fully loaded with bales of cotton or other products and a score of passengers, she might weight 1,500 tons. The mainmast rose to 115 feet, and the deck from stem to stern measured 155 feet. Thoreau accompanied Emerson to his cabin and wrote his sister Sophia this description:

> Mr. Emerson's stateroom was like a carpeted dark closet, about six feet square, with a large keyhole for a window. The window was about as big as a saucer, and the glass two inches thick, not to mention another skylight overhead in the deck, the size of an oblong doughnut, and about as opaque. . . . Such will be his lodgings for two or three weeks; and instead of a walk in Walden woods he will take a promenade on deck, where the few trees, you know, are stripped of their bark. The steam-tug carried the ship to sea against a head wind without a rag of sail being raised.[20]

The *Washington Irving* had scarcely got out of Boston harbor before the wind died down and she was becalmed for four days in the region of Cape Cod; but Saturday night a brisk west wind came up and Captain Caldwell hoisted every bit of sail he thought safe, with the result that his ship began to rival the speed of a steamship. Emerson liked to feel that he was rushing toward his destination, but he did not enjoy having the floor of his cabin sloping at a constantly changing angle of twenty to thirty degrees. At night he dreamed that someone was tipping up one end or the other of his berth. The cabin passengers included three mothers, ten children, and seven men, with sixty-five persons crowded into the steerage. The crew, besides the captain, numbered sixteen sailors.

On October 21, while still at sea, Emerson began a letter to Lidian and finished it at Liverpool. "The prattle & play of the children," he wrote, "who never seem to have been sick or suspicious of danger or even impatient of confinement one moment during the passage has been as pleasant as the song of birds, and the good fellowship of the cabin has been complete."[21] At night he dreamed of his own children. He wrote for Ellen that he had seen whales spouting, porpoises swimming and leaping by the bowsprit, and thousands of mackerel jumping out of the water. The captain claimed that they made the voyage from Boston to Liverpool in fifteen days, though Emerson counted sixteen. Either way, it was remarkable speed for a sailing vessel, and Captain Caldwell drew a "line in red ink on his chart for the encouragement or for the envy of all future navigators."

Carlyle had not learned the date of Emerson's sailing from Boston soon enough to get a letter back to him before his departure. Consequently, he sent a letter to Mr. Ireland to be delivered to Emerson immediately on his arrival in Liverpool, but through a series of unlucky coincidences Waldo did not receive the letter until he had been in Liverpool a couple of days. Carlyle had written: "Know then, my Friend, that in verity your Home while in England is *here;* and all other places, whither work or amusement may call you, are but inns and temporary lodgings . . . Come soon; come at once."[22] Learning in Manchester that his lectures would not begin for a week, Emerson took a train to London—a six-hour ride—then a cab to 5 Great Cheyne Row in Chelsea, where he arrived at ten o'clock that Monday evening. Jane opened the door, with Thomas close behind her holding a lamp over her head.

Two days later Emerson wrote Lidian that he found the Carlyles little changed in the fourteen years since he had spent the night with them at Craigenputtock. The "floodgates of Carlyle's discourse are very quickly opened, & the river is a great & constant stream." They talked until nearly two o'clock that first night, and at breakfast began all over again. In the afternoon they walked to Hyde Park, then to the palaces (about two miles from Chelsea), visited the National Gallery, and finally stopped at Chapman's shop on the Strand. Along the way Carlyle melted "all Westminster & London down into his talk & laughter as he walked."[23]

Although Emerson knew something of Carlyle's gloomy views from his letters and books, he had not suspected the depth of his friend's black pessimism. "He talks like a very unhappy man," Waldo wrote Lidian, "profoundly solitary, displeased & hindered by all men & things about him, & plainly biding his time, & meditating how to undermine & explode the whole world of nonsense which torments him." His last publication had been an edition of *Oliver Cromwell's Letters and Speeches,* and Cromwell was his current hero. One night Emerson admitted that he did not share Carlyle's admiration for Cromwell, whereupon his host rose from his chair, angry as a Norse god, and running his finger across the table between them, shouted: "Then, sir, there is a line of separation between you and me as wide as that, and as deep as the pit."[24] Emerson was beginning to understand that there was, indeed, a gulf separating them, and could never again feel that their friendship was unshakable.

On Wednesday, at the National Gallery, Emerson met Mrs. George

Bancroft, whose husband was now the United States minister to Great Britain. She invited him to breakfast at the American Embassy, 90 Eaton Square, on Friday morning, and took him in her carriage to call on the poet and famous art collector Samuel Rogers, who had known nearly everyone of prominence and was full of endless anecdotes about Scott, Wordsworth, Byron, the Duke of Wellington, Tallyrand, Mme. de Staël, Lafayette, Fox, Burke, and many others. As Emerson reported to Lidian, "crowds of high men & women had talked and feasted in these rooms in which we sat.[25] After this "private show" for Emerson's benefit, Mrs. Bancroft took him to Westminster Abbey, and then insisted on conveying him in her coach to Carlyle's door in Chelsea, "a very long way." At Carlyle's he met more notable people before catching a train in the afternoon for Liverpool.

On Saturday Emerson drank tea with James Martineau, the brother of Harriet, and heard him preach on Sunday. By Monday he was bored with Liverpool, but he was impressed—almost appalled—by the size and vitality of the men he met on the street. They all seemed "bigger & solider far than our people, more stocky, both men and women, and with a certain fixedness & determination in each person's air," unlike "the sauntering gait & roving eyes of Americans. In America you catch the eye of everyone you meet: here you catch no eye almost." He thought the "axes of an Englishman's eyes" must be "united to his backbone." But what most impressed him was the "Patagonian size" of the porters, carters, even shopkeepers. He saw no one as slender as himself. Later he would decide that British beef and ale made the difference.

Emerson gave his first lecture in Manchester on March 2, and on alternate days lectured in Liverpool, commuting by train. He engaged lodgings in both cities but made his chief residence in Manchester with a Mrs. Massey.[26] He was received with great acclaim in the newspapers, and his audiences were enthusiastic. In fact, he was a celebrity, and received invitations to lecture to many other groups. Pirated editions of his *Essays* and *Poems* had made his name well known in the British Isles.[27] One invitation he felt he could not decline was to speak at the annual Grand Soirée of the Manchester Athenaeum.[28] Its object was to raise funds for the Institutes and libraries for workingmen. Young factory workers had not shown the enthusiasm which the philanthropists had expected, and membership had been opened to clerks, shopkeepers, and even the professions. As a consequence there were now four hundred Institutes with a combined membership of a hundred thousand. Some people thought the Grand Soirée should not be held in 1847 because of the economic depression, which was worst in the industrial cities, but the officials insisted that the depression increased the need to raise money to support the educational programs.

The Grand Soirée was scheduled for November 18 in the Manchester Free Trade Hall, which could seat eight thousand people. The price of admission would be five shillings a couple. The program would include a sumptuous banquet, music for dancing provided by the Double Quadrille Band, and famous people, who would be honorary guests at the High Table. Charles Dickens declined, but among those who accepted were Richard Cobden, a hero of the working class because of his role in getting the Corn Laws (import tax on grain) repealed, and several other members of Parliament, including John Bright, Vincent Brookley, and John Bowing. Other guests would be George Cruikshank, cartoonist for *Punch;* Robert Blackwood, publisher; the dean of Manchester; and Archibald Alison, famous historian, who would be toastmaster.

Alison spoke first, reminisced sentimentally about his childhood in Shropshire, then surveyed the history of manufacturing in Manchester. Cobden was so popular that he could scarcely speak for the cheering. What he said did not matter; his presence was enough to please the crowd. Emerson spoke next, beginning slowly and hesitantly, but he soon caught the excitement of the occasion and gave one of the most successful speeches of his life. First he told Cobden he was known and admired by all the friends of free trade in America. Turning to Alison, he said he had found his *History of Europe* in the cabin of his ship and had read it on his way to England, and he could have had no better preparation. To Cruikshank he said his drawings in *Punch* were eagerly awaited twice a month in every bookstore in Boston, New York, and Philadelphia. Then, settling into his speech, Emerson said he had been taught that England was "a cold, foggy, mournful country, bearing no fruit well in open air, but robust men and virtuous women, and these, too, of a certain wonderful fibre and endurance."[29] They were inclined to be a little moody and dumpish, but "in adversity they were grand." He predicted that the "mother of nations" would grandly survive the present adversity. Emerson's speech was the hit of the evening, and *The Manchester Guardian* printed it in full next morning.

In his lectures at the Institutes and the Athenaeum Emerson's appeal was mainly to young men, many of whom became his personal friends. Some who had not yet heard him speak but had read his *Essays* (less often the *Poems*) were attracted by his ideas and wrote him letters by the "penny post," all of which he answered on his free days in Manchester. What appealed to them was the assurance that "a vaster mind and will" operated through them. "The opaque self becomes transparent with the light of the First Cause," which some people called God and Emerson called the Over-Soul. The sources of energy and intellect drawn upon by the makers of history and literature were open to all men: "This is the key to the power of the greatest men,—their spirit diffuses itself. A new quality of mind travels by night and by day, in concentric circles from its origin . . . the union of all minds appears intimate . . ."[30] These thoughts encouraged the young men to read and think—and believe in themselves.

One of Emerson's young admirers was Henry Sutton, an idealistic poet, who used a quotation from Emerson's *Essays* as an epigraph for his book, *The Evangel of Love.* Waldo wrote Lidian about this doubtful honor and called it figuring him "with saints & mystics of many colours."[31] But his new friends were not all young or poets. Wealthy manufacturers also invited him to their mansions, and by December he had begun to accept some of the invitations. He still hated evening parties, but he even attended some of those.

News of Emerson's reception led Henry Thoreau to suppose he was triumphant everywhere he went. Waldo wrote Lidian on December 1 that this was not true, for he was beginning to meet considerable opposition from the Church of England and conservative newspapers. Even the Swedenborgians denounced him. They had liked his little book on *Nature,* but his lecture on Swedenborg had alienated them because he had called their prophet a mystic and an idealist. The Congregationalists called his theory of evil as negation "false and flippant." Both the Scottish Dissenters and the Church of England were offended by his saying that God incarnates Himself in men. Emerson's reputation with these denominations was not helped by his being embraced by the Unitarians and the Secularists. British Unitarians were more liberal than American Unitarians, and very obnoxious to conservative British churches. The Secularists, "free thinkers," worshipers of God in nature, were widely regarded as atheists. George Holyoake, editor of *The Reasoner,* called himself an atheist. He had warmly welcomed Emerson to the British Isles. John Chapman, Emerson's British publisher, was a Secularist, and so was his friend George Cupples. In *The Reasoner* Cupples asked: "If Emerson be not a Christian, what are we? . . . Greek though he be, even as Plotinus . . . , Emerson is the *consequence* of Christianity." Cupples defended the Over-Soul doctrine as an attempt to awaken the soul in each person. A critic in *The English Review* replied: "Ah, poor Emerson! can *you* believe this sad twaddle?"[32]

III

By the first of December Emerson was ready to extend his lecturing itinerary to other towns and cities. On December 5 he wrote Margaret Fuller: "Tomorrow, I am to go to Nottingham & Derby, where, it seems, I have special friends."[33] At Nottingham he was the guest of four different friends on successive nights. One of these was Joseph Neuberg, a prospering German merchant. Emerson later introduced him to Carlyle, and he did valuable research in Germany for Carlyle's *Frederick the Great.* At Neuberg's house he met Philip Bailey, author of *Festus,* a version of the Faust story extremely popular in America. "But the pride of Nottingham," he declared to Lidian, was Henry Sutton, mentioned above. Sutton now confessed to him, "I like Alcott much better than I do you."[34] This candor amused Emerson, and he wished Alcott could meet his admirer. At Derby, Emerson met Herbert Spencer, the philosopher of Materialism, who professed himself a great admirer of the *Essays.*[35]

During December, Emerson shuttled back and forth between Manchester and a score or more of towns in the industrial region of England: Leicester, Preston, Chesterfield, Birmingham, Newstead, Worcester, Bradford, York, Leeds, Sheffield, Halifax, Newcastle, and other places. He enjoyed traveling on British trains: "I ride everywhere as on a cannonball (though cushioned and comforted in every manner)," he wrote Lidian on December 16 from Birmingham, "high & low over rivers & towns through mountains in tunnels of 3 miles & more at twice the speed & with half the motion of our cars & read quietly the Times Newspaper which seems to have machinized the world, for my occasions."[36] At the home of Frederick Stanwick, an engineer in Chesterfield, Emerson met George Stephenson, the inventor and perfecter of the locomotive in use on British railroads. Stanwick, in the careless way of British hosts, failed to introduce Stephenson to Emerson, but the large, ruddy, forthright man strode up to the guest, laid a heavy hand on his shoulder, gave it a friendly shake, and introduced himself. No one in Boston would have dared be so familiar with the reserved Waldo Emerson, but he loved it, and immediately liked the burly engineer, now an old man living in retirement.

Emerson always looked forward to returning to Manchester because he received his mail there, and his family was seldom out of his mind. Lidian had been faithful in writing him, and he had sent her long letters about his experiences, but they did not satisfy her. On Christmas Day he wrote her, "I fear that I shall not be able at this time to write you yet, those full and 'private' letters, which you so rightfully demand."[37] His excuse was lack of time, "so harried by this necessity of reading Lectures." He also spent much time in seeing "men & things in each town," opportunities he could not afford to miss. Probably Lidian wanted him to send assurances of his love for her, which he was psychologically unable to write. He had, indeed, not been writing "private" letters to her, for he had asked her to share his letters with their friends, including Henry Thoreau and Elizabeth Hoar, then to send them to his mother on Staten Island, since he did not often find time to write her personally.

From Lidian's latest letter Emerson had learned that his Uncle Samuel Ripley, who had aided him financially and otherwise at several crucial stages in his life, had died on November 25 in the Old Manse, where he had moved his family after the Hawthornes vacated it. He did write his Aunt Sarah a letter of condolence, in which he declared: "He was the hoop that held us all staunch with his sympathies of *family*," but he asked Lidian to send "this leaf [expressing his grief] to Mother that she may know how heartily I agree with her in all she will now feel & say of her friend & mine." To his aunt he said he hoped that Lidian, "who is sometimes slow to express her real respect, has cheered you by communicating her hearty affection for all she beheld in your husband."[38] He regarded condolences as one of his most solemn duties.

In all the three months Emerson spent in traveling, lecturing, and being entertained in the hospitable homes of industrial England, he saw very little of the lives of the poor, though he read of their conditions. Unlike Margaret Fuller, he did not seek them out. In February he saw barefooted beggars in Glasgow. He could not help noticing the pollution caused by coal-burning factories and trains. In cloudy London the sun rarely penetrated the smoke,[39] but it was worse elsewhere: "The coalsmoke makes some of the manufacturing towns, like Sheffield, Leeds, Bradford, very dirty. There the sheep are black (from smoke), & the trees black, & the human spittle black."[40] And for all his admiration for the philanthropy of leading industrialists (founders of workers' Institutes and Athenaeums), by the spring of 1848 he was wondering: "What wrong road have we taken that all the improvements of machinery have helped every body but the operative? Him they have incurably hurt."[41]

Emerson decided that, on January 29, before leaving Manchester for Edinburgh, he would give a dinner for some of his most devoted friends in his rooms on Fenny Street, a half-hour's walk from the center of town.[42] Mrs. Massey took care of the preparations, cooked the meal, and served it in his rented parlor. From Manchester he invited, first of all, Alexander Ireland, his sponsor; Dr. W. B. Hodgson, doctor of laws but at that time headmaster of a private school in Manchester; Thomas Ballantyne, editor of *The Examiner;* Francis Espinasse, a staff member of *The Examiner;* William Maccall, a former Unitarian minister; and George Dawson, a popular lecturer. All of these except Espinasse were Scots, with characteristic speech, manners, and appearance. Dr. Hodgson was the most imposing in appearance, with black hair, shaggy eyebrows, and great bushy beard. He was a neighbor on Fenny Street and helped Emerson host his party.

In addition to these local friends, Emerson invited several from other towns. Some had entertained him, and others were young men who had sought his advice and encouragement. Two were Joseph Neuberg, the Nottingham merchant, and the young poet Henry Sutton, whom Emerson had met at Neuberg's house. Another guest was George Searle Phillips of Huddersfield, who had turned to Emerson for help in overcoming his cynical despair. He was so poor that he had to walk twenty-five miles across the Yorkshire moors in the rain to attend the dinner. But the oddest character to attend was Thomas Hornblower Gill, poet, hymn writer, and would-be disciple, who had come from Birmingham the previous evening in order to be sure of a private talk with his mentor.

In writing to Lidian about his party, Emerson said only that "The day before leaving Manchester, we had a company of friends assembled at Dr. Hodgson's house and mine. . . . [Names them.] I gave them all a dinner, on Sunday. These are all men of merit, & of various virtues & ingenuities."[43] Fortunately, three of the guests published fuller accounts. To Ireland, they "were principally young men—ardent, hopeful, enthusiastic moral and religious reformers, and independent thinkers."[44] Phillips he called "a man of erratic genius . . . an inveterate smoker." Phillips years later died in a lunatic asylum in New York. Ireland called Phillips's account of the gathering "sarcastic . . . but curious for its life-like sketches of his fellow-guests." Henry Sutton, the Nottingham poet, was "One of the finest spirits assembled on that occasion." Dr. Hodgson was a "classical scholar . . . and master of several European languages," whose remarkable memory "supplied him with an inexhaustible store of witty . . . anecdotes, sparkling *bon mots,* and an infallible affluence of apt quotations." Joseph Neuberg was cultured, thoughtful, "with many admirable qualities of head and heart." Ireland was not critical and apparently liked everyone at the dinner.

But to Phillips they were a congenial odd lot of eccentrics, unrelated to each other, and few with close relations to their host. Emerson had probably not expected him to make the long journey from Huddersfield, but warmly welcomed and introduced him to his other guests—a courtesy in which the British were often negligent. Thomas Hornblower Gill was "a tall, thin, ungainly man, about thirty years of age," who spoke "in squeaks at the top of his voice, making all kinds of grimaces and strange gesticulations."[45] He had a volume of Plato in his hand and wanted to read a passage to Emerson, which he proceeded to do, with many twitches and nervous jerks. He was also nearsighted and held the book a few inches from his nose. Then, in spite of his distracting bodily contortions, he gave a brilliant commentary. When he sat down, Emerson said, "That man is a fine scholar, has a fine mind, and much real culture. He is well read in literature, in philosophy, in history; and has written rhymes, which, like my friend Ellery Channing's, are very nearly poetry."

When Henry Sutton came into the room, he appeared to Phillips as "a thin, timorous, young man; not more than twenty years old—with strange, mystic eyes, and a head and face like George Herbert's." He was a devout disciple of Emerson's, and was "tinged with his thought." A vegetarian, he lived on roots and water, "that nature and God's thought and inspiration might flow through him without impediment." He sounds a good deal like Jones Very: "a poet also, as well as a preacher and an apostle . . . the St. John of the company."

The Scotsmen tended to draw into a little group: Maccall, the ex-minister, "brilliant as a Vaux-hall exhibition—full of metaphysics and poetry," speaking "in a half musical, half savage Scotch drawl ..."; Ballantyne, who had worked his way up from the lowly trade of weaver to editor, a "hard, iron man, learned in Adam Smith, and possessed by the glitter of Carlyle"; and Ireland, a "dark, bilious man, with black hair, kind intelligent black eyes, a friendly, genial face, and a most true and affectionate nature." Dawson, the lecturer, was called a demagogue; he reminded Phillips of "Judas at the Last Supper." In his copy of Phillips's book, Ireland wrote, "A most unjust remark." Espinasse, "a dark, Shakespear-browed young man, with the general *physique* of a Spaniard," wearing spectacles, listened to everything said and made witty, sardonic comments. He was a great reader, once employed in the British Museum in London. Dawson escaped being caricatured.

When dinner was served at four o'clock, Emerson seated Sutton on his right, and Gill, "that odd compound stuff from Birmingham," on his left. Gill's nearsightedness made it difficult for him to see his plate, and in one of his spasmodic movements he knocked it into his lap. At the table there was an embarrassed silence, then a titter, and recovered gaiety after Gill rescued his plate. When wine was served he stood up to drink a toast proposed by Emerson but let the glass slip through his fingers, splattering the red liquid over the table and Phillips's white shirt front.

After dinner Emerson was urged to read his newly composed essay on Plato (probably a revision of his *Representative Men* lecture), which for Espinasse prevented the evening from being a failure. Both he and Phillips felt that the guests were too heterogeneous to be congenial, though Ireland thought the banquet had been a success in every respect. The gracious courtesy of the host had made each guest feel "that *he* was the favoured one of the party ..." After Emerson read his lecture on Plato, Phillips wandered outdoors in the rain, but finally returned, and he, Sutton, and Gill sat and talked with Emerson for the remainder of the night. Their host told them about his friends in Concord, saying of Thoreau, "you will hear of [him] by and by. He is now writing a book, most of which I have heard, called *A Week on the Concord and Merrimack Rivers.*" In the morning they went next door to Dr. Hodgson's for breakfast.[46]

IV

After resting a few days in Manchester and finishing his lecture on "Natural Aristocracy," Emerson bought a railroad ticket on February 7 to Halifax, the first stop on his way to Edinburgh. Next day he stopped at Barnard Castle, and the following at Newcastle, where he was the guest of George Crawshay, part owner of the Gateshead Iron Works. He reached Edinburgh on February 10 barely in time for his first lecture, and would not have made it if Dr. Samuel Brown had not met him at the railroad station. After delivering "Natural Aristocracy" he went home with Dr. Brown, and remained his guest until the fourteenth, when he repeated this lecture in Glasgow. Then he alternated his four lectures ("Natural Aristocracy," "Genius of the Age," "Shakespeare," and "Eloquence") between Edinburgh and Glasgow; and again between Dundee and Perth.[47]

On February 21 Emerson wrote Lidian that his audiences in Edinburgh had contained "many remarkable men & women, as I afterwards found."[48] The coincidence of the 1848 Revolution in Paris, which forced the abdication of Louis Philippe, with Emerson's arrival in Scotland caused some people to fear that his lectures might increase social unrest in the cities. One of the most apprehensive was Emerson's host in Dundee, George Gilfillan, pastor of the Calvinistic George Chapel. But he was completely won over by Emerson's charm, and defended him when the deacons of the chapel wanted to prevent him from speaking in their church. Gilfillan's enthusiasm grew, in fact, with each lecture—though in later years he would turn against Emerson.

Dundee and Perth, however, were sideshows. Emerson's greatest pleasures were experienced in Edinburgh.[49] Dr. Brown, the eminent chemist, showed him around the city, and introduced him to its most important people, many of whom invited him to dine with them. He met Robert Chambers, author of *Vestiges of Creation;* George Combe, famous phrenologist and social theorist; Francis, Lord Jeffrey, editor of *The Edinburgh Review;* and others. At the university he heard Professor John Wilson (Christopher North) lecture on moral philosophy, and William Hamilton on logic; he was not impressed. The person who did impress him was Thomas De Quincey, probably the finest living essayist in English, then in his seventieth year, a small, still handsome, white-haired man.

Emerson met De Quincey on Sunday evening at a dinner given by Mrs. Catherine Crowe, author of *The Night Side of Nature* and other short-lived works. De Quincey lived at Lass Wade, ten miles from Edinburgh, and Mrs. Crowe had had difficulty in getting an invitation to him. His three daughters took good care of him, and he was no longer addicted to opium, but he was still poor. Sunday was stormy, but he walked the ten miles in the rain and mud, and arrived soaking wet, "and though," Emerson wrote Lidian, "Mrs. Crowe's hospitality is comprehensive & minute, yet she had no pantaloons in her house." As De Quincey dried out before the open fire, he talked; and Emerson was fascinated, reminded of Ellery Channing and George Bradford—"say George's amiableness raised to the tenth power." De Quincey invited Emerson and Mrs. Crowe to dine with him in Lass Wade the following Saturday, which they did, afterward bringing their host back in Mrs. Crowe's carriage to Edinburgh to hear Emerson's lecture.

At Mrs. Crowe's dinner Emerson also met a young painter named David Scott, who had read his *Essays* and was eager to meet him. Scott had studied art in Rome, and now specialized in large allegorical paintings. He seldom did portraits from life, but he wanted to paint Emerson. The portrait, not finished during Emerson's sittings, was also allegorical to some extent, with dark clouds in the background, luminated by a bright rainbow. It can still be seen in the Concord Public Library.

Late in February Waldo said good-bye to Dr. Brown and De Quincey at the Edinburgh railroad station, then traveled to Ambleside to visit Harriet Martineau and renew his acquaintance with Wordsworth, her neighbor.[50] Wordsworth was in his seventy-seventh year, but in sound health and "full of talk." Emerson had intended to stay only one day, but Miss Martineau persuaded him to remain over another day to view the mountains and lakes with her on horseback. He then returned to Manchester, settled his debts with Mrs. Massey, and set out for London on March 3.

Emerson had recently learned from Lidian, and more fully from Henry Thoreau, that she had been gravely ill with "jaundice" (hepatitis) most of the winter. The children had also been ill, but had recovered. On February 23 Henry had written that the doctor still called every day, and Lidian was "yellow as saffron."[51] She had also had financial worries, Emerson learned to his chagrin, and had had to call on William for help. Waldo had sent money to Abel Adams, but instead of turning it over to Lidian, Adams had paid an installment on Emerson's debt to the Concord Bank and a fifty-dollar assessment for two shares of Fitchburg Railroad stock. Adams wrote him nothing but bad news about conditions in America: the continuation of the wicked war with Mexico, which was partly to blame for the scarcity of money, the failure of banks, and the generally depressed business conditions. On March 9 Emerson wrote William from London that he was sending Mr. Adams fifty pounds by the next steamer to pay his various debts, leaving himself forty pounds to live on in London. He might have to give more lectures to pay his passage home.[52]

In London everyone was excited about the revolution in France, the conservatives fearing the effect on the British poor, and the radicals being stimulated to greater exertions. Louis Philippe had sought refuge in London under the protection of the Belgian ambassador. Chartists and labor unions were sending delegates to Paris, and most of the liberal members of Parliament praised the revolutionaries across the Channel. Monckton Milnes was so enthusiastic that Thackeray satirized him in *Punch* as "Citoyen Milnes." Carlyle declaimed, " 'Woe to Jerusalem' just before the Fall," though he sympathized with the rebels. For the first time in his life he began reading the newspapers every day. Emerson was eager to see the changes in France at first hand, but Tennyson, whom he had recently met, warned him that he would never return alive if he went over.[53]

Early in March there were riots in Glasgow, which the army put down with some bloodshed, and there was agitation in Edinburgh and Manchester. The leaders of the Chartist (People's Charter) movement tried to collect six million signatures to a petition for reforms to be presented to Parliament on April 10.[54] They announced that one-half million sympathizers would assemble on Kensington Common and carry the petition to Parliament Square. These plans so frightened the authorities that Parliament placed the Duke of Wellington in charge of defense against disorder. When the day arrived, only fifty thousand people assembled, and a token delegation carried the petition to Parliament. This fiasco practically ended the Chartist movement in England, though it would probably have declined anyway because Parliament was gradually granting the reforms asked. Another reason for the Chartists' failure was that the labor unions refused to support them because the unions were not in favor of free trade (as were the Chartists).

Meanwhile, through the kindness of the Bancrofts, Carlyle, and Milnes, Emerson was meeting and being entertained by the "best" people in London: Thomas Babington Macaulay (not yet a baron), Henry Milman, Lord

Morpeth, Lord Auckland, Lady Harriet Baring, Lady Ashburton (Mrs. Carlyle's intimate friend), Charles Lyell (the geologist), and numerous others. He was elected honorary member of the Athenaeum Club, a privilege he prized, Waldo wrote Lidian, "not only because only ten foreigners are eligible at any one time, but because it gives all the rights of a member in a magnificent library, reading-room, a home to sit in & see the best company, and a coffee room . . . at cost."[55]

Emerson attended lectures at the Geological Society, the Antiquarian Society, and the Royal Institute, where he heard Michael Faraday lecture on electricity. At the Royal College of Surgeons he met the men most prominent in medicine. On the urging of both Lidian and her brother, Dr. Charles T. Jackson, he tried to interest the surgeons in Dr. Jackson's claim to the discovery of sulfuric ether. (Dr. Jackson apparently was the first to verify the anesthetic effect of ether, but a Boston dentist, William Morton, first used it in surgery and got the credit.) British physicians were not interested in the rival claims, Emerson wrote Lidian on April 6, because they had almost forgotten ether in their use of chloroform.[56]

Since his first trip to Europe, in 1833, Emerson's interest in science had continued to grow, and he missed no opportunity to talk with the best English minds in the field. Richard Owen, librarian of the Royal Society of Surgeons, showed him the Hunterian Museum, and Sir William Hooker, keeper of Kew Gardens, spent several hours on a beautiful day in April guiding him and the Bancrofts through this remarkable collection of botanical specimens from all over the world. Under these stimulations Emerson began working every day from early breakfast until two o'clock in the afternoon on what he called in a letter to Lidian "a kind of Book of Metaphysics to print at home. Does not James Walker [professor of philosohy at Harvard] want relief, & to let me be his lieutenant for one semester to his class in Locke?"[57] This book was, indeed, Emerson's most ambitious undertaking, never completed, though parts of it he would present in lectures at Harvard near the end of his life. Eventually the fragments would be published posthumously as the *Natural History of the Intellect* (1893).

Emerson's personal charm won the friendship of nearly everyone he met in London. One of his most interesting conquests was the crusty, fashionable old Crabb Robinson, who lived in a big corner house on Russell Square, near the British Museum. He was a friend of Wordsworth's, but detested Carlyle, as did Wordsworth. Robinson read Emerson's *Essays* and pronounced them an imitation of Carlyle, who imitated Coleridge, an imitator of the Germans.[58] After meeting Emerson on two or three occasions, Robinson was still prejudiced, but on April 1, at Lord Northampton's soirée, he came face-to-face with the American author and was won over instantly. He wrote his brother Thomas: "He has one of the most interesting countenances I ever beheld, a combination of intelligence and sweetness that quite disarmed me." He gave Emerson his card, and took him to the annual banquet of the Antiquarian Society. Viscount Palmerston also invited Emerson to a reception, where he met the crown prince of Prussia, as well as Isaac D'Israeli (father of the future prime minister), with whom he had a short talk. He also met the head of the London branch of the Rothschild Bank.

Recently Emerson had returned from Oxford, where he had spent two days with Arthur Hugh Clough, Fellow of Oriel College, then in his thirtieth year. At Rugby, Clough had been the favorite student of Headmaster Thomas Arnold, father of Matthew, and he had made a brilliant record at Oxford, but he was disturbed about the enforced orthodoxy of the Church of England in British universities. Clough and his friends had read Emerson's *Essays* and were eager to meet the author. Emerson had first heard of Clough through his sister in Liverpool. She wrote her brother about the visiting American, and he initiated a correspondence.[59]

On March 31 Emerson accepted Clough's invitation to visit him at Oxford.[60] There he was housed in Oriel College, where he dined with the Fellows and various "Deans and Doctors." The authorities had never heard of him, so did not fear his influence on the young men. Emerson, tall, slender, slightly stooped, made a striking contrast to ruddy, stocky Clough, but they liked each other immediately and became lifelong friends. Francis Palgrave, future professor of poetry at Oxford and editor-to-be of a famous anthology, *Golden Treasury of English Lyric Poetry,* also liked Emerson, as did James Anthony Froude, who would become Carlyle's biographer. After Emerson's return to London, Froude wrote him: "Your . . . visit here, short as it was, was not without its service to you; you left luminous traces of your presence in the words you scattered . . . In a few years I hope even here in Oxford you will see whole acres yellow with the corn of your sowing."[61]

On April 25 John Forster, editor of *The Examiner,* took Emerson to dine at Lincoln's Inn, and there he found Carlyle and Dickens, who joined them. Forster greeted Carlyle as "My Prophet!" and remarked that his passion was "Musket-worship." No women dined in Lincoln's Inn, and the conversation was uninhibited. It turned to lewdness in the London streets at night, and "Carlyle said, & the others agreed, that chastity for men was as good as given up in Europe."[62] Emerson said that in Liverpool he had asked if prostitution was as gross in the city as it appeared to be. It seemed to him a "fatal rottenness in the state," and he wondered "how any boy could grow up safe." Both Carlyle and Dickens "replied that chastity in the male sex was as good as gone in our times," and in England was so rare as to be the exception. Carlyle had heard that it was the same in America, but Emerson insisted that, "for the most part, young men of good standing & good education with us, go virgins to their nuptial bed, as truly as their brides." This was a little too much for Dickens, and he said that if his son were especially chaste he would fear he was not in good health. Emerson was rather shocked by this talk. Afterward he recorded in his Journal his present opinion of Carlyle: "no idealist in opinions, but a protectionist in political economy, aristocrat in politics, epicure in diet, goes for murder, money, punishment by death, slavery, & all the pretty abominations, tempering them with epigrams."

By the end of April, Emerson was tired of his unaccustomed social life and decided to go to Paris for three weeks.[63] He would have liked to stay longer, but he had just agreed to read six lectures in London, beginning June 6. After having about decided to give up the idea of lecturing in London, he had received a request to do so, signed by Carlyle, Dickens, Barry Cornwall, Bulwer-Lytton, and John Forster, and he had consented. These friends had assured him that he ought to clear two hundred pounds, charging one guinea for admission. As his topic he had chosen "The Mind and Manners in the Nineteenth Century," for which he would have to revise some manuscripts on hand, writing linking passages. It would be necessary, therefore, to take his manuscripts with him to Paris and continue working on them there. After seeing Tennyson twice, and Tennyson's friend Coventry Patmore, a poet who worked in the British Museum Library, and Clough several times (he was now on vacation), as well as some friends from Boston on their way to Paris, and after hearing Grisi and Alboni at the Opera, Emerson took a train to Folkstone, crossed the Channel at night to Boulogne, and arrived in Paris Sunday morning, May 7. Clough had preceded him, as had the American friends. Monckton Milnes had also come over for a close look at the revolutionaries.[64]

V

Emerson registered at the Hôtel Montmorency on the boulevard des Italiens, but after a couple of days he found lodging on the rue des Petits Augustins, on the Left Bank, for ninety francs a month. Breakfast, served in his room, was extra. At first he took his dinner at the Café Cinque Arcades in the Palais Royal for two francs plus tips, but soon discovered a more convenient "table d'hôte," served at 16 rue de Notre Dame des Victoires, "where 500 French habitués usually dine at 1 franc 60 centimes . . . an excellent place for French grammar. Nouns, verbs, adverbs, & interjections furnished gratuitously."[65]

Clough took dinner with Emerson every day, and often other British friends joined them, including Milnes, Geraldine Jewsbury (whom Jane Carlyle called "Miss Gooseberry") from Manchester, the Paulets, a Swiss merchant family from Liverpool, and once Hugh Doherty, an Irish socialist who had been forced to flee England until the excitement over the riots died down. Of the Americans in Paris, Emerson saw only Tom Appleton, the perpetual traveler from Cambridge.

When Emerson arrived in Paris, everything was peaceful. The only evidence of the February riots was the tree stumps along the avenues; the trees had been cut down to form barricades. Now the streets were filled until late at night with chattering, gesticulating, seemingly happy people. Emerson soon found that his pronunciation made it difficult to communicate with them, but they were friendly, and he felt that he gained a little skill in speech each day. He wrote in his Journal, "I have been exaggerating the English merits all winter, & disparaging the French. Now I am correcting my judgment of both, & the French have risen very fast."[66]

Two radical clubs, one headed by Armand Barbès and the other by Louis Auguste Blanqui, were still holding agitated discussions and planning further defiance of the National Assembly. On May 9, Emerson, in the company of Forster and Mrs. Paulet, tried to visit the Barbès Club, but found it closed. Next day, however, from a side box, they saw and heard it in a stormy session. On Sunday, May 14, Emerson and Forster attended the "Blanqui Club" and heard the leader's instructions to his Montagnards.[67] The furious earnestness of the conspirators was fascinating, and a little frightening. That day on the street the excitement was also intense.

Next day, about one o'clock, the followers of Barbès and Blanqui began assembling in front of the National Assembly. When they numbered several thousand, they demanded to be admitted to present a petition supporting Poland's struggle for freedom. Finally the National Guard, which seemed to Emerson to be made up of "the entire male population of Paris," drove them off. The rioters retreated to the Hôtel de Ville, where they proclaimed a new government. But about five o'clock the National Guard dispersed them and arrested the leaders—also General Courtois, commander of the Guard, on suspicion of treason.

A few days later Emerson described for Lidian the excitement and suspense of this thwarted revolt, which he witnessed from a safe distance:

> The fire & fury of the people, when they are interrupted or thwarted, are inconceivable to New England. The costumes are formidable. All France is bearded like goats & lions, then most of Paris is in some kind of uniform[:] red sash, red cap, blouse perhaps bound by red sash, brass helmet, & sword, and every body is supposed to have a pistol in his pocket.[68]

As soon as tranquillity was restored, Emerson continued his exploration of Paris—after working on his manuscripts in the morning, as he had done in London. He went several times to see the famous actress Rachel in *Phèdre* and *Mithridate*. She was of slight build, and her voice lacked resonance, but, Emerson wrote Lidian, "She deserves all her fame, and is the only good actress I have ever seen . . . you feel her genius at first sight, and trust her resources."[69] He could not catch all her words, but her acting made it easy to follow the meaning of the drama.

At the Sorbonne, Emerson heard a lecture on mathematics by Urbain Jean Joseph Leverrier, a famous astronomer. His formulas on the blackboard meant nothing to the nonmathematical Emerson, "but I saw the man." On Wednesday the great poet-statesman Lamartine was to speak to the National Assembly on the Polish question, and Richard Rush, the American ambassador, lent Emerson his pass. Lamartine, "a manly handsome greyhaired gentleman with nothing of the rust of the man of letters," spoke with ease and authority. Occasionally he refreshed himself with a sip of wine or a pinch of snuff.

To Emerson everything in Paris was dramatic and fascinating. The weather was almost ideal, unlike that of drizzly London, and everyone seemed to be out on the street, or in the well-kept public gardens, or strolling along the Seine, which was lined by broad streets on both sides, with stone bridges crossing the river at frequent intervals. The Thames was a commercial highway, but the Seine was the pride and joy of Parisians. People mingled without social distinction, stopping to converse with anyone, whether in blouse or fine coat.

Sunday, May 21, was the "fête de la Concorde, de la Paix et du Travail," a national holiday celebrating concord, peace, and labor—forerunner of the Communist May Day celebrations in the twentieth century. Delegates came from all parts of France, and from Poland, Italy, Germany, and Ireland; as many as 1,200,000, *Le Moniteur Universel* estimated. To Emerson, standing in their midst at the Champ de Mars, "it was like an immense family[;] the perfect good humour & fellowship is so habitual to them all." That night the Champs-Élysées was illuminated with "festal chandeliers" for a mile, giving the avenue the appearance of "an immense ballroom in which the countless crowds of men & women walked with ease & pleasure. It was easy to see that France is far nearer to Socialism than England . . ."[70] But Emerson was skeptical of the permanent effect of the recent changes, and he wrote in his Journal: "At the end of the year we shall take account, & see if the Revolution was worth the trees."[71]

The only regret he had was that, in spite of the sociability in the street, he met almost no French families. The one exception was that of Alexis de Tocqueville, author of the famous study of American society. Milnes was acquainted with Tocqueville, and took Emerson for a call on the family. Though both M. and Mme. de Tocqueville spoke English, she apparently caused Emerson some embarrassment, for he recorded in his Journal: "Madame de Tocqueville, who is English, tells me, that the French is so beautiful a language[,] so neat, concise, & lucid, that she can never bear to speak English."[72] More cooperative was Marie de Flavigny, Comtesse d'Agoult; she had reviewed Emerson's *Essays* under her pseudonym "Daniel Stern." She recorded in her *Mémoires* that "le moraliste Emerson" called on her.[73]

The French *grisettes* interested Emerson, as they had his priggish self in 1834, when he thought his friend Wendell Holmes was too familiar with them. Now Clough seemed to be knowledgeable on the subject. Philosophically Emerson observed in his Journal that he had no doubt the extremes of vice flourished here, but evidently nature took care of the excesses, for he observed posters on the walls everywhere advertising "La Guérison des Maladies secrètes."[74] Those *affiches* on every spot of available wall were a Parisian phenomenon. Not only advertising was thus displayed, but also official announcements—these on white paper, which the government reserved to itself.

Yes, Emerson was "thankful for Paris," and if he should ever feel "driven to seek some refuge of solitude & independency, why here is Paris."[75] Some years later Oscar Wilde would have one of his characters say, "When good Americans die they go to Paris." But it might have been said by Emerson's friend Tom Appleton, the most amusing American in Paris, and Emerson would have agreed. He had received letters from Lidian assuring him that she had recovered and that the children were well, and he was in glowing good humor. But he hated to leave Paris, and he dreaded those lectures in London.

When Emerson reached London on June 3, he felt he was not ready for his first lecture three days later at 17 Edwards Street, Portman Square, and worked furiously at the last minute, as he used to do on his sermons in Boston. *The Times* announced his lecture schedule: June 6, "Powers and Laws of Thought"; 8, "Relation of Intellect to Natural Science"; 10, "Tendencies and Duties of Men of Thought"; 13, "Politics and Socialism"; 15, "Poetry and Eloquence"; 17, "Natural Aristocracy."[76]

Attendance at the lectures was smaller than expected, but aristocrats and people of fashion came "to hear the Massachusetts Indian," as Emerson expressed it to Lidian.[77] Carlyle, of course, attended, loudly applauding at times, and the loyal Monckton Milnes; also the Duchess of Sutherland, Lord Morpeth, the Duke of Argyle, Lord Lovelace, and other notables. Most of them invited Emerson to dine, and in the round of social activities he found insufficient time to prepare each lecture to his satisfaction. At one of these dinners Mr. Bancroft introduced him to Lady Byron. Some of the nobility were alarmed by certain statements he made in "Natural Aristocracy." For example, after an unsympathetic description of the "aristocrat," he said, "who can blame the peasant if he fires his [lord's] barns."[78] Privately, Lord Morpeth told him he hoped he would leave that out next time he gave the lecture.

Emerson was disappointed by the eighty pounds he cleared from his fashionable audiences and agreed to give three more lectures in Exeter Hall for the middle class for a flat fee of thirty guineas; also, to read "The Superlative in Manners and Literature" for the Marylebone Literary and Scientific Institution at Portman Square.[79] He wrote William that he was giving the extra lectures to earn money needed for his steamship fare. On June 21, from his third-story window in John Chapman's house on the Strand, he could see on the sides of the passing vans announcements in huge red letters that Ralph Waldo Emerson would speak that evening in Exeter Hall. These made him cringe with self-conscious embarrassment.[80]

He liked his Exeter Hall audiences better than his aristocratic ones. But his social life did not decline with this shift. At one dinner party he talked again with Lyell about geology, and was introduced to Charles Babbage, professor of mathematics at Cambridge, inventor of the first calculating machine. On June 23, Chopin gave a matinee in London and sent him a complimentary ticket through their mutual friend Jane Stirling. Emerson also found time to visit some friends in the suburbs of London. In Tottenham he inspected a famous collection of landscape paintings by Turner, whom some critics called the greatest of landscape painters, and he believed them.[81] Between July 4 and 6 he visited Windsor, Eton, and Cambridge.

Finally Emerson engaged passage on the steamer *Europa* for July 15. He was now impatient to return home. He missed his children and his comfortable house in Concord. But of course, before he left England, his friends gave farewell teas and dinners for him. Carlyle had dutifully attended all his lectures, but Emerson had not called at 5 Great Cheyne Row during most of the summer. Both he and Carlyle were aware of an increasing incompatibility between them. Emerson was tired of the grumpy Scot's continual scoffing and sarcastic laughter. And Carlyle was weary of Emerson's cheerfulness and imperturbable amiability. Jane Carlyle also aggravated the situation. Her friend Miss Jewsbury in Liverpool had declared to her that Emerson's *Essays* imitated her husband's writings.[82] Jane had a jealous streak in her and she was ready to believe "Miss Gooseberry." She resented, too, all the attention Emerson had been receiving from eminent people, some of them her own friends, whom she felt to be disloyal to her husband in lionizing Emerson. Yet Thomas Carlyle was aware of the debt he owed to Emerson for his reputation in America, which had also worked to his advantage in England, and he wanted his friend's last days in Great Britain to be happy for both of them. Having long intended to visit Stonehenge, the mysterious ring of mammoth stones on Salisbury Plain left by some prehistoric people, he suggested that they make the trip together.[83]

On July 7 the two ill-matched friends set out by train for Salisbury. On the way they almost quarreled when Emerson innocently remarked that, though he had been tremendously impressed by England, he thought the nation had seen its best days and that the future belonged to America. No one abused England more often than Carlyle, but he could not bear to have anyone else, and an American at that, make such comparisons. However, Emerson refused to argue, and Carlyle calmed down.

In Salisbury they took a carriage to Amesbury, a village only two miles from Stonehenge. At Amesbury they dined at the George Inn, then walked to Stonehenge across the wide, unfenced plain. When the sun went down, a brisk wind came up. They met no one and heard no sound except the song of skylarks high in the sky. The circle of monoliths, some standing, several lying on the ground, was one of the loneliest scenes on earth, especially in the twilight. No one knew how many thousands of years those huge gray stones had stood there, or why they had been erected on this spot. Carlyle sat in the shadow of one of the trilithons and smoked his pipe. He felt subdued, and said regretfully, "I plant cypresses wherever I go, and if I am in search of pain, I cannot go wrong."[84]

As they walked back to the inn a shower came up and they got pretty thoroughly sprinkled. That night Emerson wrote in his Journal: "Gray stones on a gray evening[,] here were they[,] nettles & butter cups at their feet within the enclosure[,] larks singing over them & the wind old as they ringing among the conscious stones. . . . They understood the English language[,] these British stones[,] of the two talkers one from America one from Scotland who came up to this old ark of the race."[85]

Next morning a local antiquary, a Mr. Brown, went back with Emerson and Carlyle to Stonehenge and told them "what he knew of the 'astronomical' and 'sacrificial' stones."[86] Mr. Brown pointed out that precisely over one of the stones facing east the sun rises at the summer solstice. He thought this was a Druid astronomical observatory—a theory generally accepted today, except for the Druid part; the stones are now believed to have been set up by a people more ancient than the Druids.

Back in Salisbury, Carlyle and Emerson visited the cathedral and heard the great organ, which sounded to Carlyle "as if a monk were panting to some fine Queen of Heaven."[87] From Salisbury they proceeded to Bishopstoke, where they spent a rainy Sunday; then continued on Monday to Winchester. Emerson thought Winchester Cathedral the most impressive he had seen, except for Westminster and York. Here lay the remains of King Canute, and Alfred the Great had been both crowned and buried here, with other Saxon kings. Late in the afternoon they returned to London by train. Both felt sad because they did not expect to see each other again—though they would.

Emerson's last days in England were spent in hasty visits and hurried preparations for his journey home—buying presents, books for himself, and the usual souvenirs. On Tuesday, July 11, he visited the Charles Brays in Coventry. (Later Bray described the visit in *Phases of Opinion and Experience*.) Mr. and Mrs. Edward Flower, with Miss Marian Evans (George Eliot), drove over from Stratford-upon-Avon to meet him, then carried him back in their carriage to Stratford. Miss Evans had read Emerson's *Essays* and was already an ardent admirer, and Emerson felt drawn to her, in spite of her lack of physical beauty. "What one book do you like best?" he asked her, and she said, "Rousseau's Confessions." "So do I," he replied. "There is a point of sympathy between us."[88]

On Friday, Emerson joined his friends in Liverpool, and they gave him a send-off dinner. Clough had come to Liverpool to spend as much remaining time as possible with his deeply loved friend. On Saturday he accompanied Emerson aboard the *Europa*. As they stood on the deck, waiting for the signal for visitors to leave and the steamer to start down the Mersey, Clough said sorrowfully: "You leave all of us young Englishmen without a leader. Carlyle has led us into the desert, and he has left us there." Emerson replied: "That is what all young men in England have said to me." Placing his hand on Clough's head, he said with mock solemnity: "I ordain you Bishop of England, to go up and down among all the young men, and lead them into the promised land."[89]

CHAPTER XXIII

Lyceum Express

...I am a literary runner & Lyceum Express.[1]

I

At six-thirty on Thursday morning, July 27, 1848, Emerson's steamship *Europa* docked at Boston.[2] The voyage from England had been uneventful, except for a short delay in Halifax because of fog, and he had had pleasant companions in Tom Appleton and Tom Ward, the youngest brother of his friend Samuel Gray Ward. He arrived in Boston in time to catch the morning train to Concord, and he was anxious to join his family, see how his fruit trees were doing, and begin setting his house in order after his long absence. He was tired of traveling and felt that he never wanted to leave home again. But his homecoming was somewhat dampened by the realization that his debt to the Concord Bank was nearly as large as it had been on his departure. He would have to put in a busy lecture season, with the necessity of frequent absences from home.[3]

When he reached Concord, Emerson found Lidian in "miserable health," and before she recovered, Eddy came down with a fever (perhaps a virus, then unknown to medical science), followed by his mother's taking a "bilious turn" (another medical ambiguity). William wanted Waldo's whole family to visit him on Staten Island, but Waldo wrote: "if we came to see you tis plain we should all be detained at Quarantine pier a full week."[4] This was a grim joke because the dreaded cholera had broken out in New York, and other American cities, and New York was almost panicking with fear.

In Emerson's absence Thoreau had efficiently planted his garden and sprayed his fruit trees. His little farm had not suffered while he was away, but he had missed the satisfaction of seeing the stages of growth, and on his return in midsummer his orchard and garden lacked their usual interest for him. In the spring Thoreau had written about the fire which had damaged nearly two acres of forest on the east side of Walden Pond. The fire had been detected soon after a train passed, and everyone agreed that it had been set by sparks from the engine. In August Emerson approached the superintendent of the Fitchburg Railroad about paying for the damage, and he agreed to cut the trees for the company's use and pay Emerson their value as lumber, estimated at fifty dollars.[5] This was a satisfactory settlement, but only time could repair the aesthetic loss.

By September all members of the Emerson family had recovered their health, and the summer ended with their visiting friends at the seashore. In October Lidian and the children made a trip to Plymouth. Thoreau had rejoined his family on the day Emerson returned. Several months earlier John Thoreau had suffered a heavy financial loss when the steam mill at the dam in the center of town was set on fire by an incendiary[6] —and now Henry was trying to assist his father in making pencils at home. He also began to survey land as another source of income. In addition to these activities, he was revising *A Week on the Concord and Merrimack Rivers* and was seeking a publisher, with Emerson's advice and encouragement.

Emerson was annoyed by demands on his time which interfered with his literary plans. He had scarcely reached home before Theodore Parker began imploring his help in sustaining the life of *The Massachusetts Quarterly Review*, and listed him as "senior editor" without his consent. Emerson told him bluntly that the magazine was not worth saving and that he would not waste his time on it.[7] He did not resent helping Dr. John Carlyle, Thomas's brother, find an American publisher for his prose translation of Dante's *Inferno*, for he thought it a valuable work, but negotiations with publishers were lengthy and frustrating, and he had finally to settle for publication without royalties. Meanwhile he was having considerable trouble in finding someone to board Bulkeley. The farmer who had been keeping him had sold his farm and no longer had a suitable place for him. "He is easily irritated," Waldo wrote William on October 4, "very garrulous, and altogether no inmate for me who have no sand rope for him to twist."[8]

National affairs did not greatly concern Emerson for several months after his return from England. The war with Mexico had officially ended the previous February with the Treaty of Guadalupe Hidalgo after General Winfield Scott ("Old Fuss and Feathers") invaded Mexico. Emerson was still in England when the political conventions were held in June to nominate candidates for the presidency. Polk, in poor health, had refused renomination, and the Democratic party selected Lewis Cass of Michigan, who was tolerant of slavery and thus acceptable to the South. The Democratic platform defended the Mexican War and condemned any attempt to interfere with slavery. Another Mexican War general, William O. Butler, of Kentucky, was nominated for Vice-President.

The Whigs, like the Northern Democrats, were divided on slavery; so without attempting to adopt a platform they nominated General Zachary Taylor ("Old Rough and Ready"), a war hero who rivaled Scott in popularity. For Vice-President they chose the undistinguished Millard Fillmore, of New York. The radical faction of the New York Democrats (the "Barnburners"), who opposed any extension of slavery, had wanted Martin Van Buren nominated for President, and were embittered by the selection of Taylor and Fillmore; so they called a Free-Soil convention in Buffalo and nominated Van Buren and Charles Francis Adams, son of John Quincy Adams.

If Emerson had been at home during these political maneuvers, he might have taken more interest in the 1848 election. His sympathies should have been with the Free-Soil ticket, but neither his letters nor his Journal gives any indication that he even voted on November 7. Two days after the election he recorded: "Here has passed an Election, I think, the most dismal ever known in this country. Three great parties voting for three candidates whom they disliked."[9] If he bothered to vote at all, he probably voted Whig, as usual. He could hardly have forgiven Van Buren for having permitted the removal of the Cherokee Indians from their homeland.

The significance of the discovery of gold in California was not yet apparent to Emerson, either. The "gold rush" did not actually start until 1849, but in 1848 Stephen Foster wrote "Oh! Susannah," the song which in a short time thousands of young men were singing around the camp-fires as they traveled in caravans to California—the land of instant wealth, if they were lucky. In a few months, too, cargoes of gold would begin arriving in Boston, New York, and Philadelphia, bringing temporary prosperity to the nation and a wider market for Emerson's lectures.

II

"I write no letters in these days, in which I am a literary runner & Lyceum Express," Emerson wrote his brother William on February 3, 1849.[10] He had begun lecturing on November 22 and had accelerated his pace in February. From two lectures in November, ten in December, ten in January, he increased the number to eighteen in February and fourteen in March, then tapered off to seven in April, one in May, and one in August.[11] Never before had he been quite so active in public speaking, and he earned nearly twelve hundred dollars that winter—the last two speeches were without fee, one to the Town and Country Club in Boston and the other at a meeting of the Anti-Slavery Society in Worcester.

For subject matter Emerson drew often from his recent experiences in Great Britain, and occasionally from those in France. For variety he could use some of the lectures he had given or revised in England, especially those in the series "Mind and Manners in the Nineteenth Century." On October 2, 1848, he had written Carlyle that everyone seemed to be interested in his recent experiences, and "were obstinate to know if the English were superior to their possessions, and if the old religion warmed their hearts, & lifted a little the mountain of wealth."[12]

It was easy for him to praise England, Emerson continued in his letter to Carlyle, because "England is the country of success, & success has a great charm for me." As he prepared to lecture on "Why England Is England," or simply "England," and a few times on "London," his estimation of the British people and their institutions grew in admiration. A correspondent for *The Boston Transcript* reported from Newport: "We had last night [December 5] the pleasure of hearing Mr Ralph Waldo Emerson lecture on the subject of England; in praise of which he could not say enough. He laid it on pretty thick, I assure you."[13]

In April 1849, Emerson began a mostly new series of lectures on "Laws of the Intellect," which he had begun writing in London. Parts of these lectures show that he was still interested in the kind of ideas he had expressed in *Nature* (1836). His lectures on England, London, and the manners of his contemporary world might seem to indicate that he had turned from Neoplatonic speculation to the realities of his everyday world, and he was moving in that direction as he struggled ever harder to earn money to pay his taxes and support his family. But his continued ambition to anatomize the mind shows that he had not become a *nominalist* in any philosophical sense, in spite of his very real domestic problems. That spring Lidian was so "feeble," he wrote William on April 4, that he had decided to employ a housekeeper, a Mrs. Hill, formerly housekeeper at Brook Farm.[14] He was now supporting five servants, to William's consternation.

In his lectures on "Intellect"[15] Emerson did not attempt to explain whether a finite or an infinite mind makes the world of human consciousness. What he preached (he never ceased being a preacher) was faith in a rational cosmos as the model for a rational moral order, which he attempted to analogize in "laws" of the mind that were less psychological than ethical. Soon this faith would be tested by human laws that violated—or so he would feel—the very nature of the Intellect which he believed created and permeated nature and the human mind.

III

After living at Hillside for three and a half years, Bronson Alcott moved his family to Boston on November 17, 1848, first to Dedham Street, then at short intervals to other addresses in the city. Hillside was later sold to Nathaniel Hawthorne, to whom Emerson deeded the eight acres of land held in trust for Mrs. Alcott's use.[16] She had never been satisfied with Concord, and she also hoped that in Boston her husband might find some way to contribute more to the support of his family, "a moderate expectation," Odell Shepard remarks, since he had earned practically nothing in Concord.[17] His plan was to hold "conversations" again, and for these he rented a room at 12 West Street, next door to Elizabeth Peabody's bookshop. As it turned out, Mrs. Alcott became the main support of the family by working for a charity organization which provided aid and advice to newly arrived immigrants, mostly Irish, in need of immediate employment. She had a special talent for this work. Until the novelty wore off, audiences did come to hear Alcott's performances, and seemed about to fulfill's his wife's hopes. On December 9 he gave his first conversation on the comprehensive subject of "Man."[18] A few weeks later Emerson, who was himself lecturing on "Spirit of the Times," wrote in his Journal:

> It is not the least characteristic sign of the Times, that Alcott should have been able to collect such a good company of the best heads for two Monday Evenings, for the expressed purpose of discussing the Times. What was never done by human beings in another age, was done now; there they met to discuss their own breath, to speculate on their own navels, with eyeglasses & solar microscope, and no man wondered at them. But these very men came in the cars[,] by steam-ferry & locomotive to the meeting, & sympathized with engineers & Californians. Mad contradictions flavor all our dishes.
>
> Putnam, Whipple, Dewey, W. H. Channing, & I,—and I know not how many more,—are lecturing this winter on the *Spirit of the Times!* And now Carlyle's first pamphlet is "The Present Age."[19]

Alcott's move to Boston also set both him and Emerson to thinking about starting a new social club, though their intentions appear not to have been exactly the same. For Emerson the Town and Country Club was to be both a literary and a social organization, where congenial men could gather for talk, a dinner now and then, and sometimes a formal lecture. He also wanted a room open to members at all times, so they could drop in at leisure to meet friends or read. Alcott wanted to found another magazine, and at one time a plan was formed for James Russell Lowell to edit a *Town and Country Magazine*.

Emerson drew up and printed a prospectus, copies of which both he and Alcott sent to men they hoped to have as members, not only their personal friends but all men of prominence in Boston and surrounding towns (the "country" part of the club). They were invited to meet at ten o'clock, Tuesday morning, March 20, at 12 West Street, to organize. In sending out the prospectus Alcott referred to the proposed organization as "a Club or College, for the study and diffusion of the Ideas and Tendencies proper to the Nineteenth Century; and to concert measures, if deemed desirable, for promoting the ends of good fellowship."[20] The response was so encouraging that by May the club had more than a hundred members, and Emerson was thinking of expanding to five hundred. Alcott was appointed secretary and keeper of the clubroom. He wanted to admit women to membership, but Emerson objected, possibly hoping to keep it something like the Athenaeum in London.

At the first meeting of the club on May 2, 1849, Emerson read a paper on "Books,"[21] probably a version of a lecture he had given in England. On August 28 he wrote Henry James Sr., informing him that he had been made a member and was invited to read a paper at the November meeting.[22] Emerson had visited James several times on his trips to New York, and valued his friendship highly, though James, like Margaret Fuller, complained of Waldo's reserve. James accepted the invitation, but added, "There is nothing I dread so much as literary men, especially *our* literary men." He found stage drivers more sincere and congenial. But lest Emerson think he preferred stage drivers to him, he explained: "I never read you as an author at all. Your books are not literature but life, and criticism always strikes me, therefore, as infinitely laughable when applied to you."

As subject for his lecture James proposed "Socialism," though he feared it would shock the members of the Town and Country Club; however, it was all he had to offer. Emerson replied that "Socialism is as good a topic as a brave man who likes it can choose."[23] On November 1 Henry James read "Socialism and Civilization in Relation to the Development of the Individual Life," in which he defended his Fourieristic thesis that man is "sufficient unto himself . . . save during his minority." Civilization he regarded as inherently depraved, subjecting a man to "the domination of tutors and governors all his appointed days upon the earth."[24]

Though Emerson had a low opinion of Fourier, his ideas and James's impinged at several points. Both believed that God incarnates Himself in human beings, and that the ideal life is one of spontaneous action in response to one's own innate divinity. Both agreed that society as then constituted (James's "Civilization") did not make use of "the divine in man," and in many ways hindered it. Emerson's "self-reliance" equated easily with James's "spontaneity." But Emerson was not a socialist, because he confined his reform to the individual: awaken one to one's infinite possibilities for a better and happier life, and society will take care of itself. James would reform society and merge the *self* in it. For him, conscious selfhood was a menace to both society and individual souls, whereas for Emerson consciousness of the self was awareness of God.

Alcott wrote in his Journal: "I would as soon attend an execution as one of his [James's] lectures. He is a headsman of social evils, and shows his teeth with a grace to frighten one."[25] Emerson cared as little for rigorous argumentation as Alcott, and he wrote James the following February, after visiting him in New York, that he was "awed and distanced a little by this argumentative style" (in *Moralism and Christianity* [1850], which contained the Boston speech). He preferred James's oral to his written expression. "And moreover I find or fancy ... that you have not shed your last coat of Presbyterianism, but that a certain catechetical and legendary Jove glares at me sometimes, in your pages, which astonishes me in so sincere and successful a realist."[26]

The Town and Country Club lasted little more than a year, but it succeeded in making Emerson more sociable—even to the extent of his indulging in after-dinner cigars, a sight that horrified his friend James. For some years Emerson had been a member of the Social Circle in Concord, which had somewhat the same purpose. It was composed of twenty-five of the "solidest" men of the town and met every Tuesday evening from October to April. Emerson claimed that Harvard was a wafer compared to the solid land which his friends in the Circle represented, and he never missed a Tuesday-night meeting if he could possibly help it.[27] But however *solid* these farmers, doctors, and lawyers were, they were surpassed in talent by the members of the Boston club, though some men of talent, such as Henry Thoreau, refused to join.

The Town and Country Club was succeeded by the Saturday Club, organized in 1855, with Emerson as a charter member.[28] *The Atlantic Monthly* has often been associated with the latter, but the original purpose was entirely social. Dr. Oliver Wendell Holmes made the meetings of the club at the Parker House famous by writing about them in his *Autocrat of the Breakfast-Table.* Now when friends from England came to Boston, Emerson could invite them to dine at the Saturday Club. But no guest from abroad gave such an amusing account of a meeting as Henry James Sr.

After an evening's entertainment at the Saturday Club, James wrote to Emerson that Hawthorne "had the look all the time, to one who did n't know him, of a rogue who suddenly finds himself in a company of detectives."[29] Mr. Frederic Henry Hedge, that pivotal character in the "Transcendental Club," sat beside James, but the little man talked so softly that James scarcely heard a word of what he said, and "felt at one time very much like sending down to Mr. Parker to have him removed from the room as maliciously putting his artificial little person between me and a profitable object of study." That object, Hawthorne, "seemed to me to possess human substance and not to have dissipated it all away as that debauched Charles Norton, and the good, inoffensive, comforting Longfellow."

At one end of the table, Emerson sat with John M. Forbes, the railroad builder (and father of Emerson's future son-in-law). James was incapable of understanding a financial genius such as Mr. Forbes, and thought he looked pathetic in this intellectual company: "How he buried his eyes in his plate, and ate with such a voracity that no person should dare to ask him a question!" James said his "heart broke for him as that attenuated Charles Norton kept putting forth his long antennae toward him, stroking his face, and trying whether his eyes were shut." But for Ellery Channing, James had only kind words: "so human and good, sweet as summer, and fragrant as pine woods . . . I felt the world richer by two *men,* who had not yet lost themselves in mere members of society."

Emerson thanked James for this "happiest letter" about the club, "so nobly true in its broad lights, that one was forced to forgive the perverse shadows you choose to throw on some of our quaintest statues." He read the letter to Ellery, "who vainly endeavored to disown his joy."[30]

IV

A few days before Christmas, 1848, on his way to visit his second cousin in Boston, George Barrell Emerson, Waldo Emerson learned of George's death.[31] He had also intended to call on Dr. Nathaniel Bowditch, a trustee of the Massachusetts General Hospital, hoping to interest him in defending Dr. Charles Jackson's claim to the discovery of anesthesia. While debating with himself whether to visit Dr. Bowditch in Pemberton Square, Emerson wandered into a bookstore (possibly Miss Peabody's on West Street), and his eyes fell on a volume of poems by Arthur Hugh Clough entitled *The Bothie of Toper-na-Fuosich.* What a strange title, and Clough had never mentioned it. Of course he bought the book.

Whether Emerson called on Dr. Bowditch that day or another, his Journal does not indicate, but when he did call he found no sympathy for his brother-in-law. Since the dentist William Morton had first used ether in the Massachusetts General Hospital, the hospital staff supported his claim. Dr. Jackson's case was not helped by the fact that he had an abrasive personality. Emerson was loyal to him because Lidian was fond of her brother and always came to his defense.

In May, while spraying his fruit trees, the thought occurred to Emerson that his pear tree was a perfect symbol of the world. "I find that each man, like each plant, has his own parasite, & Dr J[ackson] has very different & formidabler & more vicious enemies than any slugs that are on my leaves."[32] Dr. Bowditch was Jackson's "curculio & F & W [not identified] his borers & knifeworms. C. Brown eat[s] him first; then Morse; then Morton." Dr. Jackson was also involved in a dispute over his commission to make a geological and mineral survey in Michigan for the U.S. government. On May 23 Waldo wrote William: "My time was sadly occupied for a fortnight in Dr Jackson's affair[.] We now get from him assurances that he is to be left undisturbed in his survey & he is expected daily from Washington[.]"[33]

This was the kind of life Emerson led these days—and would lead for the next several years: grief, distractions, wasted time, with intervals of joy and accomplishment. On January 16 he wrote Clough how he had come upon his book at a time of "frightful calamity," and had that night "a strange balance to adjust, of grief & joy."[34] He called *The Bothie* to the attention of his friends. Longfellow found it "Altogether fascinating," and Lowell liked it. Longfellow wrote further that Tom Appleton read it aloud to the delight of the family, and "In the morning I found Appleton reading it again to himself; in the afternoon, my wife doing the same, &c. . . ." What surprised Emerson was the carefree exuberance, the wit, the joy of life, in Clough's poem. At the time that the young Oxonian left him on the deck of the steamer in Liverpool, Emerson had been worried about Clough's loss of religious faith and his dissatisfaction with the academic life. But the poem assured him that Clough was strong enough to endure.

The Bothie was a pastoral narrative in hexameter meter, such as Longfellow had used in *Evangeline,* about a collegian named Philip and his friends on vacation in the Highlands of Scotland. Philip falls in love with Elspie Mackaye, the daughter of a Highland farmer, or cottager (in Gaelic *bothie* means "cottage"). He marries her in defiance of his social class, and emigrates to New Zealand to lead an agrarian life. In a letter to Emerson written in February 1849, Clough explained that at the time of their parting in Liverpool he had not even thought of writing the poem. In the same letter he also announced that he had resigned from Oxford and accepted a position with University College in London for the following October.

During the spring of 1849 Emerson himself was writing nothing of consequence, but he was editing and revising his prose (except for his two series of *Essays*). He planned to collect his early writings as *Nature, Addresses, and Lectures.* (The book would eventually become Volume I of his *Collected Works.*[35]) The contents were to be the 1836 *Nature,* four addresses ("The American Scholar," "Divinity School Address," "Literary Ethics," and "The Method of Nature"), and three lectures published in *The Dial:* "Man the Reformer," "Lecture on the Times," and "The Young American." The most significant change Emerson made in the text was dropping his motto from Plotinus, "Nature is but an image or imitation of wisdom, the last thing of the soul; nature being a thing which doth only do, but not know," for some verses of his own:

> A subtle chain of countless rings
> The next unto the farthest brings;
> The eye reads omens where it goes,
> And speaks all languages the rose;
> And, striving to be man, the worm
> Mounts through all the spires of form.

The difference between the two mottoes, or epigraphs, is at first startling, the former stressing the unconsciousness of nature and the second suggesting an evolution of dawning consciousness. Actually Emerson's new verses also derive from Plotinus. The American Hegelian philosopher William T. Harris pointed out that these lines originated in Plotinus's statement: "We might say that all beings, not only rational ones, but even irrational ones, the plants, and even the soil that bears them, aspire to attain conscious knowledge."[36] Harris also attributed to Plotinus "the suggestion of those fine poetic dreams of Schelling and Oken,—that reason dreams in the plant, and feels in the animal, and thinks in man." Whether the first epigraph was really what Plotinus said (it was supposedly written down by a disciple) is not known, but Emerson, after further exposure to European Romanticism, as well as reading and talking with Lyell the geologist about the origin of the planet, now found more appropriate the notion that though nature might be unconscious in plants or lower animals, an emerging consciousness was struggling to be born. *Nature, Addresses, and Lectures* was published by James Munroe and Company in September 1849.[37]

Emerson worked away at the text of *Representative Men* during the hot summer of 1849 and well into the fall. He felt that his lectures on Plato and Swedenborg had been superficial, and that his Shakespeare had been "uninspired."[38] Attempts to improve these chapters held up publication for several months, but *Representative Men* was finally issued by Phillips, Sampson and Company on January 1, 1850. The ideas in the book were nearly the same as the lectures described above in Chapter XX.

The difficulties Emerson experienced during this work of editing and revision were in large part domestic. In May, Ellen was severely ill with mumps, which of course the other children contracted. After her recovery, Emerson interrupted his literary work to take her to Staten Island for a long visit with her uncle and aunt, and then had to make another trip at the end of the summer to bring her back. The burning of the Court House on June 20 was no personal loss to him, but the whole town was upset by the prospect that the county court might be moved to another town—though Emerson ascertained that it would not be. The fire had been set by a man being prosecuted for selling liquor without a license.

In July, Emerson wrote Ellen that the "great heats" kept Edith and Eddy confined to the house. "Concord is a good deal burned by too much sunshine and the farmers are beginning to cut down their corn because it rolls & withers. Our corn in the garden & Warren lot is still good, but we use our pump to keep all the shrubs & my pear trees from perishing."[39] Lidian suffered more than anyone else from the heat, and in September Waldo's mother was alarmingly ill with pneumonia. She recovered, but for some time her hearing was impaired, and, in fact, her final decline had begun, and she would die November 16, 1853.

V

Edward Emerson says that *Representative Men* was "well received on both sides of the ocean. It was naturally at that time a more popular book than the *Essays* had been."[40] The second statement is more accurate than the first. In his own country Emerson's friends liked the book, and his enemies—of which he, like Dr. Jackson, had a good supply—disliked it. The negative critics judged it with their preconceived prejudices against the author's unorthodox religion and his reputed "Transcendentalism." A reviewer in *The New Englander* thought it "purely ridiculous for anyone to laborously [*sic*] write out, and gravely read to large audiences, such gratuitous absurdities."[41] But *The Literary World,* edited by Evert and George Duyckinck, welcomed the book as less visionary and metaphysical than Emerson's previous publications, and as containing more common sense.

In England the reception of *Representative Men* was equally mixed, as Emerson's lectures had been; or perhaps more accurately, the reception was more mixed, for the approval or disapproval was not only moral and religious but also literary.[42] James Froude, for example, who had been friendly on Emerson's visit to Oxford, declared that the design of the book was wrong, the author having chosen men of thought instead of action. A critic in *Sharp's London Journal* took it that Emerson's purpose was to show that virtuous men live in harmony with "the design of God—the visible manifestation of the sacred laws which are the vital force of humanity. . . ." He noted that Napoleon lacked this harmony, and that through him Emerson criticized "the age in which we live."

The Athenaeum also observed that in this book Emerson exposed "the course, the varieties, of human life, as exhibited in the world's great men." Sometime early in 1850 (exact day not indicated) Emerson complained in his Journal: "The English journals snub my new book; as indeed they have all its foregoers. Only now they say, that this last has less vigour & originality than the others. . . . The fate of my books is like the impression of my face. My acquaintances, as long as I can remember, have always said, 'Seems to me you look a little thinner than when I saw you last.' "[43]

Some reviews did not appear until summer. Carlyle wrote on July 19 that Chapman had sent him a copy on the day of publication (which was the same as in Boston): "you now get the Book offered you for a shilling, at all railway stations"—meaning in a pirated edition. In fact, Emerson's title had become so well known that when Sir Robert Peel died on July 2, newspapers called him a "representative man." Carlyle thought this ought to be some compensation for the piracy. As for his own opinion: "I found the Book a most finished clear and perfect set of *Engravings in the line manner;* portraitures full of *likeness,* and abounding in instruction and materials for reflection . . ."[44] He cared less for "Plato," and found incompleteness in "Swedenborg," though "excellent in many respects." He dissented a little over the end of all the chapters, though he "had so lustily shouted 'Hear! hear!' all the way from the beginning up to that stage."

Many reviewers compared Emerson's *Representative Men* with Carlyle's *Heroes and Hero-Worship* (1841), often to Emerson's disadvantage. Émile Montégut in *La Revue des Deux Mondes* was friendly on the whole, but he preferred Carlyle's great men to Emerson's, who is the "pagan *par excellence,* the man who holds his *grace from nature.* For Carlyle, the great man is he who has received his mission from heaven, who must express it to others with difficulty, and obtain its triumph at his own peril."[45] Emerson exhibits "the eminent types of humanity, the men who represent most powerfully the different intellectual forces of the human mind."

His book was scarcely printed before Emerson began to have some strange "after thoughts" about it. Why had he not given expression to "the greatness of the common farmer & labourer[?] A hundred times I have felt the superiority of George, & Edmund, & Barrows, & yet I continue the parrot echoes of the names of literary notabilities." George and Edmund were probably Emerson's farmer neighbors George Minott and Edmund Hosmer, but which of several Barrows he meant is not certain. Yet, "the whole human race agree to value a man precisely in proportion to his power of expression, & to the most expressive man that has existed, namely Shakspeare, they have awarded the highest place."[46]

Several months before the publication of *Representative Men,* a remarkable Swedish woman named Fredrika Bremer arrived in the United States to study American life and character, and especially to make the acquaintance of the country's leading writers, artists, and politicians. She herself was a famous novelist, admired for her depiction of average people such as she had known in Scandinavia. Her novels had been translated into many languages, including English, and were widely read in America. Walter Whitman, then editor of *The Brooklyn Eagle,* said he knew of no novels "more likely to melt and refine the human character."[47] Miss Bremer was a middle-aged woman, with plain features, simple manners, and in poor health. She had been well educated in music, art, literature, and modern languages. Intellectually, she was comparable to Margaret Fuller, about whom she had immense curiosity, but had a gentler personality and more pleasing manners.

Miss Bremer had read and admired Emerson's *Essays* and *Poems,* and wanted to meet their author. On December 4, 1849, she went out to Concord on the train with a companion. Emerson was expecting her, and walked out bareheaded in a snowstorm to meet her at his front gate. He was a younger man than she had expected, but not so handsome, with a pale complexion, dark hair, and strongly marked features. No one could have been more courteous to her, yet she thought him cold and hypercritical, "looking out for an ideal, which he never finds realized on earth."[48] He seemed to despise suffering, regarding it "as a weakness unworthy of higher natures." His poems showed that he had had sorrows and felt them deeply, but he "has only allowed himself to be bowed for a short time by these griefs." For Lidian she felt a strong affinity. "Mrs. Emerson has beautiful eyes, full of feeling, but she appears delicate, and is in character very different from her husband."

The Emersons invited Miss Bremer to return for a longer visit, and Emerson himself brought her from Boston on January 17, 1850. She stayed from Thursday evening until Monday morning. She was still somewhat repelled by her host's "eagle-like nature," but he listened attentively to everything she had to say, and she felt more at ease than she had on her initial call. "One may quarrel with Emerson's thoughts [she did], with his judgment, but not with himself. . . . He is a born nobleman."[49]

In 1850 Emerson was still, so far as he could, keeping aloof from the great social agitations of the day, and Miss Bremer held this against him. "I could desire in him warmer sympathies, larger interest in social questions that touch upon the well-being of mankind, and more feeling for the suffering and sorrowful on earth." Miss Bremer's judgment of Emerson was probably affected by the fact that she was quite ill on her arrival—she complained that the train ride was rough; European trains were smoother. But Mrs. Emerson's ministrations revived her, and she was feeling completely recovered when she left Monday morning, accompanied by Dr. Charles Jackson, who had also been a weekend guest in the Emerson home.

VI

Emerson could hardly have traveled faster in 1850 as a "Lyceum Express" than he had in 1849, but he certainly traveled farther. Beginning his lectures in Concord on January 2, he journeyed to Albany a few days later, and roundabout to New York City, where he delivered "Spirit of the Times" on January 22 and 29. Then he continued through Connecticut, Massachusetts, Maine, and back home in mid-February. He had mentioned to Henry James Sr. that he thought of returning to New York, and on March 1 James wrote that Emerson should do so and stay with him. Emerson replied: "I am balancing whether to carry my popgun and thimbleful of paper bullets to Brooklyn, to New Jersey, and to the adjacent hamlet of New York."[50]

A letter from Marcus Spring, a New York merchant and Quaker philanthropist, who owned a large estate near Perth Amboy, New Jersey, settled his decision to go. He asked James to make arrangements for tickets and newspaper announcements in New York, but "I shall go to the Astor [hotel], that I may the more unblushingly spend the whole day at your house." He had no new lectures, but suggested that "Lectures on the XIX Century" would cover anything he could offer. However, he would not promise "London," because he had already drained that lecture for "England," and would not have time to "make good these defects" in the "London" manuscript. This gives some insight into his methods.

In New York, Emerson spoke in Hope Chapel, which was larger than Clinton Hall, where he had lectured in January, but *The New York Post* reported that "the opening lecture of the new series [March 14] had one of the most crowded audiences that we have seen this season." The subject was his old standby, "Natural Aristocracy." Two days later "The Superlative in Literature, Manners, and Races" drew a smaller audience. During the remainder of the month he gave five more performances in New York, with side trips to Brooklyn, Newark, and Paterson. He brought the series in Hope Chapel to a close on April 2 with "Instinct and Inspiration," before what *The Post* called his largest audience yet, including ex-President Van Buren and other notables. The George Bancrofts, now living in New York, were present, and Waldo reported to Lidian that Mrs. Bancroft wished her to visit them in the city.[51]

During April, Emerson gave six performances in Philadelphia, but snow and rain kept him from drawing a good crowd. One newspaper reported that he "says some of the most original as well as some of the most unintelligible things of any man in the United States."[52] Though he enjoyed seeing his old schoolmate William Henry Furness, and made many new friends, including the Quaker reformer Lucretia Mott, he was bored by hotel life, and wrote in his Journal:

> I have made no note of these long weary absences at New York & Philadelphia. I am a bad traveller, & the hotels are mortifications to all sense of well being in me. The people who fill them oppress me with their excessive virility [probably the traveling salesmen], and would soon become intolerable, if it were not for a few friends, who, like women, tempered the acrid mass. Henry James was true comfort—wise, gentle, polished, with heroic manners, and a serenity like the sun.[53]

Emerson had scarcely had time to get rested at home after his tiresome stay in Philadelphia, when he received a letter from Cincinnati, with a hundred signatures, urging him to come there for a round of lectures. Many New Englanders had settled in Ohio, and Emerson's friend James Freeman Clarke had been the pastor of a Unitarian church in Cincinnati. During *The Dial*'s four years of life a surprising number of subscriptions had come from that city. On May 6 Emerson wrote William that he was debating whether to accept the invitation, which was for that month, but "I incline to refuse, as my garden wants me, & my library more."[54] But the chance to see Niagara Falls and the West was too tempting to resist.

Near the middle of May Emerson started on his long journey. The railroad had recently been extended to the Middle West, but he selected a combination of trains and steamer: first the train to Buffalo, then a lake steamer to Sandusky. Near Cleveland, however, on May 16, the steamer caught fire and hastily docked. As soon as the Cleveland Library Association learned that Emerson was one of the passengers, he was invited to give a lecture, and he agreed to do so—gratis. He was reported to have delighted a large audience, assembled on a few hours' notice, with his lecture on "England."[55] From Cincinnati he wrote Lidian on Monday, May 20:

> I left Cleveland ... on Friday evening, about 7 o'clock, in the steamer Saratoga, had a rough pleasant ride over the lake to Sandusky, about 5

hours, slept there until nearly 5 o'clock, A.M., then took the cars for the South, and travelled 218 miles to this city. Beautiful road, grand old forest, beeches, immense black walnuts, oaks, rock maples, buckeyes (horse chestnuts) in bloom, cornels [dogwood] in white flower, & red buds—a forest tree whose bloom is precisely the colour of the peach-blossom,— made all the miles rich with beauty; enormous grapevines I saw too! Most of the houses were log-huts, with log-barns. Cities are everywhere much the same thing, but this forest is very unlike ours. The land was all heavy with wood, and, of course, the poor Germans buy it with confidence that it will bear wheat & corn.[56]

Emerson had seen primeval forests in Maine, but those in Ohio had few pines. In the scattered places where the land had been cleared for cultivation, it was still so fertile that it did not need manure. Emerson was told that it was the custom, when the manure pile had grown too big, to move the barn to a new location, leaving the pile undisturbed. Near Cincinnati the wheat was, he judged, from a foot to eighteen inches tall, and the corn about six inches. Emerson thought this surprising for mid-May, about the time he would have been planting corn, but he was told the season was backward that year.

In Cincinnati, Emerson stayed at the Burnet House, "a magnificent hotel, the best & largest building of that kind I have ever seen," he wrote Lidian. Cincinnati itself had grown in ten years from 46,000 to over 100,-000 inhabitants (the census gave 115,435). Emerson lectured in the Universal Church to audiences reported as "large."[57] His five scheduled subjects ("Natural Aristocracy," "Eloquence," "Spirit of the Times," "England," and "Books") were so well received that he was persuaded to give three more lectures; but these, chosen from "The Natural History of the Intellect" manuscript begun in England, were not so successful. *The Cincinnati Gazette* pronounced them "too abstruse . . . and altogether too comprehensive in their method."[58]

On May 25 Emerson celebrated his birthday by an excursion to a place called Ancient Forest, in Warren County, where the fabled Mound Builders had constructed circular ridges extending four or five miles. The mounds had not yet been excavated, but the ancient trees, the flowering tulip poplars especially, were magnificent. "In this sylvan Persepolis, I spent my birthday with a very intelligent party of young men."[59]

On another occasion Emerson crossed the Ohio River and admired Cincinnati from the opposite shore. He was much amused by Kentucky man-ners and "tall tales":

The Kentuckian sits all day on his horse. You shall see him at the door of a country store. There he sits & talks & makes his bargains for hours, & never dismounts. When all is done, he spurs up his steed, & rides away.— The path of a tornado is traced through the forest, of the same width for miles. They tell of a child who was carried five miles by one. This was too good to leave alone. So we presently heard of a tornado which drove a plough through a field, & turned as pretty a furrow all around the field as you ever saw. This, of course, suggested to another of the company a storm in Havana where the wind blew so hard, that a man was left cling-ing to an iron lamp-post, with nothing on him but his stock & his spurs.

After Emerson's last lecture in Cincinnati, a group of his new friends invited him to join them on a trip to Mammoth Cave, in Kentucky. They left Cincinnati on June 4 aboard the steamboat *Ben Franklin*. Next morn-ing, after spending the night in Louisville, they found no coaches or horses available, but could get passage on the steamboat *Mammoth Cave,* which took them 182 miles down the Ohio River to Evansville, then 150 miles up the Green and Barren rivers to Bowling Green. This river trip extended from Wednesday afternoon to Saturday morning.[60]

Early Sunday morning the party rode in a coach for the remaining thirty-five miles, reaching the cave by seven-thirty a.m. They entered the cave without delay and penetrated it nine miles, walking the total of eigh-teen miles in fourteen hours. When they emerged at nine-thirty p.m., rain was pouring, after a violent thunderstorm which they had not heard. Emerson said they had lost one of the "days of our bright lives" (quoting a phrase from Ellery Channing's "Our Birth Days"). Next day he spent four more hours in the cave.

Unable to secure transportation back to Bowling Green, Emerson and a companion walked seven miles to Bell's Tavern, then next morning four-teen miles farther until they finally obtained a buggy to take them to Bowling Green—no mention is made of baggage. By stage, with two-hour rests, Emerson continued to Eddyville, where he took a steamboat down the Cumberland River to Paducah; then he took another steamboat down the Ohio to Cairo, where it flows into the Mississippi. Emerson's account of this trip makes it sound more exhausting than his crossing the Alps in 1834.

When steamboats began to ply the Mississippi, speculators bought up the land in Cairo, expecting it to become a great city. Even the Rothschilds are said to have invested. Houses were built and streets laid out, but in the spring the river flooded this low-lying spot, making most of it uninhabitable. When Emerson saw Cairo the houses were vacant, and the only "habitable place seemed to be (what is often seen in these rivers,) an old steamboat whose engine has been taken out & the boat moored & fitted up into the dirtiest of Ann-street boarding-houses." After taking on wood and tinkering with the engine, the captain of Emerson's boat steered out of rancid Cairo and steamed up the Mississippi.

These steamboats, Emerson observed, were no "palaces," as some later became, but were cheaply and poorly constructed, "just made to keep above the water from port to port, & generally disabled of one wheel." The wide Mississippi was a lonely river; for long stretches "no towns, no houses, no dents in the forest, no boat almost,—we met, I believe but one steamboat in the first hundred miles." Now and then he did see a mud scow, loaded with wood, lying near the shore. The captain would blow his whistle, and the scow would come out and tie up to the boat, which then would steam up the river while the wood was being transferred. Among the passengers were a number of planters, one with his family and six slaves, the butt of a pistol protruding from his breast pocket. Most of the passengers were armed. In the cabin, gamblers were playing cards and exchanging large sums of money. They professed to be entire strangers to each other, hoping to induce the naive Yankees to sit down with them.

In St. Louis, people were dying of cholera in Emerson's hotel, and as soon as possible he took another steamboat up to Galena, then a stage to Elgin, where he boarded a train which took him across the prairie to Chicago. Without pausing to explore this rapidly growing town, except for a buggy ride on the beach of Lake Michigan, Emerson "Crossed the lake to New Buffalo, [and] took the Central Michigan Railroad to Detroit. There, I found good company to Boston."[61] Among the "good company" was his friend John M. Forbes, president of the Central Michigan line. The hardships of this trip might have been enough to discourage a man nearing fifty from further ventures into mid-America, but the next year Emerson would extend his western lecture tour.

VII

Emerson arrived in Concord on Friday morning, June 28. At that very time, unknown to him, Margaret Fuller, with her young son, Angelo, and her Italian husband, the Marchese Giovanni Angelo Ossoli, were sailing to America on the merchant ship *Elizabeth,* which was heavily laden with Italian marble.[62] Margaret, a believer in omens, had had many misgivings about sailing on this ship—and even about making the trip at all. But the Italian revolution had failed, and both she and Ossoli had been ordered to flee Rome on twenty-four hours' notice. Both had participated in the lost cause, he as captain of the Civic Guards, and she as *regolatrice* (manager) of a hospital for wounded soldiers. Lewis Cass, the United States envoy in Rome, had helped the Ossolis escape to Florence, but they would have had great difficulty in supporting themselves there. Margaret's dispatches to *The New-York Daily Tribune* were frequently lost in transit, and payments were long delayed. The marchese was in disgrace with his family, the Vatican, and the Roman government. He had not previously been able to marry Margaret, a Protestant. A recent biographer thinks the marriage may have been performed in or near Florence.[63]

Despite Margaret's many misgivings, the Ossolis and a maid boarded the *Elizabeth* in Leghorn on May 17, but the voyage seemed ill-fated almost from the start. In a few days the captain was stricken with smallpox. He died on June 2 and was buried in Malta. The infant Angelo caught the infection, but recovered. Everything seemed to be going well until the night of July 18, when a hurricane blew the *Elizabeth* aground several hundred yards off the beach of Fire Island, New York, and totally wrecked her the next day.

Emerson did not learn of the tragedy until several days later. A reporter from *The Tribune* heard that a ship was in trouble off Long Island and reached the scene at about eleven o'clock on Friday morning, July 19. Around noon a lifeboat and howitzer arrived from the Fire Island Light House station, but the wind and waves made it impossible to launch the boat or shoot a line to the ship. In the afternoon the marble broke through the hold and the ship fell apart. The captain's wife and a few sailors managed to reach shore by clinging to parts of the wreckage; the body of little Angelo washed up on the sand, but Margaret and Ossoli completely disappeared. Some of her letters floated to shore in a box, but no part of her manuscript history of the Italian revolution was ever found.

Bits of information about the wreck were printed in *The Tribune* for several days before the full story was told on July 23.[64] Emerson read it that day, thought of going to the scene himself to search for Margaret's Italian revolution manuscript, but decided that Thoreau could better perform the errand. He wrote Horace Greeley, asking him to advise Henry, and next day Thoreau and William Henry Channing set out for Fire Island. They interviewed survivors and witnesses of the wreck, but found little that was new, only a few pieces of clothing. The *Tribune* reporter had taken the recovered letters to New York, dried them out, and turned them over to Horace Greeley.

For several days Emerson lamented the loss in his Journal; he could not get Margaret out of his mind. He commented on eight separate pages of his Journal:

[233] On Friday, 19 July, Margaret dies on rocks at Fire Island Beach within sight of & within 60 rods of the shore. To the last her country proves inhospitable to her; brave, eloquent, subtle, accomplished, devoted, constant soul![65]

. . . . .

[234] . . . Mrs [Sarah Bradford] Ripley thinks that the marriage with Ossoli was like that of De Stael in her widowhood with the young *De Rocca,* who was enamoured of her. And Mrs [Almira Penniman] Barlow has unshaken trust that what Margaret did, she could well defend.

. . . .

[236] . . . "Her heart, which few knew, was as great as her mind, which all knew" . . . E. H. [Elizabeth Hoar] says of Margaret . . . that she was the largest woman; & not a woman who wished to be a man.

. . . .

[238] I have lost in her my audience. I hurry now in my work admonished that I have few days left. There should be a gathering of her friends & some Beethoven should play the dirge.

. . . .

[240] . . . Mrs Barlow has the superiority to say of Margaret, that the death seems to her a fit & good conclusion to the life. Her life was romantic & exceptional: So let her death be; it sets the seal on her marriage, avoids all questions of Society, all of employment, poverty, & old age, and besides was undoubtedly predetermined when the world was created.

Mrs. Barlow was the wife of the Reverend D. H. Barlow of Lynn. There was, of course, much speculation about Margaret's marriage to the young nobleman ten years her junior. Hawthorne uncharitably refused to believe that Ossoli had married her at all. Emerson did not speculate on the question, but he realized that Boston society would be unsympathetic to her, and he wondered about her being able to support a husband (supposing him to be unqualified to support a family) and son. But such friends as Elizabeth Hoar thought her equal to any necessity. Margaret had written Emerson for advice on the publication of her history of the Italian revolution and he felt that it would be a great book.

Horace Greeley wanted Emerson to prepare a memorial volume for Margaret Fuller Ossoli. Rusk says that at first he doubted that she was important enough for such an honor,[66] but what he wrote to Sam Ward was, "it might be a work above our courage."[67] Whether he had doubts or not, he readily agreed to undertake a "Life and Letters" type of book with the assistance of Ward and William Henry Channing. Ward soon withdrew from the project, and James Freeman Clarke took his place. Emerson himself wrote to all of Margaret's known friends for letters and collected a large batch. The book, finally published in 1852 in two volumes by Phillips, Sampson and Company, Emerson's Boston publisher, was called *Memoirs of Margaret Fuller Ossoli*.

The biography was loosely thrown together, a narrative interspersed with letters, extracts from Margaret's Journals, and personal reminiscences by those who had known her. Clarke wrote of her Cambridge period, and Emerson of the years he had known her, which included most of her public life. The best-written and most enthralling section was the final account of the voyage home and the shipwreck by Channing, comparable in vividness to one of Melville's short stories. Channing exhaustively interviewed all survivors of the wreck and reconstructed in minute detail the last day of Margaret's life. One sailor offered to try to swim to shore with the baby strapped to his back, and another tried to persuade Margaret to hold on to a plank which he would push in front of him. Possibly neither of these schemes would have worked in the churning surf. At any rate, she persistently said that she would not be parted from her husband and child; if one of them perished, she wanted all to perish together. She had her wish. Channing ended his account rhetorically but with genuine bitterness:

Was this, then, thy welcome home? A howling hurricane, the pitiless sea, wreck on a sand-bar, an idle life-boat, beach-pirates, and not one friend! In those twelve hours of agony, did the last scene appear but as the fitting close for a life of storms, where no safe haven was ever in reach; where thy richest treasures were so often stranded; where even the dearest and nearest seemed always too far off, or just too late, to help. . . . It was in the Father's house that welcome awaited thee.[68]

CHAPTER XXIV

Quarrel with America

My own quarrel with America, ... the geography is sublime, but the men are not.[1]

I

Emerson had come back from England in 1848 with mixed feelings: he deeply appreciated the hospitality he had received, and he had been impressed by the display of wealth and power; but his conscience was disturbed by the evidences of inherited privilege, blind conservatism, stupid resistance to ideas, and colossal self-satisfaction. In *English Traits,* based on his lectures in the early 1850s (including "England," "London," and "The Anglo-Saxon"), he would say (1856), "England is the best of actual nations," yet "it is an old pile built in different ages, with repairs, additions, and makeshifts."[2] In his lectures, as we have seen, he emphasized the merits of England; in his book he is more realistic and critical. He says bluntly that in England the upper classes oppress the lower, the Church punishes dissenters, "Pauperism incrusts and clogs the state, and in hard times becomes hideous. . . . In cities, the children are trained to beg, until they shall be old enough to rob."[3] Parents actually poisoned their children to collect burial fees. "During the Australian emigration, multitudes were rejected by the commissioners as being too emaciated for useful colonists."

England at the time of Emerson's second visit was at, or near, the peak of her political and economic power, with colonies around the globe. She possessed the most highly developed industrial system in history, and was banker to the world. Small wonder that the leaders were puffed up with pride and arrogance and set bad examples for the poor and ignorant. All his life Emerson had preached against materialism uncontrolled by conscience, and here was materialism more crass than anything he had seen in America. English prosperity rested on steam power and machinery, and "the larger machinery of commerce. . . . 'T is not, I suppose, want of probity, so much as the tyranny of trade, which necessitates a perpetual competition of underselling, and that again a perpetual deterioration of the fabric."[4] If this trend continued, the result would be moral collapse, and Emerson feared that this might be the fate of industrial civilization in all countries. However, England should be credited with some palliatives: "A part of the money earned returns to the brain to buy schools, libraries, bishops, astronomers, chemists and artists with; and a part to repair the wrongs of this intemperate weaving, by hospitals, saving-banks, Mechanics' Institutes, public grounds and other charities and amenities."[5] Yet these were woefully inadequate, and Emerson wondered whether in her industrial progress England was not falling victim to a catastrophe to which all industrial nations might succumb.

As for his own country, Emerson had never seriously considered whether that "common catastrophe" could be its fate, though he had predicted in 1846 that swallowing Mexico would poison the United States.[6] By the time he returned from England, Mexico had been swallowed without yet producing obvious symptoms of poisoning. Of course the bitterness between the slaveholding states of the South and the free states of the North had increased, but the Mexican War had been an effect, not the main cause, of that strife.

The nation was now so divided on the question of slavery that if certain compromises between North and South had not been adopted in 1850, the Civil War might have begun then rather than eleven years later. However, no "compromise" could solve the problem, for the real conflict was over political power, and the North was growing stronger each year. Southern leaders knew that, and it made them desperate. The compromise finally adopted by the Senate in September 1850, and ratified by the House, included admitting California to the Union as a free state; dividing the land obtained from Mexico west of Texas into two territories, New Mexico and Utah, "with or without slavery, as their Constitution may prescribe"; abolishing the slave trade in the District of Columbia, but not the possession of slaves; and the enactment of a stringent law obligating every citizen to aid in the return of runaway slaves.

These restrictions on the extension of slavery did not in any way satisfy the abolitionists, and the Fugitive Slave Law angered many moderate-minded people in the North, including Emerson, though his emotions would not become violent until attempts were made to enforce the law in New England. With the admission of California as a free state, the North held an advantage of power in the Senate of two votes, and this was intolerable to Southern militants such as John C. Calhoun. But these had failed at a convention in Nashville in June 1850 to get the slaveholding states to secede from the Union. Now they agitated for rigorous enforcement of the Fugitive Slave Law.

During the summer and autumn of that year Emerson was more a disgusted spectator than an active protester. This may have been partly because for some weeks after Margaret Fuller's death he was more concerned with that tragedy than with national wrongs. Toward the end of October, however, he had a stimulating conversation with Henry Thoreau, after which he recorded his feeling about recent history: "My own quarrel with America, of course, was, that the geography is sublime, but the men are not." The junction of the two oceans had been effected by "selfishness, fraud, & conspiracy."[7]

Yet in spite of his contempt for the men who had made the United States a continental nation, Emerson still did not feel challenged to oppose them actively. Once again he took the view that providential nature may work in ways that seem hideous at close sight but are beneficial in the ultimate outcome. "As if what we find in nature, that the animalcule system is of ferocious maggot & hideous mite, who bite & tear, yet make up the fibre & texture of nobler creatures; so all the grand results of history are brought about by these disgraceful tools." By maggot and mite Emerson meant the parasitical organisms that scientists told him inhabit every animal, including the human. This paradox increased his curiosity about the origins and functions of power in physiology and social economy.

On December 6, 1850, Emerson gave a lecture in Concord on "Property," and in January and February 1851, another lecture on "Power" in Brookline, Rochester, Buffalo, and Syracuse. Then in March he pulled these into a series which included "The Laws of Success," "Wealth," "Economy," "Culture," and "Worship," to which he added "Fate" in December. These were to be key chapters in the book which he would call *The Conduct of Life* (1860).

Not only did Emerson venture into a wider geographical orbit with these lectures; he also explored new intellectual terrain. With his eyes on the actual facts of his contemporary world, he asked himself two basic questions: Why do certain men succeed in the struggle to gain wealth and influence? And, since many of these successful men are morally reprehensible, what is their function or contribution in the evolution of society?

Darwin's *Origin of Species* would not be published until 1859, but Emerson's concept of the struggle for survival in nature is suggested or implied in these lectures, and he anticipated some aspects of the movement in the next generation which would be called Social Darwinism (and in literature, Naturalism). The universe operates by the expenditure of energy, or power, Emerson says, and "Life is a search after power." However, he had not forsaken the teleology of his first book, *Nature* (1836), for he still believed that "A cultivated man, wise to know and bold to perform, is the end to which nature works, and the education of the will is the flowering and result of all this geology and astronomy."[8] In his earliest lectures on science he had said that the planet had to go through aeons of *preparation* before man could inhabit it.

Contemporary scientists were drifting away from teleology; they were more concerned with *how*, not *why*, nature works. Yet if Emerson still held on to *why*, he had nevertheless been influenced by the British scientists he had talked with and by his reading of their books. He had absorbed enough science to watch closely the actual operations of the men who succeeded in gaining and wielding social and political power. He noticed, first of all, that they all believed in causality, "that things were not by luck, but by law." They gained their ends by the expenditure of energy, judgment, and will. Even though he had complained of the display of *virility* in the hotels of New York and Philadelphia, he recognized that virility was a prerequisite for worldly success. The "vast majority of men at all times, and even ... heroes in all but certain eminent moments," are imbeciles, "victims of gravity, custom and fear." This gives force to the strong because "the multitudes have no habit of self-reliance or original action."

Sounding even more like a late-nineteenth-century Naturalist such as Frank Norris or Jack London, Emerson says "success [is] a constitutional trait ... courage, or the degree of life, is as the degree of circulation of the blood in the arteries. ... The advantage of a strong pulse is not to be supplied by any labor, art or concert."[9] He had always lamented his own deficiency in physical energy, and perhaps this only made him more aware that "The first wealth is health. Sickness is poor-spirited, and cannot serve any one: it must husband its resources to live." Robust health gives energy "to spare, runs over, and inundates the neighborhoods and creeks of other men's necessities." Yet Emerson is not a Determinist, for by right thinking an individual can do something to keep himself healthy: "The mind that is parallel with the laws of nature will be in the current of events and strong with their strength." Thus did Emerson anticipate Christian Science—or should we say he provided the source for it?

II

A few years later Walt Whitman in a poem called "This Compost" would marvel at how "such sweet things" could grow "out of such corruptions," yet nature performed the miracle. Emerson has a similar thought about the social realm:

> We prosper with such vigor that like thrifty trees, which grow in spite of ice, lice, mice and borers, we do not suffer from the profligate swarms that fatten on the national treasury. The huge animals nourish huge parasites, and the rancor of the disease attests the strength of the constitution. The same energy in the Greek *Demos* drew the remark that the evils of popular government appear greater than they are; there is compensation for them in the spirit and energy it awakens.[10]

The semibarbarian frontier communities of the United States sent crude men to represent them in Washington—"half orator, half assassin"—but such men were needed to enforce an orderly government on "the snarling majorities of German, Irish, and native millions." However undemocratic this sounds, Emerson still insists that "The instinct of the people is right." Respectable Whigs could never have accomplished what the unrespectable Presidents Jackson and Polk did:

> This power, to be sure, is not clothed in satin. 'T is the power of Lynch law, of soldiers and pirates; and it bullies the peaceable and loyal. But it brings its own antidote; and here is my point,—that all kinds of power usually emerge at the same time; good energy and bad; power of mind with physical health; the ecstasies of devotion with the exasperations of debauchery.[11]

Emerson's praise of the coarse energy of "the 'bruisers,' who have run the gauntlet of caucus and tavern through the county or state," is not without intended irony. They are better, he says, than the "snivelling opposition," by which he means New England governors and legislators who have not had the courage to oppose them. Idealists, too, who try to establish utopian communities, are practical failures, and can only succeed at all by "installing Judas as steward." The Shakers had a proverb that they always sent the Devil to market. "It is an esoteric doctrine of society that a little wickedness is good to make muscle . . ."[12]

In a certain rural town (Concord, of course) Emerson "knew a burly Boniface who for many years kept a public-house . . . He was a knave whom the town could ill spare."[13] Though a scoundrel, he was a good citizen, active in repairing roads, planting shade trees, and introducing new inventions such as the horse-drawn rake. "He girdled the trees and cut off the horses' tails of the temperance people, in the night." Yet he was "civil, fat, and easy, in his house, and precisely the most public-spirited citizen."

Emerson's son tells an anecdote relating to this "Concord publican."[14] In going to the post office one day, Emerson noticed a scurrilous caricature of Dr. Josiah Bartlett, the town's leading physician and advocate of temperance, hanging beside the tavern door. Emerson beat it to pieces with his cane. "In the afternoon a new board hung there with a rude picture of a man with hooked nose, tall hat and cane, and the inscription 'Rev. R. W. E. knocking down the sign.' " Before long, some friend of Emerson's destroyed this sign.

Had Emerson seen the caricature of himself, it is doubtful that he would have attacked it with his cane, for he had a sense of humor. Men like "Boniface" were not his kind, but he tolerated them because they had a place in society. Men with a "surcharge of arterial blood" did not enjoy lectures, books, and sermons, but they were made for war, adventure, and heroic actions: "The roisterers who are destined for infamy at home, if sent to Mexico will 'cover you with glory,' and come back heroes and generals."[15] This did not mean that he now approved of the war with Mexico. If the roistering soldiers returned as national heroes, they were not his heroes. "Physical force has no value where there is nothing else."[16] He could reject the results of the war without losing interest in the phenomena of its success.

As a young minister Emerson had preached against the evils of wealth, but now he proposes to examine the subject realistically and without apology. He is not speaking of greed, or the accumulation of property for its own sake, but economy. "Every man is a consumer, and ought to be a producer. He fails to make his place good in the world unless he not only pays his debt but also adds something to the common wealth."[17] Wealth results from the "application of mind to nature; and the art of getting rich consists not in industry, much less in saving, but in a better order, in timeliness, in being at the right spot." In other words, wealth consists in making the best use of natural resources, both for the individual and for society. No person can make full use of his abilities on a bare subsistence, and society benefits from the extension of his power over nature: "Wealth requires, besides the crust of bread and the roof,—the freedom of the city, the freedom of the earth, travelling, machinery, the benefits of science, music and fine arts, the best culture and the best company."[18]

Emerson admired the ancestors of the British (he calls them "Saxons") for their pecuniary independence: "No reliance for bread and games on the government; no clanship, no patriarchal style of living by the revenues of a chief, no marrying-on, no system of clientship suits them; but every man must pay his scot."[19] Obviously he would have no patience with a welfare state, or most systems of socialism; yet he does admit that some needs must be supplied by the state, such as libraries, museums, and parks, though personal wealth can, and should, contribute to these institutions. The providing for community needs is one of the best uses of wealth; the worst use is for personal pleasure or vanity, what Thorstein Veblen would later call "conspicuous consumption."

But Emerson does not regard speculators, who are mad to gain tyrannical control of wealth, as entirely evil. They are checked by other speculators, and in the competition they stimulate the building of factories and the construction of railroads. Of course Emerson did not foresee the evils of the "robber barons," a term not yet in use; it would be many years before the public learned of the corrupt means by which the Goulds and the Vanderbilts became millionaires. Emerson does say, however, that dishonest merchants inflate insurance rates, endanger banks, make the highways unsafe, and undermine judicial authority. But in a free economy the law of supply and demand will keep commerce efficient and honest. Though this laissez-faire philosophy would exclude "protected labor," Emerson believes that his favorite of all "laws," that of "compensation," will force the proper adjustment of wages. When American employers refuse to pay living wages to the impoverished immigrants, taxes are forced up by the increase in the "poor rates" and the cost of crime. And when politicians begin competing for their votes, these new Americans discover that they have political power, and demand better wages.

Emerson attempted to complete his theory of "wealth" in lectures on "Culture" and "Worship." By culture he meant a balanced life. Intelligence must control blind instinct. "For performance, nature has no mercy, and sacrifices the performer to get it done." *Culture* can prevent the sacrifice: "Our efficiency depends so much on our concentration, that nature usually in the instances where a marked man [that is, a man of exceptional ability] is sent into the world, overloads him with bias, sacrificing his symmetry to his working power."[20]

One manifestation of nature's overdevelopment is human conceit, egotism, a too-exclusive concern for one's own body, or talent, or reputation. "One of its annoying forms is a craving for sympathy. The sufferers parade their miseries. . . . They like sickness, because physical pain will extort some show of interest from the bystanders." It is impossible to avoid the suspicion that Emerson had his own wife partly in mind. But he also says that the "goitre of egotism is so frequent among notable persons that we must infer some strong necessity in nature which it subserves; such as we see in the sexual attraction."[21] The preservation of the species is so important "that nature has secured it at all hazards by immensely overloading the passion, at the risk of perpetual crime and disorder."

Thus Emerson sees culture as the exercise of control over one's animal inheritance, the instincts having survival value but needing artificial (or cultural) control in civilized society. A "well-made man" needs strong determination, "And the end of culture is not to destroy this, God forbid! but to train away all impediment and mixture and leave nothing but pure power." Such men are rare: "Very few of our race can be said to be yet finished men. We still carry sticking to us some remains of the preceding inferior quadruped organization. We call these millions men; but they are not yet men."[22]

Civilization, through trade, art, science, and Christianity, provides the means of becoming truly human (what later Nietzsche would call the *Übermensch,* though he would leave out Christianity). In fact, anything that "can set his dull nerves throbbing" can help a human being break out of his "tough chrysalis." Emerson sees "the future of the race hinted in the organic effort of nature to mount and meliorate." Man "will convert the Furies into Muses, and the hells into benefit."[23]

Some people who heard Emerson's lectures on "Power," "Wealth," and "Culture" told him he discussed these subjects on too low a plane. He wrote "Worship" to answer these critics, but it is doubtful that he convinced anyone not already in sympathy with his point of view. His faith was, as it had been since the "Divinity School Address," that "God builds his temples in the heart on the ruins of churches and religions."[24] He had no doubt that all old forms of religion were in decay, and that "skepticism devastates the community."[25] The age was becoming increasingly materialistic, believing only in matter and the physical sciences. Emerson himself was as interested in the sciences as anyone, but he found "the omnipresence and the almightiness [of God] in the reaction of every atom in nature." For proof he appealed to the "moral sentiment," which told him right from wrong, and strengthened his confidence that every atom depended for its existence and operation on the will of a Universal Mind. A religion capable of satisfying the present and future ages must be intellectual, with a faith in science and the scientific mind, and Emerson predicts: "There will be a new church founded on moral science; at first cold and naked, a babe in a manger again, the algebra and mathematics of ethical law, the church of men to come, without shawms, or psaltery, or sackbut; but it will have heaven and earth for its beams and rafters; science for symbol and illustration; it will fast enough gather beauty, music, picture, and poetry."[26]

III

The cheerful and optimistic tone of Emerson's lectures on "Conduct of Life" does not give any indication that at the time of writing and delivering them he was agitated about the Compromise of 1850 between the North and South on slavery problems. He was busy lecturing when Daniel Webster delivered his March 7 speech defending Clay's Compromise Bill, and did not immediately record his indignation in his Journal, though he did indicate his disgust at criticism of Senator William H. Seward for appealing in his March 11 speech to "a higher law" than the Constitution. Emerson called that criticism "the worst symptom I have noticed in our politics lately."[27] Webster's partisans sneered at "Higher-law Seward." And now Rufus Choate, Boston lawyer and United States senator, referred to "the trashy sentimentalism of our lutestring enthusiasts." A few months later Emerson was even more annoyed by these tactics: "Webster & Choate think to discredit the higher law by personalities[;] they insinuate much about transcendentalists & abstractionists & people of no weight. It is the cheap cant of lawyers & of merchants in a failing condition, & of rogues."[28] What Emerson most strongly objected to was the enforcement of the law passed in 1793 requiring the return of fugitive slaves to their owners, though laxly enforced until its revival in 1850.

In Boston, Webster's position was strongly supported by the merchants, bankers, and professional men. Near the end of March they signed a letter approving of his speech, and Emerson wrote in his Journal: "I think there never was an event half so painful occurred in Boston as the letter with 800 signatures to Webster."[29] The conduct of Boston during the siege of the British in the American Revolution had been a "day of glory," but this was a "day of imbecilities" and cowardice. Among the signers was Dr. Oliver Wendell Holmes, and many Unitarian and Episcopalian ministers. For Emerson this was a period of "Bad times"—though financially the country was prospering:

> We wake up with a painful auguring, and after exploring a little to know the cause find it is the odious news in each day's paper, the infamy that has fallen on Massachusetts, & that clouds the daylight, & takes away the comfort out of every hour. We shall never feel well again until that detestable law is nullified in Massachusetts & until the Government is assured that once for all it cannot & shall not be executed here. All I have, and all I can do shall be given & done in opposition to the execution of the law.[30]

Mr. Samuel Hoar felt so ashamed of his party and country that he "has never raised his head since Webster's speech in last March." Emerson himself felt personally betrayed: "I had praised the tone & attitude of the Country. My friends had mistrusted it." Now they say, "It is no worse than it was before; only it is manifest and acted out." But he thought it was worse, especially the cowardice in Boston. He had always been proud of Boston for that city's history and superior culture. Intelligent people in England had told him they could always distinguish a Bostonian from other Americans. But now, "Boston, through the personal influence of this New Hampshire man, must bow its proud spirit in the dust & make us irretrievably ashamed. . . . It is now as disgraceful to be a Bostonian as it was hitherto a credit."

While Webster was Secretary of State he had encouraged the Hungarians to fight for their freedom from Austria, but now he stood against liberty in his own country. On Washington's birthday he had written a letter to the celebrators in New York praising the first President for his part in obtaining America's freedom from England. "Pho! Let Mr Webster for decency's sake shut his lips once & forever on this word. The word *liberty* in the mouth of Mr Webster sounds like the word *love* in the mouth of a courtezan."[31] If Webster were in Austria, he would truckle to the Tsar of Russia, "as he does in America to the Carolinas; and hunt the Hungarians . . . as he does the fugitives of Virginia."[32] And Edward Everett, recent president of Harvard, a man whose scholarship and oratory Emerson had admired in his youth, was as hypocritical as Webster. Sarcastically Emerson suggests that Everett give copies of his orations at Concord, Lexington, Plymouth, and Bunker Hill to "beguile" the captured slave on his journey from Boston to the plantation whipping post. All the "bluster about the Union" was futile. "Before the passage of that law which Mr Webster made his own, we indulged in all the dreams which foreign nations still cherish of American destiny. . . . The Union! o yes, I prized that, other things being equal; but what is the Union to a man self condemned?"[33] "As soon as the Constitution enacts a criminal law, disunion already exists."[34] Secession would be a lesser evil than enforcing this law.

It was enforced. In April 1851, George Ticknor Curtis, United States Commissioner in Boston, ordered the return of Thomas Sims, a seventeen-year-old fugitive from a Georgia plantation, and he was captured and returned with the aid of a large military force assembled to prevent his rescue between the Boston jail and the waiting ship. On April 7, Judge Lemuel Shaw, Herman Melville's father-in-law, had refused to release Sims from prison on a writ of habeas corpus, and Emerson berated the judge for not declaring the law unconstitutional. If the Constitution permitted such atrocities, it did not deserve respect. It was almost unthinkable that "this filthy enactment was made in the 19th Century by people who could read & write. I will not obey it, by God."[35]

On May 3, 1851, Emerson delivered an address in Concord on "The Fu-

gitive Slave Law," in which he elaborated the protests made in his Journal.
"The last year," he said, "has forced us all into politics."[36] He had lived all
his life in Massachusetts, and never felt inconvenienced by any law until
now. The willingness of Bostonians to support it was shocking. After the
rescue in February of Shadrach (Frederick Williams), fugitive from Georgia, Bostonians rushed to put their names "on the list of volunteers in aid
of the marshal."[37] Emerson's audience knew that Shadrach had been
brought to Concord and concealed by Edwin Bigelow, the village black-
smith, until he could take the black fugitive to New Hampshire, where
someone else in the Underground Railroad helped him escape to Canada.
That rescue had caused a general panic in Boston, among the clergy, the
newspapers, and most of the business community. That was why when
Sims was captured, "the whole wealth and power of Boston" was arrayed
against him: "The learning of the universities, the culture of elegant society, the acumen of lawyers, the majesty of the Bench, the eloquence of
the Christian pulpit, the stoutness of Democracy, and the respectability of
the Whig party."[38] Such inhumanity made Emerson "question the value
of our civilization." In the courts "the Higher Law" had been reckoned a
joke, though Emerson said he had always heard that "the Bible constituted a part of every technical law library, and that it was a principle in law
that immoral laws are void."[39] All the great jurists from Cicero and Gro-
tius to Coke and Blackstone had affirmed this principle. Unless "those se-
ditious Ten Commandments which are the root of our European and
American civilization" could be expunged, no conscientious man could
support the Fugitive Slave Law. Moreover:

> Statute fights against Statute. By the law of Congress March 2, 1807, it is
> piracy and murder, punishable with death, to enslave a man on the coast
> of Africa. By law of Congress September, 1850, it is a high crime and mis-
> demeanor, punishable with fine and imprisonment, to resist the reënslav-
> ing a man on the coast of America. . . . What kind of legislation is that?
> What kind of constitution which covers it?[40]

The only way to resolve this conflict of statutes and morality was to
abrogate the second law, and so long as it had legal sanction it must be
disobeyed. Then abrogate it, and "confine slavery to slave states, and help
them effectively to make an end of it."[41] On August 1, 1844, in an address

delivered in Concord on the tenth anniversary of the emancipation of black slaves in the British West Indies, Emerson had proposed that the United States follow Britain's example of ending slavery by buying slaves their freedom from the plantation owners. He again recommends the same idea: "I say buy,—never conceding the right of the planter to own, but that we may acknowledge the calamity of his position, and bear a countryman's share in relieving him."[42]

Dr. John Gorham Palfrey, former dean of Harvard Divinity School, was running for Congress from Emerson's district on the Free-Soil ticket. After serving a term in Congress he had been defeated at the last election, and had decided to run again for the sake of conscience. Emerson wanted to help him, and used his Concord speech as a campaign aid to Palfrey. Among the several places in the county where he spoke was Cambridge. The Harvard authorities and many of the students were pro-South, and they gave him a raucous reception. A law student (later professor at Harvard), James B. Thayer, was one of the few in the audience in sympathy with the speaker; he gave Emerson's first biographer, James Elliot Cabot, this eyewitness description:

> The hisses, shouts, and cat-calls made it impossible for Mr. Emerson to go on. Through all this there never was a finer spectacle of dignity and composure than he presented. He stood with perfect quietness until the hubbub was over, and then went on with the next word. It was as if nothing had happened: there was no repetition, no allusion to what had been going on, no sign that he was moved, and I cannot describe with what added weight the next words fell.[43]

In the election of May 26, 1851, Palfrey carried Concord, but lost the district to Benjamin Thompson, the Whig candidate. Emerson ruefully recorded the vote in his Journal, and commented: "There is one benefit derived from the movement lately. The most polite & decorous whigs, all for church & colleges & charity, have shown their teeth unmistakeably. We shall not be deceived again."[44] A few days later he concluded bitterly that Webster did represent "the American people just as they are, with their vast material interests, materialized intellect, & low morals."[45]

On Sunday, October 24, 1852, Emerson was at Plymouth, and as he stood on the beach, looking across the hazy water toward Marshfield, he guessed that Daniel Webster had died (doubtless he had been following the senator's illness in the newspapers). Later in the day he learned that Webster had indeed died at three o'clock that morning. Death, as usual, softened Emerson's opinion, and in his Journal he wrote that "America & the world had lost the completest man. Nature had not in our days, or, not since Napoleon, cut out such a masterpiece. He brought the strength of a savage into the height of culture."[46] If only Webster had been endowed with a conscience, too. "But alas! he was the victim of his ambition; to please the South he betrayed the North, and was thrown out by both."

On March 7, 1854, Emerson commemorated the fourth anniversary of Webster's speech by giving a lecture in the New York City Tabernacle on "The Fugitive Slave Law." He had been invited to speak against Webster immediately after the senator's death, but had refused, and he had not since discussed the Fugitive Slave Law in public because the subject was taboo on the Lyceum circuit, which had taken up most of his time. But in the Tabernacle, perhaps the most-often-used antislavery forum in the nation, he could speak freely.

Though Emerson repeated in New York many of the ideas of his Concord speech of 1851, he gave a more finished and dramatic performance. Rusk calls it calmer and more philosophical than the Concord speech,[47] but the mildness was ironical. Actually, Emerson was now so bitter that he had become almost an anarchist. He said he had never suffered any personal inconvenience, or check on his free speech, until Mr. Webster "brought the Fugitive Slave Law on the country."[48] Though it was not his bill, he gave it life and soul by his support, and it "cost him his life." Webster told the people of Boston " 'they must conquer their prejudices'; that 'agitation of the subject of Slavery must be suppressed.' He did as immoral men usually do, made very low bows to the Christian Church, and went through the Sunday decorums."[49] For such hypocrisy Emerson never forgave him.

The immediate stimulus of Emerson's New York speech was the debate in Washington over the Kansas-Nebraska bill, which proposed to admit slavery into the vast territory where the Missouri Compromise of 1820 had forbidden it. This region extended from the southern border of Missouri to the Canadian border and the Rocky Mountains of the Northwest. Debate in Congress had been acrimonious. Senator George Badger of North

Carolina said he could not understand why the North was so indignant. All Southerners wanted was to be able to take their "mammies" with them when they moved to Kansas. Senator Benjamin Franklin Wade of Ohio replied: "We have not the least objection . . . to the Senator's migrating to Kansas and taking his old 'Mammy' along with him. We only insist that he shall not be empowered to *sell* her after taking her there."[50] So far, all the tactics used by the defenders of "free soil" had failed:

> The events of this month are teaching one thing plain and clear, the worthlessness of good tools to bad workmen; that official papers are of no use; resolutions of public meetings, platforms of conventions, no, nor laws, nor constitutions, any more. . . . You relied on the Missouri Compromise. That is ridden over. You relied on State sovereignty in the Free States to protect their citizens. They are driven with contempt out of the courts and out of the territory of the Slave States,—if they are so happy as to get out with their lives . . .
>
> I fear there is no reliance to be put on any kind or form of covenant, no, not on sacred forms, none on churches, none on bibles. For one would have said that a Christian would not keep slaves;—but the Christians keep slaves. Of course they will not dare to read the Bible? Won't they? They quote the Bible, quote Paul, quote Christ, to justify slavery. If slavery is good, then is lying, theft, arson, homicide, each and all good, and to be maintained by the Union societies.[51]

Nothing but individual integrity and effort could save a free society in America. Yes, minorities, too, had failed "Because they have not a real minority of one." But Emerson had not lost faith in self-reliance:

> Whenever a man has come to this mind, that there is no Church for him but his believing prayer; no Constitution but his dealing well and justly with his neighbor; no liberty but his invincible will to do right,— then certain aids and allies will promptly appear; for the constitution of the Universe is on his side. . . . Slavery is disheartening; but Nature is not so helpless but it can rid itself at last of every wrong. But the spasms of Nature are centuries and ages, and will tax the faith of short-lived men.[52]

So many assumptions are implied in these statements that it is difficult to extract the core of Emerson's reasoning. Perhaps he had partly in mind the argument advanced by some Northern conservatives that slavery would in the end prove unprofitable, even in the South, and would decline because of its economic inefficiency. But one thing is clear: Emerson wanted results *now,* though the only practical action he could suggest was to support the Anti-Slavery Society. He found one benefit in events since the passage of the Fugitive Slave Act: "Now at last we are disenchanted and shall have no more false hopes." Yet, almost contradicting his disenchantment, he predicts that Whigs, Democrats, and maybe even Southerners will join the Anti-Slavery Society. And he ends on his paradoxical notion of "Fate": ". . . I hope we have reached the end of our unbelief, have come to a belief that there is a divine Providence in the world, which will not save us but through our own coöperation."[53] There is no mistake that his philosophy is: *God helps those who help themselves.*

IV

Just as Emerson had long been an abolitionist at heart, yet delayed actually joining the Anti-Slavery Society, so also had he been reluctant to become active in the woman's rights movement. But his reasons were not exactly the same. In August 1850, Mrs. Paulina W. Davis of Providence invited him to attend and sponsor a woman's rights convention to be held in Worcester on October 23 and 24. For several weeks he delayed answering "because I had no clear answer." Finally he did write on September 18, explaining his dilemma: "The fact of the political & civil wrongs of woman I deny not. If women feel wronged, then they are wronged." But "a public convention called by women is not very agreeable to me, and the things to be agitated for do not seem to me the best." He would not hesitate to vote for franchise for women, for their legal right to hold property, "yes & be eligible to all offices as men [are]."[54]

But Emerson could not imagine that the women he admired would want the latter. He did not say it would be unladylike, but that was what he meant: "I should not wish women to wish political functions, nor, if granted assume them. I imagine that a woman whom all men would feel to be the best, would decline such privilege if offered, & feel them to be obstacles to her legitimate influence." He was obviously embarrassed by Mrs. Davis's invitation, and somewhat ashamed of his emotional reaction. He begged her not to take his remarks too seriously:

At all events, that I may not stand in the way of any right you are at liberty if you wish it to use my name as one of the inviters of the convention, though I shall not attend it, & shall regret that it is not rather a private meeting of thoughtful persons sincerely interested, instead of what a public meeting is pretty sure to be, a heartless noise which we are all ashamed of when it is over.

Lucy Stone invited Emerson to a second convention for woman's rights at Worcester the following year, and again he declined, though this time his excuse was that he could not spare the time from Margaret Fuller's *Memoirs,* which he thought the feminist leaders would understand. Margaret's *Woman in the Nineteenth Century* was still the major contribution by an American on the condition of women in society. His letter was published in *The New-York Daily Tribune* on October 17, 1851, with the report on the convention. However, in February 1853, he declined Wendell Phillips's request for his signature to a petition for another convention on woman suffrage. He objected chiefly to having the request come from Phillips. He preferred to put off further discussion of this subject until the women themselves asked for the vote.

But when he was invited to address a Woman's Rights Convention in Boston in 1855, Emerson accepted, and on September 20 he delivered an address called simply "Woman." His attitude toward women had not basically changed since 1851, but he had come around to accepting "the benefits of [public] action having for its object a benefit to the position of Woman."[55] Twentieth-century feminists would probably accuse him of holding on to his male chauvinism, but he did go further than most of his contemporaries in recognizing the equality of women with men. By equality, he meant partnership, each sex performing its natural role and respecting the other:

Man is the Will, and Woman the sentiment. In this ship of humanity, Will is the rudder, and Sentiment the sail: when Woman affects to steer, the rudder is only a masked sail. When women engage in any art or trade, it is usually as a resource, not as a primary object. The life of the affections is primary to them, so that there is usually no employment or career which they will not with their own applause and that of society quit for a suitable marriage. And they give entirely to their affections, set their whole

fortune on the die, lose themselves eagerly in the glory of their husband
and children. Man stands astonished at a magnanimity he cannot pretend
to.[56]

This attitude was, of course, typical of American society in the
mid-nineteenth century. The only difference between Emerson's view and
that of the average man of his time was that most men took woman's responsibilities to the home for granted, and were by no means "astonished"
at her "magnanimity." The difficulty which women were having in obtaining the rights they demanded shows that society did not recognize
them as Emerson did: "the right to education, to avenues of employment,
to equal rights of property, to equal rights in marriage, to the exercise of
the professions and of suffrage."[57]

Emerson also condemned the "cheap wit," from Aristophanes to Rabe-
lais, and recently of Tennyson, charging women of being victims of temperament. "Mahomet" thought they did not "have a sufficient moral or
intellectual force to control the perturbations of their physical structure.
These were all drawings of morbid anatomy, and such satire as might be
written on the tenants of a hospital or on an asylum for idiots." Emerson
almost anticipates the modern feminists' epithet "male chauvinist pig" by
saying "it would be easy for women to retaliate in kind, by painting men
from the dogs and gorillas that have worn our shape." Emerson himself is
not one of those "who believe women to be incapable of anything but to
cook, incapable of interest in [business and political] affairs." He does
admit that he, too, thinks women victims of "temperament," but of a
"finer temperament" than men have. "They have tears, and gayeties, and
faintings, and glooms and devotions to trifles. . . . They are more personal."[58]

Before condemning these stereotype characterizations, influenced by the
Aristophanes-Rabelais tradition which Emerson renounced, one might
consider that nineteenth-century society conditioned women to tears and
sentimentality, and modes of dress which might produce faintings. If the
novels of the period are an indication of reality, Emerson was not an inac-
curate observer. And his contemporary society also conditioned him to
favor the unaggressive woman, such as he had worshiped in his first wife.
To judge by the women he knew best, most did not wish "equal share
in public affairs." Yet he insists that "it is they and not we that are to de-

termine it. Let the laws be purged of every barbarous remainder, every barbarous impediment to women."[59] He had so much respect for the feminine mind and character that he thought women were better judges of their needs and mode of life than were men. His ideal is mutual freedom and faith. Then, "whatever the woman's heart is prompted to desire, the man's mind is simultaneously prompted to accomplish."[60]

V

"A man writes a lecture, & is carted round the Country at the tail of his lecture, for months, to read it," Emerson complained in his Journal in 1851.[61] As he extended his lecture territory, he had to be away from home for longer periods of time, and to endure increasing hardships in traveling and tedious hours of waiting to make train connections. Worst of all were the steamboats, slow, uncomfortable, and extremely dangerous. In 1851, after lecturing in western New York—Rochester, Buffalo, and Syracuse—then returning to Massachusetts for several engagements, he set out for Pittsburgh. On March 21 he wrote Lidian from the Monongahela House:

> I arrived here last night after a very tedious & disagreeable journey from Philadelphia by railway & canal with little food & less sleep two nights being spent in the railcars & third on the floor of a canal boat, where the cushion allowed me for a bed was crossed at the knees by another tier of sleepers as long limbed as I,—so that in the air was a wreath of legs; and the night, which was bad enough, would have been worse but that we were so thoroughly tired we could have slept standing.[62]

When Emerson had finally arrived in Pittsburgh at four p.m., he wanted nothing so much as a few hours of good sleep. He had planned to give six of his "Conduct of Life" lectures, but had hoped to revise the first, "The Laws of Success," before reading it again, and was too tired to think. He told the committee that he would perform that night if they would let him read a lecture on "England" instead of the first of the series announced, and they readily agreed. His audience was appreciative, and everyone was kind to him, but the town itself, like the industrial towns of England, was black with soft-coal smoke—"black houses black air black faces & clothes of men & women."

Under his window on the Monongahela River, "which will be [in]

Ohio in a quarter of a mile," Emerson could see a row of steamers soon to depart for Cincinnati, St. Louis, and New Orleans. He had been invited to lecture in Cincinnati again, but it was forty hours away by steamboat. A slight inducement was that he would probably have the companionship of a Mr. Mitchell, a Cincinnati astronomer, who had stopped with him at the Monongahela House. Emerson liked Mr. Mitchell, but he was eager to return to Staten Island, where he would pick up Edward and Lidian, who had been visiting William's family.

In New York on Saturday night, April 5, father, son, and wife took a steamboat to Norwich, "both Eddy & Lidian getting a sleep," Waldo wrote William the following week. A carriage took them to Framingham, then a "carry-all" the rest of the way. They arrived home just before "meeting time," and the whole family had a brief reunion before Grandma had to leave for church. Probably Lidian did not accompany her (Waldo seldom attended church services now), for she was fatigued from the journey, and, in fact, she was ill for many days afterward.

This was the last spring that Emerson's mother would enjoy her usual good health. In June she rolled out of bed one night during a nightmare and fractured her hip.[63] The doctor said she would probably never walk again, but Emerson thought him "an alarmist" and expected her to recover. She did several months later regain a limited mobility, but would never be in sound health again.

Emerson began his 1851–52 lecture season in Massachusetts, where between October 20 and the end of January he spoke thirty-five times, as well as once in Augusta, Maine. Then he did another tour of upstate New York in February, rushed back to New York City, and returned home at the end of the month. After more lecturing in Massachusetts, he returned to New York City for another round, broken by an interruption of two weeks because too many lecturers were competing for audiences at the same time.

After the New York series and a brief pause at home, Emerson traveled by train to Montreal, arriving on Saturday, April 17, 1852. That night he walked across the frozen St. Lawrence, two days before it began to thaw:

Monday morning the ice *shoved,* as they call it, & I stood on the quay & saw acres & acres of ice rolling swiftly down stream, & presently my *road* came floating down with the rest, the well beaten black straight road I had traversed. Parts of it were making mad sommersaults [*sic*] & revolutions like porpoises in the water, very cheerful to see *from the stone quay.*[64]

That evening, to "a great crowd," Emerson gave his lecture on "England," before beginning his "Conduct of Life" series. He wrote Lidian that it was "a piece of good luck" that he had begun with "England," because it was so well received that "I shall be allowed to be as stupid as I please on the 'Conduct of Life.' " A reporter declared in *The Montreal Courier* that he had never known any lecture to be so popular in Montreal. The success exhilarated Emerson and he enjoyed his stay in the French-Canadian city. A judge of the Supreme Court invited him to dinner and Emerson recorded in his Journal: "I found, on the 22 April, ten feet of old snow on each side of the carriage in riding out to Judge [Charles] Day's, 3 miles from Montreal."[65] In his letter of April 20 to Lidian he wrote, "The difficulties of going to Quebec are such, at this early season, that I shall have to postpone my visit to St Ann's Falls, I fear." On the twenty-third he spoke at the annual banquet of the St. George's Society, where many of the people reminded him of England, and still more of Scotland.

About two weeks after returning from Canada, Emerson welcomed Lajos Kossuth, hero of the Hungarian revolution of 1848 and for a few months in 1849 president of the short-lived Hungarian Republic. When Russia intervened in support of Austria, Kossuth was forced into exile, and was touring England and the United States to obtain help in his country's struggle for independence. On a beautiful day in May, Kossuth visited Lexington and Concord, speaking to large crowds in each town. A Concord mounted guard met him at the Lexington line and escorted him to Town Hall, which was packed with people waiting to see and hear him.

John S. Keyes presented him to Emerson, who gave the welcoming address. He said he had expected Kossuth to visit the birthplace of American freedom. "The man of freedom, you are also the man of Fate. You do not elect, but are elected by God and your genius to the task."[66] Kossuth spoke English with some difficulty, and Emerson could not understand all he said. Realizing that the audience was unfamiliar with the word *Österreich*, Kossuth turned to Emerson for the English equivalent, and he suggested "ostrich." Kossuth yelled "No, no!" until someone from the audience said, *"Austria."*[67] After the ceremonies Emerson entertained Kossuth in his home.

At the end of May the Hawthornes took up residence in Alcott's former home on the Lexington Road, which they renamed The Wayside. Though Emerson was sympathetic with Nathaniel Hawthorne, he still felt ill at ease with him, and the novelist's politics made their relations even more awkward. When the Democratic party nominated Franklin Pierce for the presidency and Hawthorne agreed to write a "campaign biography" for him, Emerson's tolerance was severely tried. That Hawthorne should remain loyal to his college classmate and personal friend was understandable, but that he should go so far as to defend Pierce's proslavery politics was hard to forgive. Always moved by a personal tragedy, however, Emerson was grieved to read in *The Boston Daily Advertiser* on July 31 that Hawthorne's sister Louisa had lost her life when the steamboat *Henry Clay* burned on the Hudson River July 28. Previously Mrs. Hawthorne had left some kind of petition at the Emerson house (probably having something to do with Pierce's and Hawthorne's politics), and on August 4 Emerson wrote her this curious letter:

> *Dear Madam,*
>   *I am extremely mortified, that, in an unusual press of company, & then an absence from town, I quite dropt out of mind the paper you had confided to me. It was all the more inexcusable, as I do not give my name; not having the smallest interest, unless of aversation, to the whole subject, as it now presents itself in our community. I heard with pain the dreadful story of the wreck & fire, and hoped, as long as I could, that there was mistake in the report that your sisters [sic] name was in the list. But who knows which is the shortest & most excellent way out of the calamities of the present world.*
>   *With great regard,/R. W. Emerson.*[68]

On August 18 Emerson recorded in his Journal: "Horatio Greenough came here & spent a day:—an extraordinary man—'Forty seven years of joy,' he says, 'he has lived'; and is a man of sense, of virtue, & of great elevation."[69] He thought Greenough's democracy "very deep," though not quite without crotchets. Greenough's idea was that to be beautiful architecture must be functional; beauty as embellishment "is false, childless [childish] & moribund." However, Emerson was not sure that Greenough was not better in theory than in practice; and the sculptor-critic was impatient with Emerson's "contemplations," calling them "masturbation of the brain."

During that summer Emerson's attention was mainly on his family and life in Concord. Now his mother frequently took buggy rides, and Waldo wrote William of her recovery. Ellen went to Staten Island to visit her uncle's family and became ill, causing her father much uneasiness. Of course Emerson also spent some time in reading, revising his notes on England, and answering letters. He frequently received requests for lectures during the coming season. Fanatics such as Delia Bacon wrote him about their mad ideas. She was obsessed with the conviction that the plays and poems attributed to Shakespeare had actually been written by Francis Bacon. She could not produce a shred of evidence, yet she somehow aroused Emerson's sympathy. He patiently advised her, and even wrote a letter of introduction for her to present to Carlyle when she went to England to get permission to open Shakespeare's grave, which for some insane reason she thought would contain proof of her theory. Carlyle, too, thought her mad, but he also felt moved to protect and humor her.

The most interesting of Emerson's correspondence in the summer of 1852 was with Arthur Hugh Clough. He had resigned his position with University Hall and was now only a professor of English literature in University College, which paid him but thirty pounds a year. He had found the woman he wanted to marry, but everyone told him that he should not think of marrying on less than five hundred pounds a year. He wondered if in New England he might earn enough by writing and teaching to support a wife there.[70] He was thinking of coming over to investigate the possibilities. Emerson immediately urged him to come and invited him to stay in his home until he could find suitable work. Clough, he said, could give him advice on his book about England. And he should have no difficulty in obtaining students to tutor for college entrance, or Harvard students who had been "rusticated" (temporarily suspended, and Concord was a favorite place of exile). Clough arrived on November 12 on the steamship *Canada,* with Lowell and Thackeray, the latter to begin a lecture tour in America. On the twentieth Emerson gave a dinner for Clough in Boston, attended by the best-known literary men in the region.[71]

VI

The night before Thanksgiving, Emerson left home for the most extensive tour in the West he had yet undertaken. Clough had found lodgings in

Cambridge, where he would tutor a small group of boys in Greek, and would probably not need any further assistance. Emerson was having a furnace installed in his home, and was anxious to know how well it worked, but could not wait to find out. He must be off to Cincinnati and St. Louis, stopping along the way to read lectures. In Troy, New York, he discovered that he had forgotten to bring a list of his engagements, and hastily wrote Ellen to copy it out of his *Account Book;* she was to stay out of school to do it if necessary.[72] This was the beginning of her acting as his secretary, a role which would grow with the years and her father's declining memory. From Cincinnati, December 9, he asked Lidian to write him how the new furnace was performing, and asked Ellen to report on the horse he had recently bought. If it snowed, and they wanted a sleigh, they should ask Mr. Staples to provide a good secondhand one "on the account," which implies that he had bought the horse from Sam on credit. Emerson's first Cincinnati audience was disappointing, but later ones were larger. He managed to finish writing his lecture on "Fate" (to become a chapter in *Conduct of Life*) in time to read it on December 16.

Emerson's philosophy of "Fate" developed out of his previous Neoplatonism: "The whole world is the flux of matter over the wires of thought to the poles or points where it would build."[73] Thus, "Every solid in the universe is ready to become fluid on the approach of the mind, and the power to flux it is the measure of the mind. If the wall remain adamant, it accuses the want of thought."[74] How this Theosophy impressed his Western audiences, Emerson did not record—perhaps did not know. But his emphasis on the power of will to overcome obstacles and get things done must have appealed to men who were conquering nature by determination and effort, men who believed that Fate was on their side. "Why should we fear to be crushed by savage elements, we who are made up of the same elements?"[75]

On Christmas Day, Emerson arrived in St. Louis, after an exhausting trip down the Ohio and up the Mississippi, with the constant threat of being blocked by ice. In two years the railroad would extend from Cincinnati to St. Louis, a distance of three hundred miles instead of the eight hundred by water. Emerson had enjoyed his last days in Cincinnati so much that he hoped to return again "if the same parties should summon me."[76] He enjoyed St. Louis, too, especially the companionship of "Mr

Eliot, the Unitarian minister" (William Greenleaf Eliot, a New Englander, who would become the grandfather of a major twentieth-century poet). Also, St. Louis paid him $500 for seven lectures, compared to Cincinnati's $362 net. "But I believe no thinking or reading man is here in the 95000 souls. [Mr. Eliot included?] An Abstractionist cannot live near the Mississippi River & the Iron Mountain." A Pacific Rail Road had started construction, and another to New Orleans was under way. "Such projects cannot consist with much literature, so we must excuse them if they cannot spell quite as well as Edith."[77]

While in St. Louis, Emerson wrote Ellen instructions for an unusual errand. He had learned, shortly before leaving home, that Mrs. Paulina Nash, Ellen Tucker's sister, had returned to America after a long residence in Italy:

> The beautiful Ellen Tucker, for whom you were named, died twenty two years ago. . . . Do you not wish to take the cars on the first fine morning, & go down to Cambridge, & find your way to her [Mrs. Nash's] door, & say to her that your father sends his love to her, & means to bring your mother to see her as soon as he comes home. You need not stay five minutes, but take the omnibus for Boston, & come straight home again. Write on your card Ellen L. Emerson or better, Ellen Tucker Emerson. Yes that is best, & send it up to her from the door.[78]

Tucker was his daughter's middle name, but his first wife's middle name was Louisa, and the inadvertent "L" shows the extent to which he identified his daughter with the "sainted" memory of Ellen Tucker. Of course he was also intent on erasing any remaining bitterness over the lawsuit with the Nashes in the settlement of Ellen's estate.

On January 8, 1853, Emerson boarded a steamboat for Alton, Illinois, twenty-five miles upriver; then at Alton took a train for the seventy-two miles to Springfield. On the train he met State Senator Sidney Breese, Congressman Timothy Young, and Ninian Edwards, superintendent of public instruction for Illinois (Emerson called him "Gov. Edwards," apparently confusing him with his father, who had died in 1833).[79] They invited Emerson to a party in the baggage car, where they had a case of brandy, a box of buffalo tongues, and soda biscuits. They called his attention to "eight or ten deer flying across the prairie." He also saw a prairie fire, and corn still on the stalk. The mud was so deep that a horse and wagon could not get through the fields to gather the corn. This condition often lasted into March, he was told.

In Springfield, Emerson wrote Lidian he was "in the deep mud of the prairie, misled, I fear, into this bog" by an overoptimistic editor, a New Hampshire man, F. A. Moore, who edited *The Illinois Daily Journal,* and "fancied I should glitter in the prairie & draw the prairie birds & waders."[80] The intermittent rain and thaw made the mud so deep that if he stepped off the boardwalk, he feared, he would sink to his shoulders. "My chamber is a cabin. My fellow boarders are legislators, but of Illinois, or the big bog. Two or three Governors or ex-Governors live in the house." The accommodations were miserable. "But in the prairie, we are all new men, just come, & must not stand for trifles. Tis of no use then for me to magnify mine." He feared he was wasting his time, but his three lectures on "The Anglo-Saxon," "Power," and "Culture" were favorably reported in *The Journal,* though the reporter said the lecturer was a monologist who talked to himself. Emerson may have felt that he was talking to the only person who understood him. But he did not entirely waste his time, for he received one hundred and ten dollars for the three lectures.

In his Journal Emerson tried to rationalize his observations:

> Meanness of politics, low filibusterism [*sic*], dog-men, that have not shed their canine teeth; well, don't be disgusted; 'tis the work of this River, this Mississippi River that warps the men, warps the nations, they must all obey it, chop down its woods, kill the alligator, eat the deer, shoot the wolf, "follow the river," mind the boat, plant the Missouri-corn, cure, & save, and send down stream the wild foison harvest tilth & wealth of this huge mud trough of the 2 000 miles or 10 000 miles of river. How can they be high? How can they have a day's leisure for anything but the work of the river? Every one has the mud up to his knees, & the coal of the country dinges his shirt collar. How can he be literary or grammatical?[81]

Yet Emerson could not help admiring the independence and personal dignity of these hardworking people. They "are all kings: Out on the prairie the scepter is the driving whip." The cattle drivers all had an extraordinary firmness of face and lip, and a proud bearing. "No holding a hat for opinions. But the politicians in their statehouses are truckling & adulatory." Was it different in the older states? Emerson did not make comparisons. But he thought Illinois had chosen a strange place for its seat of government. Springfield, in the midst of a rich corn belt, was built on "bottom" land. The residents "cannot build cellars under the houses, & there is mud such as I never beheld. The Capitol, a costly limestone building, sinks & cracks its walls."[82]

To get to Jacksonville, Emerson traveled thirty-five miles on a "strap-rail-road," meaning that the rails were of wood covered with flat strips of iron. For forty dollars Emerson read his lecture on "Culture." At least two members of his audience, he thought, appreciated his effort: Dr. David Prince, a community leader, and Jonathan Turner, a Yale graduate, who had recently helped formulate a plan for land-grant colleges (though it would not be enacted until 1862). But probably Jacob Strawn, a major cattle dealer in the county, was a more typical prairie man. His "ideal of a great man" was one who could stand "in the gap when a great herd of cattle are to be separated."[83] At a glance he must be able to decide instantly which to send to market and which to return to the range, and at the same time look so formidable that the cattle will not run over him. Most inhabitants of the state were engaged in raising cattle and hogs, and corn to feed them. Not many were likely to be interested in lectures on "Culture."

Emerson's next engagement was in Cleveland, where he would repeat "Culture" and "The Anglo-Saxon" on January 20 and 22. But to get there he had to return to St. Louis, travel on a steamboat to Cincinnati for nearly three days, then ride the train for twelve hours to Cleveland. When he reached there, he probably had a more literate audience. Somehow he managed to get to New York in time for a lecture on the twenty-fifth, and to Philadelphia to repeat "The Anglo-Saxon" on the twenty-seventh.

In a letter to Carlyle dated April 19, 1853, Emerson told of his second trip to mid-America. He had been most impressed by "the insatiable craving for nations of men to reap and cure its harvests." Men able to do this work abounded. "Nothing higher was to be thought of. America is incomplete. Room for us all, since it has not ended, nor given sign of ending, in bard or hero."[84] But persons of talent were apt to die early; Horatio Greenough had died two months before, "a sculptor, whose tongue was far cunninger in talk than his chisel to carve." Emerson also reported: "Clough is here . . . He begins to have pupils, and, if his courage holds out, will have as many as he wants." *Courage:* if Emerson's recent travels had taught him anything, it was respect for courage.

CHAPTER XXV

Gathering Storm

Emerson as clearly as any one, perhaps more clearly than any one at the time, saw the enormous dangers that were gathering over the Constitution.[1]
                                    —George Bancroft

I

The reminiscences of a young Virginian named Moncure Conway provide a convenient window on the personal life of Emerson in the early 1850s. Conway, tall, attractive, with dark hair, silky beard, and gracious manners, was barely twenty-one when he met Emerson on May 3, 1853. Conway had been ordained a Methodist minister in Maryland on his nineteenth birthday, March 17, 1851, the spring of the tension in Boston over the capture and return to slavery of Thomas Sims. Though all his life he had taken slavery for granted, Conway was beginning to have serious misgivings about the institution, and within a few months his conscience would not let him live in a region which not only practiced but fanatically supported slavery. He had also begun to doubt the theology he was preaching. Reading Emerson's *Essays* had attracted him to Northern Unitarians, and he had recently enrolled in the Harvard Divinity School.[2]

On his first Sunday in Boston, Conway heard Theodore Parker preach in the morning and disliked his cold intellectuality. In the afternoon he heard Father Taylor in the Seamen's Bethel and was charmed by him. Of course Taylor was also a Methodist, though he concerned himself little with dogma. When Conway introduced himself, he mentioned the name of Emerson, and Father Taylor's heart "opened wide." He said Emerson was a contributor to the Seamen's Bethel, and would, he thought, welcome a visit from a young admirer. Conway had already heard the story of

Father Taylor's defending Emerson against the complaint of the orthodox that he was leading young men to hell, by saying that if he went there he would change the climate and encourage immigration.

Conway felt timid about calling on Emerson. After alighting from the train in Concord one morning, he strolled out to the Old Manse, in the opposite direction from Emerson's house, before finding courage to knock at his door a little before twelve o'clock to ask for an afternoon appointment. A servant received his message, and Emerson's children brought back the reply that he was not in, but would return by one, and their mother wished the caller to stay for dinner. Then the children took him out to the summerhouse Alcott had built, and entertained him until he was called.[3]

Emerson received him in the library. "On learning that I was at the Divinity School and had come to Concord simply to see him, he called from his library door, 'Queeney!' Mrs. Emerson came, and I was invited to remain some days." Conway replied that he must return to the college that evening, and apologized for taking up his host's time, but Emerson seemed to have time for everyone, including his children, who came in to report on their experiences of the morning. Edith said a man next door had accused a woman (probably a servant) of stealing something, and she had struck him in the leg with a corkscrew. Her father said, "He insinuated that she was a rogue, and she insinuated the corkscrew in his leg."

Presently dinner was announced and they all went into the dining room. The children joined in the talk and Conway felt happier than he had for a long time. After the children left the table, Mrs. Emerson announced with pride that they had been christened. " 'Husband was not willing the children should be christened in the formal way, but said he would offer no objection when I could find a minister as pure and good as the children.' " When William Henry Channing came to visit them, " 'we agreed he was good enough.' "[4] She was speaking, of course, of her living children, for Waldo had been christened by Dr. Ripley before his father had grown quite so heterodox.

At the end of the meal Emerson invited Conway to walk with him to Walden Pond. While waiting for his host to make some slight preparations, Conway surveyed the library. Over the mantel hung a large copy of Michelangelo's *Parcae,* and two statuettes of Goethe were prominently displayed. The furniture was mostly antique, simple, solid. Four shelves were stacked with manuscripts—enough, Conway estimated, to fill twenty printed volumes. On a later visit he learned that Mrs. Emerson had a strong aversion to Goethe, regarding him as a man without religious faith. Edith, possibly to tease her mother, had named her handsome cat Goethe. "Emerson affected to take it seriously, and once when the cat was in the library and scratched itself, he opened the door and politely said, 'Goethe, you must retire; I don't like your manners.'"[5]

On the walk to Walden the conversation was mainly about religion. Emerson said the best recruits to the Unitarian ministry came from the more orthodox denominations:

> That was a symptom. Those from other churches, having gone through experiences and reached personal convictions strong enough to break with their past, would of course have some enthusiasm for their new faith. But the Unitarians might take note of that intimation that individual growth and experience are essential for the religious teacher.[6]

Conway said he could not understand how he himself could ever have tolerated the doctrines of "inherited depravity, blood atonement, eternal damnation for Adam's sin, and the rest." Emerson replied: "I cannot feel interested in Christianity; it is deplorable that there should be a tendency to creeds that would take men back to the chimpanzee." He said he no longer attended church services, but kept a pew for his wife and children, and supported the minister because it was useful to have "a conscientious man to sit on school committees, to help at town meetings, to attend the sick and the dead." Though this talk interested Conway very much, he was still more impressed by Emerson's radiant presence. After returning to his room in Divinity Hall, Conway wrote in his diary: "May 3. The most memorable day of my life: spent with Ralph Waldo Emerson!"[7]

Conway wanted to spend his summer vacation in Concord, and Emerson found a room for him with two maiden ladies named Hunt, cousins of Martha Hunt, whose suicide Hawthorne had described the year before in *The Blithedale Romance* (though his Zenobia has often been interpreted as Margaret Fuller). Emerson also introduced Conway to the Thoreau family, and Henry invited him to take a walk with him the next day. The following morning, however, the Thoreaus were concerned with concealing and ministering to a fugitive slave who had come to them at dawn. Henry took Conway to see him, and he recognized a slave he had known in Virginia. Seeing Conway alarmed the fugitive, but he was soon reassured and enjoyed talking about people they both knew. The next day the black man was on his way to Canada, and the postponed walk took place. Many people in Concord joked about Thoreau's imitating Emerson, but Conway thought the resemblances in voice, verbal expression, and gesture were "superficial and unconscious," acquired from listening to Emerson's lectures and conversation.[8]

One day Conway was strolling on Main Street with Emerson when Samuel Hoar passed them. He was seventy-five, tall, thin, blond, clean-shaven, with the dreamy look of a man in a Bellini painting. Emerson thought he looked like Dante and called him a saint: "he no longer dwells with us down on earth." Judge Rockwood Hoar was a complete contrast to his father. "One felt in meeting him that the glasses on those bright eyes were microscopic . . ." They made Conway feel he was about to be cross-examined on the witness stand. The judge was a Free-Soiler, but Wendell Phillips had criticized him for insufficient abolition fervor, and Emerson shared the judge's resentment.

Professor Louis Agassiz, the famous Swiss scientist teaching at Harvard, gave a lecture in Concord every year, and was always a guest of the Emersons. He talked of "spiritual evolution," but when Darwin's *Origin of Species* appeared, he refused to accept the theory of natural selection. Emerson said this theory appeared to him to be a counterpart of the "ideal development" taught by Agassiz, "Whereupon Agassiz exclaimed, 'There I cannot agree with you,' and changed the subject." Conway remembered "a curious conversation" between Agassiz and Alcott, the pure idealist:

After delighting Agassiz by repudiating the theory of the development of man from animals, he filled the professor with dismay by equally decrying the notion that God could ever have created ferocious and poisonous beasts. When Agassiz asked who could have created them, Alcott said they were the various forms of human sin. Man was the first being created. And the horrible creatures were originated by his lusts and animalisms. When Agassiz, bewildered, urged that geology proved that the animals existed before man, Alcott suggested that man might have originated them before his appearance in his present form. Agassiz having given a signal of distress, Emerson came to the rescue with some reconciling discourse on the development of life and thought, with which the professor had to be content, although there was a *soupçon* of evolution in every word our host uttered.[9]

II

In the winter of 1854, with deep snow on the ground and the temperature below zero, Conway and two other divinity students rented a sleigh and drove from Cambridge to Concord to hear Emerson give a lecture in the Town Hall. When they arrived they found the hall closed. They drove to Emerson's house and learned that the lecture had been postponed. Emerson was deeply touched that they would drive forty miles (twenty each way) in an open sleigh in such weather to hear him. A few days later he wrote Conway that he would read a lecture in his room in Divinity Hall as compensation if Conway would make the arrangements.

When rumors of the plan began to circulate, the Divinity School authorities became alarmed, fearing a repetition of the turmoil caused by Emerson's address there in 1838. But Conway tactfully explained that the reading would take place on a Saturday afternoon, when no classes were being taught, for a very small group of invited friends, and every effort would be made to avoid any appearance of its being sponsored by the school.

Because his own room was sparsely furnished, Conway borrowed Laommi Ware's. There Emerson read a lecture on "Poetry" (he had given a lecture on "Poetry and English Literature" in Philadelphia on January 10). Among the fifteen present were Mr. and Mrs. Henry Wadsworth Longfellow, James Russell Lowell, John Dwight (the music critic), Charles Eliot Norton and his sisters Jane and Grace, and Emerson's neighbor Franklin B. Sanborn. When Emerson finished reading, no one knew what to say. Spontaneously Otto Dresel, a divinity student, went to the piano and played Mendelssohn's "Songs Without Words."[10]

A long footnote by Conway in his *Autobiography* and an editorial note by Edward Emerson in *Letters and Social Aims* make it possible to identify the lecture (the introduction, at least) as substantially the text of the essay published as "Poetry and Imagination." And the remarkable thing is not what Emerson had to say about poetry but what he had to say about science—or perhaps about the link between the imagination and matter, in discussing which he anticipated some twentieth-century discoveries in atomic physics and revolutionary theories on the nature of matter.

Many atomic physicists would today agree with Emerson that "Science was false by being unpoetical."[11] What impressed Conway was Emerson's anticipation of Darwinian evolution. Conway was startled by this statement:

> The electric word pronounced by John Hunter a hundred years ago, *arrested and progressive development,* indicating the way upward from the invisible protoplasm to the highest organisms, gave the poetic key to Natural Science, of which the theories of Geoffroy Saint-Hilaire, of Oken, of Goethe, of Agassiz and Owen and Darwin in zoölogy and botany, are the fruits,—a hint whose power is not yet exhausted, showing unity and perfect order in physics.[12]

Many years later while preparing a lecture for the Royal Institute in London, Conway asked "Professors Huxley, Tyndall, and Flower (then Hunterian [Museum] lecturer) where I could find John Hunter's statement about 'arrested and progressive development.' " They searched and could not find it, and marveled that Emerson in 1854 should have known about natural selection. (Conway remarks parenthetically that the Darwin alluded to was doubtless Erasmus, not Charles.) Finally Conway himself found the idea in a note in Hunter's collected works (1835),[13] but Emerson had coined the phrase "arrested and progressive development." Actually, Emerson's saying something that resembled Darwin's theory of evolution (1859) was less remarkable than Conway thought, for Erasmus Darwin had anticipated his grandson's theories by more than half a century, and Emerson had also read Robert Chambers's *Vestiges of Creation* as early as 1845.[14] More surprising today is Emerson's statement about the impermanence and fluidity of matter:

> First innuendoes, then broad hints, then smart taps are given, suggesting that nothing stands still in Nature but death; that the creation is on wheels, in transit, always passing into something else, streaming into something higher; that matter is not what it appears;—that chemistry can

blow it all into gas. Faraday, the most exact of natural philosophers, taught that when we should arrive at the monads, or primordial elements (the supposed little cubes or prisms of which all matter was built up), we should not find cubes, or prisms, or atoms, at all, but spherules of force.[15]

The commonsense view of matter is that it is stable and inert, and that if one could penetrate to the "building blocks" one would find something like what the Greeks called *atoms* (Faraday's *monads*). But when twentieth-century physicists began probing the atom, and even more in exploring subatomic levels, they found not something stable and solid but bundles of energy (Emerson's "spherules of force") moving at incredible speeds. These bundles or knots of energy, moreover, existed in *fields* of energy, each one attracting or repulsing every other field in its region. On the subatomic level, matter is extremely volatile, dynamic, and unstable. Then some physicists, such as Niels Bohr and Robert Oppenheimer, began to perceive that this world of physical reality strongly resembles the "reality" taught for centuries by Hindu, Buddhist, Taoist, and Zen mystics. By contemplating the inner world of the mind, or consciousness, the mystics arrived at concepts startlingly parallel to those of the modern physicists when they explored the external world with sophisticated instruments. The consequences of these similarities are only beginning to affect Western concepts of reality. Of course the belief in a supernatural power directing the dance of the atoms belongs to religion rather than to science, though it is held by some scientists.

From Swedenborg (via Sampson Reed) Emerson had derived the notion that spirit and matter (nature) "correspond" one to the other, like negative and positive charges in electricity. Of course he draped this theory with his moral didacticism. But his conception of dynamic matter produced and propelled by some mysterious force (in his terminology, Reason or Divine Mind) like an electric charge no longer seems as improbable as it did in a mechanistic age. The latest theories of atomic and subatomic physics even cast doubt on the existence of elementary particles of matter. "They revealed," says Fritjof Capra, "a basic interconnection of matter, showing that energy of motion can be transferred into mass, and suggesting that particles are processes rather than objects."[16] Emerson said something like that, though going beyond Capra in his speculative interpretation:

There is one animal, one planet, one matter and one force [that is, en-ergy]. The laws of light and of heat translate into each other;—so do the laws of sound and of color; and so galvanism, electricity and magnetism are varied forms of the selfsame energy. While the student ponders this immense unity, he observes that all things in Nature, the animals, the mountain, the river, the seasons, wood, iron, stone, vapor, have a mysteri-ous relation to his thoughts and his life; their growths, decays, quality and use so curiously resemble himself, in parts and in wholes, that he is com-pelled to speak by means of them.[17]

This mysterious relation to his "thoughts" anticipates the increasing conviction of some twentieth-century physicists "that all their theories of natural phenomena, including the 'laws' they describe, are creations of the human mind; properties of our conceptual map of reality, rather than of reality itself."[18] Of course there is an implied skepticism here which does not sound like Emerson: that man can "know" only such aspects of the natural world as he can experience through his senses or through instru-ments which extend their range. There are probably aspects which he can never observe even with the most subtle instruments, and thus never "know." The Eastern mystics granted this limitation (and so did Kant!), and cheerfully accepted the "Void," pure negation, as ultimate reality. They even developed techniques for ego annihilation, for experiencing the infinite Nothingness.

Emerson was too much a child of the West to seek the Void as an ulti-mate goal, but he was increasingly fascinated by the Hindu doctrine of maya, the illusory appearance of the world. In his lecture on "Poetry" he said:

This belief that the higher use of the material world is to furnish us types or pictures to express the thoughts of the mind, is carried to its logi-cal extreme by the Hindoos, who, following Buddha, have made it the central doctrine of their religion that what we call Nature, the external world, has no real existence,—is only phenomenal. Youth, age, property, condition, events, persons,—self, even,—are successive *maias* (deceptions) through which Vishnu mocks and instructs the soul. I think Hindoo books the best gymnastics for the mind, as showing treatment.[19]

The purpose of Emerson's phenomenology is not, like that of the Orien-tal mystics, to attain a state of beatitude, but to learn how to use sensory experiences in both a philosophical and a literary way. Nature is "a vast trope" (as he had said in *Nature,* 1836). "All thinking is analogizing, and it is the use of life to learn metonymy." Hence the value of poetry. Man might be imprisoned in his senses, but "The intellect acts on these brute reports, and obtains from them results which are the essence or intellectual form of the experiences."[20] The theory of biological evolution Emerson readily accepted, but the evolution which interested him most was the "transfigurations" of matter from inanimate to animate forms, until they finally energize the mind and become knowledge:

> The atoms of the body were once nebulae, then rock, then loam, then corn, then chyme, then chyle, then blood; and now the beholding and co-energizing mind sees the same refining and ascent to the third, the seventh or the tenth power of the daily accidents which the senses report, and which make the raw material of knowledge. It was sensation; when memory came, it was experience; when mind acted, it was knowledge; when mind acted on it as knowledge, it was thought.

Fascinated as Emerson was by the "transfigurations" of atoms from stellar nebulae to chyle and blood, he never entirely succeeded in expressing this idea in a poem. He came nearest in "Song of Nature,"[21] which he began working on in 1846 and completed in 1859. The "I" of the poem is the cosmic power which hides in "solar glory": "I sit by the shining Fount of Life, / And pour the deluge still." The poet draws upon geology to describe the workings of this cosmic process:

> I wrote the past in characters
> Of rock and fire the scroll,
> The building in the coral sea,
> The planting of the coal.

The seas boiled and the granite was deposited, layer upon layer, and yet man did not appear:

> I travail in pain for him,
> My creatures travail and wait;
> His couriers come by squadrons,
> He comes not to the gate.

Several times nature molded an "image" of the ideal man, once in a Judean manger, once near the mouth of the Nile (Plotinus?), once in the "Academe" (Plato), and once "by Avon stream."

> I moulded kings and saviors,
> And bards o'er kings to rule;—
> But fell the starry influence short,
> The cup was never full.

Nature (and the poet) still expect the coming of this superman (what was called in Chapter XX "the central man"), bred "Of all the zones and countless days," and meanwhile:

> No ray is dimmed, no atom worn,
> My oldest force is good as new,
> And the fresh rose on yonder thorn
> Gives back the bending heavens in dew.

While Emerson waited for the "sunburnt world" to produce his "man," one July day in 1855 he received through the mail a book of poems called *Leaves of Grass* that gave him new hope. Here the elemental forces of nature were celebrated in fresh lyric forms by an elemental "I," part human, part myth, and symbolizing the same evolutionary "transfigurations" described in Emerson's "Song of Nature"—which of course Whitman had not read. But the great difference between Emerson's poem and Walt Whitman's "Song of Myself" (untitled in 1855) was that Emerson still expected the coming man, whereas Whitman presented him as having arrived, personified in himself, or the "I" of his poem. Whitman's theme is the ecstasy of being. The "I" is intoxicated by the fragrance of the atmosphere and vibrates with the "procreant urge of the world." He symbolizes in this "I" not only the processes and preparations for his own arrival but also the culmination, the taking possession of his birthright:

> Cycles ferried my cradle, rowing and rowing like cheerful boatmen;
> For room to me stars kept aside in their own rings,
> They sent influences to look after what was to hold me.
>
> Before I was born out of my mother generations guided me,
> My embryo has never been torpid.... nothing could overlay it;

For it the nebula cohered to an orb ... the long slow strata
    piled to rest it on ... vast vegetables gave it sustenance,
Monstrous sauroids transported it in their mouths and deposited
    it with care.

All forces have been steadily employed to complete and delight me,
Now I stand on this spot with my soul. [1160–68]

In his lecture on "Poetry" Emerson said: ". . . the best parts of many old and many new poets are simply enumerations by a person who felt the beauty of the common sights and sounds, without any attempt to draw a moral or affix a meaning."[22] This was exactly what Whitman did in "Song of Myself." Later critics would ridicule his enumerations by calling them "catalogs," but Emerson could appreciate them on his own theory—even if he was apologetic to Carlyle about the "inventories." Also he probably recognized in Whitman's style the same similarities to the prosody of Hebrew and Persian poetry which attracted Conway, whom Emerson had introduced to Persian poetry. Conway had been reading the *Desatir* before meeting Whitman, "and other books which I found he had never heard of." But his imagery "seemed like the colours of dawn reappearing in the sunset."[23]

There are many things in Whitman's poems of which Emerson might have been expected to disapprove, such as "I dote on myself ... there is that lot of me, and all so luscious." And he attempts to identify his personal self with his mythical "I":

Walt Whitman, an American, one of the roughs, a kosmos,
Disorderly fleshy and sensual ... eating drinking and breeding,
No sentimentalist ... no stander above men and women or apart
    from them. . . . no more modest than immodest. [499–501]

Outright sensuality was always offensive to Emerson, and he admitted to Conway that there were parts of *Leaves of Grass* "where I hold my nose as I read."[24] But he added, "One must not be too squeamish when a chemist brings him to a mass of filth and says, 'See, the great laws are at work here also.'" A poem called "Music," which Edward Emerson published in an appendix to his father's collected *Poems* (1904), ends with this stanza:

'T is not in the high stars alone,
   Nor in the cup of budding flowers,
   Nor in the redbreast's mellow tone,
   Nor in the bow that smiles in showers,
   But in the mud and scum of things
   There alway, alway something sings.[25]

Dr. Oliver Wendell Holmes protested against Edward Emerson's "allowing the 'mud and scum of things' to have a voice," and they certainly did not in the poems Emerson published, but his critical tolerance was wider than his practice.

The title page of Whitman's strange book did not bear the name of the author, but it was copyrighted by Walter Whitman, and distributed by Fowler and Wells in New York and Boston. (And of course the poet had named himself in the passage quoted above.) So on July 21 Emerson addressed a letter to Walter Whitman, in care of Fowler and Wells. Though this letter has often been printed, it is worth quoting again in order to call attention to Emerson's exact phrases:

Concord 21 July
Masstts. 1855

Dear Sir,

   I am not blind to the worth of the wonderful gift of "Leaves of Grass." I find it the most extraordinary piece of wit & wisdom that America has yet contributed. I am very happy in reading it, as great power makes us happy. It meets the demand I am always making of what seemed the sterile & stingy nature, as if too much handiwork or too much lymph in the temperament were making our western wits fat & mean. I give you joy of your free & brave thought. I have great joy in it. I find incomparable things said incomparably well, as they must be. I find the courage of treatment, which so delights us, & which large perception only can inspire. I greet you at the beginning of a great career, which yet must have had a long foreground somewhere for such a start. I rubbed my eyes a little to see if this sunbeam were no illusion; but the solid sense of the book is a solid certainty. It has the best merits, namely, of fortifying & encouraging.

   I did not know until I, last night, saw the book advertised in a news-

paper, that I could trust the name as real & available for a post office. I wish to see my benefactor, & have felt much like striking my tasks, & visiting New York to pay you my respects.

R. W. Emerson.[26]

Mr Walter Whitman

Whitman did not write a personal reply, but permitted Charles A. Dana to print the letter in *The New-York Daily Tribune.* Then a year later he emblazoned "I greet you at the / Beginning of A / Great Career / R. W. Emerson" on the spine of his second edition, in which he also printed a fulsome open letter, ostensibly to thank Emerson but taken up mainly with parading his own grandiose literary plans. Nevertheless, Emerson was still delighted to find in *Leaves of Grass* views of an abundantly fructifying nature, and perceptions as large and inspiring as his own. Many of the ideas were similar to Emerson's but magnified and emphasized. He did not know that Whitman had some knowledge of the "ancient Hindoo poems," though later after some of his enthusiasm had subsided, he called *Leaves of Grass* a combination of the *"Bhagavad-gita* and the *New-York Tribune."*[27]

Emerson did not see Whitman until December 11, 1855, when he lectured at the Brooklyn Athenaeum. By that time Conway had paid a visit to Whitman. Upon his graduation from Harvard, Conway accepted the pastorate of a Unitarian church in Washington, D.C., where he began his ministry in September 1854. He spent a vacation in Boston the following year. On Emerson's recommendation he bought a copy of *Leaves of Grass* at Miss Peabody's bookshop and read it on the steamboat to New York. On September 17 he wrote Emerson that he had visited Whitman in Brooklyn.

When Conway called, Whitman was not at home, but his mother said he was at Rome's printing office on Fulton Street. There Conway found him correcting proofs, probably of poems for his second edition. He looked like the engraved photograph in his book. He said Conway was the first person to visit him because of his book, and of course he was pleased. When told that the Reverend Cyrus Bartol, one of the original 'Transcendentalists," had attempted to read *Leaves of Grass* to a mixed audience and had failed, Whitman laughed. He said he had heard of someone who had tried to sell his book as pornography, but that did not amuse him. He accompanied Conway on the ferry back to New York, and on the way greeted all working-class men as personal friends. Conway thought this partly a game he played with himself, but he liked the man and wrote Emerson, "He is clearly his Book."[28]

After Whitman used the "greeting" letter to promote his second edition, Emerson told Conway that if he had known it would be published he would have qualified his praise. He thought some of Whitman's illustrations of "the great laws [of nature] at work" might have been deodorized. "However, I do not fear that any man who has eyes in his head will fail to see the genius in these poems. Those are terrible eyes to walk along Broadway. It is all there, as if in an auctioneer's catalogue."

Some of Emerson's friends later reported that Whitman's use of his letter without permission made him terribly angry, but Conway's testimony does not indicate more than annoyance, and it is probable that the witnesses colored their reports by their own feelings. Aside from Thoreau, Alcott, and Conway, nearly all of Emerson's friends were only too glad to find some excuse to attack a poet who shocked their sense of decency. Yet it was true that as time passed, Emerson had less confidence that others would see in Whitman's poems what he had seen. On May 6, 1856, he wrote Carlyle:

One book, last summer, came out in New York, a nondescript monster which yet had terrible eyes and buffalo strength, and was indisputably American,—which I thought to send you; but the book throve so badly with the few to whom I showed it, and wanted good morals so much, that I never did. Yet I believe now again, I shall. It is called *Leaves of Grass,*— was written and printed by a journeyman printer in Brooklyn, New York, named Walter Whitman; and after you have looked into it, if you think, as you may, that it is only an auctioneer's inventory of a warehouse, you can light your pipe with it.[29]

III

In the mid-1850s Emerson became both emotionally and practically involved in events growing out of the enforcement of the Fugitive Slave Law. On May 26, 1854, friends of his attempted to rescue Anthony Burns, a fugitive from Virginia, from the Court House in Boston. Burns had been arrested on a charge of robbery (a false charge, the abolitionists claimed), and while he was being held, his owner appeared and demanded his return. Wendell Phillips and Theodore Parker heard of the arrest and rushed to Burns's aid. They held a noisy mass meeting that evening in Faneuil Hall, after which a small band of men, including Parker, Alcott, and T. W. Higginson, a Unitarian minister from Worcester, broke down the door to the jail and attempted unsuccessfully to release Burns. In the melee one man was killed, by whom could never be determined. Higginson and Parker were tried for their participation in the break-in, but were finally acquitted.[30]

Emerson was not in Boston at this time—or on June 2, when Burns was escorted by sailors from a nearby U.S. Navy base to a ship waiting in the harbor to take him back to Virginia—but his sympathies were strongly aroused. On June 17 he wrote Charles Sumner, the most fiery antagonist of the slavocracy in the United States Senate, that he had just returned from Boston, where he had been "edified as never before, by the conversation of lawyers & merchants." They felt cheated and insulted by the "riff-raff of the streets" who supported the arrest of men such as Burns. "I came home with more confidence in the future of Massachusetts than I have felt for many a day."[31] He assured Sumner he would certainly be reelected to the Senate in November. Public sentiment in Massachusetts was now turning against the defenders of slavery. But Emerson still felt contempt for the state officials. "The Governor is not worth his own cockade," he wrote in his Journal. "He sits in his chair to see the laws of his Commonwealth broken, & . . . every peaceable citizen endangered[,] every patriotic citizen insulted."[32]

The previous year Emerson had experimented with poems that might encourage slaves to rebel, but found his Muse would not aid him:

> Once I wished I might rehearse
> Freedom's praises in my verse
> That the slave who caught the strain
> Should throb until he snapt his chain
> But the Spirit said, Not So,
> Speak it not, or speak it low,
> Name not idly to be said,
> Gift too precious to be prayed,
> Passion not to be expressed
> But by the heaving of the breast.[33]

Because Emerson was not permitted to speak on the slavery question in his bread-and-butter lectures, he felt guilty, and when he got a chance and a good pretext for declaring his convictions, he did so with vigor. Such an occasion was the protest meeting in the Town Hall of Concord on May 26, 1856, on "The Assault upon Mr. Sumner."[34] That spring, feelings over "bleeding Kansas" had reached the boiling point. Northern newspapers were reporting horrendous atrocities committed by invading Missourians and troops sent in by proslavery President Pierce. Leading abolitionists in New York, Boston, and even Concord (notably Samuel and Rockwood Hoar) were buying Sharps rifles to send to the defenders of the "free state."

In the United States Senate, Charles Sumner, a ruthless puritan in his moral convictions, had excoriated the South in an eight-hour speech on May 21–22. He accused Senator Andrew Butler of South Carolina of "every possible deviation from truth," and said civilization would lose nothing if South Carolina were "blotted out of existence." Butler was elderly, and Sumner in his vigor at forty-five, a handsome man with a goatee, six feet three inches in height, weighing 185 pounds. Butler's nephew, Representative Preston Brooks, had been taught from childhood that any attack on the honor of one's family or country must be avenged. Arming himself with a stout walking stick, he advanced on Senator Sumner, who was sitting at his desk in the Senate Chamber, and beat him into semiconsciousness.

Judge Hoar heard of the attack and rushed to tell Emerson on a warm May evening. Emerson's response was to deliver a speech at the protest meeting, which began:

> Mr. Chairman: I sympathize heartily with the spirit of the resolutions. The events of the last few years and months and days have taught us the lessons of centuries. I do not see how a barbarous community and a civilized community can constitute one state. I think we must get rid of slavery, or we must get rid of freedom. Life has not parity of value in the free state and the slave state.[35]

Angry as he was at the brutal assault on Sumner, Emerson insisted in his Journal that the episode was "only a leaf of the tree, it is not Sumner who must be avenged, but the tree must be cut down."[36] Though most New Englanders shared his indignation, many still refused to consider the breakup of the Union and the possibility of civil war. In his Journal Emerson wrote another sentence which he would repeat in his speech: "The hour is coming when the strongest will not be strong enough."[37] He had no doubt that "South Carolina is in earnest." The courtesy of the Carolinians was deceptive. He knew, so he wrote, "that the only reason why they do not plant a cannon before Faneuil Hall, & blow Bunker Hill monument to fragments, as a nuisance, is because they have not the power. They are fast acquiring the power, & if they get it, they will do it."[38]

During the spring of 1856 other atrocities were committed in Kansas. On May 21 the Free State headquarters in Lawrence were pillaged and burned by a proslavery mob. In retaliation a newcomer to the scene, John Brown, a Connecticut Yankee turned avenger, slew five proslavery men because, he said, they deserved to die. Then on June 2 at Black Jack he led nine determined men against twenty-three under a dashing Southern leader, Henry Pate Clay, later a cavalry commander under Confederate General J. E. B. Stuart, and forced them to surrender. The Northern abolitionists now had a hero, and emigrant aid societies sprang up all over New England. Under the guise of raising money for the relief of Kansans made destitute by marauding bandits, they supplied guns and ammunition. The Hoar family was active in these meetings, and both Samuel and Judge Rockwood began to take an increasing interest in the new Republican party, founded in Wisconsin in 1854, but expanding to the East in the summer of 1856 by uniting "Conscience Whigs" with "Free-Soil" Democrats.

At their national convention at Cincinnati in June, the Democrats nominated James Buchanan for the presidency on a platform supporting the Fugitive Slave Law and "squatter sovereignty" in Kansas (that is, slavery). The ragtag Know-Nothing party, whose main purpose was to curb the political influence of recent immigrants from Europe, nominated Millard Fillmore, who (while filling out the term of Zachary Taylor) had signed the Fugitive Slave Law in 1850.

The Republican party had scheduled its first national convention in Philadelphia for mid-June. Through the influence of the Hoars, Emerson was named as an alternate delegate for Governor George S. Boutwell, who was uncertain of attending, though he did—and Emerson took a vacation at Pigeon Cove on the coast of Massachusetts. But he had narrowly escaped taking part in the nomination of John C. Frémont. In the November election Buchanan won, though the Republicans were encouraged by the showing they made.

Meanwhile, Emerson was becoming more deeply involved in the Kansas relief meetings. On September 10 he gave one of his most impassioned speeches in Cambridge on "Affairs in Kansas."[39] He had no doubt that "all the right is on one side. We hear the screams of hunted wives and children answered by the howl of the butchers." Men from New England had been murdered: Mr. Hoppe of Somerville, Mr. Hoyt of Deerfield, Mr. Jenison of Groton, Mr. Phillips of Berkshire; and others had been imprisoned. Not only did President Pierce fail to protect the Kansas settlers; the troops he sent to keep order "armed and led the ruffians against the poor farmers." The President says: " 'Let the complainants go to the courts;' though he knows that when the poor plundered farmer comes to the court, he finds the ringleader who had robbed him dismounting from his own horse, and unbuckling his knife to sit as his judge."[40]

The President's conduct had made Emerson lose confidence not only in the national government but in almost any government: "I am glad to see that the terror at disunion and anarchy is disappearing. Massachusetts, in its heroic day, had no government—was an anarchy. Every man stood on his own feet, was his own governor; and there was no breach of peace from Cape Cod to Mount Hoosac."[41]

Of course Emerson was exaggerating, but he had always believed more in town meetings than in state or federal government. In his disillusionment he was acutely prophetic. He foresaw a "new revolution" more terrible than the American Revolution. Then the enemy was three thousand miles away. "But now, vast property, gigantic interests, family connections, webs of party, cover the land with a network that immensely multiplies the dangers of war."[42] Yet whatever the danger, it was the duty of every man and woman of conscience to send money and supplies to the good citizens of Kansas, to hold "town meetings, and resolve themselves into Committees of Safety," as they had done in the time of the American Revolution. Many years later George Bancroft, the historian and friend of Emerson, wrote of this speech:

Emerson as clearly as any one, perhaps more clearly than any one at the time, saw the enormous dangers that were gathering over the Constitution. . . . It would certainly be difficult, perhaps impossible, to find any speech made in the same year that is marked with so much courage and foresight as this of Emerson. . . . Even after the inauguration of Lincoln several months passed away before the Secretary of State or he himself saw the future as clearly as Emerson had foreshadowed it in 1856.[43]

IV

In the winter of 1857 John Brown came east to raise funds for his work in Kansas. In February he spoke at the Town Hall in Concord, and Emerson invited him to spend the night in his home. Having failed at farming and business, Brown had now found his calling in fighting slavery—a work, he believed, for which God had predestined him, and this conviction gave him incredible stamina and courage. Brown was a man of medium height and wiry build whose tanned, weather-beaten face and metallic voice conveyed his intense dedication. It was an hour, he said, to die in a good cause, and his hearers believed him. He began speaking in a calm voice, but his tone became hard and penetrating when he held up a trace chain which he said had bound one of his sons when a mountain ruffian had dragged him to prison. He had lost two sons in Kansas: one murdered and the other driven insane by his suffering at the hands of the proslavery invaders. But his remaining five would never stop fighting by his side. "One of his good points," Emerson wrote next day in his Journal, "was, the folly of the peace party in Kansas." Emerson was beginning to share that thought, too; but, he recorded, " 'tis no use to tell me, as Brown & others do, that the Southerner is not a better fighter than the Northerner."[44]

Afterward in Emerson's home the wild-eyed speaker was a charming guest. Twelve-year-old Eddie was fascinated by his talk of animals.[45] Brown said he had had three thousand sheep in Ohio, and could instantly detect a strange one. He thought a cow could communicate with her calf by a secret signal, probably by a look in the eye, when she sensed danger. He always made friends with his horse or mule, or visiting deer. He could sleep while riding his horse as easily as in bed, and his horse would look out for him.[46]

On Brown's second visit to Concord, May 8, 1859, he looked many years older. He had grown a prophet's beard, and his face was lined and drawn. He said he had suffered greatly, but was determined to see his work completed. His audience in Town Hall thought he meant to make Kansas a free state, but he was actually preparing for his doomed raid on the federal arsenal at Harpers Ferry, Virginia. Alcott, a shrewd judge of men in spite of his misty Platonism, wrote in his Journal: "Our best people listen to his words—Emerson, Thoreau, Judge Hoar, my wife—and some of them contribute something in aid of his plans without asking particulars, such confidence does he inspire with his integrity and abilities." (Judge Hoar contributed one hundred dollars; Emerson, fifty.)

Brown did take some people into his confidence, but apparently Emerson was not one of them. It was a shock to him, therefore, when telegraphic dispatches reported Brown's raid on the arsenal on October 16, 1859. With the assistance of eighteen white and black men he actually seized the arsenal, intending to distribute the weapons to Virginia slaves to use against their masters. Within a few hours U.S. Marines had captured him and most of his band. In fact, he scarcely tried to escape and had strangely bungled his operation, as if courting martyrdom.

News of the raid reached Emerson on a balmy day in October, following the annual cattle show in Concord, at which he had exhibited fruit from his orchard and made a speech to the farmers. First prize for grapes had gone, as expected, to his neighbor Ephraim Bull for his newly developed Concords, but Emerson's grapes received a third prize.[47] These pleasant experiences were quickly forgotten when the telegraph continued to bring grim news about John Brown. On October 23 Waldo wrote William: "We are all very well, in spite of the sad Harpers Ferry business, which interests us all who had Brown for our guest twice. . . . He is a true hero, but lost his head there."[48]

One of the persons who had cause to fear revelations in Brown's correspondence, seized when he was captured, was Franklin B. Sanborn, head of the Concord Academy, once taught by the Thoreau brothers and revived at Emerson's suggestion by this recent graduate of Harvard. Sanborn had also served as regional secretary of the Kansas Aid Society. He had fled to Canada once after his neighbors beat off two U.S. marshals trying to arrest him in front of his own house, and he would flee a second time after being summoned to Washington to testify in the investigation of Brown's conspiracy.

Brown was promptly tried for treason and murder and sentenced on November 1 to be hanged on December 2. At some time in that interval

Emerson started a private letter to the governor of Virginia, Henry Alexander Wise, pleading for Brown's life on the basis of insanity. (The letter was never completed, but Emerson copied a rough draft into his Journal.) Possibly the insanity plea was only a stratagem for saving the old man's life, though to William, to whom Waldo could be absolutely frank, he had said Brown "lost his head"; so he was doubtless sincere in believing that Brown was not rational—or had temporarily lost his sanity:

> The man is so transparent that all can see him through, that he had no second thought, but was the rarest of heroes[,] a pure idealist, with no by-ends of his own. He is therefore precisely what lawyers call crazy, being governed by ideas, & not by external circumstance. He has afforded them the first trait marked in the books as betraying insanity, namely, disproportion between means & ends.[49]

The plea of insanity had already been used by Brown's lawyers at his trial, and Governor Wise had insisted that the old man was sane, that he was deliberately carrying out the wishes of Northern abolitionists. Wise admitted, though, that Brown had shown great courage and strength of character.[50] Emerson probably had little confidence in his own plea, but he had intended a shrewd appeal to the governor's own self-interest. Brown's speeches in court, he pointed out, had captured the interest of the nation, and would "in due time" certainly do so in England, France, and Germany:

> It is not, I am sure, your wish to stand in the most unlucky position which history must give to the Governor who signs his death warrant. It is very easy to see that he will be a favorite of history, which plays mad pranks with dignitaries, &, if so, that he will drag gentlemen into an immortality not desireable.[51]

Although Emerson's letter failed to achieve his purpose, his sincerity is attested by the fact that he did not publish it. Finally, realizing that nothing could be done to save the old martyr's life, he turned his attention to Brown's family. On November 18 he attended a meeting in Boston at Tremont Temple "For the Relief of the Family of John Brown," and made a short speech repeating some of the ideas in his letter to Governor Wise:

It is easy to see what a favorite he will be with history . . . Indeed, it is the *reductio ad absurdum* of Slavery, when the governor of Virginia is forced to hang a man whom he declares to be a man of the most integrity, truthfulness and courage he has ever met. Is that the kind of man the gallows is built for? It were bold to affirm that there is within that broad commonwealth, at this moment, another citizen as worthy to live, and as deserving of all public and private honor, as this poor prisoner.[52]

How completely Emerson sympathized with the man calmly waiting his execution, he revealed in a lecture on "Courage" given in Boston November 8. In an interpolation he called Brown "that new saint than whom none purer or more brave was ever led by love of men into conflict and death,—the new saint awaiting his martyrdom, and who, if he shall suffer [execution], will make the gallows glorious like the cross." (This passage was omitted when the lecture was published in *Society and Solitude.*)[53]

It was Thoreau's idea to hold a memorial service in Concord on the day of Brown's execution. He met considerable opposition from unsympathetic neighbors, but the meeting was held on schedule in the Town Hall. It was attended by Rockwood Hoar, justice of the Supreme Court of Massachusetts; James Redpath, a reporter on *The New-York Daily Tribune* who was collecting material for a biography of Brown; and of course Sanborn, Alcott, Emerson, and Thoreau. They had agreed not to make impassioned speeches, but to read poems and reverently praise the martyr. Many people who came to the meeting were from nearby towns. But that night a jeering crowd burned John Brown in effigy.[54]

The memorial service was scarcely over before Sanborn received word that Francis Meriam, one of the Harpers Ferry raiders who had escaped capture, was in Boston. He had already been aided in fleeing to Canada once, but had become mentally unbalanced and returned, ignoring the price on his head. He was persuaded to escape to Canada again, but he had the crazy idea that he must talk with Mr. Emerson and took the train to Concord. That night he showed up at Sanborn's house, nearer the depot than Emerson's. Sanborn, acutely aware of the danger to himself as well as to the hunted man, stealthily set about getting him out of town. He asked Thoreau to drive a man to the South Acton station that night, without revealing who the man was. Nor did he tell Emerson, whose horse and wagon he borrowed for the trip. On the way Meriam jumped out of the wagon, saying he must see Mr. Emerson, but Thoreau persuaded him to continue the trip, and finally placed him on the train which would take him to Canada. Thoreau suspected he was aiding one of Brown's men, but he did not know this for a fact until told on his deathbed two and a half years later. In lending his horse and wagon without asking questions, Emerson had also shown his willingness to take chances on what he suspected was desperate business.[55]

CHAPTER XXVI

Works and Days

The days ... come and go like muffled and
veiled figures, sent from a distant friendly party;
but they say nothing ...[1]

I

"I have now for more than a year, I believe, ceased almost wholly to write
in my Journal, in which I formerly wrote almost daily," Emerson confessed in an undated entry (probably late spring) in his 1859 Journal. "I
see few intellectual persons, & even those to no purpose, & sometimes believe that I have no new thoughts, and that my life is quite at an end."[2] At
fifty-six Emerson was in sound health, but his continuous traveling to give
those lectures was exhausting, and only occasionally did he meet stimulating companions. That very morning, however, "came by a man with
knowledge & interests like mine, in his head, and suddenly I have
thoughts again." (The man sounds like Bronson Alcott.)

During the remainder of the year Emerson had "thoughts" for his
Journal. This may have been partly because in July he sprained his foot
coming down Mount Wachusett and had to restrict his physical activities
for several months.[3] In his confinement and boredom he turned to his
Journal again, though he did not enjoy his leisure: "When I sprained my
foot I soon found it was all one as if I had sprained my head ... Then I
thought nature had sprained her foot; and that King Lear had never
sprained his, or he would have thought there were worse evils than unkind
daughters. When I see a man unhappy, I ask, has a sprained foot brought
him to *this* pass?"[4]

Sometimes bad luck comes in tandem. Before his foot had healed,

Emerson experienced several other "frets," as he called them in a letter to William on September 8: "My two cows, which had been all summer at pasture in New Hampshire, strayed, on the return, & are not found. A windy day strewed the ground with my unripe pears. My saint of an Irishman [James Burke] has had a *spree* on a most unfitting time. More grave disaster I find in the loss of Mr Phillips, my publisher, and the loss & inconvenience that comes therefrom may be greater than I know."[5]

The most serious of these "frets" was undoubtedly the death of both senior members of his publishing firm, Moses D. Phillips and Charles Sampson. As Emerson feared, the firm failed two days after his writing William. One consequence was an interruption in the sales of *English Traits,* which had been selling steadily in England and America since its publication in 1856. The book had been both praised and damned in both countries, but controversy often helps the sale of a book.

To the present day, *English Traits* has remained one of Emerson's most readable and enjoyable books, though some critics have pointed out flaws in organization. The first chapter rehearses Emerson's experiences on his first visit to England in 1833. Though this is interesting as autobiography, his second chapter, beginning with his 1847 sea voyage, would have made a more appropriate introduction; and his speech in Manchester in November 1847 is not an appropriate conclusion. *English Traits* is a combination of travel book, historical survey (origin and growth of the British people), and sociological study, but Emerson combined these in a piquant view of the British in the eyes of a curious, observant, and kindly American critic, at a time when England was at the peak of her economic and military power. The unfailing hospitality he received gave him unique opportunities to observe and judge. Howard Mumford Jones says in his Introduction to a recent edition of *English Traits,* "no better book by an American about Victorian England (or rather Great Britain at midcentury) has ever been published."[6]

Emerson's foot was still not entirely healed when January came and it was time to start his annual hegira to the Midwest. Notes were coming due at the bank and he must earn money to pay them and meet other expenses; this was no "illusion," but a "fate" to be met head on. As his earnings increased, so did his expenses, and he never seemed to gain on them. On February 5 he wrote Lidian from Lafayette, Indiana, "My foot . . . admires railroad cars, and rewards their rest by strength & almost friskiness, on each arrival."[7] He had lectured his way through New York State, To-ronto, Ohio, into Indiana; then he went to Illinois and would proceed to Wisconsin, Michigan, and back to Zanesville, Ohio. The weather was milder that winter in the West than in New England. He was enjoying his travels, and was even being amused by his little crises.

From Milwaukee, Emerson wrote Ellen on February 10: "I had to char-ter a special train to carry me 90 miles to Michigan City, in fault of any other means to reach Chicago in time."[8] He had been scheduled to read his lecture on "Manners" at the Young Men's Christian Association in Chicago on February 6. The next night in Rockford he wore "a wet nightgown from the Chicago laundry" and caught cold. In the morning he wired to Madison, Wisconsin, "I come tonight, but doubtful of my voice." All the way on the train he sucked Brown's troches and awed the Wisconsin Senate that night (the legislature was in session) with a rich orotund voice. The sore throat did not prevent his lecturing the following three days in Milwaukee, Racine, and Kenosha.

From Niles, Michigan, Emerson wrote Edith on February 13 that he "had traveled all the day before through Wisconsin, with horses, & could not for long distances find water for them: The wells were dry, &, the people said, they had no water but snow for the house." At Kalamazoo he found "many personal friends" acquainted with his books, and a couple of professors in the college accompanied him to Marshall, to hear another lecture. But:

> My chief adventure was the necessity of riding in a buggy 48 miles to Grand Rapids; then, after lecture, 20 more, on the return, &, the next morning, getting back to Kalamazoo, in time for the train hither at 12. So I saw Michigan & its forest, and the Wolverines, pretty thoroughly.... The people are rough grisly Esaus, full of dirty strength. Every forcible [*sic*] man came from New York or New England, for all the country was settled since 1834. Very good schools however in all the large towns, & in every town, schools.[9]

In spite of his having lectured in the Midwest eight of the past ten years, Emerson still felt uncertain of his audiences. In 1854 he had written William from Chicago: "though I see many amiable & many vigorous people, I am heartily tired of wasting my time, and must learn to stay at home."[10] Of course he did not stay at home, and two years later he was still feeling discouraged because his Illinois auditors were "in all that is called cultivation . . . only ten years old."[11] He also brooded over his failures: "The climate & people are a new test for the wares of a man of letters. All his thin watery matter freezes; 'tis only the smallest portion of alcohol that remains good. At the lyceum, the stout Illinoi[s]ian, after a short trial, walks out of the hall. The Committee tell you that the people want a hearty laugh, & Stark, & Saxe, & Park Benjamin, who give them that, are heard with joy."[12] Emerson supposed he would have to accept these as "the new conditions to which I must conform."

Two of these competitors, John Godfrey Saxe and Park Benjamin, specialized in light, humorous verse. "Stark" was probably a slip of the pen (or a nickname) for Starr King, the popular young minister of the Hollis Street Church in Boston, whom Emerson had known well enough to use his first name. Carl Bode, in his history of the Lyceum, says Starr King "occupied one of the top places among the royalty of the lecture platform,"[13] from Bangor to Chicago. That Emerson seriously considered modifying his lecture to the style of these entertainers is improbable, though he did make some attempt to simplify and enliven his subject matter. His delivery belonged to his character, and that he could not change. It continued to delight some and to annoy others, especially that trick of pausing for the last word or phrase of a sentence and then seeming to stumble upon it triumphantly. In spite of his sore throat he had indeed "awed" his Madison audience, for *The Wisconsin State Journal* reported on February 9 of his Madison performance: "With no grace of gesture, there is nevertheless a charm in his manner, in the shifting expression of that New England visage of his, with the keen, seer-like eyes, and the fine, deep, musical voice, which renders him one of the most effective lecturers."[14]

On the day *The State Journal* praised Emerson, he gave a lecture on "Success" in Milwaukee which stirred up a stormy dispute between Catholics and freethinkers. Speaking of religion, he said the important thing was not the form of religion, but the faith common to all: "We see religious systems on which nations have been reared, pass away. The religion of one age is the literary entertainment of the next. . . . but central in the whirl a faith abides, which does not pass, a central doctrine which Judaism, Stoicism, Mahometism, Buddhism, Christianity all teach."[15]

The following week Father G. T. Riordan replied to Emerson's lecture by defending the infallible authority of the Papacy. The controversy followed Emerson to Kenosha, where *The Democrat* denounced him as "an infidel—an abolitionist—a monarchist."[16] Probably a monarchist because he had praised England, though his antislavery views were as strongly disliked as his presumed infidelity: "Emerson, Parker, Phillips, Garrison—and the lesser lights which revolve around them—form a moral and political cabal which is a curse to the country." This was the partisan view of an editor who might be called a premature copperhead (the term would not come into general use until a year or two later). On the whole, Emerson was so favorably received that he would be invited back to Wisconsin in 1863, 1865, and 1867, to increasingly large and appreciative audiences. Both he and they had come to understand each other better, and he ceased to feel that these trips to the prairie states were a waste of his time.

In 1860 the incipient copperheads were not confined to Wisconsin. An invitation to lecture in Philadelphia was withdrawn in March because Emerson had defended Captain John Brown.[17] Feeling about Brown was still running so high in the Quaker City that a riot was feared if a friend of his attempted to speak. There were probably more slavery sympathizers in New York City than in Philadelphia, but curiously no opposition was offered to Emerson's reading his lecture on "Manners" to the New York Christian Union on March 23, or to his speaking to the Athenaeum Club on May 10. Throughout the spring and summer of 1860 he also lectured frequently in Boston, especially on Sundays to Theodore Parker's "Fraternity" (Congregational Society), which met in the Music Hall in larger numbers than attended any of the orthodox churches. Parker had gone to Italy to regain his health, but was dying of tuberculosis in Florence.

II

While Emerson was on speaking tours, his daughters, aged twenty-one and nineteen in 1860, kept him informed about home matters. Both were prompt correspondents, though usually Ellen acted as treasurer and secretary for her father, depositing checks in the bank and paying bills. If Ellen happened to be away from home on a visit, Edith was equally reliable. They both attended Sanborn's school in Concord, with Edward, or took turns in commuting by train to Agassiz's private school for girls in Cambridge. Their mother was so frequently confined to bed with real or imagined illnesses that one of the girls had to act as housekeeper. Ellen, being the elder, usually assumed this responsibililty. As early as the autumn of 1856 Emerson had had to postpone an invitation to James Russell Lowell to dine with him because "My daughter Ellen who is grown important to my housekeeping is untimely sick for these few days."[18]

On May 1, 1859, Emerson had written Carlyle that his children gave him great contentment, making him "cling to the world on their account":

> My two girls, pupils once or now of Agassiz, are good, healthy, apprehensive, decided young people, who love life. My boy divides his time between Cicero and cricket,—knows his boat, the birds, and Walter Scott, verse and prose, through and through,—and will go to College next year. Sam Ward and I tickled each other the other day, in looking over a very good company of young people, by finding in the new-comers a marked improvement on their parents. . . .[19]

Early in April 1860, Edward was stricken by typhoid fever. On the thirteenth his father wrote William: "He still flames in the face with fever turns some hours of each day. But his symptoms are ever better, or with short interruption. . . . Ellen & Edith have been exemplary nurses."[20] It would be many weeks before Edward recovered, and in fact he would remain "delicate" for several years. But in May he was sufficiently out of danger for his father to begin taking more interest in the affairs of his friends.

One of these, Bronson Alcott, was once more a neighbor, having failed to prosper in Boston. Three years earlier, Emerson had solicited his friends to establish a fund for the relief of the Alcott family. On October 31, 1857, he himself advanced money for a house and land on the Lexington Road, a short walk from Emerson's own house on the Boston Turnpike. Knowing all too well Alcott's impracticality, Emerson had insisted that the property be held in trust by a trustee. Alcott called his new home the Orchard House, and there exercised his genius for gardening and landscaping to good effect.

Alcott had lost his third daughter, Elizabeth, to tuberculosis in the spring of 1858. Within an hour after her death the "good Emerson" had called, the best friend he had "on this planet,"[21] Alcott wrote in his Journal, though well aware of their differences in mind and temperament. The winter after that, Alcott had made a trip to St. Louis, partly to visit the Hegelian philosopher William Torrey Harris, and had been convinced "how purely Eastern I am, how little I have in common with the wild life of the West."[22] The landscape showed so little evidence of the ameliorating hand of man that it seemed to him as if mankind had not yet arrived. Thoreau doted on *wildness,* and even Emerson found romantic pleasure in it, but Alcott's taste was neoclassic. *Man* was more important than *nature.*

In 1860 Alcott was the happiest he had been since his trip to England in 1842. The previous May he had been appointed superintendent of the Concord public schools, and the town seemed pleased with his administration. In March 1860 he held a successful school festival, saying, "We spend much on our cattle and flower shows; let us each spring have a show of our children."[23] His second daughter, Louisa, was beginning to be known for her short stories. On May 23 his oldest daughter, Anna, was married in the Orchard House. In his Journal Alcott called it "a day of fair omens, sunny after showers of the days past. Apple blossoms luxuriant, and a company of true and real persons present to grace the occasion."[24] These included Mr. and Mrs. Emerson, Mr. Ephraim Bull (the grape-growing neighbor), Henry Thoreau, and relatives of the groom, John Pratt. Mrs. Alcott's brother, Samuel May, performed the ceremony. Louisa recorded a few more details in her Journal:

> We had a little feast, sent by good Mrs. Judge Shaw [Lemuel Shaw was chief justice of the Massachusetts Supreme Court]; then the old folks danced round the bridal pair on the lawn in the German fashion, making a pretty picture to remember, under our Revolutionary elm. . . . Mr. Emerson kissed her; and I thought the honor would make even matrimony endurable, for he is the god of my idolatry.[25]

For Emerson the spring and summer of 1860 were filled with a variety of personal experiences. Theodore Parker had finally paid the penalty of his overwork and self-sacrifice; he died in Florence May 10. Early in June some of his friends began urging Emerson to speak at a memorial service in Parker's Music Hall forum in Boston. At first Emerson said he would be glad to attend but would not speak, for though he honored Parker highly they were not intimate friends. But he did give an oration on June 15, in which he said Parker's experiences "were part of the history of the civil and religious liberty of his times." His mind lacked the "poetic element," but that might have "disqualified him for some of his severer offices to his generation. . . . He never kept back the truth for fear to make an enemy."[26] Emerson could think of no one else in the ministry who so valiantly insisted "that the essence of Christianity is in its practical morals; it is there for use or it is nothing." In his Journal Emerson added: "Theodore Parker has filled up all his years & days & hours. A son of the energy of New England[:] restless, eager, manly, brave, early old, contumacious, clever. I can well praise him at a spectator's distance[,] for our minds & methods were unlike,—few people more unlike."[27]

All his life Emerson had felt guilty because he did not—could not—live with such intensity as Parker. He had expressed this idea best in his poem "Days," published in 1857 in *The Atlantic Monthly:*

> Daughters of Time, the hypocritic Days,
> Muffled and dumb like barefoot dervishes,
> And marching single in an endless file,
> Bring diadems and fagots in their hands.
> To each they offer gifts after his will,
> Bread, kingdoms, stars, and sky that holds them all.
> I, in my pleached garden, watched the pomp,
> Forgot my morning wishes, hastily
> Took a few herbs and apples, and the Day
> Turned and departed silent. I, too late,
> Under her solemn fillet saw the scorn.[28]

Emerson's excuse for having forgotten his "morning wishes" was still the same he had given nearly twenty years before in another poem, called "The Day's Ration": at his birth, Fate had filled a chalice from "the seas of strength" and said: "This be thy portion, child; this chalice, / Less than a lily's, thou shalt daily draw / From my great arteries,—nor less, nor more."[29] Parker had drawn his portion with reckless disregard of his health, and had died an old man at fifty. Emerson did not consciously or deliberately spare himself from danger or sacrifice, yet some unconscious instinct protected him, as it had all his life. In appearance this trait was a sort of stoic indifference. After his birthday in May he described the "Advantages of old age" in his Journal:

I reached the other day the end of my fifty seventh year, and am easier in my mind than hitherto. I could never give much reality to evil & pain. But now when my wife says, perhaps this tumor on your shoulder is a cancer, I say, what if it is? It would not make the gentleman on his way in a cart to the gallows very unhappy, to tell him that the pain in his knee threatened a white swelling.[30]

III

Emerson's neighbor Nathaniel Hawthorne was beginning to suffer the disadvantages of old age. He had returned from Europe a broken man. After serving as consul in Liverpool from 1853 to 1857, he went to Italy, where he wrote *The Marble Faun*. Immediately upon his arrival in Boston on June 28, 1860, he had brought his family back to the house which Alcott had called Hillside and Hawthorne had renamed The Wayside. Emerson invited the Hawthorne family to a party at his house the following evening. Alcott recorded in his Journal that he had eaten strawberries and cream at the Emersons' with Hawthorne, Thoreau, Sanborn, William Hunt (the artist), John Keyes (the lawyer and politician), and Seth Cheney (another artist).[31]

Hawthorne was uncertain how he could support his family, worried about his country, and haunted by a symbolical story of an ancestral home in England which he would never be able to finish. He was no longer so partisan a Democrat, and had begun to sympathize with his antislavery neighbors, though still resentful of the spitefulness they had shown when he wrote the biography of his friend Franklin Pierce. The neighbor he found most congenial was Alcott, partly because he was so willing to offer advice on how to improve the grounds and architecture of The Wayside. But Alcott complained in his Journal that Hawthorne sat in his castle with his drawbridge up. He never called on anyone, and was seldom seen outside his gate. "Still he has a tender kindly side, and a voice that a woman might own, the hesitancy is so taking, and the tone so remote from what you expected."[32]

In August a young man named William Dean Howells was touring New England with the purpose of meeting its most famous writers. He had contributed Heinesque poems to *The Atlantic Monthly,* and his name was becoming familiar to Lowell, Longfellow, Holmes, and of course to James T. Fields, the publisher of *The Atlantic*. Howells had worked on newspapers in Ohio, and had come to the attention of Abraham Lincoln, who asked him to write his campaign biography. That was finished and was being circulated when Howells came to Concord, though no one there seemed to be aware of it.

First Howells called on Hawthorne because Lowell had written a note of introduction. Hawthorne greeted him with a somber and brooding look, "the look of a man who had dealt faithfully and therefore sorrowfully with that problem of evil which forever attracted, forever evaded him."[33] In the course of their conversation Howells noticed a copy of *The Blithedale Romance,* and said that was his favorite of Hawthorne's books: "his face lighted up, and he said he believed the Germans liked that best too."[34] They parted such good friends that Hawthorne invited Howells to call again and offered to give him a card for Emerson on which he wrote, "I find this young man worthy."

But Hawthorne had given him so much to think about that Howells waited until next day before presenting the card. Then he decided to call on Thoreau first, but that visit was a disaster. Thoreau offered him a chair on one side of the room and placed his own near the opposite wall. Howells tried to talk of Walden Pond and John Brown, but Thoreau seemed to be in a dreamy mood and refused to be drawn out of it. As Howells recalled the experience later, "It was not merely a defeat of my hopes, it was a rout, and I felt myself so scattered over the field of thought that I could hardly bring my forces together for retreat."[35] What Howells did not know was that Thoreau was dying of tuberculosis. Concern for his guest might have caused him to put the room's width between them.

With trepidation, Howells then walked across town and presented Hawthorne's card to Emerson, who opened the door himself, a tall, serene old man of about sixty, Howells guessed (actually fifty-seven), with no gray in his sandy hair, kindly eyes, and "a kind of marble youthfulness" in his intelligent face. The eyes reminded him of Lincoln's, but were shyer and less sad. Howells thought Emerson was "the most misunderstood man in America."[36] In 1860 he was a sort of "national joke," yet "his countenance expressed the patience and forbearance of a wise man to bide his time." Howells's sympathy could scarcely have been more complete, though one may wonder why he thought Emerson so misunderstood: was that what they thought of him in Ohio? Howells had read Emerson's poems and essays in *The Atlantic,* and he applauded the notorious prediction that John Brown would make "the gallows glorious like the cross."[37] Yet the interview did not go well. Emerson wanted to talk about the West, but Howells soon concluded that his host knew almost nothing about the region, in spite of his many lecture tours. This judgment, however, may have shown some of Howells's Midwestern bias.

Emerson praised Hawthorne for "personal excellence and for his fine qualities as a neighbor. 'But his last book,' he added reflectively, 'is a mere mush.'" Howells was shocked that he would join "the groundlings who were then crying out upon the indefinite close of *The Marble Faun.*" Howells regarded the moral ambiguity of the ending as proper and even inevitable for the unsolvable problem of evil. Emerson changed the subject by asking if Howells knew the poems of William Henry Channing—he must have said "William Ellery," and Howells confused the two men. Anyway, he replied that he knew them only through Poe's criticism.

" 'Whose criticism?' asked Emerson.

" 'Poe's,' I said again.

" 'Oh,' he cried out, after a moment, as if he had returned from a far search for my meaning, *'you mean the jingle man!'* "[38]

Such comments led Howells to conclude: "Emerson had, in fact, a defective sense as to specific pieces of literature; he praised extravagantly, and in the wrong place, especially among the new things, and he failed to see the worth of much that was fine and precious beside the line of his fancy." Howells, as a newspaperman, doubtless knew about Emerson's impulsive letter to Walt Whitman five years before, and he may have had this partly in mind. He did not know, of course, about Emerson's talk with Whitman on the Boston Common in March, in which Emerson had tried unsuccessfully to persuade Whitman to omit "Children of Adam" from the new edition of his poems. Howells would probably have approved Emerson's judgment in this case, for he was himself squeamish about sex, though he thought well enough of Whitman to look him up at Pfaff's restaurant in New York a few days later.

Howells left Emerson's house wondering what had gone wrong. By the time he got back to Boston, he could begin to see the comic aspects of his encounter, though he still felt wounded. At the office of *The Atlantic*, Fields wanted to hear about his adventures in Concord. When he described his incompatibility with Emerson, Fields "perfectly conceived the situation" and howled with laughter, getting "an amusement from it that I could only get through sympathy with him."[39]

A few weeks later Emerson received a visit from his old friend Henry James Sr., who had recently returned from Europe to settle in Newport so that his oldest son, William, could study painting with William Hunt. He had gone to Europe twice to give his children educational advantages which he thought America lacked. The European schools and tutors had disappointed him, too, and he now wanted to try American teachers again. He had heard favorable reports of Mr. Sanborn's school, with its bold experiments in coeducation and new methods of instruction. One of Sanborn's boarding students was a daughter of the martyred John Brown, and this fact impressed Mr. James.

The day following the trip to Concord, James described his experiences in a letter to Mrs. William Tappan, formerly Caroline Sturgis. She, too, had lived in Europe during the Jameses' expatriation, and the two families had become intimate. "Mary and I traveled forth last Wednesday," James wrote Mrs. Tappan, "bearing Wilky and Bob in our arms to surrender them to the famous Mr. Sanborn."[40] In the warm sunshine the brilliant maple, oak, and dogwood leaves "showered such splendours upon the eye as made the Champs Elysées and the Bois appear parvenus and comical." After he satisfied himself of the excellence of Sanborn's school: "Then we drove to Emerson's and waded up to our knees through a harvest of apples and pears, which, tired of their outward or carnal growth, had descended to the loving bosom of the lawn, there or elsewhere to grow inwardly meet for their heavenly rest in the veins of Ellen the saintly and others; until at last we found the cordial Pan himself in the midst of his household, breezy with hospitality and blowing exhilarating trumpets of welcome."

In November 1860 Emerson's *Conduct of Life* was finally published by Ticknor and Fields, with six thousand copies printed by December 21. It would be more accurate to say that Emerson had printed the book and commissioned the publisher to sell it for him. The contents offered not even a hint of the growing national crisis. "Wealth" and "Power" gave the book a pragmatic tone. The style was lucid, much easier to read than that of Emerson's earlier books, and appealing to a wider audience. The chapters on "Fate," "Beauty," and "Illusions" (discussed in Chapter XXIV) are among Emerson's best philosophical essays. They contain some of his most characteristic solutions to the dilemmas of life: "Thought" cannot move a mountain, only makes the proper use of it; "Beauty" has a cosmical quality which lifts an object out of its individuality and suggests its universality; whatever game Providence plays with us, "we must play no game with ourselves ...": "Leave this hypocritical prating about the masses. . . . I do not wish any mass at all, but honest men [and women] only ..."[41]

Not all criticism of *The Conduct of Life* was favorable. Someone in *The New Englander* objected to "the utter shallowness and flippancy of the judgments Emerson expresses concerning Christianity."[42] The London *Saturday Review,* which had always been unfriendly to Emerson, observed that an American audience liked to hear dreary platitudes strung together in an oration. It is to be doubted that the critic had read the book. But even Thoreau, so Alcott recorded in his Journal, "Thinks it is moderate, and wants the fire and force of the earlier books." As for Alcott's own opinion: "I told E. today [Christmas] that his essay on 'Worship' gave us the worshipful temperament but not the worship. The 'Fate' and 'Beauty' are perhaps best. I think he must write out and complement the 'Worship' ... Certainly a simple devout soul, maid or man, will not find what he seeks in that essay."[43]

Carlyle read *The Conduct of Life* in the sheets supplied him by Emerson's London publisher before he received a copy of the American edition. He wrote Emerson that it gave him more satisfaction than any other book by another living mortal. He thought it the "best of all your books," and predicted a great sale in England: "You have grown older, more pungent, piercing;—I never read from you before such lightning-gleams of meaning as are to be found here. The finale of all, that of 'Illusions' falling on us like snow-showers, but again of 'the gods sitting steadfast on their thrones' all the while,—what a *Fiat Lux* is there, into the deeps of philosophy, which the vulgar has not, which hardly three men living *have,* yet dreamt of! *Well done,* I say; and so let the matter rest."[44]

IV

Emerson felt so little concerned with the 1860 presidential election that he did not mention Abraham Lincoln's name in his Journal or letters. He did, though, take a lively interest in Massachusetts politics and supported

George S. Boutwell for governor at the Republican caucus held in Concord.[45] Of course Lincoln was scarcely known to him before his nomination. When Emerson met him in the White House in 1862, Lincoln told him he had heard him lecture in Illinois. That would probably have been in 1853, for on January 10, 11, and 12 of that year Emerson gave three lectures in Springfield, where Lincoln was practicing law. If they met at that time, Lincoln made no impression on Emerson.

In his acceptance speech on June 16, Lincoln declared, "A house divided against itself cannot stand." He would do anything to preserve the Union. Emerson, as we have seen, was quite ready to sacrifice the Union if necessary for the abolition of slavery; that was why he was slow to work up enthusiasm for Lincoln. But by the eve of the election, when Concord boys carried torches and transparencies reading "Old North Bridge, Ever True to Freedom!,"[46] Emerson had accepted the Republican ticket as the best means of attaining abolition.

On November 6 Alcott recorded in his Journal: "At Town House, and cast my vote for Lincoln and the Republican candidates generally—the first vote I ever cast for a President and State officers."[47] Thoreau refused to vote; in Alcott's words, he "Thinks a freeman cannot vote for the President, candidates, etc." Two days later Emerson wrote Charles Eliot Norton, "With joy to you in the joy of the country . . ."[48] A week later he recorded in his Journal: "The news of last Wednesday morning (7th) was sublime, the pronunciation of the masses of America against Slavery."[49] It was hardly that, as Emerson would learn in succeeding months. On December 20, South Carolina seceded from the Union, and by February 1, Mississippi, Florida, Alabama, Georgia, and Louisiana had followed, as did Texas on February 23.

On January 6, 1861, in a lecture on "Cause and Effect" read to Parker's congregation in the Music Hall, Emerson said the South was right to see that free speech endangered slavery. "And if a gag-law could reach to whispers and winks and discontented looks, why you might plant a very pretty despotism, and convert your boisterous cities into deaf-and-dumb asylums."[50] He would soon discover that free speech was not permitted in Boston, either, though the curbing was by a mob and not by elected officials. The Massachusetts Anti-Slavery Society attempted to hold its annual convention in Tremont Temple in Boston on January 24. Emerson had consented to speak to the convention, but a howling mob would not let him be heard. He had agreed to speak in loyalty to Wendell Phillips, who sometimes, almost alone, had risked his life to defend freedom: "He did me the honour to ask me to come to the meeting at Tremont Temple, and, esteeming such invitation a command, though sorely against my inclination and habit, I went, and, though I had nothing to say, showed myself. If I were dumb, yet would I have gone and mowed and muttered or made signs. The mob roared whenever I attempted to speak, and after several beginnings, I withdrew."[51]

Whether the unpredictable mood of the country influenced Emerson not to make his annual trip to the Midwest in the winter of 1861, he nowhere indicated. Possibly in the uncertainty, committees hesitated to invite him—though he did go to Buffalo, which some people in Massachusetts called "West." He continued to accept invitations from various towns in New England and to lecture frequently to Parker's "Fraternity." He was in the midst of a series in Boston on "Life and Literature" when the electrifying news came on April 13 that Fort Sumter had been fired upon by Confederate artillery the previous evening. Members of the Concord Artillery, a component of the Fifth Massachusetts Regiment, wondered how soon they would be mobilized. On Monday the fifteenth, the fort surrendered and President Lincoln called for seventy-five thousand volunteers. The Fifth Regiment was ordered to Washington.

On April 9, in his lecture in Boston on "Genius," Emerson had spoken unemotionally of "the downfall of our character-destroying civilization."[52] He was even willing to consider the advantages of the downfall: "we had opened the wrong door and let the enemy into the castle. Civilization was a mistake, and, in the circumstances, the best wisdom was an auction or a fire." Only when the nation unites "on an equal and moral contract to protect each other in humane and honest activities" can there be a civilized State. But the guns at Fort Sumter shattered these musings. Almost instantly Emerson was energized with new hope and a patriotic fervor he had never experienced before. He had planned to give a lecture in Boston April 23 on the "Doctrine of Leasts," but quickly changed it for a hastily written speech on "Civilization at a Pinch."[53]

By no means did Emerson underestimate the seriousness of war with the South, as many in the North did. He had always, as we have seen repeatedly, insisted that the Southerner was a fighting man. But now the challenge must be accepted. Finally the North could do something about the dragon coiling around the free states and squeezing the moral life out of them. "How does Heaven help us when civilization is at a pinch? Why, by a whirlwind of patriotism, not believed to exist, but now magnetizing all discordant masses under its terrific unity." It was a time for "instincts," for activity without calculation, for following "a sentiment mightier than logic, wide as light, strong as gravity." It must be felt in "the college, the bank, the farm-house, and the church." The language reminds one of Walt Whitman's recruiting poem, "Beat! Beat! Drums!," written after the first battle of Bull Run to rally a dispirited nation.[54] Emerson felt this excitement at the very beginning of hostilities:

> It is the day of the populace; they are wiser than their teachers. Every parish-steeple marks a recruiting station; every bell is a tocsin. Go into the swarming town-halls, and let yourself be played upon by the stormy winds that blow there. The interlocutions from quiet-looking citizens are of an energy of which I had no knowledge ... now we have a country again.[55]

Emerson was following his own advice and letting his emotions have free play. When his mind was in firm control he would not have made every church spire a focal point of energy. In his excitement he visited the Charlestown Navy Yard and asked to be shown around, declaring, "Sometimes gunpowder smells good."[56] And when Concord volunteers met at the railroad station on April 19, the anniversary of the "Concord Fight" at the bridge, Emerson was there to see them off. Judge Rockwood Hoar made a speech and the new Unitarian minister, the Reverend Grindall Reynolds, offered a prayer as the crowd stood in a ring, while the clink of cannon being rolled up made musical beats. Next day Emerson described the scene in a letter to Edith, who happened to be away from home. George Prescott, the commanding officer, "was an image of manly beauty.... All the families were there. They left Concord 45 men, but on the way recruits implored to join them, &, when they reached Boston, they were 64."[57]

From Boston the Fifth Regiment proceeded to Springfield, then Annapolis, Emerson following them all the way through newspaper reports. In Springfield a funeral procession stopped to cheer as they marched by. With pride Emerson copied into his Journal the opinion expressed in *The National Intelligencer* (Washington) that probably no other regiment in the country could have done what the Eighth Massachusetts Regiment did in Annapolis: "put a locomotive together, lay the rails of the broken [sabotaged] railroad, and bend the sails of a man-of-war (the frigate Constitution), which they manned."[58] However, the triumphal march of the Massachusetts soldiers came to an end in Washington, where they mired down in the incredible bungling, stupidity, and chaos of the unprepared Union military establishment, or nonestablishment.

V

The North was stunned by the humiliating defeat of the Union Army at the Battle of Bull Run. Monday, July 22, soldiers still alive and able to walk dragged themselves in the rain and mud into Washington and dropped, exhausted, in the streets. Rumors reached Concord that its Artillery Company had been cut to pieces, half of its men killed. Actually, only five were missing, and eventually these returned home after being released from Libby Prison months later.

After Bull Run, those who had escaped capture were sent home because a new army would have to be recruited and trained. Concord prepared to welcome the returning heroes with speeches and a bountiful supper, but the men were in no mood to enjoy the reception. Captain Prescott, one arm in a sling, had already addressed his men in Boston and he had nothing more to say. Corporal George Buttrick said all he wanted was a swim in the river.[59]

Emerson refused to be discouraged by the bad news. On August 4 he wrote James Elliot Cabot: "the war with its defeats & uncertainties is immensely better than what we lately called the integrity of the Republic, as amputation is better than cancer."[60] But for the men who had been in battle the war was not so simple. Captain Prescott hated war so much that he agonized over reenlisting. He consulted Reverend Reynolds, and was told his own conscience would have to be his guide. Finally he did reenlist and recruited seventy men for his company. In November they left without any fanfare. Many of the men asked themselves what they were fighting for. Mr. Emerson and Mr. Alcott said it was to destroy slavery; President Lincoln said it was to save the Union. In Boston the Concord recruits watched a column of soldiers led by Daniel Webster's son marching on State Street singing a catchy new song, "John Brown's body lies a-mould'ring in the grave."[61] In Washington, Julia Ward Howe heard this song of unknown origin and wrote "Battle Hymn of the Republic" to be sung to the same tune. *The Atlantic Monthly* printed her song in the February 1862 issue.

Emerson doubtless talked with some of the Concord veterans of Bull Run, but he would not be infected by their discouragement. On August 5 he wrote in his Journal: "The war goes on educating us to a trust in the simplicities, and to see the bankruptcy of all narrow views."[62] The important thing was to compensate the loyal states. Probably by "loyal" he meant the border states, such as Kentucky and Missouri, which had not seceded. The plan he had advocated in 1844 in his address on "Emancipation in the British West Indies," of buying the freedom of the slaves, scarcely seemed feasible now. But he thought a presidential proclamation declaring the slaves free would turn the war into a moral crusade, and at the same time cause the slaveowners to rush home to protect their property from destruction by blacks in revolt. The war made it possible to cut out "our cancerous slavery." "Better that war and defeats continue, until we have come to that amputation."[63]

The enthusiasm for war of Emerson and Henry James Sr. did not extend to encouraging their own sons to enlist—both felt they had good reasons for hesitation. James's elder sons, William and Henry, nineteen and eighteen respectively, suffered dissimilar afflictions. William was nervous, with gastrointestinal disturbances; Henry had injured his sacroiliac in September 1861. Later, in memory, Henry Jr. associated his pain with the first battle of Bull Run, perhaps because it was followed by calls for recruits which his injury kept him from answering. The two younger sons, Garth Wilkinson and Robertson, sixteen and fifteen, were more determined to volunteer. "Bob" threatened to run away and join the navy. He was so discontented that he refused to return to Mr. Sanborn's school in the autumn of 1861. "Wilkie" did finish the school year, but enlisted, with his father's consent, at the end of the spring term of 1862.

Meanwhile, Edward Emerson, seventeen, and the James boys visited each other and became great friends. On March 26, 1861, Henry James Sr. wrote Emerson: "Only one word about Edward, the good boy who smiles like opening violets, but who is not near so robust as he ought to be, because he is allowed to study too hard, in order that he may enter college one year rather than another."[64] Emerson hastened to reply that he was not pushing Edward in his preparation for college; he was thin because he had not yet recovered his strength after typhoid fever. But it seemed the right time for him to enter Harvard in the coming fall.

Edward did begin his freshman year at Harvard in September 1861, but in October his father encouraged him to return home. On November 6 he wrote William that Edward "showed himself so feeble when shut up in a college room & routine, that I have had him at home now for a fortnight & have almost decided to withdraw him altogether for this year."[65] Emerson says nothing of the war, but at Harvard students were dropping out every week to enlist, and the sensitive Edward must have been disturbed by his inability to follow their example. His eagerness to toughen himself indicates as much. He talked to his father of going to California, or working in a lumber camp in Maine, but settled for helping to survey lots for Mount Auburn Cemetery, in Cambridge.

By this time Emerson himself was beginning to feel economic distress because of the war. In a November 6, 1861, letter to William he complained that the Atlantic Bank in Boston had failed to pay a dividend. In addition, "My books have no sale this year, and the Winter Lectures will, for the most part, omit their dividends."[66] In December he wrote again: "We are all knitting socks & mittens for soldiers, writing patriotic lectures, & economizing with all our mights."[67] But the financial pinch grew worse. On January 21, 1862, Waldo wrote William that he missed the five or six hundred dollars a year his books usually yielded, and dividends from his stocks and bonds, including his Mad River and Lake Erie bonds (Sandusky, Ohio), which should pay one hundred and forty dollars a year.[68] Lidian had not been able to collect any rent on her Plymouth property. Emerson had been trying to sell a woodlot, but had found no buyers. Another letter complained again of the decline of income from his lectures, but that situation would soon begin to improve. Also his friend Abel Adams had insisted on paying Edward's expenses in college to make up for the money Emerson had lost on investments that Adams had advised him to make.

Emerson gave some lectures during January and February in Massachusetts towns, but usually for small fees, averaging about twenty-five dollars. However, the Smithsonian Association in Washington offered him eighty-four dollars for a lecture on January 31,[69] which he eagerly accepted because this was a chance, he hoped, to speak directly to the highest officials of the federal government. He had been talking with Moncure Conway, who was now lecturing and writing on abolition in Boston, and they agreed that this was his big opportunity to influence the President. Conway believed that the President could shorten the war by issuing an emancipation proclamation now: slaves would revolt, and this would cripple, perhaps even halt, the Confederate war effort. It seems in retrospect a rather naive scheme for someone who knew plantation life as Conway did. Emerson, who had not seen a plantation since his long-ago winter in Charleston and St. Augustine, was convinced anew that immediate abolition was brilliant strategy.

Both Conway and Emerson had become suspicious of Lincoln's intentions when the President removed General Frémont from his command after Frémont proclaimed freedom for all slaves in the Southwest who had taken up arms against the Missouri rebels. The President's excuse was that the general had exceeded his authority, as he doubtless had, but many Northern abolitionists began to wonder whether Lincoln was not more concerned with preserving the Union than with ending slavery. Apologists for Lincoln maintained that he was only biding his time, that he needed some military victories to give his proclamation authority. On January 17 Conway himself gave an address at the Smithsonian, in which he urged the immediate freeing of all slaves by proclamation. After the address Lincoln said to Conway, "I think the country grows in that direction daily, and I am not without hope that something of the desire of you and your friends may be accomplished."[70]

On January 18 Emerson gave his lecture on "American Civilization" in New Bedford. Then he hastily revised it, incorporating some of Conway's ideas, as he acknowledged in a note when he published the address in *The Atlantic Monthly* in April 1862. He began his address with the thesis that "Use, labor of each for all, is the health and virtue of all beings." But the conspiracy of slavery pronounced "labor disgraceful, and the well being of a man to consist in eating the fruit of other men's labor."[71] These attitudes had resulted in two states of civilization: a higher, "where labor and the tenure of land and the right of suffrage are democratical; and a lower," a military oligarchy, based on the "tenure of prisoners or slaves."[72] The latter now menaces the whole country, and must be stopped. "The evil you contend with has taken alarming proportions, and you still content yourself with parrying the blows it aims, but, as if enchanted, abstain from striking at the cause."[73] The one weapon not yet tried, Emerson contended, and the most "sure," was for Congress to abolish slavery "by edict, as part of the military defence.'. . . Then the slaves near our armies will come to us,"[74] and those farther away will hear and prepare to desert their masters. "Instantly, the armies that now confront you must run home to protect their estates, and must stay there, and your enemies will disappear."

After his address on January 31, Emerson remained in Washington for three days. The President and members of his Cabinet were so busy that, most witnesses agree, they did not attend the lecture on "American Civilization," but on February 1, 2, and 3 Emerson met almost everyone of any importance in the government, Senator Sumner acting as guide. Emerson had a short but friendly chat with the President:

> The President impressed me more favourably than I had hoped. A frank, sincere, well-meaning man, with a lawyer's habit of mind, good clear statement of his fact; correct enough, not vulgar, as described, but with a sort of boyish cheerfulness, or that kind of sincerity and jolly good meaning that our class meetings on Commencement Days show, in telling our old stories over. When he has made his remark, he looks up at you with great satisfaction, and shows all his white teeth, and laughs.[75]

On Saturday, in Mr. Seward's dingy State Department office, Emerson found Governor John A. Andrews of Massachusetts and his friend John M. Forbes. There was too much confusion in Seward's office for satisfactory conversation, but the Secretary invited Emerson to go to church with him next day and dine with him afterward. "I told him I hoped he would not demoralize me; I was not much accustomed to churches, but trusted he would carry me to a safe place."[76] Mr. Seward's church was Episcopalian. The minister was the Reverend Dr. Pyne, who had remained loyal to the Union after most of his secessionist congregation had left. The service and Dr. Pyne's sermon reminded Emerson anew of the "blind antiquity of life and thought" of the English Church. After leaving church, they called on the President, talked with his two small sons, and got a glimpse of his domestic life. When the President came in, Mr. Seward said, "You have not been to church to-day." "No," Lincoln said, "and, if we must make a frank confession, he had been reading for the first time Mr. Sumner's speech (on the Trent affair)."[77]

The *Trent* Affair was the name given to a diplomatic crisis between the United States and England which arose when the U.S.S. *San Jacinto* halted the British ship *Trent* in the Bahamas and seized James M. Mason and John Slidell, Confederate agents going to England to seek aid for the South. Both nations had become excited and threatened war, but tension had recently eased when the United States released Mason and Slidell to Great Britain. The President said he had received congratulatory messages from France and Spain on the release of the Confederate agents. He knew, he said, that Cuba sympathized with the secessionists, but Spain knew that they wanted to conquer Cuba.[78] After leaving the White House, Emerson dined at the Sewards', where the conversation continued on relations with Great Britain.

Sunday evening Emerson spent in the home of Charles Eames, former minister to Venezuela, whom he had known in New York. There he met governors, politicians, writers, and secretaries, including Lincoln's private secretaries John Hay and John Nicolay. Robert Lincoln, the President's oldest son, was there, and Emanuel Leutze, the historical painter, who was working on a mural in the Capitol for a panel called *The Emigration to the West* (the painting became *Westward the Course of Empire Takes Its Way*). Emerson had such a good time that he stayed until a late hour, forgetting that he had been invited to call that evening on Mr. Stanton, the Secretary of War.

On Monday Emerson approvingly inspected the architecture of the Capitol, then visited the Library of Congress. The assistant librarian told him that for the past twelve years "it had been under Southern domination, and as under dead men."[79] The medical and theological departments were large, but modern literature had been almost totally neglected. The library did not subscribe to *The Atlantic Monthly, The Knickerbocker Magazine,* or any New York newspaper. It did not have a single copy of the London *Saturday Review,* but had one hundred bound volumes of the London *Court Journal.*

VI

With decidedly mixed feelings about Washington, Emerson took the train to New York on Tuesday, February 4. On his arrival he found that he was expected to lecture in Brooklyn on Friday, so he remained in the city instead of returning home that week. After his return, he resumed his lectures to Parker's "Fraternity" in Boston. But his mind that spring was frequently on Henry Thoreau. Henry knew he was dying and discussed the subject calmly with his friends. Sam Staples, the constable who had jailed him for not paying his taxes, visited him on March 24, and told Emerson he had "Never spent an hour with more satisfaction. Never saw a man dying with so much pleasure and peace."[80] Everyone in Concord now seemed to love Henry and asked about him every day. On April 1 Emerson walked across Walden Pond and reported this to Henry, who said he had known the ice to hold until April 18. On the eighteenth Emerson recorded that though the day was warm, the ice had still not broken up.[81]

Thoreau died quietly on the morning of May 6. Emerson insisted that the funeral service be held in the Unitarian church, though Thoreau, like himself, had renounced his membership some years earlier. The casket was decked with spring flowers, many of them picked in the woods and fields by schoolchildren. Emerson gave the address, the choir sang an ode composed by Ellery Channing, and other friends read selections from Thoreau's writings. He was buried in the new cemetery, Sleepy Hollow, which Emerson had dedicated in 1855, saying then, "In this quiet valley, as in the palm of Nature's hand, we shall sleep well when we have finished our day."[82] The town had planted an arboretum, containing every tree native to Massachusetts, and the giant fir of California and Oregon. The trees already made a bird sanctuary. It was the perfect resting place for Henry Thoreau the naturalist.

In his Journal Emerson listed twenty volumes of translations from classic Hindu works which Thoreau had bequeathed to him from the much larger collection which his friend Thomas Cholmondeley had sent him from England (the remainder of the collection Thoreau willed to Harvard). Cholmondeley had come to Concord in 1854 to meet Emerson, but while boarding with Mrs. Thoreau had become so charmed by her son that he sent him these "Hindu Scriptures" after returning to England. Later he emigrated to Canada. Emerson recorded in his Journal for 1862 that Cholmondeley returned to Concord for a brief visit, but he did not give the date; presumably it was after Thoreau's death. As for the Hindu classics, Emerson had been reading some of them for many years (always in translation, for he knew no Sanskrit), but he valued them even more now for their associations with his friend.

Emerson polished his funeral oration on Thoreau and repeated it to Parker's "Fraternity" on June 29. That summer he also spent many hours reading and rereading Thoreau's Journals and manuscripts. Though Emerson himself was much less systematic in his observations, he shared fully Thoreau's enthusiasm for nature and delighted in his anecdotes:

> His determination on Natural History was organic. He confessed that he sometimes felt like a hound or a panther, and, if born among Indians, would have been a fell hunter. But, restrained by the Massachusetts culture, he played out the game in this mild form of botany and ichthyology. His intimacy with animals suggested what Thomas Fuller records of Butler the apiologist, that "either he had told the bees things or the bees had told him."[83]

There was personal feeling, too, in Emerson's regret that no college ever offered Thoreau an honorary degree or a professorship, and no academy invited him to membership. A few months earlier Emerson had wondered in his Journal, "Why has never the poorest country college offered me a professorship of rhetoric? I think I could have taught an orator, though I am none."[84] There were probably many reasons why neither Thoreau nor Emerson was ever offered a professorship. Colleges and academies operated by conventional and often unenlightened procedures. Both men had been very severe in their criticism of such institutions, or at times, it seemed, of any institution whatsoever. Quite rightly Emerson added of Thoreau, "Perhaps these learned bodies feared the satire of his presence."[85] In Emerson's prime, his presence would have been a reproach, too.

Emerson himself had to admit of Thoreau that "His virtues . . . sometimes ran into extremes." He was so inexorably frank that even some of his admirers called him "that terrible Thoreau."[86] He also had a "tendency to magnify the moment, to read all the laws of Nature into one object . . . To him there was no such thing as size. The pond was a small ocean; the Atlantic, a large Walden Pond."[87] Of course Emerson himself had tried to find a one-to-one relationship between nature and spirit. Similarly, Thoreau "referred every minute fact to cosmical laws." And if he found a new botanical specimen, he said all the botanists who had missed it were blockheads. "'That is to say,' we replied, 'the blockheads were not born in Concord; but who said they were? It was the misfortune of many to be born in London, or Paris, or Rome—poor fellows. . . .' "[88] But these were mere foibles. "The scale on which his studies proceeded was so large as to require longevity, and we were the less prepared for his sudden disappearance."[89] It is to be doubted that anyone will ever write a better characterization of Thoreau.

A few days after Thoreau's funeral Edward Emerson finally began his cherished trip to the West. His father had consented because Edward would have Cabot Russell for a companion. Their plan was to go by railroad and stagecoach. In July Emerson was disturbed by newspaper accounts of an Indian uprising near Salt Lake, but Edward reached San Francisco without mishap. Then he had another attack of conscience about not fighting for the Union, and started home by ship. He did not reach New York until early October, almost more dead than alive, his Uncle William thought. After a few days of rest and medical attention on Staten Island, he continued to Concord. On October 14 his father wrote William to thank him "for the kind care of my boy," and to report his condition. Edward was still tired and emaciated, but his father thought the rough sea voyage had taught him that he was not strong enough to be a soldier: "he has yielded more to this experience than to me, in consenting to go quietly to Cambridge." Yet when he arrived home "last week he took the earliest opportunity to convince me that his sole duty & necessity was to go to the war. And now he threatens that this *pis aller* of the college is only for the present distemper."[90]

Without warning, President Lincoln finally, on September 22, issued his Preliminary Emancipation Proclamation, freeing the slaves in the rebellious states, though he set January 1, 1863, for its taking effect. Emerson was overjoyed. He would have preferred the freeing of all slaves immediately, but Lincoln had been so deliberate that he did not think the President could now fail to make good on his promise. Within a few days abolitionists arranged a rally in Boston, at which Emerson was asked to speak. He gave an address on "The Emancipation Proclamation," which *The Atlantic Monthly* printed in its November issue.[91]

Emerson began by saying that states encrust themselves with such arid forms that only once in a century do we have "a poetic act," such as this proclamation. He now forgave Lincoln's extreme caution, and he liked the "firm tone" of his announcement, "without inflation or surplusage." He could now say, "we have underestimated the capacity and virtue which the

Divine Providence has made an instrument of benefit so vast." In fact, "Forget all that we thought shortcomings, every mistake, every delay. In the extreme embarrassments of his part, call these endurance, wisdom, magnanimity; illuminated, as they now are, by this dazzling success."[92] Emerson had lost every shred of displeasure or impatience with the great President.

On January 1, 1863, the day the Emancipation Proclamation went into effect, Boston held a "Jubilee Concert" in the Music Hall. Emerson wrote a "Boston Hymn," which was used to open the program. One might think that the twenty-two stanzas, rehearsing the spirit of American freedom from the Puritans to the Emancipation, would have been tedious. But if so, two stanzas near the end brought the crowd—many of its members former slaves—to their feet, shouting and singing wildly:

> To-day unbind the captive
> So only are ye unbound;
> Lift up a people from the dust,
> Trump of their rescue, sound!
>
> Pay ransom to the owner
> And fill the bag to the brim.
> Who is the owner? The slave is owner,
> And ever was. Pay him.[93]

The following July, Emerson again tapped popular sentiment in a poem. Colonel Robert Shaw resigned from the famous Fifth Massachusetts Regiment to command a black regiment, recruited from escaped slaves. Shaw was killed, with many of his brave soldiers, in an attempt to take Fort Wagner, in South Carolina, on July 18, 1863. Emerson wrote a poem in praise of "Voluntaries" "to nerve heroic boys / To hazard all in Freedom's fight." It contained a passage which immediately became famous and widely quoted:

> So nigh is grandeur to our dust,
> So near is God to man,
> When Duty whispers low, *Thou must,*
> The youth replies, *I can.*[94]

Today the best that can be said for this poem is that it completely expresses the faith and confidence of those who believed in the *righteousness* of the cause for which, after Emancipation, there was no longer any doubt that Union troops were fighting. Emerson wrote "Voluntaries" in the spirit of Julia Ward Howe's "Battle Hymn of the Republic."

CHAPTER XXVII

The Voice at Eve

Obey the voice at eve obeyed at prime ...[1]

I

On Sunday night, January 4, 1863, Emerson went to bed early in the
American Hotel at Niagara Falls, the only hotel still open in winter. He
wanted to be rested for his trip next day to Toronto, where he was scheduled to lecture in the evening. At three a.m. he was awakened by cries of
"Fire!" Clutching what clothes and possessions he could find in the dark,
he stumbled downstairs through thick smoke to find women draped in
blankets and half-clothed men standing barefoot in the icy-cold street.
They had lost everything in the raging fire, which quickly gutted the
building.[2]

Emerson had been remarkably lucky to escape with his clothing and the
precious black bag containing his lecture. His trunk was also safe because
he had left it in the town of Suspension Bridge on the Canadian side,
where he would resume his journey to Toronto, but he had lost his railroad ticket to Chicago. At the Suspension Bridge railroad station, however, he met Reuben Rice, a young man from Concord who was now an
official of the Central Michigan Railroad, and who gladly gave Emerson a
pass from Buffalo to Chicago.

These experiences were an ominous introduction to 1863, a year filled
with many unexpected events. On the fortunate side, Emerson was now
again in wide demand as a lecturer, with more invitations than he could
accept. He was especially gratified to be invited back to the Midwest:

Cleveland, Detroit, Ann Arbor, Milwaukee, Racine, Beloit, Chicago, and Indianapolis. But fate continued to mix the good with the bad. In Cleveland he had a large and appreciative audience; in Detroit, a small one, perhaps because of the bad weather, though a popular entertainer had recently attracted six hundred people. In Milwaukee one newspaper critic thought "Clubs and Conversations" one of the poorest lectures Emerson was capable of giving, and accused him of underrating his audience.[3] Actually, he was repeating old ideas in his present repertoire on "Clubs," "Third Estate in Literature," "Perpetual Forces," and similar, easily understood lectures. He was indeed making some attempt to popularize, but the truth was that he had no new ideas, except in respect to the war, and that subject was still not to be discussed on the lecture circuit.

Vexations on the road were also becoming more annoying to a man approaching his sixtieth birthday. In great haste and inconvenience he rushed from Chicago to Indianapolis on Friday, January 23, only to learn that no hall would be available until the following Monday. His agent had failed to inform him of this problem, or had not himself been informed by the lecture committee. Then in Pittsburgh, where he went next, he met with further delay, but occupied his time by visiting a steel mill, where he witnessed the molding of a fifteen-inch cannon. "'Tis a wonderful spectacle," he wrote Ellen, "& one comes to look at every one in the crowd of workmen with vast respect."[4] He had hoped to spend a night with William in New York, but snowdrifts in the Pennsylvania mountains delayed his arrival.[5] After a few hours of sleep in the St. Denis Hotel in New York, he caught a morning train for Boston; then in a few days he was off again to Montreal.

The war was never far from Emerson's mind, no matter how much he traveled or read lectures on peaceful subjects. In December the Union forces had suffered heavy losses at Fredericksburg; then they got bogged down in the futile "mud campaign" of the Potomac. But now able-bodied black men were flocking to the Union lines, as Emerson had predicted, and the great problem was what to do with them. Major George L. Stearns, of Medford, began enlisting them for the Fifty-fourth and Fifty-fifth Massachusetts Volunteer Infantry. In his Journal Emerson wrote appeals to these men which he may have intended to use in a speech. So far as is known, the speech was not delivered, but the words show his thinking at the time: *"Negro Soldiers.* If the war means Liberty to you, you should enlist. It does mean Liberty to you in the opinion of the South, for the South says, We fight to plant Slavery as our foundations."[6]

The following October this subject must have become an embarrassment to Emerson when Colonel E. N. Hallowell wrote him that he needed a second lieutenant for the Fifty-fourth Regiment and suggested that younger men than Edward Emerson had died for their country.[7] Edward would have been willing to accept the commission, but his father still thought his health was too fragile. Eventually Edward obtained his parents' permission to enlist in the Home Guard at Harvard. Emerson in his own way did what he could for the war effort. He wrote letters recommending young men of the region for commissions in the army, and lobbied for the promotion of Ethan Allen Hitchcock, of Boston, to brigadier general.

He was hurt and vexed that some of his English friends, Carlyle among them, sympathized with the South. He heard of Carlyle's pro-Confederate leaning more through rumors and newspaper reports than from his letters, which remained affectionate. Their correspondence had become less frequent, mainly because Emerson was too busy to write, but it had not ceased. In December 1862 Emerson had written Carlyle: "The war is our sole and doleful instructor. All our bright young men go into it, to be misused and sacrificed hitherto by incapable leaders." Later he wrote that "the battle for Humanity is, at this hour, in America." He regretted that Carlyle had never made "the visit to America, which in earlier years you projected or favored. It would have made it impossible that your name should be cited for one moment on the side of the enemies of mankind."[8]

The draft riots in New York City in July 1863 caused Emerson to blame "the wild Irish element, imported in the last twenty-five years into this country, and led by Romish priests, who sympathize, of course, with despotism," for much of the opposition to the war in Northern cities. He told Carlyle that Southern slaveholders, traders, and propagandists in London had filled English ears with their wishes and beliefs. He apologized for writing "a newspaper, but, in these times, 't is wonderful what sublime lessons I have once and again read on the Bulletin-boards in the streets." He meant, of course, news of the war. "I shall always respect War hereafter. The cost of life, the dreary havoc of comfort and time, are overpaid by the Vistas it opens of . . . reconstructing and uplifting Society."[9]

Of course Emerson never saw the ravages of war at first hand, as his friend Walt Whitman had. Whitman had gone down to the Fredericks burg battlefield to find his wounded brother, George. He found George not seriously wounded, but those in a worse plight aroused his compassion. Instead of returning to Brooklyn, he stayed in Washington to aid the sick and wounded in military hospitals. The government supplied competent physicians and nurses, but these had no time for personal attention to the ill and lonely men. This Walt Whitman was especially endowed to give, and with remarkable success. He tried to find a government position to support him while he did volunteer hospital visitation in his spare time. Emerson wrote a recommendation for him to the Secretary of the Treasury, Salmon P. Chase, which a friend delivered for him, but Chase had heard of the poet's notorious literary reputation and would not help him.[10] (He said, however, that he had nothing in Emerson's handwriting and would keep the letter.) Other recommendations Emerson wrote for Whitman were equally futile, but Walt managed by spartan living and part-time clerical work in the Paymaster's office to carry on his hospital work. Friends and relatives contributed money to help him buy stationery, fruit, tobacco, and books for the men in the hospitals; Emerson was one of the contributors. Louisa May Alcott was also a hospital volunteer in Washington at this time, but she gave all her time to straight nursing, until malaria made it impossible for her to continue.[11]

In May, Emerson's attention was temporarily distracted from the war by the death of his Aunt Mary in Williamsburg (now a part of Brooklyn) in the home of Augustus Parsons. For many years Mrs. Hannah Haskins Parsons, Emerson's cousin, had tried to take care of the difficult Miss Emerson, and now she accompanied the body to Concord, where the funeral service was held in the First Unitarian Church on May 4. Burial was in Sleepy Hollow Cemetery, in the plot Emerson had purchased for his family. Only a few friends attended the funeral. In a letter to William, who could not come, Emerson said he brought these friends of his aunt's home from the cemetery, "telling them I would produce all the memorabilia of the Sibyl, if they desired; they came, but did not ask for memories, and I reserved them."[12] Later he would memorialize her in a lecture for the Concord Social Circle, but in the letter to William he tried to explain what she had meant to him in his childhood. He admitted that at any time she could instantly make herself repulsive, and that few people had been able to tolerate her. But he forgave her outrageous behavior because he believed she had been a haunted genius. He still cherished her letters and diaries, overlooking "the huge alloy of theology and metaphysics." They retained the power to charm him that they had had thirty years before.

Emerson's perusal of Aunt Mary's manuscripts was interrupted by an unexpected invitation from the Secretary of War to serve on the Board of Visitors of the United States Military Academy at West Point. He reported for duty on June 1, expecting to stay for a couple of days, and was alarmed to find that he was to remain for sixteen days. He grumbled in his letters to William,[13] but stayed and conscientiously examined the course of study and interviewed cadets and their officers. John Burroughs, who was teaching school nearby, saw Emerson on the Academy grounds and thought he looked like an "alert, inquisitive farmer." On meeting Emerson next day, Burroughs was impressed by his "serene, unflinching look. Just the way his upper lip shut into his lower . . . showed to me the metal of which he was made."[14]

Emerson was "very agreeably" impressed by the discipline and industry at West Point, but recommended that "competitive examinations should be urged on the Congress, and that a severer preliminary test should be required for admission." The Academy should not, he believed, have to teach spelling and elementary English grammar. The course of study should be less superficial, with more advanced instruction in science. In his Journal Emerson made this farsighted observation: "At West Point, I saw a civilization built on powder. It is not quite creditable to our invention that all the instruction in engineering, infantry, cavalry, artillery, rigidly rests on this one accident of our chemistry, gunpowder. A new invention to-morrow would change all the art of war."[15]

In a commencement address on "The Scholar" at Waterville College in July, repeated the following month at Dartmouth, Emerson returned to the meaning of the war to the nation. Even in his now-famous "American Scholar" address in 1837, he had advocated the scholar's participation in the life of his times. He now repeated this advice for the needs of a nation at war: "The country complains loudly of the inefficiency of the army. It was badly led. But, before this, it was not the army alone, it was the population that was badly led. The clerisy, the spiritual guides, the scholars, the seers have been false to their trust."[16]

Though the war was still going badly for the North, Emerson thought he detected a new enthusiasm for liberty at work. "War, seeking for the roots of strength, comes upon the moral aspects at once," and uplifts and ennobles the age. Some said that a whole generation would be lost, but "Who would not, if it could be made certain that the new morning of universal liberty should rise on our race by the perishing of one generation,—who would not consent to die?"[17]

As the war began to approach a crisis, Emerson wrote a lecture on the "Fortune of the Republic," which he gave in Boston on December 1, 1863, and repeated eleven times by February 9, 1864. He was worried by the "careless swagger" with which America marched to power, seeming to care only for its selfish ease and little for human rights. Vast natural resources had given Americans overconfidence in their invulnerability to natural disasters. Many did not even bother to vote. Those who voted did not listen to their conscience, thereby permitting rogues to sneak into office.

Flaws in the operation of the American political system could be repaired if "the people wake and correct it with energy." Another danger was the European influences on the country: aristocratic and class-conscious, they undermined American democracy. Walt Whitman would be saying the same thing a few years later in *Democratic Vistas,* and Emerson's remedy was the same as Whitman's: "Let the passion for America cast out the passion for Europe.... What this country longs for is personalities, grand persons, to counteract its materialities." So far the United States was only a multitude of people, not yet a "new nation, the guide and lawgiver of all nations":

> Power can be generous. The very grandeur of the means which offer themselves to us should suggest grandeur in the direction of our expenditure. If our mechanic arts are unsurpassed in usefulness, if we have taught the river to make shoes and nails and carpets, and the bolt of heaven to write our letters like a Gillot pen, let these wonders work for honest humanity, for the poor, for justice, genius and the public good. Let us realize that this country, the last found, is the great charity of God to the human race.[18]

In a series of six lectures on "American Life," given in Boston in November and December 1864, Emerson continued his exhortations. He repeated three of his lectures in the series on "Education," "Social Aims," and "Resources" in other New England towns, and then took them to the

West in 1865. During the year the war ended he lectured seventy-seven times, a record surpassed only by eighty lectures in 1867, the peak year of his platform career. One reason he was so much in demand was that he had become the conscience of the nation—at least in the North and West.

After President Lincoln placed General Ulysses S. Grant in charge of the Union armies in March 1864, the North began to win battles, but at a terrible toll in human lives. The ambulance corps was hard-pressed for bandages and appealed for help. The women members of the Soldiers Aid Society in Concord responded by working long hours in the Town Hall, laundering, sewing together, and packing clean rags for use at the battlefront as bandages. Ellen Emerson foraged in Lexington and other nearby towns for contributions, only to be told in one town, "We ain't goin' to send our rags for Concord women to talk over."[19] Nevertheless, she kept the packers supplied. One of the steadiest workers was Mrs. Mike Murphy, whose "wild" Irish son had died a hero at Fredericksburg. Among some thirty bodies shipped back to Concord for burial was that of Lieutenant Ezra Ripley, grandson of Emerson's step-grandfather. In the siege at Petersburg, Virginia, Captain Prescott was mortally wounded. The Reverend Grindall Reynolds, who had refused to advise him on reenlistment, preached his funeral sermon in the First Parish Church on a bright sunny day in June.[20]

A few days earlier Nathaniel Hawthorne had been buried in Sleepy Hollow. Perhaps the war was in no way responsible for his death, though he grieved over the loss of so many young lives, and his passing seemed a part of the tragic times. His friend Franklin Pierce had taken him to New Hampshire in hopes of overcoming his mental depression, but he died on the way. On May 24, the day following Hawthorne's funeral in Concord, Emerson meditated in his Journal on the loss of a man whom he had wanted to be his friend. "It would have been a happiness, doubtless to both of us, to have come into habits of unreserved intercourse." Hawthorne was easy to talk to, only he said so little that Emerson felt he himself was saying too much. Thus communication remained clogged, and, "Now it appears that I waited too long." Emerson thought a "tragic element" in Hawthorne caused the "painful solitude of the man, which, I suppose, could not longer be endured, and he died of it."[21]

II

For the Emerson family the spring of 1865 was not all sadness, for it brought the engagement of Edith to William Hathaway Forbes, the oldest son of John Murray Forbes. William had joined the First Regiment of Cavalry, Massachusetts Volunteers, on December 26, 1861, as a second lieutenant, and had risen by valorous conduct to the rank of lieutenant colonel three years later. While he was engaged in a hand-to-hand fight during a battle with Mosby's guerrillas, his horse was shot and fell on him. Thus trapped, he was taken prisoner. He escaped from the prison at Columbia, South Carolina, in the autumn of 1863, was recaptured, but finally survived to be "exchanged" in the spring of 1865. Granted a well-merited leave, he came home in March, and promptly called on Edith Emerson in Concord.[22]

Edith and Will had been friends for four years, and his proposal was not a sudden decision. Nor was it surprising that Edith was fascinated by this handsome, mustachioed young war hero, with his military carriage and air of confidence won by leading men in battle, mild and gracious as he was in his manners to her.[23] Edith was an attractive, high-spirited girl. Unlike Ellen, she was not studious, and had protested against being sent to Professor Agassiz's school. She was sociable, gregarious, with a mind of her own, and a determination to meet life on her own terms. Will Forbes thought she was the perfect wife for him, and apparently he never had cause to change his mind. Emerson himself was delighted with the engagement, and so were the other members of his family. To a friend he wrote on March 10: "This event has brought great joy to this house, for he is a noble youth,—& perhaps none takes more delight in it than my boy Edward, who is an old firm friend of his."[24]

At the end of his furlough Colonel Forbes returned to his cavalry regiment and was present at the surrender of General Lee at Appomatox Court House on April 9. His safety gave the Emerson family an additional reason for rejoicing that the war had ended. On April 10 Emerson wrote Mrs. Tappan: "Dear Caroline, . . . what a joyful day is this . . . Mankind has appeared just now in its best attitude around Mr Lincoln—in these recent experiences—& will aid him to use sanely the immense power with which the hour clothes him."[25]

But after reading General Grant's terms of surrender, Emerson thought

they were too easy, and feared "that the high tragic historic justice which
the nation, with severest consideration, should execute, will be softened
and dissipated and toasted away at dinner-tables."[26] The President said in
Washington a few days later: no persecutions or hangings; forgive the
rebels and take them back into the Union. This did not sit well with
Emerson, who thought they ought to be punished. And if the Southern
states were permitted seats in Congress, would they not again connive
with Northern Democrats "in thwarting the will of the Government"?
The President meant well, but he was too conciliatory.

When a few days later President Lincoln was killed by an assassin's bullet, Emerson's sympathy made him forget, momentarily at least, his criticism of the surrender terms. April 19 was the anniversary of the historic
skirmish at Concord Bridge in 1775, but this year Concordians observed it
by gathering in the First Parish Church to hear Emerson deliver an address
on the late President. "In this country, on Saturday [April 15]," he said,
"every one was struck dumb, and saw at first only deep below deep, as he
meditated on the ghastly blow." Then, perhaps speaking more for himself
than the country, Emerson added that the despair was brief, because it was
realized that "his work had not perished," and "acclamations of praise for
the task he had accomplished burst out into a song of triumph."[27]

Now once again Emerson felt about Lincoln as he had in his speech on
"The Emancipation Proclamation." The late President's worth could not
be exaggerated. "In four years,—four years of battle-days,—his endurance,
his fertility of resources, his magnanimity, were sorely tried and never
found wanting." But possibly he had done his work, "this heroic deliv-
erer," and "new and uncommitted hands" might better rescue the country
from the ashes of war. Did Emerson think that perhaps a less compassion-
ate man might insist on harsher retribution for the South? Quite likely,
though of course his philosophy of evil also required a "compensation" for
every loss. He still believed, too, that "There is a serene Providence which
rules the fate of nations, . . . alike by what is called defeat or . . . victory."[28]
This was the kind of consolation he had found (or tried to find) for
the loss of his first son, and it was more emotional than intellectual.
Then, too, with the end of the war he had stopped making hard
decisions. Henceforward his life would be easier, as if Providence were
justifying his confidence, at least on the personal, if not on the national,
level.

Edith Emerson married William Forbes in her home on October 3, 1865, with the Reverend Reynolds officiating and only relatives and a few close friends present. The bride and groom settled in the Blue Hills section of Milton, near the estate of Edith's father-in-law. John Murray Forbes had built there because from his hilltop home he could see his ships arriving from China. He had started a fortune in the China trade before settling in Boston to invest his money in mines, railroads, and other profitable ventures. He was altruistic and patriotic, sharing the moral convictions of Edith's father. In 1860, when John Brown came to Boston with a price on his head, he had slept safely in Mr. Forbes's Milton home.[29]

Throughout the war John Forbes had been a frequent technical adviser to President Lincoln and his Cabinet. At the request of the Secretaries of the Navy and Treasury he had made a perilous trip to England in the spring of 1863 to prevent two armored warships, called "rams," from being delivered to the Confederate Navy. One "ram," the *Alabama,* had already been delivered, and was inflicting alarming damage on Union ships because no guns then in use could sink her. Forbes carried ten million dollars in U.S. bonds in a trunk. He was able to complete his mission successfully without using more than half the bonds; and so returned with the remaining five million in a valise, arriving in New York on the evening of July 14, during the tragic draft riots, but he reached Boston in safety.[30]

After Edith Emerson's marriage, she and Will Forbes spent a large part of every summer on Naushon Island in Buzzards Bay, near Woods Hole. The island was seven miles long and a mile and a half wide, and John Murray Forbes owned all of it. Much of it was wooded, and was well stocked with game: deer, as well as ducks, geese, and other waterfowl. It also had enough pastureland for sheep, cows, and horses; it was almost a small ranch. The large, rambling, frame house was simply furnished, but the Forbes hospitality kept it filled with family and friends. At night there were games and singing for entertainment, and in the daytime riding, driving, sailing, fishing, picnicking.[31] Both Edith and her father enjoyed Naushon, but Lidian Emerson disliked the noise and furious activity, and for several summers refused to go there.

After his discharge from the cavalry at the end of the war, Will Forbes went into business for himself and was successful from the start, investing, as his father had done, in a variety of enterprises. He was one of the first to see the commercial possibilities of the telephone, and eventually became president of Bell Telephone. Soon after his marriage he offered to manage his father-in-law's financial affairs. By this time Emerson was earning more money from his lectures and books than he ever had before, yet he still borrowed from the bank on short-term notes and worried about being in debt. In a few years, with Will's management, he was living on a comfortable income, free of debt.

Probably Emerson never knew all the ways in which his son-in-law contributed to his prosperity. For example, in 1868 Will suggested that Emerson give a series of readings from his favorite poets for young businessmen in Boston. On December 23 Emerson acknowledged receiving six hundred dollars in advance for his planned readings, "which look a little alarming to me, until they shall be earned."[32] Both Will and James T. Fields, Emerson's publisher, worked together to promote his lectures, and his earnings began to top fifteen hundred dollars for a single series. Will Forbes also began pressuring Lidian's agent, her cousin Abraham Jackson, for the collection of rents on her property in Plymouth and Boston. Will sold the Boston property for a good price. He also found that Abe Jackson had been cheating Lidian on his collections. Eventually Jackson was tried and convicted of embezzlement, for which he served a term in the penitentiary.[33]

It would be unfair to Emerson to attribute his easy postwar life entirely to his efficient and generous son-in-law. He had reached the age when a hardworking man of talent usually begins to reap his deserved rewards. His friends helped, but many of them he had won by his lectures and writings. On his trips to the Midwest Emerson always made new friends and renewed old acquaintances. During his journey from Toledo to Indiana in January 1866, he met Mr. E. B. Phillips, president of the Michigan Southern Railroad, "who told me, that his first acquaintance with me was when he had wheeled a barrel of flour to my house from the store of Charles B. Davis, whose apprentice he was."[34] From Battle Creek, Michigan, he wrote William on February 1: "In every one of these expanding towns is a knot of loving New Englanders who cherish the Lyceum out of love to the Charles & the Merrimac & Connecticut rivers." Many of them had been among the first settlers of the region, some thirty years before. "In all this swarming country, I have hardly seen anybody I ever saw before, but they treat me very kindly, and they are as anxious for the success of radical politics as the Concord people."[35] (In the postwar period many of the Democrats called the Republicans "radicals.")

In 1867 Emerson made two trips to the West, one from January through March, going as far as Minneapolis and Cedar Rapids, Iowa, and another in December to Cleveland, St. Louis, Chicago, Davenport, and stops between. At St. Paul he visited a Sioux Indian village, and in Minneapolis met his cousin Phebe Haskins, whom he had not seen for thirty years.[36] He said that if he were a young man he would like to live in Minneapolis. On February 17 he wrote Lidian that a Mississippi flood had stranded him at Port Byron for a day or two, and he did "not mean to travel westward again." (As indicated above, he did make another trip the following December.) In St. Louis he renewed his acquaintance with William Torrey Harris, editor of *The Journal of Philosophy,* and the American authority on Hegel. From Concord Emerson wrote Harris that at first sight he did not find Hegel "engaging nor at second sight satisfying. But his immense fame can not be mistaken, and I shall read and wait."[37] However, he would never be able to read Hegel with satisfaction. Alcott had complained that Hegel made his head ache, and Emerson understood.

III

From the Tremont Hotel in Chicago, Emerson wrote Ellen on February 24, 1867, that the extension of his lectures until March 19 was "very awkward, as my Poems are promised for 1 April," and here he was "eleven hundred miles & more from the printers, & so very many errata that I am bound to correct."[38] He would have to ask Mr. Fields for still another postponement. He had been carrying the proofs in his trunk, but every time he looked at them, the Muse said, "Not at home: no Sir, I do not live on railway wheels: Snatch your dinner, but not me."

To another correspondent Emerson wrote that since the previous autumn he had been collecting his "scattered verses not hitherto published in a book."[39] Among them were fourteen of his best poems published in *The Atlantic Monthly,* including "Days," "Brahma," "Two Rivers," and "Song of Nature." As late as March 6 he was still asking Fields to correct "a few errors . . . on the plates" (apparently the pages had already been stereotyped), but *May-Day and Other Poems* was finally published on April 29, 1867. This book was a small volume (16*mo,* 205 pages), containing forty-four poems. Many of them were short, but the title poem, "May-Day," ran to more than five hundred lines.[40] Its loose, almost fragmentary, structure was indicative of Emerson's method of composition.

As presented in Chapter XXI, Emerson's theory of poetry combined the Neoplatonic concept of spiritual ecstasy with the Persian ideal of intoxication of the senses, as represented by Sa'di and Hafiz. Emerson did not pretend to write his poems in a frenzy of "inspiration," but he believed that he had moments of heightened sensitivity when the channels of communication between his mind and the Divine Mind (Over-Soul or Reason) became clearer than ordinarily. These experiences usually gave him an idea or a nucleus for a poem, which he would write down in his Journal as promptly as he could. From time to time he would think of additional images or tropes which he amplified. This process might go on for years, as in the clusters which finally became the long poem "May-Day," or the more condensed "Song of Nature," begun in 1846 and finished in 1859, in which several hundred fragmentary lines became eighty-four. Sometimes he never finished the growing poem, as the twenty pages of "The Poet" in the appendix to his collected *Poems* show, though the pages contain passages as good as anything he published during his lifetime. Sometimes, luckily, the genesis of a poem was a rough nugget of ore which he was able to melt down and mold into a neat and concise poem such as "Days."

Emerson himself thought "Days" (quoted in full in Chapter XXVI) was his best poem, and eminent critics such as F. O. Matthiessen have agreed with him.[41] Its importance in the present discussion of the 1867 edition is that it serves as an allegory of Emerson's life as a poet, and of the relation of his life to his poetry. He calls the days of his life "Daughters of Time." They are hypocritical because they pass so unobtrusively and unnoticed that he forgets his youthful ambitions and settles for the mediocre things of life, symbolized by "herbs and apples." In a different context he might have valued these simple things, but here the point is that he was too easily satisfied. Too late he saw the look of scorn on the face of the goddess Day. In the same year that he published this poem in *The Atlantic Monthly* (1867), he stated this theme prosaically in a lecture called "Works and Days": "He only is rich who owns the day." The days "say nothing, and if we do not use the gifts they bring, they carry them as silently away."[42]

Since his student days at Harvard, Emerson had suffered pangs of guilt for his slothfulness and his imagined emotional coldness (a variety of sloth). Now, as a poet, he feels that he has not been sufficiently attentive to the voice of Nature and Reason. This remorse is the motif of "Days." The allegory conveys exactly the kind of life Emerson lived in his "pleached garden," and the ironical tone expresses the depth of his self-condemnation.

There is, of course, a paradox in this attitude, for Emerson's conception of his role as a poet was also that of the Aeolian harp, in which Nature (the wind) vibrates the strings of the passive instrument. In his own copy of the 1847 *Poems* he had written a sentence from Plato to serve as a motto for "Bacchus": ". . . the man who is his own master knocks in vain at the door of poetry."[43] In another poem, "My Garden," the poet is not the harp, but a listener, whose ears are too dull to catch the music:

> Wandering voices in the air
> And murmurs in the wold
> Speak what I cannot declare,
> Yet cannot all withhold.[44]

The poems of two decades collected in *May-Day* had taken shape in Emerson's imagination out of the conflict in his life between moral philosopher and lyric poet. Believing that the wisdom of Reason rose up from his unconscious into his consciousness while he was passively receptive, he found his Concord retreat the perfect place for meditation and for writing prose. But to be a poet he needed excitement, and the greatest emotional stimulations he experienced were on his walks to Walden Pond, or at the seashore, or when he gazed at the stars until he became a "transparent eyeball."

Such experiences as these were sufficient for Wordsworth, and they often satisfied Emerson. At other times, however, he felt understimulated. Had Ellen lived, she might have provided the emotional excitement he needed; Lidian obviously could not. In fact, *people* seldom stimulated Emerson except in times of social crisis, as in the events preceding and during the Civil War. Then he could write his "Boston Hymn" on the Emancipation Proclamation, or "Voluntaries" (both included in *May-Day*), but these are better as social statements than as lyrics.

Critics complained with some justification that Emerson's poems lacked human emotions. John Morley wrote: "Emerson's poetry is of that kind which springs, not from excitement of passion or feeling, but from an intellectual demand for intense and sublimated expression."[45] Morley's observation is accurate for Emerson's most intellectual poems, but ignores the kind of excitement his nature poems have. No one has understood this so well as George Woodberry:

Emerson always thinks of the process of Nature as a dance of atoms. . . . He conceives the energy of Nature as a Dionysiac force, with overflow and intoxication in it, and his imaginative symbols for it are all of this order. This incorporation of the atomic theory in his thought of the world, and also the large prominence he gives to the idea of evolution in general, and his use of scientific terms of detail, give to his poetry a characteristic tone and colour sympathetic with the age. Science, indeed, may be said to enter into the surfaces and imagery of his poetry as an integral part . . .[46]

In "May-Day" Emerson is fascinated by the sounds he hears in spring, and wonders whether they come from bird, or wind, or

> Voice of a meteor lost in day?
> Such tidings of the starry sphere
> Can this elastic air convey.[47]

But whatever the source, the combined sounds of birds, squirrels, breezes, and the cracking of the ice on the pond are tokens

> That the marble sleep is broken,
> And a change has passed on things.

Matthew Arnold complained that this poem "has no real evolution at all; it is a series of observations."[48] By "evolution" he presumably meant development or progression of thought, and that is correct, but Arnold failed to attend to what the poet did observe. It was not golden daffodils dancing beside a lake, but, as Woodberry said, the Dionysiac dance of atoms. Failure to notice the influence of science on Emerson has led most critics to look for the wrong things in his poetry, and to undervalue it accordingly. Yet anyone who has followed his career as lecturer from 1833, when he devoted his first public lectures to natural science, to his attempt from 1848 to 1879 to find a "natural history of the intellect," should be aware of the prominence of natural science in his intellectual development. In his lectures and essays the theories and facts of science are used as concepts, as illustrations of cosmic truth; in his poems more as motion (Dionysiac ecstasy); not as observation so much as empathy with the cosmic dance: "In flint and marble beats a heart."[49]

Edward Emerson said that after the publication of "May-Day" in 1867, his father "saw that the ordering of the different passages to give the advance of Spring was not quite successful," and he attempted in *Selected Poems* (1876) to improve the order, "but did not quite perfect, the arrangement."[50] However, the sequence of the seasons does not really matter, any more than it does in Thoreau's *Walden,* in which the chronology of the four seasons is not strictly observed. Spring in "May-Day," as in *Walden,* is a symbol of renewal, and a foretaste of Eden: "Hymen of element and race."[51] Like Thoreau also, Emerson plays with the paradox of concealed heat beneath the snow and ice. For this reason he praises the Northern cold, and alludes to the recent war, when Northern ice burned hotter than Southern fire.[52] It was from Thoreau, too, that Emerson borrowed the "almanack" of birds and flowers, "Exact to days, exact to hours" in their return and blooming. The message of "May-Day" is the same as that of *Walden,* which ends: "There is more day to dawn. The sun is but a morning star." With Emerson, spring is a reminder of childhood, "when life was new," and "We were quick from head to foot."[53] "May-Day" is a paean to the cosmic energy "that searches through / From Chaos of the dawning morrow."[54] Any reader who sympathizes with the Cosmic emotion of this poem will find it one of Emerson's best lyrics. The simple four-stress couplets, varied by alternating rhymes, are entirely appropriate for its spirit and substance.

As if to confound the critics who said that Emerson had only one monotonous meter, he wrote "The Adirondacs" (which follows "May-Day" in the 1867 edition) in soundly executed blank verse. This poem describes a camping trip Emerson took in the summer of 1858 with ten distinguished companions to a hunting lodge owned by the artist William J. Stillman.[55] The group included Agassiz, Judge Hoar, Sam Ward, Dr. Oliver Wendell Holmes's brother John, Dr. Jeffries Wyman (professor of comparative anatomy at Harvard), and several Boston physicians. Emerson bought a rifle, but used it only in target practice. They crossed Lake

Champlain and rode in farm carts to the upper lakes in New York. At the
north end of Follansbee Lake, the eleven men (Emerson says ten, apparently not counting himself) and their guides camped in a virgin forest,
where one pine measured fifteen feet in circumference. Here:

> Ten scholars, wonted to lie warm and soft
> In well-hung chambers daintily bestowed,
> Lie here on hemlock-boughs, like Sacs and Sioux,
> And greet unanimous the joyful change.[56]

The "scholars" find their rank reduced to "low-prized laymen," while
their guides, loggers in winter and guides in summer, are "the doctors of
the wilderness." The true doctors dissect, weigh, and analyze collected animals and plants, while Stillman paints a group picture and Emerson makes
notes for his poem. His narration is easy, detailed, and relaxed. Somewhere
in their rambles the campers meet a traveler with a newspaper announcing
that the Atlantic cable has been completed and is operating. Emerson
exults:

> Thought's new-found path
> Shall supplement henceforth all trodden ways,
> Match God's equator with a zone of art,
>
> .   .   .   .
>
> A spasm throbbing through the pedestals
> Of Alp and Andes, isle and continent,
> Urging astonished Chaos with a thrill
> To be a brain or serve the brain of man.

These learned men, playing at escape from civilization, had not escaped
after all. And when they hear someone in a log cabin playing Beethoven
on a piano, they feel that the savage enemies of civilization are being kept
at bay. With amusement Emerson observes that under the cinders of the
campfire "burned the fires of home," and when the weather turns cool,
they are glad to end their vacation:

> The prodigal sunshine rested on the land,
> The rivers gamboled onward to the sea,
> And Nature, the inscrutable and mute,
> Permitted on her infinite repose

Almost a smile to steal to cheer her sons,
As if one riddle of the Sphinx were guessed.

The poem demonstrates Emerson's seldom-used talent for irony and social observation, as well as his command of blank verse. For him it is not a
typical work. He is best known for his philosophical poems, such as
"Brahma," which he had called in his Notebook "The Song of the Soul"
(a hint which removes its supposed obscurity), using "soul" in the Hindu
sense of "Brahman" in the *Vishnu Purana* and the *Bhagavad-Gita.*[57] In
"Two Rivers" the Over-Soul is the spiritual river, the Concord Musketa-
quit [*sic*] the physical. Here Emerson handles abstractions more lucidly
than in most of his prose.

Perhaps both the poetic and the personal value of these poems can be
summed up in a glance at "Nemesis," "Fate," and "Terminus." For all his
protests against Calvinism, Emerson believed in "nemesis." No matter
where the bird flies, "it is flying home," and "The maiden fears, and fearing runs / Into the charmed snare she shuns . . ."[58] To attempt to resist
nemesis is like a woman's trying to smooth the ocean with her fan, to
soothe the "stony" (unyielding) Parcae with a prayer, or to light chaos
with a taper. The two eight-line quatrains, in couplet rhyme, are as compact as a sonnet, with a crescendo of hyperbole up to the final couplet:
"And all our struggles and our toils / Tighter wind the giant coils."

The poem "Fate" can be faulted for the overuse of generalized diction:
"mean or great," "better or worse," "doubt and fear." "Nemesis" is a better poem, at least in the use of imagery and metaphor, but "Fate" does effectively convey the idea that men carry their destiny in their character,
like an inherited gene; and they do not know whether their character is
strong or weak until it is tested. Then, "the foresight that awaits / Is the
same Genius that creates."[59]

"Terminus" shows Emerson trying to apply his philosophy of Fate to
his own life—demonstrating at the same time that his poems are even
more autobiographical than his prose (except in his Journals). At the age
of sixty-three, without protest or bitterness, he accepts the fact that he is
growing old and must economize his remaining strength:

Timely wise accept the terms,
Soften the fall with wary foot;

> A little while
> Still plan and smile,
> And,—fault of novel germs,—
> Mature the unfallen fruit.[60]

It would do no good to curse his ancestors for their "legacy of ebbing veins." He will accept his fate with stoic courage, and continue to believe that his life has a purpose in the cosmic scheme:

> As the bird trims her to the gale,
> I trim myself to the storm of time,
> I man the rudder, reef the sail,
> Obey the voice at eve obeyed at prime ...

In form this poem resembles the seventeenth-century "ode" of Abraham Cowley, with indeterminate length of line, variable metrical stresses, and no definite rhyme scheme:

> It is time to be old,
> To take in sail:—
> The god of bounds,
> Who sets to seas a shore,
> Came to me in his fatal rounds,
> And said: 'No more!
> No farther shoot
> Thy broad ambitious branches, and thy root.
> Fancy departs: no more invent;
> Contract thy firmament
> To compass of a tent. . . .'

The thought is crystal clear, but the imagery lacks unity—though the effective contrast of "firmament" and "tent" saves the poem from triteness. Both words have Old Testament connotations. "Terminus" not only shows Emerson's awareness of his physical decline, but by its unevenness gives some evidence that the decline had indeed already started. In this respect it was unconsciously "organic."

Emerson always wrote from experience, either vicarious or literally personal. The imagery of "The Harp" comes from his listening to the Aeolian harp in his own study window; that of "The Garden," from his walks to the Walden woods (the woods are his "garden"); that of "Seashore," from a week spent at Pigeon Cove in July 1856, which he described in his Journal.[61] He was better at drawing imagery from memory than from fantasy; he said himself that his strongest sense was sight. This fact makes his poems the best guide to his life—his moods, doubts, ecstasies, sympathies, his limitations in sexual love and social relations. The music of his poems is limited, and his diction seldom has the magic of surprise found in Emily Dickinson's poems. Yet Emerson's have their own elfin music and subtle paradoxes.

IV

In 1867 Emerson lost two persons very precious to him. The first was Abel Adams, the best friend he had when he was pastor of the Second Church in Boston; the two men never lost their love for each other. Adams died on July 7, leaving in his will two thousand dollars to Emerson and one thousand to each of his children. He had also, it will be recalled, paid Edward's expenses at Harvard. Emerson wrote Mrs. Adams that "from the first day when I saw him in 1828, until you left Boston for Brookline, your home was always one of my homes, & long my only home."[62]

Less than three weeks later (July 26) Mrs. Sarah Bradford Ripley died.[63] It was she who had corresponded with Waldo while he was in the Boston Public Latin School, encouraged him to write poems, and taken him horseback riding. As the wife of his kind Uncle Samuel, she had continued to be one of his most loyal friends. A still more painful loss came the following year when William Emerson, Waldo's oldest brother, died in New York on September 13. He had lost his wife six months earlier, and had not been well himself for several years. Waldo had begged him to retire to Concord, and had once picked out a small farm for him. Now they would never be together except in Sleepy Hollow, where William was buried in the plot Waldo had purchased for his family. Concord was the one spot on earth that Emerson loved most, and he wanted as much of his family together there as possible, in life and death.

Concord, however, was no longer quite the safe and peaceful village it had been before the Civil War. Boston was overrun by destitute immigrants, and the crime of the city had spread to the countryside. On August

24, 1868, Emerson had written William: "For the last week I have been sitting at home alone, Lidian & Edward being at Milton, as well as Ellen gone. I cannot leave home too for the village is annoyed lately with night robberies, successful or otherwise, but not allowing venerable heads of families to wander much."[64]

Neither death nor robberies could permanently disturb the even tenor of Emerson's life in his declining years. Both his character and his philosophy protected him. Also, honors that he valued for personal or sentimental reasons began to fall upon him. At commencement in 1866 Harvard awarded him the LL.D. degree, and the alumni elected him to the Board of Overseers. The following year he was chosen orator for the annual Phi Beta Kappa meeting, exactly thirty years after his "American Scholar" address. Possibly some members of the Divinity School faculty had not yet forgiven him for his 1838 address, but Emerson felt that his exile had ended. For the next eight years he would work hard to fulfill his duties as an overseer, serving on committees, examining the methods of teaching foreign languages, weighing the merits of the university's grading system, and debating ways to modernize the curriculum.

In March 1869, after heated discussions in meetings of the overseers, Charles W. Eliot was elected president of Harvard.[65] Emerson and a majority of the members of the board expected him to usher in a new, more progressive and liberal era. One of Eliot's innovative ideas was to invite distinguished men outside the faculty to give noncredit lectures to advanced students. Among the first to be invited was Emerson, to lecture on philosophy. He had hoped for many years to write a book on the "Natural History of the Intellect," and (as has been noted) actually made a beginning in London in the summer of 1848. He had also lectured on the general theme, and now, he thought, this opportunity to expand his ideas could be the stimulus he needed to complete the book. Fortunately he had a year to prepare for a series of sixteen lectures.

In the meantime, Emerson's *Society and Solitude* was published in February 1870 by Fields, Osgood, and Company. It contained twelve essays, slightly revised versions of lectures he had given over a number of years. They were significant for several reasons, but especially for showing how well Emerson had adapted his art to his audiences. He had simplified his style, avoided metaphysical subjects, and focused his attention on topics of interest to a large number of people: domestic life, farming, making the most of daily experiences, the right use of books and clubs, the wise balance of solitude and sociability, the advantages of old age. Even in the essay on "Civilization," inculcating the doctrine that "Civilization depends on morality," Emerson enlivened his didacticism by comments, sometimes humorous, on recent technological marvels:

> We had letters to send: couriers could not go fast enough nor far enough; broke their wagons, foundered their horses; bad roads in spring, snowdrifts in winter, heats in summer; could not get the horses out of a walk. But we found out that the air and earth were full of Electricity, and always going our way,—just the way we wanted to send. *Would he take a message?* Just as lief as not; had nothing else to do; would carry it in no time.[66]

Carlyle thought *Society and Solitude* Emerson's best book: "Such brevity, simplicity, softness, homely grace; with such penetrating meaning, *soft* enough, but irresistible, going down to the depths and up to the heights, as *silent electricity* goes."[67] Other readers liked it, too, both British and American. Emerson noted in his Journal on March 15, 1870: "My new book sells faster, it appears, than either of its foregoers." However, he did not assume that it was necessarily selling on its merits, but on the fact that "Old age is a good advertisement. Your name has been seen so often that your book must be worth buying."[68]

When Emerson gave his first Harvard lecture, on April 26, 1870, he was faced immediately by an insuperable paradox: believing, as he did, that the human mind is a projection or emanation of an all-pervading supernatural Mind, how could it be *natural* or have a *history?* In "Song of Nature" the "I" personifies this Mind:

> Mine are the night and morning,
> The pits of air, the gulf of space,
> The sportive sun, the gibbous moon,
> The innumerable days.[69]

Emerson's concept of "nature," as observed in Chapter XIII, like Carlyle's in *Sartor Resartus,* is not natural but supernatural. How, then, could there be a "natural history" (either natural or historical) of something timeless and infinite? Still believing, as he had long ago in *Nature,* that every natural fact has its exact counterpart in the spiritual world, Emerson hoped to anatomize intellect by finding in this realm parallels to the "laws of nature."[70] But of course the physical scientists had been successful precisely because they confined themselves to the material or external world, to phenomena which could be measured and weighed. They might speculate on the subjective world, and even hold "over-beliefs" about it, but these formed no part of their *science.* There can be a science of the brain, or even of psychology (mental behavior) and sociology (social behavior). But *mind* has always baffled the scientists, and some have even denied its existence. Parapsychology is still playing elementary games with cards and other simple devices to prove a statistical possibility of thought-transference.

Emerson was well aware of the difficulties in his proposal, and knew he could not use the "systematic form" of the scientists. In fact, he had always distrusted systems, logic, and metaphysics. He distrusted metaphysics because, he thought, philosophers too often divorced their abstractions from actual experience. One of the paradoxes in Emerson's Idealism is that he grounds it on empiricism: "Metaphysics must be perpetually reinforced by life; must be the observations of a working man on working men; must be biography,—the record of some law whose working was surprised by the observer in natural action."[71]

Though introspection would appear to be subjective, and therefore suspect by natural scientists, it is also experience (empirical), and by introspection of his own consciousness Emerson anticipated some of the insights into the subconscious of Charcot, Janet, William James, and even of Freud—though he had more in common with Jung than with Freud. In Chapter XV (section III) Emerson's anticipation of James's "stream-of-consciousness" was mentioned. James may even have borrowed this metaphor from Emerson.

Less useful, but no less thought-provoking, is Emerson's statement (also previously quoted) that "Consciousness is but a taper in the great night; but the taper at which all the illumination of human arts and sciences are kindled."[72] This is another example showing that Emerson's contribution to this subject was as a poet. He was a master of metaphor, but not, as he had always admitted, an analytical thinker. He even defines the intellectual man as one who "can make an object of every sensation, perception and intuition."[73] If he confuses analogy with law, it is because he thinks and feels in tropes; and his tropes are ultimately analogies for something which he feels is deeper in nature than the conscious mind fully understands. "The poet works to an end above his will, and by means, too, which are out of his will. . . . The Muse may be defined, *Supervoluntary ends effected by supervoluntary means.*" There are no rules for writing a poem, and labor cannot produce one. "It is miraculous at all points."[74]

So it is also with Emerson's "powers and laws of thought." *Memory,* for instance, is a mysterious power "that binds the conscious life together," but it has its vagaries and interruptions as if it had a personality all its own:

> One sometimes asks himself, Is it possible that it is only a visitor, not a resident? Is it some old aunt who goes in and out of the house, and occasionally recites anecdotes of old times and persons which I recognize as having heard before, and she being gone again I search in vain for any trace of the anecdotes?[75]

The conclusion to Emerson's ramblings (and here that epithet, often applied to his lectures and essays, is deserved) on the "Natural History of the Intellect" is: "Keep the intellect sacred. . . . Go sit with the hermit in you, who knows more than you do." This advice is familiar. In the sermons he preached to his Boston congregation in the Second Church, he had advised his parishioners to listen to the voice within their own breasts. And he was consistent in making the "intellect" unconscious ("the hermit in you"), and the conscious self an unsafe teacher.

Shall we say, then, that Emerson as a thinker was a mystic and a poet, no philosopher? Most critics do say this, but it depends on what one means by "philosopher." George Santayana, himself both a poet and a philosopher, wrote of Emerson:

> His heart was fixed on eternal things, and he was in no sense a prophet for his age or country. He belonged by nature to that mystical company of devout souls that recognize no particular home and are dispersed throughout history, although not without intercommunication. He felt his affinity to the Hindus and the Persians, to the Platonists and the Stoics. Like them he remains "a friend and aider of those who would live in the spirit." If not a star of the first magnitude, he is certainly a fixed star in the firmament of philosophy. Alone as yet [1900] among Americans, he may be

said to have won a place there, if not by the originality of his thought, at least by the originality and beauty of the expression he gave to thoughts that are old and imperishable.[76]

On the first centennial of Emerson's birth William James gave an address in Concord which revealed his deep affection for this elusive friend of his father's (elusive in his father's estimation). James, the philosopher of Pragmatism, Pluralism, and Radical Empiricism, appreciated individual facts as much as Emerson did. The author of classic essays on "The Sentiment of Rationality," "The Will to Believe," and a monumental treatise on *Varieties of Religious Experience,* called Emerson a "seer":

> For Emerson the individual fact and moment were indeed suffused with absolute radiance, but it was upon a condition that saved the situation—they must be worthy specimens,—sincere, authentic, archetypal; they must have made connection with what he calls the Moral Sentiment, they must in some way act as symbolic mouthpieces of the Universe's meaning. To know just which thing does act in this way, and which thing fails to make the true connection, is the secret (somewhat incommunicable, it must be confessed) of seership, and doubtless we must not expect of the seer too rigorous a consistency. Emerson himself was a real seer. He could perceive the full squalor of the individual fact, but he could also see the transfiguration. . . . His life was one long conversation with the invisible divine, expressing itself through individuals and particulars: "So nigh is grandeur to our dust, so near is God to man!"[77]

John Dewey, another Pragmatist, but in many ways quite different from James, wrote in 1929: "It is said that Emerson is not a philosopher. I find this denegation false or true according as it is said in blame or praise—according to the reasons proffered." The critic who dismisses Emerson as only a writer of maxims and proverbs is himself unable to follow "a logic that is finely wrought," such as Emerson explained: "We want in every man a logic; we cannot pardon the absence of it, but it must not be spoken. Logic is the procession or proportionate unfolding of the intuition; but its virtue is as silent method; the moment it would appear as propositions and have separate value, it is worthless."[78]

Dewey says he is not acquainted with any writer "whose movement of thought is more compact and unified, nor one who combines more adequately diversity of intellectual attack with concentration of form and effect." This may resemble poetry more than it resembles what is usually called philosophy; but then, Dewey says, it is petty to raise fences between poet and philosopher. "Emerson is not only a philosopher, but . . . the Philosopher of Democracy," and Dewey predicts that this fact will be recognized in the twentieth century:

> One century bears but a slender ratio to twenty-five; it is not safe to predict. But at least, thinking of Emerson as the one citizen of the New World fit to have his name uttered in the same breath with that of Plato, one may without presumption believe that even if Emerson has no system, none the less he is the prophet and herald of any system which democracy may henceforth construct and hold by, and that when democracy has articulated itself, it will have no difficulty in finding itself already proposed in Emerson.[79]

Dewey was speaking of Emerson's writings as a whole. He did not specifically mention "Natural History of the Intellect," which is difficult to call anything but a failure. It has some excellent paragraphs, but they were largely salvaged from previous lectures and essays—the thought if not the exact words. It was a failure not only because Emerson had set himself an unattainable goal but also because his memory was failing. Months before he began reading these lectures at Harvard in April 1870, he had struggled to organize his papers to construct a coherent discourse; the task was beyond his powers. After the first lecture he almost despaired of continuing, but rallied his courage and went on bravely.

To make his undertaking more difficult, Emerson was greatly occupied with university affairs, attending committee meetings, and trying to raise money from his college class for the construction of Memorial Hall, to be dedicated to Harvard men who had lost their lives in the war. Carlyle about this time offered to donate to Harvard the library he had accumulated in writing his biographies of Cromwell and Frederick the Great, and Emerson was the go-between. He consulted officials until the gift was accepted and formally acknowledged. These activities and reading lectures three times a week were extremely exhausting for a man of his age. There were sixteen lectures in the course, for which Harvard paid him the pittance of $8.75 per lecture. With delight and relief, Emerson wrote Carlyle on June 17: "Well, it is now ended, and has no shining side but this one, that materials are collected and a possibility shown me how a repetition of the course next year—which is appointed—will enable me partly out of these materials, and partly by large rejection of these, and by large addition to them, to construct a fair report of what I have read and thought on the subject."[80]

But the repetition of the course, with changes, in the spring of 1871 was even less of a success. By the time he had read the fourteenth lecture, Emerson was overcome with fatigue and decided to end the course abruptly. His family and John Forbes were greatly worried about his health, and Mr. Forbes proposed that Emerson join him on a six-week trip to California for relaxation and relief from his exhausting committee meetings. Emerson eagerly accepted.

CHAPTER XXVIII

Beneath the Ice

Over the winter glaciers,
  I see the summer glow,
And through the wild-piled snow-drift
  The warm rosebuds below.[1]

I

Few men in America had traveled more on railroads than Waldo Emerson, but he had never before ridden in a private car. When John Forbes's party to California assembled in Chicago on April 14, 1871, having arrived in small groups from Boston, they boarded a private car, the *Huron,* which Mr. Forbes had leased from George Pullman. Mr. Pullman himself had stocked the car with food for the trip and was on hand to greet the travelers. He assured Emerson that the *Huron* was so well constructed that it "would bear being rolled over and over," though he could not guarantee what would happen if it left the track in the Sierra Nevadas, where the drop would be hundreds of feet straight down. Submitting his bill of fare to Mr. Forbes, he said that "We could have as good a dinner as we could get at Parker's if we would only order it,—he would warrant *that.*"[2]

The passengers were Mr. and Mrs. John Forbes, their daughter Alice, Mrs. George Russell (a Boston friend), Will and Edith, Emerson, James B. Thayer (husband of one of Emerson's Uncle Samuel Ripley's daughters, and a recent Law School graduate of Harvard), and finally Garth Wilkinson James (one of the younger sons of Henry James), who had been badly wounded in the recent war. Thayer was historian of the trip and would publish *A Western Journey with Mr. Emerson* in 1884.

Emerson himself kept no record of the trip, though he jotted down in his Journal a few items from memory after his return. From the comments of others it is obvious that the journey rejuvenated him. He took along a few books to avoid boredom, and prudently, a batch of lecture manuscripts just in case he might have invitations to read them, but he scarcely looked at them during the trip out. In his purple satchel he also carried manuscript sheets of *Parnassus,* the anthology of his favorite poems on which he and Edith had been collaborating. The journey was so exhilarating for him that he talked all day long and sometimes into the night. His memory had improved, and he took keen interest in everything he saw and people he met at the stops along the way.

At Council Bluffs the Pullman car was switched onto a sidetrack for Saturday night. Next morning Emerson and Thayer, both early risers, explored the town in the Sunday-morning sunshine before breakfast, which was usually delayed to accommodate the late sleepers. After breakfast the *Huron* was ferried across the Missouri River. A bridge was being built, but was still far from completed. After leaving Omaha with their Pullman coupled to a Union Pacific train, they found the prairie uninteresting: "this poor, flat, worn-out common,"[3] Emerson called it. But when they started to climb the Rocky Mountains, they began to see wildlife and trees. A few years earlier they would have seen herds of buffalo on the plains, but on the whole trip they saw only one, and it was in captivity. At Ogden, Utah, the *Huron* was separated from the Union Pacific train and was pulled by another engine for a side trip to Salt Lake City.

It was late afternoon when the party arrived there. Someone came through the car distributing bills announcing a melodrama in the theater that night, and seven of the party, including Emerson, decided to see *Marriage by Moonlight; or the Wild Cat's Revenge.* The bill boasted that "a real pile-driver" would be on the stage. In the performance, ruffians captured the hero while he was drunk, and placed his head under the hammer of the pile driver, but as the weight descended, the heroine, called "Wild Cat," sprang forth and rescued him. What Emerson thought of this dramatic amusement is not on record.[4]

Next morning Emerson liked the tree-lined streets, with little streams of water gurgling beside them. The countryside was completely barren of trees, but the Mormons had planted them in their town and piped water down from the mountains to create a flourishing oasis. Emerson admired their industry and ingenuity. In the afternoon the men of the party joined him in calling on Brigham Young; the women refused to go. They found

Young with cloak on and hat in hand, ready for a journey in his carriage, but he received them briefly and talked with them. Thayer thought he looked like a stout stage driver, clean-shaven except for reddish chin-whiskers touched with gray. "His mouth was close, his nose somewhat aquiline, his eye quiet but cunning, his manner good, and steady."[5] Emerson asked him if any books gave a truthful impression of his opinions. He said "none," but when his secretary mentioned *Answers to Questions,* he admitted that was as good as any. "He gave no sign of knowing who Mr. Emerson was; but the secretary soon turned to one of us, and with a motion toward Mr. Emerson, inquired, in a public way: 'Is this the justly celebrated Ralph Waldo Emerson?' and then to Mr. Emerson: 'I have read a great many of your books.' We were then desired to enter our names in a register, and so took our leave."[6]

That afternoon the *Huron* returned to Ogden and then began the remaining nine hundred miles to San Francisco. The talk kept reverting to the Mormons. Someone said they impressed simple people by their imaginative use of the Bible. "Yes," replied Emerson, "it is an after-clap of Puritanism. But one would think that after this Father Abraham could go no further."[7]

Carlyle was also greatly interested in Brigham Young, and he had asked Emerson to write him immediately on his return if he had seen him. Emerson would report from Concord that they had paid him a visit and that Young had "received us with quiet uncommitting courtesy . . . Our interview was peaceable enough, and rather mended my impression of the man; and, after our visit, I read in the Deseret newspaper his Speech to his people on the previous Sunday. It avoided religion, but was full of Franklinian good sense."[8]

In the same letter to Carlyle, Emerson expressed his delight with California. Some of the mountains reached the altitude of Mont Blanc, and the state in its six hundred miles of latitude produced not only apples, pears, and peaches, but in addition figs, oranges, and bananas. "But the climate chiefly surprised me. The Almanac said April; but the day said June;—and day after day for six weeks uninterrupted sunshine." Everywhere the countryside was covered with flowers, most of them unknown to Emerson outside greenhouses. The birds were familiar, but with brighter plumage. On the plains, before reaching San Francisco, he had seen antelope, elk, jackrabbits, gophers, and even a pair of wolves. Yet in one letter to Lidian he wrote: "There is an awe & terror lying over this new garden—all empty as yet of any adequate people, yet with this assured future in American hands,—unequalled in climate & production . . . I should think no young man would come back from it."[9]

On their arrival in San Francisco, Friday, April 21, Mr. Forbes took his guests to the Occidental Hotel. Next morning Dr. Horatio Stebbins, pastor of the Unitarian church, called at the hotel to invite Emerson to speak in his church Sunday evening. He accepted and read his lecture on "Immortality." Though no public announcement was made until the day of the lecture, *The Evening Bulletin* reported next day that the audience was large. Three days later Emerson read "Society in America"; on April 29, "Resources"; and on May 1, "Greatness."[10] For the four lectures he received five hundred dollars. After returning from an excursion, he read a fifth lecture on "Chivalry"; and in Oakland on May 18, a lecture on "Hospitality" (reported as "Homes and How to Make Them Happy"). In a letter to Lidian and Ellen, he called Oakland "the Brooklyn of San Fr." He was as happy as the proverbial busman.

Emerson's trip to the Yosemite Valley was a real safari: half a day on the train, two in a covered wagon drawn by four horses, then two and a half days on horseback to the deep forest—and of course the return in reverse order. At Mirror Lake, which reflected Half Dome, the great mountain beside it, Emerson said, "This valley is the only place that comes up to the brag about it."[11] Nevada Falls reminded him of the flight of horses in William Hunt's painting *The Queen of Night.* On Sunday as they rode back, Emerson said, "This we must call *the Lord's day:* we seldom read such leaves in the Bible."[12]

While still in the Yosemite Valley, Emerson received an enthusiastic letter from a young man of thirty-three who was working at a sawmill in the valley. He was John Muir, later to become famous for his nature writings, but then unknown. He had graduated from the University of Wisconsin and had shown great ingenuity in mechanical inventions; but he wanted to live close to nature and he had found his ideal place in California. Emerson rode his piebald mustang over to the sawmill to meet Muir, was charmed, and invited him to join a horseback party next day in exploring the famous Mariposa Grove of sequoias. Muir was already an expert on the big trees and was delighted to accept the invitation. After they had seen the forest, Muir urged Emerson to camp there with him and get to know the trees better, but he declined. Muir remained behind, and later wrote Emerson that he had slept that night in the bark of a fallen sequoia.

The inn at which Emerson's party stopped on the way back from the forest was operated by Galen Clarke, "a solid, sensible man from New Hampshire," whom the state had appointed keeper of the big trees.[13] He asked Emerson to choose a tree to be labeled in memory of his visit. He chose a medium-sized sequoia, which would continue to grow for centuries, and named it Samoset, for the Plymouth sachem who had befriended the Pilgrims. Mr. Clarke promised to have a nameplate made and placed on the tree.

Later, on a thirty-mile horseback ride, one of the younger members of the party asked Thayer, "How *can* Mr. Emerson be so agreeable, all the time, without getting tired!" Thayer's only explanation was that Emerson seemed to believe in an immortal life so strongly that he had adjusted his conduct accordingly.[14] A simpler explanation would be that he had thrown off his worries (though before returning home he would learn that Edward was ill). He was amiable by nature, had resigned himself to his infirmities, and resolved not to let them affect his disposition.

On May 15 Emerson and his friends returned to San Francisco. In the remaining days there, they explored Chinatown and attended—or Emerson and Thayer did—a notorious theater, said to be the favorite of the miners, "the lowest thing in the city." Probably it was some kind of burlesque theater. Emerson and Thayer found it "flat and dreary."[15]

On the nineteenth Emerson and most of the Forbes party started east by way of Lake Tahoe. After spending a day there, they were picked up by the *Huron*. When Emerson reached Concord on May 30, he received a rude shock. Edward's illness had been diagnosed by Dr. Bartlett as a varioloid infection and the house had been quarantined. Emerson could talk to his wife, son, and daughter only from the yard. Cousin Elizabeth Ripley solved his immediate problem of where to live by offering to board him at the Manse until the quarantine was lifted.[16]

As soon as it was, Ellen and Lidian went visiting and Edward went to Edith's home to recuperate. There he developed an abscess which had to be lanced, but after that minor operation he gained strength rapidly. Meanwhile his father continued to take his meals at the Manse and work in his study at home. Before leaving, Lidian had locked his bedroom door and hidden the key, but he managed to pick the lock. By September Edward had recovered sufficiently to go to England, on his way to Berlin, where he planned to study medicine.

John Muir would not let Emerson forget California. He wrote begging him to return for a longer exploration of the Yosemite Valley. He said he "would willingly walk all the way to your Concord if so I could have you for a companion."[17] Emerson's favorable opinion of Muir is indicated in a list which he compiled of *"My Men,"*[18] containing eighteen names, beginning with Carlyle and ending with John Muir. But in October it was another Californian, Bret Harte, who visited Concord. At dinner he challenged Emerson's statement in *Society and Solitude*: " 'T is wonderful how soon a piano gets into a log hut on the frontier,"[19] to be followed by a Latin grammar and other civilizing influences. Harte said, "It is the gamblers who bring in the music to California. It is the prostitute who brings in the New York fashions of dress there, and so throughout." Emerson replied that he spoke "from Pilgrim experience, and knew on good grounds the resistless culture that religion effects."[20] Harte was not persuaded.

Then Mrs. Emerson said, "Mr. Harte I wanted to ask you if you have really witnessed the instances of disinterested feelings which you describe, in rough people, or rather whether you knew that such have been by personal experience?" (Less politely, and more colloquially: Were his kindhearted whores and honest gamblers only figments of his imagination?) Of course Harte insisted that they were real or he would not have put them in his stories, but Edith found his answer unsatisfactory and Ellen thought he had "created his tales out of the whole cloth."[21]

Surprisingly, Lidian was not as unpleasant to Bret Harte as she could be to others. John Weiss, a Unitarian minister of the region, had dined in Boston with Emerson a few years earlier, and recorded in his Journal afterward: "Mrs. Emerson, who is styled good-naturedly by her husband as the last survivor of the Nicene Council — gave us a good deal of her Bibliolatry. That he can live with her is either the seal of approval or of condemnation upon his philosophy."[22] Possibly she thought Harte was beyond redemption—as she had decided her husband was.

II

Though Emerson had fully intended not to make another lecture trip to the Midwest, the great Chicago fire of October 8, 1871, made him change his mind. He had the same consuming curiosity to see the damage that he had had in 1848 to witness the expected revolution in France. Not lacking for invitations, he went out to Chicago and read "Nature and Art" there on November 27. In mid-December he recorded in his Journal: "Home again from Chicago, Quincy, Springfield, and Dubuque, which I had not believed I should see again, yet found it easier to visit than before, and the kindest reception in each city."[23]

In January 1872 Emerson gave four lectures at the Peabody Institute in Baltimore for four hundred dollars. He read "Poetry and Imagination" and other lectures in his repertoire. He also made two appearances in Washington, where Senator Sumner entertained him and took him on a round of visits to government officials. John Burroughs heard of a scheduled lecture in Baltimore and went over to hear it, taking along Walt Whitman. They had a short talk with Emerson before he began reading, but were disappointed in the lecture.

Later, in Washington, Burroughs happened to meet Emerson at the railway station just as he was about to board a train for Baltimore. As Burroughs recalled the brief talk: "He thought Walt's friends ought to quarrel a little more with him, and insist on his being a little more tame and orderly—more mindful of the requirements of beauty, of art, of culture, etc."[24] Burroughs was surprised and a little disgusted, but the train started before he could complain to Emerson. Whitman was also disappointed in the lecture Emerson gave in Washington on "Homes and Hospitality" from his ancient manuscript. In writing a few days later to Edward Dowden, the Irish Shakespeare critic, he said: "He draws on the same themes as twenty-five years ago."[25] Whitman compared this to the fourth infusion of tea from the same leaves.

Though Emerson had nothing new to say, his influence had continued to grow. Asked to address the students of Howard University, Emerson chose to talk to them about books, and praised especially George Herbert's *Poems*. The students said their library did not have a copy, and he promised to send them one as soon as he returned to Boston. Meanwhile his talk was reported in the newspapers, and when he tried to find a copy of the book in Boston, he was told, "Since your speech was published, there has been such a demand [for Herbert's *Poems*] that they are sold out, and none left in Boston."[26] (Later he found a copy for the students.)

In April, Emerson was persuaded to give another series of readings in Boston from his favorite poets, with short discussions of the selections. These performances were even better attended than his readings in 1869, a peak year. However, his memory had still further deteriorated, and once he read a poem which he had forgotten he had read five minutes before. Ellen, who now regularly accompanied him, was alarmed and begged him to let her help keep the pages in order, but he calmly replied: "Things that go wrong about these lectures don't disturb me, because I know that everyone knows that I am worn out and passed by, and that it is only my old friends come for friendship's sake to have one last season with me."[27]

On his sixty-ninth birthday (May 25, 1872) Emerson happened to find himself, after a round of errands, on Summer Street in Boston. Where Nathaniel Goddard's pasture had been, with its long wooden fence, now stood a block of granite buildings. He thought of his Aunt Mary, who had known everyone of importance in Boston. From her he had learned their histories: "It is now nearly a hundred years since she was born, and the founders of the oldest families that are still notable were known to her as retail-merchants, milliners, tailors, distillers, as well as the ministers, lawyers, and doctors of the time."[28] He remembered his aunt as a realist, who knew "a great man or 'a whale-hearted woman' ... from a successful money-maker." These memories prompted Emerson to write in his Journal: "If I live another year, I think I shall cite still the last stanza of my own poem, 'The World-Soul.'" It reads:

> Spring still makes spring in the mind
> When sixty years are told;
> Love wakes anew this throbbing heart,
> And we are never old.
> Over the winter glaciers
> I see the summer glow,
> And through the wild-piled snowdrift
> The warm rosebuds below.[29]

Early in July Emerson read two lectures ("Character" and "Greatness") at Amherst College. Ellen was with him, and they were well entertained at the president's house. It seemed that he could continue this sort of life indefinitely. But soon after his return home, disaster came without warning. As on other occasions of extreme emotional stress, such as the death of Ellen and of Waldo Jr., Emerson's entry in his Journal was laconic: "Wednesday, July 24 / House burned."[30]

Around five-thirty that Wednesday morning Emerson was awakened by the crackling sound of fire in the wall of his bedroom, and he could see flames where the fire had already eaten through. He jumped out of bed, ran downstairs and out into a pouring rain to his front gate in his nightgown, shouting as loudly as he could for help. Almost immediately neighbors came running to his aid, and in a few minutes the Concord fire department arrived. The fire had started in the attic—set, some members of the family believed, by an overturned kerosene lamp carried by a prowling Irish maid employed the day before.[31]

Neighbors managed to save most of the furniture and other valuables. After Emerson's study was already filled with black smoke, boys ran in and, by holding their breath, saved his books and manuscripts; only a few pages of Aunt Mary's diaries got scorched around the edges. Ellen was away visiting friends, and Edward was in England. Edith and her husband had just left him in London and were on their way back to America; even John Forbes was on his yacht, returning home from the Azores. Thus, only Waldo, Lidian, and the servants were at home.

By eight-thirty the firemen and the rain, which had continued, had finally extinguished the fire, leaving the walls standing without a roof for the main part of the house. Several neighbors offered to take the Emersons in, but they accepted Elizabeth Ripley's urgent invitation to stay with her in the Manse.

As soon as Emerson's Harvard classmate Francis Cabot Lowell, a wealthy manufacturer, heard of the disaster, he came to offer the use of his large home in Waltham, but Lidian and Waldo preferred to remain in the Manse. Another friend, Dr. Le Baron Russell, formerly of Plymouth, but now a prosperous physician in Boston, had been considering establishing a fund to relieve Emerson from having to lecture for a living. He consulted mutual friends and quickly raised a purse of twelve thousand dollars, which he conveyed anonymously through Judge Hoar. At first Emerson wanted to reject this aid, but the judge convinced him that he would disappoint his friends if he did not accept their gift.[32] Meanwhile his library had been housed in the Court House, which was not at that time being used by the county, and in a few days Emerson began trying to sort out his books and papers. Friends remarked on how well he had borne the shock of the fire.

But the effect of the shock was merely delayed. About two weeks later Emerson became ill, with a low fever, a cough, and extreme fatigue. His family thought a few days at Rye Beach might help him, and he went there with Ellen; then they visited relatives at Waterford, Maine, where Aunt Mary had lived.[33] But Emerson's exhaustion and depression continued. He began feeling that he did not have long to live, and worried about his manuscripts. Edward was not a scholar and had his own career in medicine to think of. Either James Elliot Cabot or Dr. Frederic Hedge would be the ideal literary editor, but Emerson did not want either of them to neglect his own work for him.

One reason for these worries was that Emerson had promised a British publisher, John Camden Hotten, that he would edit a volume of his uncollected writings. He had made the promise mainly to divert Hotten from pirating some of his early essays, and Hotten had promised to desist if Emerson would edit the book for him. But now Emerson found sustained mental effort impossible. This problem of the edition would not be solved until two years later, when Emerson's family persuaded him to mention the idea to Mr. Cabot. To Emerson's surprise, Cabot said he would be delighted to accept the assignment. It was Cabot, therefore, who put together *Letters and Social Aims,* which contains the two valuable essays on "Poetry and Imagination" and "Persian Poetry." Meanwhile Hotten had died, and the book was published by Osgood in Boston, 1876.

After his return from the Azores, John Forbes urged Emerson, Lidian, and Ellen to join him on Naushon Island, which they did in September. There Emerson was persuaded to take a long trip while his home was being repaired under the supervision of friends. Having long been curious about Egypt, he thought he would like to go there. Doubtless, both John and Will Forbes saw to it that he had ample funds for the trip, and he now more readily accepted help. Ellen was to accompany him; Lidian was in no condition to travel, she thought, and preferred to stay with Edith.

III

While waiting in New York for the steamship *Wyoming* to sail on Wednesday, October 23, Emerson attended a dinner for James Anthony Froude and attempted to speak in his praise, but was embarrassed because he could not remember the words he wanted to say. However, he quickly forgot the incident in the excitement of sailing out into the ocean and encountering a storm on the second day. Ellen was seasick, but he was not. Ocean travel had always been good for his health, and this trip seemed auspicious. But Ellen was his only congenial companion, for the ship was loaded with missionaries of several denominations, most of them going to India. In his shipboard letter to Lidian, Emerson said that on Sunday he heard two sermons and many hymns, "But the liberal ocean sings louder, & makes us all of one church."[34]

Edward, having returned from Berlin, met his father and sister at Liverpool on November 3. Next day they visited historic Chester before proceeding to London.[35] On the fifth they breakfasted with the bishop of Chester, and Emerson was invited to attend a meeting of the Archaeological, Architectural and Historical Society that evening. There he was urged to second the thanks to the chairman "that we may have the opportunity of just hearing your voice." Emerson made a short speech so easily and coherently that his children felt much encouraged about his health.

In London, Emerson and Ellen took rooms at 17 Down Street, where James Russell Lowell had stayed before going to France. As soon as his presence was known, he received numerous invitations from old friends and new. Because Ellen was not invited, he declined "a great dinner" at the Inner Temple, where he would be seated "with the most learned men in England and the Queen of Holland at a small round table."[36] But he dined with American friends, Charles Eliot Norton, Moncure Conway, and William Henry Channing.

Of course Emerson promptly called on Carlyle and was received with a bear hug. For two or three hours Carlyle talked excitedly in his Scots accent. Ellen did not meet him until several days later because she had sprained her ankle and walked with great difficulty. When she met him at last, she could scarcely understand a word the burly Scotsman said. She wanted to see Canterbury, and Emerson consented to go when Edward left for America on November 13. Emerson was loath to leave London; he said he wanted to settle down in one spot and rest—just luxuriate in the feeling that there was nothing he had to do. Once in Canterbury, he suggested that they stay there. Ellen liked Canterbury, too, but she had left home to take her father to Egypt, and when she had a duty to perform, nothing could stop her.

In Paris, Lowell had reserved rooms for them at the Hôtel de Lorraine, where he and John Holmes, Dr. O. W. Holmes's restless brother, were living *en pension*. Ellen was elated to find that she could make herself understood in French. Her father was less successful, but the hotel was comfortable and he liked the people they met, who included several members of the Chamber of Deputies. Henry James Jr. called and took Emerson to the Louvre. Lowell also took him and Ellen sightseeing almost every day. The only disturbing experience they had was reading in *Le Figaro* of a great fire in Boston which had extended to sections that Emerson had known as a boy. Ellen wrote her mother that on Sunday her father actually enjoyed attending church at the Chapelle Évangélique de l'Étoile. Again Emerson suggested that they prolong their stay, but Ellen said they must move on.

Before leaving Paris, Emerson employed a Swiss traveling servant, Curnex,[37] to manage the trip to Egypt, and he proved to be thoroughly competent and reliable. They left Paris on November 21 and enjoyed the journey by train through southern France to Nice, where they took a steamer to Genoa. They docked there at night, too late for Emerson to pay his "respects to the memory of Columbus." Then they continued by another steamer to Leghorn, and by land to Florence, where they paused for three or four days. Emerson was content to visit the Uffizi gallery, but Ellen went sightseeing. He was delighted when she became as enamored of Santa Croce as he had been in 1833. At the time Florence was almost inundated by distinguished foreigners, but *La Nazione* noted that Emerson, "one of the most distinguished poets and philosophers of America," had stopped in Florence on his way to the Orient.

Neither Emerson nor Ellen could speak Italian with any facility, but on the train to Rome they combined their scant knowledge to concoct a sentence in Italian. Then Emerson carefully addressed it to a gentleman in the compartment, with such success that they were immediately overwhelmed with a flood of incomprehensible words. They had to apologize for their incompetence. In Rome, however, they had so many English-speaking friends that their linguistic deficiencies were no great handicap. Curnex engaged a pension for them in the Piazza di Spagna, where Emerson had stayed thirty-nine years earlier. Sam Ward had only recently left Rome for Egypt, but he had alerted his son-in-law, Baron von Hoffmann, to their arrival, and the baron gave them every assistance they needed or could possibly wish, including the hospitality of his Villa Celimontana. He took them sightseeing every day in his carriage. They also made British and American friends; Rome in those years was always full of Americans.

On December 18 Emerson and Ellen took a steamer to Naples, and three days later another, called the *Nil,* to Alexandria. Two days of the voyage were stormy, and the berths were constructed crosswise of the ship, so that every wave rolled their occupants back and forth. As a consequence Emerson and Ellen were weary when they finally reached Alexandria on Christmas Day. Without Curnex's able assistance they would have had great difficulty getting past the beggars, camels, donkeys, and aggressive hawkers of services to tourists.

The Emersons paused in Alexandria long enough to wade through the mud to Pompey's Pillar and Cleopatra's Needle.[38] Then they continued by boat through the delta country to Cairo, while Emerson lamented having left his beautiful America to see this dismal marsh. Ellen wrote her family that he kept up a stream of witty invective all the way to Cairo. He pretended to think groups of people standing on shore looking at the water were preparing to drown themselves. The weather was depressing, too, hazy, cool—fifty-eight degrees—and Emerson always preferred warm, sunny weather.

Cairo had some pleasant surprises for Emerson, and one disappointment: Sam Ward had left on a trip up the Nile. But George Bancroft, at that time American ambassador to Germany, was staying in the New Hotel, where the Emersons had rooms.[39] Bancroft took them to breakfast with the khedive, or viceroy, of Egypt, a title conferred on Ishmail Pasha by the sultan of Turkey. Bancroft also arranged for the founder of the Museum of Egypt, Auguste-Édouard Mariette, a famous Egyptologist, to show them its treasures. Mariette had excavated the tombs of Apis bulls and cleared debris from ancient temples and the great Sphinx. When a few days later Emerson and Ellen moved to Shepheard's Hotel, they found Charles Godfrey Leland, who was gathering material for his Egyptian sketchbook; also George Boker, a poet whom Emerson had met in Philadelphia. Boker was now American minister to Turkey and a close friend of the khedive's.

Ellen invited her new friends to celebrate New Year's with her, exchanging gifts and verses and observing the day by Concord, not Cairo, time.

For some weeks, travel to the Upper Nile had been banned because of an outbreak of cholera, but early in January 1873 the quarantine was lifted, and Ellen was eager to begin their trip. The Emersons, a family named Whitewell (father, mother, and two daughters), and a Miss Farquhar hired a dragoman and a dahabeah, the *Aurora,* to take them up the Nile, to Thebes, Luxor, perhaps as far as Aswân, just below the First Cataract.[40] The dahabeah would have, besides their dragoman, a captain and first mate, two cooks, a factotum boy, two waiters, and ten oarsmen, who would row when the lateen sail failed for lack of wind. The party left Cairo on January 7 in sixty-degree weather with overcast skies. The shores of the Nile were lined at intervals with palm trees, but in general the scenery was bleak and monotonous. Emerson was bored, and nearly all the passengers except Ellen were somnolent. After his return to Cairo, Emerson wrote in his Journal (one of the few times during the trip when he wrote anything):

> All this journey is a perpetual humiliation, satirizing and whipping our ignorance. The people despise us because we are helpless babies who cannot speak or understand a word they say; the sphinxes scorn dunces; the obelisks, the temple walls, defy us with their histories which we cannot spell. Every new object only makes new questions which each traveller asks of the other, and none of us can answer, and each sinks lower in the opinion of his companion. The people, whether in the boat, or out of it, are a perpetual study for the excellence and grace of their forms and motions. . . . Every group of the country people on the shores, as seen from our dahabeah, look like the ancient philosophers going to the School of Athens.[41]

The most enjoyable part of this Nile voyage for Emerson was the stops for passengers to go ashore and stretch their legs. He liked to rent a donkey and ride around with his long legs nearly touching the ground. He developed a real affection for donkeys. He also began to enjoy the trip more when he saw the ruins at Thebes, especially the great temple at Karnak. During an inspection of one of the tombs the party met Georg Ebers, a German Egyptologist, who explained some of the mysterious hieroglyphics to them. At Luxor the British consul competed with the American consul in serving Emerson's party. The British won by providing donkeys to take them to Philae. This was one of the places Emerson had said before leaving home that he wanted to see because he had read somewhere that the god Osiris was buried there. Of course he failed to find the tomb of the mythical Osiris, but Philae had beautiful gardens, in addition to the temples, palaces, and huge pylons. At Abydos the German Egyptologist told Emerson that Osiris had once been worshiped there.[42]

Emerson had hoped to catch up with Sam Ward at Aswân, but there he learned that Ward had continued on to the Second Cataract. At Aswân, though, Emerson met a British admirer, George L. Owen, who told him that he "had been his idol and his guide from his earliest youth." Then on the return to Luxor the Emersons met the Roosevelt family in their dahabeah. The Roosevelts invited them to lunch and sent their small private boat for them. In a letter to her family Ellen described the experience: "Almost before we were ready," she said, "the pretty little light boat the Roosevelt children used was waiting alongside, and we were rowed over to the Abou Erdan, by Theodore whose round red cheeks, honest blue eyes, and perfectly brilliant teeth make him a handsome boy, though plain."[43] Though Theodore was accompanied by two sailors, he assisted them by rowing himself with sculling oars. The Emersons were much taken with the whole Roosevelt family, but especially with the exuberant children.

On the return trip down the Nile, the party finally abandoned the dahabeah and took a train to Cairo to avoid missing the steamer from Alexandria to Naples. A storm delayed its sailing for several days, but they finally left Alexandria on February 19. Emerson's health had improved, and he told Ellen that Egypt had been exactly what he had needed. He had especially enjoyed the freedom from responsibilities—no books to write, no lectures to prepare, or even letters to write, though he did send two or three. He might have added that Ellen made all decisions for him. Though most of the passengers on the voyage were seasick at times, they were a congenial lot. They were well aware that they had a famous companion and asked him to read poems to them. He had brought the *Parnassus* (or at least part of it), and he read aloud some of his favorite poems, as he did again in Rome a few days later. One of the poems he read in Rome was Henry Timrod's "Ode" on the graves of the Confederate dead.[44] Time was healing the wounds of that terrible war.

In Rome the Emersons were again lavishly entertained for two weeks.

Henry James Jr., Sarah Clarke, and Elizabeth Hoar were now in Rome, as well as many other American and British friends. Emerson felt no urge to hasten home, but the methodical Ellen insisted on leaving March 10. They stopped again briefly in Florence, where Emerson met Herman Grimm, a German critic and art historian, with whom he had corresponded but whom he had never seen. Grimm had long been one of Emerson's great admirers, and he delighted Ellen by telling her that he had expected her father to look like a man of seventy (which he was) instead of a man of fifty.

Back in Paris by March 15, Emerson and Ellen were again charmed by the city and the people. They attended the theater, visited the Louvre, with Emerson acting as guide this time, and dined with Mme. and M. Auguste Laugel, in whose home they met Taine and Turgenev. Finding that Emerson had not read the last volume of his *Histoire de la Littérature Anglaise*, Taine next day sent an inscribed copy to his hotel.[45]

On April 5 Ellen and her father were back in London, and the social madness started all over again.[46] Emerson began once more to suffer lapses of memory, which he had not had in Egypt or on the Continent. They were overwhelmed with invitations, and Emerson had to decline many. But he breakfasted with Gladstone, lunched with Lord Russell, and visited with Thomas Huxley, John Tyndall, James Anthony Froude, the Duke of Bedford, and others. Moncure Conway wanted to give a banquet for him, but he begged off. Professor Max Müller, the great philologist and authority on comparative religion, induced the vice-chancellor of Oxford to invite him to give two lectures, but Emerson wisely declined, though he did accept Max Müller's invitation to visit him at Oxford. There he and Ellen met John Ruskin; Professor Benjamin Jowett, the Greek scholar; and the eccentric mathematics professor Charles Dodgson (Lewis Carroll), author of *Alice in Wonderland*.[47] Emerson heard Ruskin lecture and had a long conversation with him in his home. He did not like Ruskin's gloomy view of the nineteenth century and modern civilization. He seemed as morbid as Carlyle.

In Chepstow, Emerson and Ellen were the guests of Lord and Lady Amberley, who showed them Tintern Abbey, made famous by Wordsworth. At Warwick Edward Flower met them and took them to Stratford-upon-Avon, as he had taken Emerson in 1848.[48] On a hasty visit to Edinburgh Emerson also renewed friendship with several people who had been kind to him on his lecture tour twenty-five years before. Of course on returning to London for the last time he called again on Carlyle, now all alone in his big house. Both realized that they would not see each other again, but they knew their friendship would endure.

On the way to Liverpool Emerson stayed two days with the friend who had made his former visit to England possible, Alexander Ireland. Then on May 15 Emerson and Ellen sailed from Liverpool on the Cunard liner *Olympus*.[49] Charles Eliot Norton was returning on the same ship, and Emerson needed no other companion for the voyage. Norton kept a record of his friend's conversation, and on his seventieth birthday (May 25) presented him with a poem, which began, "Blest of the higher gods are they who die / Ere youth is fled," and ended, "And, thou, though full of days, shalt die in youth." Next day, near sunset, they saw the Boston shore. In spite of the recent disastrous fire, extending as far as Emerson's birthplace, it looked beautiful to the travelers on shipboard.

Edith and Will Forbes met them at the gangplank. Edith had been instructed to delay their return to Concord until afternoon so that preparations could be completed for a homecoming welcome. Emerson did not mind the delay, though completely unaware of its cause. He could always find business in Boston to attend to, and friends to see. Someone, probably Will, telegraphed Concord that they would arrive on the three thirty train, and someone in Concord, probably Judge Hoar, telegraphed the president of the railroad to instruct the engineer to blow his whistle from Walden woods to the station.[50]

When the train pulled in with whistle screaming, Emerson was surprised to see a crowd as large as had gathered for the departure of the soldiers for the war.[51] He asked if it was a holiday, and could not understand that they were celebrating his return. As he alighted from the train, a brass band played "Home, Sweet Home." He scarcely had time to embrace Lidian before they were both swept into John Forbes's open barouche. Ellen was guided to a second carriage in which Mr. Alcott, his daughter Louisa, and Judge and Mrs. Rockwood Hoar were waiting. Then carriages and people on foot paraded down Main Street, turned into the Cambridge Turnpike, and stopped at a hugh floral arch over Emerson's front gate. Construction of this decoration had been one of the reasons for the requested delay to an afternoon train. Emerson and Lidian then walked from the gate to their front door between rows of schoolchildren singing welcoming songs. In a few minutes Emerson came back to the gate to thank his neighbors "for this trick of sympathy to catch an old gentleman returned from his wanderings." The crowd gave three cheers.[52]

Inside the house Emerson found everything restored just as it had been before the fire. Even his books and manuscripts were in their accustomed places in his study. Lidian thought she had never seen a happier man. That evening Alcott returned with a copy of his *Concord Days,* bound in leather, which he presented to Emerson as a delayed birthday gift.

IV

After his return from Egypt, Emerson made no attempt to resume lecturing, though he responded to requests for his appearance on special occasions, such as the dedication of the Concord Public Library in 1873, or the centennial anniversary of the Boston Tea Party in Faneuil Hall the same year, when he read his poem on "Boston." He was the principal speaker at the unveiling of *The Minute Man,* mounted at Concord Bridge on April 17, 1875, the centennial of the "first shot" he had commemorated in his "Concord Hymn." A local sculptor, Daniel C. French, had cast the statue in bronze, and the town had made a great occasion of the dedication. Among the distinguished guests were President Grant and the governor of Massachusetts, with their escorting military regiments. James Elliot Cabot believed this was the last address (or lecture) Emerson ever wrote.[53] (It is not included in his *Works.*)

In the summer of 1873 Emerson received a copy of Max Müller's *Introduction to the Science of Religion,* dedicated to him in memory of his May visit, and in gratitude for twenty-five years of constant refreshment from his writings. In his letter of thanks (August 4), Emerson said he had been reading Max Müller's books for many years, but the essays in this volume were all new to him. If he had known they were being published in *Fraser's Magazine,* he would have read them as they came out.[54] However, in his Journal he admitted to some difficulty now in following Max Müller's deductions from his Oriental sources.[55]

In the spring of 1876 Emerson was pleased when he was invited by the joint literary societies of the University of Virginia to speak at commencement on June 28. He hoped the invitation signified the passing of Southern bitterness toward the North. After an exhausting journey, accompanied by Ellen, he arrived in very hot weather. Next day he read his lecture on "The National and Permanent Functions of the Scholar." But the audience was inattentive and noisy, and after half an hour Emerson found a concluding sentence and stopped. A Richmond newspaper printed an unfriendly report of the lecture,[56] indicating that sectional feeling was still very much alive. Emerson never complained of the treatment he had received; in fact, he said that the faculty had been most courteous, and some professors told him how much his books had meant to them. The following day on the train he was surprised by friendly greetings from Southerners who recognized him, introduced themselves, and expressed their admiration for him. They were on their way to the Philadelphia Centennial Exhibition.

Several years previously, in New York, Emerson had met a young poet named Emma Lazarus, whose life and verse interested him. She sent her poems to him for criticism, and he tried to advise and encourage her literary growth. In the summer of 1876 she wrote him an urgent invitation to visit her in New York, and he replied that an old man fears most his friends: "It is not them," he wrote, "that he is willing to distress with his perpetual forgetfulness of the right word for the name of book or fact or person he is eager to recall, but which refuses to come. I have grown silent to my own household under this vexation, & cannot afflict dear friends with my tied tongue."[57]

But sometimes Emerson could not remain in the seclusion of his home. The Boston Public Latin School, which he had attended, wanted him to participate in the celebration of the centennial anniversary of its reopening on November 8, 1776, when the British troops evacuated Boston. Emerson prepared a short speech, which began: "I dare not attempt to say anything to you, because in my old age I am forgetting the word I should speak. I cannot remember anybody's name; not even my recollections of the Latin School. I have therefore guarded against absolute silence by bringing you a few reminiscences which I have written."[58]

This condition gradually grew worse. Until the end of his second term on the Harvard Board of Overseers, Emerson continued to attend meetings regularly, to listen attentively, and to vote, but he seldom tried to say anything. Everyone understood and sympathized, and he never lost the ability to laugh at himself. If he could not say "chair," he called it "the thing you sit on." Sometimes his circumlocutions were witty, as when he could not recall the word "umbrella" and said, "I can't tell its name, but I can tell its history. Strangers take it away."[59] In 1878 he promised to read a lecture at the Concord Lyceum, but remarked of the prospect: "A queer occasion it will be,—a lecturer who has no idea of what he is lecturing about, and an audience who don't know what he *can* mean."[60]

When the Unitarian church in Concord, New Hampshire, planned to observe its fiftieth anniversary on September 30, 1879, Emerson, its first minister (temporary) was invited to attend. He went up on the twenty-ninth and did not remember until next morning that the evening before was the fiftieth anniversary of his marriage to Ellen Tucker. He immediately set out to find her house, and was confused when it was not where it had been. Then Ellen's stepbrother, Colonel Kent, told him it had been moved, and led him to it. Emerson took no part in the church's commemorative services except to read a hymn. He stumbled a little over some of the words, but his audience was pleased with the feeling he put into his reading.[61]

Emerson's last appearance before the Concord Lyceum was on February 4, 1880. The secretary had discovered that it was his one hundredth lecture to this society, and when he entered the room, everyone stood up to honor him. He managed to read, without much difficulty, an 1867 manuscript on "Historic Notes of Life and Letters in Massachusetts."[62] This was his next-to-last appearance before an audience. On February 10, 1881, in Boston, he read some paragraphs on "Carlyle" to the Massachusetts Historical Society, of which he was a member. Unable to write an address, he read a letter he had written Carlyle in 1848 and some passages from his Journals.[63]

A deeply concerned witness of Emerson's aphasia was Walt Whitman in September 1881. He had come to Boston to read proof on a new edition of *Leaves of Grass* to be published in the fall by James R. Osgood. Frank Sanborn had happened to meet him in Boston, and he invited the poet to be his houseguest in Concord over a weekend. Whitman had not been invited to Concord in 1860, when he was in Boston seeing his third edition through the press, because Mrs. Alcott, Mrs. Thoreau, and Mrs. Emerson all objected to having that scandalous man in their houses. But now, perhaps because Sanborn was his host, neither Mrs. Alcott nor Mrs. Emerson (Mrs. Thoreau had died) offered objections. There would later be a furor over the new edition, but that was not anticipated by his Concord friends.

On Saturday afternoon Sanborn brought Whitman on the train from Boston to his home on Main Street, and invited Mr. and Mrs. Emerson, Alcott and Alcott's daughter Louisa to meet his guest that evening. There was much talk about Margaret Fuller, Thoreau, Horace Greeley, and the younger William Ellery Channing, but Whitman was content to listen and observe his idol. After the guests had departed he wrote a memorandum of this "blessed evening with Emerson":

My seat and the relative arrangement were such that, without being rude, . . . I could just look squarely at E., which I did a good part of the two hours. On entering, he had spoken very briefly and politely to several of the company, then settled himself in his chair, a trifle push'd back, and, though a listener and apparently an alert one, remain'd silent through the whole talk and discussion. A lady friend [Louisa May Alcott] quietly took a seat next him, to give special attention. A good color in his face, eyes clear, with the well-known expression of sweetness, and the old clear-peering aspect quite the same.[64]

Mrs. Emerson's prejudices against Whitman had so completely disappeared that she invited him to dinner at her house next day. That dinner Whitman enjoyed as much as the evening before. He sat beside Mrs. Emerson and talked to her about Thoreau, to her great delight. Besides Mr. and Mrs. Sanborn, only the family was present: Ellen, Edward, and Edward's wife (he had married Annie Keyes in 1874). Again Whitman noticed in Emerson "a healthy color in the cheeks, and good light in the eyes, cheery expression, and just the amount of talking that best suited, namely, a word or short phrase only where needed, and almost always with a smile." Many of Emerson's friends had commented on the wonderful "lighting-up" of his face when he was pleased. In making the statue of him two years earlier, Daniel French had looked for that "glorifying expression," and thought he had finally caught it. (The statue may still be seen in the Concord Public Library.) But Emerson said, with his usual modesty, after one of the sittings, "The trouble is, the more it resembles me, the worse it looks."[65]

During the six months following Mrs. Emerson's dinner for Walt Whitman, Emerson continued to live quietly and apparently happily. He had begun to attend church once more, and this, of course, pleased his wife—and his daughters, too, for they were moderately orthodox. In 1880 a man named Joseph Cook had started a rumor that Emerson had recanted his radicalism and rejoined the Church. Emerson asked his son to refute the charge, and Edward wrote Mr. Cook a letter, which he also printed in *The Boston Index,* stating that "Ralph Waldo Emerson has not joined any church, nor has he retracted any views expressed in his writings after his withdrawal from the ministry."[66] He had continued to support the Free Religious Association, which met in Boston from time to time, and had spoken at several meetings. He believed that Christianity was the best of all religions, but he wanted free discussion of every variety of religious thinking.

Longfellow died on March 24, 1882, and Ellen took her father to the funeral in Cambridge. He had never been intimate with Longfellow and had reservations about his poetry, but he respected and liked his gentle personality. After returning to the coffin a second time to look at the corpse, Emerson asked Ellen, "Where are we? What house? And who is the sleeper?"[67] Moncure Conway, who was not present, was the source of the story that Emerson said, "That gentleman was a sweet, beautiful soul, but I have entirely forgotten his name." Though the words may not be accurate, they are similar in purport to Ellen's eyewitness report. She also recorded that in the evening her father had forgotten where they had been: "Father learned of Mr. Longfellow's death once more, and was very sad about it. The next day, he remembered everything."[68] Such are the vagaries of senile dementia.

On Sunday, April 16, Emerson went to church—the same church where he had heard Dr. Ripley preach in his youth—both morning and evening. The next day he had a cold, but insisted that it was nothing of importance. He tried to cure it by long walks in the cool spring air—one is reminded of Ellen Tucker Emerson's carriage rides in the raw winter winds before her death. He spent most of the day in his study, banked the fire in his fireplace at night, and climbed the stairs to his bedroom as usual, until the cold turned into pneumonia.

On Saturday, April 22, Alcott recorded in his Journal: "Call at Emerson's and find him confined to his bed, having exposed himself to our chilly winds without his overcoat, and [is] threatened with pneumonia."[69] On Monday Alcott called again, and found him "quite ill, and fears are entertained that his illness may prove fatal." On Wednesday, Emerson greeted Alcott with, "You are quite well?" He replied, "Yes," but his concern was for Emerson. Alcott left him with the sad feeling that he might not see his friend alive again.

To the end Emerson was not delirious, but at times his mind wandered. Part of the time he thought he was not at home and wondered where he was. Once he was heard to murmur, "Oh that beautiful boy!" Dr. James Putnam came out frequently from Boston to see him, and his son, Dr. Edward Emerson, watched him closely. On Thursday he suffered great pain from the pneumonia, with difficulty in breathing, and in the afternoon Dr. Putnam gave him ether. He died under its influence that evening at eight-fifty. At nine the bell of the Unitarian church began tolling seventy-nine strokes.

Emerson's boyhood companion, Dr. William Furness, came up from Philadelphia, and on Sunday, April 30, conducted a private service for the family.[70] Then the casket was taken to the Unitarian church, where Emerson's friend for many years, the Reverend James Clarke, preached the funeral sermon and Alcott read his sonnet to Emerson. In dedicating Sleepy Hollow Cemetery in 1855, it will be recalled, Emerson had said, "In this quiet valley, as in the palm of Nature's hand, we shall sleep well when we have finished our day." He was buried near the top of an eastern hill. A pine tree stood at the head of his grave, and later a large granite boulder, which he had selected, was placed in front of it, with Emerson's words carved on it:

> The passive master lent his hand
> To the vast soul that o'er him planned.

In Sleepy Hollow, Waldo Emerson rested with other members of his family: his mother, two of his brothers, his first son, his sister-in-law Susan Emerson, and Aunt Mary; there were markers for his brothers Edward and Charles. To the west, on the same hill, were the graves of Thoreau and Hawthorne.

On April 28 *The New York Times* gave three columns on its first page and more than two inside to the death, funeral, and works of Emerson. The anonymous writer declared: "His influence has in all likelihood been greater upon the American, and in less degree upon the English, mind than any other writer in the Nation." *The New York World, The Sun,* and *The Post* also carried long notices, and of course the Boston papers, but none gave as much space as *The Times* or so well summed up Emerson's significance: "Emerson appears to have acted his own definition of a philosophy—he reported to his own mind the constitution of the universe."

GENEALOGY

SOURCES OF ILLUSTRATIONS

NOTES

INDEX

Genealogy

Generations

1st   Thomas Emerson (d. Mendon, Mass., 1666)

2nd   Joseph Emerson (1620–80) m. Elizabeth Bulkeley*

3rd   Edward Emerson (1670–1743) m. Rebecca Waldo

4th   Joseph Emerson (1700–67) m. Mary Moody in 1721

5th   William Emerson (1743–76) m. Phebe Bliss (1741–1825) in 1766†

6th   William Emerson (1769–1811) m. Ruth Haskins (1768–1853) in 1797
        Phebe Bliss (1798–1800)
        John Clarke (1799–1807)
        William (1801–68)
        Ralph Waldo (1803–82)
        Edward Bliss (1805–34)
        Robert Bulkeley (1807–59)
        Charles Chauncy (1808–36)
        Mary Caroline (1811–14)

7th   Ralph Waldo Emerson m. Ellen Tucker (1811–31) in 1829
        m. Lydia (Lidian) Jackson (1802–92) in 1835
        Waldo (1836–42)
        Ellen Tucker (1839–1909)
        Edith (1841–1929) m. William H. Forbes (1840–97) in 1865
        Edward Waldo (1844–1930) m. Annie S. Keyes (1847–1928) in 1874

---

* Elizabeth Bulkeley was the great-granddaughter of a Waldo of London, perhaps of Cornelius, and the granddaughter of Peter Bulkeley, one of the founders of Concord, Mass.
† Phebe Bliss Emerson m. Ezra Ripley (1751–1841), RWE's stepgrandfather, in 1780.

Sources of Illustrations

Frontispiece, drawing of Emerson made in 1857 by Samuel Rowse, reproduced in *The Works of Ralph Waldo Emerson* (Boston, 1883). 1. First Church, from David Greene Haskins, *Ralph Waldo Emerson: His Maternal Ancestors* (Boston, 1887). 2. Reverend William Emerson, Haskins. 3. Ruth Haskins Emerson, from miniature *c.* 1840 by unknown artist, *Journals of Ralph Waldo Emerson* (1909). 4. Haskins house, Haskins. 5. Old Manse, *Works* (1883). 6. Miniature of Emerson painted by Mrs. Richard Hildreth in 1844, *Journals* (1909). 7. Ellen Tucker, from miniature painted in 1829 by unknown artist, *Journals* (1909). 8. Miniature of William (brother) by unknown artist in 1834, *Journals* (1909). 9. Second Church, Haskins. 10. Crayon of Emerson *c.* 1846 by unknown artist, *Journals* (1909). 11. Silhouette of Dr. Ezra Ripley *c.* 1841, *Journals* (1909). 12. Silhouette of Mary Moody Emerson, *Journals* (1909). 13. Silhouette of Charles (brother), *Journals* (1909). 14. Caricature by Christopher Cranch, by permission of F. DeWolfe Miller (*Christopher Pearse Cranch and His Caricatures of New England Transcendentalism* [1951]), the Harvard University Press, and the Houghton Library. 15. Photograph of Emerson in 1862, *Works* (1883). 16. Daguerreotype of Waldo (son), *Journals* (1909). 17. Lidian and Waldo, *Journals* (1909). 18. Emerson with Edward and Edith, *Journals* (1909). 19. Home in Concord, *Works* (1883). 20. Elizabeth Hoar, from crayon by A. Hartwell, *Journals* (1909). 21. Ellen (daughter), from 1860 daguerreotype, *Journals* (1909). 22. From painting of Margaret Fuller Ossoli in Rome by William Hicks, *Journals* (1909). 23. Photograph of Emerson in 1874, *Works* (1883). 24. Emerson's grave, photo by author, 1969. Quotation from "The Problem."

Notes

Symbols Used in Notes

AJ   *Journals of Bronson Alcott.* Odell Shepard, ed. (Boston: Little, Brown & Co., 1938).

AL   *The Letters of Bronson Alcott.* Richard L. Herrnstadt, ed. (Ames: Iowa State University Press, 1969).

C&E   *Correspondence of Carlyle and Emerson,* 2 vols. Charles Eliot Norton, ed. (Boston: James E. Osgood & Co., 1883).

CW   *The Collected Works of Ralph Waldo Emerson,* Vol. I. Robert E. Spiller and Alfred R. Ferguson, eds. (Cambridge: Harvard University Press, 1971).

EL   *Early Lectures of Ralph Waldo Emerson,* 3 vols. Stephen E. Whicher, Robert E. Spiller, and Wallace E. Williams, eds. (Cambridge: Harvard University Press, 1964–72).

HL   Houghton Library, Harvard University, unpublished manuscript.

J   *Journals of Ralph Waldo Emerson,* 10 vols. Edward W. Emerson, ed. (Cambridge: Riverside Press, 1909–1914).

JMN   *The Journals and Miscellaneous Notebooks of Ralph Waldo Emerson,* Vols. I–XIV. William H. Gilman, Alfred R. Ferguson, George P. Clark, Merrell R. Davis, Harrison Hayford, Ralph Orth, J. E. Parsons, Merton M. Sealts, and A. W. Plumstead, eds. (Cambridge: Harvard University Press, 1960–78).

L   *Letters of Ralph Waldo Emerson,* 6 vols. Ralph L. Rusk, ed. (New York: Columbia University Press, 1939).

OFL   *One First Love: The Letters of Ellen Louisa Tucker to Ralph Waldo Emerson.* Edith W. Gregg, ed. (Cambridge: Harvard University Press, 1962).

W   *The Complete Works,* 12 vols. Edward W. Emerson, ed. (Boston: Houghton Mifflin Co., 1903-1904).

YES   *Young Emerson Speaks: Unpublished Discourses on Many Subjects.* Arthur Cushman McGiffert Jr., ed. (Boston: Houghton Mifflin Co., 1938).

Abbreviations for Secondary Sources

Barber   Samuel Barber, *Boston Common: A Diary of Notable Events,* pamphlet n.p. (Boston: privately printed, 1914).

Bartlett   Willliam Irving Bartlett, *Jones Very, Emerson's "Brave Saint"* (Durham: Duke University Press, 1942).

Cabot   James Elliot Cabot, *A Memoir of Ralph Waldo Emerson, 2 vols. (Boston: Houghton Mifflin Co., 1887).*

Charvat   *William Charvat, Emerson's American Lecture Engagements: A Chronological List* (New York: New York Public Library, 1961).

Collection   Milton Konvitz and Stephen Whicher, eds., *Emerson: A Collection of Critical Essays* (Englewood Cliffs, N.J.: Prentice-Hall, 1962).

Conway,   Moncure Daniel Conway, *Autobiography, Memories and Expe-*
  Autobiography   *riences,* 2 vols. (Boston: Houghton Mifflin Co., 1904).

Conway,   Moncure Daniel Conway, *Emerson at Home and Abroad* (Bos-
  Emerson   ton: Houghton Mifflin Co., 1883).

Cooke   George Willis Cooke, *Ralph Waldo Emerson: Life, Writings, and Philosophy* (Boston: James R. Osgood & Co., 1882).

Ellen   Ellen Emerson's biography of Lidian Jackson Emerson, unpublished manuscript in Houghton Library, Harvard University.

Haskins   David Greene Haskins, *Ralph Waldo Emerson: His Maternal Ancestors* (Boston: Cupples, Upham & Co., 1887).

Holmes   Oliver Wendell Holmes, *Ralph Waldo Emerson* (Boston: Houghton Mifflin Co., 1885).

Ireland   Alexander Ireland, *Ralph Waldo Emerson: His Life, Genius and Writings* (London, 1882; reprint ed., Port Washington, N.Y.: Kennikat Press, 1972).

Miller,   Perry Miller, ed., *The Transcendentalists* (Cambridge: Harvard
  Transcenden-   University Press, 1950).
  talists

Morison   Samuel Eliot Morison, *Three Centuries of Harvard* (Cambridge: Harvard University Press, 1936).

Perry	Ralph Barton Perry, *The Thought and Character of William James,* 2 vols. (Boston: Little, Brown & Co., 1935).
Pommer	Henry F. Pommer, *Emerson's First Marriage* (Carbondale: Southern Illinois University Press, 1967).
Recognition	Milton R. Konvitz, ed., *The Recognition of Ralph Waldo Emerson: Selected Criticism since 1837* (Ann Arbor: University of Michigan Press, 1972).
Rusk	Ralph L. Rusk, *The Life of Ralph Waldo Emerson* (New York: Charles Scribner's Sons, 1949).
Scudder, *Concord*	Townsend Scudder, *Concord, American Town* (Boston: Little, Brown & Co., 1947).
Scudder, *Lonely Wayfaring Man*	Townsend Scudder, *The Lonely Wayfaring Man: Emerson and Some Englishmen* (New York: Oxford University Press, 1936).
Shepard	Odell Shepard, *Pedlar's Progress: The Life of Bronson Alcott* (Boston: Little, Brown & Co., 1937).
Tolman	George Tolman, *Mary Moody Emerson* (privately printed, 1929).
Whitehill	Walter Muir Whitehill, *Boston: A Topographical History,* 2d rev. ed. enl. (Cambridge: Harvard University Press, 1968).
Wright	Conrad Wright, *The Beginnings of Unitarianism in America* (Boston: Beacon Press, 1955).

Preface

1. Rusk, 37–38; cf. *L,* I, 37.
2. Rusk, 13.
3. See Chap. VIII, sec. II.
4. *CW,* I, 89.
5. *EL,* I, 1–83.
6. Garry Wills, *Inventing America: Jefferson's Declaration of Independence* (New York: Doubleday & Co., 1978), 176f.
7. HL: "Feasting, Humiliation and Prayer," sermon preached Apr. 7, 1831.
8. Whitehill, 113.
9. *JMN,* III, 78.
10. *W,* IX, 8.
11. Cf. G. W. Allen, "Emerson and the Unconscious," *American Transcendentalist Quarterly* XIX (Summer 1973): 26–30.
12. Erich Fromm, *The Forgotten Language* (New York: Grove Press, 1951), 142.

13. *W*, X, 7–8.
14. *EL*, II, 250.
15. Cabot, II, 683.
16. Fritjof Capra, *The Tao of Physics* (New York: Bantam Books, 1977).
17. *W*, XI, 87.
18. *W*, XI, 97.
19. *W*, XI, 235.
20. *W*, XI, 315f.
21. *W*, II, 81.
22. Hyatt Waggoner, *Emerson as Poet* (Princeton, N.J.: Princeton University Press, 1974); Harold Bloom, *The Ringers in the Tower: Studies in Romantic Tradition* (Chicago: University of Chicago Press, 1971), Chap. 16; Roy Harvey Pearce, *The Continuity of American Poetry* (Princeton, N.J.: Princeton University Press, 1961), 153–63; Joel Porte, *The Representative Man: Ralph Waldo Emerson in His Time* (New York: Oxford University Press, 1979).
23. See Chap. XIX, sec. V.
24. See Chap. XXI.
25. *Recognition*, 132.
26. See note 22, above.
27. Bloom, 217f.
28. *Collection*, 29.

PART ONE

CHAPTER I
The Voice in the Garden

1. *L*, IV, 179.
2. *L*, IV, 179.
3. Cabot, I, 23.
4. Cabot, I, 41.
5. Cabot, I, 27.
6. Haskins, 83.
7. Rusk, 13.
8. Haskins, 54.
9. Whitehill, 27.
10. Wright, 8.
11. Haskins, 38f.
12. Haskins, 43.
13. Cabot, I, 35.
14. Cabot, I, 17.

15. Cabot, I, 21.
16. Cabot, I, 2.
17. Cabot, I, 26.
18. Cabot, I, 29.
19. Cabot, I, 5.
20. Cabot, I, 34.
21. *J*, X, 133.
22. Rusk, 40–41.
23. *JMN,* VII, 253.
24. Haskins, 78.
25. Cabot, I, 7.
26. Haskins, 45; Holmes, 42.
27. Haskins, 60–62.
28. Barber (by years, n.p.).
29. Barber.
30. Holmes, 13.
31. Cabot, I, 26.
32. Rusk, 29.
33. Cabot, I, 27.
34. Cabot, I, 28; HL.

CHAPTER II
The Hoop That Holds

1. *W,* VII, 121.
2. *W,* X, 407.
3. Cabot, I, 10.
4. Tolman, 2–3.
5. "The Old Manse," in *Mosses from an Old Manse* (1846).
6. HL: WE to MME, Apr. 10, 1806.
7. Wright, 222.
8. HL: Tolman transcriptions, unpublished.
9. Rusk, 31.
10. Tolman, 12–13.
11. Cabot, I, 43n.
12. Rusk, 37.
13. Conway, *Autobiography,* I, 146.
14. *L,* I, 6.
15. Haskins, 27.
16. Haskins, 4–7.
17. Rusk, 38.
18. Cabot, I, 43.
19. Cabot, I, 41–42.

20. HL.
21. Scudder, *Concord,* 5–16; *W,* XI, 61–64.
22. Edward Waldo Emerson, *A Chaplain of the Revolution* (Boston: Massachusetts Historical Society, 1970), 24 pp.
23. *W,* X, 385.
24. *W,* X, 387.
25. *L,* I, 9.
26. Cabot, I, 47.
27. Rusk, 54.
28. Cabot, I, 47.
29. *L,* I, 10.
30. *L,* I, 17.
31. Rusk, 55.
32. Rusk, 69.
33. Rusk, 60.
34. *L,* I, 47.
35. *L,* I, 19.
36. Cabot, I, 48.
37. Whitehill, 73–94.
38. Cabot, I, 44n.
39. See Chap. XIII.
40. Rusk, 55.
41. William James, *Varieties of Religious Experience* (London: Longman, Green, 1902).
42. *JMN,* IV, 348.
43. *L,* I, 39.
44. Cabot, I, 51.
45. Rusk, 62.

CHAPTER III
Two Educations at Harvard

1. Miller, *Transcendentalists,* 12.
2. Rusk, 66.
3. *L,* I, 50.
4. *L,* I, 51.
5. *L,* I, 45.
6. *L,* I, 47.
7. Morison, 187–89.
8. Morison, 190–91.
9. Morison, 195.
10. Cabot, I, 50.
11. Morison, 200.

12. Morison, 195–221.
13. Morison, 195f.
14. *L*, I, 48–49.
15. Holmes, 47.
16. *L*, I, 59.
17. *L*, I, 55.
18. Cabot, II, 54–55.
19. *L*, I, 69.
20. Morison, 200.
21. *L*, I, 69.
22. *L*, I, 75.
23. *L*, I, 67.
24. Morison, 208f.
25. *L*, I, 76.
26. Cabot, I, 85.
27. *JMN*, I, 244.
28. *JMN*, I, 3.
29. *JMN*, I, 4.
30. *JMN*, I, 264–68.
31. *JMN*, I, 7n–8.
32. *L*, I, 89.
33. Morison, 227.
34. *JMN*, VIII, 269–70.
35. *JMN*, I, 13.
36. Edward T. Channing, *Lectures Read to the Seniors in Harvard College,* ed. Dorothy I. Anderson and Waldo W. Braden (Carbondale: Southern Illinois University Press, 1969), 1.
37. Morison, 216.
38. *JMN*, I, 15.
39. *JMN*, I, 206f.
40. *JMN*, I, 22.
41. *JMN*, I, 39.
42. *JMN*, I, 41.
43. *JMN*, I, 299.
44. *JMN*, I, 35.
45. *JMN*, I, 23n.
46. *JMN*, I, 18.
47. *JMN*, I, 24.
48. *JMN*, I, 51.
49. *JMN*, I, 52.
50. Kenneth Walter Cameron, *Indian Superstition: A Dissertation on Emerson's Orientalism at Harvard* (Hanover, N.H.: Friends of the Dartmouth Library, 1954), 17.

51. Cameron, 20.
52. Cameron, 49–53.
53. *L*, I, 99.
54. *L*, I, 63n.
55. *JMN*, I, 356.
56. *L*, I, 101.

CHAPTER IV
The Dupe of Hope

1. *JMN*, II, 241.
2. Cabot, I, 70.
3. Cabot, I, 70.
4. Place of torment, *Paradise Lost*, Bk. I.
5. *L*, I, 104.
6. *JMN*, II, 373n.
7. *JMN*, I, 94.
8. *JMN*, I, 133.
9. *JMN*, I, 134.
10. *JMN*, I, 304n.
11. Wright, 45–58.
12. Wright, 187f.
13. *JMN*, II, 160–61.
14. Wright, 155.
15. *Memoir of William Ellery Channing* (Boston: Wm. Crosby & H. P. Nichols, 1848), II, 49.
16. *Memoir of Channing*, I, 345–46.
17. *Memoir of Channing*, I, 418.
18. *Memoir of Channing*, I, 272.
19. *JMN*, I, 152.
20. *JMN*, II, 5.
21. *JMN*, II, 83.
22. *JMN*, II, 49.
23. *JMN*, II, 64.
24. *JMN*, II, 65.
25. *JMN*, II, 84.
26. *JMN*, II, 86.
27. *JMN*, II, 112.
28. *JMN*, II, 113.
29. *JMN*, II, 115.
30. *L*, I, 121.
31. *JMN*, II, 121.
32. *JMN*, II, 125.

33. *JMN*, II, 129.
34. *JMN*, II, 127.
35. *JMN*, II, 131.
36. Cabot, I, 83–84.
37. Rusk, 100.
38. Miller, *Transcendentalists*, 103.
39. *JMN*, V, 358.
40. *L*, I, 133.
41. *JMN*, II, 226; see *L*, I, 139.
42. *JMN*, II, 181.
43. *L*, I, 141n.
44. *L*, I, 137; *JMN*, II, 162.
45. *JMN*, II, 190.
46. *JMN*, II, 196.
47. *JMN*, II, 223.
48. *JMN*, II, 237.
49. *JMN*, II, 231.
50. *JMN*, II, 239.
51. *JMN*, II, 241–42.
52. *JMN*, II, 242.
53. *JMN*, II, 238–42.
54. *L*, I, 143.
55. Dr. Ethel E. Wortis: unpublished letters from William Emerson to his family, owned by Dr. Wortis; WE to I. Fessenden, Letter Box 18, Aug. 8, 1824; see also *L*, I, 161n.
56. *L*, I, 152n.
57. *L*, I, 149.
58. *L*, I, 149.
59. *L*, I, 160–61n.
60. *L*, I, 159.
61. *L*, I, 154.
62. Cabot, I, 105.
63. *JMN*, II, 382.
64. *JMN*, II, 384.

CHAPTER V
House of Pain

1. *J*, II, 180.
2. *JMN*, II, 309.
3. *W*, IX, 385.
4. *L*, I, 158.
5. *L*, I, 158n.

6. *JMN*, II, 330.
7. *JMN*, II, 333.
8. *JMN*, II, 332.
9. Morison, 241–44.
10. Cabot, I, 111.
11. Rusk, 111.
12. Cabot, I, 112.
13. HL: MS. Autob.: "1825 Oct. 18 Wm arrived after two years' absence. Oct. 23 Edward sailed Sunday morning."
14. *J*, IX, 236.
15. *L*, I, 164.
16. Rusk, 113.
17. *L*, I, 163.
18. *L*, I, 165.
19. Haskins, 110; *L*, I, 164n.
20. *JMN*, III, 13.
21. *JMN*, III, 15.
22. *L*, I, 166.
23. *L*, I, 168.
24. HL: CCE to MME, Sept. 12, 1825.
25. Cabot, I, 115.
26. *L*, I, 170.
27. *L*, I, 170.
28. *L*, I, 172–73n.
29. *L*, I, 173.
30. *L*, I, 176.
31. Rusk, 87.
32. Miller, *Transcendentalists*, 49–53.
33. Second ed. (Boston: Adonis Howard, 1829), page numbers given in brackets.
34. *JMN*, III, 45.
35. *L*, I, 176.
36. *J*, II, 98n.
37. *L*, I, 177; HL: MS. Autob.
38. *L*, I, 178.
39. *L*, I, 184.
40. Rusk, 119.
41. *L*, I, 180.
42. *L*, I, 179n.
43. *JMN*, III, 57.
44. *JMN*, III, 59.
45. *JMN*, III, 60.

46. *L*, I, 184.
47. *L*, I, 185.
48. *L*, I, 187.
49. *L*, I, 189.
50. *JMN*, III, 89.
51. *JMN*, III, 117.
52. *JMN*, III, 116.
53. *JMN*, III, 115.
54. *JMN*, III, 116.
55. *JMN*, III, 63.
56. *JMN*, III, 67.
57. *JMN*, III, 68.
58. *JMN*, III, 70.
59. *JMN*, III, 72.
60. *JMN*, III, 73.
61. *JMN*, III, 77.
62. *JMN*, III, 72.
63. *JMN*, III, 77n.
64. *L*, I, 194.
65. *JMN*, III, 77.
66. *JMN*, III, 78.
67. *J*, II, 187f.
68. *J*, II, 183; *L*, I, 195.
69. *L*, I, 198.
70. *L*, I, 200.
71. *L*, I, 201n.

CHAPTER VI
The Ordained Heart

1. *J*, II, 257.
2. *L*, I, 202.
3. Rusk, 124.
4. *J*, II, 208–209.
5. *L*, I, 201–202.
6. *L*, I, 204.
7. *L*, I, 209.
8. *L*, I, 210.
9. *L*, I, 207.
10. *L*, I, 212.
11. Cabot, I, 138–39.
12. *YES*, 13.

13. *YES,* 16.
14. *YES,* 17, 20.
15. *L,* I, 222n.
16. Pommer, 6.
17. *JMN,* III, 99.
18. *L,* I, 224.
19. Bacon, "Of Friendship."
20. *JMN,* III, 25.
21. Bacon, "Of Love."
22. *L,* I, 225.
23. *L,* I, 227.
24. *L,* I, 230.
25. *L,* I, 233.
26. *JMN,* III, 105.
27. *JMN,* III, 121.
28. *JMN,* III, 127.
29. *JMN,* III, 129.
30. *JMN,* III, 130.
31. *L,* I, 235n.
32. *L,* I, 236.
33. Listed in *L,* I, 237; HL.
34. HL: RWE to WE, July 3, 1828; in part, Cabot, I, 140–41.
35. *L,* I, 237.
36. *L,* I, 240.
37. *L,* I, 237.
38. *JMN,* III, 137.
39. *JMN,* III, 143.
40. *JMN,* III, 144.
41. *JMN,* III, 146.
42. *JMN,* III, 147.
43. *JMN,* III, 99.
44. *JMN,* III, 147.
45. *Plutarch's Morals,* ed. William W. Goodwin, intro. Ralph Waldo Emerson (Boston, 1874), IV, 274. (In 1828 Emerson used Taylor's translation.)
46. Plutarch quoted in John S. Harrison, *The Teachers of Emerson* (New York, 1910; reprint ed., New York: Haskell House, 1969), 166; *Plutarch's Morals,* IV, 294–95.
47. Pommer, 8.
48. *L,* I, 256.
49. Pommer, 9.
50. Pommer, 12.
51. *JMN,* III, 148–49.

CHAPTER VII
The New Eye of the Priest

1. *JMN*, III, 152.
2. *JMN*, III, 149–50.
3. *L*, I, 258.
4. *J*, II, 259.
5. Listed in *L*, I, 258; nearly complete, *J*, II, 258–60.
6. Pommer, 12.
7. *L*, I, 259.
8. Pommer, 13.
9. *L*, I, 261.
10. *L*, I, 262.
11. *L*, I, 265.
12. Rusk, 137.
13. Whitehill, 28, 32.
14. Whitehill, 112–13.
15. *L*, I, 260n.
16. *L*, I, 266n.
17. *JMN*, IX, 29.
18. *L*, I, 267.
19. *L*, I, 270n.
20. *YES*, xxxi; see also *J*, II, 294.
21. *YES*, 24–25.
22. *JMN*, III, 182.
23. *JMN*, III, 152.
24. *YES*, 29.
25. *YES*, 32.
26. *JMN*, III, 197.
27. *JMN*, III, 171.
28. *YES*, xviii.
29. *L*, I, 268.
30. *OFL*, 25.
31. *OFL*, 37.
32. *OFL*, 18.
33. *OFL*, 21.
34. *OFL*, 30.
35. *OFL*, 34.
36. *OFL*, 32.
37. *OFL*, 53.
38. *YES*, 40.
39. *OFL*, 55.

40. *OFL,* 57.
41. *OFL,* 60.
42. *OFL,* 75–76.
43. *OFL,* 78.
44. *OFL,* 84.
45. *OFL,* 86.
46. Pommer, 15.
47. *L,* I, 276.
48. *OFL,* 91.
49. *OFL,* 93–94.
50. *OFL,* 95.
51. *OFL,* 96, 99.
52. *L,* I, 282.
53. *L,* I, 283.
54. *L,* I, 285n.
55. *L,* I, 287.
56. *L,* I, 288.
57. *L,* I, 287.
58. *L,* I, 289.

CHAPTER VIII
The Heavenly Stair

1. *W,* IX, 107, 108, 109–110, 114, 115.
2. Pommer, 31.
3. *OFL,* 114; variant in *JMN,* III, 181.
4. *OFL,* 112.
5. *OFL,* 111.
6. *OFL,* 115.
7. *L,* I, 294.
8. *L,* I, 295.
9. *L,* I, 296.
10. *L,* I, 297n.
11. *L,* I, 298.
12. *OFL,* 126.
13. *OFL,* 128.
14. *YES,* 67–74.
15. *YES,* 70.
16. Cabot, I, 169.
17. *L,* I, 302.
18. *OFL,* 127.
19. *OFL,* 129.
20. *OFL,* 157.

21. *OFL,* 131.
22. *L,* I, 302.
23. *JMN,* III, 198.
24. *L,* I, 307n.
25. *L,* I, 307.
26. *L,* I, 302.
27. *OFL,* 134.
28. *L,* I, 310.
29. *L,* I, 313.
30. *L,* I, 314.
31. *OFL,* 136.
32. *OFL,* 135.
33. *OFL,* 137.
34. *YES,* 127.
35. *OFL,* 137.
36. *JMN,* III, 193.
37. *JMN,* III, 181.
38. *JMN,* III, 164n.
39. *JMN,* III, 167.
40. *JMN,* III, 187.
41. *JMN,* III, 167.
42. William James, *Varieties of Religious Experience* (London: Longman, Green, 1902), 516–17.
43. *JMN,* III, 168.
44. *JMN,* III, 177.
45. *JMN,* III, 179.
46. *JMN,* III, 198–99.
47. *JMN,* III, 217.
48. *JMN,* III, 214.
49. *JMN,* III, 215–16.
50. *JMN,* III, 216.
51. *JMN,* III, 217.
52. *YES,* 105.
53. *YES,* 112–19.
54. *OFL,* 161.
55. Pommer, 47.
56. *L,* I, 316.
57. *L,* I, 317.
58. Pommer, 48.
59. *L,* I, 318n.
60. Pommer, 48.
61. Pommer, 49.
62. *L,* I, 318.

63. *JMN*, III, 227.
64. *JMN*, III, 226–27.
65. *JMN*, III, 228.
66. *JMN*, III, 230–31.
67. *YES*, 139, 142, 143.
68. *YES*, 143–44.

CHAPTER IX
The Law of Compensation

1. *JMN*, III, 303.
2. *JMN*, III, 226.
3. *JMN*, III, 244.
4. *JMN*, III, 246.
5. *JMN*, III, 253.
6. *JMN*, III, 255.
7. *JMN*, III, 256.
8. *JMN*, III, 303.
9. *JMN*, III, 266.
10. *JMN*, III, 263n.
11. *JMN*, III, 268.
12. *JMN*, III, 273.
13. *JMN*, III, 274.
14. *JMN*, III, 269.
15. *JMN*, III, 279.
16. *JMN*, III, 259.
17. *JMN*, III, 290.
18. *JMN*, III, 286.
19. *JMN*, III, 292.
20. *JMN*, III, 327n.
21. *JMN*, III, 266.
22. *JMN*, III, 294.
23. *JMN*, III, 251n.
24. *JMN*, III, 313.
25. *JMN*, III, 312.
26. Edwin S. Hodgin, *One Hundred Years of Unitarianism in New England* (1924).
27. *JMN*, III, 318–19.
28. *JMN*, III, 324.
29. *JMN*, III, 309.
30. *OFL*, 149.
31. *JMN*, III, 311.
32. *L*, I, 330.

33. *L*, I, 332n.
34. *L*, I, 349.
35. *L*, I, 335.
36. *L*, I, 333.
37. *L*, I, 337n.
38. *L*, I, 336.
39. *L*, I, 341.
40. HL.
41. HL.
42. *JMN*, IV, 4.
43. *JMN*, IV, 6.
44. *JMN*, IV, 7.
45. Pommer, 55.
46. *JMN*, III, 226.
47. *JMN*, IV, 60.
48. Haskins, 45; Cabot, I, 172.
49. *JMN*, III, 317.
50. *JMN*, III, 321.
51. *JMN*, IV, 9.
52. *JMN*, IV, 25n.
53. *L*, I, 343.
54. *JMN*, IV, 24 (Laplace's *Mécanique céleste*, trans. Mary Somerville, 1831).
55. *YES*, 170–79.
56. *JMN*, IV, 27.
57. *YES*, 54–59.
58. *JMN*, III, 318.
59. *JMN*, IV, 27.
60. *L*, I, 352–53n.
61. *L*, I, 353n.
62. *JMN*, IV, 27.
63. *L*, I, 353n.
64. *JMN*, IV, 29.
65. *JMN*, IV, 30.
66. *JMN*, IV, 32.
67. *L*, I, 354n.
68. *JMN*, IV, 33.
69. *JMN*, IV, 34.
70. *L*, I, 352.
71. *L*, I, 355.
72. *L*, I, 352n.
73. *W*, XI, 3–25.
74. *W*, XI, 7.
75. *W*, XI, 10–11.

76. *W*, XI, 14.
77. *W*, XI, 17.
78. *W*, XI, 24.
79. *L*, I, 355.
80. *L*, I, 356n.
81. *YES*, 180–90.
82. *L*, I, 356n.
83. *L*, I, 357–58.
84. Cabot, I, 173.
85. *L*, I, 360.
86. Cabot, I, 174–75.
87. *L*, I, 359.
88. Cabot, II, 685–88.

CHAPTER X
Wayfaring Man

1. Ireland, 49.
2. *JMN*, IV, 59.
3. *L*, I, 359.
4. *JMN*, IV, 102.
5. *L*, I, 360n.
6. *JMN*, IV, 102–103.
7. *JMN*, IV, 111.
8. *JMN*, IV, 105–106.
9. *JMN*, IV, 107.
10. *JMN*, IV, 111.
11. *JMN*, IV, 112.
12. *JMN*, IV, 115.
13. *JMN*, IV, 116.
14. *JMN*, IV, 120.
15. *JMN*, IV, 131.
16. *JMN*, IV, 133.
17. *JMN*, IV, 138.
18. Rusk, 175.
19. *JMN*, IV, 142.
20. *L*, I, 367.
21. *JMN*, IV, 148.
22. *JMN*, IV, 149.
23. *JMN*, IV, 150.
24. *JMN*, IV, 153.
25. *JMN*, IV, 155.
26. *JMN*, IV, 156.

27. *JMN*, IV, 177.
28. *JMN*, IV, 164.
29. *JMN*, IV, 166; see Howard Hibbard, *Michelangelo* (New York: Harper & Row, 1975), 158.
30. *JMN*, IV, 168.
31. *JMN*, IV, 72.
32. *W*, V, 5.
33. Scudder, *Concord*, 7–10.
34. *JMN*, IV, 174.
35. *Edinburgh Review* LIV (Dec. 1831).
36. *JMN*, IV, 177.
37. *JMN*, IV, 180–82.
38. *JMN*, IV, 183.
39. *JMN*, IV, 186.
40. *JMN*, IV, 192f.
41. *JMN*, IV, 194.
42. *JMN*, IV, 196.
43. *JMN*, IV, 198.
44. Eleanor M. Tilton, *Amiable Autocrat: A Biography of Dr. Oliver Wendell Holmes* (New York: Henry Schuman, 1947), 90.
45. *JMN*, IV, 199–200.
46. *JMN*, IV, 201.
47. *JMN*, IV, 203.
48. *JMN*, IV, 204.
49. *JMN*, IV, 205, 413; *L*, I, 392.
50. *JMN*, IV, 414.
51. *W*, V, 4.
52. Rusk, 189.
53. *JMN*, IV, 411–12.
54. *JMN*, IV, 408; *W*, V, 10.
55. *W*, V, 14.
56. *JMN*, IV, 414.
57. Cabot, I, 195; Ireland, 141.
58. Scudder, *Concord*, 18f.
59. *JMN*, IV, 217.
60. *JMN*, IV, 217.
61. *JMN*, IV, 219.
62. Scudder, *Concord*, 20.
63. *L*, I, 394.
64. *JMN*, IV, 221.
65. *JMN*, IV, 219.
66. James Anthony Froude, *Thomas Carlyle: A History of His Life in London, 1834–1881* (New York: Charles Scribner's Sons, 1884), II, 290–91.

67. *JMN,* IV, 222f.
68. *JMN,* IV, 226.
69. *JMN,* IV, 236.
70. *JMN,* IV, 237.
71. *JMN,* IV, 238.
72. *JMN,* IV, 247.
73. *L,* I, 396n.
74. *L,* I, 397.

CHAPTER XI
Ancestral Fields

1. *JMN,* IV, 335.
2. *JMN,* IV, 253.
3. *JMN,* IV, 254.
4. *JMN,* IV, 269.
5. *L,* I, 411, 412.
6. *L,* I, 399n; *JMN,* IV, 97n.
7. Quoted in Cabot, I, 208.
8. *L,* I, 397n; *EL,* I, 5–26.
9. *JMN,* IV, 311.
10. *EL,* I, 11.
11. *EL,* I, 23.
12. *EL,* I, 25n.
13. Quoted in *EL,* I, 25.
14. *EL,* I, 26.
15. Cf. *Man's Place in Nature,* trans. René Hague (New York: Harper & Row, 1966); *The Phenomenon of Man,* trans. Bernard Wall (New York: Harper & Row, 1961).
16. Charvat, 15.
17. Cabot, I, 215.
18. *L,* I, 378.
19. *L,* I, 400.
20. *L,* I, 400n.
21. *L,* I, 400.
22. Conway, *Emerson,* 66.
23. *JMN,* IV, 263–64.
24. *JMN,* IV, 264n.
25. *JMN,* IV, 274.
26. *JMN,* IV, 275.
27. *JMN,* IV, 277.
28. *JMN,* IV, 318.
29. *JMN,* IV, 309–310.
30. *JMN,* IV, 274.

31. *JMN,* IV, 279.
32. *L,* I, 413n.
33. *JMN,* IV, 277, 296.
34. *L,* I, 416.
35. *JMN,* IV, 390.
36. *JMN,* IV, 391.
37. *L,* I, 417n.
38. *W,* IX, 398.
39. *L,* I, 419.
40. Conway, *Emerson,* 67.
41. *L,* I, 420.
42. *L,* I, 421.
43. *JMN,* IV, 325.
44. *L,* I, 409–410.
45. *JMN,* IV, 327.
46. *The Diary of Philip Hone,* ed. Bayard Tuckerman (New York: Dodd, Mead & Co., 1889), I, 117.
47. *JMN,* IV, 333.
48. *JMN,* IV, 335.
49. *JMN,* IV, 331.
50. *L,* I, 423.
51. *JMN,* IV, 384.
52. *JMN,* IV, 338.
53. *JMN,* IV, 349–50.
54. *JMN,* IV, 358.
55. *JMN,* IV, 359.
56. *JMN,* V, 21.
57. *JMN,* IV, 351.
58. *L,* I, 429.
59. *JMN,* IV, 352.
60. *JMN,* IV, 359.
61. *JMN,* IV, 373.
62. *JMN,* V, 11.
63. *JMN,* IV, 362.
64. Charvat, 7.
65. *C&E,* I, 18.
66. *C&E,* I, 13.
67. *C&E,* I, 15.
68. *C&E,* I, 20.
69. *C&E,* I, 27.
70. *C&E,* I, 29.
71. *C&E,* I, 32.
72. *C&E,* I, 49.

73. Ellen, 75.
74. Ellen, 83.
75. Ellen, 96.
76. Ellen, 84.
77. Rusk, 211; *JMN*, V, 28.
78. *JMN*, V, 14.
79. Ellen, 84.
80. HL.
81. Rusk, 212f.
82. Rusk, 213.
83. *L*, I, 434.
84. *L*, I, 436.
85. *L*, I, 435.
86. *L*, I, 438.
87. *L*, I, 439n.
88. *L*, I, 440.
89. *L*, I, 442.
90. *L*, I, 436n.
91. Ellen, 88.
92. *L*, I, 447.
93. *L*, I, 452n.
94. Rusk, 221.

CHAPTER XII
Stars over Concord

1. *JMN*, V, 83.
2. *JMN*, V, 81.
3. *W*, XI, 552f.
4. *W*, XI, 27–86.
5. *W*, XI, 30.
6. *W*, XI, 46–47.
7. *W*, XI, 50f.
8. *W*, XI, 61.
9. *W*, XI, 71–72.
10. *W*, XI, 83.
11. *W*, XI, 84.
12. *L*, I, 453n.
13. Cabot, I, 236.
14. Ellen, 96–100.
15. *The Emerson House* (pamphlet, n.d.), distributed at the Emerson House in Concord. (Both Emerson's house in Concord and Lydia Jackson Emerson's in Plymouth—the Winslow House—are open to the public.)

16. Scudder, *Concord,* 155–57.
17. Ellen.
18. *L,* I, 447.
19. Rusk, 225.
20. HL: LE to LJB, Sept. 22, 1835; quoted in part in Rusk, 225.
21. Cabot, I, 237.
22. *JMN,* V, 90.
23. Rusk, 228.
24. *JMN,* V, 86.
25. *JMN,* V, 113.
26. Vol. I, 375 (1877); quoted in part in *L,* II, 24n.
27. Quoted in Cooke, 103.
28. Rusk, 229.
29. Rusk, 229.
30. Shepard, 25f.
31. Shepard, 184.
32. *JMN,* V, 98.
33. Shepard, 181.
34. *JMN,* V, 175.
35. *JMN,* V, 63.
36. Shepard, 173.
37. *JMN,* V, 178.
38. *L,* II, 5.
39. *C&E,* I, 80.
40. *C&E,* I, 68.
41. *C&E,* I, 82–83.
42. *C&E,* I, 84–85.
43. *EL,* I, 217.
44. *EL,* I, 219.
45. *EL,* I, 219–20.
46. *JMN,* V, 60.
47. *JMN,* V, 66–70.
48. *EL,* I, 220.
49. *EL,* I, 221.
50. *EL,* I, 224–25.
51. *EL,* I, 226.
52. *EL,* I, 228.
53. *EL,* I, 229.
54. *EL,* I, 332.
55. *EL,* I, 347.
56. *EL,* I, 385; cf. *W,* I, 20–22.
57. *JMN,* V, 145.
58. Rusk, 228.

59. *L,* II, 9.
60. *L,* II, 12.
61. *L,* II, 14.
62. *L,* II, 16.
63. *L,* II, 17–18.
64. *L,* II, 20.
65. *L,* II, 21–22.
66. *L,* II, 25.
67. *JMN,* V, 151.
68. *JMN,* V, 153.
69. *JMN,* V, 154.
70. *JMN,* V, 157.

CHAPTER XIII
Waking the Giant

1. *JMN,* V, 161; Plotinus, *Ennead,* IV, viii, 1.
2. *JMN,* V, 160.
3. *L,* II, 31.
4. Vol. I, 13–16 (July 1840).
5. *JMN,* V, 171.
6. *JMN,* V, 174.
7. *JMN,* V, 179.
8. *JMN,* V, 189.
9. *JMN,* V, 161–62.
10. *JMN,* V, 176.
11. *The Philosophy of Plotinus, Representative Books from the Enneads,* sel. and trans. Joseph Katz (New York: Appleton-Century-Crofts, 1950), xv.
12. *JMN,* V, 179–80.
13. *Ennead,* V, i, 2; see John S. Harrison, *The Teachers of Emerson* (New York, 1910), 248.
14. *JMN,* V, 180.
15. *JMN,* V, 182–83.
16. *Nature* (Boston: James Munroe & Co., 1836; facsimile ed. with intro. by Warner Berthoff, San Francisco: Chandler Publishing Co., 1968), 94.
17. *JMN,* V, 183.
18. *JMN,* V, 184.
19. *EL,* I, 23.
20. *EL,* I, 48.
21. *JMN,* V, 25.

22. *JMN,* V, 40.
23. *L,* I, 447.
24. *JMN,* V, 182.
25. *L,* II, 26.
26. *L,* II, 32.
27. *L,* II, 28.
28. *C&E,* I, 99.
29. *Nature,* xxxvi.
30. *Nature,* 7.
31. *C&E,* I, 99.
32. *Emerson's Nature: Origin, Growth, Meaning,* ed. Merton M. Sealts Jr. and Alfred R. Ferguson (New York: Dodd, Mead & Co., 1969), 90.
33. *W,* I, [1].
34. *Nature,* 12–13.
35. Cabot, I, 44n.
36. *JMN,* IV, 355.
37. *JMN,* V, 18.
38. Jonathan Bishop, *Emerson on the Soul* (Cambridge: Harvard University Press, 1964), 15, 199.
39. F. DeWolfe Miller, *Christopher Pearse Cranch: And His Caricatures of New England Transcendentalism* (Cambridge: Harvard University Press, 1951).
40. William James, *Varieties of Religious Experience* (London: Longman, Green, 1902), 381.
41. *Nature,* 16.
42. *Nature,* 30.
43. *Nature,* 44.
44. *Nature,* 47.
45. *Nature,* 49.
46. *Nature,* 50.
47. *Goethe's Botanical Writings,* trans. Bertha Mueller (Honolulu: University of Hawaii Press, 1952), 31–105.
48. *Goethe's Botanical Writings,* 10.
49. *Goethe's Botanical Writings,* 12.
50. *Nature,* 58.
51. *Nature,* 60.
52. *Nature,* 61–62.
53. *Nature,* 63.
54. *Nature,* 65.
55. *Nature,* 70.
56. *Nature,* 72.
57. *Nature,* 73.
58. *Nature,* 74.
59. *Nature,* 75.

60. *Nature,* 77–78.
61. *Nature,* 79.
62. *Nature,* 80.
63. *EL,* II, 250.
64. Rusk, 81.
65. *Nature,* 81.
66. *Emerson's Nature,* 76.
67. *Emerson's Nature,* 78.
68. *Emerson's Nature,* 89.
69. *Emerson's Nature,* 106.
70. *Emerson's Nature,* 81.
71. *Emerson's Nature,* 87.
72. *L,* II, 36n.
73. *L,* II, 42.
74. Mason Wade, *Margaret Fuller: Whetstone of Genius* (New York: Viking Press, 1940), Chap. II.
75. *Memoirs of Margaret Fuller Ossoli,* ed. Ralph Waldo Emerson et al. (Boston: Phillips, Sampson & Co., 1852), I, 202.
76. *L,* II, 30, 32n.
77. *JMN,* V, 188, 190.
78. *L,* II, 46.
79. *L,* II, 36–37.
80. *L,* II, 36n. (Apparently the visit was not made.)
81. *L,* II, 41.
82. *L,* II, 35.
83. *JMN,* V, 194.
84. *JMN,* V, 196.
85. *JMN,* V, 208.
86. *JMN,* V, 216.
87. *JMN,* V, 234.
88. *JMN,* V, 234–35.
89. *JMN,* V, 246–47.
90. *L,* II, 46.
91. *JMN,* V, 293.
92. *L,* II, 50.
93. Ellen, 127.
94. *L,* II, 43.
95. *EL,* II, 9.
96. *EL,* II, 11.
97. *EL,* II, 12.
98. *EL,* II, 19.
99. *EL,* II, 20.
100. *EL,* II, 25.

101. *EL*, II, 35.
102. Eleanor Tilton, *Amiable Autocrat: A Biography of Dr. Oliver Wendell Holmes* (New York: Henry Schuman, 1947), 255.
103. *EL*, II, 36.
104. *EL*, II, 43.
105. *EL*, II, 44.
106. *EL*, II, 44–45.
107. *EL*, II, 54.
108. *EL*, II, 49.
109. *EL*, II, 63.
110. *EL*, II, 57.
111. *EL*, II, 174–75.
112. *EL*, II, 182.
113. *JMN*, V, 286.
114. *L*, II, 64.

CHAPTER XIV
Uriel's Voice of Scorn

1. *W*, IX, 15.
2. *JMN*, V, 304.
3. *JMN*, V, 327.
4. *L*, II, 86, 97n.
5. *L*, II, 89.
6. *JMN*, V, 331.
7. *JMN*, V, 333.
8. Shepard, 186.
9. Shepard, 193–94.
10. *L*, II, 61.
11. *L*, II, 75.
12. *AJ*, 89.
13. *AJ*, 91.
14. *L*, II, 76.
15. Shepard, 204.
16. *EL*, II, 196.
17. *EL*, II, 197–98.
18. *L*, II, 81.
19. *L*, II, 85n.
20. *L*, II, 88.
21. *L*, II, 94n.
22. *JMN*, V, 347.
23. *"The American Scholar" Today*, ed. C. David Mead (New York: Dodd, Mead & Co., 1970), 45.

24. *"American Scholar" Today*, 38.
25. *"American Scholar" Today*, 41.
26. *JMN*, V, 373.
27. *W*, I, 81.
28. Holmes, 115.
29. *W*, I, 88.
30. *W*, I, 90.
31. *W*, I, 91–93.
32. *W*, I, 98.
33. *W*, I, 105.
34. *W*, I, 106.
35. *W*, I, 111–12.
36. *W*, I, 113.
37. *W*, I, 115.
38. *"American Scholar" Today*, 47–48.
39. *JMN*, V, 411.
40. *C&E*, I, 141–42.
41. *C&E*, I, 129–30.
42. *C&E*, I, 133.
43. *C&E*, I, 137.
44. *L*, II, 121.
45. HL: LE to LB, Feb. 4, 1838.
46. *EL*, II, 216.
47. *EL*, II, 230.
48. *EL*, II, 240–42.
49. *EL*, II, 242.
50. *EL*, II, 250.
51. *EL*, II, 251.
52. *EL*, II, 254.
53. *EL*, II, 257.
54. *EL*, II, 264.
55. *EL*, II, 266.
56. *EL*, II, 288.
57. *EL*, II, 338.
58. *W*, II, 425–26.
59. *EL*, II, 336.
60. Eleanor M. Tilton, "Emerson's Lecture Schedule—1837–1838—Revised," *Harvard Library Bulletin* XXI (Oct. 1973):391n.
61. *EL*, II, 343.
62. *EL*, II, 355.
63. *EL*, II, 358.
64. Tilton, 389–90.
65. Tilton, 391.

66. Tilton, 388.
67. *L*, II, 110.
68. *C&E*, I, 161.
69. *L*, II, 113–14.
70. *JMN*, V, 442.
71. *JMN*, V, 456.
72. *JMN*, V, 465.
73. *JMN*, V, 502–503.
74. F. B. Sanborn, *Henry David Thoreau* (Boston: Houghton Mifflin Co., 1917), 58.
75. Walter Harding, *The Days of Henry Thoreau* (New York: Alfred A. Knopf, 1965), 71.
76. *JMN*, V, 453–54.
77. *W*, IX, 44.
78. Bartlett, 45.
79. Miller, *Transcendentalists*, 343–44.
80. *JMN*, V, 475.
81. *W*, XI, 91–92.
82. *JMN*, V, 437.
83. *JMN*, V, 505.
84. Cooke, 61; also in *W*, XI, 151–76.
85. *JMN*, V, 471.
86. *W*, I, 420.
87. Conway, *Autobiography*, I, 169.
88. Miller, *Transcendentalists*, 23–24.
89. Wright, 6.
90. *W*, I, 137.
91. *W*, I, 128–29, 141–44.
92. *C&E*, I, 174.

CHAPTER XV
Vanishing Gods

1. *JMN*, VII, 215.
2. Cooke, 76.
3. *C&E*, I, 190.
4. *W*, I, 152–87.
5. *W*, I, 186.
6. Cooke, 69.
7. *L*, II, 150.
8. *L*, II, 149n.
9. Cooke, 70.
10. Cooke, 72.

11.   *L*, II, 167.
12.   Cooke, 74.
13.   *L*, II, 162.
14.   *C&E*, I, 183.
15.   *C&E*, I, 184.
16.   *JMN*, VII, 65, 95.
17.   *JMN*, VII, 96.
18.   *JMN*, VII, 98.
19.   *JMN*, VII, 110–11.
20.   *JMN*, VII, 139–40.
21.   *L*, II, 147n.
22.   *L*, II, 159.
23.   Bartlett, 50.
24.   Bartlett, 51.
25.   Bartlett, 52.
26.   *L*, II, 164.
27.   *JMN*, VII, 116–17.
28.   *JMN*, VII, 123.
29.   *AJ*, 113.
30.   *JMN*, VII, 124.
31.   *JMN*, VII, 122.
32.   *L*, II, 171.
33.   Miller, *Transcendentalists*, 344.
34.   Miller, *Transcendentalists*, 347.
35.   Miller, *Transcendentalists*, 351.
36.   Miller, *Transcendentalists*, 354.
37.   *L*, II, 173.
38.   *JMN*, VII, 132.
39.   *JMN*, VII, 70.
40.   *JMN*, VII, 134.
41.   *L*, II, 172.
42.   *EL*, III, 5.
43.   *EL*, III, 11.
44.   *EL*, III, 15–16.
45.   Samuel Enoch Stumpf, *Socrates to Sartre: A History of Philosophy* (New York: McGraw-Hill Book Co., 1975), 39.
46.   *EL*, III, 5–6.
47.   *EL*, III, 19.
48.   *EL*, II, 250.
49.   William James, *Psychology: Briefer Course* (New York: Henry Holt & Co., 1892), Chap. XI.
50.   *EL*, III, 27.

51. *EL,* III, 35.
52. *EL,* III, 52.
53. *EL,* III, 64.
54. *EL,* III, 67.
55. *EL,* III, 71.
56. *EL,* III, 74.
57. *EL,* III, 79.
58. *EL,* III, 100.
59. *EL,* III, 103–137.
60. *EL,* III, 110.
61. *EL,* III, 112.
62. *EL,* III, 113–14.
63. *EL,* III, 111.
64. See *JMN,* V, 382.
65. *EL,* III, 114.
66. *EL,* III, 122.
67. *EL,* III, 123.
68. *EL,* III, 135.
69. *EL,* III, 140.
70. *EL,* III, 151.
71. *EL,* III, 155.
72. *EL,* III, 156.
73. *EL,* III, 167.
74. *L,* II, 163.
75. *L,* II, 178n.
76. *L,* II, 185.
77. *JMN,* VII, 170.
78. Ellen, 124.
79. *JMN,* VII, 184.
80. *JMN,* VII, 197.
81. *JMN,* VII, 204.
82. *JMN,* VII, 213.
83. *L,* II, 204.
84. *JMN,* VII, 213.
85. *JMN,* VII, 189.
86. *JMN,* VII, 224.
87. *JMN,* VII, 306.
88. *JMN,* VII, 301.
89. *JMN,* VII, 273.
90. *JMN,* VII, 259.
91. *C&E,* I, 246.
92. *C&E,* I, 141.

93. *C&E,* I, 263.
94. James Pope-Hennessey, *Monckton Milnes: The Flight of Youth, 1851–1885*
     (London: Constable, 1951), 38, 114–15, 133–34.
95. *C&E,* I, 162.
96. *JMN,* VII, 324.
97. *JMN,* VII, 230–31.
98. *JMN,* VII, 201–202.
99. *JMN,* VII, 220.
100. *JMN,* VII, 221.
101. *JMN,* VII, 235n.
102. *JMN,* VII, 237–38.
103. *JMN,* VII, 215.

CHAPTER XVI
Hodiernal Facts

1.   *JMN,* VII, 388.
2.   *L,* II, 217.
3.   *JMN,* VII, 265.
4.   *JMN,* VII, 268.
5.   *JMN,* VII, 283.
6.   *JMN,* VII, 270.
7.   *JMN,* VII, 301.
8.   *JMN,* VII, 300.
9.   *EL,* III, 187.
10. *EL,* III, 194.
11. *EL,* II, 276.
12. *EL,* II, 274.
13. *EL,* III, 263.
14. *L,* II, 255–56.
15. *JMN,* VII, 339.
16. Cabot, II, 400.
17. *L,* II, 272n.
18. *L,* II, 266.
18a. *L,* II, 310n.
19. *JMN,* VII, 342.
20. *Dial,* II, 251.
21. Shepard, 282.
22. Shepard, 283.
23. *W,* X, 584.
24. *Dial,* III, 112; *W,* X, 374.
25. *JMN,* VII, 539.
26. *W,* X, 376.

27. *L*, II, 300.
28. *Letters from Ralph Waldo Emerson to a Friend*, ed. Charles Eliot Norton (Boston: Houghton Mifflin Co., 1899), 19–20.
29. *L*, II, 304.
30. *L*, II, 325.
31. *L*, II, 326–27.
32. Bell Gale Chevigny, *The Woman and the Myth: Margaret Fuller's Life and Writings* (Old Westbury, N.Y.: The Feminist Press, 1976), 109.
33. Chevigny, 111.
34. Chevigny, 113.
35. Chevigny, 116.
36. *Memoirs of Margaret Fuller Ossoli*, ed. Ralph Waldo Emerson et al. (Boston: Phillips, Sampson & Co., 1852), I, 281.
37. *L*, II, 327–28.
38. *JMN*, VII, 400; Chevigny, 125.
39. *L*, II, 352–53.
40. *L*, II, 343—fragment; HL: letter, Oct. 3, 1840.
41. *W*, II, 181, 184.
42. *W*, II, 208, 211.
43. Chevigny, 105; HL: CS, unpublished.
44. The group met when Hedge came to Boston from Maine.
45. *L*, II, 229.
46. Madeleine B. Stern, *The Life of Margaret Fuller* (New York: E. P. Dutton & Co., 1942), 181–84.
47. *L*, I, 270n.
48. *L*, II, 287.
49. *Dial*, I, 1, 3.
50. *L*, II, 324n.
51. *C&E*, I, 298.
52. *JMN*, VII, 395; *C&E*, I, 304.
53. *JMN*, VII, 388.
54. *JMN*, VII, 378, 379n.
55. *JMN*, VII, 403.
56. *JMN*, VII, 488.
57. *Dial*, I, 215.
58. *Dial*, I, 149.
59. *JMN*, VII, 350.
60. *JMN*, VII, 360.
61. *JMN*, VII, 404.
62. *JMN*, VII, 407.
63. *JMN*, VII, 408.
64. Henry W. Sams, *Autobiography of Brook Farm* (Englewood Cliffs, N.J.: Prentice-Hall, 1958), 5–8.

65. *L*, II, 365.
66. *L*, II, 369.
67. Cabot, II, 437.
68. *L*, II, 371.
69. *L*, II, 389.

PART TWO

CHAPTER XVII
Idealism in 1842

1. *W*, I, 329.
2. *JMN*, VII, 411.
3. *L*, II, 376.
4. Edmund G. Berry, *Emerson's Plutarch* (Cambridge: Harvard University Press, 1961), 35f.
5. *W*, IV, 162.
6. *Selected Essays by Montaigne* (the Charles Cotton–W. C. Hazlitt Translation), rev. ed. with intro. by Blanchard Bates (New York: Modern Library, 1949), xxxi.
7. *W*, IV, 168.
8. *Green Hills of Africa,* Chap. I.
9. *W*, II, 4.
10. *W*, II, 25–26.
11. *W*, II, 28.
12. *W*, II, 36.
13. *W*, II, 36–37.
14. *W*, II, 41.
15. *W*, II, 45.
16. *W*, II, 47.
17. *W*, II, 50.
18. *W*, II, 51–52.
19. *W*, II, 57.
20. *W*, II, 61.
21. *W*, II, 62.
22. *W*, II, 79.
23. *W*, II, 81.
24. *W*, II, 58.
25. *W*, II, 58–59.
26. See Chap. XIII.
27. *Ennead,* IV, ii.
28. Samuel Enoch Stumpf, *Socrates to Sartre: A History of Philosophy* (New York: McGraw-Hill Book Co., 1975), 141.

29. Holmes, 173.
30. *W*, II, 267.
31. *W*, II, 268.
32. *W*, II, 280.
33. *W*, II, 288.
34. *W*, II, 292.
35. *W*, II, 296.
36. *W*, II, 297.
37. *W*, II, 326.
38. *W*, II, 332.
39. Erich Fromm, *The Forgotten Language* (New York: Grove Press, 1951), 140–42.
40. Friedrich Nietzsche, *The Gay Science,* trans. with commentary by Walter Kaufmann (New York: Vintage Books, 1974), 7.
41. *W*, II, 224.
42. *W*, II, 250.
43. *W*, II, 252.
44. *W*, II, 351.
45. *W*, II, 367.
46. *W*, II, 368.
47. Cooke, 109–112.
48. *W*, II, 376–77.
49. William J. Sowder, *Emerson's Impact on the British Isles and Canada* (Charlottesville: University of Virginia Press, 1966), 1.
50. Cooke, 112.
51. Quoted in Cooke, 111.
52. *JMN*, VII, 431.
53. *JMN*, VII, 413.
54. *JMN*, VII, 424.
55. *JMN*, VII, 435.
56. *JMN*, VII, 440.
57. *JMN*, VII, 442.
58. *JMN*, VII, 447.
59. Walter Harding, *The Days of Henry Thoreau* (New York: Alfred A. Knopf, 1965), 127f.
60. *JMN*, VII, 454.
61. *W*, II, 56.
62. *L*, II, 403.
63. *L*, II, 421.
64. *L*, II, 434.
65. *W*, I, 197.
66. *W*, I, 198.
67. *W*, I, 200.

68. *W*, I, 203.
69. *W*, I, 208.
70. *W*, I, 209–210.
71. *W*, I, 222–23.
72. *L*, II, 444.
73. *C&E*, I, 345.
74. *JMN*, VIII, 103.
75. *JMN*, VIII, 105.
76. *JMN*, VIII, 88.
77. *JMN*, VIII, 96.
78. *JMN*, VIII, 109.
79. *L*, II, 456n.
80. *JMN*, VIII, 110.
81. *JMN*, VIII, 111.
82. *JMN*, VIII, 142.
83. *JMN*, VIII, 125–26.
84. Ellen, 161.
85. *W*, I, 298.
86. *W*, I, 319.
87. *W*, I, 299.
88. *W*, I, 338.
89. *W*, I, 329.
90. *W*, I, 331.
91. *W*, I, 334.
92. *W*, I, 335.
93. John S. Harrison, *The Teachers of Emerson* (New York, 1910; reprint ed., New York: Haskell House, 1969), 288.
94. *W*, I, 340.
95. Stumpf, 312.
96. *W*, I, 342.
97. *W*, I, 344–47.
98. *W*, I, 357.

CHAPTER XVIII
Saturnalia of Faith

1. *JMN*, VIII, 313.
2. *L*, II, 466.
3. Charvat, 19.
4. *L*, III, 4.
5. *L*, III, 9.
6. *JMN*, VIII, 163.
7. *JMN*, VIII, 166.

8. *L*, III, 9.
9. *L*, III, 10.
10. *W*, IX, 148.
11. *JMN*, VIII, 205.
12. Ellen, 162.
13. *JMN*, VIII, 182–83.
14. *L*, III, 12.
15. *L*, III, 19.
16. *JMN*, VIII, 209.
17. *JMN*, VIII, 210.
18. *Walt Whitman of the New York Aurora, Editor at Twenty-two: A Collection of Recently Discovered Writings*, ed. Joseph Jay Rubin and Charles H. Brown (State College, Pa.: Bald Eagle Press, 1950), 105.
19. *L*, III, 26.
20. Gay Wilson Allen, *William James, A Biography* (New York: Viking Press, 1967), 13.
21. *JMN*, VIII, 235.
22. *JMN*, III, 26.
23. *L*, III, 38n; Joel Myerson, "An Annotated List of Contributions to the Boston Dial," *Studies in Bibliography: Papers of the Bibliographical Society of Virginia* XXVI (1973): 133–66.
24. *JMN*, VIII, 271–75.
25. *American Note-Book*, Oct. 10, 1842.
26. Bell Gale Chevigny, *The Woman and the Myth: Margaret Fuller's Life and Writings* (Old Westbury, N.Y.: The Feminist Press, 1976), 127.
27. Chevigny, 129.
28. Chevigny, 131.
29. *L*, III, 51.
30. Shepard, 300.
31. Shepard, 325.
32. *AJ*, 161.
33. *C&E*, I, 366.
34. *AJ*, 161–62.
35. Shepard, 317.
36. *AL*, 88.
37. *C&E*, II, 8.
38. Shepard, 321.
39. Rusk, 297.
40. *AL*, 90.
41. *C&E*, II, 24.
42. Shepard, 340–41.
43. *Dial*, III, 227.
44. *Dial*, III, 218.

45. *L*, III, 96.
46. *JMN*, VIII, 313.
47. *JMN*, VIII, 329.
48. Shepard, 356.
49. *W*, III, 351n.
50. *JMN*, VIII, 433.
51. *JMN*, VIII, 375.
52. *W*, XI, 85.
53. *Dial*, IV, 135.
54. Shepard, 373–76.
55. *Dial*, IV, 164.
56. *JMN*, VIII, 390.

CHAPTER XIX
Western Gymnosophist

1. *C&E*, II, 81.
2. Walter Harding, *The Days of Henry Thoreau* (New York: Alfred A. Knopf, 1965), 145; *L*, III, 158.
3. Ellen.
4. *The Correspondence of Henry David Thoreau*, ed. Walter Harding and Carl Bode (New York: New York University Press, 1958), 103.
5. Ellen.
6. *Correspondence of Thoreau*, 112f.
7. *The James Family: A Group Biography*, ed. F. O. Matthiessen (New York: Alfred A. Knopf, 1948), 43.
8. Harding, 140–41.
9. *The Works of Thoreau*, ed. Henry S. Canby (Boston: Houghton Mifflin Co., 1937), 776.
10. *Works of Thoreau*, 785.
11. *JMN*, IX, 7.
12. *Correspondence of Thoreau*, 137.
13. Harding, 157f.
14. *W*, I, 361.
15. *W*, I, 363.
16. *W*, I, 365.
17. *W*, I, 371.
18. *W*, I, 377.
19. *W*, I, 380.
20. *L*, III, 243.
21. *Dial*, IV, 512.
22. *JMN*, IX, 86.
23. *JMN*, IX, 89.

24. *L*, III, 256.
25. Scudder, *Concord*, 190.
26. *C&E*, II, 77.
27. *L*, III, 262–63.
28. Harding, 176.
29. *W*, XI, 99f.
30. *W*, XI, 142.
31. *W*, XI, 140.
32. *W*, XI, 130.
33. *W*, XI, 132–34.
34. *W*, XI, 138.
35. F. B. Sanborn, *The Personality of Emerson* (Boston: Goodspeed, 1903), 125–26.
36. Slight variation in *Letters from Ralph Waldo Emerson to a Friend*, ed. Charles Eliot Norton (Boston: Houghton Mifflin Co., 1899), 56–59.
37. *JMN*, IX, 161.
38. *W*, III, 196.
39. *W*, IX, 309.
40. J. D. Johannan, "Emerson's Translations of Persian Poetry from German Sources," *American Literature* XIV (Jan. 1943): 407–420. Revised and updated in *Persian Poetry in England and America: A Two Hundred Year History* (Delmar, N.Y.: Caravan Books, 1977).
41. *W*, III, 5.
42. *W*, III, 24.
43. *W*, III, 8.
44. *W*, III, 20.
45. *W*, III, 15.
46. *W*, III, 18, 22.
47. *W*, III, 17.
48. *W*, III, 34.
49. *W*, III, 26.
50. *W*, III, 28, 29.
51. *W*, III, 40.
52. *W*, III, 39.
53. *W*, III, 41.
54. *W*, III, 37.
55. *W*, III, 42.
56. *W*, III, 45.
57. *W*, III, 50.
58. *W*, III, 54.
59. *W*, III, 55.
60. *W*, III, 64.
61. *W*, III, 58.

62. *W*, III, 59.
63. *W*, III, 61.
64. *W*, III, 69.
65. *W*, III, 71, 72.
66. *W*, III, 72–73.
67. *W*, III, 75.
68. *W*, III, 77.
69. *W*, III, 81.
70. *W*, III, 84.
71. *W*, III, 86.
72. *W*, III, 128.
73. *W*, III, 137.
74. *W*, III, 155.
75. *W*, III, 178.
76. *W*, III, 180.
77. *W*, III, 182.
78. *W*, III, 215.
79. *W*, III, 221.
80. *W*, III, 226.
81. *W*, III, 284.
82. *C&E*, II, 80.
83. *C&E*, II, 85.
84. Cooke, 113.

CHAPTER XX
The Central Man

1. *JMN*, IX, 395.
2. *W*, I, 370.
3. *JMN*, IX, 74.
4. Quoted in Bernard DeVoto, *The Year of Decision 1846* (Boston: Little, Brown & Co., 1943), 10.
5. Chap. IV.
6. *JMN*, IX, 412.
7. *JMN*, IX, 425.
8. *JMN*, IX, 430.
9. *JMN*, IX, 426.
10. *JMN*, IX, 445.
11. *JMN*, IX, 437.
12. *JMN*, IX, 446.
13. *JMN*, IX, 447.
14. *L*, III, 292.
15. Walter Harding, *The Days of Henry Thoreau* (New York: Alfred A. Knopf, 1965), 179f.

16. *The Works of Thoreau,* ed. Henry S. Canby (Boston: Houghton Mifflin Co., 1937), 668.
17. *Works of Thoreau,* 195.
18. *L,* III, 290.
19. HL.
20. HL.
21. HL.
22. HL.
23. Mason Wade, *Margaret Fuller: Whetstone of Genius* (New York: Viking Press, 1940), 142–43.
24. Wade, 143.
25. Bell Gale Chevigny, *The Woman and the Myth: Margaret Fuller's Life and Writings* (Old Westbury, N.Y.: The Feminist Press, 1976), 291.
26. *W,* IV, 3–35.
27. William J. Sowder, *Emerson's Impact on the British Isles and Canada* (Charlottesville: University of Virginia Press, 1966), 32–33.
28. Holmes, 197.
29. *W,* IV, 3.
30. *W,* IV, 8–9.
31. *W,* IV, 12, 20.
32. *W,* IV, 19.
33. *W,* IV, 31, 32.
34. *W,* IV, 39–40.
35. *W,* IV, 42.
36. *W,* IV, 53.
37. *W,* IV, 55–57.
38. *W,* IV, 74, 76.
39. *W,* IV, 82, 88.
40. *W,* III 34.
41. *W,* IV, 126, 127.
42. *W,* IV, 128–29.
43. *W,* IV, 130, 137, 138.
44. *W,* IV, 138.
45. *W,* IV, 142–43.
46. *W,* IV, 165–66.
47. *W,* IV, 172.
48. *W,* IV, 174.
49. *W,* IV, 174–76.
50. *W,* IV, 189.
51. *W,* IV, 193.
52. *W,* IV, 195–96.
53. *W,* IV, 199.
54. *W,* IV, 200.

55. *W,* IV, 202.
56. *W,* IV, 210, 212, 213.
57. *W,* IV, 215, 216, 217.
58. *W,* IV, 218.
59. *W,* IV, 227–28.
60. *W,* IV, 256.
61. *W,* IV, 257–58.
62. *W,* IV, 261.
63. *W,* IV, 270.
64. *W,* IV, 271–72.
65. *W,* IV, 278–79.
66. *W,* IV, 284–88.
67. *JMN,* IX, 395.
68. *W,* I, 71.
69. *W,* I, 76.
70. *L,* III, 341.

CHAPTER XXI
The *Gai Science*

1. *W,* VIII, 37.
2. *L,* III, 366.
3. *L,* III, 366n.
4. *Massachusetts Quarterly Review,* I, 276.
5. Margaret Fuller, *Papers on Literature and Art,* new ed., combined with Part II: *Art and Literature,* ed. Arthur B. Fuller (Boston: Roberts Brothers, 1874), 308.
6. HL.
7. *C&E,* II, 119.
8. *C&E,* II, 122.
9. *JMN,* IX, 456–57, 461–64.
10. *JMN,* VIII, 8.
11. *EL,* III, 368.
12. *W,* VIII, 36–37.
13. Friedrich Nietzsche, *The Gay Science,* trans. with commentary by Walter Kaufmann (New York: Vintage Books, 1974).
14. Nietzsche, 9.
15. *EL,* III, 368n.
16. Nietzsche, 6.
17. *JMN,* VIII, 378–79.
18. *JMN,* IX, 399n.
19. *Poems* (1847 edition; not in later editions), 209–210.
20. *Poems* (1847), 212–13.

21. *J*, X, 166.
22. *JMN*, IX, 398.
23. J. D. Johannan, "Emerson's Translations of Persian Poetry from German Sources," *American Literature* XIV (Jan. 1943): 35.
24. *W*, IX, 121.
25. *W*, IX, 403n.
26. *W*, IX, 385–87.
27. Harold Bloom, *The Ringers in the Tower: Studies in Romantic Tradition* (Chicago: University of Chicago Press, 1971), 220.
28. *JMN*, IV, 291.
29. *JMN*, V, 327.
30. *W*, IX, 420n.
31. *W*, IX, 20 (variations in punctuation in 1847 and later editions).
32. William Sloane Kennedy, "Clews to Emerson's Mystic Verse," *The American Author* (June 1903): 205.
33. *W*, IX, 416n.
34. In 1847 the line read: "Stuff their nine brains in his hat . . ."
35. *W*, IX, 408n.
36. Johannan, 37–38.
37. Reuben Levy, *An Introduction to Persian Literature* (New York: Columbia University Press, 1969), 123, 175–76.
38. *Encyclopaedia Britannica* (1974 ed.), IX, 944.
39. *W*, I, 13, 68–69.
40. Manuscript in the Berg Collection, New York Public Library.
41. *JMN*, VIII, 425.
42. *W*, IV, 70.
43. *Poems* (1847), 177; "For" omitted in *W*, IX, 118.
44. *W*, IX, 424n.
45. *Poems* (1847), 99.
46. *Poems* (1847), 97; canceled in 1876 revision.
47. John Jay Chapman, *Emerson and Other Essays* (New York: Charles Scribner's Sons, 1898; reprint ed., New York: AMS Press, 1965), 94.
48. Johannan, 35.
49. *The Correspondence of Henry David Thoreau*, ed. Walter Harding and Carl Bode (New York: New York University Press, 1958), 145–46.
50. *W*, IX, 88.

CHAPTER XXII
England Revisited

1. *W*, V, 25.
2. Ireland, 140.
3. *L*, III, 379n.

4. Ireland, 197.
5. *L,* III, 371–72.
6. *JMN,* X, 28.
7. *JMN,* X, 29.
8. *JMN,* X, 80.
9. *JMN,* X, 93.
10. *JMN,* X, 131.
11. Shepard, 413–15; *AJ,* 197.
12. *C&E,* II, 125.
13. *Memoirs of Margaret Fuller Ossoli,* ed. Ralph Waldo Emerson et al. (Boston: Phillips, Sampson & Co., 1852), II, 185.
14. *Memoirs of Ossoli,* II, 187.
15. Bell Gale Chevigny, *The Woman and the Myth: Margaret Fuller's Life and Writings* (Old Westbury, N.Y.: The Feminist Press, 1976), 348f.
16. Leopold Wellisz, *The Friendship of Margaret Fuller d'Ossoli and Adam Mickiewicz* (New York: Polish Book Importing Co., 1947), 13.
17. *L,* III, 400.
18. *L,* III, 407 and n.
19. *W,* V, 26.
20. *The Correspondence of Henry David Thoreau,* ed. Walter Harding and Carl Bode (New York: New York University Press, 1958), 187.
21. *L,* III, 420.
22. *C&E,* II, 145–46.
23. *L,* III, 423.
24. *L,* III, 460; Rusk, 355.
25. *L,* III, 425–27.
26. *L,* III, 437.
27. William J. Sowder, *Emerson's Impact on the British Isles and Canada* (Charlottesville: University of Virginia Press, 1966), 60f.
28. Scudder, *Lonely Wayfaring Man,* 74.
29. Scudder, *Lonely Wayfaring Man,* 84.
30. *W,* IV, 33, 35.
31. *L,* III, 444.
32. Sowder, 12, 15.
33. *L,* III, 446.
34. *L,* III, 451.
35. *L,* III, 447n.
36. *L,* III, 452–53.
37. *L,* III, 454.
38. *L,* III, 453, 457.
39. *L,* III, 425.
40. *JMN,* X, 193.
41. *JMN,* X, 312.

42. Scudder, *Lonely Wayfaring Man,* 86f.
43. *L,* IV, 15.
44. Ireland, 162–65.
45. Scudder, *Lonely Wayfaring Man,* 90.
46. Scudder, *Lonely Wayfaring Man,* 91–95.
47. Townsend Scudder III, "Emerson's British Lectures, 1847–1848," Part I: *American Literature* VII (Mar. 1935): 178.
48. *L,* IV, 18.
49. *L,* IV, 21f.
50. *JMN,* X, 421, 558.
51. *Correspondence of Thoreau,* 207.
52. *L,* IV, 36–37.
53. *L,* IV, 74.
54. *Encyclopaedia Britannica* (1895 ed.), VIII, 366.
55. *L,* IV, 42.
56. *L,* IV, 51.
57. *L,* IV, 63.
58. Scudder, *Lonely Wayfaring Man,* 139.
59. *Emerson-Clough Letters,* ed. Howard F. Lowry and Ralph Leslie Rusk (Cleveland: Rowfant Club, 1934; reprint ed., Hamden, Conn.: Archon Books, 1968), No. 1 (unpaged).
60. Scudder, *Lonely Wayfaring Man,* 68–69.
61. Scudder, *Lonely Wayfaring Man,* 70.
62. *JMN,* X, 550.
63. *L,* IV, 65.
64. Scudder, *Lonely Wayfaring Man,* 135; *L.,* IV, 72f.
65. *JMN,* X, 270.
66. *JMN,* X, 327.
67. *L,* IV, 72n.
68. *L,* IV, 73.
69. *L,* IV, 73, 77.
70. *L,* IV, 77.
71. *JMN,* X, 267.
72. *JMN,* X, 266.
73. *L,* IV, 78n.
74. *JMN,* X, 271.
75. *JMN,* X, 272.
76. *L,* IV, 80n.
77. *L,* IV, 85.
78. *L,* IV, 86n.
79. *L,* IV, 103.
80. *L,* IV, 87.
81. *L,* IV, 93.

82. Scudder, *Lonely Wayfaring Man,* 110.
83. Scudder, *Lonely Wayfaring Man,* 150–53.
84. *W,* V, 279.
85. *JMN,* X, 431.
86. *W,* V, 280.
87. *W,* V, 286.
88. Scudder, *Lonely Wayfaring Man,* 112.
89. Edward E. Hale, *Ralph Waldo Emerson* (Boston: J. Stilman Smith & Co., 1893), 14.

CHAPTER XXIII
Lyceum Express

1. *L,* IV, 131.
2. *L,* IV, 101n.
3. *L,* IV, 102.
4. *L,* IV, 105.
5. *L,* IV, 81n, 109–110.
6. *The Correspondence of Henry David Thoreau,* ed. Walter Harding and Carl Bode (New York: New York University Press, 1958), 225–26.
7. *L,* IV, 106–108.
8. *L,* IV, 116.
9. *JMN,* XI, 47.
10. *L,* IV, 131.
11. Charvat.
12. *L,* IV, 115.
13. *L,* IV, 125n.
14. *L,* IV, 136.
15. *W,* XII, 3.
16. *L,* IV, 234n.
17. Shepard, 421.
18. *AJ,* 198.
19. *JMN,* XI, 226.
20. *AL,* 147.
21. *L,* IV, 143; Shepard, 443.
22. Perry, I, 57.
23. Perry, I, 59.
24. Text in F. O. Matthiessen, *The James Family: A Group Biography* (New York: Alfred A. Knopf, 1940), 50.
25. *AJ,* 242.
26. Perry, I, 62.

27. Edward Emerson, *Emerson in Concord* (Boston: Houghton Mifflin Co., 1890), 146.
28. *The Early Years of the Saturday Club: 1855–1870,* ed. Edward Waldo Emerson (Boston and New York: Houghton Mifflin Co., 1918), 4f.
29. Perry, I, 88.
30. Perry, I, 93.
31. *JMN,* XI, 63.
32. *JMN,* XI, 111.
33. *L,* IV, 146.
34. *Emerson–Clough Letters,* ed. Howard F. Lowry and Ralph Leslie Rusk (Cleveland: Rowfant Club, 1934; reprint ed., Hamden, Conn.: Archon Books, 1968), No. 7 (unpaged).
35. The edition cited in these notes as *CW,* the first volume of a new *Collected Works,* Vol. I ed. Robert E. Spiller and Alfred R. Ferguson (Cambridge: Harvard University Press, 1971).
36. *W,* I, 404n.
37. *CW,* I, xxxiii.
38. *L,* IV, 149.
39. *L,* IV, 156–57.
40. *W,* IV, 299n.
41. Cooke, 118.
42. William J. Sowder, *Emerson's Impact on the British Isles and Canada* (Charlottesville: University of Virginia Press, 1966), 32–35.
43. *JMN,* XI, 214–15.
44. *C&E,* II, 188.
45. Cooke, 120.
46. *JMN,* XI, 192–93.
47. G. W. Allen, *The Solitary Singer: A Critical Biography of Walt Whitman* (New York: Macmillan Co., 1955), 81.
48. Fredrika Bremer, *America of the Fifties: Letters of Fredrika Bremer* (New York: American Scandinavian Foundation, 1924), 43.
49. Bremer, 61.
50. Perry, I, 67.
51. *L,* IV, 83–84 and n.
52. Charvat, 25.
53. *W,* XI, 248.
54. *L,* IV, 201.
55. Charvat, 25.
56. *L,* IV, 203.
57. *L,* IV, 204n.
58. *L,* IV, 205n.
59. *JMN,* XI, 512.

60. *L,* IV, 212.
61. *L,* IV, 217.
62. *Memoirs of Margaret Fuller Ossoli,* ed. Ralph Waldo Emerson et al. (Boston: Phillips, Sampson & Co., 1852), II, 338f.
63. Joseph Jay Deiss, *The Roman Years of Margaret Fuller* (New York: Thomas Y. Crowell, 1969), 291–92.
64. *L,* IV, 219n.
65. *JMN,* XI, 256–59.
66. Rusk, 378.
67. *L,* IV, 222.
68. *Memoirs of Ossoli,* II, 352.

CHAPTER XXIV
Quarrel with America

1. *JMN,* XI, 284.
2. *W,* V, 299.
3. *W,* V, 300.
4. *W,* V, 168.
5. *W,* V, 169–70.
6. *JMN,* IX, 430.
7. *JMN,* XI, 284.
8. *W,* VI, 53–54.
9. *W,* VI, 55–56.
10. *W,* VI, 62.
11. *W,* VI, 63–64.
12. *W,* VI, 66.
13. *W,* VI, 67.
14. *W,* VI, 357n.
15. *W,* VI, 69.
16. *W,* VI, 70.
17. *W,* VI, 85.
18. *W,* VI, 89.
19. *W,* VI, 90.
20. *W,* VI, 131.
21. *W,* VI, 134.
22. *W,* VI, 165.
23. *W,* VI, 166.
24. *W,* VI, 204.
25. *W,* VI, 214.
26. *W,* VI, 241.
27. *JMN,* XI, 248.

28. *JMN*, XI, 258–59.
29. *JMN*, XI, 249.
30. *JMN*, XI, 343–44.
31. *JMN*, XI, 346.
32. *JMN*, XI, 348.
33. *JMN*, XI, 348–49.
34. *JMN*, XI, 410.
35. *JMN*, XI, 412.
36. *W*, XI, 179.
37. *W*, XI, 181.
38. *W*, XI, 185.
39. *W*, XI, 190.
40. *W*, XI, 195.
41. *W*, XI, 207.
42. *W*, XI, 208.
43. Cabot, II, 286.
44. *JMN*, XI, 380.
45. *JMN*, XI, 385.
46. *JMN*, XIII, 111.
47. Rusk, 369.
48. *W*, XI, 219.
49. *W*, XI, 228.
50. Richard O. Boyer, *The Legend of John Brown: A Biography and a History* (New York: Alfred A. Knopf, 1973), 109.
51. *W*, XI, 232–34.
52. *W*, XI, 236, 238.
53. *W*, XI, 244.
54. *L*, IV, 230.
55. *W*, XI, 405.
56. *W*, XI, 407.
57. *W*, XI, 416.
58. *W*, XI, 417.
59. *W*, XI, 424.
60. *W*, XI, 426.
61. *JMN*, XI, 446.
62. *L*, IV, 245–46.
63. *L*, IV, 252–53.
64. *L*, IV, 291.
65. *JMN*, XIII, 23.
66. *W*, XI, 397.
67. Rusk, 368.
68. *L*, IV, 301.

69. *JMN,* XIII, 85.
70. *Emerson-Clough Letters,* ed. Howard F. Lowry and Ralph Leslie Rusk (Cleveland: Rowfant Club, 1934; reprint ed., Hamden, Conn.: Archon Books, 1968), No. 10 (unpaged).
71. *L,* IV, 323n.
72. *L,* IV, 326.
73. *W,* VI, 44.
74. *W,* VI, 43.
75. *W,* VI, 49.
76. *L,* IV, 337.
77. *L,* IV, 339.
78. *L,* IV, 337–38.
79. *JMN,* XI, 527n.
80. *L,* IV, 342.
81. *JMN,* XI, 528.
82. *JMN,* XI, 530.
83. *JMN,* XI, 532.
84. *C&E,* II, 218.

CHAPTER XXV
Gathering Storm

1. *W,* XI, 597n.
2. Conway, *Autobiography,* I, 130.
3. Conway, *Autobiography,* I, 135.
4. Conway, *Autobiography,* I, 136.
5. Conway, *Autobiography,* I, 147.
6. Conway, *Autobiography,* I, 137.
7. Conway, *Autobiography,* I, 139.
8. Conway, *Autobiography,* I, 143.
9. Conway, *Autobiography,* I, 152–53.
10. Conway, *Autobiography,* I, 168.
11. *W,* VIII, 10.
12. *W,* VIII, 7.
13. Conway, *Autobiography,* I, 168n.
14. *L,* III, 283.
15. *W,* VIII, 4.
16. Fritjof Capra, *The Tao of Physics* (New York: Bantam Books, 1977), 275.
17. *W,* VIII, 8–9.
18. Capra, 277.
19. *W,* VIII, 14–15.
20. *W,* VIII, 24.
21. *W,* IX, 244–47.
22. *W,* VIII, 22–23.

23. Conway, *Autobiography*, I, 218.
24. Conway, *Autobiography*, I, 216–17.
25. *W*, IX, 365.
26. Original in Feinberg Collection, Library of Congress; text from facsimile.
27. G. W. Allen, *The Solitary Singer: A Critical Biography of Walt Whitman* (New York: Macmillan Co., 1955), 141.
28. Conway, *Autobiography*, I, 216.
29. *C&E*, II, 251.
30. Conway, *Autobiography*, I, 175f.
31. *L*, IV, 448.
32. *JMN*, XIV, 422.
33. *JMN*, XIII, 232.
34. *W*, XI, 245–52.
35. *W*, XI, 247.
36. *JMN*, XIV, 92.
37. *JMN*, XIV, 94.
38. *JMN*, XIV, 95.
39. *W*, XI, 255.
40. *W*, XI, 261.
41. *W*, XI, 262.
42. *W*, XI, 263.
43. *W*, XI, 597n.
44. *JMN*, XIV, 125–27.
45. *JMN*, XIV, 126.
46. Scudder, *Concord*, 213.
47. Scudder, *Concord*, 215.
48. *L*, V, 178.
49. *JMN*, XIV, 334.
50. Elbert B. Smith, *The Death of Slavery: The United States, 1837–65* (Chicago: University of Chicago Press, 1967), 158.
51. *JMN*, XIV, 334.
52. *W*, XI, 269–70.
53. *W*, VII, 427.
54. Henry Seidel Canby, *Thoreau* (Boston: Houghton Mifflin Co., 1939), 391.
55. F. B. Sanborn, *Henry David Thoreau* (Boston and New York: Houghton Mifflin Co., 1917), 291–94.

CHAPTER XXVI
Works and Days

1. *W*, VII, 168.
2. *JMN*, XIV, 248.
3. *L*, V, 161.

4. *JMN,* XIV, 312.

5. *L,* V, 172.

6. *English Traits,* ed. Howard Mumford Jones (Cambridge: Harvard University Press, 1966), ix.

7. *L,* V, 195.

8. *L,* V, 196.

9. *L,* V, 199–200.

10. *L,* IV, 427.

11. *L,* V, 4.

12. *JMN,* XIV, 27–28.

13. Carl Bode, *American Lyceum: Town Meeting of the Mind* (Carbondale: Southern Illinois University Press, 1968), 210.

14. C. E. Schorer, "Emerson and the Wisconsin Lyceum," *American Literature* XXIV (Jan. 1953): 467.

15. *W,* VII, 443.

16. Schorer, 168–69.

17. *L,* V, 205–206.

18. *L,* V, 39.

19. *C&E,* II, 271.

20. *L,* V, 211.

21. *AJ,* 302, 319.

22. *AJ,* 313.

23. *AJ,* 324.

24. *AJ,* 326.

25. *AJ,* 327n.

26. *W,* XI, 285–89.

27. *JMN,* XIV, 352–53.

28. *W,* IX, 228.

29. *W,* IX, 138.

30. *JMN,* XIV, 355–56.

31. *AJ,* 328.

32. *AJ,* 336.

33. William Dean Howells, *Literary Friends and Acquaintance* (New York: Harper Brothers, 1900), 51.

34. Howells, 55.

35. Howells, 59–60.

36. Howells, 61.

37. Howells, 62.

38. Howells, 63.

39. Howells, 65.

40. Quoted in Henry James, *Notes of a Son and Brother* (New York: Charles Scribner's Sons, 1914), 222.

41. *W,* VI, 249.

42. *W,* VI, 336n.
43. *AJ,* 331.
44. *C&E,* II, 276.
45. *L,* V, 228n.
46. Scudder, *Concord,* 224.
47. *AJ,* 330.
48. *L,* V, 229.
49. *JMN,* XIV, 363.
50. Cabot, II, 772.
51. *J,* IX, 305.
52. Cabot, II, 602–604.
53. Cabot, II, 600.
54. Published in *Harper's Weekly* and *New York Leader,* Sept. 28, 1861.
55. Cabot, II, 600.
56. Cabot, II, 601.
57. *L,* V, 246.
58. *J,* IX, 325.
59. Scudder, *Concord,* 241.
60. *L,* V, 253.
61. Scudder, *Concord,* 243.
62. *J,* IX, 330.
63. *J,* IX, 335–36.
64. Perry, I, 91.
65. *L,* V, 256.
66. *L,* V, 257.
67. *L,* V, 259.
68. *L,* V, 263.
69. Conway, *Autobiography,* I, 347f; Charvat, 38.
70. Conway, *Autobiography,* I, 345.
71. *W,* XI, 297.
72. *W,* XI, 298–99.
73. *W,* XI, 300.
74. *W,* XI, 305, 609n.
75. *J,* IX, 375.
76. *J,* IX, 385.
77. *J,* IX, 387.
78. *J,* IX, 388.
79. *J,* IX, 395.
80. *J,* IX, 413.
81. *J,* IX, 416.
82. *J,* IX, 434.
83. *W,* XI, 471–72.
84. *J,* IX, 413.

85. *W,* X, 472.
86. *W,* X, 478.
87. *W,* X, 479.
88. *W,* X, 480.
89. *W,* X, 484.
90. *L,* V, 291.
91. *W,* XI, 313–26.
92. *W,* XI, 317.
93. *W,* IX, 203–204.
94. *W,* IX, 207.

CHAPTER XXVII
The Voice at Eve

1.   *W,* IX, 252.
2.   *L,* V, 304.
3.   *L,* V, 308n.
4.   *L,* V, 311.
5.   *L,* V, 312.
6.   *J,* IX, 484.
7.   Rusk, 422.
8.   *C&E,* II, 280–85.
9.   *C&E,* II, 287–88.
10. Rusk, 423.
11. *AJ,* 353.
12. *L,* V, 326.
13. *L,* V, 328.
14. Cabot, II, 613; *L,* IV, 329n.
15. *J,* IX, 518.
16. *W,* X, 254.
17. *W,* X, 257–58.
18. *W,* XI, 539–40.
19. Scudder, *Concord,* 261.
20. Scudder, *Concord,* 262.
21. *J,* X, 40.
22. *L,* V, 258n.
23. *J,* X, 92.
24. *L,* V, 408–409.
25. *L,* V, 412.
26. *J,* X, 94.
27. *W,* XI, 329–30.
28. *W,* XI, 335–37.

29. *Dictionary of American Biography* (New York: Charles Scribner's Sons, 1935), III, 508.

30. *Letters and Recollections of John Murray Forbes,* ed. Sarah Forbes Hughes (Boston: Houghton Mifflin Co., 1899), 1-66.

31. Descriptions supplied by Edith W. Gregg (unpublished).

32. *L,* VI, 48.

33. Rusk, 431.

34. *L,* V, 451.

35. *L,* V, 455.

36. *L,* V, 494n.

37. *L,* V, 521.

38. *L,* V, 505.

39. *L,* V, 506.

40. Carl F. Strauch, "The Sources of Emerson's 'Song of Nature,' " *Harvard Library Bulletin* IX (1955): 300-334.

41. F. O. Matthiessen, *The American Renaissance* (New York: Oxford University Press, 1941), 59.

42. *W,* VII, 168.

43. Matthiessen, 59.

44. *W,* IX, 231.

45. *Recognition,* 80.

46. *Recognition,* 132.

47. *W,* IX, 163.

48. *Recognition,* 69.

49. *W,* IX, 165.

50. *W,* IX, 455.

51. *W,* IX, 172.

52. *W,* IX, 168.

53. *W,* IX, 177.

54. *W,* IX, 181.

55. *W,* IX, 461n.

56. *W,* IX, 184.

57. *W,* IX, 195, 464-67n.

58. *W,* IX, 196.

59. *W,* IV, 197.

60. *W,* IX, 251-52.

61. *JMN,* XIV, 100-101.

62. *L,* V, 529.

63. *J,* X, 207.

64. *L,* VI, 30.

65. Morison, 327.

66. *W,* VII, 27-28.

67. *C&E*, II, 324.
68. *J*, X, 312.
69. *W*, IX, 244.
70. *W*, XII, 3–4.
71. *W*, XII, 13.
72. *W*, XII, 65.
73. *W*, XII, 38–39.
74. *W*, XII, 71–72.
75. *W*, XII, 97.
76. *Collection*, 38.
77. *Collection*, 22–23.
78. *Collection*, 24.
79. *Collection*, 29.
80. *C&E*, II, 327.

CHAPTER XXVIII
Beneath the Ice

1.   *W*, IX, 19.
2.   James Bradley Thayer, *A Western Journey with Mr. Emerson* (Boston, 1884; reprint ed., Port Washington, N.Y.: Kennikat Press, 1971), 11.
3.   Thayer, 22.
4.   Thayer, 28.
5.   Thayer, 34.
6.   Thayer, 36.
7.   Thayer, 39–40.
8.   *C&E*, II, 344–45.
9.   *L*, VI, 158.
10. Charvat, 47.
11. Thayer, 76.
12. Thayer, 82.
13. Thayer, 100.
14. Thayer, 96.
15. Thayer, 120.
16. *L*, VI, 162; *C&E*, II, 343.
17. *L*, VI, 156.
18. *J*, X, 357.
19. *W*, VII, 21.
20. *J*, X, 363.
21. Rusk, 449.
22. Journal, 1861–67, entry of Oct. 14, 1866, Mass Hist. Soc.
23. *J*, X, 371.

24. Clara Barrus, *Whitman and Burroughs: Comrades* (Boston: Houghton Mifflin Co., 1931), 65.
25. Barrus, 66.
26. *J*, X, 378.
27. *J*, X, 379.
28. *J*, X, 383.
29. *J*, X, 384n; *W*, IX, 19.
30. *J*, X, 386.
31. *J*, X, 386–90.
32. Cabot, II, 703–709.
33. *L*, VI, 217.
34. *L*, VI, 225.
35. *J*, X, 395.
36. Rusk, 461.
37. Rusk, 462.
38. Rusk, 464.
39. *J*, X, 406.
40. Rusk, 466.
41. *J*, X, 407–408.
42. Rusk, 470.
43. Quoted in Rusk, 470.
44. Rusk, 472.
45. *L*, VI, 228n.
46. *L*, VI, 237f.
47. *J*, X, 417.
48. *J*, X, 418.
49. *L*, VI, 243n.
50. Cabot, II, 664.
51. Scudder, *Concord*, 269.
52. *AJ*, 433.
53. Cabot, II, 668.
54. *L*, VI, 245.
55. *J*, X, 420.
56. Cabot, II, 773–75.
57. *L*, VI, 296.
58. Cabot, II, 677.
59. Cabot, II, 652.
60. Cabot, II, 670.
61. Cabot, II, 680.
62. Charvat, 48.
63. *J*, X, 476; Cabot, II, 680.
64. Walt Whitman, *Specimen Days*, Vol. I of *Prose Works*, ed. Floyd Stovall (New York: New York University Press, 1963–64), 279.

65. Cabot, II, 679.
66. Rusk, 504.
67. Rusk, 506.
68. Rusk, 507.
69. *AJ,* 533.
70. Rusk, 508.

Index

NOTE: This Index does not include pages 673–734. (Genealogy, Sources of Illustrations, and Notes). Abbreviations: *q*, quoted; *q.v.*, which see in Index. The titles of Emerson's books, essays, lectures, poems, and sermons are given throughout in individual entries; they do not appear under the entry for Emerson. Subentries, as well as the main-entry page references, are integrated and listed in order of appearance in the biography, which is chronological.